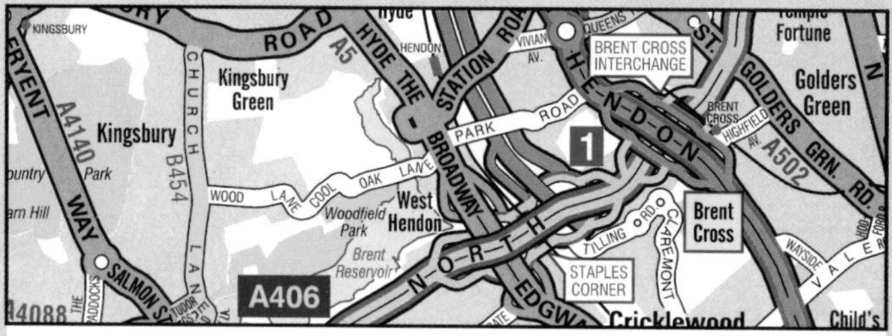

MOTORI LONDON

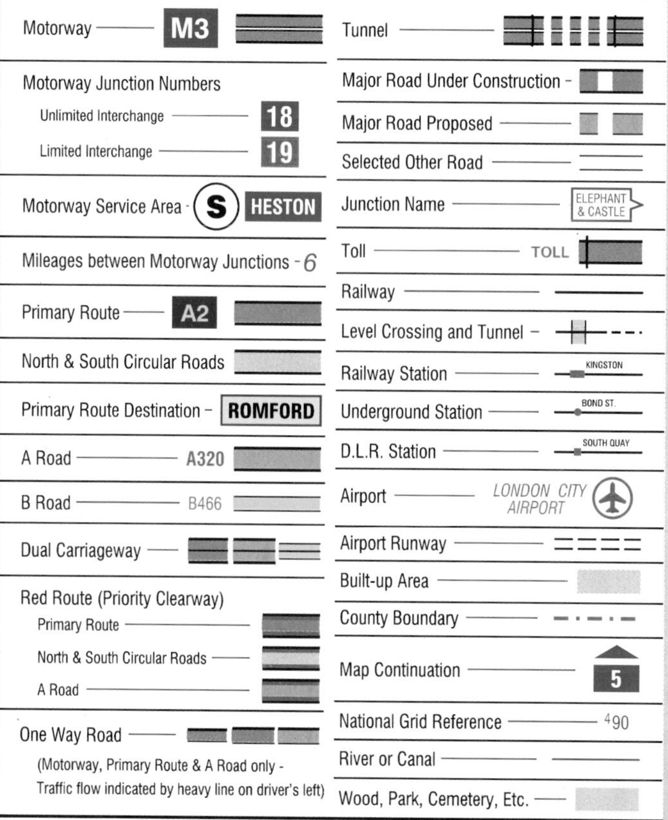

London Main Routes at 1" to 1 mile

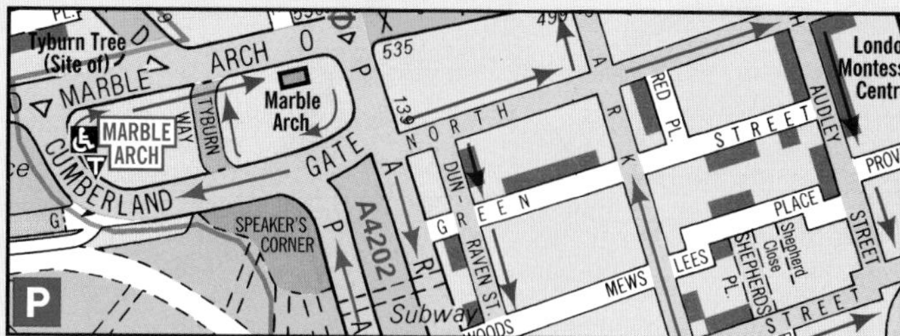

Motorway	**M3**	
Motorway Junction Numbers		
Unlimited Interchange	**18**	
Limited Interchange	**19**	
Motorway Service Area	**(S) HESTON**	
Mileages between Motorway Junctions - 6		
Primary Route	**A2**	
North & South Circular Roads		
Primary Route Destination -	**ROMFORD**	
A Road	A320	
B Road	B466	
Dual Carriageway		
Red Route (Priority Clearway)		
Primary Route		
North & South Circular Roads		
A Road		
One Way Road		

(Motorway, Primary Route & A Road only -
Traffic flow indicated by heavy line on driver's left)

Tunnel	
Major Road Under Construction -	
Major Road Proposed	
Selected Other Road	
Junction Name	ELEPHANT & CASTLE
Toll	TOLL
Railway	
Level Crossing and Tunnel -	
Railway Station	KINGSTON
Underground Station	BOND ST.
D.L.R. Station	SOUTH QUAY
Airport	LONDON CITY AIRPORT ✈
Airport Runway	
Built-up Area	
County Boundary	
Map Continuation	5
National Grid Reference	490
River or Canal	
Wood, Park, Cemetery, Etc.	

Scale: 1:63,360
1 inch (2.54cm) to 1 mile or 1.58 cm to 1 kilometre

0 .... 1 .... 2 Miles
0 ...... 1 ...... 2 ...... 3 Kilometres

Major Sporting Venues

Cricket	|||	Rugby	
Football	⚽	Tennis	
Golf Course	9 9 Hole — 18 18 Hole	Stadium	
Horse Racing		Place of Interest	• Windsor Castle
Motor Racing	🏁	Viewpoint	180° – 360°

Central London at 9" to 1 mile

Motorway	A40(M)	
A Road	A10	
B Road	B326	
Dual Carriageway		
One Way Street		
Restricted Access		
Pedestrianized Road		
House Numbers (A & B Roads only)	34 62	
Parking Meters		
Car Park	**P**	
Junction Name	MARBLE ARCH	
Police Car Pound		
Borough Boundary		
Postal Boundary		

Buildings	
Educational Establishment	
Hospital or Health Centre	
Leisure or Recreational Facility	
Open to the Public	
Place of Interest	
Shopping Centre or Market	
Other Selected Buildings	
Cinema	🎞
Fire Station	■
Information Centre	🄸
Map Continuation	75
National Grid Reference	178
Police Station	▲
Post Office	★
Railway Station	
Railway Station Entrance	
Railway Station	⇄
Underground	⊖
Docklands Light Railway	DLR
Theatre	😃
Toilet	▽
Toilet with Disabled Facilities	♿

Scale: 1:7,040
9 inches (22.86 cm) to 1 mile or 14.2 cm to 1 kilometre

0 .. 100 .. 200 .. 300 Yards .. ¼ Mile
0 .. 100 .. 200 .. 300 .. 400 Metres

Geographers' A-Z Map Company Limited

Head Office : Fairfield Road, Borough Green, Sevenoaks, Kent TN15 8PP Tel: 01732 781000
Showrooms : 44 Gray's Inn Road, London WC1X 8HX Tel: 0171 440 9500

The Maps in this Atlas are based upon the Ordnance Survey Mapping with the permission
of the Controller of Her Majesty's Stationery Office. © Crown Copyright (399000).

EDITION 2 1999

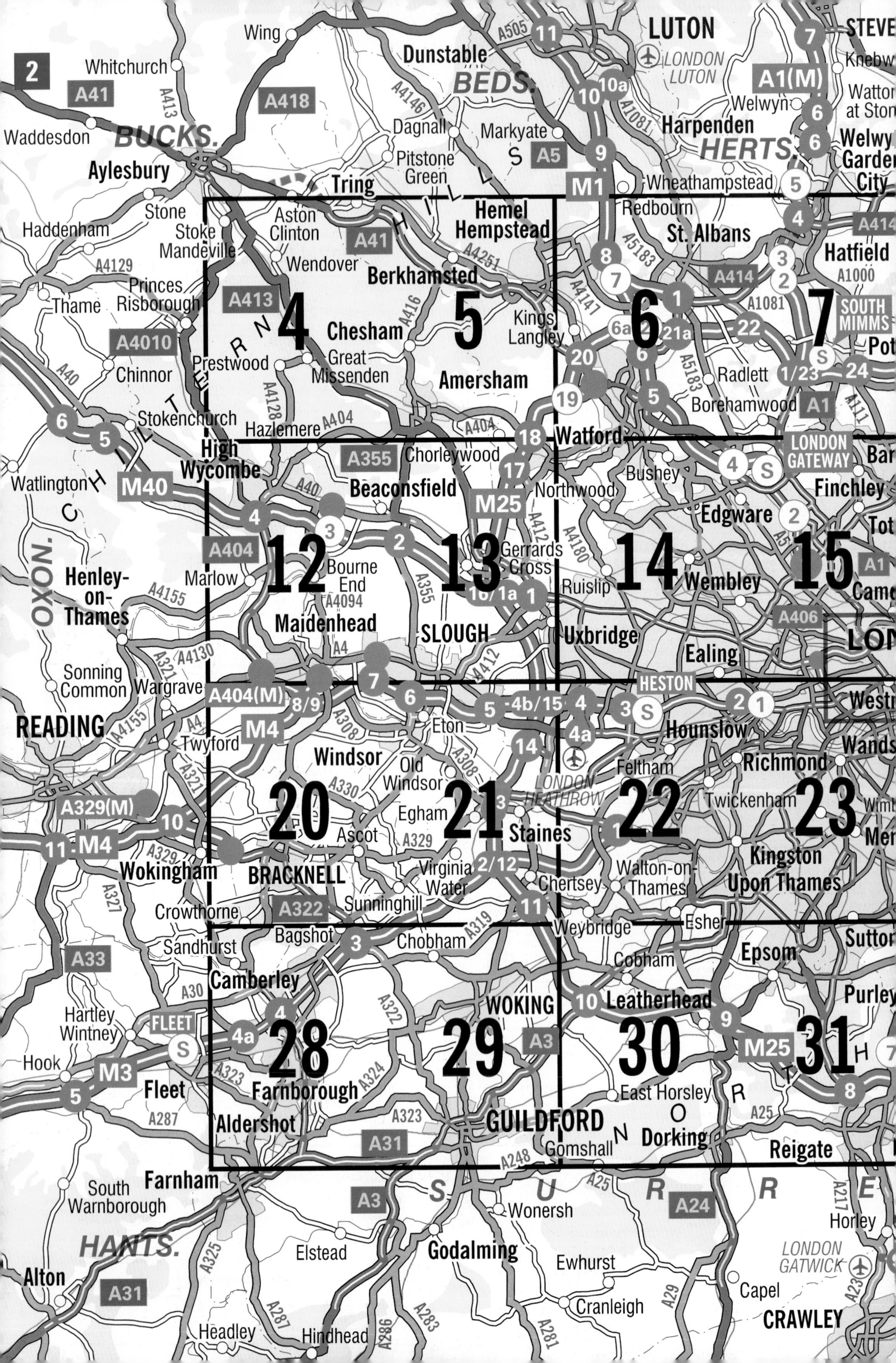
LUTON
Dunstable
BEDS.
BUCKS.
HERTS.
Aylesbury
Tring
Hemel Hempstead
St. Albans
Hatfield
Harpenden
Berkhamsted
Chesham
Amersham
Watford
High Wycombe
Beaconsfield
Marlow
Maidenhead
SLOUGH
Uxbridge
Ealing
Wembley
Edgware
Finchley
READING
Windsor
Staines
Hounslow
Richmond
Kingston Upon Thames
Wokingham
BRACKNELL
Camberley
Farnborough
Aldershot
Fleet
WOKING
GUILDFORD
Leatherhead
Epsom
Dorking
Reigate
Farnham
Godalming
CRAWLEY
Alton
HANTS.
OXON.
4
5
6
7
12
13
14
15
20
21
22
23
28
29
30
31

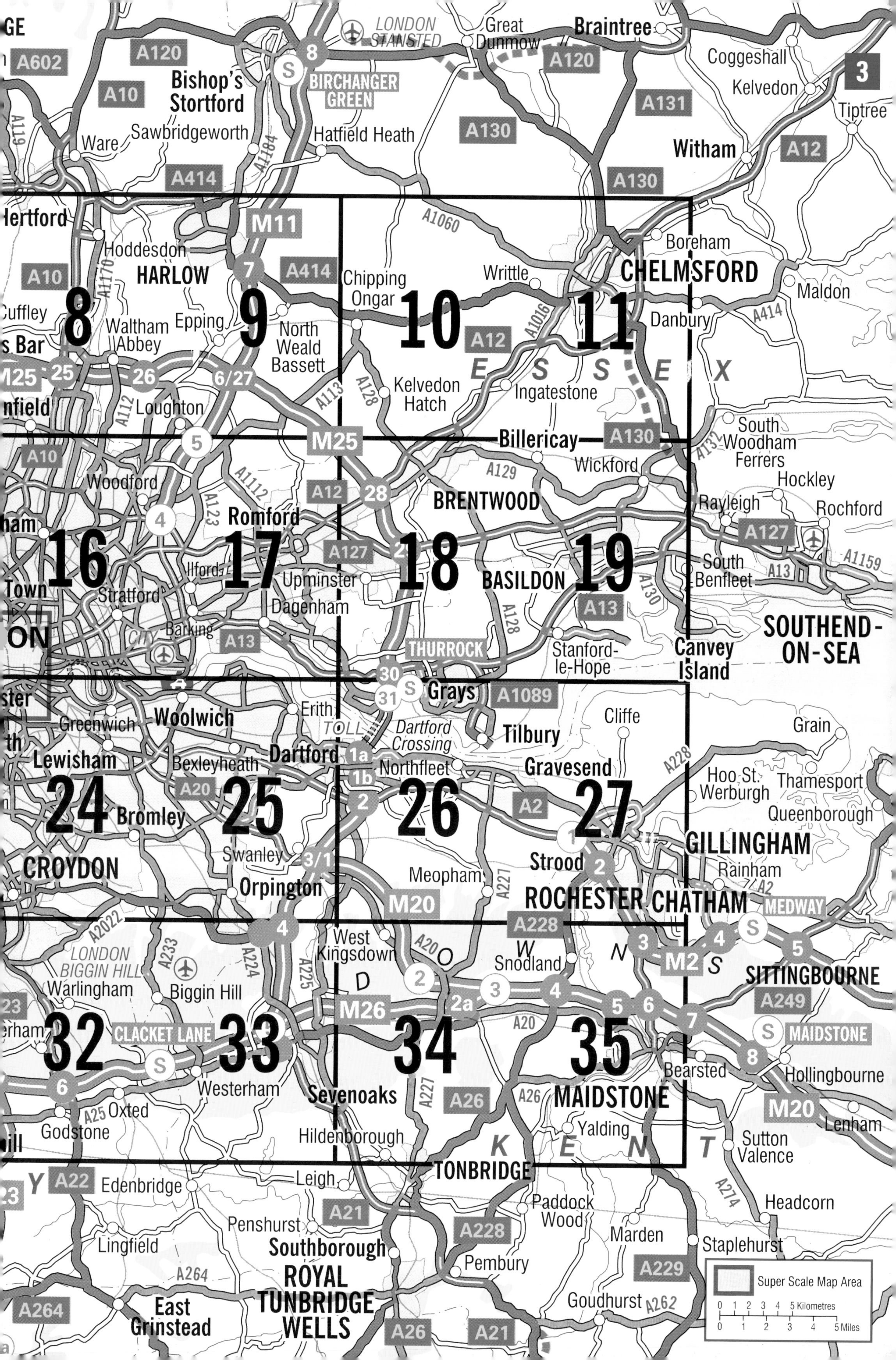

3
Braintree
Great Dunmow
LONDON STANSTED
Bishop's Stortford
Sawbridgeworth
Ware
Hatfield Heath
Coggeshall
Kelvedon
Tiptree
Witham
Hertford
Hoddesdon
HARLOW
Chipping Ongar
Writtle
Boreham
CHELMSFORD
Maldon
Danbury
Cuffley
Waltham Abbey
Epping
North Weald Bassett
Kelvedon Hatch
Ingatestone
ESSEX
Loughton
Billericay
Wickford
South Woodham Ferrers
Hockley
Rayleigh
Rochford
Woodford
Romford
BRENTWOOD
Ilford
Upminster
Dagenham
BASILDON
South Benfleet
Stratford
Barking
CITY
THURROCK
Stanford-le-Hope
Canvey Island
SOUTHEND-ON-SEA
Grays
Tilbury
Erith
Cliffe
Grain
Greenwich
Woolwich
Dartford Crossing
TOLL
Lewisham
Bexleyheath
Dartford
Northfleet
Gravesend
Hoo St. Werburgh
Thamesport
Queenborough
Bromley
GILLINGHAM
Swanley
Strood
Rainham
CROYDON
Orpington
Meopham
ROCHESTER
CHATHAM
MEDWAY
West Kingsdown
Snodland
LONDON BIGGIN HILL
Warlingham
Biggin Hill
SITTINGBOURNE
CLACKET LANE
MAIDSTONE
Westerham
Bearsted
Hollingbourne
Oxted
Godstone
Sevenoaks
MAIDSTONE
Lenham
Yalding
Hildenborough
Sutton Valence
KENT
Edenbridge
Leigh
TONBRIDGE
Paddock Wood
Headcorn
Penshurst
Marden
Lingfield
Southborough
Staplehurst
Pembury
ROYAL TUNBRIDGE WELLS
East Grinstead
Goudhurst
8 9 10 11 16 17 18 19 24 25 26 27 32 33 34 35
Super Scale Map Area
0 1 2 3 4 5 Kilometres
0 1 2 3 4 5 Miles

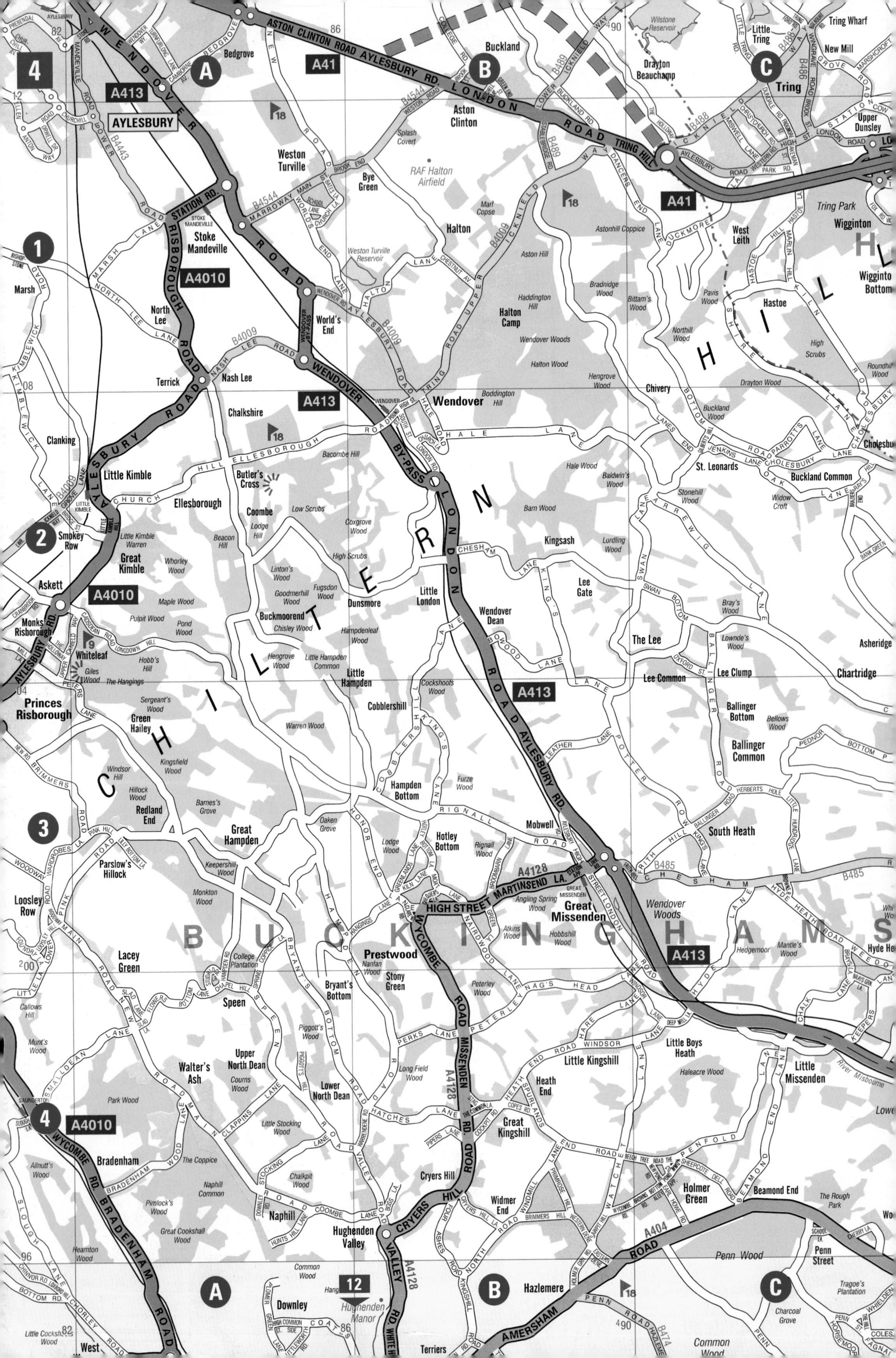

4
AYLESBURY
A413
A41
A4010
A4128
A404
B4009
B4544
B489
B488
B486
B485
B4443
ASTON CLINTON ROAD AYLESBURY RD. LONDON ROAD TRING HILL
WENDOVER ROAD
STATION RD.
RISBOROUGH ROAD
AYLESBURY ROAD
WENDOVER BY-PASS
LONDON ROAD AYLESBURY RD.
HIGH STREET MARTINSEND LA.
WYCOMBE ROAD
MISSENDEN ROAD
CRYERS HILL ROAD
WYCOMBE RD. BRADENHAM ROAD
AMERSHAM ROAD
Bedgrove
Buckland
Aston Clinton
Weston Turville
Bye Green
RAF Halton Airfield
Halton
Weston Turville Reservoir
Stoke Mandeville
Marsh
North Lee
World's End
Terrick
Nash Lee
Chalkshire
Wendover
Halton Camp
Wendover Woods
Halton Wood
Clanking
Little Kimble
Butler's Cross
Ellesborough
Coombe
Smokey Row
Great Kimble
Askett
Monks Risborough
Whiteleaf
Princes Risborough
Green Hailey
Dunsmore
Little London
Wendover Dean
Kingsash
Lee Gate
The Lee
Lee Common
Lee Clump
Chartridge
Little Hampden
Cobblershill
Hampden Bottom
Hotley Bottom
Great Hampden
Redland End
Parslow's Hillock
Loosley Row
Lacey Green
Speen
Prestwood
Stony Green
Bryant's Bottom
Great Missenden
Mobwell
South Heath
Ballinger Bottom
Ballinger Common
Hyde Heath
Little Boys Heath
Little Kingshill
Heath End
Great Kingshill
Little Missenden
Holmer Green
Beamond End
Penn Street
Penn Wood
Hazlemere
Widmer End
Cryers Hill
Hughenden Valley
Naphill
Walter's Ash
Upper North Dean
Lower North Dean
Bradenham
Downley
Hughenden Manor
Terriers
West
Drayton Beauchamp
Wilstone Reservoir
Little Tring
Tring
Tring Wharf
New Mill
Upper Dunsley
Tring Park
Wigginton
Wigginton Bottom
West Leith
Hastoe
Chivery
St. Leonards
Buckland Common
Cholesbury
Asheridge
CHILTERN HILLS
BUCKINGHAMSHIRE
A B C
1 2 3 4
12

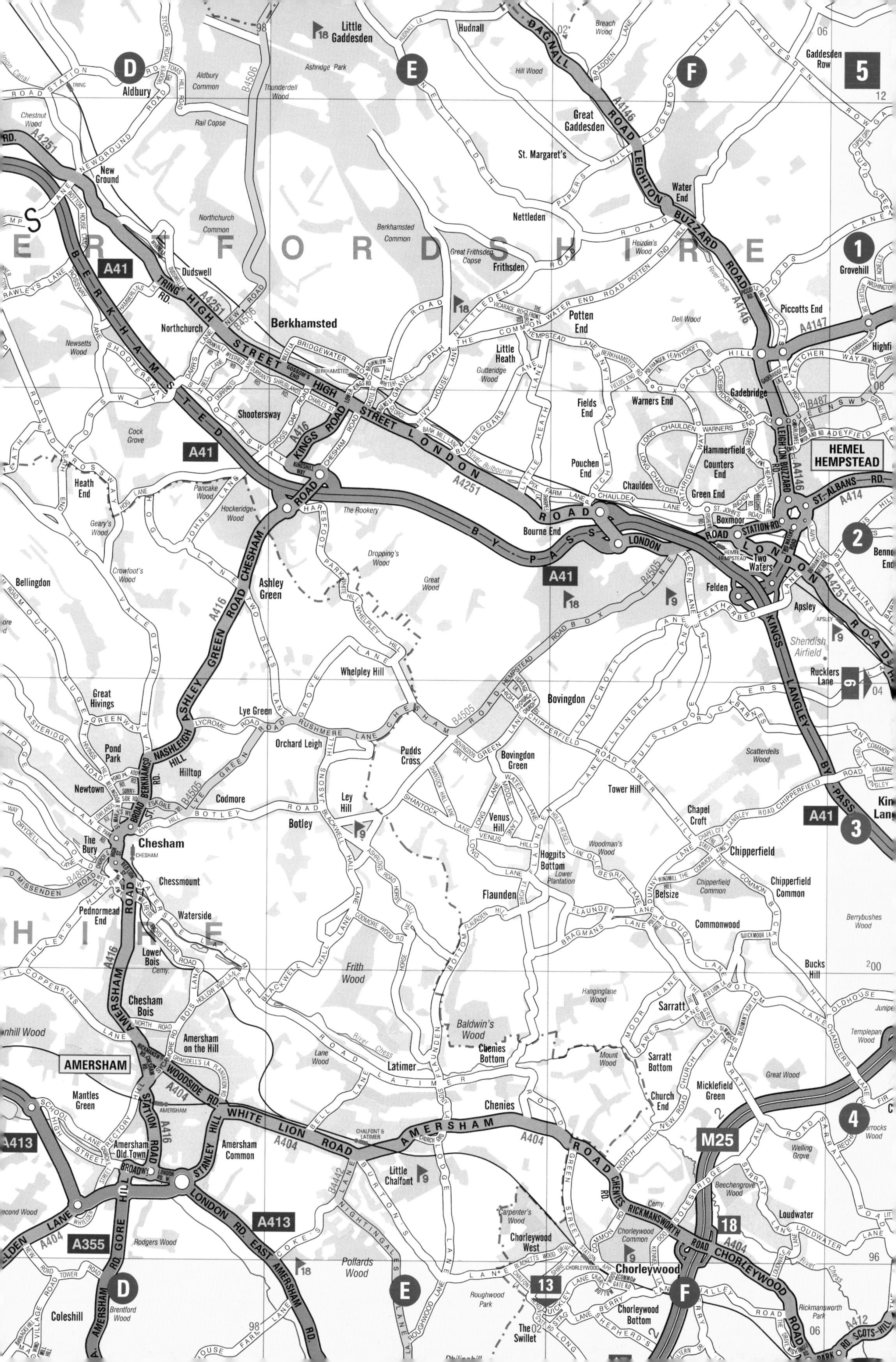
5
D
E
F
Little Gaddesden
Hudnall
Aldbury
Aldbury Common
Ashridge Park
Thunderdell Wood
Hill Wood
Breach Wood
Gaddesden Row
Chestnut Wood
Rail Copse
Great Gaddesden
St. Margaret's
New Ground
Water End
Nettleden
Northchurch Common
Berkhamsted Common
Great Frithsden Copse
Frithsden
Heizdin's Wood
HERTFORDSHIRE
1
Grovehill
Dudswell
Northchurch
Berkhamsted
Potten End
Dell Wood
Piccotts End
Highfield
Newsetts Wood
Little Heath
Gutteridge Wood
Fields End
Warners End
Gadebridge
Shootersway
Cock Grove
Pouchen End
Hammerfield
Counters End
HEMEL HEMPSTEAD
Chaulden
Green End
Heath End
Pancake Wood
Hockeridge Wood
Geary's Wood
The Rookery
Bourne End
Boxmoor
2
Two Waters
Felden
Apsley
Bennetts End
Bellingdon
Crowfoot's Wood
Dropping's Wood
Ashley Green
Great Wood
Shendish Airfield
Rucklers Lane
Whelpley Hill
Great Hivings
Lye Green
Bovingdon
Orchard Leigh
Pudds Cross
Pond Park
Bovingdon Green
Scatterdells Wood
Hilltop
Newtown
Codmore
Tower Hill
Ley Hill
Chapel Croft
Botley
Venus Hill
The Bury
Chesham
Chipperfield
3
Woodman's Wood
Hogpits Bottom
Lower Plantation
Chessmount
Chipperfield Common
Flaunden
Belsize
Pednormead End
Waterside
Commonwood
Berrybushes Wood
Frith Wood
Lower Bois
Bucks Hill
Hanginglane Wood
Chesham Bois
Sarratt
Baldwin's Wood
Amersham on the Hill
Templepan Wood
Chenies Bottom
Mount Wood
Sarratt Bottom
Lane Wood
Latimer
AMERSHAM
Great Wood
Mantles Green
Chenies
Church End
Micklefield Green
4
Amersham Old Town
Amersham Common
Little Chalfont
Welling Grove
Beechengrove Wood
Loudwater
Carpenter's Wood
Chorleywood Common
Rodgers Wood
Chorleywood West
Pollards Wood
Chorleywood
Roughwood Park
Chorleywood Bottom
Rickmansworth Park
Coleshill
Brentford Wood
The Swillet
A41
A4251
A4146
A4147
A414
A416
B4505
B4506
B485
A404
A413
A355
M25
A412
18
13

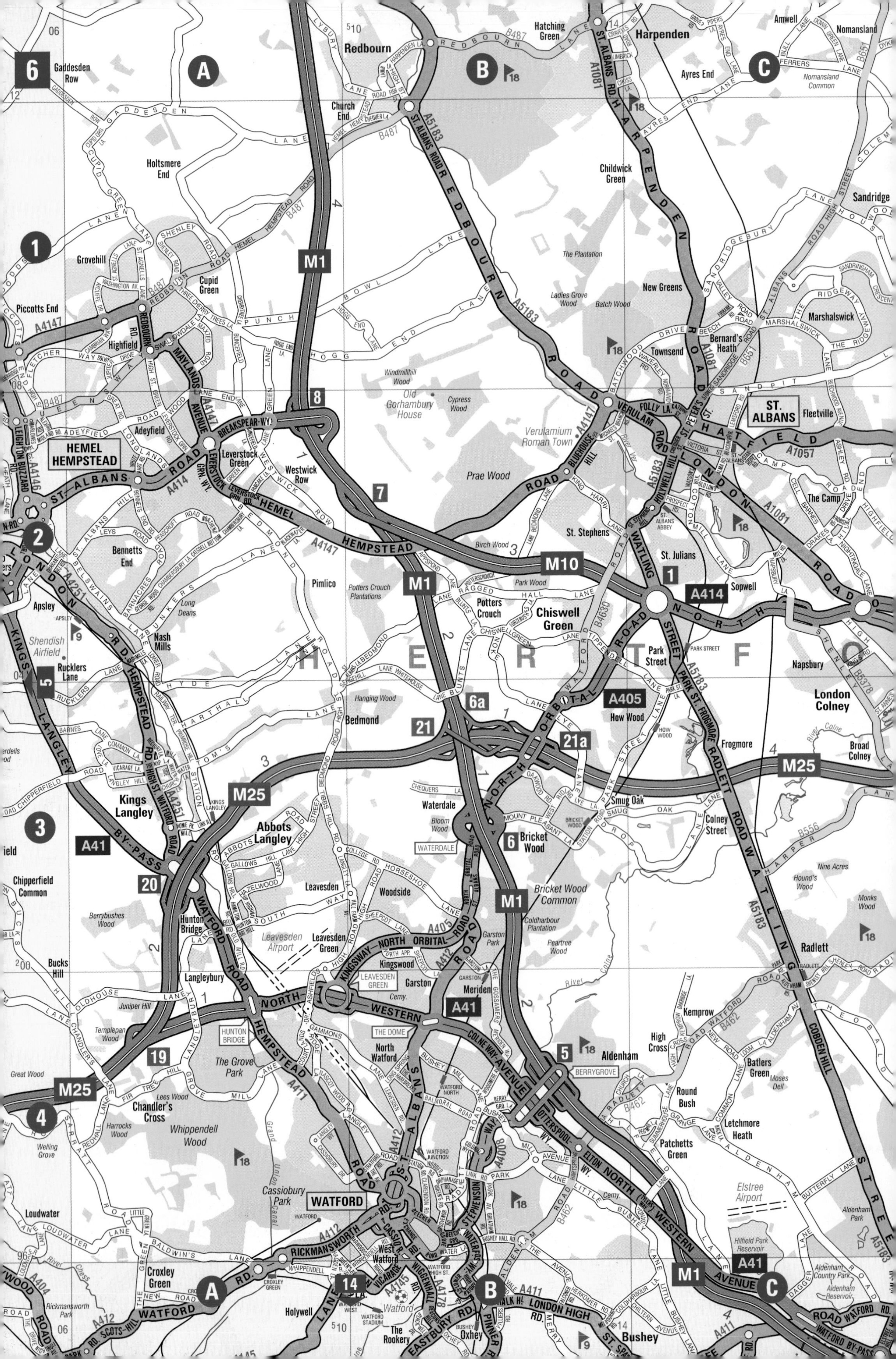

6
Gaddesden Row
Redbourn
Hatching Green
Harpenden
Amwell
Nomansland
Nomansland Common
Ayres End
Church End
Holtsmere End
Childwick Green
Sandridge
Grovehill
Cupid Green
The Plantation
New Greens
Marshalswick
Piccotts End
Highfield
Ladies Grove Wood
Batch Wood
Bernard's Heath
Townsend
Windmillhill Wood
Old Gorhambury House
Cypress Wood
HEMEL HEMPSTEAD
Adeyfield
Leverstock Green
Westwick Row
Verulamium Roman Town
ST. ALBANS
Fleetville
Prae Wood
The Camp
Bennetts End
St. Stephens
Birch Wood
St. Julians
Sopwell
Pimlico
Potters Crouch Plantations
Park Wood
Potters Crouch
Chiswell Green
Apsley
Long Deans
Shendish Airfield
Nash Mills
Park Street
Napsbury
Rucklers Lane
Hanging Wood
Bedmond
How Wood
London Colney
Frogmore
Broad Colney
Kings Langley
Waterdale
Bloom Wood
Smug Oak
Colney Street
Abbots Langley
Bricket Wood
Chipperfield Common
Leavesden
Woodside
Bricket Wood Common
Nine Acres
Hound's Wood
Monks Wood
Berrybushes Wood
Hunton Bridge
Coldharbour Plantation
Leavesden Airport
Leavesden Green
Garston Park
Peartree Wood
Radlett
Bucks Hill
Langleybury
Kingswood
Garston
Meriden
Juniper Hill
Kemprow
Templepan Wood
North Watford
High Cross
Aldenham
The Grove Park
Batlers Green
Moses Dell
Great Wood
Round Bush
Lees Wood
Chandler's Cross
Whippendell Wood
Harrocks Wood
Welling Grove
Letchmore Heath
Patchetts Green
Elstree Airport
Cassiobury Park
WATFORD
Loudwater
Aldenham Park
Hilfield Park Reservoir
West Watford
Croxley Green
Aldenham Country Park
Aldenham Reservoir
Rickmansworth Park
Holywell
Watford
The Rookery
Oxhey
Bushey
M1
M10
M25
A41
A405
A414
A4147
A5183
A1081
A1057
A4251
A412
A411

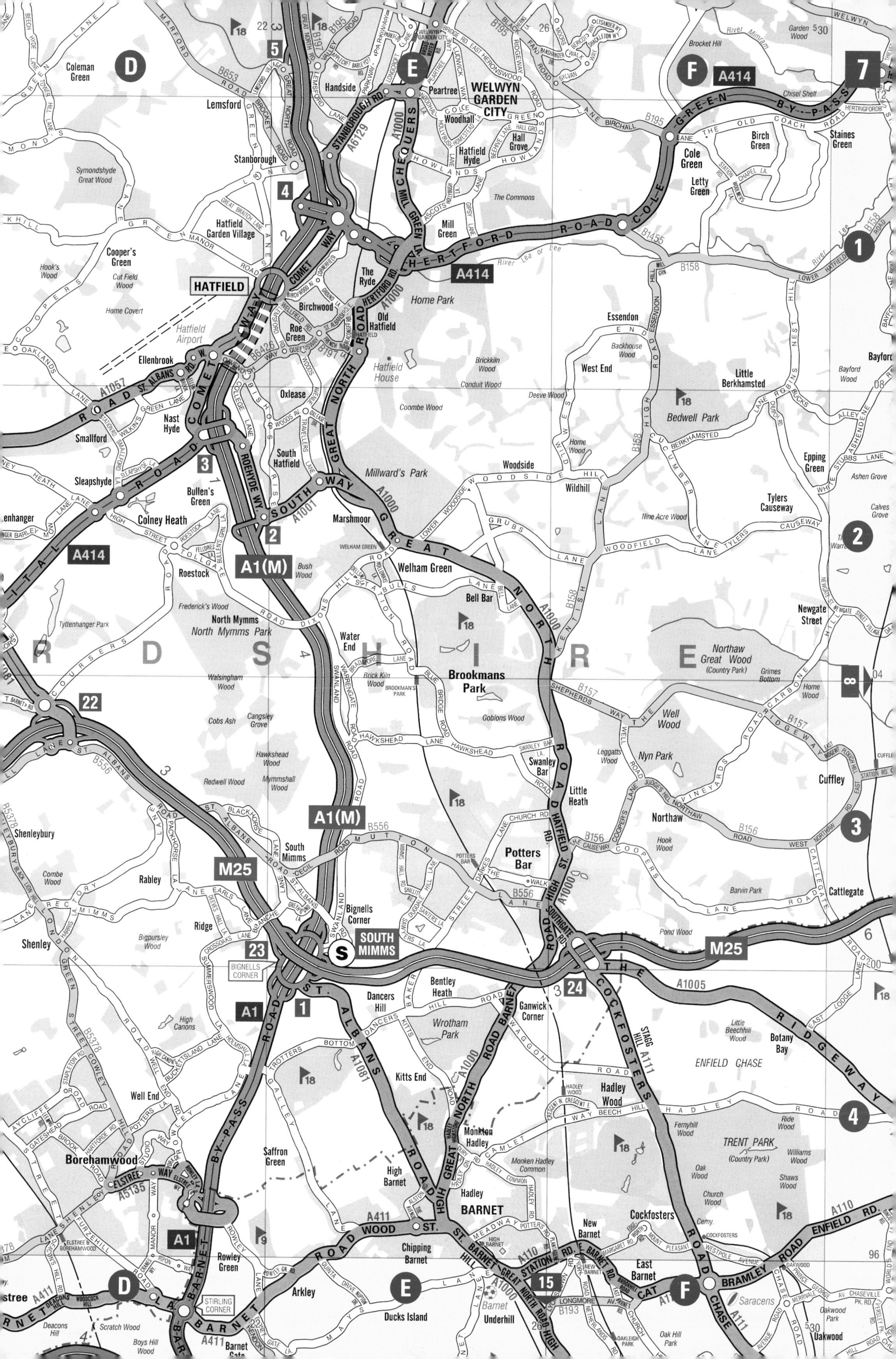

D
E
F
7
Coleman Green
Lemsford
Handside
Peartree
WELWYN GARDEN CITY
Woodhall
Hatfield Hyde
Hall Grove
Stanborough
Brocket Hill
A414
Birch Green
Cole Green
Letty Green
Staines Green
Symondshyde Great Wood
Hatfield Garden Village
Mill Green
The Commons
Cooper's Green
Hook's Wood
Cut Field Wood
HATFIELD
The Ryde
Birchwood
Home Park
Home Covert
Hatfield Airport
Roe Green
Old Hatfield
Essendon
Backhouse Wood
Ellenbrook
Hatfield House
Brickkiln Wood
Conduit Wood
West End
Little Berkhamsted
Bayford Wood
Oxlease
Coombe Wood
Deeve Wood
Bedwell Park
Smallford
Nast Hyde
South Hatfield
Home Wood
Epping Green
Ashen Grove
Sleapshyde
Bullen's Green
Colney Heath
Millward's Park
Woodside
Wildhill
Tylers Causeway
Calves Grove
Marshmoor
Nine Acre Wood
1
2
3
4
5
22
23
24
A414
A1(M)
Roestock
Bush Wood
Welham Green
Bell Bar
Frederick's Wood
Tyttenhanger Park
North Mymms
North Mymms Park
Newgate Street
Water End
Northaw Great Wood (Country Park)
Grimes Bottom
Brick Kiln Wood
Brookmans Park
Home Wood
Walsingham Wood
Well Wood
Cobs Ash
Cangsley Grove
Gobions Wood
Nyn Park
Leggatts Wood
Swanley Bar
Hawkshead Wood
Mymmshall Wood
Redwell Wood
Cuffley
Little Heath
Northaw
Shenleybury
South Mimms
Potters Bar
Hook Wood
M25
Combe Wood
Rabley
Cattlegate
Barvin Park
Ridge
Bignells Corner
SOUTH MIMMS
Bigpursley Wood
Shenley
Pond Wood
BIGNELLS CORNER
Dancers Hill
Bentley Heath
Ganwick Corner
A1005
A1
High Canons
Wrotham Park
Little Beechhill Wood
Botany Bay
Enfield Chase
Kitts End
Hadley Wood
Well End
Fernyhill Wood
Ride Wood
Monken Hadley
Monken Hadley Common
Trent Park (Country Park)
Williams Wood
Saffron Green
Borehamwood
High Barnet
Oak Wood
Shaws Wood
Church Wood
Hadley
BARNET
Cockfosters
New Barnet
A411
Chipping Barnet
Rowley Green
East Barnet
Arkley
15
STIRLING CORNER
Ducks Island
Barnet
Underhill
Oak Hill Park
Saracens
Oakwood Park
Oakwood
Scratch Wood
Deacons Hill
Boys Hill Wood
A1000
A111
A110
B556
B158
B157
B156
R D S H I R E

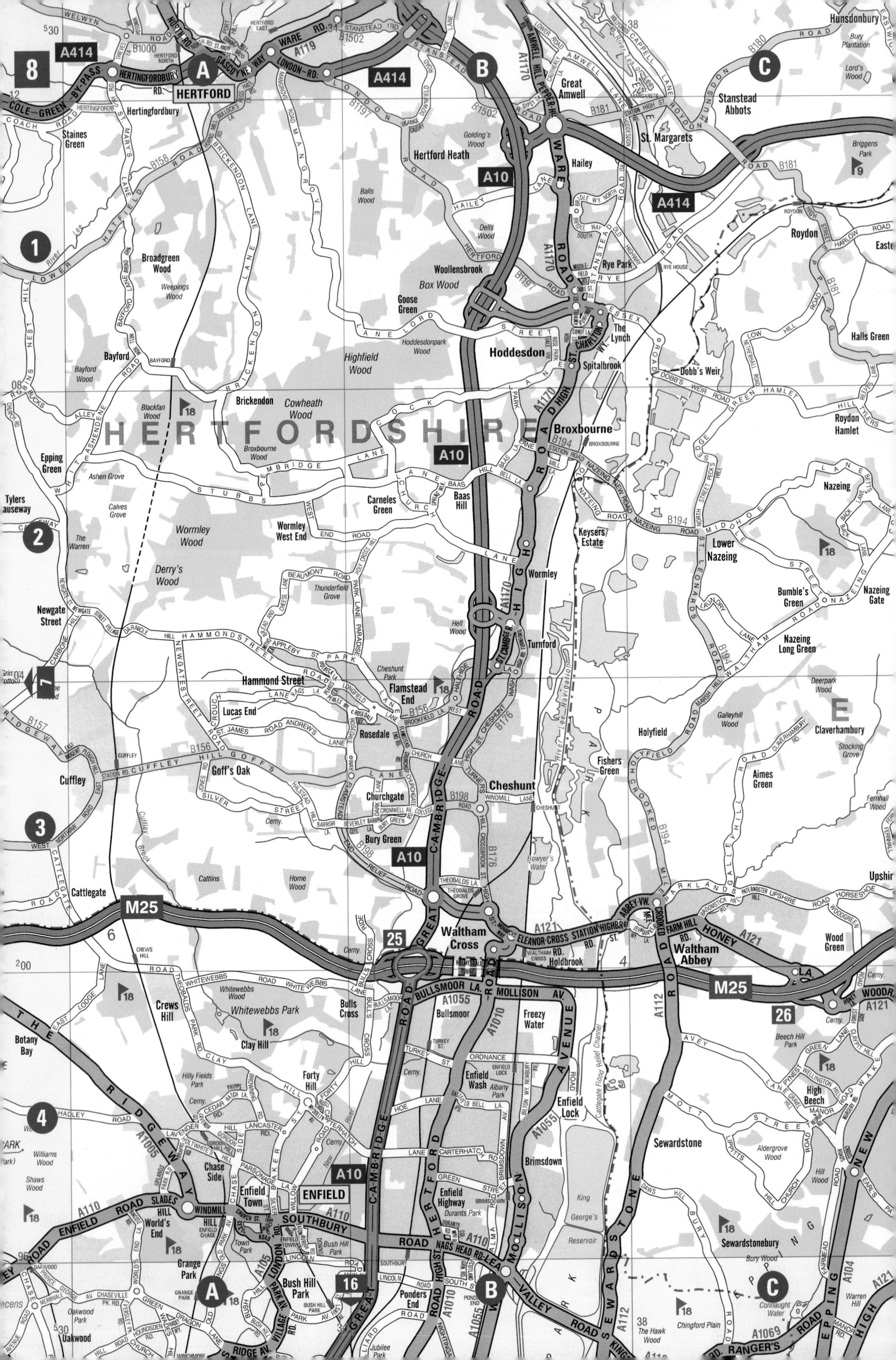

8
A414
HERTINGFORDBURY
HERTFORD
Hertingfordbury
COLE-GREEN BY-PASS
Staines Green
B158
B1000
A119
WARE RD.
LONDON RD.
GASCOYNE WAY
A414
B1502
B1197
Hertford Heath
Golding's Wood
Balls Wood
A10
A1170
B181
Great Amwell
St. Margarets
Stanstead Abbots
Hunsdonbury
Bury Plantation
Lord's Wood
Briggens Park
A414
Hailey
Roydon
Dells Wood
Woollensbrook
Box Wood
Rye Park
Goose Green
The Lynch
Hoddesdon
Spitalbrook
Highfield Wood
Hoddesdonpark Wood
Dobb's Weir
Halls Green
Broadgreen Wood
Weepings Wood
Bayford
Bayford Wood
Brickendon
Cowheath Wood
Blackfan Wood
HERTFORDSHIRE
Broxbourne Wood
Broxbourne
Roydon Hamlet
A10
B194
Epping Green
Ashen Grove
Tylers Causeway
Calves Grove
Wormley Wood
The Warren
Carneles Green
Baas Hill
Wormley West End
Keysers Estate
Nazeing
Lower Nazeing
Derry's Wood
Wormley
Bumble's Green
Nazeing Gate
Newgate Street
Thunderfield Grove
Hell Wood
Turnford
Nazeing Long Green
Hammond Street
Cheshunt Park
Flamstead End
Deerpark Wood
Lucas End
Rosedale
Galleyhill Wood
Holyfield
Claverhambury
B157
B156
B176
Cuffley
Goff's Oak
Fishers Green
Aimes Green
Stocking Grove
Cheshunt
Churchgate
Fernhall Wood
Cemy.
Bury Green
B198
Bowyer's Water
A10
B194
Cattlins
Home Wood
Upshire
Cattlegate
M25
Waltham Cross
Holdbrook
Waltham Abbey
A121
Wood Green
25
Crews Hill
Whitewebbs Wood
Whitewebbs Park
Bulls Cross
A1055
Bullsmoor
A1010
Freezy Water
A112
M25
26
Botany Bay
Clay Hill
Beech Hill Park
Hilly Fields Park
Forty Hill
Enfield Wash
Albany Park
High Beech
Enfield Lock
Sewardstone
Aldergrove Wood
Williams Wood
Shaws Wood
A1005
Chase Side
Brimsdown
Hill Wood
A10
ENFIELD
Enfield Town
Enfield Highway
Durants Park
King George's Reservoir
A110
World's End
Town Park
Bush Hill Park
Sewardstonebury
Bury Wood
Grange Park
Bush Hill Park
16
Ponders End
Connaught Water
Warren Hill
Oakwood Park
Oakwood
Chingford Plain
The Hawk Wood
Jubilee Park
A1069
A104
A1055
A112

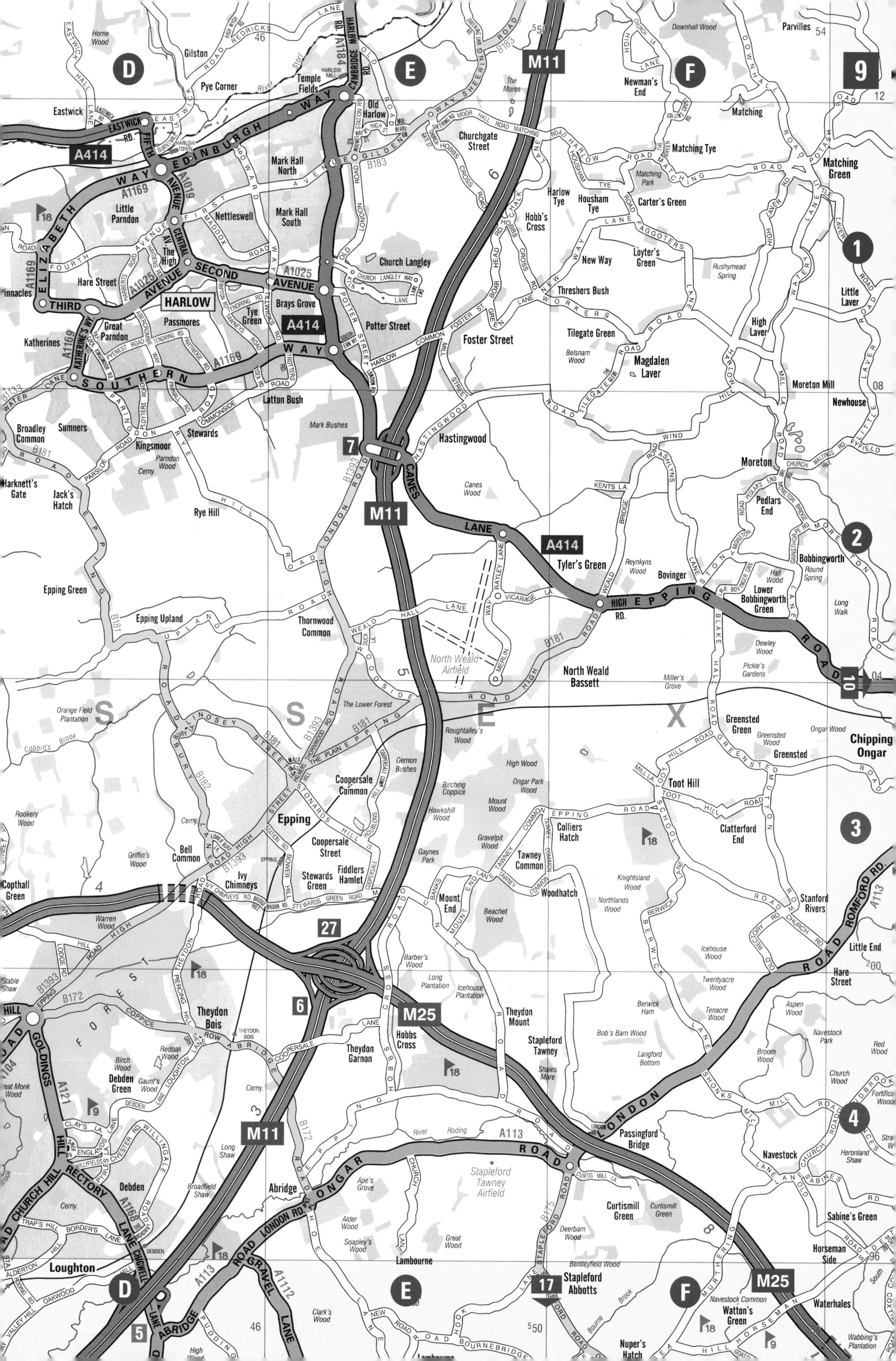

9
D
E
F
1
2
3
4
M11
M25
A414
A1169
A1019
A1025
A1184
B183
B181
B1393
B182
B172
A113
A121
A1168
A1112
B175
7
27
6
5
17
10
Home Wood
Gilston
Eastwick
Pye Corner
Temple Fields
Harlow Mill
Old Harlow
The Mores
Downhall Wood
Parvilles
Newman's End
Matching
Matching Tye
Matching Green
Matching Park
Churchgate Street
Mark Hall North
Mark Hall South
Little Parndon
Nettleswell
The High
Harlow Tye
Housham Tye
Carter's Green
Hobb's Cross
Loyter's Green
New Way
Rushymead Spring
Little Laver
Church Langley
Hare Street
Pinnacles
HARLOW
Brays Grove
Tye Green
Passmores
Great Parndon
Katherines
Potter Street
Foster Street
Threshers Bush
Tilegate Green
Belsnam Wood
Magdalen Laver
High Laver
Moreton Mill
Newhouse
Latton Bush
Mark Bushes
Broadley Common
Sumners
Stewards
Kingsmoor
Parndon Wood
Hastingwood
Moreton
Harknett's Gate
Jack's Hatch
Rye Hill
Canes Wood
Pedlars End
Tyler's Green
Reynkyns Wood
Bovinger
Bobbingworth
Hall Wood
Round Spring
Lower Bobbingworth Green
Long Walk
Epping Green
Epping Upland
Thornwood Common
North Weald Airfield
North Weald Bassett
Miller's Grove
Dewley Wood
Pickle's Gardens
Orange Field Plantation
The Lower Forest
Roughtalley's Wood
Greensted Green
Greensted Wood
Ongar Wood
Chipping Ongar
Greensted
Cobbin's Brook
Gernon Bushes
Coopersale Common
High Wood
Ongar Park Wood
Birching Coppice
Toot Hill
Mount Wood
Hawkshill Wood
Epping
Colliers Hatch
Clatterford End
Rookery Wood
Gravelpit Wood
Tawney Common
Coopersale Street
Gaynes Park
Bell Common
Griffin's Wood
Ivy Chimneys
Stewards Green
Fiddlers Hamlet
Woodhatch
Knightsland Wood
Northlands Wood
Copthall Green
Mount End
Beachet Wood
Stanford Rivers
Warren Wood
Barber's Wood
Icehouse Wood
Little End
Hare Street
Long Plantation
Icehouse Plantation
Twentyacre Wood
Stable Shaw
Theydon Bois
Theydon Mount
Berwick Ham
Tenacre Wood
Aspen Wood
Navestock Park
Hobbs Cross
Red Wood
Redoak Wood
Theydon Garnon
Stapleford Tawney
Bob's Barn Wood
Birch Wood
Debden Green
Gaunt's Wood
Shales Mere
Langford Bottom
Broom Wood
Church Wood
Great Monk Wood
Cemy.
River Roding
Passingford Bridge
Navestock
Heronland Shaw
Long Shaw
Debden
Broadfield Shaw
Abridge
Ape's Grove
Stapleford Tawney Airfield
Curtismill Green
Alder Wood
Soapley's Wood
Great Wood
Deerbarn Wood
Sabine's Green
Loughton
Lambourne
Bentleyfield Wood
Horseman Side
Stapleford Abbotts
Navestock Common
Watton's Green
Waterhales
Clark's Wood
Nuper's Hatch
Wabbing's Plantation
Lambourne
ESSEX

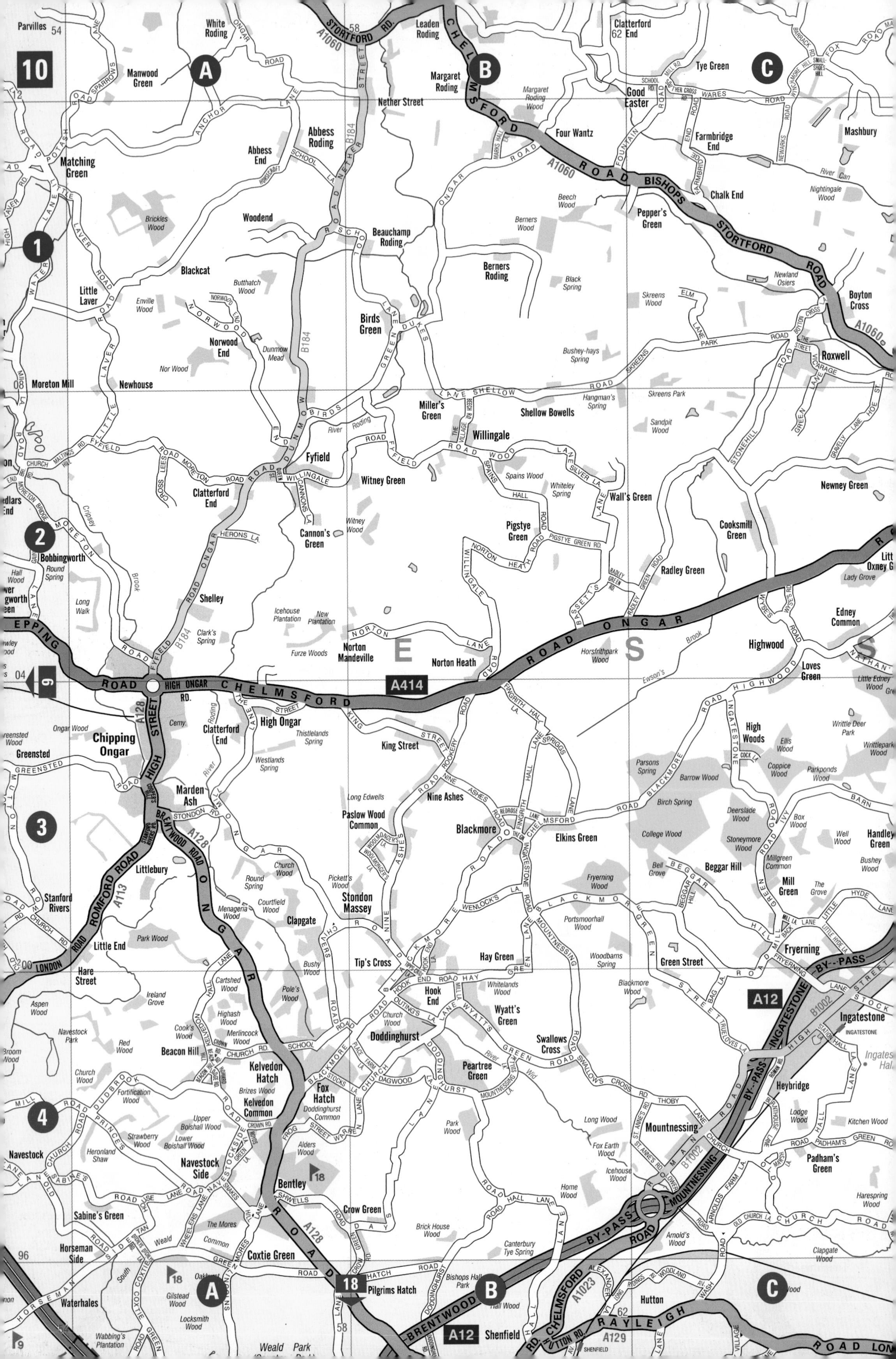
10
A
B
C
1
2
3
4
Parvilles
White Roding
Manwood Green
Leaden Roding
Margaret Roding
Clatterford End
Tye Green
Nether Street
Good Easter
Four Wantz
Farmbridge End
Mashbury
Matching Green
Abbess Roding
Abbess End
Chalk End
Pepper's Green
Brickles Wood
Woodend
Beauchamp Roding
Berners Roding
Blackcat
Little Laver
Butthatch Wood
Enville Wood
Birds Green
Boyton Cross
Norwood End
Dunmow Mead
Nor Wood
Roxwell
Moreton Mill
Newhouse
Miller's Green
Shellow Bowells
Willingale
Fyfield
Witney Green
Clatterford End
Spains Wood
Whiteley Spring
Wall's Green
Newney Green
Bobbingworth
Cannon's Green
Witney Wood
Pigstye Green
Cooksmill Green
Radley Green
Shelley
Icehouse Plantation
New Plantation
Norton Mandeville
Norton Heath
Horsfrithpark Wood
Highwood
Edney Common
Loves Green
A414
CHELMSFORD ROAD
ONGAR ROAD
Chipping Ongar
High Ongar
King Street
Greensted
Ongar Wood
Clatterford End
Thistlelands Spring
Westlands Spring
High Woods
Marden Ash
Nine Ashes
Blackmore
Elkins Green
Paslow Wood Common
Long Edwells
Littlebury
Stanford Rivers
Stondon Massey
Clapgate
Beggar Hill
Mill Green
Handley Green
Fryerning
Little End
Park Wood
Tip's Cross
Hay Green
Green Street
Hare Street
Hook End
Wyatt's Green
Doddinghurst
Swallows Cross
A12
Ingatestone
Beacon Hill
Kelvedon Hatch
Kelvedon Common
Fox Hatch
Peartree Green
Heybridge
Mountnessing
Navestock
Navestock Side
Padham's Green
Bentley
Sabine's Green
Crow Green
Coxtie Green
Horseman Side
Waterhales
Pilgrims Hatch
Hutton
Shenfield
Weald Park
A128
A113
A1060
B184
A129
A1023
18
9

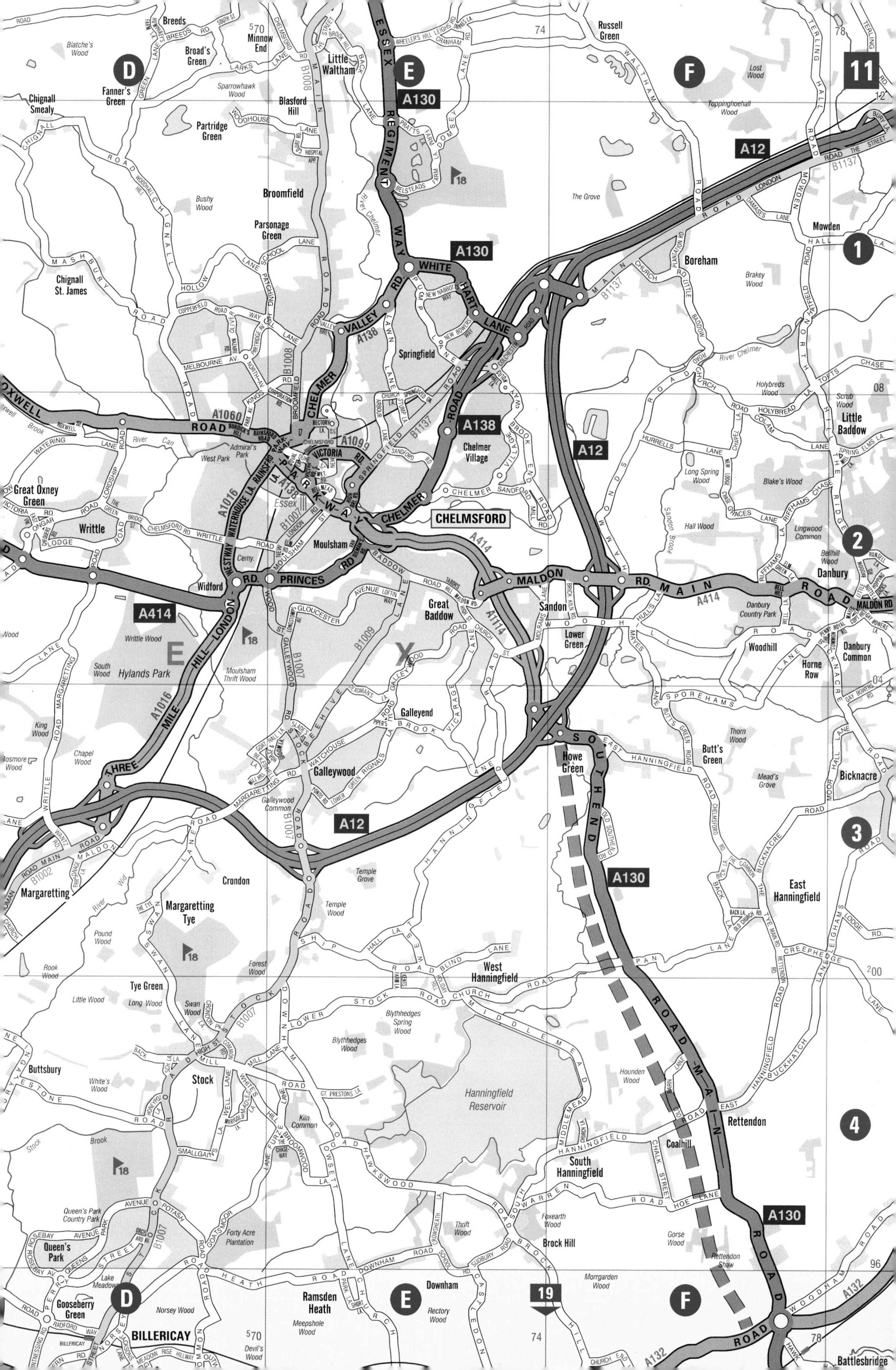
D
E
F
1
2
3
4
570
74
78
12
08
04
200
96
Breeds
Minnow End
Broad's Green
Blatche's Wood
Fanner's Green
Chignall Smealy
Sparrowhawk Wood
Little Waltham
Blasford Hill
Partridge Green
Russell Green
Lost Wood
Toppinghoehall Wood
A130
A12
B1137
B1008
Broomfield
Bushy Wood
Parsonage Green
The Grove
Mowden
Boreham
Brakey Wood
Chignall St. James
Springfield
River Chelmer
Holybreds Wood
Scrub Wood
Little Baddow
A138
A1060
A1099
A414
A1016
A1114
B1007
B1009
Great Oxney Green
Writtle
West Park
Admiral's Park
Chelmer Village
CHELMSFORD
Moulsham
Widford
Cemy.
Essex
Sandon
Long Spring Wood
Hall Wood
Blake's Wood
Lingwood Common
Bellhill Wood
Danbury
Danbury Country Park
Great Baddow
Lower Green
Woodhill
Horne Row
Danbury Common
Writtle Wood
South Wood
Hylands Park
Moulsham Thrift Wood
King Wood
Bosmore Wood
Chapel Wood
Galleyend
Galleywood
Galleywood Common
Howe Green
Thorn Wood
Butt's Green
Mead's Grove
Bicknacre
Margaretting
Crondon
Temple Grove
Temple Wood
East Hanningfield
Margaretting Tye
Pound Wood
Rook Wood
Forest Wood
West Hanningfield
Tye Green
Little Wood
Long Wood
Swan Wood
Blythhedges Spring Wood
Blythhedges Wood
Buttsbury
Stock
White's Wood
Hounden Wood
Hanningfield Reservoir
Kiln Common
Rettendon
Coalhill
South Hanningfield
Queen's Park Country Park
Queen's Park
Forty Acre Plantation
Thrift Wood
Foxearth Wood
Brock Hill
Gorse Wood
Rettendon Shaw
Lake Meadow
Gooseberry Green
Norsey Wood
BILLERICAY
Ramsden Heath
Meepshole Wood
Downham
Rectory Wood
Morrgarden Wood
Devil's Wood
Battlesbridge
A132
19

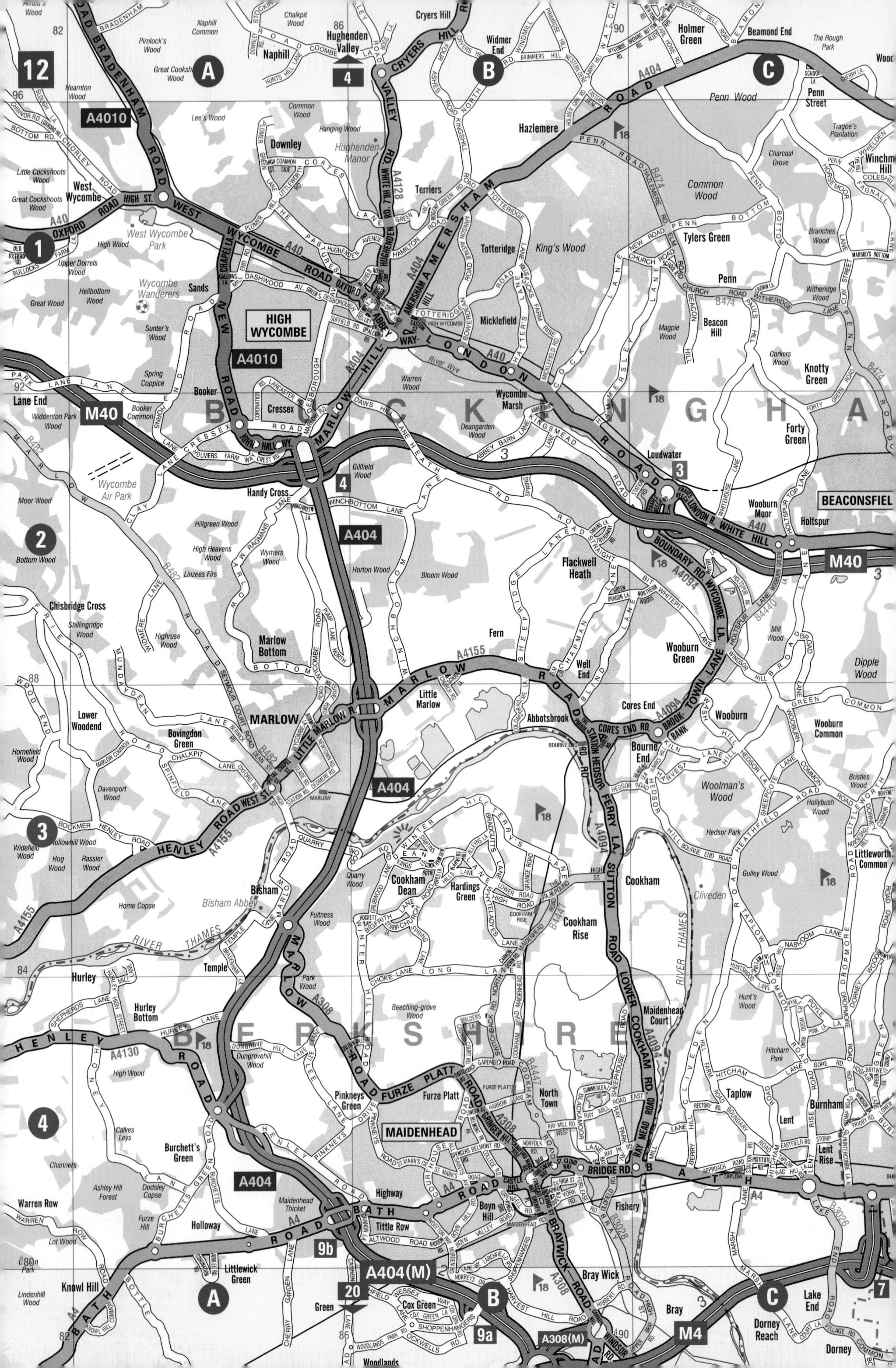

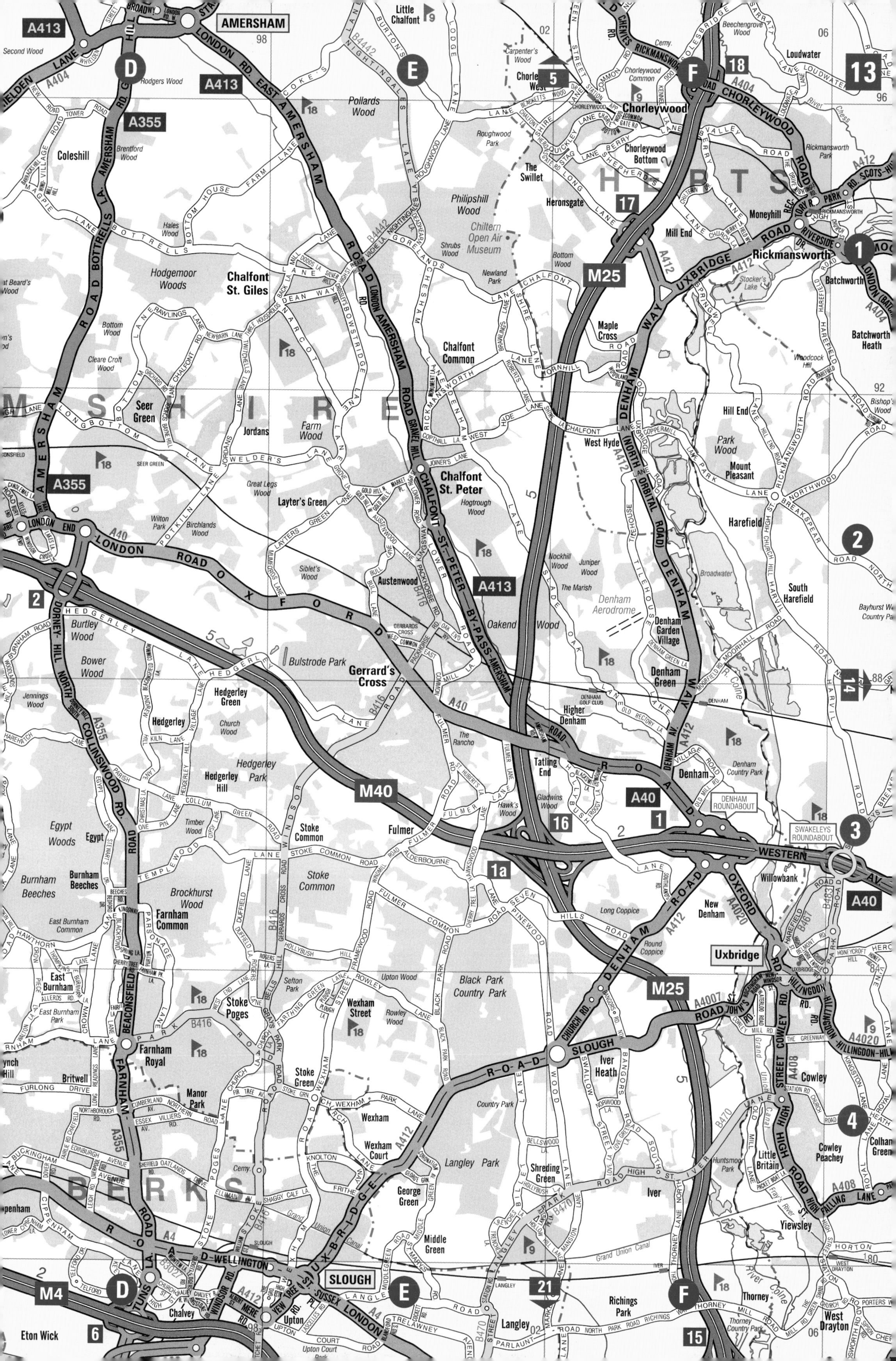
13
AMERSHAM
A413
A404
A355
A412
A40
A413
M25
M40
M4
A4
A4020
A4007
A408
B416
B470
B4442
B483
B467
B3027
Little Chalfont
Second Wood
Rodgers Wood
Coleshill
Brentford Wood
Pollards Wood
Carpenter's Wood
Chorleywood
Chorleywood Common
Chorleywood Bottom
Beechengrove Wood
Loudwater
Rickmansworth Park
Roughwood Park
The Swillet
Heronsgate
Philipshill Wood
Chiltern Open Air Museum
Shrubs Wood
Newland Park
Bottom Wood
Hales Wood
Hodgemoor Woods
Chalfont St. Giles
Moneyhill
Mill End
Rickmansworth
Batchworth
Stocker's Lake
Batchworth Heath
Maple Cross
Chalfont Common
Woodcock Hill
Bottom Wood
Cleare Croft Wood
Seer Green
Jordans
Farm Wood
West Hyde
Hill End
Park Wood
Mount Pleasant
Bishop's Wood
HERTS
Chalfont St. Peter
Great Legs Wood
Layter's Green
Hogtrough Wood
Wilton Park
Birchlands Wood
Harefield
South Harefield
Nockhill Wood
Juniper Wood
The Marish
Broadwater
Denham Aerodrome
Siblet's Wood
Austenwood
Burtley Wood
Bower Wood
Bulstrode Park
Gerrard's Cross
Oakend Wood
Denham Garden Village
Denham Green
Bayhurst Wood Country Park
Jennings Wood
Hedgerley Green
Hedgerley
Church Wood
Higher Denham
The Rancho
Tatling End
Denham
Denham Country Park
Hedgerley Park
Hedgerley Hill
Gladwins Wood
Hawk's Wood
DENHAM ROUNDABOUT
SWAKELEYS ROUNDABOUT
Egypt Woods
Egypt
Timber Wood
Stoke Common
Fulmer
Burnham Beeches
Brockhurst Wood
Willowbank
East Burnham Common
Farnham Common
Long Coppice
New Denham
Round Coppice
Uxbridge
East Burnham
Sefton Park
Upton Wood
Black Park Country Park
East Burnham Park
Stoke Poges
Wexham Street
Rowley Wood
Farnham Royal
Iver Heath
Cowley
Britwell
Manor Park
Stoke Green
Wexham
Country Park
Wexham Court
Langley Park
Shredding Green
Little Britain
Huntsmoor Park
Cowley Peachey
BERKS
George Green
Iver
Yiewsley
Middle Green
Grand Union Canal
Chalvey
SLOUGH
Upton
Upton Court Park
Richings Park
Thorney
Thorney Country Park
West Drayton
Langley
Eton Wick

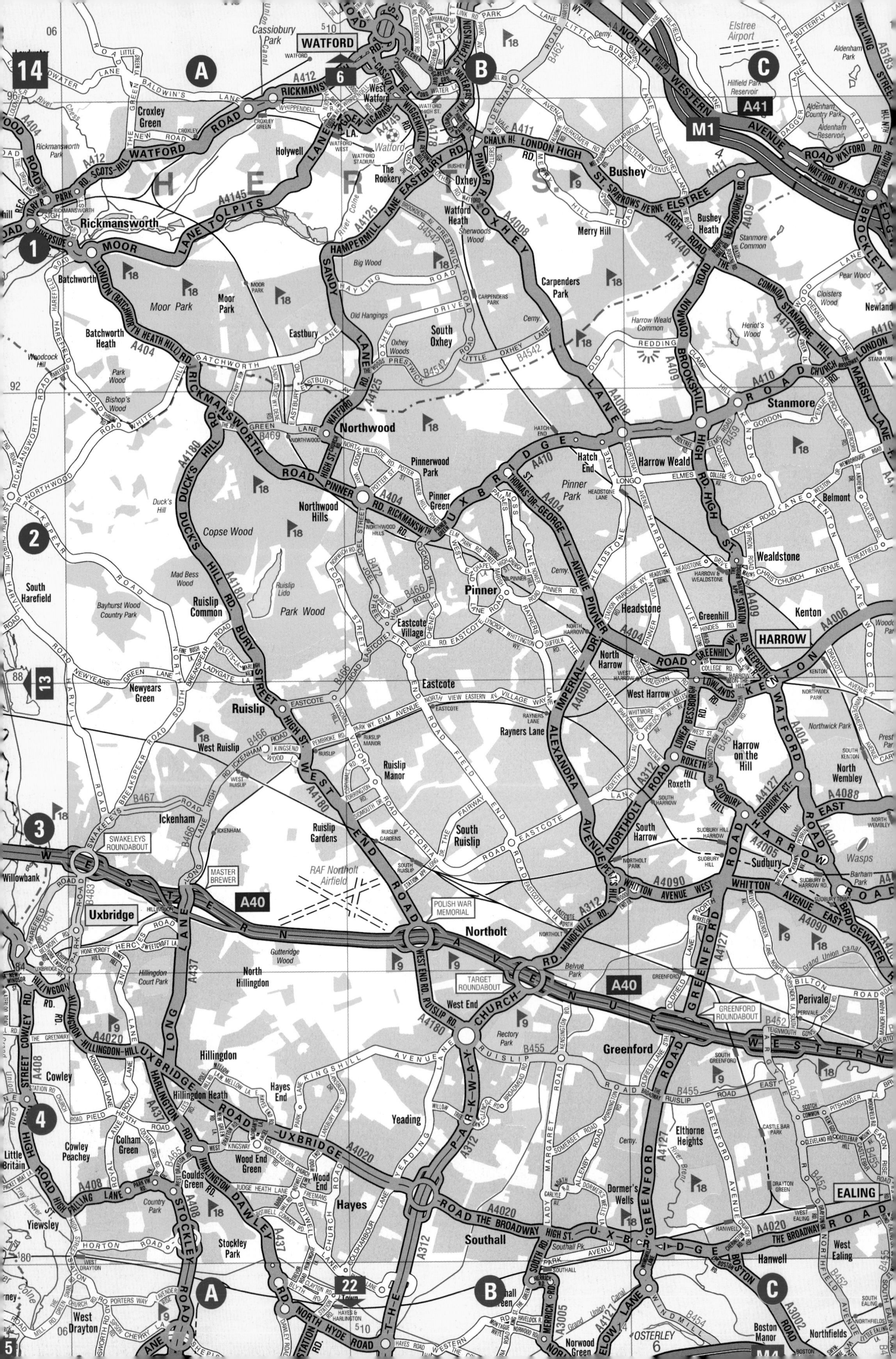
14
WATFORD
Cassiobury Park
Croxley Green
Rickmansworth
Batchworth
Batchworth Heath
Moor Park
Eastbury
Holywell
West Watford
The Rookery
Oxhey
South Oxhey
Watford Heath
Bushey
Bushey Heath
Merry Hill
Carpenders Park
Stanmore
Stanmore Common
Harrow Weald
Hatch End
Elstree Airport
Hilfield Park Reservoir
Aldenham Park
Aldenham Country Park
Aldenham Reservoir
Northwood
Northwood Hills
Pinnerwood Park
Pinner Green
Pinner
Pinner Park
Headstone
Wealdstone
Belmont
Kenton
HARROW
Harrow on the Hill
North Harrow
West Harrow
Rayners Lane
Eastcote
Eastcote Village
Ruislip
Ruislip Common
Ruislip Manor
Ruislip Gardens
South Ruislip
West Ruislip
Ickenham
Newyears Green
South Harefield
Copse Wood
Park Wood
Ruislip Lido
Bayhurst Wood Country Park
Mad Bess Wood
Duck's Hill
Northwick Park
North Wembley
Sudbury
Wasps
Roxeth
South Harrow
Northolt
RAF Northolt Airfield
POLISH WAR MEMORIAL
TARGET ROUNDABOUT
SWAKELEYS ROUNDABOUT
MASTER BREWER
GREENFORD ROUNDABOUT
Uxbridge
Willowbank
North Hillingdon
Hillingdon
Hillingdon Heath
Cowley
Cowley Peachey
Colham Green
Goulds Green
Wood End Green
Hayes End
Yeading
Hayes
Stockley Park
Yiewsley
West Drayton
Little Britain
Greenford
Perivale
Elthorne Heights
Dormer's Wells
Southall
West End
Rectory Park
Hanwell
West Ealing
EALING
Northfields
Boston Manor
Norwood Green
OSTERLEY
M1
A40
A41
M4
Grand Union Canal
River Colne
River Brent
H E R T S.

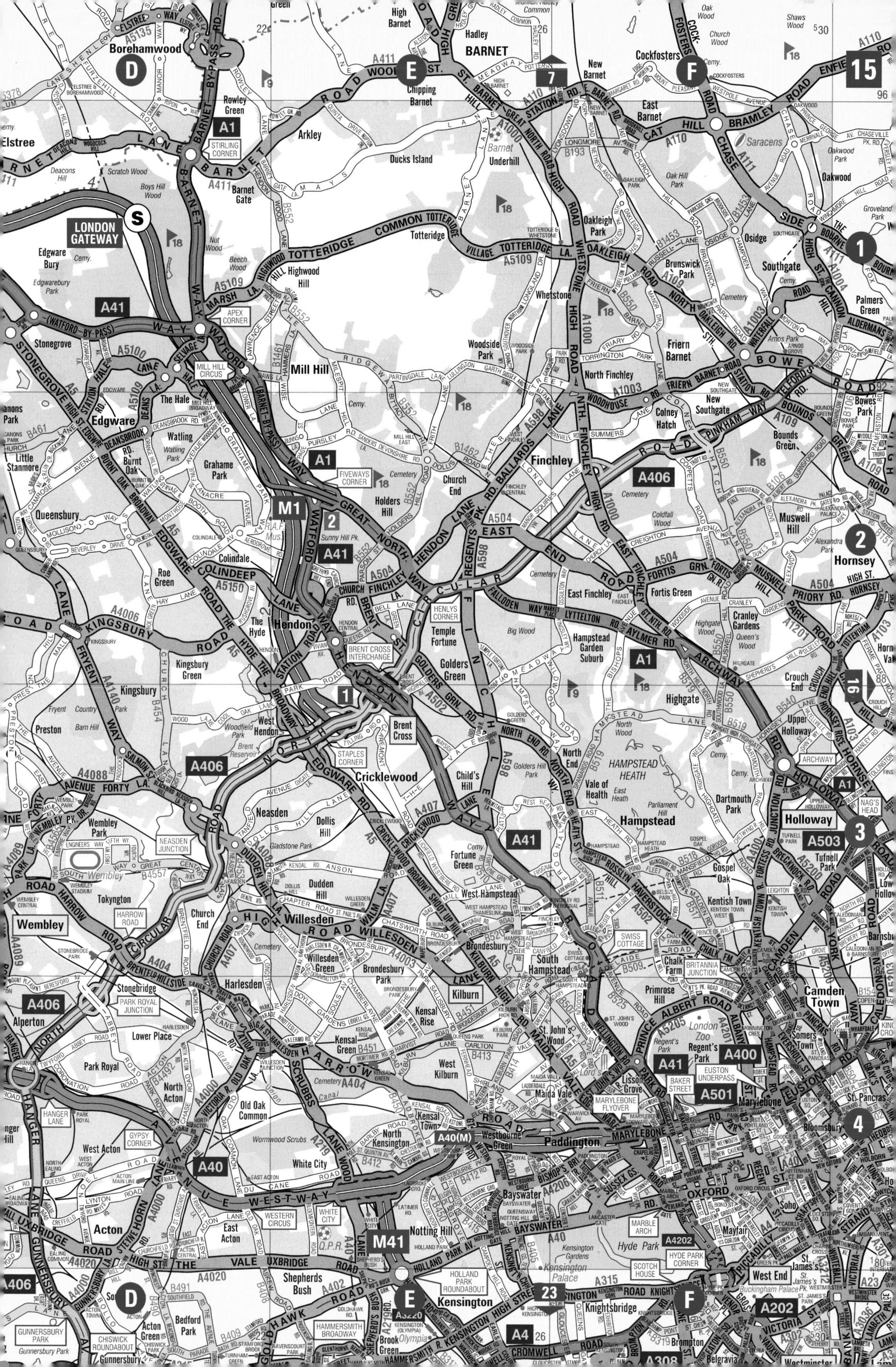

15
Borehamwood
Elstree
Rowley Green
Arkley
Chipping Barnet
High Barnet
Hadley
BARNET
New Barnet
Cockfosters
East Barnet
Barnet Gate
Ducks Island
Underhill
Totteridge
Oakleigh Park
Osidge
Southgate
Oakwood
Palmers Green
Brunswick Park
Whetstone
Woodside Park
Friern Barnet
North Finchley
New Southgate
Bowes Park
Bounds Green
Colney Hatch
Finchley
Church End
Mill Hill
Highwood Hill
LONDON GATEWAY
Edgware Bury
Stonegrove
Edgware
The Hale
Little Stanmore
Burnt Oak
Watling Park
Grahame Park
Holders Hill
Queensbury
Colindale
Roe Green
Hendon
The Hyde
Kingsbury Green
Kingsbury
Preston
West Hendon
Temple Fortune
Golders Green
Hampstead Garden Suburb
East Finchley
Fortis Green
Muswell Hill
Hornsey
Crouch End
Highgate
Upper Holloway
Brent Cross
Cricklewood
Child's Hill
North End
Vale of Health
HAMPSTEAD HEATH
Hampstead
Dartmouth Park
Holloway
Tufnell Park
Gospel Oak
Kentish Town
Neasden
Dollis Hill
Wembley Park
Wembley
Tokyngton
Dudden Hill
Willesden
Church End
Fortune Green
West Hampstead
Brondesbury
South Hampstead
Chalk Farm
Primrose Hill
Camden Town
Somers Town
St. Pancras
Bloomsbury
Willesden Green
Brondesbury Park
Kilburn
Kensal Rise
Harlesden
Stonebridge
Alperton
Lower Place
Park Royal
North Acton
Kensal Green
West Kilburn
St. John's Wood
Maida Vale
Lisson Grove
Regent's Park
Marylebone
Paddington
Westbourne Green
Kensal Town
North Kensington
Old Oak Common
White City
West Acton
Acton
East Acton
Notting Hill
Bayswater
OXFORD
Soho
Mayfair
Hyde Park
Kensington Gardens
Kensington Palace
West End
St. James's
Shepherds Bush
Kensington
Knightsbridge
Brompton
Bedford Park
Acton Green
Gunnersbury
Brook Green
Belgravia
A1
A41
A406
A5
M1
A40
A40(M)
M41
A400
A501
A503
A504
A598
A1000
A109
A110
A111
A4
A202
A315
A4020
A4000

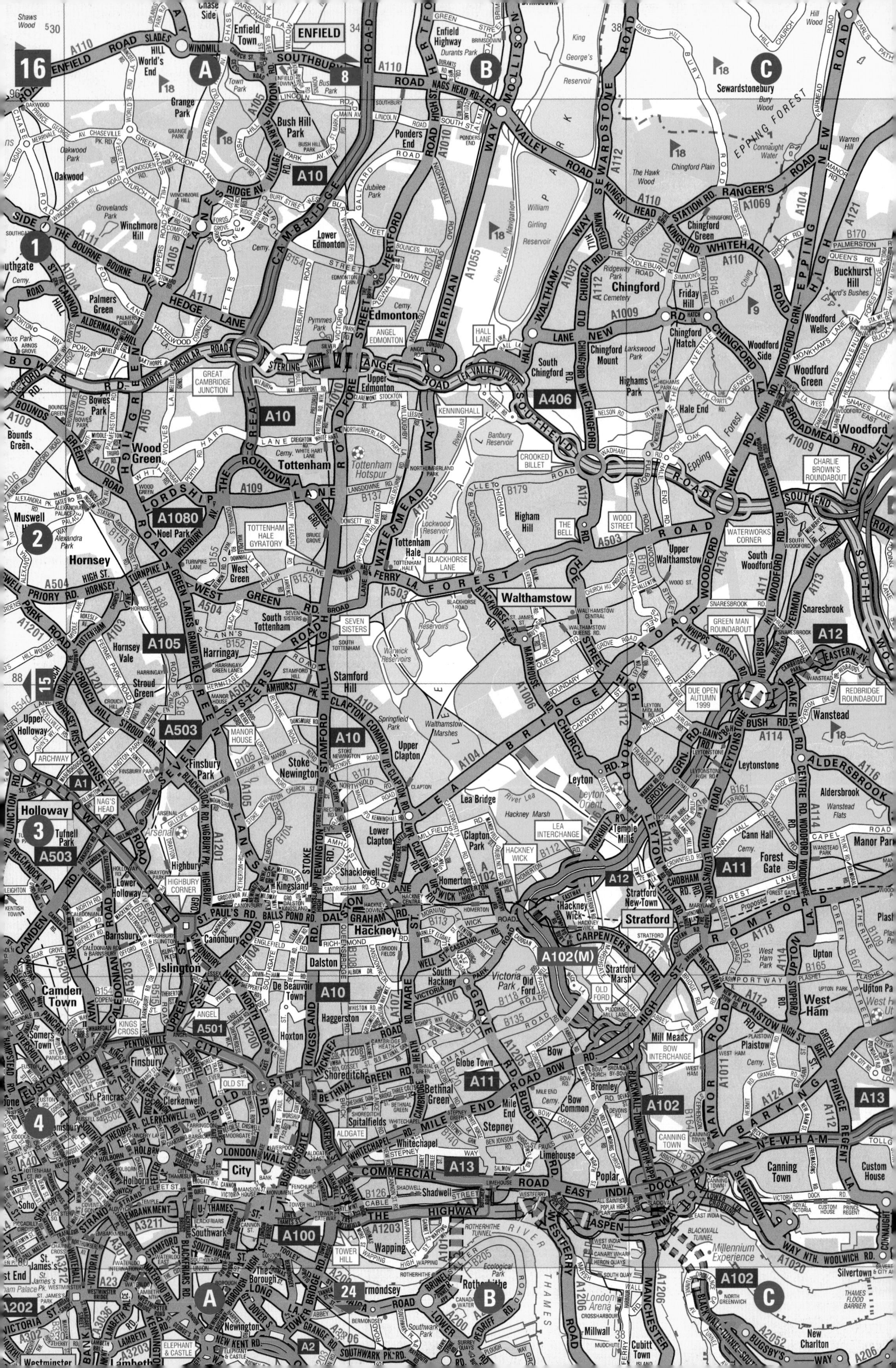
16
15
8
24
A
B
C
1
2
3
4
ENFIELD
Enfield Town
Enfield Highway
Durants Park
Southbury
World's End
Grange Park
Bush Hill Park
Ponders End
King George's Reservoir
Sewardstonebury
Bury Wood
EPPING FOREST
Connaught Water
Chingford Plain
The Hawk Wood
Oakwood
Winchmore Hill
Grovelands Park
Lower Edmonton
Jubilee Park
William Girling Reservoir
River Lee Navigation
Chingford Green
Chingford
Ridgeway Park
Friday Hill
Buckhurst Hill
Lord's Bushes
Southgate
Palmers Green
Edmonton
Pymmes Park
ANGEL EDMONTON
HALL LANE
South Chingford
Chingford Mount
Larkswood Park
Chingford Hatch
Woodford Wells
Woodford Side
Woodford Green
Woodford
Highams Park
Hale End
Epping Forest
Bowes Park
Bounds Green
GREAT CAMBRIDGE JUNCTION
Upper Edmonton
KENNINGHALL
Banbury Reservoir
CROOKED BILLET
CHARLIE BROWN'S ROUNDABOUT
Wood Green
Tottenham
Tottenham Hotspur
Muswell Hill
Alexandra Park
Hornsey
Noel Park
TOTTENHAM HALE GYRATORY
West Green
Tottenham Hale
BLACKHORSE LANE
Lockwood Reservoir
Higham Hill
THE BELL
WOOD STREET
WATERWORKS CORNER
Upper Walthamstow
South Woodford
Walthamstow
SEVEN SISTERS
South Tottenham
Harringay
Hornsey Vale
Stroud Green
Stamford Hill
Warwick Reservoirs
GREEN MAN ROUNDABOUT
Snaresbrook
REDBRIDGE ROUNDABOUT
Wanstead
DUE OPEN AUTUMN 1999
Upper Holloway
ARCHWAY
MANOR HOUSE
Springfield Park
Walthamstow Marshes
Upper Clapton
Stoke Newington
Finsbury Park
Leyton
Leyton Orient
Lea Bridge
Hackney Marsh
Leytonstone
Aldersbrook
Wanstead Flats
Holloway
NAG'S HEAD
Tufnell Park
Arsenal
Lower Clapton
Clapton Park
LEA INTERCHANGE
Temple Mills
HACKNEY WICK
Canning Hall
Forest Gate
Manor Park
Highbury
HIGHBURY CORNER
Lower Holloway
Kingsland
Shacklewell
Homerton
Hackney Wick
Stratford New Town
Stratford
Dalston
Hackney
Barnsbury
Canonbury
Islington
Camden Town
De Beauvoir Town
Haggerston
Victoria Park
Old Ford
OLD FORD
Stratford Marsh
West Ham Park
Upton
Plashet
Upton Park
West Ham
Somers Town
KINGS CROSS
ANGEL
Hoxton
Pentonville
Finsbury
Clerkenwell
Shoreditch
Bethnal Green
Globe Town
Bow
Mill Meads
BOW INTERCHANGE
Plaistow
EUSTON
St. Pancras
Bloomsbury
Spitalfields
ALDGATE
Whitechapel
Mile End
Stepney
Bow Common
Bromley
Limehouse
Poplar
CANNING TOWN
Canning Town
Custom House
Holborn
LONDON WALL
City
Shadwell
Soho
Southwark
TOWER HILL
Wapping
Rotherhithe Tunnel
Blackwall Tunnel
Millennium Experience
Ecological Park
Rotherhithe
Bermondsey
The Borough
Canada Water
Southwark Park
London Arena
Crossharbour
Millwall
Mudchute
Cubitt Town
North Greenwich
Silvertown
Thames Flood Barrier
New Charlton
St. James's
Westminster
Lambeth
Newington
ELEPHANT & CASTLE
Surrey Quays
RIVER THAMES
A10
A406
A1080
A105
A503
A1
A12
A11
A13
A102(M)
A102
A501
A100
A2
A202
A110
A1009
A104
A112
A114
A116
A118
NORTH CIRCULAR ROAD
COMMERCIAL ROAD
THE HIGHWAY
EAST INDIA DOCK RD.
MILE END RD.
ROMFORD ROAD
FOREST ROAD
LEA BRIDGE ROAD
SEVEN SISTERS ROAD
GREEN LANES
NEWHAM WAY
BARKING RD.

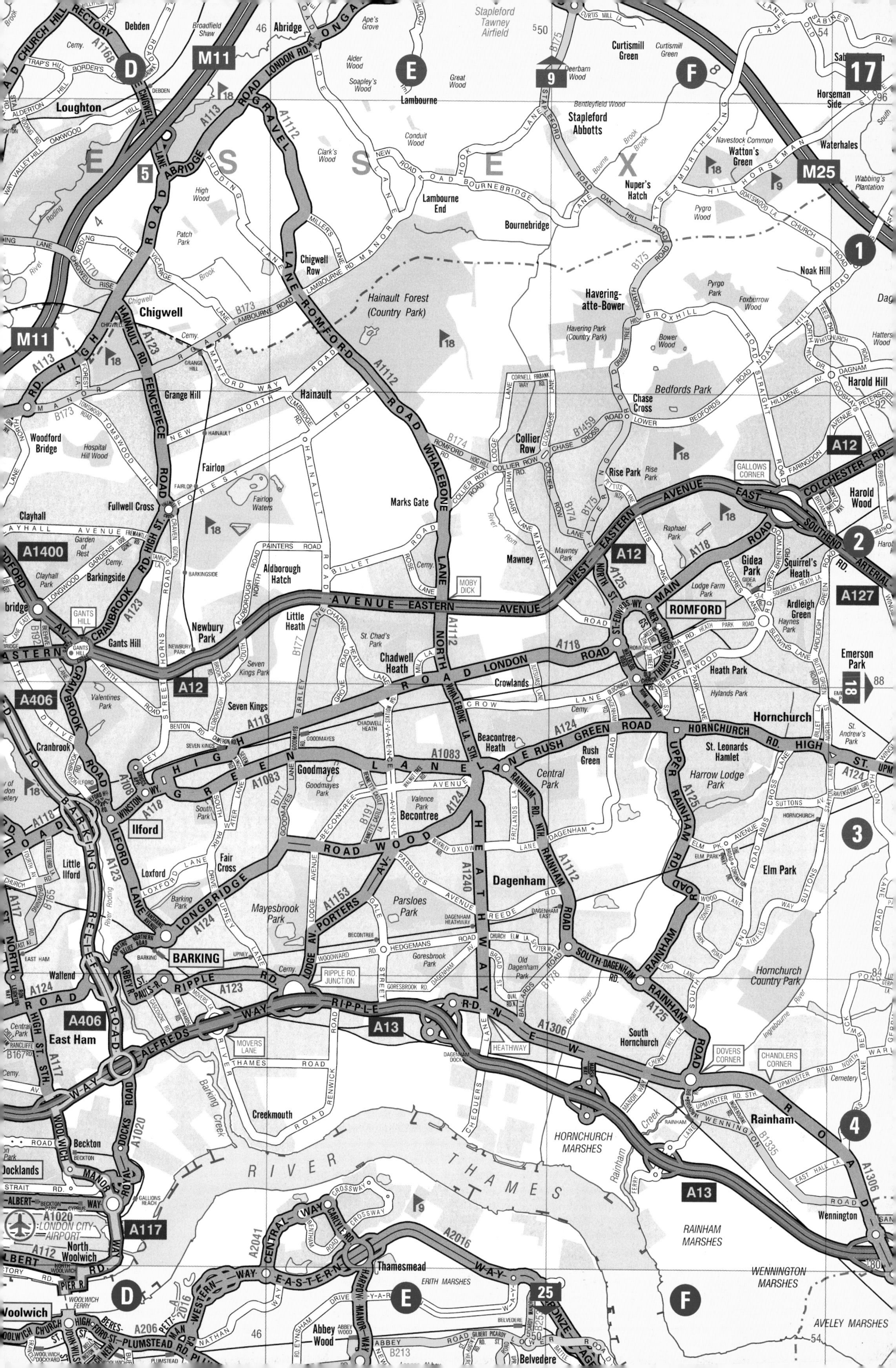

17
E S S E X
Debden
Abridge
Loughton
Chigwell
Chigwell Row
Lambourne
Lambourne End
Stapleford Abbotts
Stapleford Tawney Airfield
Curtismill Green
Bournebridge
Nuper's Hatch
Navestock Common
Watton's Green
Horseman Side
Waterhales
Noak Hill
Havering-atte-Bower
Hainault Forest (Country Park)
Hainault
Grange Hill
Woodford Bridge
Fairlop
Fullwell Cross
Clayhall
Barkingside
Gants Hill
Newbury Park
Aldborough Hatch
Marks Gate
Collier Row
Rise Park
Chase Cross
Bedfords Park
Harold Hill
Harold Wood
Gidea Park
Squirrel's Heath
Ardleigh Green
ROMFORD
Emerson Park
Hornchurch
Mawney
Little Heath
Chadwell Heath
Seven Kings
Crowlands
Goodmayes
Becontree
Beacontree Heath
Rush Green
St. Leonards Hamlet
Harrow Lodge Park
Elm Park
Ilford
Little Ilford
Loxford
Fair Cross
Dagenham
BARKING
East Ham
Wallend
Beckton
Creekmouth
South Hornchurch
Rainham
Wennington
Hornchurch Country Park
HORNCHURCH MARSHES
RAINHAM MARSHES
WENNINGTON MARSHES
AVELEY MARSHES
RIVER THAMES
North Woolwich
Woolwich
Thamesmead
ERITH MARSHES
Abbey Wood
Belvedere
LONDON CITY AIRPORT
M11
M25
A12
A13
A406
A1400
A127
A117

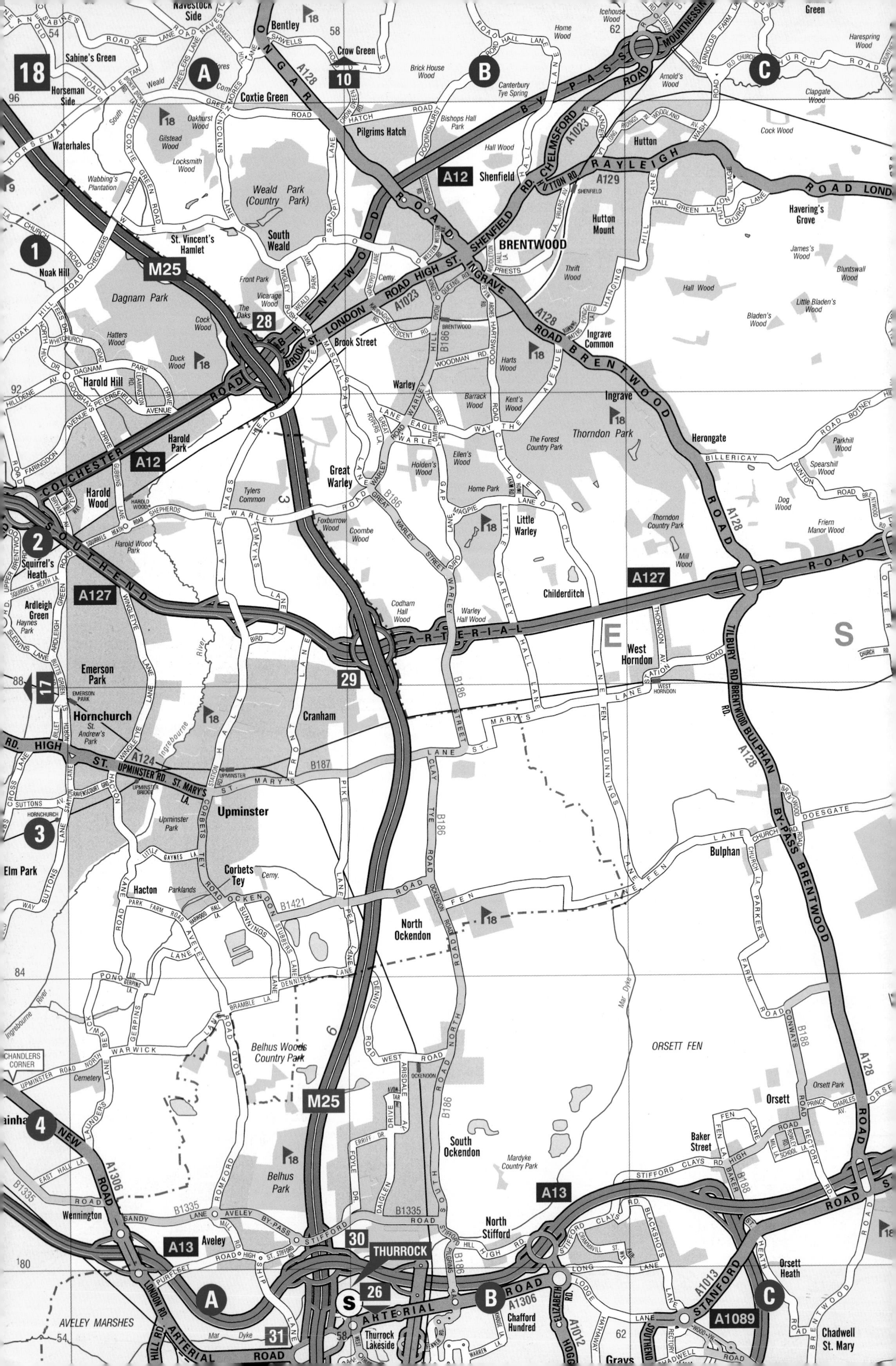

18
Navestock Side
Bentley
Crow Green
10
Sabine's Green
Horseman Side
Coxtie Green
Pilgrims Hatch
Shenfield
Hutton
Waterhales
Oakhurst Wood
Gilstead Wood
Locksmith Wood
Wabbing's Plantation
Weald Park (Country Park)
St. Vincent's Hamlet
South Weald
Noak Hill
Dagnam Park
Front Park
Vicarage Wood
The Oaks
28
Brook Street
Cock Wood
Hatters Wood
Duck Wood
Harold Hill
Harold Park
Harold Wood
Harold Wood Park
Squirrel's Heath
Ardleigh Green
Haynes Park
Emerson Park
Hornchurch
St. Andrew's Park
Upminster
Upminster Park
Corbets Tey
Hacton
Parklands
Elm Park
Tylers Common
Foxburrow Wood
Coombe Wood
Great Warley
Warley
Holden's Wood
Ellen's Wood
Barrack Wood
Kent's Wood
Harts Wood
Home Park
Little Warley
Codham Hall Wood
Warley Hall Wood
Childerditch
Cranham
29
BRENTWOOD
Hutton Mount
Thrift Wood
Ingrave Common
Ingrave
Thorndon Park
The Forest Country Park
Thorndon Country Park
Mill Wood
Herongate
Parkhill Wood
Spearshill Wood
Dog Wood
Friern Manor Wood
West Horndon
Havering's Grove
James's Wood
Bluntswall Wood
Hall Wood
Little Bladen's Wood
Bladen's Wood
Cock Wood
Clapgate Wood
Arnold's Wood
Haresping Wood
Icehouse Wood
Home Wood
Brick House Wood
Canterbury Tye Spring
Bishops Hall Park
Bulphan
North Ockendon
Belhus Woods Country Park
Orsett Fen
Orsett
Orsett Park
Baker Street
South Ockendon
Mardyke Country Park
Belhus Park
Wennington
Aveley
North Stifford
Chafford Hundred
Thurrock Lakeside
THURROCK
26
30
31
Aveley Marshes
Orsett Heath
Chadwell St. Mary
Grays
Chandlers Corner
Cemetery
M25
A12
A127
A128
A129
A1023
A124
A13
A1306
A1013
A1012
A1089
B186
B187
B1421
B1335
B188
17

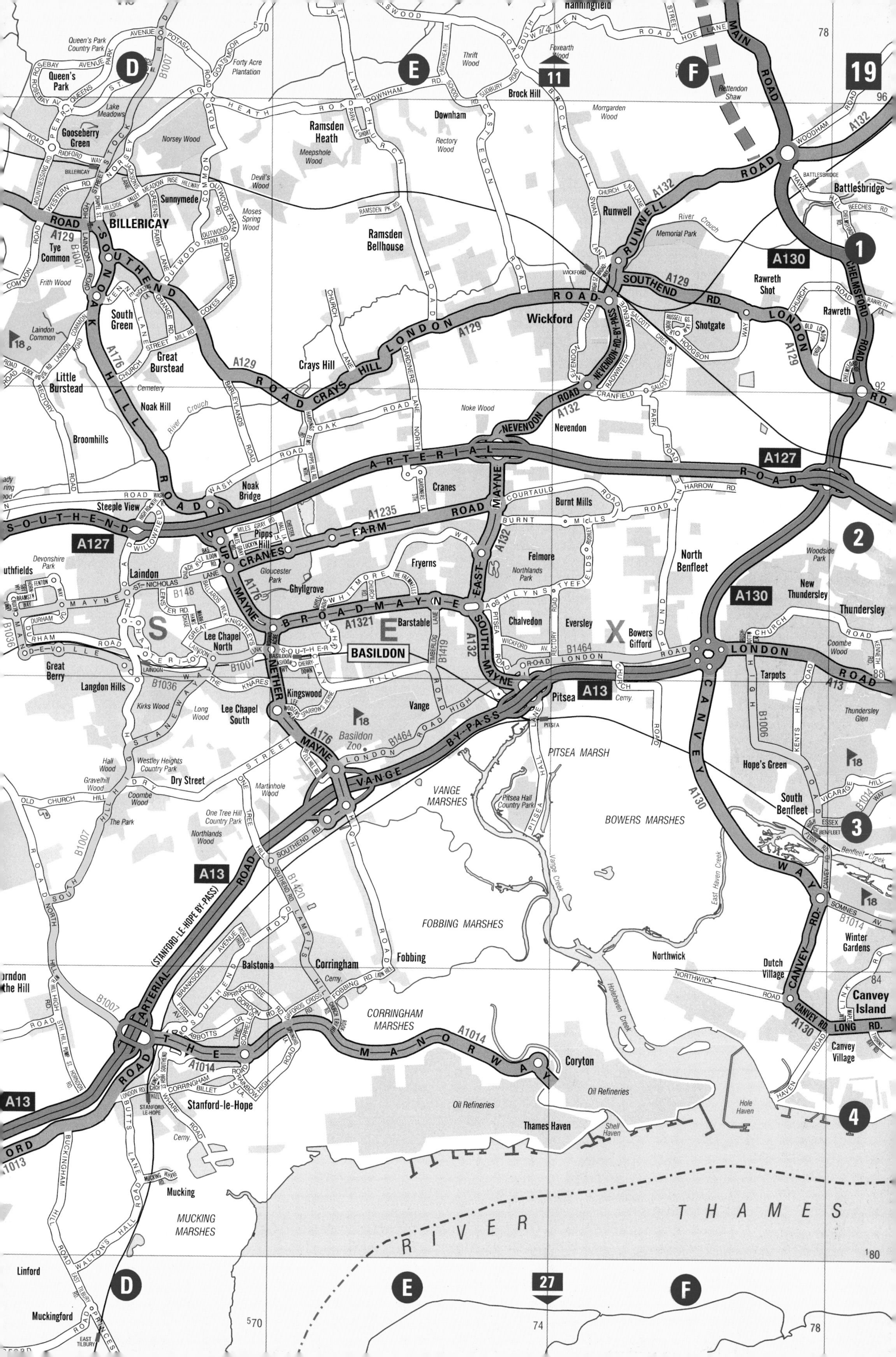

Queen's Park Country Park
Queen's Park
Gooseberry Green
Lake Meadows
Norsey Wood
Forty Acre Plantation
Ramsden Heath
Meepshole Wood
Downham
Rectory Wood
Thrift Wood
Foxearth Wood
Brock Hill
Rettendon Shaw
Morrgarden Wood
Battlesbridge
Sunnymede
BILLERICAY
Tye Common
Frith Wood
Devil's Wood
Moses Spring Wood
Ramsden Bellhouse
Runwell
Memorial Park
River Crouch
Rawreth Shot
Rawreth
Wickford
Shotgate
South Green
Laindon Common
Great Burstead
Little Burstead
Cemetery
Noak Hill
Broomhills
Crays Hill
Noke Wood
Nevendon
Noak Bridge
Cranes
Burnt Mills
Steeple View
Pipps Hill
Devonshire Park
Laindon
Gloucester Park
Ghyllgrove
Fryerns
Felmore
Northlands Park
North Benfleet
Woodside Park
New Thundersley
Thundersley
Lee Chapel North
Barstable
BASILDON
Chalvedon
Eversley
Bowers Gifford
Coombe Wood
Great Berry
Langdon Hills
Kirks Wood
Long Wood
Lee Chapel South
Kingswood
Vange
Pitsea
Tarpots
Thundersley Glen
Basildon Zoo
Hall Wood
Westley Heights Country Park
Dry Street
Gravelhill Wood
Coombe Wood
The Park
Martinhole Wood
One Tree Hill Country Park
Northlands Wood
PITSEA MARSH
Pitsea Hall Country Park
VANGE MARSHES
BOWERS MARSHES
Hope's Green
South Benfleet
Benfleet Creek
FOBBING MARSHES
Balstonia
Corringham
Fobbing
Northwick
Winter Gardens
Dutch Village
Canvey Island
Canvey Village
CORRINGHAM MARSHES
Coryton
Oil Refineries
Thames Haven
Shell Haven
Hole Haven
Stanford-le-Hope
Mucking
MUCKING MARSHES
RIVER THAMES
Linford
Muckingford
A127
A129
A130
A132
A13
A176
A1235
A1321
A1014
B1007
B1464
27
11

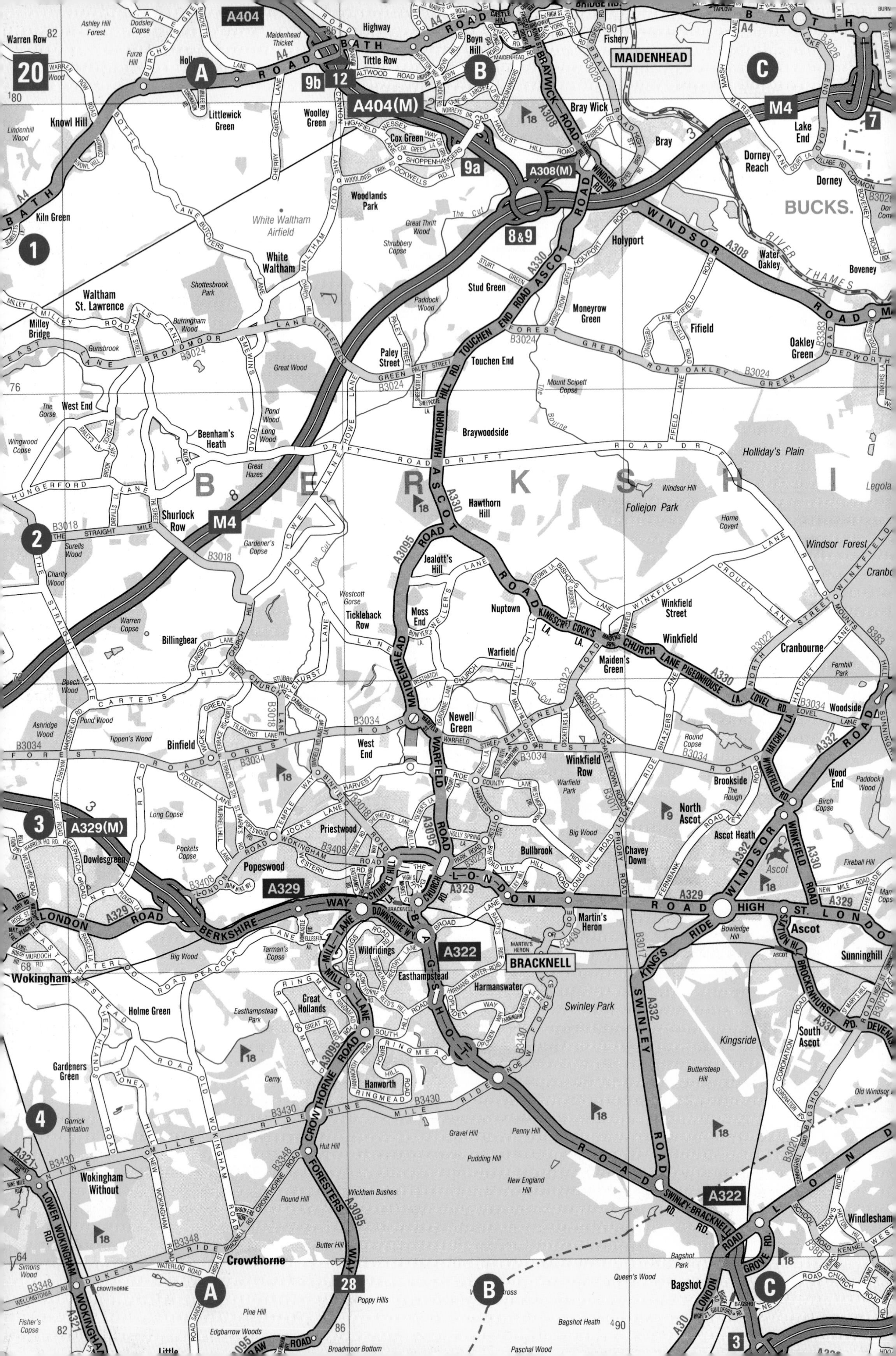

20
Warren Row
Ashley Hill Forest
Dodsley Copse
A404
Maidenhead Thicket
Highway
Boyn Hill
MAIDENHEAD
Fishery
Furze Hill
Holly
A
BATH ROAD
Tittle Row
9b
12
B
C
A4
Littlewick Green
Woolley Green
A404(M)
Knowl Hill
Lindenhill Wood
Cox Green
Bray Wick
Bray
M4
Lake End
Dorney Reach
Dorney
7
9a
A308(M)
BUCKS.
Kiln Green
White Waltham Airfield
Woodlands Park
Great Thrift Wood
The Cut
8&9
Holyport
1
Shrubbery Copse
White Waltham
Water Oakley
Boveney
RIVER THAMES
Waltham St. Lawrence
Shottesbrook Park
Stud Green
Moneyrow Green
Fifield
Milley Bridge
Burringham Wood
Paddock Wood
Gunsbrook
BROADMOOR LANE
B3024
Great Wood
Paley Street
Touchen End
Oakley Green
76
West End
The Gorse
Pond Wood
Long Wood
Mount Scipett Copse
The Bourne
Braywoodside
Wingwood Copse
Beenham's Heath
Great Hazes
DRIFT ROAD
Holliday's Plain
HUNGERFORD LANE
B E R K S H I
Hawthorn Hill
Windsor Hill
Foliejon Park
Legola
2
B3018
THE STRAIGHT MILE
Shurlock Row
M4
Surells Wood
Charity Wood
Gardener's Copse
Jealott's Hill
Home Covert
Windsor Forest
Cranbo
Warren Copse
Billingbear
Westcott Gorse
Tickleback Row
Moss End
Nuptown
Winkfield Street
Winkfield
Cranbourne
Warfield
Maiden's Green
Fernhill Park
Beech Wood
Ashridge Wood
Pond Wood
Tippen's Wood
Binfield
West End
Newell Green
Woodside
B3034
FOREST ROAD
Winkfield Row
Warfield Park
Round Copse
Brookside
The Rough
Wood End
Paddock Wood
Birch Copse
3
A329(M)
Long Copse
Priestwood
North Ascot
Ascot Heath
Dowlesgreen
Pockets Copse
Popeswood
Big Wood
Bullbrook
Chavey Down
Ascot
Fireball Hill
A329
LONDON ROAD
Martin's Heron
Bowledge Hill
Sunninghill
Wokingham
68
Big Wood
Tarman's Copse
Wildridings
A322
Easthampstead
BRACKNELL
Harmanswater
Holme Green
Great Hollands
Easthampstead Park
Swinley Park
South Ascot
Kingsride
Gardeners Green
Cemy.
Hanworth
Buttersteep Hill
Old Windsor
4
Gorrick Plantation
NINE MILE RIDE
B3430
Gravel Hill
Penny Hill
Hut Hill
Pudding Hill
Wokingham Without
New England Hill
Round Hill
Wickham Bushes
A322
Windlesham
Butter Hill
Bagshot Park
64
Simons Wood
Crowthorne
A
28
B
Queen's Wood
Bagshot
C
Poppy Hills
Pine Hill
Fisher's Copse
82
86
Edgbarrow Woods
Bagshot Heath
490
Broadmoor Bottom
Paschal Wood
3
A321
A3095
A30

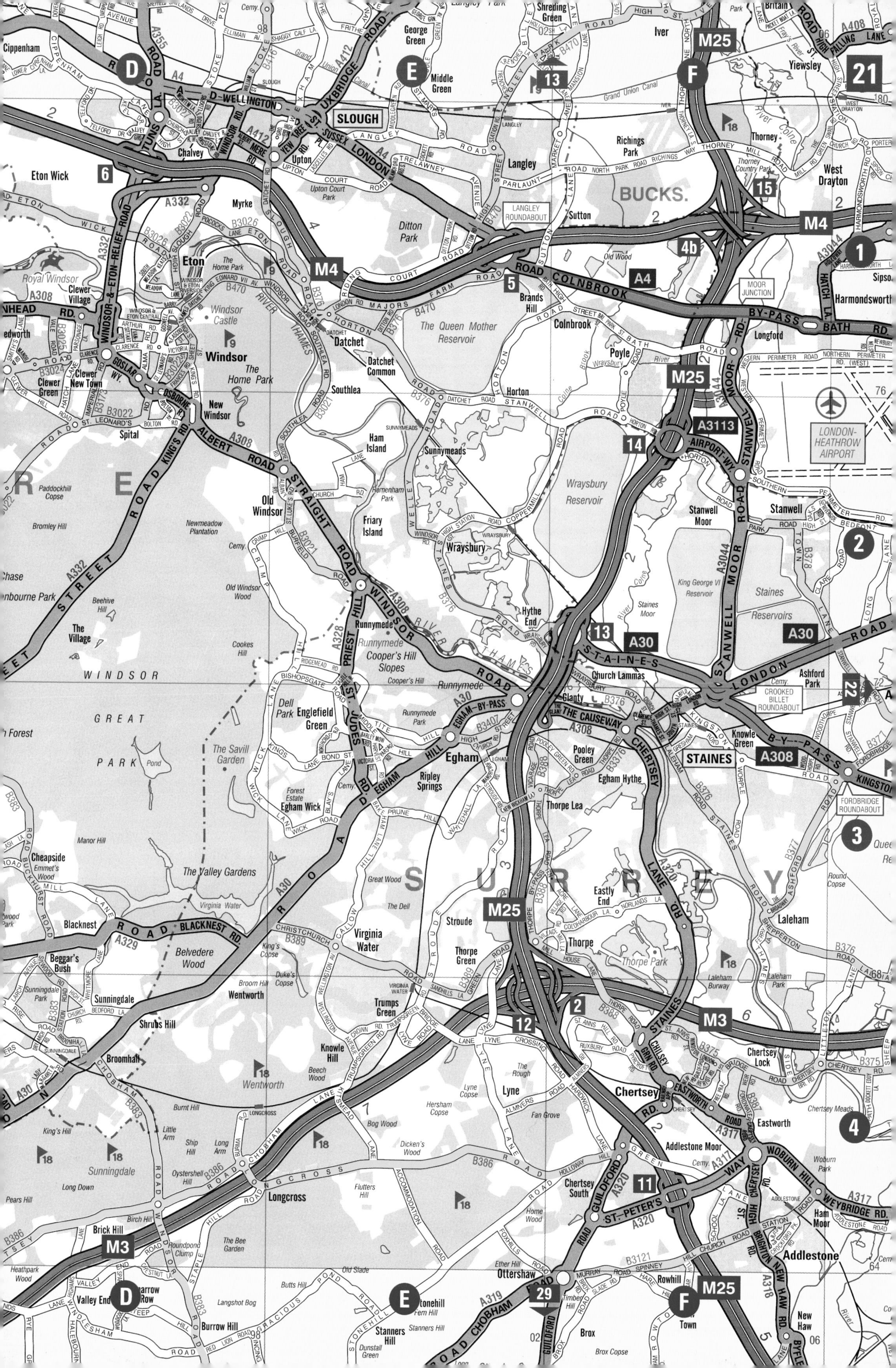

21
Cippenham
Slough
George Green
Middle Green
Iver
Shreding Green
Yiewsley
West Drayton
Thorney
Richings Park
Langley
Upton
Chalvey
Eton Wick
Eton
Myrke
Ditton Park
Sutton
BUCKS.
Colnbrook
Brands Hill
Poyle
Harmondsworth
Sipson
Longford
Royal Windsor
Clewer Village
Windsor
Windsor Castle
The Home Park
Datchet
Datchet Common
Southlea
Horton
The Queen Mother Reservoir
Clewer Green
Clewer New Town
New Windsor
Spital
Ham Island
Sunnymeads
Wraysbury Reservoir
LONDON-HEATHROW AIRPORT
Stanwell
Stanwell Moor
King George VI Reservoir
Staines Reservoirs
Staines Moor
Old Windsor
Friary Island
Wraysbury
Hythe End
Runnymede
Cooper's Hill Slopes
Ashford Park
CROOKED BILLET ROUNDABOUT
Church Lammas
Glanty
STAINES
Knowle Green
Pooley Green
Egham Hythe
Thorpe Lea
Egham
Englefield Green
Dell Park
Egham Wick
Ripley Springs
WINDSOR GREAT PARK
The Savill Garden
The Village
Cheapside
The Valley Gardens
Virginia Water
Blacknest
Beggar's Bush
Sunningdale
Belvedere Wood
Wentworth
Shrubs Hill
Broomhall
Great Wood
Stroude
Thorpe Green
Thorpe
Thorpe Park
Eastly End
Laleham
Laleham Burway
Laleham Park
SURREY
Trumps Green
Knowle Hill
Lyne
Chertsey
Chertsey Lock
Chertsey Meads
Eastworth
Addlestone Moor
Addlestone
Ham Moor
Woburn Park
Longcross
Chertsey South
Ottershaw
Rowhill
Brick Hill
Valley End
Burrow Hill
Stanners Hill
Brox
New Haw
FORDBRIDGE ROUNDABOUT
LANGLEY ROUNDABOUT
MOOR JUNCTION
M4
M25
M3
A30
A308
A4
A3113
22

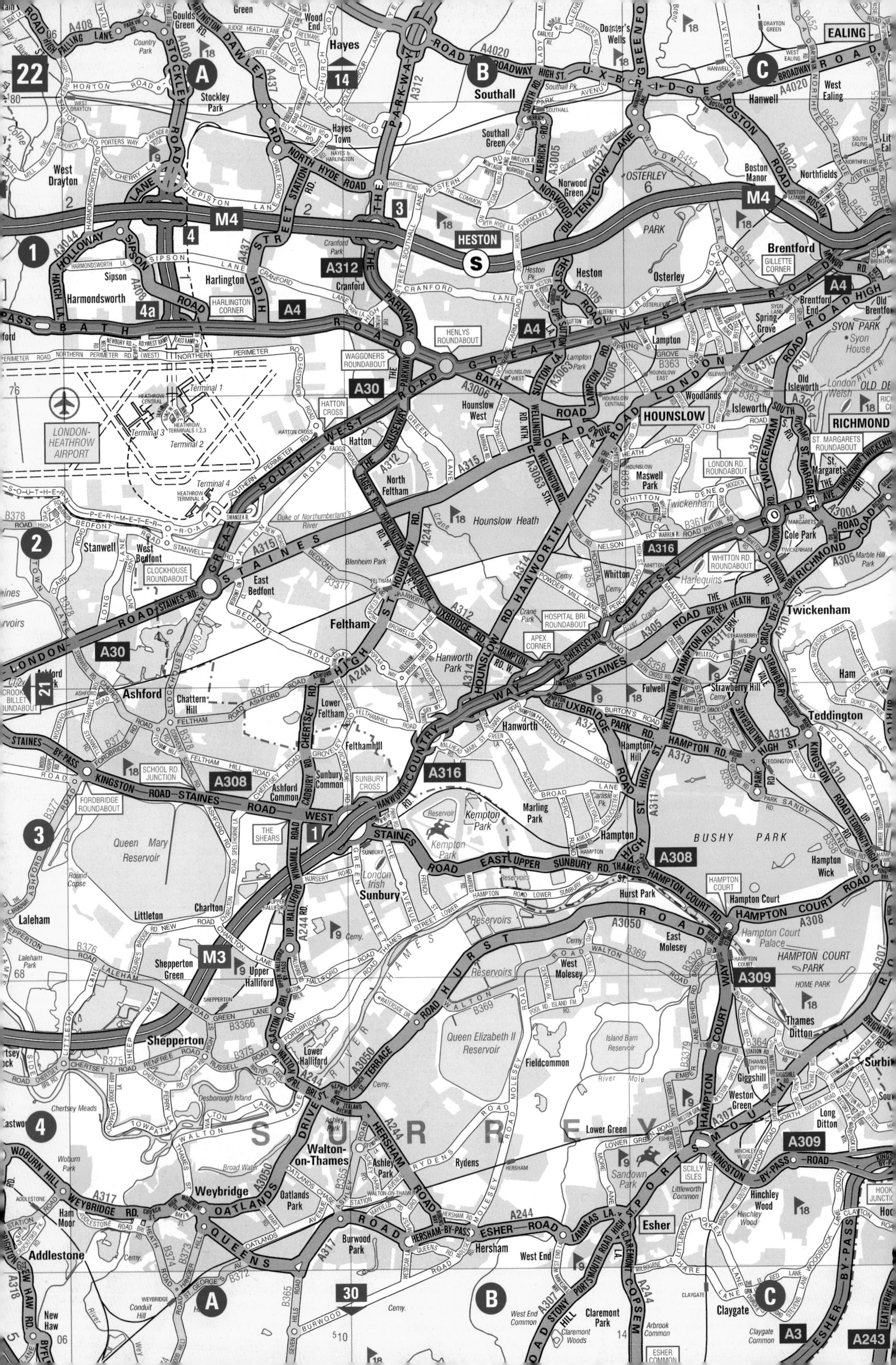

22
A
B
C
1
2
3
4
Hayes
14
30
21
M4
M3
A4
A30
A312
A316
A308
A309
A3
A243
S U R R E Y
EALING
Southall
Hanwell
West Ealing
Northfields
Boston Manor
Brentford
GILLETTE CORNER
Brentford End
Syon Park
Syon House
Old Isleworth
RICHMOND
ST. MARGARETS ROUNDABOUT
St. Margarets
Twickenham
Ham
Teddington
Hampton Wick
Bushy Park
Hampton Court
Hampton Court Palace
HAMPTON COURT PARK
HOME PARK
Thames Ditton
Giggshill
Weston Green
Long Ditton
Hinchley Wood
Claygate
Claygate Common
Esher
SCILLY ISLES
Littleworth Common
Sandown Park
Lower Green
Claremont Park
West End
West End Common
Arbrook Common
Hersham
Rydens
Walton-on-Thames
Ashley Park
Oatlands Park
Burwood Park
Weybridge
Addlestone
Ham Moor
New Haw
Woburn Park
Chertsey Meads
Desborough Island
Shepperton
Shepperton Green
Upper Halliford
Lower Halliford
Littleton
Charlton
Laleham
Laleham Park
Queen Mary Reservoir
Round Copse
Queen Elizabeth II Reservoir
Island Barn Reservoir
Fieldcommon
West Molesey
East Molesey
Hurst Park
Sunbury
Sunbury Common
SUNBURY CROSS
THE SHEARS
Kempton Park
Hampton
Hampton Hill
Marling Park
Hanworth
Feltham
Lower Feltham
Felthamhill
Hanworth Park
Ashford
Ashford Common
Chattern Hill
SCHOOL RD. JUNCTION
FORDBRIDGE ROUNDABOUT
CROOKED BILLET ROUNDABOUT
Stanwell
West Bedfont
CLOCKHOUSE ROUNDABOUT
East Bedfont
Hatton
HATTON CROSS
North Feltham
LONDON-HEATHROW AIRPORT
Terminal 1
Terminal 2
Terminal 3
Terminal 4
Hounslow Heath
Hounslow West
HOUNSLOW
Heston
HESTON
Osterley
OSTERLEY PARK
Lampton
Spring Grove
Isleworth
Woodlands
Maswell Park
LONDON RD. ROUNDABOUT
Whitton
WHITTON RD. ROUNDABOUT
Harlequins
Cole Park
Crane Park
HOSPITAL BRI. ROUNDABOUT
APEX CORNER
Fulwell
Strawberry Hill
HENLYS ROUNDABOUT
WAGGONERS ROUNDABOUT
Cranford
Cranford Park
Harlington
HARLINGTON CORNER
Sipson
Harmondsworth
West Drayton
Stockley Park
Hayes Town
Southall Green
Norwood Green
Dormer's Wells

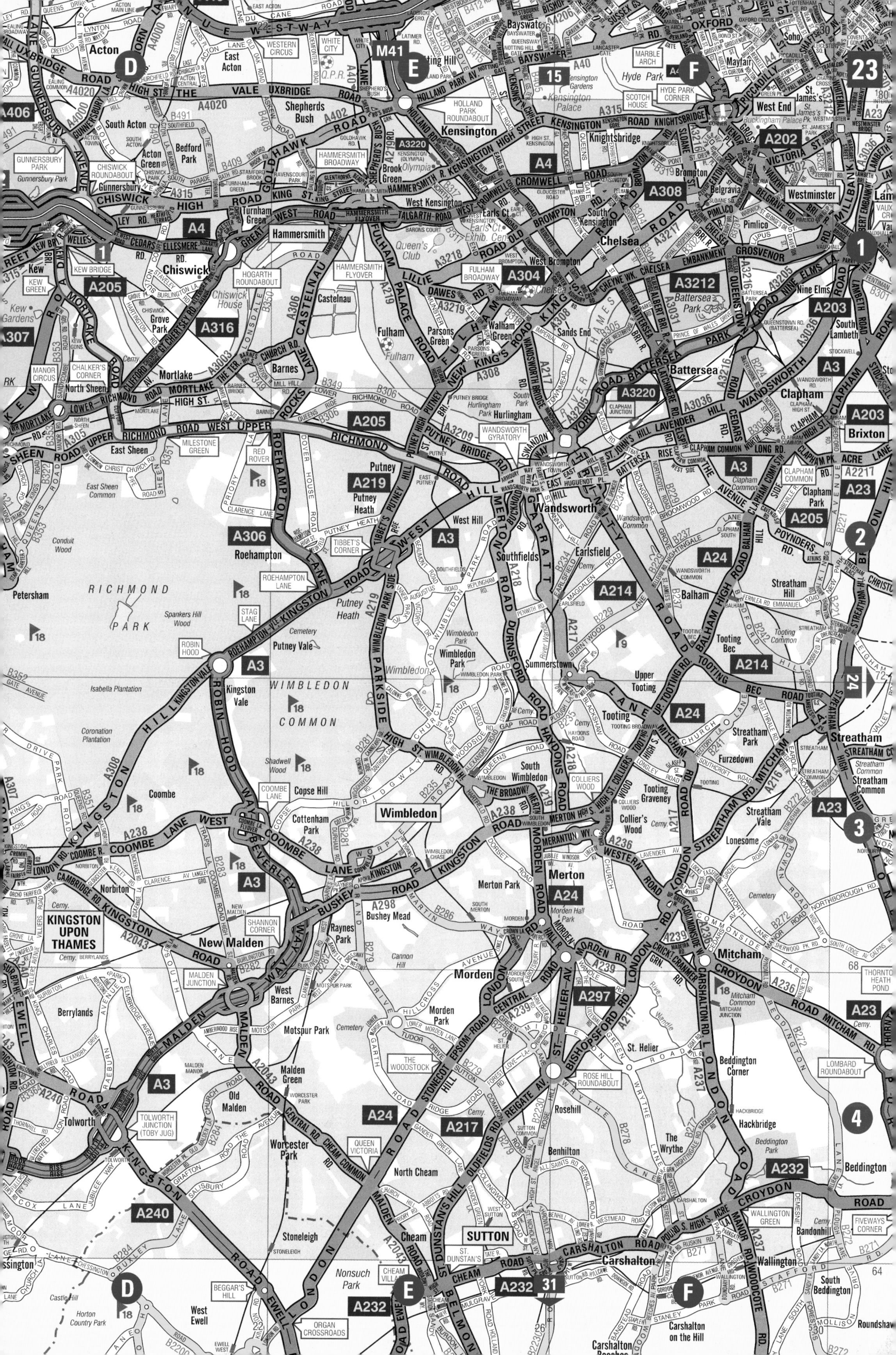

Acton
East Acton
Shepherds Bush
White City
Notting Hill
Bayswater
Kensington Gardens
Kensington Palace
Hyde Park
Marble Arch
Oxford
Mayfair
Soho
West End
St. James's
Buckingham Palace
Westminster
Kensington
Holland Park Roundabout
Knightsbridge
Hyde Park Corner
Brompton
Belgravia
Pimlico
Chelsea
South Kensington
Earls Ct.
West Kensington
West Brompton
Hammersmith
Hammersmith Broadway
Hammersmith Flyover
Brook Green
Olympia
Queen's Club
Fulham
Fulham Broadway
Parsons Green
Walham Green
Sands End
Hurlingham
Battersea
Battersea Park
Nine Elms
Vauxhall
Lambeth
South Lambeth
Clapham
Clapham Junction
Clapham Common
Clapham Park
Brixton
Stockwell
Wandsworth
Wandsworth Gyratory
Wandsworth Common
Earlsfield
Southfields
Summerstown
Balham
Tooting Bec
Upper Tooting
Tooting
Tooting Graveney
Streatham
Streatham Hill
Streatham Park
Streatham Common
Streatham Vale
Furzedown
Lonesome
Mitcham
Mitcham Common
Collier's Wood
Merton
Merton Park
Morden
Morden Hall Park
South Wimbledon
Wimbledon
Wimbledon Park
Wimbledon Common
Putney
Putney Heath
Putney Vale
West Hill
Roehampton
Richmond Park
Kingston Vale
Coombe
Copse Hill
Cottenham Park
Raynes Park
Bushey Mead
Norbiton
Kingston upon Thames
New Malden
Malden Junction
Motspur Park
West Barnes
Berrylands
Old Malden
Malden Green
Worcester Park
Tolworth
Tolworth Junction (Toby Jug)
Chessington
Stoneleigh
West Ewell
North Cheam
Cheam
Nonsuch Park
Sutton
Rosehill
Rose Hill Roundabout
St. Helier
Benhilton
Carshalton
Carshalton on the Hill
The Wrythe
Hackbridge
Beddington Corner
Beddington
Wallington
South Beddington
Bandonhill
Lombard Roundabout
Thornton Heath Pond
Fiveways Corner
Petersham
East Sheen
East Sheen Common
North Sheen
Mortlake
Barnes
Castelnau
Chiswick
Chiswick House
Chiswick Roundabout
Hogarth Roundabout
Gunnersbury
Gunnersbury Park
South Acton
Acton Green
Bedford Park
Kew
Kew Gardens
Kew Bridge
Turnham Green
Roehampton Lane
Robin Hood
Stag Lane
Tibbet's Corner
Red Rover
Milestone Green
Chalker's Corner
Manor Circus
Shannon Corner
Coombe Lane
Queen Victoria
The Woodstock
Beggar's Hill
Organ Crossroads
Cheam Village
St. Dunstan's
Wallington Green
Horton Country Park
Conduit Wood
Spankers Hill Wood
Isabella Plantation
Coronation Plantation
Shadwell Wood
Cannon Hill
A4
A40
A4020
A406
A315
A205
A316
A306
A3
A308
A3220
A304
A3212
A202
A203
A219
A24
A214
A217
A23
A232
A240
A238
A297
A236
A239
A2043
A298
A307
M41
15
23
24
31
64
68
72

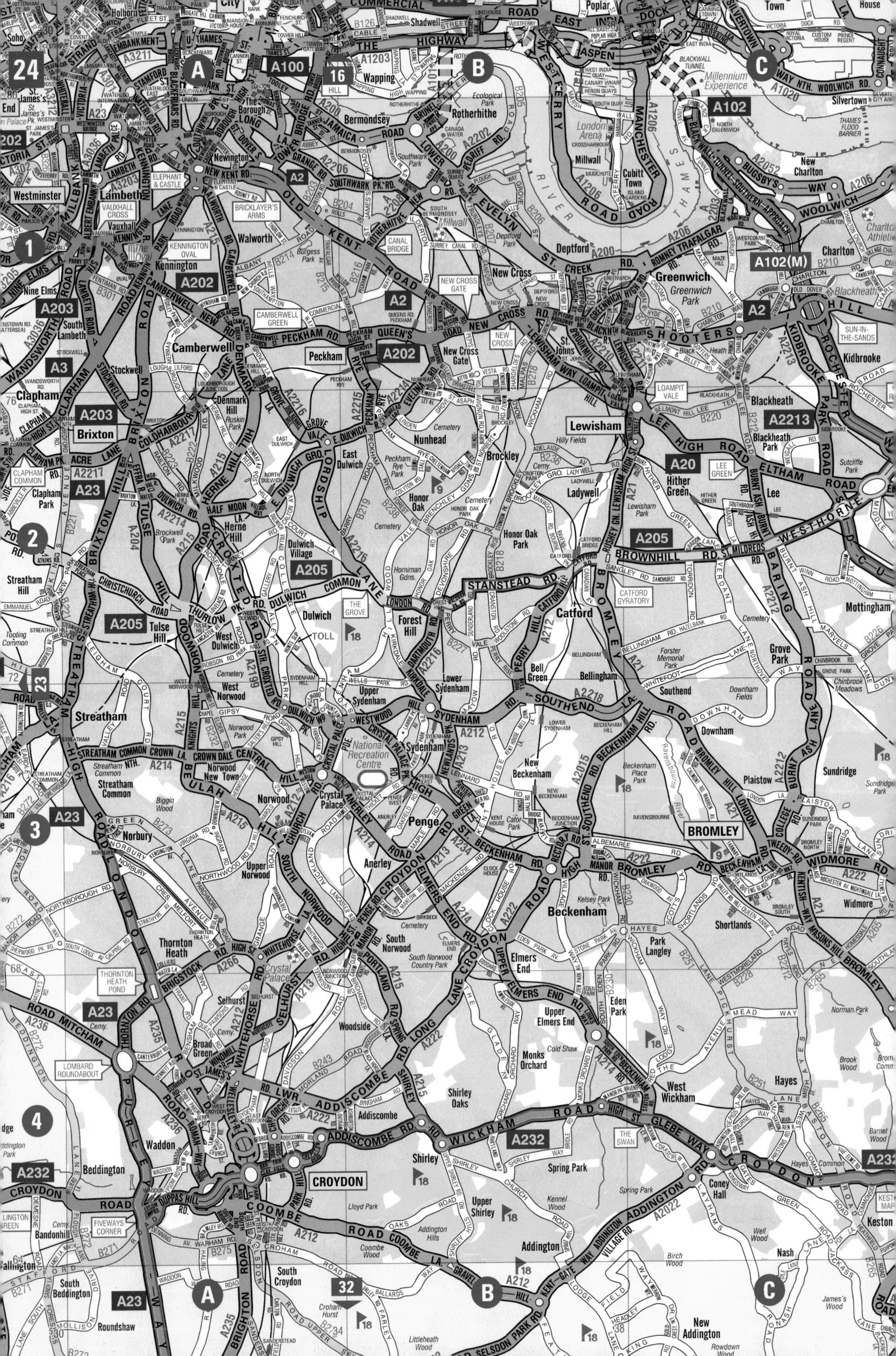

24
A
B
C
16
32
23
1
2
3
4
A100
A102
A102(M)
A2
A202
A203
A3
A23
A205
A20
A2213
A232
Westminster
Lambeth
Vauxhall
Kennington
Walworth
Camberwell
Peckham
Brixton
Clapham
Stockwell
South Lambeth
Nine Elms
Bermondsey
Rotherhithe
Wapping
Shadwell
Newington
Deptford
New Cross
New Cross Gate
Greenwich
Blackheath
Charlton
Kidbrooke
Lewisham
Brockley
Nunhead
East Dulwich
Dulwich
Dulwich Village
Herne Hill
Denmark Hill
Tulse Hill
West Dulwich
West Norwood
Streatham
Streatham Hill
Streatham Common
Norbury
Thornton Heath
Norwood
Upper Norwood
South Norwood
Crystal Palace
Penge
Anerley
Sydenham
Lower Sydenham
Upper Sydenham
Forest Hill
Honor Oak
Honor Oak Park
Catford
Bellingham
Bell Green
Ladywell
Hither Green
Lee
Grove Park
Mottingham
Southend
Downham
Plaistow
Sundridge
Bromley
Widmore
Shortlands
Beckenham
New Beckenham
Elmers End
Upper Elmers End
Eden Park
Park Langley
West Wickham
Hayes
Keston
Coney Hall
Monks Orchard
Shirley
Shirley Oaks
Upper Shirley
Addiscombe
Woodside
Selhurst
Broad Green
Croydon
Waddon
Beddington
Bandonhill
South Beddington
Roundshaw
South Croydon
Addington
New Addington
Spring Park
Millwall
Cubitt Town
Silvertown
New Charlton
Millennium Experience
Blackwall Tunnel
Lombard Roundabout
Fiveways Corner
Thornton Heath Pond
The Swan
Elephant & Castle
Bricklayer's Arms
Canal Bridge
Camberwell Green
Kennington Oval
Vauxhall Cross
Loampit Vale
Lee Green
Catford Gyratory
Sun-in-the-Sands
The Grove
National Recreation Centre

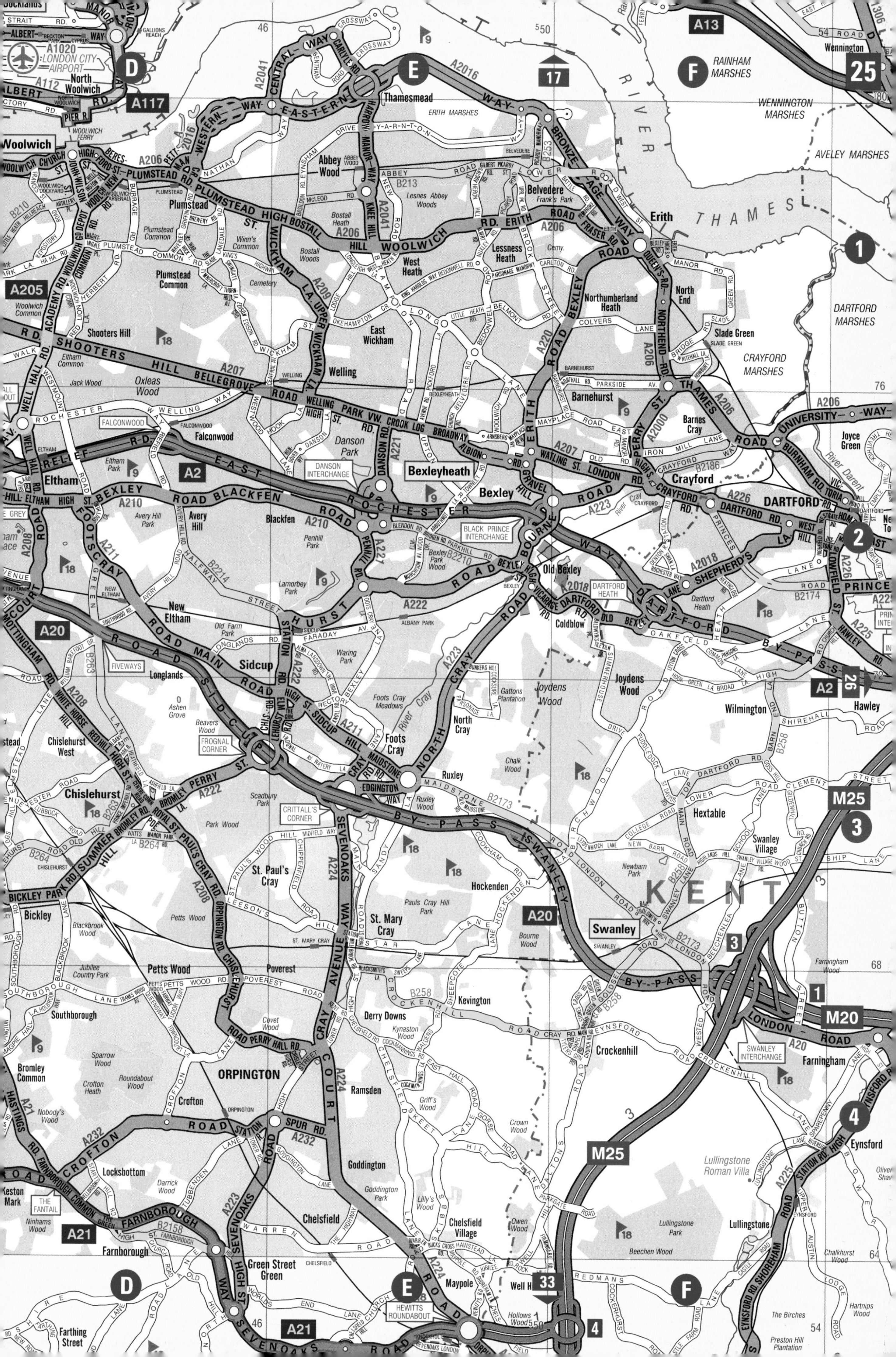

25
A13
Wennington
RAINHAM MARSHES
WENNINGTON MARSHES
AVELEY MARSHES
THAMES
RIVER
DARTFORD MARSHES
CRAYFORD MARSHES
LONDON CITY AIRPORT
North Woolwich
Woolwich
A117
A205
A206
A2016
A2041
A207
A2
A20
A21
A208
A209
A210
A211
A220
A221
A222
A223
A224
A225
A226
A232
A2000
A2018
M25
M20
B213
B253
B258
B2173
B2174
B2186
B2158
17
33
Thamesmead
ERITH MARSHES
Abbey Wood
Lesnes Abbey Woods
Belvedere
Erith
Plumstead
Plumstead Common
Winn's Common
Bostall Heath
Bostall Woods
West Heath
Lessness Heath
Northumberland Heath
North End
Slade Green
Woolwich Common
Shooters Hill
Eltham Common
Oxleas Wood
Jack Wood
East Wickham
Welling
Falconwood
Barnehurst
Barnes Cray
Joyce Green
Eltham
Eltham Park
Danson Park
DANSON INTERCHANGE
Bexleyheath
Bexley
Crayford
DARTFORD
Avery Hill Park
Avery Hill
Blackfen
Penhill Park
BLACK PRINCE INTERCHANGE
Bexley Park Wood
Old Bexley
DARTFORD HEATH
Dartford Heath
Lamorbey Park
New Eltham
Old Farm Park
Longlands
Sidcup
Waring Park
Coldblow
FIVEWAYS
Joydens Wood
Gattons Plantation
Wilmington
Hawley
Chislehurst West
Ashen Grove
Beavers Wood
FROGNAL CORNER
Foots Cray Meadows
Foots Cray
North Cray
River Cray
Chalk Wood
Chislehurst
Scadbury Park
Ruxley
Ruxley Wood
CRITTALL'S CORNER
Park Wood
Hextable
Swanley Village
St. Paul's Cray
Hockenden
Newbarn Park
KENT
Bickley
Blackbrook Wood
Petts Wood
Pauls Cray Hill Park
St. Mary Cray
Bourne Wood
Swanley
Jubilee Country Park
Poverest
Kevington
Farningham Wood
Southborough
Derry Downs
Covet Wood
Kynaston Wood
SWANLEY INTERCHANGE
Farningham
Bromley Common
Sparrow Wood
Crofton Heath
Roundabout Wood
ORPINGTON
Ramsden
Crockenhill
Nobody's Wood
Crofton
Griff's Wood
Crown Wood
Eynsford
Lullingstone Roman Villa
Locksbottom
Darrick Wood
Goddington
Goddington Park
Keston Mark
THE FANTAIL
Ninhams Wood
Lilly's Wood
Chelsfield
Chelsfield Village
Owen Wood
Lullingstone
Lullingstone Park
Beechen Wood
Farnborough
Green Street Green
Maypole
Well Hill
Chalkhurst Wood
HEWITTS ROUNDABOUT
Hollows Wood
Farthing Street
The Birches
Hartnips Wood
Preston Hill Plantation
46
50
54
76
72
68
64

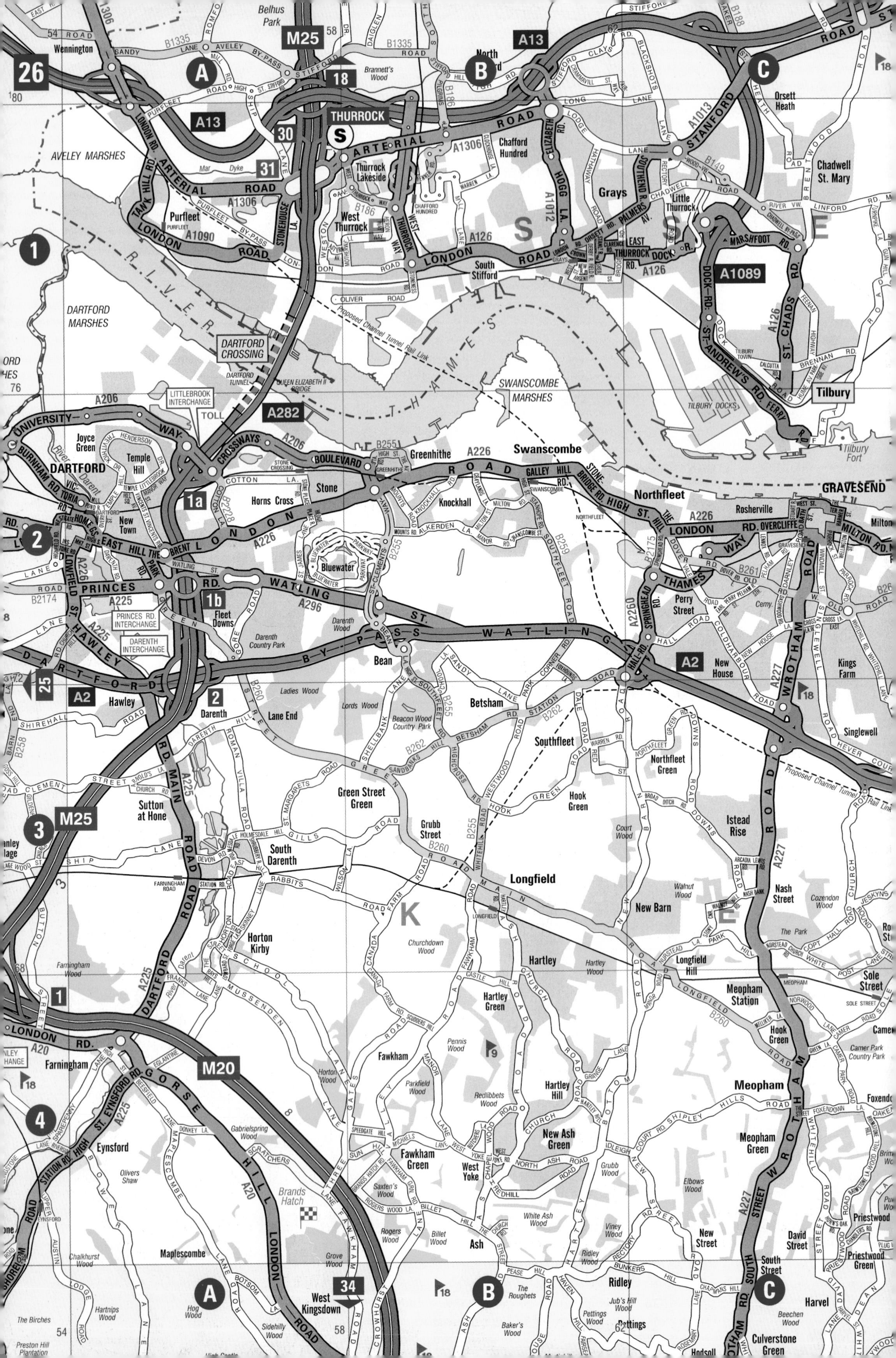
26
Belhus Park
M25
A13
Wennington
B1335
Aveley By-Pass
Brannett's Wood
North Stifford
18
Orsett Heath
Thurrock
30
31
Aveley Marshes
Purfleet
A1306
A1090
Chafford Hundred
Thurrock Lakeside
West Thurrock
Grays
Little Thurrock
Chadwell St. Mary
A1012
A1013
B149
A1089
A126
South Stifford
Dartford Marshes
Dartford Crossing
Dartford Tunnel
Queen Elizabeth II Bridge
Proposed Channel Tunnel Rail Link
River Thames
Swanscombe Marshes
Tilbury Docks
Tilbury
Tilbury Fort
Littlebrook Interchange
A206
A282
Toll
Joyce Green
Temple Hill
Dartford
Crossways
Greenhithe
Swanscombe
A226
Stone
Horns Cross
Knockhall
Northfleet
Gravesend
Rosherville
1a
B2228
New Town
Bluewater
B255
B259
B2175
B261
Perry Street
Princes Rd. Interchange
Darenth Interchange
A225
A296
1b
Fleet Downs
Darenth Country Park
Darenth Wood
Bean
Watling St.
A2
New House
Kings Farm
25
Hawley
Darenth
Lane End
Ladies Wood
Lords Wood
Beacon Wood Country Park
Betsham
B262
Southfleet
Northfleet Green
Singlewell
B2174
B258
Sutton at Hone
M25
Green Street Green
Hook Green
Istead Rise
South Darenth
Grubb Street
B260
Longfield
Nash Street
Horton Kirby
K
Churchdown Wood
New Barn
Walnut Wood
Cozendon Wood
Court Wood
Farningham Wood
Hartley
Hartley Wood
Longfield Hill
Meopham Station
Sole Street
Hartley Green
Hook Green
A227
M20
A20
Farningham
Fawkham
Pennis Wood
Parkfield Wood
Horton Wood
Hartley Hill
Redlibbets Wood
Meopham
Camer Park Country Park
Eynsford
Gabrielspring Wood
New Ash Green
Meopham Green
Olivers Shaw
Fawkham Green
West Yoke
Grubb Wood
Elbows Wood
Brands Hatch
Saxten's Wood
White Ash Wood
Rogers Wood
Billet Wood
Ash
Viney Wood
New Street
Maplescombe
Chalkhurst Wood
Grove Wood
Ridley Wood
David Street
Priestwood
Priestwood Green
Ridley
South Street
Hartnips Wood
Hog Wood
West Kingsdown
34
The Roughets
Jub's Hill Wood
Harvel
Beechen Wood
The Birches
Sidehilly Wood
Baker's Wood
Pettings Wood
Pettings
Culverstone Green
Preston Hill Plantation
Hodsoll
A
B
C
E
S
1
2
3
4
54
58
62
76
80

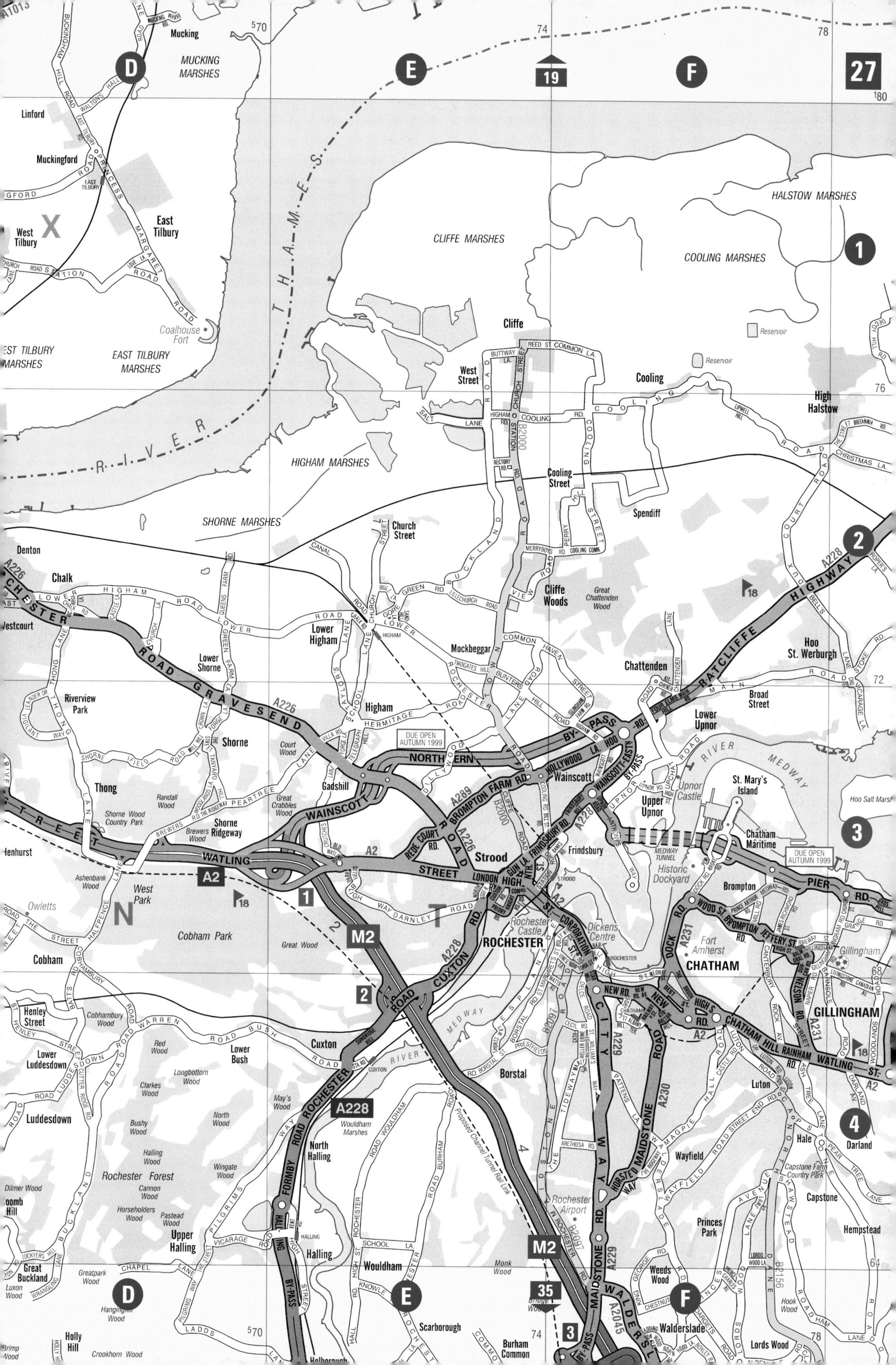
Mucking
MUCKING MARSHES
Linford
Muckingford
East Tilbury
West Tilbury
Coalhouse Fort
EAST TILBURY MARSHES
RIVER THAMES
CLIFFE MARSHES
COOLING MARSHES
HALSTOW MARSHES
HIGHAM MARSHES
SHORNE MARSHES
Cliffe
West Street
Cooling
High Halstow
Cooling Street
Spendiff
Church Street
Denton
Chalk
Westcourt
Lower Higham
Mockbeggar
Cliffe Woods
Great Chattenden Wood
Chattenden
Hoo St. Werburgh
Broad Street
Lower Shorne
Riverview Park
Higham
Shorne
Court Wood
Thong
Randall Wood
Shorne Wood Country Park
Gadshill
Great Crabbles Wood
Shorne Ridgeway
Brewers Wood
Wainscott
Lower Upnor
Upper Upnor
Upnor Castle
St. Mary's Island
Hoo Salt Marsh
Chatham Maritime
Frindsbury
Strood
Henhurst
Ashenbank Wood
West Park
Owletts
Cobham Park
Great Wood
Cobham
Rochester Castle
ROCHESTER
Dickens Centre
Historic Dockyard
Fort Amherst
CHATHAM
Brompton
Gillingham
GILLINGHAM
Henley Street
Cobhambury Wood
Lower Luddesdown
Red Wood
Cuxton
Lower Bush
Longbottom Wood
Clarkes Wood
Luddesdown
Bushy Wood
North Wood
May's Wood
Wouldham Marshes
Borstal
Luton
Darland
Hale
Wayfield
Capstone Farm Country Park
Capstone
Hempstead
Princes Park
Halling Wood
Wingate Wood
Rochester Forest
Cannon Wood
North Halling
Horseholders Wood
Pastead Wood
Upper Halling
Rochester Airport
Dilmer Wood
Great Buckland
Luxon Wood
Greatpark Wood
Hangingfield Wood
Holly Hill
Crookhorn Wood
Halling
Wouldham
Monk Wood
Scarborough
Burham Common
Weeds Wood
Walderslade
Hook Wood
Lords Wood
Holborough
A2
M2
A226
A228
A229
A230
A231
A289
A2045
B2000
B2097
B2156
WATLING STREET
GRAVESEND ROAD
RATCLIFFE HIGHWAY
NORTHERN BY-PASS
WAINSCOTT
MEDWAY TUNNEL
DUE OPEN AUTUMN 1999
Proposed Channel Tunnel Rail Link
RIVER MEDWAY
D
E
F
19
35
1
2
3
4
X
N
T

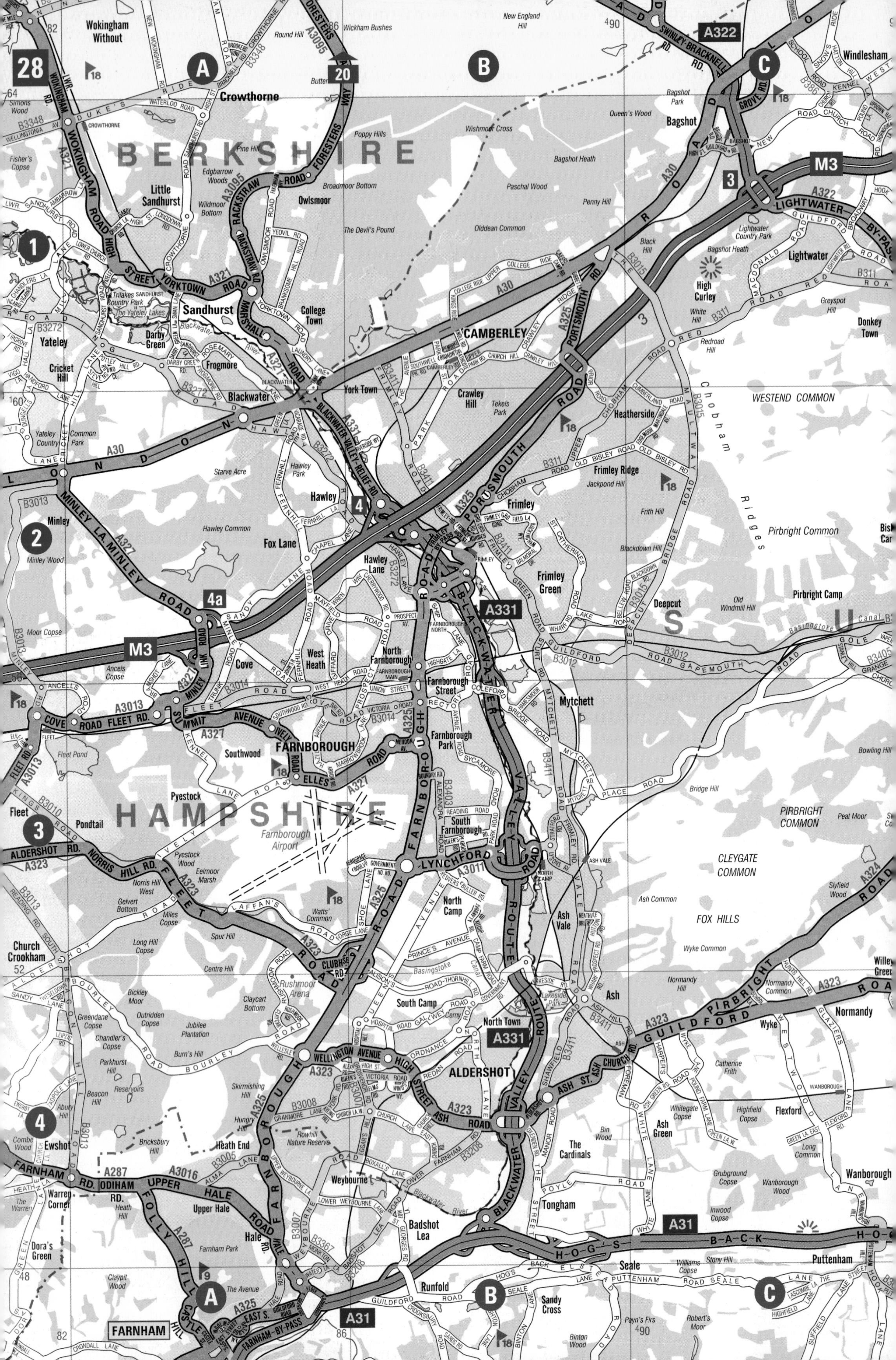
28
A
B
C
1
2
3
4
BERKSHIRE
HAMPSHIRE
Wokingham Without
Crowthorne
Wickham Bushes
Round Hill
New England Hill
Windlesham
Bagshot Park
Bagshot
Queen's Wood
Wishmoor Cross
Poppy Hills
Pine Hill
Edgbarrow Woods
Little Sandhurst
Wildmoor Bottom
Owlsmoor
Broadmoor Bottom
Bagshot Heath
Paschal Wood
Penny Hill
Olddean Common
The Devil's Pound
Black Hill
Lightwater Country Park
Lightwater
High Curley
White Hill
Greyspot Hill
Donkey Town
Redroad Hill
Sandhurst
College Town
Trilakes Sandhurst Country Park
The Yateley Lakes
Yateley
Darby Green
Frogmore
Cricket Hill
Blackwater
York Town
CAMBERLEY
Crawley Hill
Tekels Park
Heatherside
WESTEND COMMON
Chobham Ridges
Yateley Country Park
Starve Acre
Hawley Park
Hawley
Frimley Ridge
Jackpond Hill
Frith Hill
Minley
Minley Wood
Hawley Common
Fox Lane
Hawley Lane
Frimley
Frimley Green
Blackdown Hill
Pirbright Common
Deepcut
Old Windmill Hill
Pirbright Camp
Moor Copse
West Heath
North Farnborough
Cove
Ancels Copse
Farnborough Street
Mytchett
Southwood
FARNBOROUGH
Farnborough Park
Fleet Pond
Fleet
Pyestock
Pondtail
Farnborough Airport
South Farnborough
Bridge Hill
PIRBRIGHT COMMON
Peat Moor
Pyestock Wood
Eelmoor Marsh
Norris Hill West
Gelvert Bottom
Miles Copse
Watts' Common
North Camp
Ash Vale
CLEYGATE COMMON
Ash Common
FOX HILLS
Slyfield Wood
Church Crookham
Spur Hill
Long Hill Copse
Centre Hill
Wyke Common
Rushmoor Arena
Bickley Moor
Claycart Bottom
Normandy Hill
Normandy Common
Ash
Normandy
Wyke
South Camp
North Town
Greendane Copse
Outridden Copse
Jubilee Plantation
Chandler's Copse
Burn's Hill
Parkhurst Hill
Reservoirs
ALDERSHOT
Catherine Frith
Beacon Hill
Skirmishing Hill
Whitegate Copse
Highfield Copse
Flexford
Ash Green
Abury Hill
Combe Wood
Ewshot
Hungry Hill
Bricksbury Hill
Heath End
Rowhill Nature Reserve
Bin Wood
The Cardinals
Long Common
Weybourne
Grubground Copse
Wanborough Wood
Wanborough
The Warren
Warren Corner
Heath Hill
Upper Hale
Tongham
Inwood Copse
Hale
Badshot Lea
Dora's Green
Farnham Park
Seale
Williams Copse
Stony Hill
Puttenham
Claypit Wood
The Avenue
Runfold
Sandy Cross
Payn's Firs
Robert's Moor
Binton Wood
FARNHAM
M3
A30
A31
A322
A323
A324
A325
A327
A331
A3013
A3016
A3095
A287
A321
A3011
B3008
B3007
B3012
B3013
B3015
B3272
B3348
B3411
B3403
B3005
B3010
B3014
B3208
B3367
B311
B3405
B3386
20
3
4
4a
LONDON ROAD
HOG'S BACK
BLACKWATER VALLEY RELIEF RD.
BLACKWATER VALLEY ROUTE
FARNBOROUGH ROAD
PORTSMOUTH ROAD
GUILDFORD ROAD
Basingstoke Canal
Blackwater River
82
86
490
64
60
56
52
48

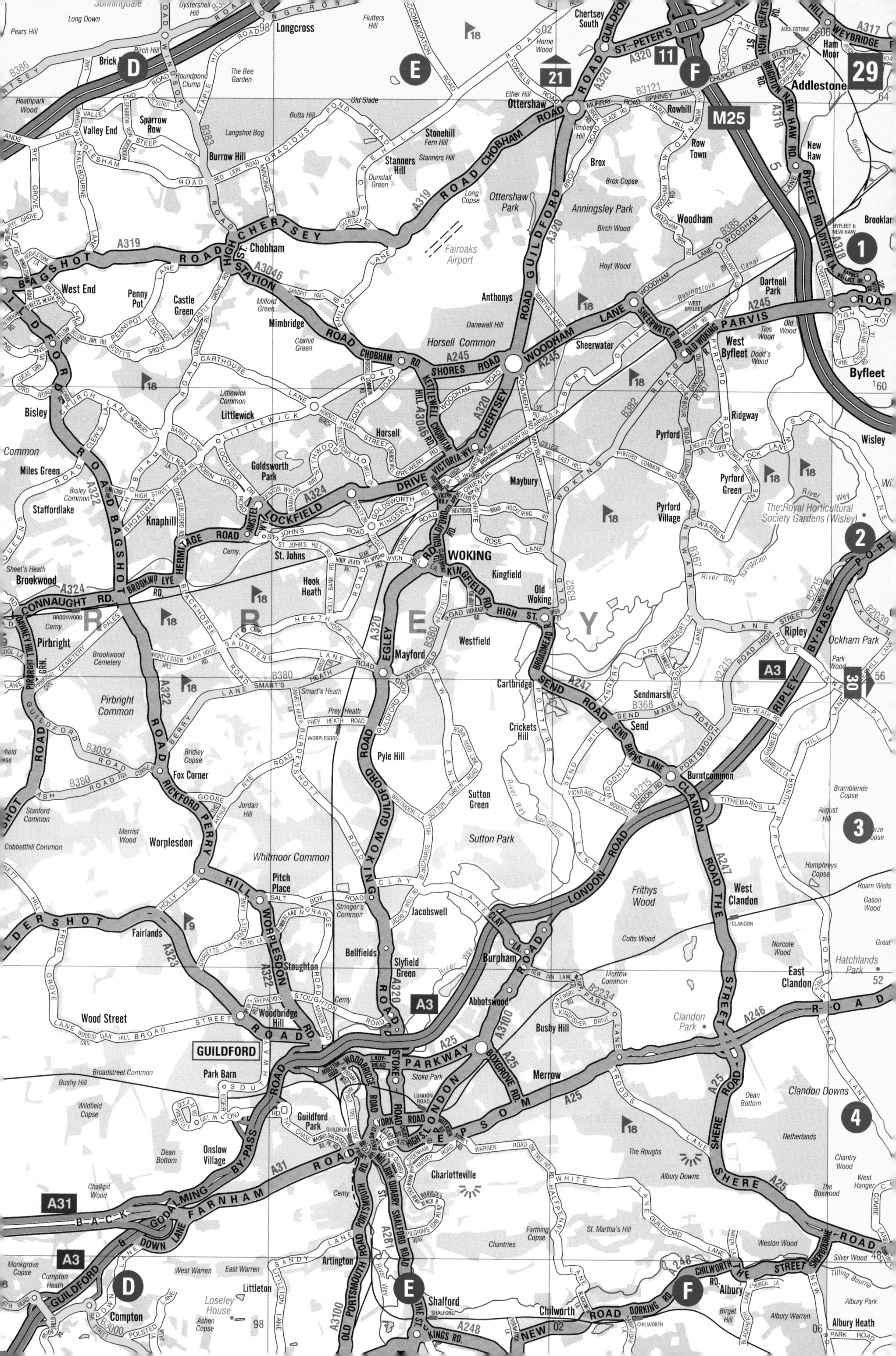

29
Longcross
Chertsey South
Ottershaw
Addlestone
Ham Moor
Rowhill
Row Town
New Haw
Brox
Woodham
Byfleet
West Byfleet
Dartnell Park
Sheerwater
Anthonys
Horsell Common
Fairoaks Airport
Ottershaw Park
Anningsley Park
Stonehill
Stanners Hill
Chobham
Burrow Hill
Sparrow Row
Valley End
Brick Hill
West End
Penny Pot
Castle Green
Mimbridge
Bisley
Littlewick
Horsell
Goldsworth Park
Knaphill
Staffordlake
Miles Green
Brookwood
Pirbright
Pirbright Common
St. Johns
Hook Heath
WOKING
Kingfield
Old Woking
Westfield
Mayford
Maybury
Pyrford
Pyrford Village
Pyrford Green
Ridgway
Wisley
The Royal Horticultural Society Gardens (Wisley)
Ripley
Ockham Park
Send
Sendmarsh
Cartbridge
Burntcommon
Crickets Hill
Pyle Hill
Sutton Green
Sutton Park
Worplesdon
Fox Corner
Whitmoor Common
Pitch Place
Jacobswell
Fairlands
Stoughton
Bellfields
Slyfield Green
Burpham
Abbotswood
West Clandon
East Clandon
Merrow
Bushy Hill
Wood Street
Woodbridge Hill
GUILDFORD
Park Barn
Guildford Park
Onslow Village
Charlotteville
Stoke Park
Artington
Littleton
Compton
Shalford
Chilworth
Albury
Albury Heath
Clandon Downs
Netherlands
SURREY
M25
A3
A31
A320
A322
A324
A245
A246
A247
A25
A248
A281
A3100
A319
A3046
A318

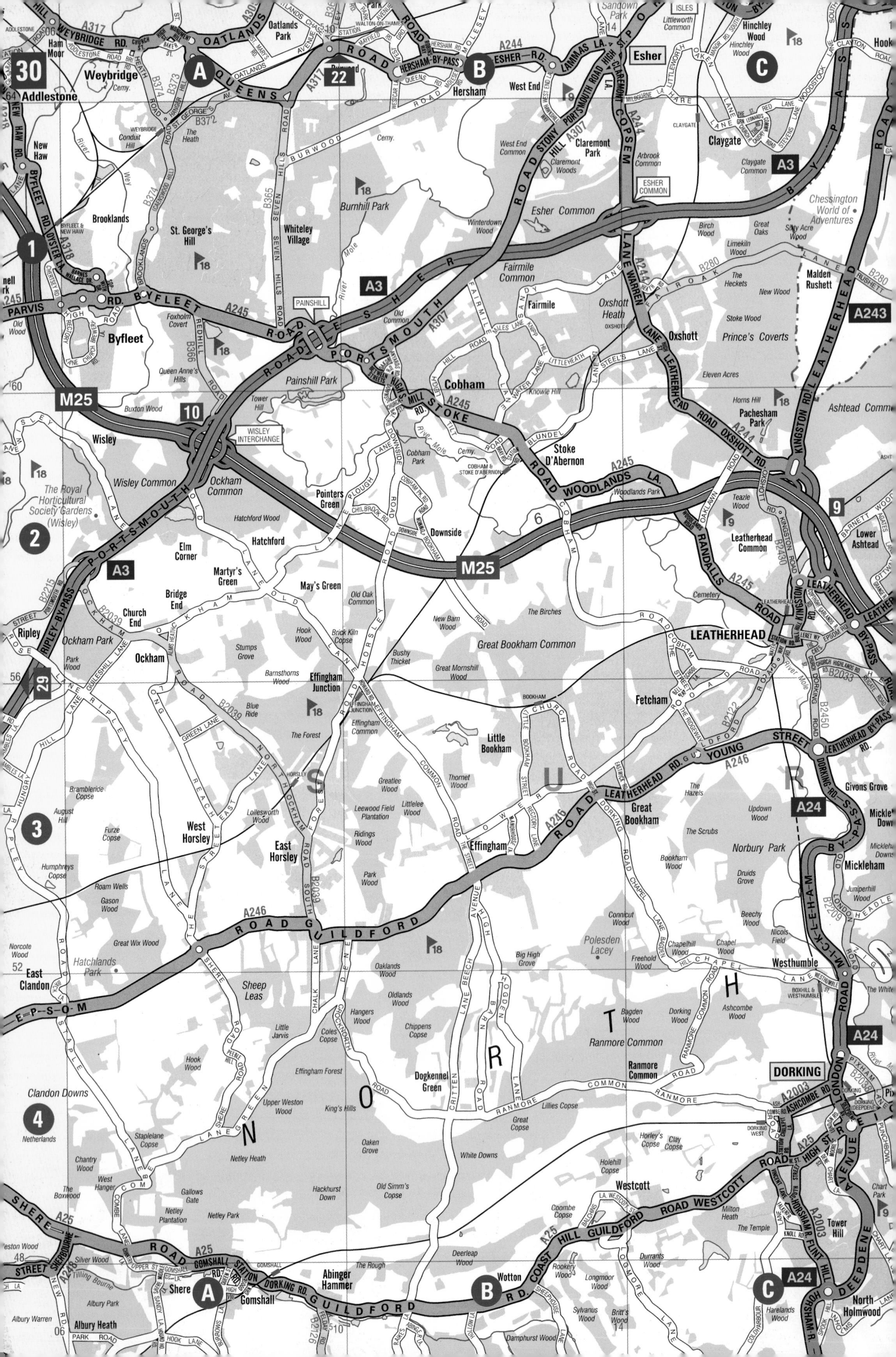

30
Addlestone
Weybridge
Ham Moor
New Haw
Oatlands Park
Walton-on-Thames
Hersham
Esher
West End
Hinchley Wood
Claygate
Littleworth Common
Sandown Park
Brooklands
St. George's Hill
Whiteley Village
Burnhill Park
Claremont Park
Esher Common
Arbrook Common
Winterdown Wood
Fairmile Common
Fairmile
Oxshott Heath
Oxshott
Prince's Coverts
Chessington World of Adventures
Malden Rushett
Birch Wood
Great Oaks
Limekiln Wood
The Heckets
New Wood
Stoke Wood
Eleven Acres
Horns Hill
Pachesham Park
Ashtead Common
Byfleet
Foxholm Covert
Queen Anne's Hills
Painshill
Painshill Park
Cobham
Knowle Hill
Stoke D'Abernon
Cobham Park
Downside
Pointers Green
Woodlands Park
Teazle Wood
Leatherhead Common
Lower Ashtead
Wisley
Wisley Interchange
Wisley Common
The Royal Horticultural Society Gardens (Wisley)
Ockham Common
Hatchford Wood
Hatchford
Elm Corner
Martyr's Green
Bridge End
Church End
Ripley
Ockham Park
Ockham
May's Green
Old Oak Common
New Barn Wood
The Birches
Great Bookham Common
Hook Wood
Brick Kiln Copse
Stumps Grove
Barnsthorns Wood
Effingham Junction
Bushy Thicket
Great Mornshill Wood
Cemetery
LEATHERHEAD
Fetcham
Blue Ride
The Forest
Effingham Common
Little Bookham
Thornet Wood
Greatlee Wood
Leewood Field Plantation
Littlelee Wood
Ridings Wood
Park Wood
Effingham
Great Bookham
The Hazels
Updown Wood
The Scrubs
Norbury Park
Givons Grove
Mickleham Downs
Mickleham
Bramblebride Copse
August Hill
Furze Copse
West Horsley
Lollesworth Wood
East Horsley
Humphreys Copse
Roam Wells
Gason Wood
Great Wix Wood
Norcote Wood
Hatchlands Park
East Clandon
Sheep Leas
Oaklands Wood
Oldlands Wood
Hangers Wood
Chippens Copse
Coles Copse
Little Jarvis
Big High Grove
Polesden Lacey
Connicut Wood
Freehold Wood
Chapelhill Wood
Chapel Wood
Bookham Wood
Druids Grove
Juniperhill Wood
Beechy Wood
Nicols Field
Westhumble
Ashcombe Wood
Bagden Wood
Dorking Wood
Ranmore Common
Dogkennel Green
Lillies Copse
Great Copse
DORKING
Hook Wood
Effingham Forest
Upper Weston Wood
King's Hills
Clandon Downs
Netherlands
Staplelane Copse
Netley Heath
Oaken Grove
White Downs
Horley's Copse
Clay Copse
Holehill Copse
Westcott
Chantry Wood
West Hanger
The Boxwood
Gallows Gate
Netley Plantation
Netley Park
Hackhurst Down
Old Simm's Copse
Coombe Copse
Milton Heath
The Temple
Tower Hill
Silver Wood
Tilling Bourne
Shere
Gomshall
The Rough
Abinger Hammer
Deerleap Wood
Wotton
Rookery Wood
Durrants Wood
Longmoor Wood
Sylvanus Wood
Britt's Wood
Harelands Wood
North Holmwood
Albury Park
Albury Heath
Albury Warren
Damphurst Wood
M25
A3
A24
A243
A25
A246
A245
A244
A307
A317
SURREY
NORTH

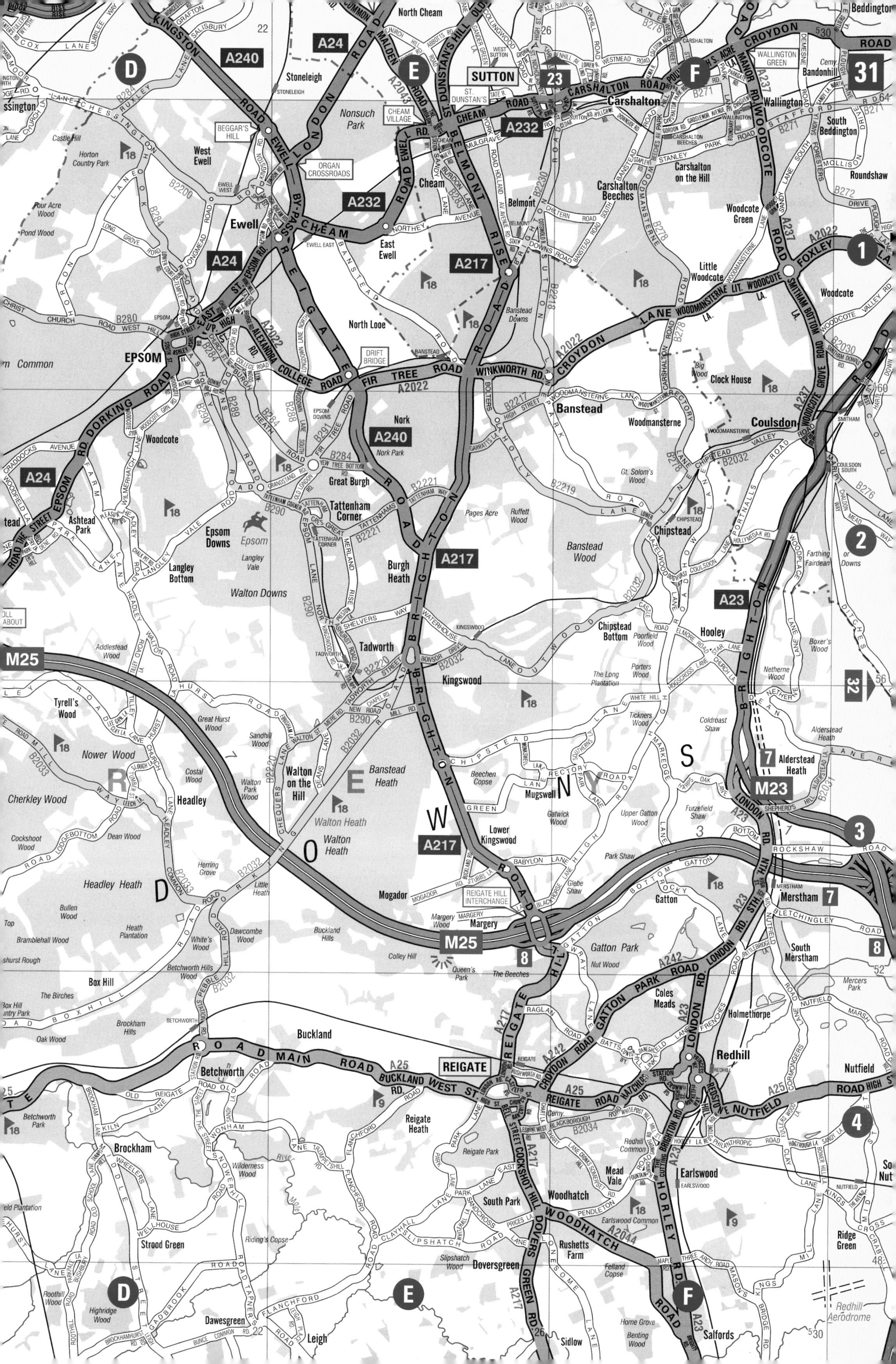
31
North Cheam
Beddington
Stoneleigh
Nonsuch Park
CHEAM VILLAGE
SUTTON
WEST SUTTON
ST. DUNSTAN'S
Carshalton
WALLINGTON GREEN
Bandonhill
Wallington
South Beddington
Roundshaw
BEGGAR'S HILL
ORGAN CROSSROADS
West Ewell
Horton Country Park
Castle Hill
Cheam
Belmont
Carshalton Beeches
Carshalton on the Hill
Woodcote Green
Four Acre Wood
Pond Wood
Ewell
East Ewell
Little Woodcote
Woodcote
North Looe
DRIFT BRIDGE
EPSOM
Epsom Common
Banstead Downs
Big Wood
Clock House
Banstead
Woodmansterne
Coulsdon
Nork
Nork Park
Woodcote
Great Burgh
Tattenham Corner
Epsom Downs
Epsom
Langley Vale
Langley Bottom
Ashtead Park
Gt. Solom's Wood
Pages Acre
Ruffett Wood
Banstead Wood
Chipstead
Farthing Fairdean
Burgh Heath
Walton Downs
Chipstead Bottom
Poorfield Wood
Hooley
Boxer's Wood
Addlestead Wood
Tadworth
Kingswood
The Long Plantation
Porters Wood
Netherne Wood
Tyrell's Wood
Great Hurst Wood
Sandhill Wood
Tickners Wood
Coldroast Shaw
Alderstead Heath
Nower Wood
Cherkley Wood
Costal Wood
Walton Park Wood
Headley
Walton on the Hill
Banstead Heath
Beechen Copse
Mugswell
Gatwick Wood
Upper Gatton Wood
Furzefield Shaw
Walton Heath
Lower Kingswood
Cockshoot Wood
Dean Wood
Park Shaw
Headley Heath
Herring Grove
Little Heath
Glebe Shaw
Gatton
Merstham
Mogador
REIGATE HILL INTERCHANGE
Margery Wood
Margery
Bullen Wood
Heath Plantation
Dawcombe Wood
Buckland Hills
Bramblehall Wood
White's Wood
Colley Hill
Gatton Park
Nut Wood
South Merstham
Mercers Park
Queen's Park
The Beeches
Betchworth Hills Wood
Box Hill
The Birches
Box Hill Country Park
Brockham Hills
Coles Meads
Holmethorpe
Oak Wood
Buckland
Redhill
Nutfield
Betchworth
REIGATE
Betchworth Park
Reigate Heath
Brockham
Wilderness Wood
Reigate Park
Redhill Common
Mead Vale
Earlswood
South Park
Woodhatch
Earlswood Common
Strood Green
Riding's Copse
Slipshatch Wood
Doversgreen
Rushetts Farm
Felland Copse
Ridge Green
Roothill Wood
Highridge Wood
Dawesgreen
Leigh
Home Grove
Benting Wood
Sidlow
Salfords
Redhill Aerodrome
M25
M23
A24
A240
A232
A217
A2022
A237
A23
A25
A242
A2044
B2032
B2033
B2034
B2219
B2221
B2220
B290
B284
B280
B278
B2230
B2218
B2200
B271
B272
B276
B2031
B2030
23
32
1
2
3
4
7
8
9
18
D
E
F

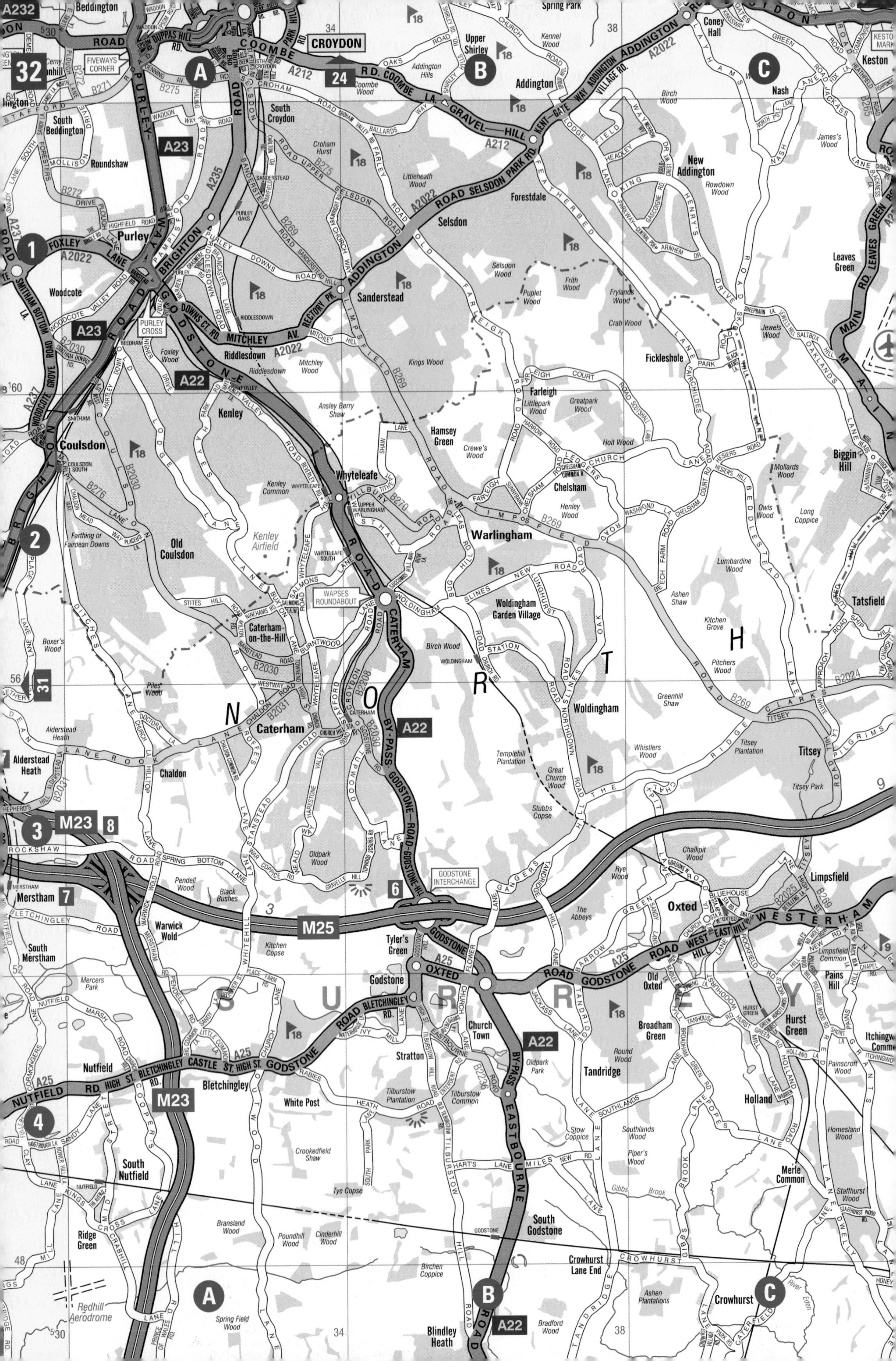
32
31
24
A
B
C
1
2
3
4
Croydon
Beddington
South Beddington
Roundshaw
Purley
Woodcote
Coulsdon
Old Coulsdon
Kenley
Riddlesdown
Sanderstead
South Croydon
Selsdon
Forestdale
Addington
Upper Shirley
New Addington
Coney Hall
Keston
Nash
Leaves Green
Biggin Hill
Farleigh
Chelsham
Hamsey Green
Warlingham
Whyteleafe
Woldingham Garden Village
Woldingham
Fickleshole
Tatsfield
Titsey
Limpsfield
Oxted
Old Oxted
Caterham-on-the-Hill
Caterham
Chaldon
Alderstead Heath
Merstham
South Merstham
Warwick Wold
Tyler's Green
Godstone
Church Town
Bletchingley
Nutfield
South Nutfield
Ridge Green
Stratton
White Post
South Godstone
Tandridge
Broadham Green
Hurst Green
Holland
Merle Common
Crowhurst
Crowhurst Lane End
Blindley Heath
Pains Hill
Redhill Aerodrome
Kenley Airfield
Fiveways Corner
Purley Cross
Wapses Roundabout
Godstone Interchange
Surrey
North
A23
A22
A25
A232
A212
A2022
A235
A237
B269
B270
B2030
B2031
B2208
B2024
B2025
M23
M25
Brighton Road
Godstone Road
Caterham By-Pass
Eastbourne Road
Godstone By-Pass
Eastbourne By-Pass
Westerham Road
Main Road
Limpsfield Road
Addington Road
Selsdon Park Road
Coombe Road
Mitchley Av.
Foxley Lane
Smitham Bottom La.
Woodcote Grove Road
Woodcote Valley Road
Downs Ct. Rd.
Rectory Pk.
Gravel Hill
Kent Gate Way
Addington Village Rd.
Layhams Road
Featherbed Lane
Farleigh Road
Chelsham Road
Clarks Lane
Ridge
Pilgrims
Titsey Hill
Approach Road
Croydon Road
Chaldon Road
Rook Lane
Church Lane
Spring Bottom Lane
War Coppice Rd
Stanstead
Rockshaw
Bletchingley Road
Nutfield Road
Castle St.
High St.
Crowhurst
Selsdon Wood
Puplet Wood
Frith Wood
Frylands Wood
Crab Wood
Kings Wood
Mitchley Wood
Foxley Wood
Croham Hurst
Littleheath Wood
Addington Hills
Coombe Wood
Kennel Wood
Birch Wood
Rowdown Wood
James's Wood
Jewels Wood
Mollards Wood
Owls Wood
Long Coppice
Lumbardine Wood
Ashen Shaw
Kitchen Grove
Pitchers Wood
Greenhill Shaw
Whistlers Wood
Titsey Plantation
Titsey Park
Templehill Plantation
Great Church Wood
Stubbs Copse
Chalkpit Wood
Rye Wood
The Abbeys
Littlepark Wood
Greatpark Wood
Holt Wood
Henley Wood
Crewe's Wood
Ansley Berry Shaw
Kenley Common
Farthing or Fairdean Downs
Boxer's Wood
Piles Wood
Alderstead Heath
Oldpark Wood
Pendell Wood
Black Bushes
Kitchen Copse
Mercers Park
Round Wood
Oldpark Park
Tilburstow Plantation
Tilburstow Common
Crookedfield Shaw
Tye Copse
Bransland Wood
Poundhill Wood
Cinderhill Wood
Birchen Coppice
Spring Field Wood
Bradford Wood
Ashen Plantations
Stow Coppice
Southlands Wood
Piper's Wood
Painscroft Wood
Homesland Wood
Staffhurst Wood
Limpsfield Common
Spring Park
34
38
56
52
48
64
60
530
9
8
7
6

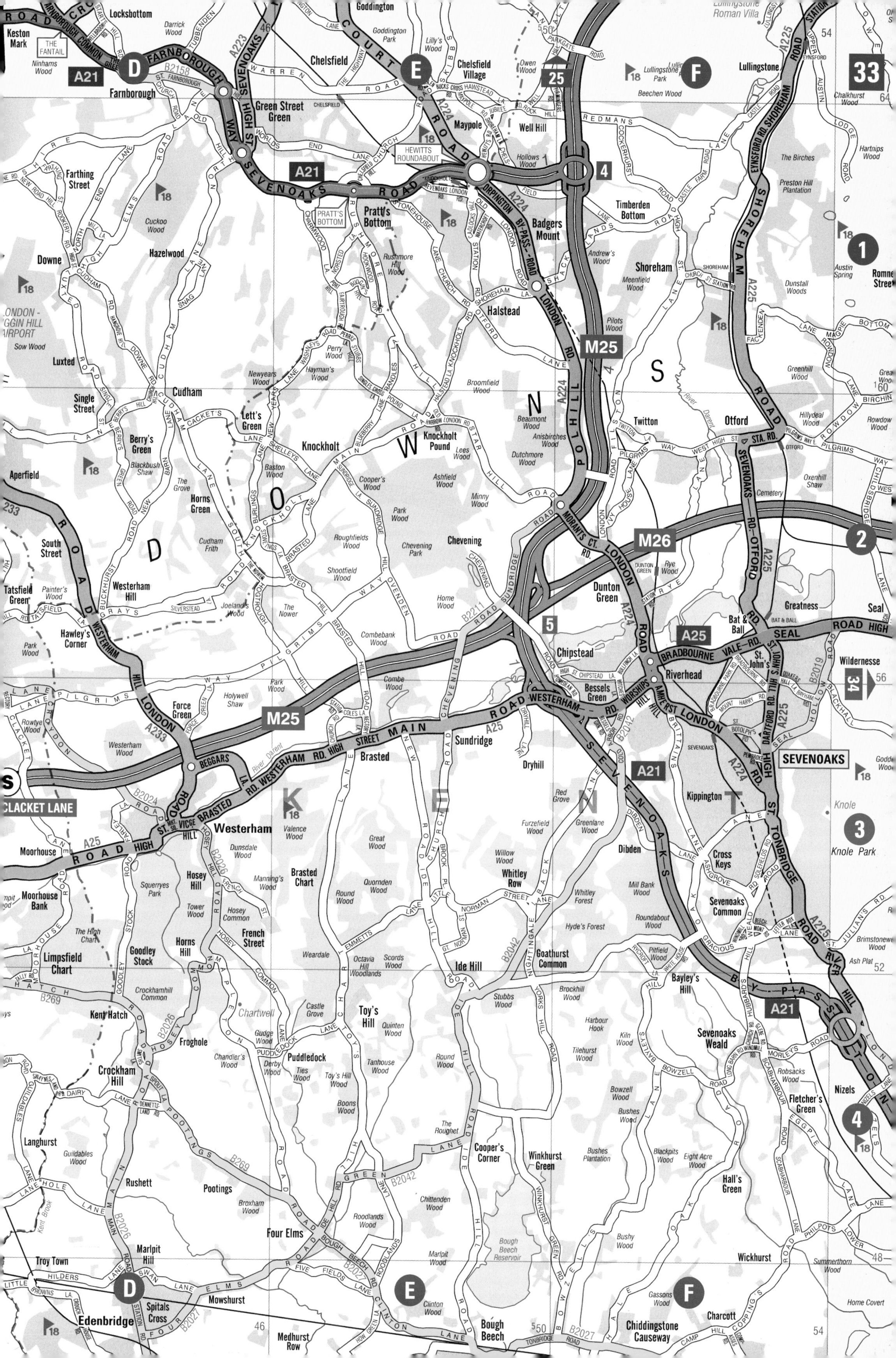
Keston Mark
Locksbottom
Farnborough
A21
Goddington
Chelsfield
Chelsfield Village
Lullingstone Roman Villa
Lullingstone
Lullingstone Park
Beechen Wood
Green Street Green
Maypole
Well Hill
Hewitts Roundabout
25
4
Farthing Street
Cuckoo Wood
Pratt's Bottom
Badgers Mount
Timberden Bottom
Shoreham
Downe
Hazelwood
Halstead
Biggin Hill Airport
Sow Wood
Luxted
Single Street
Cudham
Lett's Green
Knockholt
Knockholt Pound
M25
Twitton
Otford
Berry's Green
Aperfield
Horns Green
Chevening
Chevening Park
M26
Dunton Green
South Street
Cudham Frith
Westerham Hill
Tatsfield Green
Hawley's Corner
Chipstead
Bessels Green
Riverhead
St. John's
Bat & Ball
Greatness
Seal
Wildernesse
Force Green
A25
Sundridge
Brasted
Dryhill
Sevenoaks
Clacket Lane
Westerham
Moorhouse
Moorhouse Bank
Kippington
Cross Keys
Dibden
Knole
Knole Park
Hosey Hill
Brasted Chart
Whitley Row
Sevenoaks Common
French Street
Limpsfield Chart
Goodley Stock
Horns Hill
Ide Hill
Goathurst Common
Bayley's Hill
Kent Hatch
Chartwell
Toy's Hill
Sevenoaks Weald
Froghole
Puddledock
Crockham Hill
Nizels
Fletcher's Green
Langhurst
Cooper's Corner
Winkhurst Green
Rushett
Pootings
Hall's Green
Four Elms
Troy Town
Marlpit Hill
Wickhurst
Mowshurst
Spitals Cross
Edenbridge
Bough Beech
Bough Beech Reservoir
Chiddingstone Causeway
Charcott
Medhurst Row
34
D
E
F
1
2
3
4

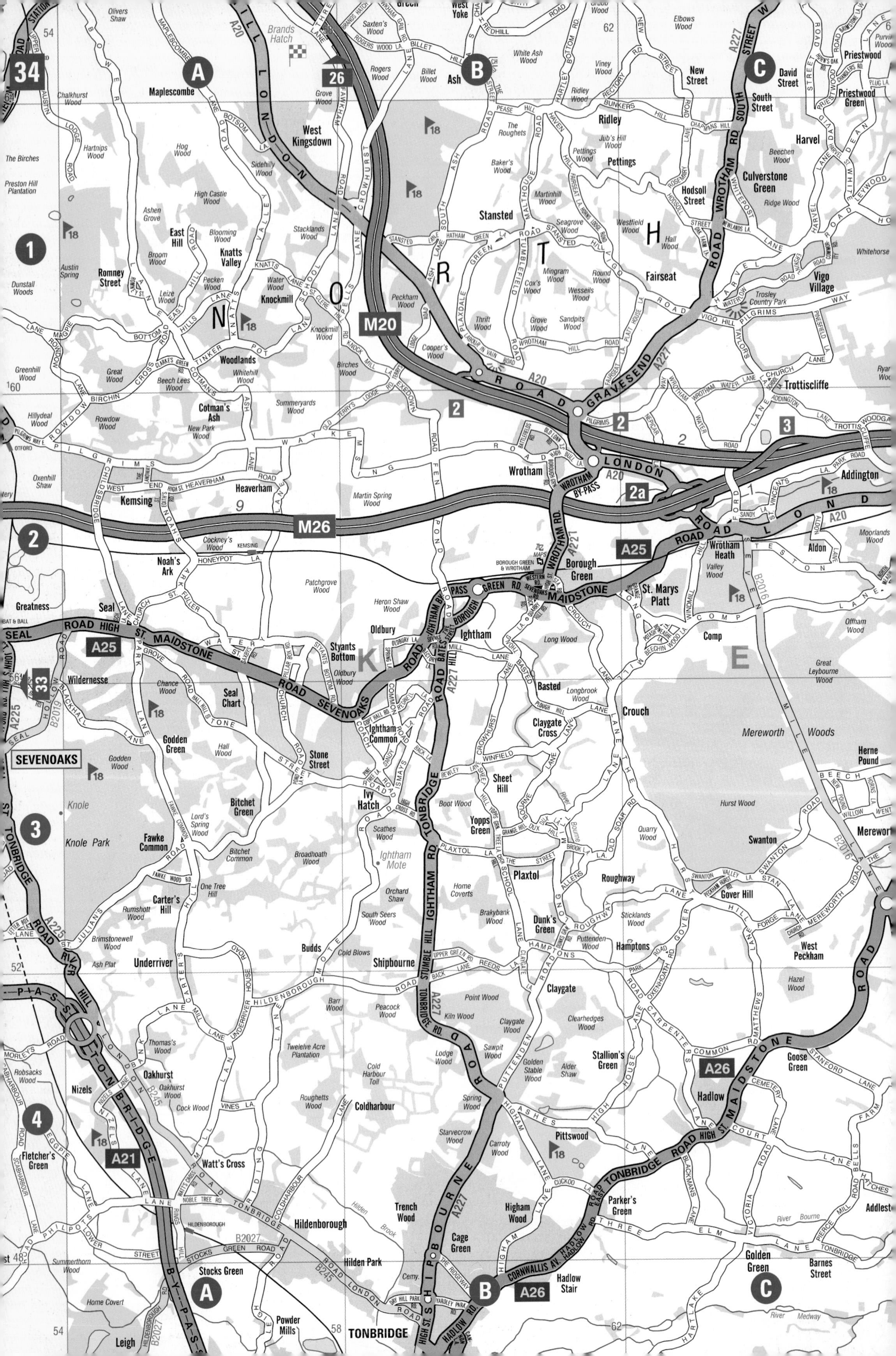

34
Maplescombe
West Kingsdown
Ash
Ridley
New Street
David Street
South Street
Priestwood
Harvel
Culverstone Green
Hodsoll Street
Pettings
Stansted
Fairseat
Vigo Village
Trottiscliffe
Addington
Wrotham
Heaverham
Kemsing
Noah's Ark
Seal
Borough Green
St. Marys Platt
Wrotham Heath
Ightham
Oldbury
Styants Bottom
Ivy Hatch
Ightham Common
Stone Street
Seal Chart
Godden Green
Wildernesse
SEVENOAKS
Knole Park
Fawke Common
Carter's Hill
Underriver
Plaxtol
Basted
Crouch
Comp
Mereworth Woods
Shipbourne
Dunk's Green
Hamptons
Claygate
Hadlow
Golden Green
Barnes Street
Hildenborough
Tonbridge
Leigh
Stocks Green
Watt's Cross
Nizels
Fletcher's Green
Oakhurst
M20
M26
A20
A25
A26
A21
A227
A225

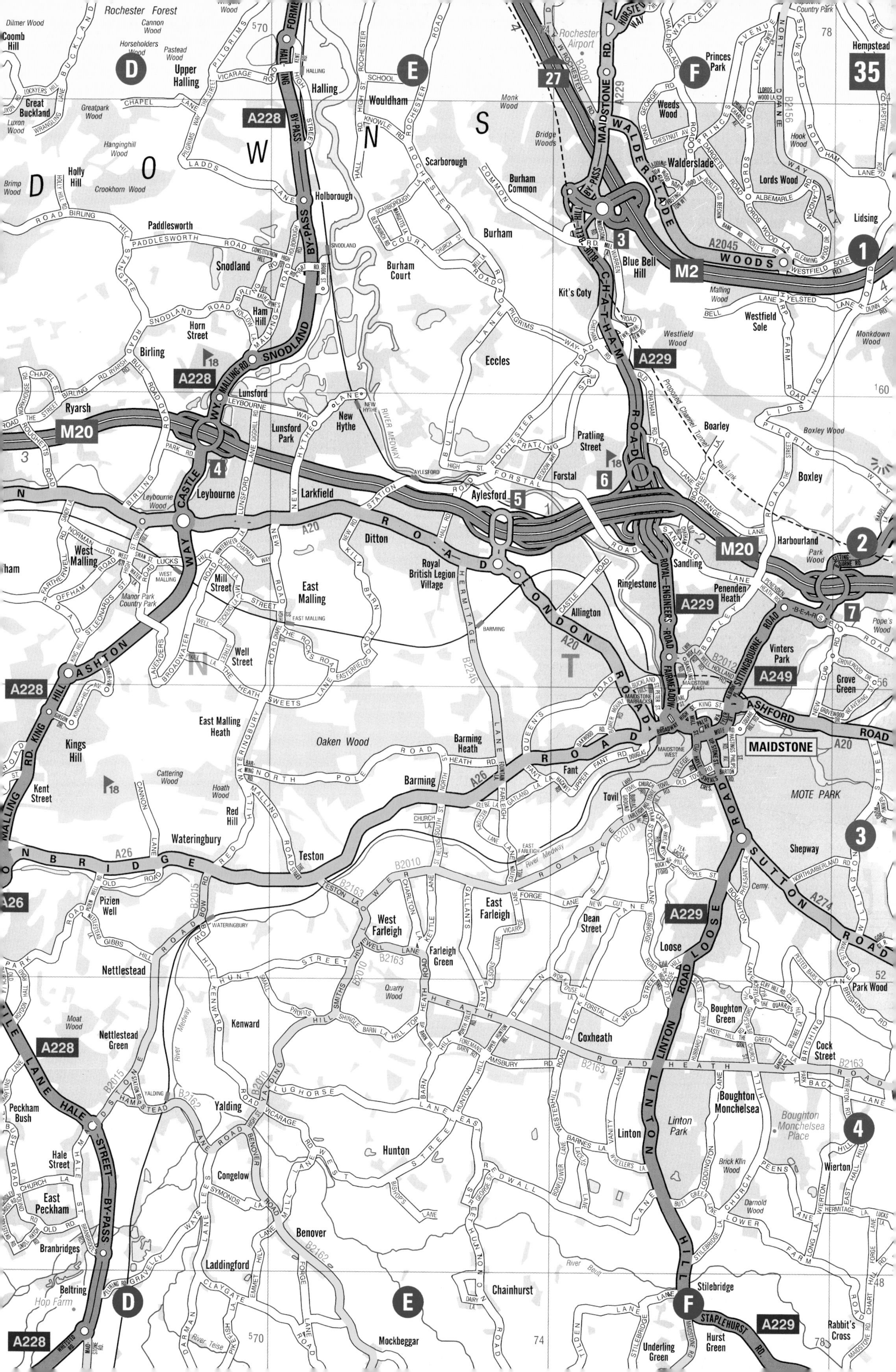
35
Rochester Forest
Upper Halling
Halling
Wouldham
Rochester Airport
Princes Park
Great Buckland
Walderslade
Lords Wood
Lidsing
Hempstead
Holly Hill
Paddlesworth
Holborough
Burham Common
Burham
Scarborough
Snodland
Burham Court
Blue Bell Hill
Kit's Coty
Westfield Sole
Ham Hill
Horn Street
Birling
Eccles
Ryarsh
Lunsford
New Hythe
Lunsford Park
Pratling Street
Boarley
Boxley
Leybourne
Larkfield
Aylesford
Forstal
Ditton
Harbourland
West Malling
Mill Street
East Malling
Royal British Legion Village
Sandling
Ringlestone
Penenden Heath
Allington
Vinters Park
Grove Green
Well Street
Kings Hill
East Malling Heath
Oaken Wood
Barming Heath
MAIDSTONE
Fant
Barming
Tovil
MOTE PARK
Kent Street
Red Hill
Wateringbury
Teston
Shepway
Pizien Well
West Farleigh
East Farleigh
Dean Street
Loose
Nettlestead
Farleigh Green
Park Wood
Kenward
Boughton Green
Coxheath
Cock Street
Nettlestead Green
Peckham Bush
Yalding
Hunton
Boughton Monchelsea
Linton
Linton Park
Hale Street
Congelow
Wierton
East Peckham
Benover
Branbridges
Laddingford
Chainhurst
Stilebridge
Beltring
Mockbeggar
Underling Green
Hurst Green
Rabbit's Cross
M20
M2
A228
A229
A20
A26
A249
A274
B2010
B2015
B2162
B2163

INDEX TO STREETS, PLACES AND AREAS, NAMED JUNCTIONS AND SELECTED TOURIST INFORMATION

HOW TO USE THIS INDEX

1. Each street name is followed by its Postal District (or if outside the London Postal District, by its Posttown or Postal Locality) and then by its map reference; e.g. Abbey Barn La. *High W* —2B **12** is in the High Wycombe Posttown and is to be found in square 2B on page **12**. The page number being shown in bold type.
A strict alphabetical order is followed in which Av., Rd., St., etc. (though abbreviated) are read in full and as part of the street name; e.g. Ash Chu. Rd. appears after Ashburton Rd. but before Ashcombe Rd.

2. Places and areas are shown in the index in **bold type**, the map reference referring to the actual map square in which the town or area is located and not to the place name; eg. **Abbess End. —1A 10**

3. With the now general usage of Postcodes for addressing mail, it is not recommended that this index is used for such a purpose.

GENERAL ABBREVIATIONS

All : Alley
App : Approach
Arc : Arcade
Av : Avenue
Bk : Back
Boulevd : Boulevard
Bri : Bridge
B'way : Broadway
Bldgs : Buildings
Bus : Business
Cvn : Caravan
Cen : Centre
Chu : Church
Chyd : Churchyard
Circ : Circle
Cir : Circus
Clo : Close
Comn : Common
Cotts : Cottages
Ct : Court
Cres : Crescent
Cft : Croft
Dri : Drive
E : East
Embkmt : Embankment
Est : Estate
Fld : Field
Gdns : Gardens
Gth : Garth
Ga : Gate
Gt : Great
Grn : Green
Gro : Grove
Ho : House
Ind : Industrial
Junct : Junction
La : Lane
Lit : Little
Lwr : Lower
Mc : Mac
Mnr : Manor
Mans : Mansions
Mkt : Market
Mdw : Meadow
M : Mews
Mt : Mount
N : North
Pal : Palace
Pde : Parade
Pk : Park
Pas : Passage
Pl : Place
Quad : Quadrant
Res : Residential
Ri : Rise
Rd : Road
Shop : Shopping
S : South
Sq : Square
Sta : Station
St : Street
Ter : Terrace
Trad : Trading
Up : Upper
Va : Vale
Vw : View
Vs : Villas
Wlk : Walk
W : West
Yd : Yard

POSTTOWN AND POSTAL LOCALITY ABBREVIATIONS

Ab R : Abbess Roding
Ab L : Abbots Langley
Ab C : Abinger Common
Ab H : Abinger Hammer
Abr : Abridge
Adtn : Addington
Alb : Albury
Ald : Aldbury
Alder : Aldershot
Amer : Amersham
Art : Artington
Asc : Ascot
Ash : Ash (nr. Aldershot)
As : Ash (nr. Sevenoaks)
Ashf : Ashford
Ash G : Ashley Green
Asht : Ashtead
Ash V : Ash Vale
Ast C : Aston Clinton
Ave : Aveley
Ayl : Aylesbury
Ayle : Aylesford
Badg M : Badgers Mount
Bad L : Badshot Lea
Bag : Bagshot
Bans : Banstead
Bark : Barking
B'side : Barkingside
Barm : Barming
Barn : Barnet
Bas : Basildon
B Hth : Batchworth Heath
Bat : Battlesbridge
B'frd : Bayford
Beac : Beaconsfield
Bean : Bean
Beau R : Beauchamp Roding
Beck : Beckenham
Bedd : Beddington
Bedm : Bedmond
Bell : Bellingdon
Belv : Belvedere
Ben : Benfleet
Berk : Berkhamsted
Berr G : Berrys Green
Bet : Betchworth
Bex : Bexley
Bexh : Bexleyheath
Big H : Biggin Hill
Bill : Billericay
B'bear : Billingbear
Binf : Binfield
Birl : Birling
Bish : Bisham
Bisl : Bisley
B'more : Blackmore
B'water : Blackwater
Bled R : Bledloe Ridge
Blet : Bletchingley
Blue B : Blue Bell Hill
Bookh : Bookham
Bore : Boreham
Borwd : Borehamwood
Bor G : Borough Green
Bough B : Bough Beech
Bou M : Boughton Monchelsea
Bour E : Bourne End
Bov : Bovingdon
Boxl : Boxley
Brack : Bracknell
Brmly : Bramley
Bras : Brasted
Bray : Bray
Braz E : Braziers End
Bred : Bredhurst
Bren : Brentford
Brtwd : Brentwood
Brick : Brickendon
Brock : Brockham
Brom : Bromley
Brook P : Brooklands Ind. Pk.
Brk P : Brookmans Park
Brkwd : Brookwood
Broom : Broomfield
Brox : Broxbourne
Buck H : Buckhurst Hill
Bkld : Buckland (nr. Aylesbury)
Buck : Buckland (nr. Reigate)
Bulp : Bulphan
Bur G : Burchetts Green
Bur : Burcott
Burh : Burham
Burn : Burnham
Bush : Bushey
But C : Butlers Cross
Byfl : Byfleet
Camb : Camberley
Can I : Canvey Island
Cars : Carshalton
Cat : Caterham
Chad H : Chadwell Heath
Chal G : Chalfont St Giles
Chal P : Chalfont St Peter
Chalv : Chalvey
Chan X : Chandlers Cross
Chart : Chartridge
Cha S : Chart Sutton
Chat : Chatham
Chatt : Chattenden
Cheam : Cheam
Chelm : Chelmsford
Chels : Chelsfield
Cher : Chertsey
Che : Chesham
Ches B : Chesham Bois
Chesh : Cheshunt
Chess : Chessington
Chev : Chevening
Chid : Chiddingstone
Chid C : Chiddingstone Causeway
Chig S : Chignal Smealey
Chig : Chigwell
Chil : Chilworth
Chfd : Chipperfield
Chip : Chipstead
Chst : Chislehurst
Chob : Chobham
C'bry : Cholesbury
Chor : Chorleywood
C Crook : Church Crookham
Cipp : Cippenham
Clay : Claygate
Cli : Cliffe
Cobh : Cobham (nr. Esher)
Cob : Cobham (nr. Strood)
Cockf : Cockfosters
Col G : Cole Green
Coles : Coleshill
Coll S : Collier Street
Coln : Colnbrook
Col H : Colney Heath
Comp : Compton
Cook : Cookham
C'ing : Cooling
Coop : Coopersale
Corr : Corringham
Coul : Coulsdon
Cow : Cowley
Cox : Coxheath
Cran : Cranford
Cray : Crayford
Cray H : Crays Hill
Cre P : Cressex Business Park
Crock : Crockenhill
Crock H : Crockham Hill
Crou : Crouch
Crow : Crowhurst
Crowt : Crowthorne
Crox G : Croxley Green
Croy : Croydon
Cud : Cudham
Cuff : Cuffley
Culv : Culverstone
Cux : Cuxton
Dag : Dagenham
Dan : Danbury
Dart : Dartford
Dat : Datchet
Deep : Deepcut
Den : Denham
Det : Detling
Dit : Ditton
Dodd : Doddinghurst
Dork : Dorking
Dor : Dorney
Dor R : Dorney Reach
Dow : Downe
D'ham : Downham
D'ley : Downley
D'side : Downside
Down : Downswood
Dud : Dudswell
D Grn : Dunks Green
Dun : Dunton
Dun G : Dunton Green
E Clan : East Clandon
E Far : East Farleigh
E Han : East Hanningfield
E Hor : East Horsley
E Mal : East Malling
E Mol : East Molesey
E Peck : East Peckham
E Til : East Tilbury
E'wck : Eastwick
Eccl : Eccles
Eden : Edenbridge
Edgw : Edgware
Eff : Effingham
Eff J : Effingham Junction
Egh : Egham
Els : Elstree
Enf : Enfield
Epp : Epping
Epp G : Epping Green
Eps : Epsom
Eri : Erith
Esh : Esher
Ess : Essendon
Eton : Eton
Ewe : Ewell
Ews : Ewshot
Eyns : Eynsford
Fair : Fairseat
Farn : Farnborough
Farnh : Farnham
Farn C : Farnham Common
Farn R : Farnham Royal
F'ham : Farningham
Fawk : Fawkham
Fel : Felden
Felt : Feltham
Fet : Fetcham
Fif : Fifield
Finch : Finchampstead
Five G : Five Oak Green
F Hth : Flackwell Heath
Flau : Flaunden
Fleet : Fleet
Fob : Fobbing
Four E : Four Elms
Frim : Frimley
Frim G : Frimley Green
Frog : Frogmore
Fry : Fryerning
Ful : Fulmer
Fyf : Fyfield
Gad R : Gaddesden Row
Gall : Galleywood
G Grn : George Green
Ger X : Gerrards Cross
Gid P : Gidea Park
Gill : Gillingham
God : Godstone
G Oak : Goffs Oak
Gold G : Golden Green
Gom : Gomshall
Good E : Good Easter
Grav : Gravesend
Grays : Grays
Gt Amw : Great Amwell
Gt Bad : Great Baddow
Gt Gad : Great Gaddesden
Gt Kim : Great Kimble
Gt Kin : Great Kingshill
Gt Miss : Great Missenden
Gt Wal : Great Waldingfield
Gt Walt : Great Waltham
Gt War : Great Warley
Gnfd : Greenford
Grnh : Greenhithe
Grn St : Green Street Green
Guild : Guildford
Had : Hadleigh
Hdlw : Hadlow
Hail : Hailey
Hall : Halling
H'std : Halstead (nr. Braintree)
Hals : Halstead (nr. Otford)
Hal : Halton
Hamp : Hampton
Hamp H : Hampton Hill
Hamp W : Hampton Wick
Hand : Handcross
Hanw : Hanworth
Hare : Harefield
Hare H : Hare Hatch
Harl : Harlington
H'low : Harlow
Harm : Harmondsworth
Hpdn : Harpenden
H'shm : Harrietsham
Harr : Harrow
Hart : Hartley
Hasl : Haslemere
H'wd : Hastingwood
Hast : Hastoe
Hat : Hatfield
Hat H : Hatfield Heath
Hat P : Hatfield Peverel
Hav : Havering-atte-Bower
Hawr : Hawridge
Hay : Hayes
H'ley : Headley
Hedg : Hedgerley
Hem : Hempstead
Hem H : Hemel Hempstead
Hem I : Hemel Hempstead Ind. Est.
Heron : Herongate
Hert : Hertford
Hert H : Hertford Heath
Hever : Hever
Hex : Hextable
High : Higham
H Bee : High Beech
High Bar : High Barnet
H Hals : High Halstow
H Lav : High Laver
H Ong : High Ongar
Hghwd : Highwood
High W : High Wycombe
Hild : Hildenborough
Hod : Hoddesdon
Hods : Hodsoll Street
Holm G : Holmer Green
Holyp : Holyport
Hoo : Hoo
Hook E : Hook End
Hool : Hooley
Horn : Hornchurch
Horn H : Horndon-on-the-Hill
Hors : Horsell
Hort : Horton
Hort K : Horton Kirby
Houn : Hounslow
H Grn : Howe Green
Hugh : Hughenden
Hugh V : Hughenden Valley
Hunt : Hunton
Hur : Hurley
Hut : Hutton
Hyde H : Hyde Heath
Ide H : Ide Hill
Igh : Ightham
Ilf : Ilford
Ing : Ingatestone
Ingve : Ingrave
Iswth : Isleworth
Iver : Iver
Ivy H : Ivy Hatch
Jor : Jordans
Kel C : Kelvedon Common
Kel H : Kelvedon Hatch
Kems : Kemsing
Kenl : Kenley
Kes : Keston
Kiln G : Kiln Green
King H : Kings Hill
K Lan : Kings Langley
King T : Kingston upon Thames
Kgswd : Kingswood
Knap : Knaphill
Knat : Knatts Valley
Knock : Knockholt
Knot : Knotty Green
Know H : Knowl Hill
Lac G : Lacey Green
Ladd : Laddingford
Lain : Laindon
Lale : Laleham
L End : Lane End
Lang H : Langdon Hills
Langl : Langley
Lark : Larkfield
Lea R : Leaden Roding
Lea : Leatherhead
Leav : Leavesden
Lee : Leedon
Leeds : Leeds
Lee G : Lee Gate
L'gh : Leigh (nr. Reigate)
Leigh : Leigh (nr. Tonbridge)
Lem : Lemsford
Let H : Letchmore Heath
Let G : Letty Green
Leyb : Leybourne
Light : Lightwater
Limp : Limpsfield
Linf : Linford
Ling : Lingfield
Lin : Linton
L Bad : Little Baddow
L Berk : Little Berkhamsted
L Bur : Little Burstead
L Chal : Little Chalfont
L Gad : Little Gaddesden
Lit H : Little Heath (nr. Berkhamsted)
L Hth : Little Heath (nr. Romford)
L Kim : Little Kimble
L Kin : Little Kingshill
L Mar : Little Marlow
L Sand : Little Sandhurst
L Walt : Little Waltham
L War : Little Warley
L Grn : Littlewick Green
Lon C : London Colney
H'row A : London Heathrow Airport
Longc : Longcross
Long : Longfield
Loose : Loose
L Row : Loosley Row
Loud : Loudwater
Lou : Loughton
Lwr K : Lower Kingswood
Lwr U : Lower Upnor
Ludd : Luddesdown
Lyne : Lyne
M'head : Maidenhead
Maid : Maidstone
Mard : Marden
Mar R : Margaret Roding
Marg : Margaretting
Mar : Marlow
Mash : Mashbury
Mat G : Matching Green
Mat T : Matching Tye
Mayf : Mayford
Medm : Medmenham
Meop : Meopham
Mere : Mereworth
Mers : Merstham
Mick : Mickleham
Mitc : Mitcham
Mon R : Monks Risborough
Mord : Morden
More : Moreton
Mount : Mountnessing
Myt : Mytchett
Nap : Naphill
Nash : Nash
Nave : Navestock
N'side : Navestockside
Naze : Nazeing
Nett : Nettlestead
New Ad : New Addington
New Ash : New Ash Green
New S : Newgate Street
New H : New Haw
N Mald : New Malden
Noak H : Noak Hill
Norm : Normandy
N Asc : North Ascot
N'thaw : Northaw
N Ben : North Benfleet
N'chu : Northchurch
N Dean : North Dean
N'fleet : Northfleet
N Har : North Harrow
N Holm : North Holmwood
N Mym : North Mymms
N'holt : Northolt
N Stif : North Stifford
N Wea : North Weald
N'wd : Northwood
Nup : Nuptown
Nutf : Nutfield
Oak G : Oakley Green
Ock : Ockham
Off : Offham
Old Win : Old Windsor
Old Wok : Old Woking
Ong : Ongar
Orch : Orchard Leigh
Orp : Orpington
Ors : Orsett
Otf : Otford
Otham : Otham
Ott : Ottershaw
Out : Outwood
Oxs : Oxshott
Oxt : Oxted
Pad W : Paddock Wood
Par H : Parslows Hillock
Penn : Penn
Penn S : Penn Street
Pic E : Piccotts End
Pid : Piddington
Pil H : Pilgrims Hatch
Pim : Pimlico
Pinn : Pinner
Pirb : Pirbright
Pits : Pitsea
Platt : Platt
Plax : Plaxtol
Pott E : Potten End
Pot B : Potters Bar
Pot C : Potters Crouch
Prat B : Pratts Bottom
P'wd : Prestwood
P Ris : Princes Risborough
Purf : Purfleet
Purl : Purley
Putt : Puttenham
Pyr : Pyrford
Rad : Radlett
R'ge : Radnage
Rain : Rainham
Rams H : Ramsden Heath
Ran C : Ranmore Common
Raw : Rawreth
Ray : Rayleigh
Redb : Redbourn
Red : Redhill
Red A : Redhill Aerodrome
Reig : Reigate
Ret C : Rettendon Common
Rich : Richmond
Rick : Rickmansworth
Ridge : Ridge
Rip : Ripley
Roch : Rochester
Romf : Romford
Rough : Roughway
Rox : Roxwell
Roy : Roydon
Ruis : Ruislip
Runf : Runfold
Runw : Runwell
Rya : Ryarsh
St Alb : St Albans
St L : St Leonards
St M : St Mary Cray
St P : St Pauls Cray
Salf : Salfords
Sand : Sandhurst
S'ing : Sandling
S'don : Sandon
Sandr : Sandridge
Sarr : Sarratt
S'ton : Saunderton
Saw : Sawbridgeworth
Seal : Seal
Seale : Seale
Send : Send
Sev : Sevenoaks
Shalf : Shalford
Srng : Sheering
Shenf : Shenfield
Shenl : Shenley
Shep : Shepperton
Shere : Shere
S'brne : Shipbourne
Shor : Shoreham
Shorne : Shorne
Short : Shortlands
Shur R : Shurlock Row
Sidc : Sidcup
Slou : Slough
Smal : Smallford
Snod : Snodland
S'hall : Southall
S Croy : South Croydon
S Dar : South Darenth
S'fleet : Southfleet
S God : South Godstone
S Han : South Hanningfield
S Nut : South Nutfield
S Ock : South Ockendon
S Pk : South Park
S Wea : South Weald
Sole S : Sole Street
Speen : Speen
Spri : Springfield
Stai : Staines
Stan H : Stanford-le-Hope
Stan : Stanmore
Stan A : Stanstead Abbotts
Stans : Stansted
Stanw : Stanwell
Stap A : Stapleford Abbotts
S'hrst : Staplehurst
Stock : Stock
Stoke D : Stoke D'abernon
Stoke M : Stoke Mandeville
Stok : Stokenchurch
Stoke P : Stoke Poges
Ston M : Stondon Massey
Stone : Stone
Strood : Strood
Str G : Strood Green
Sun : Sunbury-on-Thames
Sund : Sundridge
S'dale : Sunningdale
S'hill : Sunninghill
Surb : Surbiton
Sur R : Surrey Research Park
Sutt : Sutton
S at H : Sutton at Hone
Sut G : Sutton Green
Swan : Swanley
Swans : Swanscombe
Tad : Tadworth
Tand : Tandridge
Tap : Taplow
Tats : Tatsfield
Tedd : Teddington
Terl : Terling
Ter : Terrick
Tstn : Teston
Th Dit : Thames Ditton
They B : Theydon Bois
They G : Theydon Garnon
They M : Theydon Mount
T Hth : Thornton Heath
Thorn : Thornwood
Thr B : Threshers Bush
Til : Tilbury
T'sey : Titsey
Tonb : Tonbridge
Tong : Tongham
Ton : Tonwell
Toot : Toot Hill
Tovil : Tovil
Tring : Tring
Tros : Trottiscliffe
Twic : Twickenham
Tyngr : Tyttenhanger
Under : Underriver
Upm : Upminster
Upnor : Upnor
Up H'ing : Upper Halling
Uxb : Uxbridge
Van : Vange
Vir W : Virginia Water
Wain : Wainscott
W'slde : Walderslade
Wall : Wallington
Wal A : Waltham Abbey
Wal X : Waltham Cross
Wal L : Waltham St Lawrence
W on T : Walton-on-Thames
Wanb : Wanborough
Ware : Ware
Warf : Warfield
War : Warley
Warl : Warlingham
Wat E : Water End
W'bury : Wateringbury
Wat : Watford
Weald : Weald
W'stone : Wealdstone
Weav : Weavering
Well : Welling
Wel G : Welwyn Garden City
Wemb : Wembley
Wen : Wennington
W Byf : West Byfleet
W Cla : West Clandon
Westc : Westcott
W Dray : West Drayton
W End : West End
W'ham : Westerham
W Far : West Farleigh
W Han : West Hanningfield
W Horn : West Hornden
W H'dn : West Horndon
W Hor : West Horsley
Westh : Westhumble
W King : West Kingsdown
W Mal : West Malling
W Mol : West Molesey
W'ton T : Weston Turville
W Peck : West Peckham
W Thur : West Thurrock
W Til : West Tilbury
W Wick : West Wickham
W Wyc : West Wycombe
Wheat : Wheathampstead
Wtlf : Whiteleaf
Whit : Whitton
Whyt : Whyteleafe
Wid : Widford

Posttown and Postal Locality Abbreviations

Wig : Wigginton
Will : Willingale
Winch H : Winchmore Hill
W'sham : Windlesham

Wind : Windsor
Wink : Winkfield
Wink R : Winkfield Row
Wok : Woking

Wokgm : Wokingham
Wold : Woldingham
Wbrn G : Wooburn Green
Wbrn M : Wooburn Moor

Wdhm : Woodham
Wdrow : Woodrow
Wood S : Wood Street Village
Wor Pk : Worcester Park

Worm : Wormley
Worp : Worplesdon
Wott : Wotton
Woul : Wouldham

Wray : Wraysbury
Writ : Writtle
Wro : Wrotham
Wro H : Wrotham Heath

Wy G : Wyatts Green
Yald : Yalding
Yiew : Yiewsley

INDEX

Betsham Rd.—Butt Grn. La.

Betsham Rd. S'fleet —3B 26
Betts La. Naze —2C 8
Between Streets. Cobh —1B 30
Beulah Hill. SE19 —3A 24
Beulah Rd. T Hth —3A 24
Beverley Dri. Egdwd —2D 15
Beverley Gdns. Chesh —3B 8
Beverley Rd. Dag —3E 17
Beverley Rd. Whyt —2A 32
Beverley Way. SW20 & N Mald —3D 23
Bewley La. Plax —3B 34
Bexley. —2E 25
Bexleyheath. —2E 25
Bexley High St. Bex —2E 25
Bexley La. Sidc —3E 25
Bexley Rd. SE9 —2D 25
Bexley Rd. Eri —1F 25 (in two parts)
Beynon Rd. Cars —4F 23
Bickley. —3D 25
Bickley Pk. Rd. Brom —3D 25
Bickley Rd. Brom —3C 24
Bicknacre. —3F 11
Bicknacre Rd. Dan —2F 11
Bicknacre Rd. E Han —3F 11
Big Comn. La. Blet —4A 32
Bigfrith La. Cook —3B 12
Biggin Hill. —2C 32
Biggin Hill Airport. —1C 32
Bignells Corner. —3E 7
Bignells Corner. (Junct.) —3E 7
Billericay. —1D 19
Billericay Rd. Heron & Bill —2C 18
Billet Hill. As —4B 26
Billet La. Berk —1E 5
Billet La. Horn —3F 17
Billet La. Slou & Iver —4E 13
Billet La. Stan H —4D 19
Billet Rd. E17 —2B 16
Billet Rd. Romf —2E 17
Billingbear. —2A 20
Billingbear La. Binf —2A 20
Bill St. Rd. Roch —3E 27
Bilton Rd. Gnfd —4C 14
Bilton Way. Enf —4B 8
Bincote Rd. Enf —4A 8
Binfield. —3A 20
Binfield Rd. Brack —3A 20
Binfield Rd. Wokgm —3A 20
Bingham Rd. Croy —4B 24
Binton La. Seale —4B 28
Birchall La. Col G —1F 7
Birchanger Rd. SE25 —4B 24
Birch Green. —1F 7
Birch Hill Rd. Brack —4B 20
Birchin Cross Rd. Knat —2A 34
Birch La. Flau —3E 5
Birchwood. —1E 7
Birchwood Av. Hat —1E 7
Birchwood Rd. Swan & Dart —3F 25
Bird La. Gt War —2B 18
Bird La. Upm —2A 18
Birds Green. —1B 10
Birds Grn. Will —2A 10
Birkbeck Rd. W3 —4D 15
Birling. —1D 35
Birling Hill. Snod —1D 35
Birling Rd. Rya —2D 35
Birling Rd. Snod —1D 35
Birling Rd. W Mal —2D 35
Bisham. —3A 12
Bisham Abbey. —3A 12
Bishops Av., The. N2 —3F 15
Bishop's Bri. W2 —4E 15
Bishopsford Rd. Mord —4F 23
Bishopsgate. EC3 —4A 16
Bishopsgate Rd. Egh —2E 21
Bishop's La. Hunt —4E 35
Bishop's La. Wink —2B 20
Bishops Rise. Hat —2D 7
Bishops Stortford Rd. Rox —1C 10
Bishopstone. Ayl —1A 4
Bishop's Way. E2 —4B 16
Bisley. —2D 29
Bisley Camp. —2C 28
Bitchet Green. —3A 34
Bittacy Hill. NW7 —2F 15
Blackamoor La. M'head —4B 12
Blackbird Hill. NW9 —3D 15
Blackborough Rd. Reig —4F 31
Black Boy La. N15 —2A 16
Blackbrook La. Brom —4D 25
Blackbrook Rd. Dork —4C 30
Black Bush La. Horn H —4C 18
Blackcat. —1A 10
Blackdown Rd. Deep —2C 28
Blacketts Wood Dri. Chor —1E 13
Black Fan Rd. Wel G —1E 7
Blackfen. —2E 25
Blackfen Rd. Sidc —2D 25
Blackfriars Bri. SE1 —4A 16
Blackfriars Rd. SE1 —4A 16
Blackhall La. Sev —3A 34
Blackheath. —2C 24
Blackheath Hill. SE10 —1C 24
Blackheath La. Alb —4F 29
Blackheath Park. —2C 24
Blackheath Rd. SE8 —1B 24
Blackheath Rugby Ground. —1C 24
Blackheath Village. SE3 —1C 24
Blackhorse Lane. (Junct.) —2B 16
Blackhorse La. E17 —2B 16
Black Horse La. Croy —4B 24
Blackhorse La. Pot B —3D 7
Blackhorse La. Tad —3E 31
Blackhorse Rd. E17 —2B 16
Blackhorse Rd. Wok —2D 29
Black Lion Hill. Shenl —3D 7
Blackmans La. Hdlw —4C 34
Blackmans La. Warl —1C 32
Blackmore. —3B 10
Blackmore Rd. B'more & Fry —3B 10
Blackmore Rd. Ing & Hghwd —3C 10
Blackmore Rd. Kel H & Ing —4A 10
Blackness La. Kes —1C 32
Blacknest. —3D 21
Blacknest Rd. Asc & Vir W —3D 21
Black Pk. Rd. Slou —4E 13
Blackpond La. Slou —3D 13
Black Prince Interchange. (Junct.) —2E 25
Blackshaw Rd. SW17 —3F 23
Blackshots La. Grays —4C 18
Blacksmith La. Chil —4F 29
Blacksmiths La. Den —3F 13
Blacksmith's La. Orp —4E 25
Blackstock Rd. N4 & N5 —3A 16
Blackstroud La. E. Light —1C 28
Blackwall La. SE10 —1C 24 (in two parts)
Blackwall Tunnel Northen App. E3 & E14 —4C 16
Blackwall Tunnel Southern App. SE10 —1C 24
Blackwater. —2A 28
Blackwater La. Hem H —2A 6
Blackwater Valley Relief Rd. Camb —2A 28
Blackwater Valley Route. Farnh & Alder —4B 28
Blackwell Dri. Wat —1B 14
Blackwell Hall La. Che —3E 5
Blake Hall Gardens. —2F 9
Blake Hall Rd. E11 —3C 16
Blake Hall Rd. Ong —2F 9
Blake Hall War Museum. —2F 9
Blakeney Rd. Beck —3B 24
Blanchards Hill. Guild —3E 29
Blanch La. Pot B —3D 7
Blandford Rd. S. Slou —1E 21
Blasford Hill. —1E 11
Blay's La. Egh —3E 21
Blendon Rd. Bex —2E 25
Bletchingley. —4A 32
Bletchingley Rd. God —4B 32
Bletchingley Rd. Mers —3F 31
Bletchingley Rd. Nutf —4A 32
Blighton La. Farnh —4B 28
Bligh Way. Roch —3E 27
Blind La. Bour E & F Hth —3B 12
Blind La. W Han —3E 11
Blindley Heath. —4B 32
Bloemfontein Rd. W12 —4E 15
Bloomsbury St. WC1 —4F 15
Blue Anchor La. W Til —1C 26
Blue Bell Hill. —1F 35
Blue Bell Hill By-Pass. W'slde —1F 35
Blueberry La. Knock —2E 33
Blue Bri. Rd. Brk P —2E 7
Blue Circle Heritage Centre. —2B 26
Bluehouse Hill. St Alb —2B 6
Bluehouse La. Oxt —3C 32
Bluewater. —2A 26
Bluewater Parkway. Grnh —2A 26
Blundel La. Stoke D —2B 30
Blunts La. Pot C —2B 6
Blyth Rd. Hay —1A 22
Boarley. —2F 35
Boarley La. S'lng —2F 35 (in two parts)
Bobbingworth. —2F 9
Bobmore La. Mar —3A 12
Bockingford La. Maid —3F 35
Bockmer. Mar —3A 12
Bois La. Amer —4D 5
Bois Moor Rd. Che —3D 5
Boley Hill. Roch —3F 27
Boleyn Rd. N16 —3A 16
Bolingbroke Gro. SW11 —2F 23
Bollo La. W3 & W4 —1D 23
Bolters La. Bans —1E 31
Bolton Av. Wind —2D 21
Bolton Rd. Wind —2D 21
Boltons La. Wok —2F 29
Bolton St. W1 —4F 15
Bond St. W5 —4C 14
Bond St. Egh —3E 21
Bond Way. SW8 —1A 24
Bonner Rd. E2 —4B 16
Bonsor Dri. Tad —2E 31
Booker. —2A 12
Bookham Rd. D'side —2B 30
Booth Rd. HA8 —2D 15
Border's La. Lou —4D 9
Boreham. —1F 11
Borehamwood. —4D 7
Borough Green. —2B 34
Borough Grn. Rd. Igh —2B 34
Borough Grn. Rd. Wro —2B 34
Borough High St. SE1 —1A 24
Borough Rd. SE1 —1A 24
Borough Rd. Iswth —1C 22
Borough, The. —1A 24
Borstal. —4E 27
Borstal Rd. Roch —4E 27
Borstal St. Roch —4E 27
Boss La. Hugh V —4B 4
Bostall Hill. SE18 —1E 25
Boston Manor. —1C 22
Boston Mnr. Rd. Bren —1C 22
Boston Rd. W7 —1C 22
Botany Bay. —4F 7
Botley. —3E 5
Botley Rd. Che —3D 5
Botney Hill Rd. L Bur —2C 18
Botsom La. W King —1A 34
Bottle La. L Grn —1A 20
Bottle La. Warf —2A 20
Bottlescrew Hill. Bou M —4F 35
Bottom All. Holm G —4C 4
Bottom Ho. Farm La. Chal G —1D 13
Bottom Ho. La. New G —1D 5
Bottom La. K Lan —4F 5
Bottom La. Seer —2D 13
Bottom Rd. R'ge —1A 12
Bottom Rd. St L & Buck C —2C 4
Bottrells La. Coles & Chal G —1D 13
Botwell Comn. Rd. Hay —4A 14
Botwell La. Hay —4A 14
Bough Beech. —4E 33
Bough Beech Rd. Four E —4E 33
Boughton Green. —4F 35
Boughton La. Maid —3F 35
Boughton Monchelsea. —4F 35
Boughton Monchelsea Place. —4F 35
Bounces Rd. N9 —1B 16
Boundary Rd. E13 —4C 16
Boundary Rd. E17 —3B 16
Boundary Rd. NW8 —4E 15
Boundary Rd. Cars —1F 31
Boundary Rd. Farn —3B 28
Boundary Rd. Loud & Wbrn G —2C 12
Boundary Rd. Tap —4C 12
Bounds Green. —2F 15
Bounds Grn. Rd. N11 & N22 —2F 15
Bourley Rd. C Crook & Alder —4A 28
Bournebridge. —1E 17
Bournebridge La. Stap A —1E 17
Bourne End. —3C 12 **(nr. Cores End)**
Bourne End. —2E 5 **(nr. Hemel Hempstead)**
Bourne End Rd. Bour E —3C 12
Bourne Hill. N13 —1A 16
Bourne La. Sev —3B 34
Bourne Rd. Bex & Dart —2E 25
Bourne, The. N14 —1F 15
Bourne Way. Brom —4C 24
Boveney. —1C 20
Boveney Rd. Dor —1C 20
Boveney Wood La. Burn —3C 12
Bovingdon. —3E 5
Bovingdon Green. —3E 5 **(nr. Bovingdon)**
Bovingdon Green. —3A 12 **(nr. Marlow)**
Bovingdon Grn. La. Hem H —3E 5
Bovinger. —2F 9
Bow. —4B 16
Bow Common. —4B 16
Bow Comn. La. E3 —4B 16
Boweashe La. Sev —2C 34
Bowerdean Rd. High W —1B 12
Bower Hill. Epp —3E 9
Bower Hill La. S Nut —4F 31
Bower La. Eyns & Sev —4A 26
Bower Mt. Rd. Maid —3F 35
Bowers Gifford. —2F 19
Bowes Park. —2A 16
Bowes Rd. N11 & N13 —1F 15
Bow Interchange. (Junct.) —4C 16
Bowood La. Wen —2B 4
Bow Rd. E3 —4B 16
Bow Rd. W'bury —3D 35
Bow St. WC2 —4A 16
Bowstridge La. Chal G —1E 13
Bowyer's La. Warf —2B 20
Bowzell Rd. Weald —4F 33
Bowzell's La. Chid C —4F 33
Boxall's La. Alder —4B 28
Boxgrove Rd. Guild —4E 29
Box Hill. —4D 31
Boxhill Rd. Tad —4D 31
Box La. Hem H —2F 5
Boxley. —2F 35
Boxley Rd. Boxl —2F 35
Boxley Rd. Chat —1F 35
Boxley Rd. W'slde —1F 35
Boxmoor. —2F 5
Boxted. Hem H —1F 5
Boxtree Rd. Harr —2C 14
Boyn Hill. —4B 12
Boyn Hill Rd. M'head —4B 12
Boyn Valley Rd. M'head —4B 12
Boyton Cross. —1C 10
Boyton Cross La. Rox —1C 10
Bracknell. —3B 20
Bracknell Rd. Bag —4C 20
Bracknell Rd. Crowt —4A 20
Bracknell Rd. Warf —3B 20
Bradbourne Pk. Rd. Sev —3F 33
Bradbourne Rd. Sev —2F 33
Bradbourne Vale Rd. Sev —2F 33
Bradcutts La. Cook —3B 12
Bradden La. Gad R —1F 5
Bradenham. —4A 4
Bradenham La. Mar —3A 12
Bradenham Rd. W Wyc —4A 4
Bradenham Wood La. Walt A —4A 4
Bradmore La. Brk P —2E 7
Bragmans La. Rick —3F 5
Braham St. E1 —4A 16
Bramble La. Upm —4A 18
Bramley Hill. S Croy —4A 24
Bramley Rd. N14 —1F 15
Brampton Rd. Bexh —1E 25
Bramshot La. Fleet —3A 28
Bramston Way. Lain —2D 19
Branbridges. —4D 35
Branbridges Rd. E Peck —4D 35 (in two parts)
Brancaster La. Purl —1A 32
Branch Hill. NW3 —3F 15
Branch Rd. St Alb —2B 6
Brands Hatch Motor Racing Circuit. —4A 26
Brands Hatch Rd. Fawk —4B 26
Brands Hill. —1E 21
Branksome Av. Stan H —4D 19
Branksome Hill Rd. Camb —1A 28
Brasted. —3E 33
Brasted Chart. —3E 33
Brasted Hill. Knock & W'ham —2E 33
Brasted Hill Rd. Bras —2E 33
Brasted La. Knock —2E 33
Brasted Rd. W'ham —3D 33
Brawlings La. Ger X —1E 13
Bray. —1C 20
Bray Rd. M'head —4B 12
Bray Rd. Stoke D —2B 30
Brays Grn. La. Hyde H —4C 4
Brays Grove. —1E 9
Brays La. Hyde H —3C 4
Bray Wick. —1B 20
Braywick Rd. M'head —4B 12
Braywoodside. —2B 20
Braziers End. Braz E —2C 4
Braziers La. Wink R —3C 20
Bread and Cheese La. Chesh —2A 8
Breakspear Rd. Ruis —2A 14
Breakspear Rd. N. Hare —2F 13
Breakspear Rd. S. Uxb —3A 14
Breakspear Way. Hem H —2A 6
Brecknock Rd. N19 & N7 —3F 15
Breeds Rd. Gt Walt —1D 11
Brenchley Gdns. SE23 —2B 24
Brennan Rd. Til —1C 26
Brent Cross. —3E 15
Brent Cross Interchange. (Junct.) —2E 15
Brentfield. NW10 —3D 15
Brentfield Rd. NW10 —3D 15
Brentford End. —1C 22
Brentford F.C. —1C 22
Brentmoor Rd. W End —1D 29
Brent St. NW4 —2E 15
Brent, The. Dart —2A 26
Brentwood. —1B 18
Brentwood By-Pass. Brtwd —1A 18
Brentwood Rd. Bulp & Grays —3C 18
Brentwood Rd. Grays —1C 26
Brentwood Rd. Heron —2C 18
Brentwood Rd. Ingve —1B 18
Brentwood Rd. Ong —3A 10
Brentwood Rd. Romf —2F 17
Brentwood Rd. W H'dn —3C 18
Brewers Rd. Shorne —3D 27
Brewer St. Blet —4A 32
Brewery La. Byfl —1A 30
Brewery Rd. N7 —3A 16
Brewery Rd. SE18 —1D 25
Brewery Rd. Wok —2E 29
Brickendon. —1A 8
Brickendon La. Brick —1A 8
Bricket Wood. —3B 6
Brick Hill. —4D 21
Brick Kiln La. Oxt —3C 32
Brick Kiln Rd. S'don —2F 11
Brick La. E1 —4A 16
Bricklayer's Arms. (Junct.) —1A 24
Bridge End. —2A 30
Bridge Hill. Epp —3D 9
Bridge La. Vir W —4E 21
Bridgen Rd. Bex —2E 25
Bridge Rd. E15 —4C 16
Bridge Rd. N22 —2A 16
Bridge Rd. Bag —1C 28
Bridge Rd. Beck —3B 24
Bridge Rd. Cher —4F 21
Bridge Rd. Chess —4D 23
Bridge Rd. E Mol —3C 22
Bridge Rd. Eps —1D 31
Bridge Rd. Eri —1F 25
Bridge Rd. Farn —3A 28
Bridge Rd. Grays —1B 26
Bridge Rd. Houn —2C 22
Bridge Rd. K Lan —3A 6
Bridge Rd. M'head —4B 12
Bridge Rd. More —2F 9
Bridge Rd. Rain —4F 17
Bridge Rd. Wemb —3D 15
Bridge Rd. Wey —4A 22
Bridge Rd. E. Wel G —1E 7
Bridge St. Coln —1F 21
Bridge St. Gt Kim —2A 4
Bridge St. Guild —4E 29
Bridge St. Pinn —2B 14
Bridge St. W on T —4A 22
Bridge St. Writ —2D 11
Bridge, The. Harr —2C 14
Bridgewater Rd. Berk —1E 5
Bridgewater Rd. Wemb —3C 14
Bridle Rd. Croy —4B 24 (in two parts)
Bridle Rd. Pinn —2B 14
Bridle Rd., The. Purl —1A 32
Bridle Way N. Hod —1B 8
Bridle Way S. Hod —1B 8
Bridport Rd. N18 —2A 16
Brighton Rd. Add —4F 21
Brighton Rd. Bans —2E 31
Brighton Rd. Hool & Coul —3F 31
Brighton Rd. Purl & S Croy —1A 32
Brighton Rd. Red —4F 31
Brighton Rd. Salf —4F 31
Brighton Rd. Surb —4C 22
Brighton Rd. Tad & Bans —2E 31
Brigstock Rd. T Hth —4A 24
Brimmers Hill. Wid E —4B 4
Brimmers Rd. P Ris —3A 4
Brimsdown. —4B 8
Brimsdown Av. Enf —4B 8
Brimstone Hill. Meop —4C 26
Brimstone La. Meop —4C 26
Brishing La. Bou M —4F 35
Brishing Rd. Cha S —4F 35
Britannia Rd. H Hals —2F 27
Brittains La. Sev —3F 33
Brittania Junction. (Junct.) —3F 15
Britwell. —4D 13
Britwell Rd. Slou —4C 12
Brixton. —2A 24
Brixton Hill. SW2 —2A 24
Brixton Rd. SW9 —2A 24
Brixton Water La. SW2 —2A 24
Broad Colney. —3C 6
Broad Ditch Rd. Meop —3C 26
Broadfields Av. Edgw —1D 15
Broad Grn. B'frd —1A 8
Broadgreen Wood. —1A 8
Broadham Green. —4C 32
Broadham Grn. Rd. Oxt —4C 32
Broadhurst Gdns. NW6 —3E 15
Broad La. N15 —2A 16
Broad La. Brack —3B 20
Broad La. Dart —3F 25
Broad La. Hamp —3B 22
Broad La. Wbrn G & Beac —2C 12
Broadley Common. —2D 9
Broadmayne. Bas —2E 19
Broadmead Rd. Hay & N'holt —4B 14
Broadmead Rd. Send —2E 29
Broadmead Rd. Wfd G —2C 16
Broadmoor La. Wal L & White —1A 20
Broad Sanctuary. SW1 —1F 23
Broad's Green. —1D 11
Broad Street. —3F 27
Broad St. Che —3D 5
Broad St. Dag —3E 17
Broad St. Guild —4D 29
Broad St. Tedd —3C 22
Broadview Gardens. —4C 34
Broad Wlk. SE3 —1C 24
Broadwater Rd. Wel G —1E 7
Broadwater Rd. W Mal —2D 35
Broadway. E15 —3C 16 (in two parts)
Broadway. Amer —4D 5
Broadway. Bexh —2E 25
Broadway. Knap —2D 29
Broadway. M'head —4B 12
Broadway. Maid —3F 35
Broadway. Rain —4F 17
Broadway. Surb —4D 23
Broadway. Swan —4F 25
Broadway. W'fd —1F 19
Broadway Mkt. E2 —4B 16
Broadway Rd. Light & W'sham —1C 28
Broadway, The. N8 —2A 16
Broadway, The. N9 —1B 16
Broadway, The. NW7 —1D 15
Broadway, The. NW9 —2D 15
Broadway, The. SW19 —3E 23
Broadway, The. W13 —4C 14
Broadway, The. Cheam —1E 31
Broadway, The. Gnfd —4C 14
Broadway, The. Horn —3F 17
Broadway, The. Lou —4D 9
Broadway, The. S'hall —4B 14
Broadway, The. Stai —3F 21
Broadway, The. Stan —1C 14
Broadway, The. Wok —2E 29
Brockenhurst Rd. Asc —3C 20
Brocket Rd. Lem & Wel G —1D 7
Brockham. —4D 31
Brockhamhurst Rd. Bet —4D 31
Brockham La. Brock —4D 31
Brock Hill. —4E 11
Brock Hill. Runw —4E 11
Brockley. —2B 24
Brockley Gro. SE4 —2B 24
Brockley Hill. Stan —1C 14
Brockley Rise. SE23 —2B 24
Brockley Rd. SE23 —2B 24
Brock Rd. Ilf —2D 17
Bromley. —4B 16 **(nr. Bow)**
Bromley. —3C 24 **(nr. Chislehurst)**
Bromley Common. —4D 25
Bromley Comn. Brom —3C 24
Bromley Hill. Brom —3C 24
Bromley La. Chst —3D 25
Bromley Museum. —4E 25
Bromley Rd. SE6 & Brom —2B 24
Bromley Rd. Beck & Brom —3B 24
Bromley Rd. Chst —3D 25
Brompton. —1F 23 **(nr. Belgravia)**
Brompton. —3F 27 **(nr. Chatham)**
Brompton Farm Rd. Roch —3E 27
Brompton Rd. SW3 —1F 23
Brompton Rd. Gill —3F 27
Brondesbury. —3E 15
Brondesbury Pk. NW2 & NW6 —3E 15
Brondesbury Park. —3E 15
Brondesbury Rd. NW6 —4E 15
Bronze Age Way. Eri —1F 25
Brookbank. Wbrn G —3C 12
Brookdene Av. Wat —1B 14
Brook End. W'ton T —1A 4
Brook End Rd. Chelm —2E 11
Brookers Row. Crowt —4A 20
Brookfield La. W. Chesh —3B 8
Brook Green. —1E 23
Brook Hill. L Walt —1E 11
Brookhill Rd. Barn —1F 15
Brooklands. —1A 30
Brooklands Rd. Wey —1A 30
Brook La. Gall —3E 11
Brook La. Plax —3B 34
Brook La. Wal L —2A 20
Brookmans Park. —3E 7
Brookmill Rd. SE8 —1B 24
Brook Pl. Ide H —3E 33
Brook Rd. Borwd —4D 7
Brook Rd. Buck H —1C 16
Brook Rd. Epp —3E 9
Brook Rd. Ilf —2D 17
Brooksby's Wlk. E9 —3B 16
Brookshill. Harr —1C 14
Brookside. —3C 20
Brookside S. EN4 —1F 15
Brook Street. —1A 18
Brookwood. —2D 29
Brook St. Ast C —1B 4
Brook St. Belv & Eri —1E 25
Brook St. Brtwd —1A 18
Brook St. Snod —1E 35
Brook St. Tring —1C 4
Brook, The. Chat —3F 27
Brookwood Lye Rd. Wok —2D 29
Broombarn La. Gt Miss —3B 4
Broomfield. —1E 11
Broomfield Av. N13 —1A 16
Broomfield Rd. N13 —1A 16
Broomfield Rd. Chelm —2E 11
Broomhall. —4D 21
Broomhall La. Asc —4D 21
Broomhill Rd. Wfd G —2C 16 (in two parts)
Broomhills. —2D 19
Broom Rd. Tedd —3C 22
Broomstick Hall Rd. Wal A —3C 8
Broomwood La. Stock & Rams H —4E 11
Broomwood Rd. SW11 —2F 23
Browells La. Felt —2B 22
Brownhill Rd. SE6 —2C 24
Browning Rd. E12 —3D 17
Browning Rd. Enf —4A 8
Brownlow Rd. N11 —2A 16
Brownlow Rd. Berk —1E 5
Browns La. Eden —4D 33
Brown's Rd. Holm G —4C 4
Browns Rd. Hyde E —3C 4
Brownswood Rd. N4 —3A 16
Brox. —1F 29
Broxbourne. —2B 8
Broxhill Rd. Hav —1F 17
Brox Rd. Ott —1F 29
Bruce Gro. N17 —2A 16
Brunel Rd. SE16 —1B 24
Brunswick Av. N11 —1F 15
Brunswick Park. —1F 15
Brunswick Pk. Rd. N11 —1F 15
Brunswick Rd. W5 —4C 14
Bruton St. W1 —4F 15
Bryant Av. Romf —2F 17
Bryant's Bottom. —4A 4
Bryant's Bottom Rd. Gt Miss —3A 4
Bucketsland La. Borwd —4D 7
Buckhatch La. Ret C —4F 11
Buckhold Rd. SW18 —2E 23
Buckhurst Hill. —1C 16
Buckhurst Rd. Asc —3D 21
Buckhurst Rd. W'ham —2D 33
Buckhurst Way. Buck H —1C 16
Buckingham Av. Slou —4D 13
Buckingham Hill Rd. Stan H —4F 19
Buckingham Palace. —1F 23
Buckingham Pal. Rd. SW1 —1F 23
Buckingham Rd. N22 —2A 16
Buckingham Rd. Edgw —2D 15
Buckingham Way. Frim —2B 28
Buckland. —1B 4 **(nr. Aston Clinton)**
Buckland. —4E 31 **(nr. Reigate)**
Buckland Common. —2C 4
Buckland Cres. NW3 —3F 15
Buckland Hill. Maid —2F 35
Buckland Rd. Buck —1B 4
Buckland Rd. High —2E 27
Buckland Rd. Lwr K —3E 31
Buckland Rd. Ludd —4D 27
Buckland Rd. Reig —4E 31
Buckmoorend. —2A 4
Bucks All. L Berk —2F 7
Bucks Cross Rd. Orp —4E 25
Bucks Hill. —4F 5
Bucks Hill. K Lan —3F 5
Budds. —3A 34
Budgin's Hill. Prat B —1E 33
Bug Hill. Wold & Warl —2B 32
Bugsby's Way. SE10 & SE7 —1C 24
Bulbeggers La. God —4B 32
Bulbourne Rd. Tring —1C 4
Bullbeggars La. Berk —2E 5
Bullbeggars La. Wok —2E 29
Bullbrook. —3B 20
Bullen La. E Peck —4D 35
Bullen's Green. —2D 7
Bullen's Grn. La. Col H —2D 7
Buller Rd. Alder —3B 28
Bullfinch La. Sev —2F 33
Bull Hill. Lea —2C 30
Bull La. N18 —1A 16
Bull La. Brack —3B 20
Bull La. Chal P —2E 13
Bull La. Eccl —2E 35
Bull La. High —2E 27
Bull La. Wheat —1C 6
Bull La. Wro —2B 34
Bullocks Farm La. W Wyc —1A 12
Bullock's La. Hert —1A 8
Bull Rd. Birl —1D 35
Bulls Cross. —4B 8
Bull's Cross. Enf —4B 8
Bulls Cross Ride. Wal X —4B 8
Bulls Farm Rd. Tonb —4C 34
Bulls La. Brk P —2E 7
Bullsmoor. —4B 8
Bullsmoor La. Enf —4B 8
Bulphan. —3C 18
Bulphan By-Pass. W H'dn & Bulp —3C 18
Bulstrode La. Chfd & Hem H —3F 5
Bumble's Green. —2C 8
Bunce Comn. Rd. Leigh —4D 31
Buncefield La. Hem H —1A 6
Bunhill Row. EC1 —4A 16
Bunkers Hill. Sev —4B 26
Bunkers Hill. Sidc —2E 25
Bunkers La. Pim & Hem H —2A 6
Bunns La. NW7 —2D 15
Bunters Hill Rd. Cli —2E 27
Burchett's Green. —4A 12
Burchetts Grn. Rd. Bur G —4A 12
Burchetts La. Bur G —4A 12
Burdenshott Rd. Worp —3E 29
Burdett Rd. E3 & E14 —4B 16
Burdon La. Sutt —1E 31
Burfield Rd. Old Win —2E 21
Burford St. Hod —1B 8
Burgh Heath. —2E 31
Burgh Heath Rd. Eps —1D 31
Burghley Rd. SW19 —3E 23
Burham. —1E 35
Burham Common. —1E 35
Burham Court. —1E 35
Burial Ground La. Tovil —3F 35
Burleigh Rd. Enf —4A 8
Burlings La. Knock —2D 33
Burlington La. W4 —1D 23
Burlington Rd. N Mald —3D 23
Burlington Rd. W. N Mald —3E 23
Burma Rd. Wok —4D 21
Burnham. —4C 12
Burnham Beeches. —3D 13
Burnham La. Slou —4C 12
Burnham Rd. Beac —2D 13
Burnham Rd. Dart —2F 25
Burnham Rd. Woul —4E 27
Burnhouse La. Ing —4C 10
Burnt Ash Hill. SE12 —2C 24 (in two parts)
Burnt Ash La. Brom —3C 24
Burnt Ash Rd. SE12 —2C 24
Burntcommon. —3F 29
Burntmill La. H'low —1D 9
Burnt Mills. —2E 19
Burnt Mills Rd. Bas & N Ben —2E 19
Burnt Oak. —2D 15
Burnt Oak B'way. Edgw —2D 15
Burnt Pollard La. Light —1D 29
Burntwood La. SW17 —2F 23
Burntwood La. Cat —2A 32
Burpham. —4E 29
Burrage Rd. SE18 —1D 25
Burroughs, The. NW4 —2E 15
Burrow Hill. —1D 29
Burrows La. Gom —4A 30
Burton's La. Chal G & Rick —4E 5
Burton's Rd. Hamp —3B 22
Burwood Park. —4B 22
Burwood Rd. W on T —1A 30
Bury Farm Centre. —3D 9
Bury Green. —3B 8
Bury Grn. Rd. Chesh —3B 8
Bury La. Epp —3D 9
Bury La. Hat P —1F 11
Bury Rd. E4 —4C 8
Bury St. N9 —1A 16
Bury St. Ruis —2A 14
Bury, The. —3D 5
Busbridge Rd. Loose —3F 35
Bushbury Rd. Brock —4D 31
Bushey. —1B 14
Bushey Hall Rd. Bush —4B 6
Bushey Heath. —1C 14
Bushey Mead. —3E 23
Bushey Mill La. Wat —4B 6
Bushey Rd. SW20 —3E 23
Bush Hill. N21 —1A 16
Bush Hill Park. —1A 16
Bush Hill Rd. N21 —1A 16
Bush Rd. E11 —3C 16
Bush Rd. SE16 —1B 24
Bush Rd. Cux —4D 27
Bush Rd. E Peck —4D 35
Bushy Hill. —4F 29
Butcher Row. E1 —4B 16
Butchers La. Mere —3C 34
Butchers La. New Ash —4B 26
Butchers La. White —1A 20
Butler's Cross. —2A 4
Butterfly La. Els —4C 6
Butt Grn. La. Lint —4F 35

Button St.—Clarence Av.

Button St. Swan —3F 25
Buttsbury. Ing —4C 10
Butt's Green. —3F 11
Butts Grn. Rd. Horn —2F 17
Butt's Grn. Rd. S'don —3F 11
Butts La. Stan H —4D 19
Buttway La. Cli —1E 27
Buxton La. Cat —2A 32
Buxton Link. Lain —2D 19
Bye Green. —1B 4
Byfleet. —1A 30
Byfleet Rd. New Haw —1F 29
Byfleet Rd. Wey & Cob —1A 30
Byron Rd. W'stone —2C 14

Cabbagehill La. Warf —3A 20
Cable St. E1 —4B 16
Cacket's La. Cud —2D 33
Cadbury Rd. Sun —3A 22
Cadlocks Hill. Hals —1E 33
Cadogan Ter. E9 —3B 16
Cadsdean Rd. Wtlf —2A 4
Caenswood Hill. Wey —1A 30
Caesars Camp Rd. Camb —1B 28
Cage Green. —4B 34
Calcutta Rd. Til —1C 26
Caledonian Rd. N1 & N7 —4A 16
Callin's La. Shur R —2A 20
Callow Hill. Vir W —3E 21
Calmont Rd. Brom —3C 24
Calonne Rd. SW19 —3E 23
Calthorpe St. WC1 —4A 16
Calton Av. SE21 —2A 24
Camberley. —1B 28
Camberwell. —1A 24
Camberwell Chu. St. SE5 —1A 24
Camberwell Green. (Junct.) —1A 24
Camberwell Grn. SE5 —1A 24
Camberwell New Rd. SW9 —1A 24
Camberwell Rd. SE5 —1A 24
Camborne Av. Ayl —1A 4
Cambrian Way. Hem H —1A 6
Cambridge Gdns. W10 —4E 15
Cambridge Heath Rd. E1 & E2 —4B 16
Cambridge Pk. E11 —3C 16
Cambridge Rd. SE25 —3B 24
Cambridge Rd. SW11 —1F 23
Cambridge Rd. H'low —1E 9
Cambridge Rd. King T —3D 23
Camden High St. NW1 —4F 15
Camden Pk. Rd. NW1 —3F 15
Camden Rd. NW1 & N7 —3F 15
Camden St. NW1 —4F 15
Camden Town. —4F 15
Camer. —4C 26
Cameron Rd. Ilf —3D 17
Camer Pk. Rd. Meop —4C 26
Camer Rd. Meop —4C 26
Camlet Way. Barn —4E 7
Campbell Rd. E3 —4B 16
Campden Hill Rd. W8 —4E 15
Camp Farm Rd. Alder —3B 28
Camp Hill. Chid C —4F 33
Camphill Rd. W Byf —1F 29
Camp Rd. St Alb —2C 6
Camp, The. —2C 6
Camrose Av. Edgw —2D 15
Canada Farm Rd. S Dar & Dart —3B 26
Canadian Av. SE6 —2B 24
Canadian Av. Gill —4F 27
Canal Bridge. (Junct.) —1B 24
Canal Rd. High —2E 27
Canberra Rd. SE7 —1C 24
Candlemas La. Beac —2D 13
Canes La. H'wd —2E 9
Canfield Gdns. NW6 —3E 15
Canham Rd. SE25 —3A 24
Cann Hall. —3C 16
Cann Hall Rd. E11 —3C 16
Canning Town. —4C 16
Canning Town. (Junct.) —4C 16
Cannizaro Rd. SW19 —3E 23
Cannon Ct. Rd. M'head —4B 12
Cannon Hill. N14 —1A 16
Cannon Hill. M'head —1B 20
Cannon La. M'head —4B 12
Cannon La. Tonb —4B 34
Cannon La. W'bury —3D 35
Cannon's Green. —2A 10
Cannons La. Fyf —2A 10
Cannon St. EC4 —4A 16
Cannon St. Rd. E1 —4B 16
Canonbury. —3A 16
Canonbury Pk. N. N1 —3A 16
Canonbury Rd. N1 —3A 16
Canons Park. —2D 15
Canterbury Rd. Croy —4A 24
Canterbury St. Gill —3F 27
Canvey Island. —4F 19
Canvey Rd. Can I —4F 19
Canvey Village. —4F 19
Canvey Way. Pits & Can I —3F 19
Capel Manor Gardens. —4B 8
Capel Rd. E7 —3C 16
Cappell La. Stan A —1C 8
Capstone. —4F 27
Capstone Rd. Chat & H'std —4F 27
Capworth St. E10 —3B 16
Carbone Hill. N'thaw —3F 7
Cardinals, The. —4B 28
Carlton Av. E. Wemb —3C 14
Carlton Rd. Eri —1E 25
Carlton Rd. S Croy —1A 32
Carlton Vale. NW6 —4E 15
Carlyle Av. S'hall —4B 14
Carlyle Rd. SE28 —4E 17
Carmichael Rd. SE25 —4B 24
Carneles Green. —2B 8
Carpenders Park. —1B 14
Carpenters La. Hdlw —4C 34
Carpenter's Rd. E15 —3B 16
Carshalton. —4F 23
Carshalton Beeches. —1F 31
Carshalton on the Hill. —1F 31
Carshalton Pk. Rd. Cars —1F 31
Carshalton Rd. Bans —1F 31
Carshalton Rd. Mitc —4F 23
Carshalton Rd. Sutt & Cars —4F 23
Cartbridge. —3E 29
Carterhatch La. Enf —4A 8
Carterhatch Rd. Enf —4B 8
Carter's Green. —1F 9
Carter's Hill. —3A 34
Carter's Hill. B'bear —3A 20
Carter's Hill. Under —4A 34
Carthouse La. Wok —1D 29
Cassiobury Dri. Wat —4A 6
Cassio Rd. Wat —4B 6
Cassland Rd. E9 —3B 16
Castelnau. —1E 23
Castelnau. SW13 —1E 23
Castlebar Hill. W5 —4C 14
Castlebar Rd. W5 —4C 14
Castledon Rd. D'ham & W'fd —1E 19
Castle Farm Rd. Sev —1F 33
Castlefield Rd. Reig —4E 31
Castle Green. —1D 29
Castle Gro. Rd. Chob —1D 29
Castle Hill. Farnh —4A 28
Castle Hill. Hart —4B 26
Castle Hill. M'head —4B 12
Castle Hill Rd. Egh —2E 21
Castle La. Grav —2D 27
Castle Rd. Chat —4F 27
Castle Rd. Coul —2F 31
Castle Rd. Maid —2F 35
Castle Rd. Sev & Dart —1F 33
Castle St. Berk —2E 5
Castle St. Blet —4A 32
Castle St. Farnh —4A 28
Castleton Av. Wemb —3D 15
Castle Way. Felt —3B 22
Castle Way. Leyb —2D 35
Caterfield La. Crow —4C 32
Caterham. —3A 32
Caterham By-Pass. Cat —2B 32
Caterham-on-the-Hill. —2A 32
Cater Museum. —1D 19
Catford. —2B 24
Catford Gyratory. (Junct.) —2B 24
Catford Hill. SE6 —2B 24
Catford Rd. SE6 —2B 24
Cathall Rd. E11 —3C 16
Catherine St. Roch —4F 27
Catherine St. St Alb —2C 6
Cat Hill. Barn —1F 15
Catsdell Bottom. Hem H —2A 6
Cattlegate. —3F 7
Cattlegate Rd. N'thaw & Enf —3F 7
Causeway, The. Clay —1C 30
Causeway, The. Felt & Houn —2B 22
Causeway, The. Hghwd —2C 10
Causeway, The. Pot B —3F 7
Causeway, The. Stai —3F 21
Cautherly La. Gt Amw —1B 8
Cave Hill. Maid —3F 35
Cavendish Rd. NW6 —3E 15
Cavendish Rd. SW12 —2F 23
Cavendish Sq. W1 —4F 15
Cavendish Way. Hat —1D 7
Cazenove Rd. N16 —3A 16
Cecil Rd. Enf —4A 8
Cecil Rd. Pot B —3E 7
Cecil Rd. Roch —4F 27
Cedar Rd. Enf —4A 8
Cedar Rd. Sutt —1F 31
Cedars Av. Mitc —3F 23
Cedars Rd. SW4 —2F 23
Cedars Rd. W4 —1D 23
Cell Barnes La. St Alb —2C 6
Cemetery La. Hdlw —4C 34
Cemetery Pales. Brkwd —2D 29
Central Av. H'low —1D 9
Central Av. Well —1E 25
Central Av. W Mol —3B 22
Central Hill. SE19 —3A 24
Central Pde. New Ad —1C 32
Central Pk. Rd. E13 —4C 16
Central Rd. Mord —4E 23
Central Rd. Wor Pk —4E 23
Central St. EC1 —4A 16
Central Way. SE28 —4E 17
Centre Comn. Rd. Chst —3D 25
Centre Rd. E11 & E7 —3C 16
Chadwell By-Pass. Grays —1C 26
Chadwell Heath. —2E 17
Chadwell Heath La. Chad H —2E 17
Chadwell Rd. Grays —1C 26
Chadwell St Mary. —1C 26
Chafford Hundred. —1B 26
Chainhurst. —4E 35
Chaldon. —3A 32
Chaldon Comn. Rd. Cat —3A 32
Chaldon Rd. Cat —3A 32
Chaldon Way. Coul —2A 32
Chalfont Common. —1E 13
Chalfont La. Ger X & Rick —2F 13
Chalfont La. Rick —1E 13
Chalfont Rd. Ger X & Rick —1E 13
Chalfont Rd. Seer —1D 13
Chalfont St Giles. —1E 13
Chalfont St Peter. —2E 13
Chalfont St Peter By-Pass. Ger X —2E 13
Chalk. —2D 27
Chalk End. —1C 10
Chalker's Corner. (Junct.) —2D 23
Chalk Farm. —3F 15
Chalk Farm Rd. NW1 —3F 15
Chalk Hill. Wat —1B 14
Chalk La. E Hor —4A 30
Chalk La. H'low —1E 9
Chalk La. Hyde H —4C 4
Chalkpit La. Dork —4C 30
Chalkpit La. Mar —3A 12
Chalkpit La. Oxt —3C 32
Chalk Pit Rd. Eps —2D 31
Chalk Pit Way. Sutt —1F 31
Chalk Rd. Grav —2D 27
Chalk Rd. High —2E 27
Chalkshire. —2A 4
Chalk St. Ret C —4F 11
Chalvedon. —2E 19
Chalvey. —1D 21
Chalvey Gro. Slou —1D 21
Chalvey Rd. E. Slou —1D 21
Chalvey Rd. W. Slou —1D 21
Chamberlayne Rd. NW6 —4E 15
Chambersbury La. Hem H (in two parts) —2A 6
Chambers La. NW10 —3E 15
Champion Pk. SE5 —2A 24
Chancery La. WC2 —4A 16
Chanctonbury Way. N12 —1E 15
Chandlers Corner. (Junct.) —4F 17
Chandler's Cross. —4A 6
Chandlers La. Crowt —1A 28
Chandlers La. Rick —4A 6
Chandlers Rd. Meop —4C 26
Chantry La. Shere —4A 30
Chapel Croft. —3F 5
Chapel Croft. Chfd —3F 5
Chapel Hill. Speen —4A 4
Chapel La. Bookh —3C 30
Chapel La. Farn —2A 28
Chapel La. Hall —1D 35
Chapel La. High W —1A 12
Chapel La. Let G —1F 7
Chapel La. L Bad —2F 11
Chapel La. Pinn —2B 14
Chapel La. Westh —3C 30
Chapel Rd. SE27 —3A 24
Chapel Rd. Ilf —3D 17
Chapel Rd. Oxt —3C 32
Chapel Rd. Tad —3E 31
Chapel St. NW1 —4F 15
Chapel St. Bill —1D 19
Chapel St. E Mal —2E 35
Chapel St. Mar —3A 12
Chapel St. Rya —1D 35
Chapel St. W Mal —1D 35
Chapel Wood Rd. As & Sev —4B 26
Chapman La. Bour E & F Hth —2B 12
Chapman Rd. E9 —3B 16
Chapmans Hill. Meop —1C 34
Chapman Way. E Mal —2D 35
Chapter Rd. NW2 —3E 15
Charcott. —4F 33
Charing Cross Rd. WC2 —4F 15
Charles St. Berk —2E 5
Charlie Brown's Roundabout. (Junct.) —2C 16
Charlotteville. —4E 29
Charlton. —3A 22
(nr. Shepperton)
Charlton. —1C 24
(nr. Woolwich)
Charlton Athletic F.C. —1C 24
Charlton Chu. La. SE7 —1C 24
Charlton La. Shep —3A 22
Charlton La. W Far —3E 35
Charlton Pk. La. SE7 —1C 24
Charlton Pk. Rd. SE7 —1C 24
Charlton Rd. SE3 & SE7 —1C 24
Charlton Rd. Shep —3A 22
Charlton Way. SE10 —1C 24
Charlton Way. Hod —1B 8
Charmwood La. Orp —1E 33
Charterhouse St. EC1 —4A 16
Charter Rd., The. Wfd G —2C 16
Charters Rd. Asc —4C 20
Charters Rd. Wfd G —2C 16
Chart La. Dork —4C 30
Chart La. Reig —4F 31
Chart La. W'ham —4E 33
Chart La. S. Dork —4C 30
Chartridge. —3C 4
Chartridge La. Che —3C 4
Chartwell. —4D 33
Chase Cross. —2F 17
Chase Cross Rd. Romf —2F 17
Chase Rd. N14 —1F 15
Chase Rd. NW10 —4D 15
Chase Side. —4A 8
Chase Side. N14 —1F 15
Chase Side. Enf —4A 8
Chase, The. Guild —4E 29
Chaseville Pk. Rd. N21 —1A 16
Chaseway, The. Stock —4E 11
Chatfield. Slou —4D 13
Chatham. —4F 27
Chatham Hill. Chat —4F 27
Chatham Maritime. —3F 27
Chatham Rd. Blue B —1F 35
Chatham Rd. S'ing —1F 35
Chatsworth Rd. E5 —3B 16
Chatsworth Rd. NW2 —3E 15
Chattenden. —2F 27
Chattenden La. Chatt —2F 27
Chattern Hill. —3A 22
Chaulden. —2F 5
Chaulden La. Hem H —2F 5
Chavey Down. —3B 20
Chavey Down Rd. Wink —3B 20
Cheam. —1E 31
Cheam Comn. Rd. Wor Pk —4E 23
Cheam Rd. Eps & Sutt —1E 31
Cheam Rd. Sutt —1E 31
Cheam Village. (Junct.) —1E 31
Cheapside. —3D 21
Cheapside Rd. Asc —3C 20
Chelmer Rd. Chelm —2E 11
Chelmer Valley Rd. Chelm —2E 11
Chelmer Village. —2E 11
Chelmer Village Way. Chelm —2E 11
Chelmsford. —2E 11
Chelmsford Cathedral. —2E 11
Chelmsford & Essex Museum. —2E 11
Chelmsford Rd. B'more —3B 10
Chelmsford Rd. E Han —3F 11
Chelmsford Rd. Gt Walt —1E 11
Chelmsford Rd. Lea R & Mar R —1B 10
Chelmsford Rd. Ong —3A 10
Chelmsford Rd. Raw —1F 19
Chelmsford Rd. Shenf —1B 18
Chelmsford Rd. Writ —2D 11
Chelsea. —1F 23
Chelsea Bri. SW1 & SW8 —1F 23
Chelsea Bri. Rd. SW1 —1F 23
Chelsea Embkmt. SW3 —1F 23
Chelsea F.C. —1E 23
Chelsfield. —4E 25
Chelsfield Hill. Orp —1E 33
Chelsfield La. Badg M —1E 33
Chelsfield La. Orp —4E 25
Chelsfield Rd. Orp —4E 25
Chelsfield Village. —4E 25
Chelsham. —2B 32
Chelsham Comn. Rd. Warl —2B 32
Chelsham Ct. Rd. Warl —2C 32
Chelsham Rd. Warl —2B 32
Cheltenham Gdns. E6 —4D 17
Cheltenham Rd. SE22 —2B 24
Cheney St. Pinn —2B 14
Chenies. —4E 5
Chenies Bottom. —4E 5
Chenies Rd. Chor —4F 5
Chenies St. WC1 —4F 15
Chepstow Rd. W2 —4E 15
Chepstow Rd. Croy —4A 24
Chepstow Vs. W11 —4E 15
Chequer La. Redb —1B 6
Chequers. Wel G —1E 7
Chequers La. Dag —4E 17
Chequers La. P'wd —3B 4
Chequers La. Tad —3E 31
Chequers La. Wat —3B 6
Chequers Rd. Romf & S Wea —1A 18
Chequers Rd. Writ —2D 11
Chequer St. St Alb —2C 6
Cherington Rd. W7 —4C 14
Cherrydown E. Bas —2E 19
Cherry Garden La. M'head —1A 20
Cherry La. Amer —4C 4
Cherry La. W Dray —1A 22
Cherry La. Wdrow —4C 4
Cherry Orchard Rd. Croy —4A 24
Cherry Tree La. Ful —3E 13
Cherrytree La. Hem H —1A 6
Cherry Tree La. Rain —4F 17
Cherry Tree Rd. Farn R —3D 13
Cherrywood Rd. Farn —2B 28
Chertsey. —4F 21
Chertsey Bri. Rd. Cher —4F 21
Chertsey La. Stai —3F 21
Chertsey Lock. —4F 21
Chertsey Rd. Add —4F 21
Chertsey Rd. Ashf & Sun —3A 22
Chertsey Rd. Byfl —1F 29
Chertsey Rd. Chob —1D 29
Chertsey Rd. Felt —3A 22
Chertsey Rd. Shep —4A 22
Chertsey Rd. Twic —2B 22
Chertsey Rd. W'sham & Wok —1C 28
Chertsey Rd. Wok —2E 29
Chertsey South. —4F 21
Chertsey St. Guild —4E 29
Chesham. —3D 5
Chesham Bois. —4D 5
Chesham La. Chal G & Ger X —1E 13
Chesham La. Wen D —2B 4
Chesham Pl. SW1 —1F 23
Chesham Rd. Amer —4D 5
Chesham Rd. Ash G & Berk —2D 5
Chesham Rd. Bell —2D 5
Chesham Rd. Bov —3E 5
Chesham Rd. Che —3C 4
Chesham Rd. Gt Miss —3C 4
Chesham Rd. Wig —1C 4
Cheshire St. E2 —4B 16
Cheshunt. —3B 8
Cheshunt Wash. Chesh —3B 8
Chessington. —4D 23
Chessington Rd. Eps —1D 31
Chessington World of Adventures. —1C 30
Chessmount. —3D 5
Chester Hall La. Bas —2E 19
Chester Rd. Lou —4D 9
Chesterton Rd. W10 —4E 15
Chestnut Av. Chat —1F 35
Chestnut Av. Hal —1B 4
Chestnut La. Wok —4D 21
Chetwynd Rd. NW5 —3F 15
Chevening. —2E 33
Chevening Rd. NW6 —4E 15
Chevening Rd. Chev —2E 33
Chevening Rd. Sund —3E 33
Cheyne Wlk. SW10 & SW3 —1F 23
Chichele Rd. NW2 —3E 15
Chiddingstone Causeway. —4F 33
Chidley Cross Rd. E Peck —4D 35
Chignall Rd. Chelm —1D 11
Chignall Rd. Chig S —1D 11
Chignall St James. —1D 11
Chignall Smealy. —1D 11
Chigwell. —1D 17
Chigwell La. Lou & Chig —4D 9
Chigwell Rise. Chig —1D 17
Chigwell Rd. E18 & Wfd G —2C 16
Chigwell Row. —1E 17
Chilbrook Rd. D'side —2B 30
Childerditch. —2B 18
Childerditch La. L War —2B 18
Childsbridge La. Sev —2A 34
Child's Hill. —3E 15
Childwick Green. —1B 6
Chilsey Grn. Rd. Cher —4F 21
Chiltern Av. Bush —1C 14
Chiltern Dri. Rick —1F 13
Chiltern Open Air Museum. —1E 13
Chiltern Rd. Sutt —1E 31
Chilworth. —4F 29
Chilworth Rd. Alb —4F 29
Chinbrook Rd. SE12 —2C 24
Chingford. —1C 16
Chingford Green. —1C 16
Chingford Hatch. —1C 16
Chingford La. Wfd G —1C 16
Chingford Mount. —1B 16
Chingford Mt. Rd. E4 —1B 16
Chingford Rd. E4 & E17 —2B 16
Chinnor Rd. Bled R —1A 12
Chippendale Way. Uxb —3F 13
Chippenham Rd. W9 —4E 15
Chipperfield. —3F 5
Chipperfield Common. —3F 5
Chipperfield Rd. Hem H —3E 5
Chipperfield Rd. K Lan —3F 5
Chipperfield Rd. Orp —3E 25
Chipping Barnet. —4E 7
Chipping Ongar. —3A 10
Chipstead. —2F 31
(nr. Coulsdon)
Chipstead. —2F 33
(nr. Sevenoaks)
Chipstead Bottom. —2F 31
Chipstead La. Sev —2F 33
Chipstead La. Tad & Coul —3E 31
Chipstead Valley Rd. Coul —2F 31
Chisbridge Cross. —2A 12
Chislehurst. —3D 25
Chislehurst Rd. Brom & Chst —3D 25
Chislehurst Rd. Orp —3D 25
Chislehurst Rd. Sidc —3E 25
Chislehurst West. —3D 25
Chiswell Green. —2B 6
Chiswellgreen La. St Alb —2B 6
Chiswell St. EC2 —4A 16
Chiswick. —1D 23
Chiswick Bri. W4 —1D 23
Chiswick High Rd. Bren & W4 —1D 23
Chiswick House. —1D 23
Chiswick La. N. W4 —1D 23
Chiswick Roundabout. (Junct.) —1D 23
Chivers Rd. Ston M —3A 10
Chivery. —2C 4
Chobham. —1D 29
Chobham La. Wok & Vir W —4D 21
Chobham Rd. E15 —3C 16
Chobham Rd. Asc & Wok —4D 21
Chobham Rd. Frim —2B 28
Chobham Rd. Knap —2D 29
Chobham Rd. Ott —1E 29
Chobham Rd. Wok —2E 29
Chobham Rd. Wok —1E 29
Choke La. M'head —4B 12
Cholesbury. —2C 4
Cholesbury La. C'bry —2C 4
Cholesbury Rd. Wig —2C 4
Chorley Rd. W Wyc —1A 12
Chorleywood. —1F 13
Chorleywood Bottom. —1F 13
Chorleywood Bottom. Rick —1F 13
Chorleywood Rd. Rick —1F 13
Chorleywood West. —4E 5
Chrisp St. E14 —4B 16
(in two parts)
Christchurch Av. Harr —2C 14
Christchurch Rd. SW2 —2A 24
Christ Chu. Rd. SW14 —2D 23
Christchurch Rd. SW19 —3F 23
Christ Chu. Rd. Eps —1D 31
Christchurch Rd. Tring —1C 4
Christchurch Rd. Vir W —3E 21
Christmas La. Farn C —3D 13
Christmas La. H Hals —2F 27
Church Cres. E9 —3B 16
Church Crookham. —3A 28
Church Elm La. Dag —3E 17
Church End. —2E 15
(nr. Finchley)
Church End. —3D 15
(nr. Neasden)
Church End. —2A 30
(nr. Ockham)
Church End. —1B 6
(nr. Redbourn)
Church End. —4F 5
(nr. Sarratt)
Church End. NW4 —2E 15
Church End La. Runw —1F 19
Churchfield Rd. W3 —4D 15
Churchgate. —3B 8
Churchgate. Chesh —3B 8
Churchgate Rd. Chesh —3B 8
Churchgate Street. —1E 9
Churchgate St. H'low —1E 9
Church Gro. Amer —4E 5
Church Gro. King T —3C 22
Church Hill. E17 —2B 16
Church Hill. N21 —1A 16
Church Hill. Alder —4B 28
Church Hill. Bas —2D 19
Church Hill. Camb —1B 28
Church Hill. Cat —3A 32
Church Hill. Cud —2D 33
Church Hill. Dart —2A 26
Church Hill. Hare —2F 13
Church Hill. H'shm —4F 35
Church Hill. Hors —2E 29
Church Hill. L Kim & Ell —2A 4
Church Hill. Lou —4D 9
Church Hill. Plax —3B 34
Church Hill. Pyr —2F 29
Church Hill. Red —4A 32
Church Hill. Shur R —2A 20
Church Hill. Stan H —4D 19
Church Hill. Tats —2C 32
Church Hill. White —1A 20
Church Hill Rd. Barn —1F 15
Church Hill Rd. Sutt —4E 23
Churchill Av. Ayl —1A 4
Church Lammas. —2F 21
Church La. N2 —2F 15
Church La. N8 —2A 16
Church La. NW9 —2D 15
Church La. SW17 —3F 23
Church La. Alb —4F 29
Church La. Ald —4B 6
Church La. Barm —3E 35
Church La. Binf —3B 20
Church La. Bisl —2D 29
Church La. Blet —4A 32
Church La. Bov —3E 5
Church La. Brox —2B 8
Church La. Bulp —3C 18
Church La. Cat —3A 32
Church La. Chelm —2E 11
Church La. Chesh —3B 8
Church La. Chess —1D 31
Church La. Coul —2F 31
Church La. Cray H —1E 19
Church La. Dodd —4B 10
Church La. E Peck —4D 35
Church La. Ews —4A 28
Church La. God —4B 32
Church La. Grav —2D 27
Church La. H'ley —3D 31
Church La. Hut —1C 18
Church La. K Lan —3A 6
Church La. Marg —3D 11
Church La. Oxt —3C 32
Church La. Pinn —2B 14
Church La. Pirb —2C 28
Church La. Rick —1F 13
Church La. Romf —4E 9
Church La. Sarr —4F 5
Church La. S Han —4F 11
Church La. Stoke P —4D 13
Church La. Tros —1C 34
Church La. Warf —2A 20
Church La. Warl —2B 32
Church La. Wen —2B 4
Church La. W'ham —2C 32
Church La. Wex —4E 13
Church La. Wind —2C 20
Church La. W'ton T —1A 4
Church La. E. Alder —4B 28
Church La. W. Alder —4A 28
Church Langley. —1E 9
Church Langley Way. H'low —1E 9
Church Rd. E10 —3B 16
Church Rd. E12 —3D 17
Church Rd. NW4 —2E 15
Church Rd. NW10 —3D 15
Church Rd. SE19 —3A 24
Church Rd. SW13 —1E 23
Church Rd. SW19 & Mitc
(Merton) —3F 23
Church Rd. SW19 —3E 23
(Wimbledon)
Church Rd. W7 —4C 14
Church Rd. Add —4F 21
Church Rd. Alder —4B 28
Church Rd. Asc —4D 21
Church Rd. Ashf —2A 22
Church Rd. As —4B 26
Church Rd. Bas —2E 19
Church Rd. Bexh —2E 25
Church Rd. Bookh —3B 30
Church Rd. Brack —3B 20
Church Rd. Bulp —3C 18
(in two parts)
Church Rd. Byfl —1A 30
Church Rd. Cat —3A 32
Church Rd. Chels —1E 33
Church Rd. Clay —1C 30
Church Rd. Cob —3C 26
Church Rd. Cook —3B 12
Church Rd. Corr —4E 19
Church Rd. Crowt —1A 28
Church Rd. Dun —2C 18
Church Rd. Egh —3E 21
Church Rd. Eps —1D 31
Church Rd. Farn —4D 25
Church Rd. Frim —2B 28
Church Rd. Had —2F 19
Church Rd. Hals —1E 33
Church Rd. Hart —4B 26
Church Rd. Hay —4A 14
Church Rd. H Bee —4C 8
Church Rd. Houn —1B 22
Church Rd. Igh —3A 34
Church Rd. Iver —4F 13
Church Rd. Kel H —4A 10
Church Rd. Kes —1C 32
Church Rd. Lea —2C 30
Church Rd. L Berk —2F 7
Church Rd. L Gad —1E 5
Church Rd. Mar —2B 12
Church Rd. More —2F 9
Church Rd. Mount & Ing —4C 10
Church Rd. Nave —4F 9
Church Rd. Noak H —1F 17
Church Rd. N'holt —4B 14
Church Rd. N'wd —2A 14
Church Rd. Ong —3F 9
Church Rd. Penn —1C 12
Church Rd. Pits —2F 19
Church Rd. Pot B —3E 7
Church Rd. Rams H —1E 19
Church Rd. Raw —1F 19
Church Rd. Red —4F 31
Church Rd. Rich —2D 23
Church Rd. Sev —4F 33
Church Rd. Shep —4A 22
Church Rd. Short —3C 24
Church Rd. Stan —1C 14
Church Rd. Sund —3E 33
Church Rd. Surb —4C 22
Church Rd. S at H —3A 26
Church Rd. Swan —4F 25
(Crockenhill)
Church Rd. Swan —3F 25
(Swanley Village)
Church Rd. Tedd —3C 22
Church Rd. Til —1D 27
Church Rd. Tovil —3F 35
Church Rd. Uxb —4F 13
Church Rd. W Dray —1A 22
Church Rd. W'ham —3E 33
Church Rd. W Han —4E 11
Church Rd. W Mal —2C 34
Church Rd. W Peck —3C 34
Church Rd. W'sham —1C 28
Church Rd. Wind —2E 21
Church Rd. Wold —2B 32
Church Rd. Wor Pk —4D 23
Church Street. —2E 27
Church St. N9 —1A 16
Church St. Amer —4D 5
Church St. Bill —1D 19
Church St. Bou M —4F 35
Church St. Bov —3E 5
Church St. Bur —1E 35
Church St. Che —3D 5
Church St. Cli —2E 27
Church St. Cobh —2B 30
Church St. Croy —4A 24
Church St. Enf —4B 8
Church St. Eps —1D 31
Church St. Gill —3F 27
Church St. Gt Bad —2E 11
Church St. Hamp —3C 22
Church St. High —2E 27
Church St. High W —1B 12
Church St. Hoo —2F 27
Church St. Lea —2C 30
Church St. Loose —3F 35
Church St. Reig —4E 31
Church St. Rick —1A 14
Church St. Seal —2A 34
Church St. Shor —1F 33
Church St. Slou —1D 21
Church St. Stai —3F 21
Church St. W on T —4B 22
Church St. Wey —4A 22
Church St. W. Wok —2E 29
Church Town. —4B 32
Church Wlk. Hay —4A 14
Church Way. S Croy —1A 32
Cippenham. —4D 13
Cippenham La. Slou —4D 13
Circus Rd. NW8 —4F 15
City. —4A 16
City Rd. EC1 —4A 16
City Way. Roch —4F 27
Clacket La. W'ham —3D 33
Clacton Rd. E13 —4C 16
Clamp Hill. Stan —1C 14
Clandon Park. —4F 29
Clandon Rd. Chat —1F 35
Clandon Rd. Send & Guild —3F 29
Clanking. —2A 4
Clapgate. —3A 10
Clapham. —2F 23
Clapham Common. (Junct.) —2F 23
Clapham Comn. N. Side. SW4 —2F 23
Clapham Comn. S. Side. SW4 —2F 23
Clapham Comn. W. Side. SW4 —2F 23
Clapham High St. SW4 —2F 23
Clapham Junction. —2F 23
Clapham Park. —2F 23
Clapham Pk. Rd. SW4 —2F 23
Clapham Rd. SW9 —2A 24
Clappins La. N Dean & Nap —4A 4
Clapton Comn. N16 —3A 16
Clapton Park. —3B 16
Clare La. E Mal —2D 35
Claremont Av. N Mald —4E 23
Claremont Av. Wok —2E 29
Claremont La. Esh —4B 22
Claremont Park. —1B 30
Claremont Rd. NW2 —3E 15
Claremont Rd. Surb —4D 23
Claremont St. N18 —2B 16
Clarence Av. N Mald —3D 23

Clarence La.—Dora's Green

Clarence La. SW15 —2D 23
Clarence Rd. Grays —1B 26
Clarence Rd. Wind —1D 21
Clarence St. King T —3D 23
Clarence St. Stai —3F 21
Clarendon Rd. W11 —4E 15
Clarendon Rd. P'wd —3B 4
Clarendon Rd. Wat —4B 6
Clare Rd. Stai —2F 21
Clarke's Grn. Rd. Sev —1A 34
Clarks La. Warl & W'ham —3C 32
Clatterford End. —2A 10 (nr. Fyfield)
Clatterford End. —1C 10 (nr. Good Easter)
Clatterford End. —3A 10 (nr. High Ongar)
Clatterford End. —3F 9 (nr. North Weald Bassett)
Claverhambury. —3C 8
Claverhambury Rd. Wal A —3C 8
Claverton St. SW1 —1F 23
Claycart Rd. Alder —4A 28
Claygate. —1C 30 (nr. Esher)
Claygate. —4B 34 (nr. Shipbourne)
Claygate Cross. —3B 34
Claygate La. S'brne —3B 34
Claygate La. Th Dit —4C 22
Claygate Rd. Ladd —4D 35
Clayhall. —2D 17
Clayhall Av. Ilf —2D 17
Clayhall La. Reig —4E 31
Clay Hill. —4A 8
Clay Hill. Enf —4A 8
Clay Hill Rd. Bas —2E 19
Clay La. Guild —3E 29
Clay La. H'ley —3D 31
Clay La. High W —2A 12
Clay La. S Nut —4F 31
Claypit Hill. Wal A —4C 8
Clay's La. Lou —4D 9
Clay St. Knot —1C 12
Clayton Rd. Chess —4C 22
Clayton Rd. Hay —1A 22
Clay Tye Rd. Upm —3B 18
Clement St. Swan & Dart —3F 25
Clerkenwell. —4A 16
Clerkenwell Rd. EC1 —4A 16
Cleveland Rd. W13 —4C 14
Cleveland St. W1 —4F 15
Cleve Rd. NW6 —3E 15
Clewer Green. —1D 21
Clewer Hill Rd. Wind —1D 21
Clewer New Town. —1D 21
Clewer Village. —1D 21
Clew's La. Bisl —2D 29
Cliffe. —1E 27
Cliffe Rd. Roch —3E 27
Cliffe Woods. —2E 27
Cliff Hill. Bou M —4F 35
Cliff Hill Rd. Bou M —4F 35
Clifford Av. SW14 —1D 23 (in two parts)
Clifford Rd. SE25 —3B 24
Clifton Gdns. W9 —4F 15
Clinton La. Bough B —4E 33
Cliveden. —3C 12
Cliveden Pl. SW1 —1F 23
Cliveden Rd. Tap —4C 12
Clive Rd. Gt War —2B 18
Clock House. —1F 31
Clockhouse La. Ashf & Felt —3A 22
Clockhouse La. N Stif —1B 26 (in two parts)
Clockhouse La. Romf —2E 17
Clock Ho. Rd. Beck —3B 24
Clock Ho. Rd. L Bur —1D 19
Clockhouse Roundabout. (Junct.) —2A 22
Clubhouse Rd. Alder —3A 28
Coach Rd. Sev —3B 34
Coalhill. —4F 11
Coalhouse Fort & Thameside Aviation Museum. —1D 27
Coast Hill. Westc —4B 30
Coates La. D'ley —1A 12
Cobbett Hill. Norm —3D 29
Cobblershill. —3B 4
Cobblershill La. Gt Miss —3B 4
Cobden Hill. Rad —4C 6
Cobham. —1B 30 (nr. Esher)
Cobham. —3D 27 (nr. Henley Street)
Cobham. —3D 27 (nr. Meopham)
Cobhambury Rd. Cob —3D 27
Cobham Hall. —3D 27
Cobham Pk. Rd. Cobh —2B 30
Cobham Rd. Stoke D & Lea —2B 30
Coborn Rd. E3 —4B 16
Cockerhurst Rd. Shor —1F 33
Cockett Rd. Slou —1E 21
Cockfosters. —4F 7
Cockfosters Rd. Pot B & Barn —4F 7
Cock La. Hghwd —3C 10 (in two parts)
Cock La. High W & Penn —1B 12
Cock La. Hod —2B 8
Cockmannings La. Orp —4E 25
Cockmannings Rd. Orp —4E 25
Cockpit Rd. Gt Kin —4B 4
Cockshot Hill. Reig —4E 31
Cock's La. Warf —2B 20
Cock Street. —4F 35
Cocksure La. Sidc —2E 25
Codmore. —3D 5
Codmore Wood Rd. Che —3E 5
Coke's La. Chal G —4E 5
Colam La. L Bad —2F 11
Colchester Rd. Romf —2F 17
Colchester Rd. Spri —1E 11
Cold Arbor Rd. Sev —3F 33
Coldblow. —2F 25
Coldharbour. —4B 34
Coldharbour La. SW9 & SE5 —2A 24
Coldharbour La. Bush —1B 14
Coldharbour La. Dork —4C 30
Coldharbour La. Egh —3F 21
Coldharbour La. Hay —4B 14
Coldharbour La. Hild —4A 34
Coldharbour Rd. N'fleet —2C 26
Coldharbour Rd. W Byf & Wok —1F 29
Coldmoorholme La. Bour E —3B 12
Coldrum Long Barrow. —1C 34
Coleford Bri. Rd. Myt —3B 28
Cole Green. —1E 7
Cole Grn. By-Pass. Col G & Hert —1F 7
Cole Grn. La. Wel G —1E 7
Coleman Green. —1D 7
Coleman Grn. La. Wheat —1C 6
Cole Park. —2C 22
Coleshill. —1D 13
Coleshill La. Winch H —1C 12
Coles La. Bras —3E 33
Coles Meads. —4F 31
Colham Green. —4A 14
Colham Grn. Rd. Uxb —4A 14
Colindale. —2D 15
Colindale Av. NW9 —2D 15
Colindeep La. NW9 & NW4 —2D 15
College Av. Harr —2C 14
College Cres. NW3 —3F 15
College Hill Rd. Harr —2C 14
College La. Hat —2D 7
College Ride. Camb —1B 28
College Rd. SE21 & SE19 —2A 24
College Rd. Ab L —3B 6
College Rd. Ast C —1B 4
College Rd. Brom —3C 24
College Rd. Chesh —3B 8
College Rd. Eps —1D 31
College Rd. Harr —2C 14
College Rd. Iswth —1C 22
College Rd. M'head —4B 12
College Rd. Maid —3F 35
College Rd. Swan —3F 25
College Rd. Wok —2E 29
College St. NW1 —3F 15
College Town. —1A 28
Collier Row. —2E 17
Collier Row La. Romf —2E 17
Collier Row Rd. Romf —2E 17
Colliers Hatch. —3F 9
Colliers Water La. T Hth —4A 24
Collier's Wood. —3F 23
Colliers Wood. (Junct.) —3F 23
Collingwood Rd. Sutt —4E 23
Collinswood Rd. Farn C —3D 13
Collum Grn. Rd. Slou —3D 13
Colmore Rd. Enf —4B 8
Colnbrook. —1F 21
Colnbrook By-Pass. Slou & W Dray —1F 21
Colne Way. Wat —4B 6
Colney Hatch. —2F 15
Colney Hatch La. N11 & N10 —2F 15
Colney Heath. —2D 7
Colney Heath La. St Alb —2D 7
Colney Street. —3C 6
Colonial Way. Wat —4B 6
Colston Av. Cars —4F 23
Columbia Rd. E2 —4A 16
Colyers La. Eri —1F 25
Colyton Rd. SE22 —2B 24
Combe La. Brmly —4A 30
Comet Way. Hat —2D 7
Commercial Rd. E1 & E14 —4B 16
Commercial Rd. Roch —3E 27 (in two parts)
Commercial St. E1 —4A 16
Commercial Way. SE5 —1A 24
Common Ga. Rd. Rick —1F 13
Common La. Burn —3C 12
Common La. Cli —2E 27
Common La. Cli —1F 27
Common La. Dart —2F 25
Common La. K Lan —3A 6
Common La. Let H & Rad —4C 6
Common Rd. Chat —1E 35
Common Rd. Chor —4F 5
Common Rd. Clay —1C 30
Common Rd. Hdlw —4C 34
Common Rd. Igh —3B 34
Common Rd. Stan —1C 14
Common Rd. Wal A —2D 9
Common Rd. Wind —1C 20
Common Side. D'ley —1A 12
Commonside. Kes —4C 24
Commonside E. Mitc —3F 23
Commonside Rd. H'low —2D 9
Commonside W. Mitc —3F 23
Common, The. W5 —4D 15
Common, The. Dan —2F 11
Common, The. E Han —3F 11
Common, The. Gt Kin —4B 4
Common, The. Holm G —4C 4
Common, The. K Lan —3F 5
Common, The. Pott E —1E 5
Common, The. S'hall —1B 22
Common, The. Stan —1C 14
Commonwood. —3F 5
Commority Rd. Meop —1C 34
Comp. —2C 34
Compasses Rd. Leigh —4F 33
Comp La. Platt & W Mal —2C 34
Compton. —4D 29
Compton Rd. N21 —1A 16
Conduit La. N18 —1B 16
Conduit La. Hod —1B 8
Conduit St. W1 —4F 15
Coney Hall. —4C 24
Coney Hill Rd. W Wick —4C 24
Congelow. —4D 35
Coningsby La. Fif —1C 20
Coniston Way. Reig —4F 31
Connaught Bri. E16 —4C 16
Connaught Gdns. N13 —1A 16
Connaught Rd. Brkwd —2D 29
Connaught St. W2 —4F 15
Constitution Hill. Snod —1D 35
Convent Rd. Ashf —3A 22
Conways Rd. Ors —4C 18
Cookham. —3B 12
Cookham Dean. —3B 12
Cookham Dean Bottom. Cook —3B 12
Cookham Rise. —3B 12
Cookham Rd. M'head —4B 12
Cookham Rd. Swan —3E 25
Cooksmill Green. —2C 10
Cooling. —2F 27
Cooling Comn. Cli —2F 27
Cooling Rd. Cli —2E 27 (in two parts)
Cooling Rd. Roch —3E 27
Cooling Street. —2F 27
Cooling St. Cli —2F 27
Cool Oak La. NW9 —3D 15
Coombe. —3D 23 (nr. Kingston Upon Thames)
Coombe. —2A 4 (nr. Wendover)
Coombe Lane. (Junct.) —3D 23
Coombe La. SW20 —3E 23
Coombe La. Croy —4B 24
Coombe La. Hugh & Nap —4A 4
Coombe La. Flyover. King T & SW20 —3D 23
Coombe La. W. King T —3D 23
Coombe Rd. Croy —4A 24
Coombe Rd. King T —3D 23
Coombe Rd. N Mald —3D 23
Coombe St. Hem H —2F 5
Coomb Hill. —4D 27
Coopersale Common. —3E 9
Coopersale Comn. Coop —3E 9
Coopersale La. They B —4E 9
Coopersale Street. —3E 9
Cooper's Corner. —4E 33
Cooper's Green. —1D 7
Coopers Grn. La. St Alb & Hat —1D 7
Cooper's Hill. Ong —3A 10
Coopers Hill Rd. S Nut —4A 32
Cooper's La. Pot B —3F 7
Cooper's La. W Til —1C 26
Coopers La. Rd. Pot B —3F 7
Copenhagen St. N1 —4A 16
Copes Rd. Gt Kin —4B 4
Copperfield Rd. Chelm —1D 11
Copperkins La. Amer —4D 5
Coppermill La. Rick & Uxb —2F 13
Coppermill Rd. Wray —2E 21
Coppetts Rd. N10 —2F 15
Coppice Row. They B —4D 9
Copping's Rd. Leigh —4F 33
Copse Hill. —3E 23
Copse Hill. SW20 —3E 23
Copsem La. Esh & Lea —1B 30
Copthall Green. —3C 8
Copthall La. Chal P —2E 13
Copt Hall La. Cob —3C 26
Copt Hall Rd. Igh —3B 34
Copt Hill. Dan —2F 11
Copthorne Rd. Lea —2C 30
Corbets Tey. —3A 18
Corbets Tey Rd. Upm —3A 18
Cores End. —3B 12
Cores End Rd. Bour E —3B 12
Corkscrew Hill. W Wick —4C 24
Cormongers La. Nutf —4F 31
Cornell Way. Romf —1E 17
Cornerfield. Hat —1E 7
Cornwall Cres. W11 —4E 15
Cornwallis Av. Gill —4F 27 (in two parts)
Cornwallis Av. Tonb —4B 34
Cornwall Rd. Ruis —3B 14
Coronation Av. G Grn —4E 13
Coronation Dri. Horn —3F 17
Coronation Rd. NW10 —4D 15
Coronation Rd. Asc —4C 20
Coronation Rd. Cre P —2A 12
Coronation Rd. L Grn —4A 12
Corporation Rd. Chelm —1E 11
Corporation St. Roch —3F 27
Corringham. —4E 19
Corringham Rd. Stan H & Corr —4D 19 (in two parts)
Coryton. —4E 19
Cotman's Ash. —2A 34
Cotman's Ash La. Kems —1A 34
Coton St. E14 —4C 16
Cotswold Rd. Sutt —1E 31
Cottenham Park. —3E 23
Cottenham Pk. Rd. SW20 —3E 23
Cotton La. Dart & Grnh —2A 26
Cottonmill La. St Alb —2C 6
Coulsdon. —2F 31
Coulsdon La. Coul —2F 31
Coulsdon Rd. Coul & Cat —2A 32
Counters End. —2F 5
Country Way. Hanw —3B 22
County La. Warf —3B 20
Coursers Rd. Col H —3D 7
Courtauld Rd. Bas —2E 19
Courtenay Av. Harr —2C 14
Courthill Rd. SE13 —2C 24
Courthouse Rd. M'head —4B 12
Courtlands Dri. Wat —4A 6
Court La. SE21 —2A 24
Court La. Burn —4C 12
Court La. Dor —1C 20
Court La. Hdlw —4C 34
Court Rd. SE9 —2D 25
Court Rd. Broom —1E 11
Court Rd. Bur —1E 35
Court Rd. Orp —4E 25
Coval La. Chelm —2E 11
Cove. —2A 28
Cove Rd. Farn —3A 28
Cove Rd. Fleet —3A 28
Cowbridge. Hert —1A 8
Cow La. Tring —1C 4
Cowley. —4F 13
Cowley Hill. Borwd —4D 7
Cowley Mill Rd. Uxb —4F 13
Cowley Peachey. —4F 13
Cowley Rd. Uxb —4F 13
Cow Watering La. Writ —2D 11
Coxes Farm Rd. Bill —1D 19
Cox Green. —1B 20
Cox Grn. La. M'head —1B 20
Cox Grn. Rd. M'head —1B 20
Coxheath. —4F 35
Cox La. Chess —4D 23
Coxtie Green. —1A 18
Coxtie Grn. Rd. Brtwd —1A 18
Crabhill La. S Nut —4A 32
Craddocks Av. Asht —2D 31
Crammavill St. Grays —4B 18
Cranbourne. —2C 20
Cranbrook. —3D 17
Cranbrook Rd. Ilf —2D 17
Cranes. —2E 19
Cranes Farm Rd. Bas —2D 19
Cranes Way. Borwd —1D 15
Cranfield Pk. Rd. W'fd —2F 19
Cranford. —1B 22
Cranford La. Hay —1A 22
Cranford La. Houn —1B 22
Cranham. —3A 18
Cranham Rd. L Walt —1E 11
Cranley Gardens. —2F 15
Cranley Gdns. N10 —2F 15
Cranmer Rd. Mitc —3F 23
Cranmore La. Alder —4A 28
Cranston Rd. SE23 —2B 24
Craufurd Rise. M'head —4B 12
Cravells Rd. Hpdn —1B 6
Craven Gdns. Ilf —2D 17
Craven Hill. W2 —4F 15
Craven Pk. NW10 —4D 15
Craven Pk. Rd. NW10 —4D 15
Craven Rd. W2 —4F 15
Crawley Hill. —1B 28
Crawley Hill. Camb —1B 28
Crawley Ridge. Camb —1B 28
Crawley's La. Wig —1D 5
Cray Av. Orp —4E 25
Crayford. —2F 25
Crayford Rd. Dart —2F 25
Crayford Way. Dart —2F 25
Craylands La. Swans —2B 26
Cray Rd. Sidc —3E 25
Cray Rd. Swan —4F 25
Crays Hill. —2E 19
Crays Hill. Bill —2E 19
Creekmouth. —4D 17
Creek Rd. SE8 & SE10 —1B 24
Creek Rd. E Mol —3C 22
Creephedge La. E Han —3F 11
Creffield Rd. W5 & W3 —4D 15
Creighton Av. N2 & N10 —2F 15
Creighton Rd. N17 —2A 16
Cremorne Rd. SW10 —1F 23
Crescent E. Barn —4F 7
Crescent Rd. War —1B 18
Crescent, The. Lea —2C 30
Crescent W. Barn —4F 7
Cressex. —2A 12
Cressex Rd. High W —2A 12
Crest Rd. Hand —2A 12
Crews Hill. —4A 8
Cricketers La. Warf —3B 20
Cricketfield Rd. E5 —3B 16
Cricket Grn. Mitc —3F 23
Cricket Hill. —1A 28
Cricket Hill La. B'water —2A 28
Crickets Hill. —3E 29
Cricklewood. —3E 15
Cricklewood B'way. NW2 —3E 15
Cricklewood La. NW2 —3E 15
Crimp Hill. Wind & Egh —2D 21
Cripple St. Maid —3F 35
Crittall's Corner. (Junct.) —3E 25
Critten La. Dork —4B 30
Crockenhill. —4F 25
Crockenhill La. Swan & Eyns —4F 25
Crockenhill Rd. Orp & W Wick —4E 25
Crockford Pk. Rd. Add —4F 21
Crockham Hill. —4D 33
Crocknorth Rd. E Hor & Dork —4A 30
Crofton. —4D 25
Crofton La. Orp —4D 25
Crofton Rd. Orp —4D 25
Croham Rd. S Croy —4A 24
Croham Valley Rd. S Croy —1B 32
Cromwell Av. Chesh —3B 8
Cromwell Rd. SW5 & SW7 —1E 23
Cromwell Rd. Houn —2B 22
Cromwell Rd. King T —3D 23
Cromwell Rd. Red —4F 31
Crondall La. Farnh —4A 28
Crondon. —3D 11
Crondon Pk. La. Stock —4D 11
Cronks Hill. Reig —4F 31
Crooked Billet. (Junct.) —2B 16
Crooked Billet Roundabout. (Junct.) —3F 21
Crooked Mile. Wal A —3C 8
Crook Log. Bexh —2E 25
Crooksbury Rd. Farnh —4B 28
Croom's Hill. SE10 —1C 24
Crossbrook St. Chesh —3B 8
Cross Deep. Twic —2C 22
Cross Keys. —3F 33
Cross Lances Rd. Houn —2B 22
Cross La. Beac —2D 13
Cross La. Hpdn —1B 6
Cross La. E. Grav —2C 26
Cross La. W. Grav —2C 26
Cross Lees. More —2A 10
Crossley's Hill. Chal G —1E 13
Cross Oak Rd. Berk —2E 5
Crossoaks La. Borwd & Pot B —3D 7
Cross Rd. Brom —4D 25
Cross Rd. Tad —2E 31
Cross Roads. Lou —4C 8
Cross St. N1 —4A 16
Crossway. SE28 —4E 17
Crossway. SW20 —3E 23
Crossways Boulevd. Dart —2A 26
Crouch. —3B 34
Crouch End. —2F 15
Crouch End Hill. N8 —3F 15
Crouch Hill. N8 & N4 —2A 16
Crouch Ho. Rd. Eden —4D 33
Crouch La. Bor G —2B 34
Crouch La. Chesh —3A 8
Crouch La. Wink —2C 20
Crowbrook Rd. P Ris —2A 4
Crow Green. —4B 10
Crow Grn. Rd. Pil H —1B 18
Crowhurst. —4C 32
Crowhurst La. Crow —4C 32
Crowhurst La. Igh —3B 34
Crowhurst La. W King —1B 34
Crowhurst Lane End. —4B 32
Crowhurst Village Rd. Crow —4C 32
Crowlands. —3E 17
Crow La. Romf —3E 17
Crown Dale. SE19 —3A 24
Crowndale Rd. NW1 —4F 15
Crownfield Rd. E15 —3C 16
Crown Hill. Wal A & Epp —3D 9
Crown La. SW16 —3A 24
Crown La. Brom —4C 24
Crown La. Farn R —4D 13
Crown La. Mord —3E 23
Crown La. Penn —1C 12
Crown La. Shorne —3D 27
Crown Rd. Grays —1B 26
Crown Rd. Kel H —4A 10
Crown Rd. Mord —3E 23
Crown Rd. N'side —4A 10
Crown Rd. Sutt —4E 23
Crown Rd. Twic —2C 22
Crown Rd. Vir W —4E 21
Crown St. W3 —4D 15
Crow Piece La. Farn R —3D 13
Crowsheath La. D'ham —4E 11
Crowthorne. —1A 28
Crowthorne Rd. Brack —4B 20
Crowthorne Rd. Crowt & Brack —4A 20
Crowthorne Rd. Sand —1A 28
Croxley Green. —1A 14
Croxted Rd. SE24 & SE21 —2A 24
Croydon. —4A 24
Croydon La. Bans —1F 31
Croydon Rd. SE20 —3B 24
Croydon Rd. Beck —4B 24
Croydon Rd. Cat —3B 32
Croydon Rd. Kes —4C 24
Croydon Rd. Mitc & Croy —3F 23
Croydon Rd. Reig —4E 31
Croydon Rd. Wall & Croy —4F 23
Croydon Rd. W'ham —3D 33
Croydon Rd. W Wick & Brom —4C 24
Crutches La. Roch & Strd —3E 27
Cryers Hill. —4B 4
Cryers Hill La. Cry H —4B 4
Cryers Hill Rd. Cry H —4B 4
Crystal Palace. —3A 24
Crystal Palace F.C. —3A 24
Crystal Pal. Pde. SE19 —3A 24
Crystal Pal. Pk. Rd. SE26 —3B 24
Cubitt Town. —1C 24
Cuckoo Hill. Pinn —2B 14
Cuckoo La. Tonb —4B 34
Cucumber La. Ess —2F 7
Cudham. —2D 33
Cudham La. N. Cud & Orp —1D 33
Cudham La. S. Sev —2D 33
Cudham Rd. Orp —1D 33
Cuffley. —3A 8
Cuffley Hill. Chesh —3A 8
Culver Gro. Stan —2C 14
Culverstone Green. —1C 34
Cumberland Av. Guild —3E 29
Cumberland Av. Slou —4D 13
Cumberland Ga. W1 —4F 15
Cumberland Rd. Camb —2C 28
Cumberland Rd. Stan —2D 15
Cupid Green. —1A 6
Cupid Grn. La. Hem H —1A 6
Curriers La. Slou —3C 12
Curtain Rd. EC2 —4A 16
Curtismill Green. —4F 9
Curzon St. W1 —4F 15
Custom House. —4C 16
Cuton Hall La. Spri —1E 11
Cutter Ridge Rd. Ludd —4D 27
Cut, The. SE1 —1A 24
Cutting, The. Red —4F 31
Cutty Sark. —1C 24
Cuxton. —4E 27
Cuxton Rd. Roch —3E 27

Dagenham. —3E 17
Dagenham Av. Dag —4E 17 (in two parts)
Dagenham Rd. Romf & Dag —3F 17
Dagger La. Borwd —1C 14
Dagnall Rd. Gt Gad —1E 5
Dagnam Pk. Dri. Romf —1A 18
Dagwood La. Dodd —4B 10
Daiglen Dri. S Ock —4B 18
Dairy La. Crock H —4D 33
Dairy La. Mard —4E 35
Dale Rd. S'fleet —3B 26
Dalling Rd. W6 —1E 23
Dalston. —3A 16
Dalston La. E8 —3A 16
Daltons Rd. Orp & W Wick —4F 25
Damases La. Bore —1F 11
Dames Rd. E7 —3C 16
Danbury. —2F 11
Danbury Common. —2F 11
Dancers End La. Tring —1B 4
Dancers Hill. —4E 7
Dancers Hill Rd. Barn —4E 7
Daneshill. Red —4F 31
Danson Interchange. (Junct.) —2E 25
Danson La. Well —2E 25
Danson Rd. Bex & Bexh —2E 25 (in two parts)
Darby Green. —1A 28
Darby Grn. La. B'water —1A 28
Darby Grn. Rd. B'water —1A 28
Darenth. —3A 26
Darenth Hill. Dart —3A 26
Darenth Interchange. (Junct.) —2A 26
Darenth Rd. Dart —2A 26
Dargets Rd. Chat —1F 35
Darkes La. Pot B —3E 7
Dark La. Chesh —3B 8
Dark La. Gt War —1A 18
Darland. —4F 27
Darland Av. Gill —4F 27
Darman La. Pad W & Ladd —4D 35
Darnicle Hill. Chesh —2A 8
Darnley Rd. E8 —3B 16
Darnley Rd. Grav —2C 26 (in two parts)
Darnley Rd. Roch —3E 27
Darr's La. N'chu —1D 5
Dartford. —2A 26
Dartford Borough Museum. —2A 26
Dartford By-Pass. Bex & Dart —2F 25
Dartford Heath. (Junct.) —2F 25
Dartford Rd. Bex —2F 25
Dartford Rd. Dart —2F 25
Dartford Rd. F'ham —4A 26 (in two parts)
Dartford Rd. Sev —3F 33
Dartmouth Hill. SE13 —1C 24
Dartmouth Park. —3F 15
Dartmouth Pk. Hill. N19 —3F 15
Dartmouth Rd. SE26 & SE23 —2B 24
Dartnell Park. —1F 29
Darvills La. Shur R —2A 20
Dashwood Av. High W —1A 12
Dashwood Rd. Grav —2C 26
Datchet. —1E 21
Datchet Common. —1E 21
Datchet Rd. Hort —2E 21
Datchet Rd. Old Win —2E 21
Datchet Rd. Slou —1D 21
Datchet Rd. Wind —1D 21
Daubeney Rd. E5 —3B 16
Davidson Rd. Croy —4A 24
David Street. —4C 26
David St. Meop —4C 26
Dawesgreen. —4D 31
Dawes La. Sarr —4F 5
Dawes Rd. SW6 —1E 23
Dawley Rd. Hay —4A 14
Dawney Hill. Pirb —2D 29
Daws Hill. E4 —4C 8
Daws Hill La. High W —2B 12
Daws La. NW7 —1D 15
Days La. Pil H —4B 10
Deacons Hill. Borwd —1D 15
Deacons Hill. Wat —1B 14
Deacons Hill Rd. Els —4D 7
Deadhearn La. Chal G —1E 13
Deadman's Ash La. Sarr —4F 5
Deadman's La. Chelm —3E 11
Dean La. Cook —3B 12
Dean La. Meop —1C 34
Dean La. Red —3F 31
Dean Rd. Meop —4C 26
Deansbrook Rd. Edgw —2D 15
Deans La. Edgw —2D 15
Deans La. Tad —3E 31
Dean Street. —4E 35
Dean St. W1 —4F 15
Dean St. E Far —4E 35
Dean St. Mar —3A 12
Dean Way. Chal G —1E 13
Debden. —4D 9
Debden Green. —4D 9
Debden La. Lou —4D 9
De Beauvoir Rd. N1 —4A 16
De Beauvoir Town. —4A 16
Decoy Hill Rd. H Hals —1F 27
Dedmere Rd. Mar —3A 12
Dedworth. —1D 21
Dedworth Rd. Wind —1C 20
Deepcut. —2C 28
Deepcut Bri. Rd. Deep —2C 28
Deepdene Av. Dork —4C 30
Deep Mill La. L Kin —4C 4
Deeves Hall La. Pot B —3D 7
Delancey St. NW1 —4F 15
Delce Rd. Roch —4F 27
Dellsome La. N Mym —2E 7
Demesne Rd. Wall —4F 23
Dene Rd. Asht —2D 31
Dene Rd. N'wd —2A 14
Dene St. Dork —4C 30
Denham. —3F 13
Denham Aerodrome. —2F 13
Denham Av. Den —3F 13
Denham Garden Village. —2F 13
Denham Green. —2F 13
Denham Grn. La. Den —2F 13
Denham La. Chal P —2E 13
Denham Rd. Iver & Uxb —3F 13
Denham Roundabout. (Junct.) —3F 13
Denham Way. Den & Rick —2F 13
Denmark Hill. —2A 24
Denmark Hill. SE5 —1A 24
Dennett Rd. Croy —4A 24
Dennettsland Rd. Crock H —4D 33
Denning Av. Croy —4A 24
Dennises La. Upm —4A 18
Dennis La. Stan —1C 14
Dennis Rd. S Ock —4B 18
Densham Rd. E15 —4C 16
Denton. —2D 27
Denton Rd. Dart —2F 25
Denton Way. Wok —2D 29
Denzil Rd. NW10 —3D 15
Deptford. —1B 24
Deptford Bri. SE8 —1B 24
Deptford B'way. SE14 —1B 24
Deptford Chu. St. SE8 —1B 24
Deptford High St. SE8 —1B 24
Derby Rd. Croy —4A 24
Derby Rd. Grays —1B 26
Deringwood Dri. Down —3F 35
Derry Downs. —4E 25
Desborough Av. High W —2A 12
Desborough Rd. High W —1A 12
Detillens La. Oxt —3C 32
Devas St. E3 —4B 16
Devenish Rd. Asc —4C 20
Deville Way. Lain —2D 19
Devon Rd. S Dar —3A 26
Devonshire Rd. NW7 —2E 15
Devonshire Rd. SE23 —2B 24
Devons Rd. E3 —4B 16
Dibden. —3F 33
Dibden La. Ide H & Sev —3F 33
Dickens Centre. —3F 27
Dickerage La. N Mald —3D 23
Dickerage Rd. King T —3D 23
Dillywood La. Roch & High —3E 27
Dimmocks La. Sarr —4F 5
Ditches La. Coul & Cat —2A 32
Ditton. —2E 35
Ditton Hill. Surb —4C 22
Ditton Hill Rd. Surb —4C 22
Ditton Pk. Rd. Slou —1E 21
Ditton Rd. Slou —1E 21 (nr. Horton Rd.)
Ditton Rd. Slou —1E 21 (nr. Riding Ct. Rd.)
Ditton Rd. Surb —4C 22
Dixons Hill Rd. N Mym —2E 7
Dobb's Weir Rd. Hod —1C 8
Dockett Eddy La. Shep —4A 22
Docklands. —4D 17
Dock Rd. Chat —3F 27
Dock Rd. Grays & Til —1C 26
Dock St. E1 —4B 16
Doctors La. Cat —3A 32
Doddinghurst. —4B 10
Doddinghurst Rd. Brtwd —4B 10
Dodds La. Chal G —1E 13
Dodds La. Pic E —1F 5
Doesgate La. Bulp —3C 18
Dogflud Way. Farnh —4A 28
Doghurst La. Coul —2F 31
Dogkennel Green. —4B 30
Dog Kennel Hill. SE22 —2A 24
Dog Kennel La. Chor —4F 5
Dollis Hill. —3E 15
Dollis Rd. NW7 & N3 —2E 15
Dolls Hill La. NW2 —3D 15
Dome, The. (Junct.) —4B 6
Domsey La. L Walt —1E 11
Doncastle Rd. Brack —3A 20
Donkey La. F'ham —4A 26
Donkey Town. —1C 28
Donnington Rd. NW10 —4E 15
Dora's Green. —4A 28

Dora's Grn. La.—Foxley La.

Dora's Grn. La. *Farnh* —4A 28
Dorchester Gro. *W4* —1D 23
Dorking Rd. *Bookh* —3B 30
Dorking Rd. *Chil* —4F 29
Dorking Rd. *Eps* —2D 31
Dorking Rd. *Gom & Ab H* —4A 30
Dorking Rd. *Lea* —2C 30
Dorking Rd. *Tad* —3D 31
Dormer's Wells. —4B 14
Dormer's Wells La. *S'hall* —4B 14
Dorney. —1C 20
Dorney Hill N. *Beac* —2D 13
Dorney Hill S. *Slou* —3D 13
Dorney Reach. —1C 20
Dorney Wood Rd. *Burn* —3C 12
Dorset Rd. *SW19* —3E 23
Douglas Rd. *Maid* —3F 35
Dover Ho. Rd. *SW15* —2E 23
Dover Rd. *N'fleet* —2C 26
Dover Rd. *Slou* —4D 13
Dover Rd. E. *Grav* —2C 26
Dovers Corner. (Junct.) —4F 17
Doversgreen. —4E 31
Dovers Grn. Rd. *Reig* —4E 31
Dowlesgreen. —3A 20
Downe. —1D 33
Downe Rd. *Cud* —1D 33
Downe Rd. *Kes* —1D 33
Downfield Rd. *Hert H* —1B 8
Down Grn. La. *Wheat* —1C 6
Downhall Rd. *Mat G* —1F 9
Downham. —3C 24
(nr. Bromley)
Downham. —1E 19
(nr. Ramsden Heath)
Downham Rd. *N1* —4A 16
Downham Rd. *Rams H* —4E 11
Downham Rd. *Stock* —4E 11
Downham Way. *Brom* —3C 24
Downhills Pk. Rd. *N17* —2A 16
Down House. —1D 33
Down La. *Comp* —4D 29
Downley. —1A 12
Downley Rd. *Nap* —4A 4
Downs Ct. Rd. *Purl* —1A 32
Downs Hill Rd. *Eps* —2D 31
Downshills Way. *N17* —2A 16
Downshire Way. *Brack* —3B 20
Downside. —2B 30
Downside Bri. Rd. *Cobh* —2B 30
Downside Comn. Rd. *D'side* —2B 30
Downside Rd. *D'side* —2B 30
Downside Rd. *Sutt* —1F 31
Downs Rd. *Enf* —4A 8
Downs Rd. *Eps* —1D 31
Downs Rd. *Grav* —3C 26
Downs Rd. *Sutt* —1E 31
Downsview Rd. *SE19* —3A 24
Dowsett La. *Rams H* —4E 11
Dowsett Rd. *N17* —2B 16
Doyle Gdns. *NW10* —4E 15
Drake's Dri. *St Alb* —2C 6
Drakes La. *L Walt* —1E 11
Drapers Rd. *Enf* —4A 8
Draycott Av. *Harr* —2C 14
Drayton Beauchamp. —1C 4
Drayton Gdns. *SW10* —1F 23
Drayton Grn. Rd. *W13* —4C 14
Drayton Pk. *N5* —3A 16
Drewstead Rd. *SW16* —2F 23
Drift Bridge. (Junct.) —1E 31
Drift Rd. *M'head* —2A 20
Drive, The. *Gt War* —2B 18
Drive, The. *Ilf* —2D 17
Drive, The. *Mord* —4F 23
Drive, The. *Reach* —1F 13
Drive, The. *Sidc* —2E 25
Drop La. *Brick* —3B 6
Dropmore Rd. *Burn* —4C 12
Druid St. *SE1* —1A 24
Drury La. *WC2* —4A 16
Drury Way. *NW10* —3D 15
Dry Arch Rd. *Asc* —4D 21
Drydell La. *Che* —3D 5
Dryhill. —3E 33
Dryhill La. *Sund* —3E 33
Dry Hill Pk. Rd. *Tonb* —4B 34
Dry Street. —3D 19
Dry St. *Bas* —3D 19
Du Cane Rd. *W12* —4D 15
Duck La. *Thorn* —2E 9
Duckmore La. *Tring* —1C 4
Duck's Hill Rd. *N'wd* —2A 14
Ducks Island. —1E 15
Dudbrook Rd. *Kel C* —4A 10
Dudden Hill. —3E 15
Dudden Hill La. *NW10* —3D 15
Dudswell. —1D 5
Dudswell La. *Dud* —1D 5
Duffield La. *Stoke P* —3D 13
Dugdale Hill La. *Pot B* —3E 7
Duke's Av. *N10* —2F 15
Dukes Av. *Rich & King T* —3C 22
Dukes La. *Will* —1B 10
Duke's Ride. *Crowt* —1A 28
Duke St. *Chelm* —2E 11
Duke St. *Hod* —1B 8
Dulwich. —2A 24
Dulwich Comn. *SE21* —2A 24
Dulwich Rd. *SE24* —2A 24
Dulwich Village. —2A 24
Dulwich Village. *SE21* —2A 24
Dulwich Wood Pk. *SE19* —3A 24
Dunbar Rd. *N22* —2A 16
Dunbridge St. *E2* —4B 16
Duncan Rd. *Gill* —3F 27
Dundale Rd. *Tring* —1C 4
Dungells La. *B'water* —2A 28
Dungrove Hill La. *M'head* —4A 12
Dunkery Rd. *SE12* —3C 24
Dunk's Green. —3B 34
Dunks Grn. Rd. *S'brne* —3B 34
Dunmow Rd. *Fyf* —2A 10
Dunnings La. *W H'dn & Upm* —3B 18
Dunn St. Rd. *Bred* —1F 35
Dunny La. *Chfd* —3F 5
Dunsmore. —2B 4
Dunsmure Rd. *N16* —3A 16
Dunton Green. —2F 33
Dunton Rd. *SE1* —1A 24
Dunton Rd. *Bill & Bas* —2C 18
Dunton Rd. *Dun* —2C 18
Duppas Hill Rd. *Croy* —4A 24
Durants Rd. *Enf* —4B 8
Durham Rd. *SW20* —3E 23
Durham Rd. *Lain & Bas* —2D 19
Durnsford Rd. *N22* —2F 15
Durnsford Rd. *SW19* —2E 23
Durrants Hill Rd. *Hem H* —2F 5
Durrants La. *Berk* —2D 5
Durrants Rd. *Berk* —1D 5
Dury Rd. *Barn* —4E 7
Dutch Cottage Museum. —4F 19
Dutch Village. —4F 19
Dux Ct. Rd. *Hoo* —2F 27
Dux Hill. *Plax* —3B 34
Dux La. *Plax* —3B 34
Dwelly La. *Eden* —4C 32
Dyke La. *Wheat* —1C 6
Dytchleys La. *N'side* —4A 10
Dytchleys Rd. *Brtwd* —4A 10

Eagle Way. *Gt War* —2B 18
Eagle Wharf Rd. *N1* —4A 16
Ealing. —4C 14
Ealing Common. (Junct.) —4D 15
Ealing Grn. *W5* —4C 14
Ealing Rd. *Bren* —1C 22
Ealing Rd. *Wemb* —3D 15
Eardley Rd. *SW16* —3F 23
Earl Howe Rd. *Holm G* —4C 4
Earl Rd. *N'fleet* —2C 26
Earls Court. —1E 23
Earls Court Exhibition Centre. —1E 23
Earls Ct. Rd. *W8 & SW5* —1E 23
Earlsfield. —2F 23
Earlsfield Rd. *SW18* —2F 23
Earl's La. *Pot B* —3D 7
Earl's Path. *Lou* —4C 8
Earl St. *Maid* —3F 35
Earlswood. —4F 31
East Acton. —4D 15
E. Acton La. *W3* —4D 15
East Av. *E12* —3D 17
East Barnet. —1F 15
E. Barnet Rd. *Barn* —4F 7
East Bedfont. —2A 22
Eastbourne Rd. *God* —4B 32
Eastbourne Rd. *S God* —4B 32
Eastbourne Ter. *W2* —4F 15
East Burnham. —3D 13
E. Burnham La. *Farn R* —4D 13
Eastbury. —1A 14
Eastbury Av. *N'wd* —1A 14
Eastbury Rd. *N'wd* —2A 14
Eastbury Rd. *Wat* —1B 14
E. Churchfield Rd. *W3* —4D 15
Eastchurch Rd. *H'row A* —1A 22
East Clandon. —4F 29
East Comn. *Ger X* —2E 13
Eastcote. —3B 14
Eastcote High Rd. *Pinn* —2B 14
Eastcote La. *Harr* —3B 14
Eastcote La. *N'holt* —3B 14
Eastcote La. N. *N'holt* —3B 14
Eastcote Rd. *Pinn* —2B 14
Eastcote Rd. *Ruis* —3A 14
Eastcote Village. —2B 14
East Dulwich. —2B 24
E. Dulwich Gro. *SE21* —2A 24
E. Dulwich Rd. *SE22 & SE15* —2A 24
Eastend. —1C 8
E. End Rd. *N3 & N2* —2E 15
Easter Av. *Grays* —1A 26
Easterfields. *E Mal* —2E 35
Eastern Av. *E11 & Ilf* —2C 16
Eastern Av. *Pinn* —3B 14
Eastern Av. E. *Romf* —2F 17
Eastern Av. W. *Romf* —2E 17
(in two parts)
Eastern Dene. *Hasl* —4B 4
Eastern Way. *SE28 & Eri* —1E 25
East Ewell. —1E 31
East Farleigh. —3E 35
Eastferry Rd. *E14* —1B 24
Eastfield Rd. *Burn* —4C 12
Eastfield Rd. *Enf* —4B 8
Eastfields Rd. *Mitc* —3F 23
East Finchley. —2F 15
E. Hall Hill. *Bou M* —4F 35
E. Hall La. *Wen* —4F 17
E. Hall Rd. *Orp* —4E 25
East Ham. —4D 17
Easthampstead. —4B 20
Easthampstead Rd. *Brack* —3B 20
Easthampstead Rd. *Wokgm* —3A 20
East Hanningfield. —3F 11
E. Hanningfield Rd. *H Grn & E Han* —3F 11
E. Hanningfield Rd. *Ret C* —4F 11
E. Heath Rd. *NW3* —3F 15
East Hill. —1A 34
East Hill. *SW18* —2F 23
East Hill. *Dart* —2A 26
East Hill. *Oxt* —3C 32
East Hill. *S Dar* —3A 26
East Hill. *Wok* —2F 29
E. Hill Rd. *Knat* —1A 34
E. Hill Rd. *Oxt* —3C 32
East Horsley. —3A 30
E. India Dock Rd. *E14* —4B 16
East La. *Wal L* —1A 20
East La. *Wemb* —3C 14
East La. *W Hor* —3A 30
E. Lodge La. *Enf* —4F 7
Eastly End. —3F 21
East Malling. —2E 35
East Malling Heath. —3D 35
E. Mayne. *Bas* —2E 19
E. Milton Rd. *Grav* —2C 26
East Molesey. —3C 22
Easton St. *High W* —1B 12
East Peckham. —4D 35
East Ramp. *H'row A* —1A 22
E. Ridgeway. *Cuff* —3A 8
East Rd. *EC1* —4A 16
E. Rochester Way. *Sidc & Bex* —2D 25
E. Row. *Roch* —3F 27
East Sheen. —2D 23
E. Smithfield. *E1* —4A 16
East St. *Eps* —1D 31
East St. *Farnh* —4A 28
East St. *Hunt* —4E 35
E. Thurrock Rd. *Grays* —1C 26
East Tilbury. —1D 27
E. Tilbury Rd. *Linf* —1D 27
East View. *Writ* —2D 11
East Way. *E9* —3B 16
Eastwick. —1D 9
Eastwick Hall La. *E'wck* —1D 9
East Wickham. —1E 25
Eastwick Rd. *Bookh* —3B 30
Eastwick Rd. *H'low* —1D 9
Eastworth. —4F 21
Eastworth Rd. *Cher* —4F 21
Eaton Ri. *W5* —4C 14
Eaton Rd. *Enf* —4A 8
Eaton Sq. *SW1* —1F 23
Ebbisham Rd. *Tad* —3E 31
Ebury Bri. Rd. *SW1* —1F 23
Eccles. —1E 35
Eccleston St. *SW1* —1F 23
Echo Pit Rd. *Guild* —4E 29
Edenbridge. —4D 33
Eden Park. —4B 24
Eden Pk. Av. *Beck* —3B 24
(in two parts)
Edgehill Rd. *Purl* —1A 32
Edgemoor Rd. *Frim* —2C 28
Edgeworth Rd. *Barn* —4F 7
Edgington Way. *Sidc* —3E 25
Edgware. —2D 15
Edgware Bury. —1D 15
Edgwarebury La. *Edgw* —1D 15
Edgware Rd. *NW2* —3E 15
Edgware Rd. *NW9* —2D 15
Edgware Rd. *W2 & W9* —4F 15
Edgware Way. *Edgw* —1C 14
Edinburgh Av. *Slou* —4D 13
Edinburgh Way. *H'low* —1D 9
Edison Gro. *SE18* —1D 25
Edison Rd. *SE18 & Well* —1D 25
Edith Gro. *SW10* —1F 23
Edmonton. —1B 16
Edney Common. —2C 10
Edward St. *SE14 & SE8* —1B 24
Effingham. —3B 30
Effingham Comn. Rd. *Eff* —3B 30
Effingham Junction. —3B 30
Effingham Rd. *Surb* —4C 22
Effra Rd. *SW2* —2A 24
Egerton Dri. *SE10* —1B 24
Egerton Rd. *Guild* —4D 29
Eggar's Hill. *Alder* —4B 28
Eggpie La. *Weald* —4F 33
Egham. —3E 21
Egham By-Pass. *Egh* —3E 21
Egham Hill. *Egh* —3E 21
Egham Hythe. —3F 21
Egham Wick. —3E 21
Eglantine La. *F'ham* —4A 26
Egley Rd. *Wok* —2E 29
Egypt. —3D 13
Egypt La. *Farn C* —3D 13
Elder Rd. *SE27* —3A 24
Eleanor Cross Rd. *Wal X* —3B 8
Elephant & Castle. (Junct.) —1A 24
Elgin Av. *W9* —4E 15
Elgin Cres. *W11* —4E 15
Elizabeth Rd. *Grays* —1B 26
Elizabeth Way. *H'low* —1D 9
Elkins Green. —3B 10
Elkstone Rd. *W10* —4E 15
Ellenbrook. —1D 7
Ellenbrook La. *Hat* —1D 7
Ellen Rd. *Ayl* —1A 4
Ellesborough. —2A 4
Ellesborough Rd. *But C & Wen* —2A 4
Ellesfield Av. *Brack* —3A 20
Ellesmere Rd. *W4* —1D 23
Elles Rd. *Farn* —3A 28
Elliman Av. *Slou* —4D 13
Elm Av. *Ruis* —3B 14
Elmbridge Av. *Surb* —4D 23
Elmbridge Rd. *Ilf* —2E 17
Elm Corner. —2A 30
Elmers End. —3B 24
Elmers End Rd. *SE20 & Beck* —3B 24
Elm Grn. La. *Dan* —2F 11
Elm La. *Bour E* —2B 12
Elm La. *Rox* —1C 10
Elmore Rd. *Coul* —2F 31
Elm Park. —3F 17
Elm Pk. Av. *Horn* —3F 17
Elm Pk. Rd. *Pinn* —2B 14
Elm Rd. *Chelm* —2E 11
Elm Rd. *Penn* —1C 12
Elm Rd. *Sidc* —3E 25
Elmshott La. *Slou* —4D 13
Elms Perrin. *Wemb* —3C 14
Elms Rd. *Alder* —4B 28
Elms Rd. *Harr* —2C 14
Elmstead. —3D 25
Elmstead La. *Chst* —3D 25
Elmwood Av. *Felt* —2B 22
Elmwood Dri. *Bex* —2E 25
Elsdale St. *E9* —3B 16
Elspeth Rd. *SW11* —2F 23
Elstead Rd. *Seale* —4B 28
Elstree. —1C 14
Elstree Airport. —4C 6
Elstree Hill N. *Els* —1C 14
Elstree Hill S. *Els* —1C 14
Elstree Rd. *Bush & Borwd* —1C 14
Elstree Way. *Borwd* —4D 7
Eltham. —2D 25
Eltham High St. *SE9* —2D 25
Eltham Hill. *SE9* —2C 24
Eltham Place. —2D 25
Eltham Rd. *SE12 & SE9* —2C 24
Elthorne Heights. —4C 14
Elton Way. *Wat* —4B 6
Elvetham Rd. *Fleet* —3A 28
Embercourt Rd. *Th Dit* —4C 22
Ember La. *Esh & E Mol* —4C 22
Emerson Park. —2A 18
Emmanuel Rd. *SW12* —2F 23
Emmet Hill La. *Ladd* —4D 35
Emmetts. —3E 33
Emmetts La. *W'ham* —3E 33
Empire Way. *Wemb* —3D 15
Endell St. *WC2* —4A 16
Endlebury Rd. *E4* —1C 16
Endwell Rd. *SE4* —1B 24
Endymion Rd. *N4* —3A 16
Enfield. —4A 8
Enfield Highway. —4B 8
Enfield Lock. —4B 8
Enfield Rd. *Enf* —4A 8
Enfield Town. —4A 8
Enfield Wash. —4B 8
Engineers Way. *Wemb* —3D 15
Englands La. *NW3* —3F 15
Englands La. *Lou* —4D 9
Englefield Green. —3E 21
Englefield Rd. *N1* —3A 16
Engliff La. *Wok* —2F 29
Enterdent Rd. *God* —4B 32
Epping. —3E 9
Epping Forest District Museum. —3C 8
Epping Green. —2D 9
(nr. Epping Upland)
Epping Green. —2F 7
(nr. Tylers Causeway)
Epping New Rd. *Buck H & Lou* —1C 16
Epping Rd. *Epp* —3E 9
(Epping)
Epping Rd. *Epp* —4D 9
(Epping Forest)
Epping Rd. *Ong* —2F 9
Epping Rd. *Roy & Epp G* —1C 8
Epping Rd. *Toot* —3F 9
Epping Upland. —2D 9
Epsom. —1D 31
Epsom Downs. —2D 31
Epsom La. N. *Eps & Tad* —2E 31
Epsom Racecourse. —2D 31
Epsom Rd. *Asht* —2D 31
Epsom Rd. *Croy* —4A 24
Epsom Rd. *Eps* —1D 31
Epsom Rd. *Guild & Eff* —4E 29
Epsom Rd. *Lea* —2C 30
Epsom Rd. *Sutt & Mord* —4E 23
Erith. —1F 25
Erith High St. *Eri* —1F 25
Erith Museum. —1F 25
(off Walnut Tree Rd.)
Erith Rd. *Belv & Eri* —1E 25
Erith Rd. *Bexh & N Hth* —2E 25
Erriff Dri. *S Ock* —4B 18
Erskine Rd. *Meop* —1C 34
Esher. —4B 22
Esher By-Pass. *Chess* —4C 22
Esher By-Pass. *Esh & Cob* —1B 30
Esher By-Pass. *Lea* —1C 30
Esher Common. (Junct.) —1C 30
Esher Rd. *E Mol* —4C 22
Esher Rd. *W on T* —4B 22
Eskdale Av. *Che* —3D 5
Esplanade. *Roch* —4E 27
Essendon. —1E 7
Essendon Hill. *Ess* —1F 7
Essex Av. *Slou* —4D 13
Essex Regiment Way. *L Walt & Chelm* —1E 11
Essex Rd. *E10 & E11* —2C 16
Essex Rd. *N1* —4A 16
Essex Rd. *Hod* —1B 8
(in two parts)
Essex Rd. S. *E11* —3C 16
Essex Way. *Ben* —3F 19
Eton. —1D 21
Eton Rd. *Dat* —1D 21
Eton St. *Rich* —2D 23
Eton Wick. —1D 21
Eton Wick Rd. *Wind* —1D 21
Euston Av. *Wat* —1A 14
Euston Rd. *NW1* —4F 15
Euston Underpass. (Junct.) —4F 15
Evelina Rd. *SE15* —2B 24
Evelyn St. *SE8* —1B 24
Evering Rd. *N16 & E5* —3A 16
Eve Rd. *Wok* —2E 29
Eversholt St. *NW1* —4F 15
Eversley. —2F 19
Eversley Pk. Rd. *N21* —1A 16
Ewell. —1D 31
Ewell By-Pass. *Eps* —1E 31
Ewell La. *W Far* —3E 35
Ewell Rd. *Surb* —4C 22
(Long Ditton)
Ewell Rd. *Surb* —4D 23
(Surbiton)
Ewell Rd. *Sutt* —1E 31
Ewshot. —4A 28
Ewshot La. *Ews* —4A 28
Exchange Rd. *Wat* —4B 6
Exedown Rd. *Sev* —1B 34
Exhibition Rd. *SW7* —1F 23
Eynsford. —4A 26
Eynsford Castle. —4A 26
Eynsford Rd. *F'ham* —4A 26
Eynsford Rd. *Sev* —1F 33
Eynsford Rd. *Swan* —4F 25
Eynsham Dri. *SE2* —1E 25

Fackenden La. *Shor* —1F 33
Factory Rd. *E16* —1D 25
Faggoters La. *Mat T* —1F 9
Fagg's Rd. *Felt* —2A 22
Fagnall La. *Winch H* —1C 12
Fairchildes Rd. *Warl* —1C 32
Fair Cross. —3D 17
Fairfield Av. *Stai* —3F 21
Fairfield La. *Farn R* —4D 13
Fairfield N. *King T* —3D 23
Fairfield Rd. *E3* —4B 16
Fairfield Rd. *Croy* —4A 24
Fairfield S. *King T* —3D 23
Fairfield St. *SW18* —2E 23
Fairlands. —3D 29
Fair La. *Coul* —3F 31
Fairlie Rd. *Slou* —4D 13
Fairlop. —2D 17
Fairlop Rd. *E11* —3C 16
Fairmeadow. *Maid* —2F 35
Fairmead Rd. *Lou* —1C 16
Fairmile. —1B 30
Fairmile La. *Cobh* —1B 30
Fairoak La. *Oxs & Chess* —1C 30
Fairoaks Airport. —1E 29
Fairseat. —1C 34
Fairseat La. *Fair* —1B 34
Fairseat La. *Wro* —1B 34
Fairtrough Rd. *Orp* —1E 33
Fairway. *Grays* —4B 18
Fairway. *Orp* —4D 25
Fairway, The. *Ruis* —3B 14
Fakenham Way. *Camb* —1A 28
Falconer Rd. *Bush* —1B 14
Falconwood. —2D 25
Falconwood. (Junct.) —2D 25
Falkland Rd. *Dork* —4C 30
Falling La. *W Dray* —4A 14
Falloden Way. *NW11* —2E 15
Falmouth Av. *E4* —1C 16
Fane Way. *M'head* —1B 20
Fanner's Green. —1D 11
Fanshawe Av. *Bark* —3D 17
Fant. —3F 35
Fantail, The. (Junct.) —4D 25
Fant La. *Maid* —3E 35
Faraday Av. *Sidc* —2E 25
Faringdon Av. *Romf* —2F 17
Farleigh. —2B 32
Farleigh Ct. Rd. *Warl* —1B 32
Farleigh Green. —3E 35
Farleigh Hill. *Tovil* —3F 35
Farleigh La. *Maid* —3E 35
Farleigh Rd. *Warl* —2B 32
Farley La. *W'ham* —3D 33
Farley Rd. *S Croy* —1B 32
Farmbridge End. —1C 10
Farm Hill Rd. *Wal A* —3C 8
Farm La. *Asht & Eps* —2D 31
Farm Rd. *N21* —1A 16
Farm Rd. *Mord* —4E 23
Farm Way. *Buck H* —1C 16
Farnaby Rd. *Brom* —3C 24
Farnborough. —3B 28
(nr. Aldershot)
Farnborough. —4D 25
(nr. Orpington)
Farnborough Airport. —3B 28
Farnborough Comn. *Orp* —4D 25
Farnborough Hill. *Orp* —4D 25
Farnborough Park. —3B 28
Farnborough Rd. *Alder* —4A 28
Farnborough Rd. *Farn* —3B 28
Farnborough Rd. *Farnh* —4A 28
Farnborough Street. —2B 28
Farnborough Way. *Orp* —4D 25
Farnham. —4A 28
Farnham By-Pass. *Farnh* —4A 28
Farnham Common. —3D 13
Farnham La. *Slou* —4D 13
Farnham Pk. La. *Farn R* —4D 13
Farnham Rd. *Ews* —4A 28
Farnham Rd. *Guild* —4D 29
Farnham Rd. *Slou* —4D 13
Farnham Royal. —4D 13
Farningham. —4A 26
Farningham. *Brack* —4B 20
Farquhar Rd. *SE19* —3A 24
Farringdon Rd. *EC1* —4A 16
Fartherwell Rd. *W Mal* —2D 35
Farthing Grn. La. *Stoke P* —4E 13
Farthing Street. —1D 33
Farthing St. *Orp* —1D 33
Fassett Rd. *King T* —3D 23
Faversham Rd. *Mord* —4E 23
Fawke Common. —3A 34
Fawke Comn. *Under* —3A 34
Fawke Wood Rd. *Sev* —3A 34
Fawkham. —4B 26
Fawkham Green. —4B 26
Fawkham Grn. Rd. *Fawk* —4B 26
Fawkham Rd. *Fawk & W King* —4A 26
Fawkham Rd. *Long* —3B 26
Featherbed La. *Croy & Warl* —1B 32
Featherbed La. *Hem H* —2F 5
Feenan Highway. *Til* —1C 26
Felday Rd. *Ab H* —4A 30
Felden. —2F 5
Felden La. *Fel* —2F 5
Fellowes La. *Col H* —2D 7
Fellow Grn. *W End* —1D 29
Felmore. —2E 19
Feltham. —2B 22
Felthambrook Way. *Felt* —2B 22
Felthamhill. —3A 22
Feltham Hill Rd. *Ashf* —3A 22
Felthamhill Rd. *Felt* —3B 22
Feltham Rd. *Ashf* —3A 22
Fencepiece Rd. *Chig & Ilf* —1D 17
Fen La. *Ors* —4C 18
Fen La. *Upm* —3B 18
Fen La. *W Horn* —3B 18
Fenner Rd. *Grays* —1B 26
Fenns La. *W End* —1D 29
Fennycroft Rd. *Hem H* —1F 5
Fen Pond Rd. *Igh* —2B 34
Fentiman Rd. *SW8* —1A 24
Fenton Way. *Bas* —2D 19
Ferme Pk. Rd. *N8 & N4* —2A 16
Fern. —2B 12
Fernbank Rd. *Asc* —3C 20
Fernhall La. *Wal A* —3C 8
Fernhead Rd. *W9* —4E 15
Fernhill La. *B'water* —2A 28
Fernhill Rd. *B'water & Farn* —2A 28
Fernlea Rd. *SW12* —2F 23
Ferrers La. *Hpdn & Wheat* —1C 6
Ferry La. *N17* —2B 16
Ferry La. *Bour E* —3B 12
Ferry La. *Lale* —3F 21
Ferry La. *Rain* —4F 17
Ferry La. *Shep* —4A 22
Ferry Rd. *Ben* —3F 19
Ferry Rd. *Til* —2C 26
Fetcham. —3C 30
Fetter La. *EC4* —4A 16
Fickleshole. —1C 32
Fiddlers Hamlet. —3E 9
Fieldcommon. —4B 22
Field End Rd. *Pinn & Ruis* —2B 14
Field La. *Frim* —2B 28
Fields End. —2F 5
Fields End La. *Hem H* —1F 5
Field Way. *New Ad* —1B 32
Field Way. *Rick* —1F 13
Fife Rd. *SW14* —2D 23
Fifield. —1C 20
Fifield La. *Wink* —2C 20
Fifield Rd. *Fif* —1C 20
Fifth Av. *H'low* —1D 9
Fifth Cross Rd. *Twic* —2C 22
Fifth Way. *Wemb* —3D 15
Filston La. *Sev* —2F 33
Finchley. —2E 15
Finchley La. *NW4* —2E 15
Finchley Rd. *NW11, NW3 & NW8* —2E 15
Fine Bush La. *Hare* —2A 14
Fingrith Hall La. *Ing* —3B 10
(in two parts)
Finsbury. —4A 16
Finsbury Park. —3A 16
Firbank Rd. *Romf* —1E 17
Firbank Rd. *St Alb* —1C 6
Firgrove Rd. *B'water* —1A 28
Firmingers Rd. *Orp* —4E 25
Firs La. *N21 & N21* —1A 16
First Av. *Enf* —1A 16
First Av. *H'low* —1D 9
First Av. *Stan H* —4D 19
First Way. *Wemb* —3D 15
Fir Tree Av. *Stoke P* —4D 13
Fir Tree Hill. *Chan X* —4A 6
Fir Tree Rd. *Eps & Bans* —2E 31
Fishers Green. —3B 8
Fishery. —4B 12
Fishery Rd. *Hem H* —2F 5
Fishponds Rd. *Kes* —4C 24
Fish St. *Redb* —1B 6
Fitzjohn's Av. *NW3* —3F 15
Five Elms Rd. *Brom* —4C 24
Five Fields La. *Four E* —4E 33
Fiveways. (Junct.) —2D 25
Fiveways Corner. (Junct.)
(nr. Croydon) —4A 24
Fiveways Corner. (Junct.)
(nr. Hendon) —2E 15
Flackwell Heath. —2B 12
Flamstead End. —3B 8
Flamstead End Relief Rd. *Chesh & Wal X* —3A 8
Flamstead End Rd. *Chesh* —3B 8
Flanchford Rd. *L'gh* —4E 31
Flanchford Rd. *Reig* —4E 31
Flaunden. —3E 5
Flaunden Bottom. *Che & Hem H* —4E 5
Flaunden Hill. *Flau* —3E 5
Flaunden La. *Hem H* —3E 5
Flaunden La. *Rick* —3F 5
Fleece Rd. *Surb* —4C 22
Fleet. —3A 28
Fleet Downs. —2A 26
Fleet Rd. *NW3* —3F 15
Fleet Rd. *Farn & Alder* —3A 28
Fleet Rd. *Fleet* —3A 28
Fleet St. *EC4* —4A 16
Fleetville. —2C 6
Fletcher's Green. —4F 33
Fletcher Way. *Hem H* —1F 5
Flexford. —4C 28
Flexford Rd. *Norm* —4C 28
Flint Hill. *Dork* —4C 30
Florence Rd. *SE14* —1B 24
Flower La. *NW7* —2D 15
Flower La. *God* —3B 32
Flowers Bottom La. *Speen* —4A 4
Floyd's La. *Wok* —2F 29
Fobbing. —4E 19
Fobbing Rd. *Corr* —4E 19
Folder's La. *Brack* —3B 20
Folly Hill. *Farnh* —4A 28
Folly La. *St Alb* —2C 6
Fonthill Rd. *N4* —3A 16
Foots Cray. —3E 25
Foots Cray La. *Sidc* —2E 25
Footscray Rd. *SE9* —2D 25
Force Green. —3D 33
Force Grn. La. *W'ham* —3D 33
Fordbridge Rd. *Ashf* —3A 22
Fordbridge Rd. *Shep & Sun* —4A 22
Fordbridge Roundabout. (Junct.) —3A 22
Ford La. *Rain* —3F 17
Ford La. *Tros* —2C 34
Ford Rd. *Wok* —2D 29
Fords Gro. *N21* —1A 16
Fordwater Rd. *Cher* —4F 21
Foreman Rd. *Ash* —4B 28
Foremans Barn Rd. *Maid* —4E 35
Forestdale. —1B 32
Forest Dri. *E12* —3C 16
Forest Edge. *Buck H* —1C 16
Foresters Dri. *Wall* —1F 31
Foresters Way. *Crowt* —4A 20
Forest Gate. —3C 16
Forest Grn. Rd. *Fif* —1B 20
Forest Hill. —2B 24
Forest Hill Rd. *SE22 & SE23* —2B 24
Forest La. *E15 & E7* —3C 16
Forest La. *Chig* —1D 17
Fore St. *N18 & N9* —2B 16
Fore St. *Pinn* —2A 14
Forest Rd. *E17* —2B 16
Forest Rd. *Felt* —2B 22
Forest Rd. *Ilf* —2D 17
Forest Rd. *Lea* —3A 30
Forest Rd. *Lou* —4C 8
Forest Rd. *Sutt* —4E 23
Forest Rd. *Wink R & N Asc* —3B 20
Forest Rd. *Wokgm* —3A 20
Forest Side. *E4* —1C 16
Forest Side. *Wal A* —4C 8
Forge La. *Alder* —3A 28
Forge La. *E Far* —3E 35
Forge La. *High* —3E 27
Forge La. *Hort K* —3A 26
Forge La. *Leeds* —4F 35
Forge La. *Maid* —3C 34
Forge La. *Shorne* —3D 27
Forge La. *Yald* —4E 35
Forlease Rd. *M'head* —4B 12
Formby Rd. *Hall* —4E 27
Forstal. —2E 35
Forstal La. *Cox* —4F 35
Forstal Rd. *Ayle & Sandl* —2E 35
Fort Amherst. —3F 27
Fortess Rd. *NW5* —3F 15
Fortis Grn. *N2 & N10* —2F 15
Fortis Green. —2F 15
Fortis Grn. Rd. *N10* —2F 15
Fort Luton. —4F 27
Fort Pitt Hill. *Chat* —4F 27
Fort Rd. *Til* —2C 26
Fortune Green. —3E 15
Fortune Grn. *NW6* —3E 15
Forty Av. *Wemb* —3D 15
Forty Green. —2C 12
Forty Grn. Rd. *Knot* —2C 12
Forty Hall. —4A 8
Forty Hill. —4A 8
Forty Hill. *Enf* —4A 8
Forty La. *Wemb* —3D 15
Foster Street. —1E 9
Foster St. *H'low* —1E 9
Fostington Way. *W'slde* —1F 35
Foundry La. *L Row* —3A 4
Fountain Dri. *SE19* —3A 24
Fountain La. *Maid* —3E 35
Fountain Rd. *Red* —4F 31
Four Ashes Rd. *Cry H* —4B 4
Four Elms. —4E 33
Four Elms Hill. *Chatt* —3F 27
Four Elms Rd. *Eden* —4D 33
Fourth Av. *E12* —3D 17
Fourth Av. *H'low* —1D 9
Fourth Way. *Wemb* —3D 15
Four Wantz. —1B 10
Fox Corner. —3D 29
Fox Corner. *Worp* —3D 29
Foxendown. —4C 26
Foxendown La. *Meop* —4C 26
Fox Hatch. —4A 10
Foxhills Rd. *Ott* —4E 21
Foxhounds La. *S'fleet* —2B 26
Fox Lane. —2A 28
Fox La. *N13* —1A 16
Fox La. *Kes* —4C 24
Foxley Hill Rd. *Purl* —1A 32
Foxley La. *Binf* —3B 20
Foxley La. *Purl* —1F 31

Foxley Rd.—Hampton

Foxley Rd. SW9 —1A 24
Fox Rd. Mash —1C 10
Fox Rd. Wig —1C 4
Foyle Dri. S Ock —4B 18
Framewood Rd. Slou —3E 13
Frances Rd. Wind —1D 21
Frances St. SE18 —1D 25
Francis Rd. E10 —3C 16
Franks La. Hort K —4A 26
Franks Wood Av. Orp —4D 25
Frant Rd. T Hth —4A 24
Frascati Way. M'head —4B 12
Fraser Rd. Eri —1F 25
Freelands Rd. Brom —3C 24
Freemans La. Hay —4A 14
Freemasons Rd. E16 —4C 16
Free Prae Rd. Cher —4F 21
Freezy Water. —4B 8
Fremantle Rd. Ilf —2D 17
Fremnells, The. Bas —2E 19
Frenches Rd. Red —4F 31
French Horn La. Hat —1E 7
French Street. —3D 33
French St. Sun —3B 22
Frendsbury Rd. SE4 —2B 24
Friars Av. Shenf —1B 18
Friars Pl. La. W3 —4D 15
Friars Stile Rd. Rich —2D 23
Friars, The. —2E 35
Friary Bri. Guild —4E 29
Friary Island. —2E 21
Friary Rd. N12 —1F 15
Friary Rd. W3 —4D 15
Friday Hill. —1C 16
Friday Hill. E4 —1C 16
Friern Barnet. —1F 15
Friern Barnet La. N20 & N11 —1F 15
Friern Barnet Rd. N11 —1F 15
Frieth Rd. Medm —2A 12
Frimley. —2B 28
Frimley By-Pass. Frim —2B 28
Frimley Green. —2B 28
Frimley Grn. Rd. Frim G —2B 28
Frimley Gro. Gdns. Frim —2B 28
Frimley High St. Frim —2B 28
Frimley Ridge. —2B 28
Frimley Rd. Ash V —3B 28
Frimley Rd. Camb & Frim —1B 28
Frindsbury. —3F 27
Frindsbury Hill. Roch —3F 27
Frindsbury Rd. Strood —3E 27
Frithe, The. Slou —4E 13
Frith Hill. Gt Miss —3B 4
Frith La. NW7 —2E 15
Frith Rd. Croy —4A 24
Frithsden. —1E 5
Frizlands La. Dag —3E 17
Frobisher Rd. St Alb —2C 6
Frog Gro. La. Wood S —3D 29
Froggy La. Uxb —3F 13
Froghole. —4D 33
Frogmoor. High W —1B 12
Frogmore. —3C 6
(nr. St Albans)
Frogmore. —1A 28
(nr. Sandhurst)
Frogmore. St Alb —3C 6
Frogmore Rd. B'water —1A 28
Frogmore St. Tring —1C 4
Frognal. NW3 —3F 15
Frognal Av. Sidc —3E 25
Frognal Corner. (Junct.) —3D 25
Frognal La. NW3 —3E 15
Frog St. Kel H —4A 10
Front La. Upm —3A 18
Front, The. Pott E —1E 5
Fryent Way. NW9 —2D 15
Fryerning. —3C 10
Fryerning La. Ing —3C 10
Fryerns. —2E 19
Fulbourne Rd. E17 —2C 16
Fulham. —1E 23
Fulham Broadway. (Junct.) —1E 23
Fulham F.C. —1E 23
Fulham High St. SW6 —1E 23
Fulham Pal. Rd. W6 & SW6 —1E 23
Fulham Rd. SW6, SW10 & SW3 —1E 23
Fuller's Hill. Che —3D 5
Fuller St. Sev —2A 34
Fullers Way N. Surb —4D 23
Fullers Way S. Chess —4D 23
Fullers Wood La. S Nut —4F 31
Fullwell Cross. —2D 17
Fullwell Cross. Ilf —2D 17
Fulmer. —3E 13
Fulmer Comn. Rd. Ful & Iver —3E 13
Fulmer La. Ful & Ger X —3E 13
Fulmer Rd. Ful & Ger X —3E 13
Fulwell. —3C 22
Fulwell Rd. Tedd —3C 22
Furlong Rd. Bour E —3B 12
Furness Rd. Mord —4E 23
Furzebushes La. St Alb —2B 6
Furzedown. —3F 23
Furzehill Rd. Borwd —4D 7
Furze La. Stock —4E 11
Furze Platt. —4B 12
Furze Platt Rd. M'head —4B 12
Fyfield. —2A 10
Fyfield Rd. More —2A 10
Fyfield Rd. Ong —2A 10
Fyfield Rd. Will —2B 10

Gadbrook Rd. Bet —4D 31
Gaddesden La. Redb —1A 6
Gaddesden Row. —1F 5
Gaddesden Row. Gad R —1F 5
Gadebridge. —1F 5
Gadebridge La. Hem H —1F 5
Gadebridge Rd. Hem H —1F 5
Gadshill. —3E 27
Gads Hill. Gill —3F 27
Gainsborough Rd. E11 —3C 16
Gainsborough Rd. N12 —1E 15
Gainsthorpe Rd. Ong —2F 9
Gale St. Dag —3E 17
Gallants La. E Far —3E 35
Gallery Rd. SE21 —2A 24
Galleyend. —3E 11
Galley Hill. Hem H —1F 5
Galley Hill Rd. Swans & N'fleet —2B 26
Galleyhill Rd. Wal A —3C 8
Galley La. Barn —4E 7
Galleywood. —3E 11
Galleywood Rd. Chelm —2E 11
Galleywood Rd. Gt Bad —2E 11
Galliard Rd. N9 —1B 16
Gallows Corner. (Junct.) —2F 17
Gallows Hill. K Lan —3A 6
Gallows Hill La. Ab L —3A 6
Gallows La. High W —1A 12
Gallwey Rd. Alder —4B 28
Gallys Rd. Wind —1C 20
Galpins Rd. T Hth —3A 24
Galsworthy Rd. King T —3D 23
Gambles La. Wok —3F 29
Gammons La. Wat —4A 6
Gander Grn. La. Sutt —4E 23
Gandy's La. Bou M —4F 35
Gangers Hill. God —3B 32
Gannondown Rd. Cook —3B 12
Gants Hill. —2D 17
Gants Hill. (Junct.) —2D 17
Gants Hill Cross. Ilf —2D 17
Ganwick Corner. —4E 7
Gapemouth Rd. Pirb —2C 28
Gap Rd. SW19 —3E 23
Gardeners Green. —4A 20
Gardens, The. Harr —2C 14
Gardiners La. N. Cray H —1E 19
Gardiners La. S. Bas —2E 19
Gardner Rd. M'head —4B 12
Garfield Rd. Add —4F 21
Garlands Rd. Lea —2C 30
Garnet St. E1 —4B 16
Garrad's Rd. SW16 —2F 23
Garratt La. SW18 & SW17 —2E 23
Garratts La. Bans —2E 31
Garrison La. Chess —1C 30
Garson's La. Warf —2B 20
Garston. —4B 6
Garston La. Wat —3B 6
Garth Rd. Mord —4E 23
Gascoigne Rd. Bark —4D 17
Gascoigne Rd. New Ad —1C 32
Gascoyne Rd. E9 —3B 16
Gascoyne Way. Hert —1A 8
Gaston Bri. Rd. Shep —4A 22
Gates Grn. Rd. W Wick & Brom —4C 24
Gateshead Rd. Borwd —4D 7
Gatland La. Maid —3E 35
Gatton. —3F 31
Gatton Bottom. Reig & Red —3F 31
Gatton Pk. Rd. Reig & Red —4F 31
Gay Bowers La. Dan —2F 11
Gellatly Rd. SE15 —1B 24
General Wolfe Rd. SE10 —1C 24
George V Av. Pinn —2B 14
George Green. —4E 13
George Grn. Slou —4E 13
George La. E18 —2C 16
(in two parts)
George St. W1 —4F 15
George St. Berk —2E 5
George St. Croy —4A 24
George St. Hunt —4E 35
George St. Rich —2C 22
George Wood Rd. Hem H —2A 6
Germain St. Che —3D 5
Gerpins La. Upm —4A 18
Gerrard's Cross. —2E 13
Gerrards Cross Rd. Stoke P —3E 13
Gervase Rd. Edgw —2D 15
Ghyllgrove. —2E 19
Ghyllgrove. Bas —2E 19
Gibbet La. Camb —1B 28
Gibbon Rd. SE15 —1B 24
Gibbs Brook La. Oxt —4C 32
Gibbs Hill. Nett —3D 35
Gibraltar Hill. Chat —4F 27
Gibson Dri. King H —3D 35
Gidea Park. —2F 17
Giffard Dri. Farn —2A 28
Giffords Cross Rd. Corr —4E 19
Gigghill Rd. Leyb —2D 35
Giggshill. —4C 22
Giggshill Rd. Th Dit —4C 22
Gilbert Rd. Belv —1E 25
Gilbert's Hill. St L —2C 4
Gildenhill Rd. Swan —3F 25
Gilden Way. H'low —1E 9
Gill Av. Guild —4D 29
Gillespie Rd. N5 —3A 16
Gillette Corner. (Junct.) —1C 22
Gillingham. —3F 27
Gillingham F.C. —3F 27
Gillingham Rd. Gill —3F 27
Gills Rd. S Dar & Dart —3A 26
Gilston. —1D 9
Giltspur St. EC4 —4A 16
Gipsy Hill. SE19 —3A 24
Gipsy La. Wel G —1E 7
Gipsy Rd. SE27 —3A 24
Givons Grove. —3C 30
Glade Rd. Mar —3A 12
Glade, The. Croy —4B 24
Glanty. —3F 21
Glanty, The. Egh —3F 21
Glasford St. SW17 —3F 23
Glassmill La. Brom —3C 24
Glaziers La. Norm —4C 28
Gleaming Wood Dri. Chat —1F 35
Glebe La. Maid —3E 35
Glebe Rd. Weald —4F 33
Glebe Way. W Wick —4C 24
Glencoe Rd. Hay —4B 14
Glenthorne Rd. W6 —1E 23
Globe Rd. E2 & E1 —4B 16
Globe Town. —4B 16
Gloucester Av. NW1 —4F 15
Gloucester Av. Chelm —2E 11
Gloucester Pl. NW1 & W1 —4F 15
Gloucester Rd. SW7 —1F 23
Gloucester Rd. Hamp —3B 22
Gloucester Rd. King T —3D 23
Gloucester Ter. W2 —4E 15
Goat Hall La. Chelm —3D 11
Goathurst Common. —3E 33
Goat Rd. Mitc —4F 23
Goatsmoor La. Bill & Stock —4D 11
Goatswood La. Nave —1F 17
Goddard Rd. Beck —3B 24
Godden Green. —3A 34
Goddington. —4E 25
Goddington La. Orp —4E 25
Godstone. —4B 32
Godstone By-Pass. God —3B 32
Godstone Hill. Cat & God —3B 32
Godstone Interchange. (Junct.) —3B 32
Godstone Rd. Blet —4A 32
Godstone Rd. Cat —3B 32
Godstone Rd. Oxt —4B 32
Godstone Rd. Purl & Whyt —1A 32
Goffers Rd. SE3 —1C 24
Goff's La. Chesh —3A 8
Goff's Oak. —3A 8
Goldcrest Way. New Ad —1C 32
Golden Ball La. M'head —4A 12
Golden Green. —4C 34
Golden La. EC1 —4A 16
Golders Green. —2E 15
Golders Grn. Rd. NW11 —2E 15
Goldhawk Rd. W6 & W12 —1D 23
Gold Hill E. Chal P —2E 13
Gold Hill N. Chal P —2E 13
Gold Hill W. Chal P —2E 13
Goldings Hill. Lou —4D 9
Goldsel Rd. Swan —4F 25
Goldsmith Rd. W3 —4D 15
Goldsmith's Row. E2 —4B 16
Gold St. Sole S —4C 26
Goldsworth Park. —2D 29
Goldsworth Rd. Wok —2E 29
Gole Rd. Pirb —2C 28
Golf Ho. Rd. Oxt —3C 32
Gomshall. —4A 30
Gomshall La. Shere —4A 30
Gomshall Rd. Gom —4A 30
Good Easter. —1C 10
Goodge St. W1 —4F 15
Goodley Stock. —3D 33
Goodley Stock Rd. Crock H & W'ham —4D 33
Goodmayes. —3E 17
Goodmayes La. Ilf —3E 17
Goodmayes Rd. Ilf —3E 17
Goods Way. NW1 —4A 16
Goodwyns Vale. N10 —2F 15
Gooseberry Green. —1D 19
Goose Green. —4C 34
(nr. Hadlow)
Goose Green. —1B 8
(nr. Hoddesdon)
Goose Grn. Gom & Brmly —4A 30
Goose La. Wok —2E 29
Goose Rye Rd. Worp —3D 29
Gooshays Dri. Romf —1A 18
Gordon Av. Stan —2C 14
Gordon Hill. Enf —4A 8
Gordon Ho. Rd. NW5 —3F 15
Gordon Rd. Cars —1F 31
Gordon Rd. Corr —4D 19
Gordon Sq. WC1 —4F 15
Gordons Way. Oxt —3C 32
Gore Ct. Rd. Otham —3F 35
Gore Grn. La. High —2E 27
Gore Hill. Amer —4D 5
Gorelands La. Chal G & Ger X —1E 13
Gore Rd. Burn —4C 12
Gore Rd. Dart —2A 26
Goresbrook Rd. Dag —4E 17
Gorse Hill. F'ham —4A 26
Gorse Rd. Orp —4E 25
Goslar Way. Wind —1D 21
Gospel Oak. —3F 15
Gosport Rd. E17 —2B 16
Gossamers, The. Wat —4B 6
Gosset St. E2 —4B 16
Goss Hill. Swan —3F 25
Gossom's End. Berk —1E 5
Goswell Rd. EC1 —4A 16
Goswell Rd. Wind —1D 21
Goulds Green. —4A 14
Gover Hill. Rough —3C 34
Gover Hill. —3C 34
Government Ho. Rd. Alder —3B 28
Government Rd. Alder —4B 28
Gower St. WC1 —4F 15
Graces La. L Bad —2F 11
Gracious La. Sev —3F 33
Gracious Pond Rd. Chob —1D 29
Grafton Rd. Wor Pk —4D 23
Grahame Park. —2D 15
Grahame Pk. Way. NW7 & NW9 —2D 15
Graham Rd. E8 —3B 16
Grand depot Rd. SE18 —1D 25
Grand Dri. SW20 —3E 23
Grand Pde. N4 —2A 16
Grandstand Rd. Eps —2E 31
Grange Hill. —2D 17
Grange Hill. Plax —3B 34
Grange La. Hart —4B 26
Grange La. Let H —4C 8
Grange La. S'ing —2F 35
(in two parts)
Grange Park. —1A 16
Grange Rd. E16 —4C 16
Grange Rd. SE1 —1A 24
Grange Rd. Bill —1D 19
Grange Rd. Cook —3B 12
Grange Rd. Gill —3F 27
(in two parts)
Grange Rd. Guild —3E 29
Grange Rd. Lea —2C 30
Grange Rd. Pirb —2C 28
Grange Rd. Platt —2C 34
Grange Rd. T Hth & SE19 —3A 24
Grants La. Oxt —4C 32
Granville Rd. N12 —2F 15
Granville Rd. N'chu —1D 5
Grasmere Rd. Purl —1A 32
Gravel Hill. N3 —2E 15
Gravel Hill. Bexh —2E 25
Gravel Hill. Chal P —2E 13
Gravel Hill. Croy —1B 32
Gravel Hill. Lou —4C 8
Gravel La. Chig —1E 17
Gravelly Hill. Cat —3A 32
Gravelly Ways. Ladd —4D 35
Gravel Path. Berk —2E 5
Gravel Rd. Brom —4D 25
Gravesend. —2C 26
Gravesend Rd. High —3E 27
Gravesend Rd. Roch —3E 27
Gravesend Rd. Shorne —3D 27
Gravesend Rd. Wro —2B 34
Gravetts La. Guild —3D 29
Grays. —1B 26
Gray's Inn Rd. WC1 —4A 16
Grays Pk. Rd. Stoke P —4E 13
Grays Rd. W'ham & Sev —2D 33
Great Amwell. —1B 8
Great Baddow. —2E 11
Great Berry. —2D 19
Great Bookham. —3B 30
Gt. Braitch La. Hat —1D 7
Great Buckland. —1D 35
Great Burgh. —2E 31
Great Burstead. —1D 19
Great Cambridge Junction. (Junct.) —1A 16
Gt. Cambridge Rd. N9 —1A 16
Gt. Cambridge Rd. N17 & N18 —2A 16
Gt. Cambridge Rd. Enf & Wal X —1A 16
Gt. Central Way. Wemb & NW10 —3D 15
Gt. Chertsey Rd. W4 —1D 23
Gt. Chertsey Rd. Felt & Twic —2B 22
Great Comp Garden. —2C 34
Gt. Dover St. SE1 —1A 24
Gt. Eastern Rd. E15 —3C 16
Gt. Eastern St. EC2 —4A 16
Great Gaddesden. —1F 5
Great Hampden. —3A 4
Greatham Rd. Bush —4B 6
Great Hivings. —3D 5
Great Hollands. —4A 20
Gt. Hollands Rd. Brack —4A 20
Great Kimble. —2A 4
Great Kingshill. —4B 4
Gt. Knightleys. Bas —2D 19
Gt. Marlborough St. W1 —4F 15
Great Missenden. —3B 4
Greatness. —2F 33
Gt. Norman St. Sev —3E 33
Gt. North Rd. N2 & N6 —2F 15
Gt. North Rd. Barn —1E 15
Gt. North Rd. Brk P —2E 7
Gt. North Rd. Hat & Pot B —2E 7
Gt. North Rd. High Bar —4E 7
Gt. North Rd. Wel G —1E 7
(in two parts)
Gt. North Way. NW4 —2E 15
Great Oxney Green. —2D 11
Great Parndon. —1D 9
Gt. Portland St. W1 —4F 15
Gt. Prestons La. Stock —4E 11
Gt. Queen St. WC2 —4A 16
Great Rd. Hem H —2A 6
Gt. Ropers La. War —2B 18
Gt. South W. Rd. Felt & Houn —2A 22
Gt. Tattenhams. Eps —2E 31
Great Warley. —2B 18
Gt. Warley St. Gt War —2B 18
Gt. Western Rd. W9 & W11 —4E 15
Gt. West Rd. W4 & W6 (Chiswick) —1D 23
Gt. West Rd. W4 —1D 23 (Gunnersbury)
Gt. West Rd. Houn & Iswth —1B 22
Grn. Common La. Beac —3C 12
Green Comn. La. Wbrn G —3C 12
Green Ct. Rd. Swan —4F 25
Green Dene. E Hor —4A 30
Green Dragon La. N21 —1A 16
Green Dragon La. F Hth —2B 12
Green End. —2F 5
Green End St. Ast C —1B 4
Green Farm La. Shorne —2D 27
Greenford. —4C 14
Greenford Av. W7 —4C 14
Greenford Rd. S'hall & Harr —4C 14
Greenford Roundabout. (Junct.) —4C 14
Greengate St. E13 —4C 16
Green Hailey. —3A 4
Greenhill. —2C 14
Green Hill. High W —1B 12
Greenhill Pk. NW10 —4D 15
Greenhill Way. Harr —2C 14
Greenhithe. —2B 26
Greenhurst La. Oxt —4C 32
Greenlands La. P'wd —3B 4
Green La. NW4 —2E 15
Green La. SE9 & Chst —2D 25
Green La. SE20 —3B 24
Green La. SW16 & T Hth —3A 24
Green La. B'water —2A 28
Green La. Bou M —4F 35
Green La. Bov —3E 5
Green La. Burn —4C 12
Green La. Cher & Add —4F 21
Green La. Felt —3B 22
Green La. Four E —4E 33
Green La. Hem H —2A 6
Green La. Houn —2B 22
Green La. Ilf & Dag —3D 17
Green La. Kel H —4A 10
Green La. Meop —4C 26
Green La. Mord —4E 23
Green La. N'wd —2A 14
Green La. Ock —3A 30
Green La. P'wd —3B 4
Green La. Rox —2C 10
(in two parts)
Green La. Shep —4A 22
Green La. Stan —1C 14
Green La. Tad & Coul —3E 31
Green La. Thr B —1E 9
Green La. Uxb —4A 14
Green La. E. Norm —4C 28
Green Lanes. N4 & N16 —2A 16
Green Lanes. N8 —2A 16
Green Lanes. N13 & N21 —2A 16
Green Lanes. Lem & Hat —1D 7
Green La. W. Ash —4C 28
Green Man Roundabout. (Junct.) —2C 16
Green Rd. Dart —3B 26
Green Rd. High W —1B 12
Green Rd. Vir W & Egh —4E 21
Greens Farm La. Bill —1D 19
Greensted. —3F 9
Greensted Green. —3F 9
Greensted Rd. Ong —3F 9
Green Street. —4C 10
Green St. E7 & E13 —3C 16
Green St. Dart —2A 26
Green St. Enf —4B 8
Green St. High W —1A 12
Green St. Ing —3C 10
Green St. Rick —4F 5
Green St. Shenl —3D 7
Green St. Sun —3B 22
Green Street Green. —3B 26
(nr. Dartford)
Green Street Green. —1D 33
(nr. Orpington)
Green, The. E4 —1C 16
Green, The. N9 —1B 16
Green, The. N14 —1F 15
Green, The. N21 —1A 16
Green, The. B'more —3B 10
Green, The. Bou M —4F 35
Green, The. Clay —1C 30
Green, The. Crox G —1A 14
Green, The. Orp —4D 25
Green, The. Sarr —4F 5
Green, The. Sidc —3E 25
Green, The. S'hall —1B 22
Green, The. They B —4D 9
Green, The. Til —1C 26
Green, The. Twic —2C 22
Green, The. Warl —2B 32
Green, The. W Dray —1F 21
Green, The. Writ —2D 11
Green Wlk. Wfd G —2D 17
Greenway. Che —3D 5
Greenway, The. Uxb —4F 13
Greenwich. —1C 24
Greenwich Borough Museum. (off Speranza St.) —1D 25
Greenwich High Rd. SE8 —1B 24
Greenwich S. St. SE10 —1C 24
Green Wrythe La. Cars —4F 23
Grenfell Pl. M'head —4B 12
Grenfell Rd. M'head —4B 12
Gresham Rd. Houn —1C 22
Gresham Rd. Stai —3F 21
Greville Pl. NW6 —4E 15
Greyhound Hill. NW4 —2E 15
Greyhound La. SW16 —3F 23
Greyhound La. Pot B —3E 7
Greyhound Ter. SW16 —3F 23
Griffin Rd. SE18 —1D 25
Griggs App. Ilf —3D 17
Grimsdell's La. Amer —4D 5
Gringer Hill. M'head —4B 12
Grosvenor Av. N5 —3A 16
Grosvenor Av. Cars —1F 31
Grosvenor Gdns. SW1 —1F 23
Grosvenor Pl. SW1 —1F 23
Grosvenor Rd. N10 —2F 15
Grosvenor Rd. SW1 —1F 23
Grosvenor Rd. Alder —4B 28
Grosvenor Rd. Wall —1F 31
Grosvenor Rd. Wat —4B 6
Grosvenor St. W1 —4F 15
Ground La. Hat —1E 7
Grove Av. N10 —2F 15
Grove Cres. King T —3D 23
Grove Cross Rd. Frim —2B 28
Grove End Rd. NW8 —4F 15
Grove Green. —2F 35
Grove Grn. Rd. E10 & E11 —3C 16
Grove Heath Rd. Rip —3F 29
Grovehill. —1A 6
Grove La. SE5 —1A 24
Grove La. Chal P —2E 13
Grove La. Che —3E 5
Grove La. Gt Kim —2A 4
Grove La. King T —3D 23
Groveley Rd. Sun & Felt —3A 22
Grove Mill La. Rick & Wat —4A 6
Grove Park. —2C 24
(nr. Bromley)
Grove Park. —1D 23
(nr. Chiswick)
Grove Pk. Rd. SE12 —2C 24
Grove Pk. Rd. W4 —1D 23
Grove Rd. E9 —4B 16
Grove Rd. E17 —2B 16
Grove Rd. Bag —1C 28
Grove Rd. Burn —4C 12
Grove Rd. Hpdn —1C 6
Grove Rd. Houn —2B 22
Grove Rd. Mitc —3F 23
Grove Rd. Romf —3E 17
Grove Rd. Seal —2A 34
Grove Rd. Sutt —1E 31
Grove Rd. Tring —1C 4
Grove St. SE8 —1B 24
Grove, The. (Junct.) —2B 24
Grove, The. E15 —3C 16
Grove, The. Iswth —1C 22
Grove, The. Slou —1E 21
Grove Vale. SE22 —2A 24
Grovewood Dri. Maid —2F 35
Grubb St. —3B 26
Grubs La. Hat —2E 7
Grubwood La. Cook —3B 12
Gubbins La. Romf —2A 18
Guildables La. Eden —4D 33
Guildford. —4E 29
Guildford & Godalming By-Pass Rd. Comp & Guild —4D 29
Guildford La. Alb —4F 29
Guildford Park. —4E 29
Guildford Pk. Rd. Guild —4E 29
Guildford Rd. Ab C —4A 30
Guildford Rd. Ash & Norm —4C 28
Guildford Rd. Bag —1C 28
Guildford Rd. Bag —1C 28
Guildford Rd. Farnh —4A 28
Guildford Rd. Fet —3C 30
Guildford Rd. Frim G —2B 28
Guildford Rd. Guild & Wok —3E 29
Guildford Rd. Lea —3A 30
Guildford Rd. Light & Wok —1C 28
Guildford Rd. Mayf —2E 29
Guildford Rd. Norm —4C 28
Guildford Rd. Pirb & Guild —3D 29
Guildford Rd. Runf —4B 28
Guildford Rd. Westc —4B 30
Guildford Rd. Wok & Cher —1E 29
Guildford St. Cher —4F 21
Guileshill La. Ock —2A 30
Guilford St. WC1 —4A 16
Gun Hill. W Til —1C 26
Gun La. Strood —3E 27
Gunnersbury. —1D 23
Gunnersbury Av. W5 & W3 —4D 15
Gunnersbury Dri. W5 —1D 23
Gunnersbury La. W3 —1D 23
Gunnersbury Park. (Junct.) —1D 23
Gunter Gro. SW10 —1F 23
Gypsy Corner. (Junct.) —4D 15
Gypsy La. Gt Amw —1B 8
Gypsy La. Stoke P —3D 13
Gyratory Rd. Wat —1B 14

Hackbridge. —4F 23
Hackbridge Rd. Wall —4F 23
Hackney. —3B 16
Hackney Rd. E2 —4A 16
Hackney Rd. Maid —3F 35
Hackney Wick. —3B 16
Hackney Wick. (Junct.) —3B 16
Hacton. —3A 18
Hacton La. Horn & Upm —3A 18
Haddon Rd. M'head —4B 12
Hadley. —4E 7
Hadley Comn. Barn —4E 7
Hadley Grn. Rd. Barn —4E 7
Hadley Highstone. Barn —4E 7
Hadley Rd. Barn —4E 7
Hadley Rd. Cockf & Enf —4F 7
Hadley Way. N21 —1A 16
Hadley Wood. —4F 7
Hadlow. —4C 34
Hadlow Rd. Tonb —4B 34
(in two parts)
Hadlow Rd. E. Tonb —4B 34
Hadlow Stair. —4B 34
Hagden La. Wat —4A 6
(in two parts)
Haggerston. —4A 16
Hag Hill La. Tap —4C 12
Ha Ha Rd. SE18 —1D 25
Hailey. —1B 8
Hailey La. Hail —1B 8
Hainault. —2E 17
Hainault Rd. E10 —3C 16
Hainault Rd. Chig —1D 17
Hainault Rd. Romf —2E 17
Hale. —4A 28
(nr. Farnham)
Hale. —4F 27
(nr. Gillingham)
Halebourne La. Wok —1D 29
Hale End. —2C 16
Hale End Rd. E4 & E17 —2C 16
Hale La. Edgw & NW7 —1D 15
Hale La. Wen —2B 4
Hale Oak Rd. Chid & Weald —4F 33
Hale Oak Rd. Weald —4F 33
Hale Rd. N17 —2B 16
Hale Rd. Farnh —4A 28
Hale Rd. Hert —1A 8
Hale Rd. Wen —2B 4
Hale Street. —4D 35
Hale St. E Peck —4D 35
Hale, The. —2D 15
Half Acre. Bren —1C 22
Halfhide La. Chesh —3B 8
Half Moon La. SE24 —2A 24
Halfpence La. Cob —3D 27
Halfpenny La. Guild —4F 29
Halfway St. Sidc —2D 25
Haling Pk. Rd. S Croy —4A 24
Hall Grn. La. Hut —1C 18
Hall Gro. —1E 7
Hall Gro. Wel G —1E 7
Hall Hill. Oxt —4C 32
Hall Hill. Sev —3A 34
Halliford Rd. Shep & Sun —4A 22
Halliford St. N1 —3A 16
Halling. —4E 27
Halling By-Pass. Hall —4E 27
Hall Lane. (Junct.) —1B 16
Hall La. E4 —1B 16
Hall La. B'water —1A 28
Hall La. Ing —4C 10
Hall La. Shenf —4B 10
Hall La. Upm —3A 18
Hall Place. —2F 25
Hall Rd. E11 —3C 16
Hall Rd. NW8 —4F 15
Hall Rd. Ayle —2E 35
Hall Rd. Iswth —2C 22
Hall Rd. N'fleet —2C 26
Hall Rd. Woul —1E 35
Halls Green. —1C 8
(nr. Roydon)
Hall's Green. —4F 33
(nr. Sevenoaks Weald)
Halls La. Wal L —1A 20
Halstead. —1E 33
Halstead Hill. Chesh —3A 8
Halstead La. Knock —2E 33
Halstead Rd. N21 —1A 16
Halton. —1B 4
Halton Camp. —1B 4
Halton La. Wen —1B 4
Ham. —2C 22
Hamberlins La. N'chu —1D 5
Ham Comn. Rich —2C 22
Hamesmoor Rd. Myt —3B 28
Ham Ga. Av. Rich —2D 23
Hamilton Rd. High W —1B 12
Hamilton Rd. K Lan —3A 6
Ham Island. —2E 21
Ham La. Gill —1F 35
Ham La. Old Win —2E 21
Hamlet Hill. Roy —2C 8
Hamlet Rd. SE19 —3A 24
Hammerfield. —2F 5
Hammers La. NW7 —1E 15
Hammersley La. High W & Penn —2B 12
Hammersmith. —1E 23
Hammersmith Broadway. (Junct.) —1E 23
Hammersmith Flyover. (Junct.) —1E 23
Hammersmith Flyover. W6 —1E 23
Hammersmith Rd. W6 & W14 —1E 23
Hammond's La. Sandr —1C 6
Hammonds Rd. S'don & L Bad —2F 11
Hammond Street. —3A 8
Hammondstreet Rd. Chesh —2A 8
Ham Moor. —4F 21
Hampden Bottom. —3B 4
Hampden Rd. P'wd —3A 4
Hampden Rd. Speen —4A 4
Hampden Way. N14 —1F 15
Hampermill La. Wat —1B 14
Hampstead. —3F 15
Hampstead Garden Suburb. —2F 15
Hampstead High St. NW3 —3F 15
Hampstead La. NW3 & N6 —3F 15
Hampstead La. Yald —4D 35
Hampstead Rd. NW1 —4F 15
Hampstead Way. NW11 —2E 15
Hampton. —3B 22

Hampton Court—Hildenborough Rd.

Hampton Court. —3C 22
Hampton Court. (Junct.) —3C 22
Hampton Ct. Bri. E Mol —3C 22
Hampton Court Palace. —3C 22
Hampton Ct. Rd. E Mol & King T —3C 22
Hampton Ct. Rd. Hamp & E Mol —3C 22
Hampton Ct. Way. Th Dit & E Mol —4C 22
Hampton Hill. —3C 22
Hampton La. Felt —3B 22
Hampton Rd. Tedd —3C 22
Hampton Rd. Twic —2C 22
Hampton Rd. E. Felt —3B 22
Hampton Rd. W. Felt —2B 22
Hamptons. —3C 34
Hamptons Rd. D Grn —3B 34
Hampton Wick. —3C 22
Hamsey Green. —2B 32
Ham St. Rich —2C 22
Handcroft Rd. Croy —4A 24
Handford La. B'water —1A 28
Handley Green. —3C 10
Handside. —1E 7
Handy Cross. —2A 12
Hanger Hill. Wey —1A 30
Hanger Hill. —4D 15
Hanger Lane. (Junct.) —4D 15
Hanger La. HA0 —4D 15
Hanging Hill La. Hut —1B 18
Hangings La. P'wd —3B 4
Hangrove Hill. Orp —1D 33
Hanley Rd. N4 —3A 16
Hanover Pk. SE15 —1B 24
Hanwell. —4C 14
Hanworth. —4B 20
(nr. Bracknell)
Hanworth. —3B 22
(nr. Feltham)
Hanworth Rd. Brack —4B 20
Hanworth Rd. Felt —2B 22
Hanworth Rd. Hamp —3B 22
Hanworth Rd. Houn —2B 22
Hanworth Rd. Sun —3B 22
(in two parts)
Harberts Rd. H'low —1D 9
Harbet Rd. N18 & E4 —2B 16
Harbourland. —2F 35
Hardings Dean. —3B 12
Hardings Elms Rd. Cray H —2E 19
Hardwick La. Lyne —4F 21
Hare & Billet Rd. SE10 —1C 24
Harebreaks, The. Wat —4B 6
Harefield. —2F 13
Harefield Rd. Rick —1F 13
Harefield Rd. Uxb —3F 13
Harehatch La. Slou —3D 13
Hare Hill. Add —1F 29
Hare La. Clay —4C 22
Hare La. L Kin —4B 4
Haresfoot Pk. Berk —2E 5
Harestone Valley Rd. Cat —3A 32
Hare Street. —1D 9
(nr. Harlow)
Hare Street. —4A 10
(nr. Little End)
Hareward Rd. Guild —4F 29
Harfield Rd. Sun —3B 22
Harlequins R.U.F.C. —2C 22
Harlesden. —4D 15
Harlesden Rd. NW10 —4E 15
Harleyford Rd. SE11 —1A 24
Harlington. —1A 22
Harlington Corner. (Junct.) —1A 22
Harlington Rd. Uxb —4A 14
Harlington Rd. E. Felt —2B 22
Harlington Rd. W. Felt —2B 22
Harlow. —1D 9
Harlow Comn. H'low —1E 9
Harlow Museum. —1D 9
Harlow Rd. Mat T —1F 9
Harlow Rd. More —1F 9
Harlow Rd. Roy —1C 8
Harlow Rd. Saw —1E 9
Harmanswater. —3B 20
Harmans Water Rd. Brack —4B 20
Harmer St. Grav —2C 26
Harmondsworth. —1F 21
Harmondsworth La. W Dray —1A 22
Harmondsworth Rd. W Dray —1A 22
Harold Hill. —1A 18
Harold Park. —2A 18
Harold Rd. SE19 —3A 24
Harold Wood. —2A 18
Harpenden. —1B 6
Harpenden La. Redb —1B 6
Harpenden Rd. St Alb —1B 6
Harper La. Rad —3C 6
Harper Rd. SE1 —1A 24
Harper's Rd. Ash —4C 28
Harp Farm Rd. Boxl —1F 35
Harple La. Det —2F 35
Harps Oak La. Red —3F 31
Harringay. —2A 16
Harris La. Shenl —3D 7
Harrow. —2C 14
Harrow La. M'head —4B 12
Harrow Mnr. Way. SE28 —1E 25
Harrow on the Hill. —3C 14
Harrow Road. (Junct.) —3D 15
Harrow Rd. E11 —3C 16
Harrow Rd. NW10, W10 & W9 —4E 15
Harrow Rd. Knock —2E 33
Harrow Rd. N Ben —2F 19
Harrow Rd. Warl —2B 32
Harrow Rd. Wemb —3C 14
(Sudbury)
Harrow Rd. Wemb —3D 15
(Wembley)
Harrow View. Harr —2C 14
Harrow Weald. —2C 14
Hartfield Rd. SW19 —3E 23
Hartforde Rd. Borwd —4D 7
Harthall La. K Lan & Hem H —3A 6
Hartington Rd. W4 —1D 23
Hartlake Rd. Gold G —4C 34
Hartland Way. Croy —4B 24
Hartley. —3B 26
Hartley Bottom Rd. Sev & Hart —1B 34
Hartley Down. Purl —2A 32
Hartley Green. —4B 26
Hartley Hill. —4B 26
Hartley Hill. Hart —4B 26
Hartley Rd. Long —3B 26
Hart Rd. Ben —2F 19
Hart's La. S God —4B 32
Hartspring La. Wat —4B 6
Hartswood Rd. War & Brtwd —1B 18
Harvel. —1C 34
Harvel La. Meop —1C 34
Harvel Rd. Fair —1C 34
Harvel St. Meop —1C 34
Harvest Hill. Bour E —3C 12
Harvest Hill Rd. M'head —1B 20
Harvest Ride. Brack —3B 20
Harvest Rd. Egh —3E 21
Harvey Rd. Guild —4E 29
Harvil Rd. Hare & Uxb —2F 13
Harvist Rd. NW6 —4E 15
Harwood Hall La. Upm —3A 18
Harwood Rd. SW6 —1E 23
Harwoods Rd. Wat —4B 6
Haselbury Rd. N18 & N9 —1A 16
Haste Hill Rd. Bou M —4F 35
Hastings Rd. Brom —4D 25
Hastings Rd. Maid —3F 35
Hastingwood. —2E 9
Hastingwood Rd. H'wd —2E 9
Hastoe. —1C 4
Hastoe Hill. Hast —1C 4
Hastoe La. Hast —1C 4
Hatch End. —2B 14
Hatches Farm Rd. L Bur —1C 18
Hatches La. E Peck —4C 34
Hatches La. Gt Kin —4B 4
Hatchet La. N Asc —3C 20
Hatchford. —2A 30
Hatching Green. —1B 6
Hatchlands Park. —3A 30
Hatchlands Rd. Red —4F 31
Hatch La. E4 —1C 16
(in two parts)
Hatch La. W Dray —1F 21
Hatch La. Wind —2D 21
Hatch Rd. Pil H —1B 18
Hatfield. —1E 7
Hatfield Airport. —1D 7
Hatfield Garden Village. —1D 7
Hatfield House. —1F 7
Hatfield Hyde. —1E 7
Hatfield Rd. L Bad —1F 11
Hatfield Rd. Pot B —3F 7
Hatfield Rd. St Alb & Smal —2C 6
Hatham Grn. La. Stans —1B 34
Hathaway Rd. Grays —1B 26
Hatherley Gdns. E6 —4C 16
Hatterill. Lain —2D 19
Hatter's La. High W —1B 12
Hatton. —2B 22
Hatton Cross. (Junct.) —2A 22
Hatton Garden. EC1 —4A 16
Hatton Hill. W'sham —4C 20
Hatton Rd. Felt —2A 22
Havelock Rd. N17 —2B 16
Havelock Rd. S'hall —1B 22
Haven Grn. W5 —4C 14
Haven Hill. Hods —1B 34
Haven Rd. Can I —4F 19
Haven St. Wain —2E 27
Havering-atte-Bower. —1F 17
Havering Rd. Romf —2F 17
Havering's Grove. —1C 18
Haverstock Hill. NW3 —3F 15
Haviker St. Coll S —4E 35
Hawk Hill. Bat —1F 19
Hawkhurst Gdns. Chess —4D 23
Hawkshead La. N Mym —3C 7
Hawkshead Rd. Pot B —3E 7
Hawks Hill. Bour E —3C 12
Hawkshill Way. Esh —1B 30
Hawks Rd. King T —3D 23
Hawkstone Rd. SE16 —1B 24
Hawkswood La. Slou & Ger X —3E 13
Hawkswood Rd. D'ham —4E 11
Hawley. —3A 26
(nr. Dartford)
Hawley. —2A 28
(nr. Farnborough)
Hawley Lane. —2B 28
Hawley La. Farn —2B 28
Hawley Rd. NW1 —3F 15
Hawley Rd. B'water —2A 28
Hawley Rd. Dart —2A 26
Hawley's Corner. —2D 33
Hawstead La. Orp —4E 25
Hawthorn Hill. —2B 20
Hawthorn Hill Rd. Holyp —2B 20
Hawthorn La. Farn C —3D 13
Hawthorn Rd. NW10 —3E 15
Haydens Rd. H'low —1D 9
Haydons Rd. SW19 —3E 23
Hayes. —4C 24
(nr. Bromley)
Hayes. —4A 14
(nr. Uxbridge)
Hayes End. —4A 14
Hayes End Rd. Hay —4A 14
Hayes Hill Farm. —3C 8
Hayes Hill Rd. Brom —4C 24
Hayes La. Beck —3C 24
Hayes La. Brom —4C 24
Hayes La. Kenl —2A 32
(in two parts)
Hayes Rd. Brom —3C 24
Hayes Rd. S'hall —1B 22
Hayes St. Brom —4C 24
Hayes Town. —1A 22
Hay Green. —3B 10
Hay Grn. La. Hook E & B'more —4B 10
Hay La. NW9 —2D 15
Hayle Rd. Maid —3F 35
Hayley Grn. Warf —3B 20
Hayling Rd. Wat —1B 14
Haymarket. SW1 —4F 15
Haymill Rd. Slou —4C 12
Hazel Av. Farn —3A 28
Hazelbank Rd. SE6 —2C 24
Hazellville Rd. N19 —3F 15
Hazelwood. —1D 33
Hazelwood Rd. N13 —1A 16
Hazelwood La. Ab L —3A 6
Hazelwood La. Binf —3A 20
Hazelwood La. Coul —2F 31
Hazlemere. —1B 12
Hazlemere Rd. Penn —1C 12
Headley. —3D 31
Headley Comn. Rd. H'ley & Tad —3D 31
Headley Dri. New Ad —1B 32
Headley Rd. Dork —3C 30
Headley Rd. Eps —2D 31
Headley Rd. Lea & Eps —2C 30
Headstone. —2C 14
Headstone Dri. Harr —2C 14
Headstone Gdns. Harr —2C 14
Headstone La. Harr —2B 14
Headstone Rd. Harr —2C 14
Heathbourne Rd. Bush & Stan —1C 14
Heathclose Rd. Dart —2F 25
Heathcote Rd. Camb —1B 28
Heath End. —4A 28
(nr. Aldershot)
Heath End. —4B 4
(nr. Great Kingshill)
Heath End. —2D 5
(nr. Shootersway)
Heath End. Berk —2D 5
Heath End Rd. F Hth —2B 12
Heath End Rd. Gt Kin —4B 4
Heatherside. —2C 28
Heathfield La. Chst —3D 25
Heathfield Rd. Burn —3C 12
Heathfield Rd. Kes —4C 24
Heathfield Ter. W4 —1D 23
Heath Ho. Rd. Wok —2D 29
Heathlands Rd. Wokgm —4A 20
Heath La. Dart —2F 25
Heath La. Ews —4A 28
Heath La. Hem H —2F 5
Heath Park. —2F 17
Heath Pk. Rd. Romf —2F 17
Heath Rd. Grays —4C 18
Heath Rd. Houn —2C 22
Heath Rd. Maid —3E 35
Heath Rd. Oxs —1C 30
Heath Rd. Rams H —1D 19
Heath Rd. Twic —2C 22
Heath Rd. W Far & Cox —4E 35
Heath Rd. Wey —4A 22
Heathrow Airport (London). —2A 22
Heathside Cres. Wok —2E 29
Heathside Rd. Wok —2E 29
Heath St. NW3 —3F 15
Heath, The. E Mal —2D 35
Heathvale Bri. Rd. Ash V —3B 28
Heathway. (Junct.) —4E 17
Heathway. Dag —3E 17
Heavens Lea. Bour E —3C 12
Heaverham. —2A 34
Heaverham Rd. Kems —2A 34
Hedge La. N13 —1A 16
Hedgemans Rd. Dag —3E 17
Hedge Pl. Rd. Grnh —2A 26
Hedgerley. —3D 13
Hedgerley Green. —3D 13
Hedgerley Hill. —3D 13
Hedgerley Hill. Hedg —3D 13
Hedgerley La. Beac & Ger X —2D 13
Hedsor Hill. Bour E —3C 12
Hedsor La. Wbrn G —3C 12
Hedsor Rd. Bour E —3B 12
Hemel Hempstead. —1A 6
Hemel Hempstead Rd. Hem H & St Alb —2A 6
Hemel Hempstead Rd. Redb —1A 6
Hemp La. Wig —1D 5
Hempstead. —4F 27
Hempstead La. L Hth & Pott E —1E 5
Hempstead Rd. Bov —2E 5
Hempstead Rd. Hem —1F 35
Hempstead Rd. K Lan —2A 6
Hempstead Rd. Wat —4A 6
Henderson Dri. Dart —2A 26
Hendon. —2E 15
Hendon La. N3 —2E 15
Hendon Way. NW4 & NW2 —2E 15
Hendon Wood La. EN5 —1D 15
Henhurst. —3D 27
Henhurst Rd. Sole S —3C 26
Henley Rd. Hur & M'head —4A 12
Henley Rd. Medm —3A 12
Henley Street. —4D 27
Henley St. Ludd —4D 27
Henlys Corner. (Junct.) —2E 15
Henlys Roundabout. (Junct.) —1B 22
Henniker Gdns. E6 —4C 16
Henrys Rd. Wfd G —2C 16
Hepworth Way. W on T —4A 22
Herbert Rd. SE18 —1D 25
Herberts Hole. S Hth —3C 4
Hercies Rd. Uxb —3A 14
Heriot Rd. Cher —4F 21
Herkomer Rd. Bush —1B 14
Hermitage La. NW2 —3E 15
Hermitage La. SW16 —3A 24
Hermitage La. Ayle & Barm —2E 35
Hermitage La. Bou M —4F 35
Hermitage Rd. N4 & N15 —3A 16
Hermitage Rd. SE19 —3A 24
Hermitage Rd. High —3E 27
Hermitage Rd. Wok —2D 29
Hermit Rd. E16 —4C 16
Hermon Hill. E11 & E18 —2C 16
Herne Hill. —2A 24
Herne Hill. SE24 —2A 24
Herne Hill Rd. SE24 —2A 24
Herne Pound. —3C 34
Herns La. Wel G —1E 7
Herongate. —2C 18
Heron Hill. Belv —1E 25
Heronsgate. —1F 13
Heronsgate Rd. Chor —1E 13
Herons La. Fyf —2A 10
(in two parts)
Heronswood Rd. Wel G —1E 7
Heron Way. Grays —1B 26
Hersham. —4B 22
Hersham By-Pass. W on T —4B 22
Hersham Rd. W on T —4B 22
Hertford. —1A 8
Hertford Heath. —1B 8
Hertford Museum. —1A 8
Hertford Rd. N9 —1B 16
Hertford Rd. Enf —4B 8
Hertford Rd. Hat —1E 7
Hertford Rd. Hod —1B 8
Hertingfordbury. —1A 8
Hertingfordbury Rd. Hert —1A 8
(in two parts)
Hesiers Hill. Warl —2C 32
Hesiers Rd. Warl —2C 32
Heston. —1B 22
Heston Rd. Houn —1B 22
Hever Ct. Rd. Grav —3C 26
Hewitts Rd. Orp —1E 33
Hewitts Roundabout. (Junct.) —1E 33
Hextable. —3F 25
Heybridge. —4C 10
Hibbert Rd. M'head —1B 20
Hibernia Rd. Houn —2B 22
Hicks Farm Rise. High W —1B 12
Hickstars La. Bill —1D 19
Higham. —2E 27
Higham Hill. —2B 16
Higham Hill Rd. E17 —2B 16
Higham La. Tonb —4B 34
Higham Rd. Cli —2E 27
Higham Rd. Wain —3F 27
Highams La. Chob —1D 29
Highams Park. —1C 16
Higham Wood. —4B 34
High Banks. Loose —3F 35
High Barnet. —4E 7
High Barn Rd. Eff & Dork —3B 30
High Beech. —4C 8
High Bri. Rd. Chelm —2E 11
Highbridge St. Wal A —3B 8
(in two parts)
Highbury. —3A 16
Highbury Corner. (Junct.) —3A 16
Highbury Gro. N5 —3A 16
Highbury Pk. N5 —3A 16
High Canons. Borwd —4D 7
High Cross. —4C 6
High Cross. Ald —4C 6
High Cross Rd. Ivy H —3B 34
Highcross Rd. S'fleet —3B 26
High Curley. —1C 28
High Elms Rd. Dow —1D 33
Higher Denham. —3F 13
Higher Dri. Purl —1A 32
Highfield. —1A 6
Highfield Av. NW11 —3E 15
Highfield La. M'head —1B 20
Highfield La. Putt —4C 28
Highfield La. Tyngr —2C 6
Highfield Rd. Dart —2F 25
Highfield Rd. Felt —2B 22
Highfield Rd. Purl —1A 32
Highgate. —3F 15
Highgate High St. N6 —3F 15
Highgate Hill. N6 & N19 —3F 15
Highgate La. Farn —2B 28
Highgate Rd. N6 & NW5 —3F 15
Highgate W. Hill. N6 —3F 15
High Halstow. —2F 27
High Holborn. WC1 —4A 16
High Ho. La. Hdlw —4B 34
Highlands Hill. Swan —3F 25
Highlands Rd. Lea —2C 30
High La. Srng —1F 9
High Laver. —1F 9
High Laver Rd. Mat G —1F 9
High Ongar. —3A 10
High Ongar Rd. Ong —3A 10
High Rd. E18 —2C 16
High Rd. N15 & N17 —2A 16
High Rd. N22 —2A 16
High Rd. NW10 —3D 15
High Rd. Ben —2F 19
High Rd. Bush —1C 14
High Rd. Byfl —1A 30
High Rd. Chesh —2B 8
High Rd. Chig —1D 17
High Rd. Cook —3B 12
High Rd. Cow —4F 13
High Rd. Dart —2F 25
High Rd. Epp —3D 9
High Rd. Ess —2F 7
High Rd. Harr —2C 14
High Rd. Horn H —3E 19
High Rd. Ilf & Romf —3D 17
(in five parts)
High Rd. Lang H & Lain —3D 19
(in two parts)
High Rd. Leav —3A 6
High Rd. N Stif —4B 18
High Rd. N Wea —3E 9
High Rd. Ors —4C 18
High Rd. Reig & Coul —3F 31
High Rd. Stan H —4D 19
High Rd. Thorn —2E 9
High Rd. Uxb —3A 14
High Rd. Van & Pits —3E 19
High Rd. Wemb —3D 15
High Rd. Wfd G & Lou —1C 16
High Rd. Worm & Brox —2B 8
High Rd. E. Finchley. N2 —2F 15
High Rd. Leyton. E10 —3C 16
High Rd. Leytonstone. E15 & E11 —3C 16
High Rd. N. Lain —2D 19
High Rd. N. Finchley. N12 —1F 15
High Rd. Turnford. Chesh —2B 8
High Rd. Whetstone. N20 —1F 15
High Rd. Woodford Grn. Wfd G & E18 —2C 16
High St. Abbots Langley, Ab L —3A 6
High St. Acton, W3 —4D 15
High St. Addlestone, Add —4F 21
High St. Aldershot, Alder —4B 28
High St. Amersham, Amer —4D 5
High St. Ascot, Asc —3C 20
High St. Aveley, Ave —4A 18
High St. Aylesford, Ayle —2E 35
High St. Bagshot, Bag —1C 28
High St. Banstead, Bans —2E 31
High St. Barkingside, B'side —2D 17
High St. Barnet, Barn —4E 7
High St. Bean, Bean —2B 26
High St. Beckenham, Beck —3B 24
High St. Bedmond, Bedm —3A 6
High St. Benfleet, Ben —3F 19
High St. Berkhamsted, Berk —1D 5
High St. Billericay, Bill —1D 19
High St. Bletchingley, Blet —4A 32
High St. Borough Green, Bor G —2B 34
High St. Bovingdon, Bov —3E 5
High St. Bracknell, Brack —3B 20
High St. Brasted, Bras —3E 33
High St. Bray, Bray —1C 20
High St. Brentford, Bren —1C 22
High St. Brentwood, Brtwd —1B 18
High St. Bromley, Brom —3C 24
High St. Burnham, Burn —4C 12
High St. Bushey, Bush —1B 14
High St. Carshalton, Cars —4F 23
High St. Caterham, Cat —3A 32
High St. Chalfont St Giles, Chal G —1E 13
High St. Chalfont St Peter, Chal P —2E 13
High St. Chalvey, Chalv —1D 21
High St. Chatham, Chat —4F 27
(in two parts)
High St. Cheam, Cheam —1E 31
High St. Chesham, Che —3D 5
High St. Cheshunt, Chesh —3B 8
High St. Chipping Ongar, Ong —3A 10
High St. Chipstead, Chip —2F 33
High St. Chislehurst, Chst —3D 25
High St. Chobham, Chob —1D 29
High St. Cobham, Cobh —1B 30
High St. Colliers Wood. SW19 —3F 23
High St. Colnbrook, Coln —1F 21
High St. Colney Heath, Col H —2D 7
High St. Cookham, Cook —3B 12
High St. Cowley, Cow —4F 13
High St. Cranford, Cran —1B 22
High St. Crayford, Cray —2F 25
High St. Crowthorne, Crowt —1A 28
High St. Croydon, Croy —4A 24
High St. Dartford, Dart —2A 26
High St. Datchet, Dat —1E 21
High St. Dorking, Dork —4C 30
High St. Downe, Dow —1D 33
High St. Downley, D'ley —1A 12
High St. Ealing, W5 —4C 14
High St. East Malling, E Mal —2E 35
High St. Edgware, Edgw —2D 15
High St. Egham, Egh —3E 21
High St. Elstree, Els —1C 14
High St. Epping, Epp —3D 9
High St. Epsom, Eps —1D 31
High St. Esher, Esh —4B 22
High St. Eton, Eton —1D 21
High St. Ewell, Ewe —1D 31
High St. Eynsford, Eyns —4A 26
High St. Farnborough, Farn —4D 25
High St. Farningham, F'ham —4A 26
High St. Feltham, Felt —2B 22
High St. Gillingham, Gill —3F 27
(in four parts)
High St. Godstone, God —4B 32
High St. Great Baddow, Gt Bad —2E 11
High St. Great Bookham, Bookh —3B 30
High St. Great Missenden, Gt Miss —3B 4
High St. Greenhithe, Grnh —2B 26
High St. Green Street Green, Grn St —1D 33
High St. Guildford, Guild —4E 29
(in two parts)
High St. Hadlow, Hdlw —4C 34
High St. Halling, Hall —4E 27
High St. Hampton, Hamp —3C 22
High St. Hampton Hill, Hamp H —3C 22
High St. Hampton Wick, Hamp W —3C 22
High St. Harefield, Hare —2F 13
High St. Harlesden. NW10 —4D 15
High St. Harlington, Harl —1A 22
High St. Harlow, H'low —1E 9
(in two parts)
High St. Harrow on the Hill, Harr —3C 14
High St. Hemel Hempstead, Hem H —2F 5
High St. High Wycombe, High W —1B 12
High St. Hoddesdon, Hod —2B 8
High St. Hornchurch, Horn —3F 17
High St. Hornsey, N8 —2A 16
High St. Horsell, Hors —2E 29
High St. Ingatestone, Ing —4C 10
High St. Iver, Iver —4F 13
High St. Kemsing, Kems —2A 34
High St. Kings Langley, K Lan —3A 6
High St. Kingston upon Thames, King T —3C 22
High St. Knaphill, Knap —2D 29
High St. Langley, Langl —1E 21
High St. Limpsfield, Limp —3C 32
High St. Little Sandhurst, L Sand —1A 28
High St. London Colney, Lon C —2C 6
High St. Maidenhead, M'head —4B 12
High St. Maidstone, Maid —3F 35
High St. Marlow, Mar —3A 12
High St. Merstham, Mers —3F 31
High St. New Malden, N Mald —3D 23
High St. Northfleet, N'fleet —2B 26
High St. Northwood, N'wd —2A 14
High St. Nutfield, Nutf —4A 32
High St. Old Oxted, Oxt —3C 32
High St. Old Woking, Old Wok —2E 29
High St. Orpington, Orp —4E 25
High St. Otford, Otf —2F 33
High St. Oxshott, Oxs —1C 30
High St. Penge, SE20 —3B 24
High St. Pinner, Pinn —2B 14
High St. Ponders End, Enf —1B 16
High St. Potters Bar, Pot B —3F 7
High St. Prestwood, P'wd —3B 4
High St. Redbourn, Redb —1B 6
High St. Redhill, Red —4F 31
High St. Reigate, Reig —4E 31
High St. Rickmansworth, Rick —1F 13
High St. Ripley, Rip —2F 29
High St. Rochester, Roch —3F 27
(in two parts)
High St. Roydon, Roy —1C 8
High St. Ruislip, Ruis —3A 14
High St. St Mary Cray, St M —4E 25
High St. Sandhurst, Sand —1A 28
High St. Sandridge, Sandr —1C 6
High St. Seal, Seal —2A 34
High St. Sevenoaks, Sev —3F 33
High St. Shepperton, Shep —4A 22
High St. Shoreham, Shor —1F 33
High St. Sidcup, Sidc —3E 25
High St. Slough, Slou —1E 21
High St. Snodland, Snod —1E 35
(in two parts)
High St. Southall, S'hall —4B 14
High St. Southgate, N14 —1F 15
High St. South Norwood, SE25 —3A 24
High St. Staines, Stai —3F 21
High St. Stanford-le-Hope, Stan H —4D 19
High St. Stanstead Abbots, Stan A —1C 8
High St. Stanwell, Stanw —2F 21
High St. Stock, Stock —4D 11
High St. Stratford, E15 —4C 16
High St. Strood, Strood —3E 27
High St. Sunningdale, S'dale —4D 21
High St. Sunninghill, S'hill —4C 20
High St. Sutton, Sutt —4E 23
High St. Swanley, Swan —3F 25
High St. Swanscombe, Swans —2B 26
High St. Teddington, Tedd —3C 22
High St. Thames Ditton, Th Dit —4C 22
High St. Thornton Heath, T Hth —3A 24
High St. Tonbridge, Tonb —4B 34
High St. Tring, Tring —1C 4
High St. Upper Upnor, Upnor —3F 27
High St. Uxbridge, Uxb —3F 13
High St. Waltham Cross, Wal X —3B 8
High St. Wanstead, E11 —2C 16
High St. Wealdstone, W'stone —2C 14
High St. Wendover, Wen —2B 4
High St. Westerham, W'ham —3D 33
High St. West Ham, E13 —4C 16
High St. West Malling, W Mal —2D 35
High St. West Molesey, W Mol —4B 22
High St. West Wickham, W Wick —4B 24
High St. West Wycombe, W Wyc —1A 12
High St. Weybridge, Wey —4A 22
High St. Whitton, Whit —2C 22
High St. Wickford, W'fd —1F 19
High St. Wimbledon, SW19 —3E 23
High St. Windsor, Wind —1D 21
High St. Woking, Wok —2E 29
High St. Woolwich, SE18 —1D 25
High St. Wouldham, Woul —1E 35
High St. Wraysbury, Wray —2E 21
High St. Wrotham, Wro —2B 34
High St. Yalding, Yald —4D 35
High St. Yiewsley, Yiew —4F 13
High St. Grn. Hem H —1A 6
High St. N. E12 & E6 —3D 17
High St. S. E6 —4D 17
High, The. —1D 9
High View. Gom —4A 30
Highway. —4B 12
Highway, The. E1 —4B 16
Highway, The. Orp —4E 25
Highwood. —2C 10
Highwood Hill. —1E 15
Highwood Hill. NW7 —1D 15
(in two parts)
Highwood Rd. Hghwd & Ed C —3C 10
(in two parts)
High Woods. —3C 10
High Wych Rd. Saw —1D 9
High Wycombe. —1B 12
Hildenborough. —4A 34
Hildenborough Rd. Leigh —4A 34
Hildenborough Rd. S'brne —4A 34

Manor Rd.—N. Circular Rd.

Manor Rd. N16 —3A 16
Manor Rd. SE25 —3B 24
Manor Rd. Abr —1E 17
Manor Rd. Beck —3B 24
Manor Rd. Bren —1C 22
Manor Rd. Dart —2F 25
Manor Rd. Eri —1F 25
Manor Rd. Guild —4E 29
Manor Rd. Hat —1D 7
Manor Rd. H Bee —4C 8
Manor Rd. Long —4C 26
Manor Rd. Lou —1C 16
Manor Rd. Mitc —3F 23
Manor Rd. Rich —2D 23
Manor Rd. Swans —2B 26
Manor Rd. Tedd —3C 22
Manor Rd. Tong & Alder —4B 28
Manor Rd. Wall —4F 23
Manor Rd. Wind —1D 21
Manor Rd. Wfd G & Chig —2D 17
Manor Rd. N. Esh & Th Dit —4C 22
Manor Rd. S. Esh —4C 22
Manor View. N3 —2E 15
Manor Way. Borwd —4D 7
Manor Way. Rain —4F 17
Manorway, The. Stan H —4D 19
Mansell St. EC3 —4A 16
Mansfield Hill. E4 —1B 16
Mansfield Rd. NW3 —3F 15
Mansion La. Iver —4F 13
Mantle Rd. SE4 —2B 24
Mantles Green. —4D 5
Manwood Green. —1A 10
Manwood Rd. SE4 —2B 24
Mapesbury Rd. NW2 —3E 15
Maple Cross. —1F 13
Maple Rd. SE20 —3B 24
Maple Rd. Red —4F 31
Maple Rd. Surb —4C 22
Maplescombe. —4A 26
Maplescombe La. F'ham & Sev —4A 26
Mapleton Rd. W'ham & Eden —3D 33
Maple Way. Can I —4F 19
Marble Arch. (Junct.) —4F 15
Marcilly Rd. SW18 —2F 23
Marden Ash. —3A 10
Mare St. E8 —4B 16
Marford Rd. Wheat & Lem —1D 7
Margaret Rd. Barn —4F 7
Margaret Roding. —1B 10
Margaretting. —3D 11
Margaretting Rd. Gall —3D 11
Margaretting Rd. Writ —3D 11
Margaretting Tye. —3D 11
Margery. —3E 31
Margery La. Tad —3E 31
Margery St. WC1 —4A 16
Margetts La. Bur —1E 35
Marigold La. Stock —4D 11
Markedge La. Coul & Reig —3F 31
Marketfield Way. Red —4F 31
Market La. Slou —1F 21
Market Pl. NW11 —2E 15
Market Pl. Abr —4E 9
Market Pl. Chal P —2E 13
Market Pl. Wokgm —3A 20
Market Rd. N7 —3A 16
Market Rd. Chelm —2E 11
Market Sq. Brom —3C 24
Market Sq. W'ham —3D 33
Market St. Brack —3B 20
Market St. Dart —2A 26
Mark Hall Cycle Museum & Gardens. —1E 9
Mark Hall Gardens. —1E 9
Mark Hall North. —1E 9
Mark Hall South. —1E 9
Markhams Chase. Bas —2D 19
Markhouse Rd. E17 —2B 16
Marks Gate. —2E 17
Marks Hall La. Mar R —1B 10
Marlborough Av. Ruis —2A 14
Marlborough Rd. N19 —3F 15
Marling Park. —3B 22
Marlin Hill. Wig —1C 4
Marlow. —3A 12
Marlow Bottom. —2A 12
Marlow Bottom. Mar —2A 12
Marlow Comn. Mar —3A 12
Marlowes. Hem H —2F 5
Marlow Hill. High W —2A 12
Marlow Rd. SE20 —3B 24
Marlow Rd. Bish —3A 12
Marlow Rd. High W —2A 12
Marlow Rd. L End —2A 12
Marlow Rd. L Mar & Bour —3B 12
Marlow Rd. M'head —4B 12
Marlow Rd. Mar —3A 12
Marlpit Hill. —4D 33
Marlpit La. Coul —2A 32
Marrod's Bottom. Amer —1C 12
Marroway. W'ton T —1A 4
Marrowbrook La. Farn —3A 28
Marsh. —1A 4
Marshall Rd. Camb —1A 28
Marshalswick La. St Alb —1C 6
Marshalwick. —1C 6
Marsham St. SW1 —1F 23
Marshcroft La. Tring —1C 4
Marshfoot Rd. Grays —1C 26
Marshgate La. E15 —3B 16
Marsh Hill. E9 —3B 16
Marsh Hill. Wal A —3C 8
Marsh La. NW7 —1D 15
Marsh La. Dor R & Tap —4C 12
Marsh La. Stoke M —1A 4
Marsh La. Stan —1C 14
Marshmoor. —2E 7
Marsh Rd. Pinn —2B 14
Marsh Wall. E14 —1B 24
Martindale Av. Camb —2C 28
Martindale Rd. Houn —2B 22
Martinsend La. Gt Miss —3B 4
Martin's Heron. —3B 20
Martins La. E Peck —4D 35
Martin Way. SW20 & Mord —3E 23
Martyr's Green. —2A 30
Martyr's La. Wok —1E 29
Marvels La. SE12 —2C 24
Marylebone. —4F 15
Marylebone Flyover. (Junct.) —4F 15
Marylebone High St. W1 —4F 15
Marylebone Rd. NW1 —4F 15
Mascalls La. Gt War —1A 18
Mashbury. —1C 10
Mashbury Rd. Gt Wal —1D 11
Masons Av. Harr —2C 14
Mason's Bri. Rd. Red —4F 31
Masons Hill. Brom —3C 24
Master Brewer. (Junct.) —3A 14
Maswell Park. —2C 22
Matching. —1F 9
Matching Green. —1A 10
Matching Rd. H'low —1E 9
Matching Tye. —1F 9
Matthews La. Hdlw —4C 34
Matthias Rd. N16 —3A 16
Maultway, The. Camb —1B 28
Maury Rd. N16 —3B 16
Mawney. —2E 17
Mawney Rd. Romf —2E 17
Maxted Rd. Hem I —1A 6
Maybank Av. Wemb —3C 14
Maybury. —2F 29
Maybury Hill. Wok —2E 29
Maybury Rd. Wok —2E 29
Mayes La. Dan —2F 11
Mayes La. S'don —2F 11
Mayes Rd. N22 —2A 16
Mayfair. —4F 15
Mayfield Rd. W3 —4D 15
Mayfield Rd. Farn —2A 28
Mayfield Rd. S Croy —1A 32
Mayfield Rd. W on T —4B 22
Mayford. —2E 29
Maygrove Rd. NW6 —3E 15
Maylands Av. Hem H —1A 6
Mayow Rd. SE26 & SE23 —3B 24
Mayplace Rd. E. Bexh —2E 25
Mayplace Rd. W. Bexh —2E 25
Maypole. —1E 33
Maypole Rd. Orp —4E 25
May's Green. —2A 30
Mays La. Barn —1E 15
Maze Hill. SE10 & SE3 —1C 24
Meadow La. Eton —1D 21
Meadow Rise. Bill —1D 19
Mead Vale. —4F 31
Meadway. NW11 —2E 15
Meadway. Barn —4E 7
Mead Way. Brom —4C 24
Mead Way. Coul —2A 32
Meadway. Twic —2C 22
Medfield St. SW15 —2E 23
Medhurst Row. —4E 33
Median Rd. E5 —3B 16
Medlar St. SE5 —1A 24
Medway Rd. Gill —3F 27 (in two parts)
Medway St. Chat —3F 27
Melbourne Av. Chelm —1D 11
Melbourne Rd. Bush —1B 14
Melfort Rd. T Hth —3A 24
Melliker La. Meop —4C 26
Mellow La. E. Hay —4A 14
Mellow La. W. Uxb —4A 14
Melton St. NW1 —4F 15
Melville Av. Gnfd —3C 14
Melville Gdns. N13 —2A 16
Meopham. —4C 26
Meopham Green. —4C 26
Meopham Station. —4C 26
Meopham Windmill. —4C 26
Merantun Way. SW19 —3F 23
Mercian Way. Slou —4C 12
Mercury Gdns. Romf —2F 17
Mere Rd. Slou —1D 21
Mere Rd. Tad —3E 31
Mereworth. —3C 34
Mereworth Rd. Maid —3C 34
Meriden. —4B 6
Meriden Way. Wat —4B 6
Meridian Way. N18 & Enf —1B 16
Merland Rise. Eps & Tad —2E 31
Merle Common. —4C 32
Merlin Cres. Edgw —2D 15
Merlin Way. N Wea —2E 9
Merrick Rd. S'hall —1B 22
Merrivale. N14 —1F 15
Merrow. —4E 29
Merrow La. Guild —4F 29
Merrow Way. New Ad —1C 32
Merryboys Rd. Cli —2E 27
Merry Hill. —1B 14
Merry Hill Rd. Bush —1B 14
Merstham. —3F 31
Merstham Rd. Red —3A 32
Merton. —3F 23
Merton High St. SW19 —3F 23
Merton Park. —3E 23
Merton Rd. SW18 —2E 23
Merton Rd. SW19 —3E 23
Merttins Rd. SE15 —2B 24
Meudon Av. Farn —3B 28
Mewshurst. —4D 33
Michaels La. Fawk & Sev —4B 26
Micklefield. —1B 12
Micklefield Green. —4F 5
Micklefield Rd. High W —1B 12
Mickleham. —3C 30
Mickleham By-Pass. Mick —3C 30
Mickleham Downs. —3C 30
Middlefield Rd. Hod —1B 8
Middle Green. —4E 13
Middle Grn. Slou —4E 13
Middlegreen Rd. Slou —1E 21
Middle Hill. Egh —3E 21
Middle La. N8 —2A 16
Middle La. Bov —3E 5
Middlemead. S Han —4E 11
Middle Pk. Av. SE9 —2C 24
Middle St. Brock —4D 31
Middle St. Naze —2C 8
Middle St. Shere —4A 30
Middleton Hall La. Brtwd —1B 18
Middleton Rd. Mord & Cars —4E 23
Midfield Way. Orp —3E 25
Midland Rd. NW1 —4F 15
Midland Rd. Hem H —2F 5
Midleton Rd. Guild —4E 29
Mid St. S Nut —4A 32
Milbourne La. Esh —1C 30
Mildmay Gro. N1 —3A 16
Mildmay Pk. N1 —3A 16
Mile End. —4B 16
Mile End Rd. E1 & E3 —4B 16
Mile Ho. La. St Alb —2C 6
Miles Gray Rd. Bas —2D 19
Miles Green. —2D 29
Miles La. Cobh —1B 30
Miles La. S God —4B 32
Milespit Hill. NW7 —1E 15
Milestone Green. (Junct.) —2D 23
Milkwood Rd. SE24 —2A 24
Millbank. SW1 —1A 24
Mill Bri. Hert —1A 8
Millbrook. Guild —4E 29
Millbrook Rd. St M —3E 25
Mill End. —1F 13
Mill End Rd. High W —1A 12
Millennium Dome. —4C 16
Miller's Green. —2B 10
Miller's La. Chig —1E 17
Milley Bridge. —1A 20
Milley La. Hare H —1A 20
Milley Rd. Wal L —1A 20
Millfields. Che —3D 5
Millfields Rd. E5 —3B 16
Mill Green. —3C 10
(nr. Ingatestone)
Mill Green. —1E 7
(nr. Welwyn Garden City)
Mill Grn. Hat —1F 7
Mill Grn. La. Wel G & Mill G —1E 7
Mill Grn. Rd. Ing —3C 10
Mill Grn. Rd. Mitc —4F 23
Mill Hill. —1E 15
Mill Hill. W3 —1D 23
Mill Hill. Chelm —3D 11
Mill Hill. Tovil —3F 35
Mill Hill Circus. (Junct.) —1D 15
Mill Hill La. Shorne —3D 27
Mill Hill Rd. SW13 —1E 23
Mill Ho. La. Egh & Cher —3F 21
Mill La. NW6 —3E 15
Mill La. Asc —3D 21
Mill La. B'water —1A 28
Mill La. Blue B —1F 35
Mill La. Brack —3A 20
Mill La. Brox —2B 8
Mill La. Chal G —1E 13
Mill La. Dan —2F 11
Mill La. Egh —3F 21
Mill La. Ger X —2E 13
Mill La. Grays —1B 26
Mill La. Hild —4A 34
Mill La. Hook E —4B 10
Mill La. Hur —4A 12
Mill La. Igh —2B 34
Mill La. Ing —3C 10
Mill La. K Lan —3A 6
Mill La. L Bad —2F 11
Mill La. Mon R —2A 4
Mill La. More —1F 9
Mill La. Nave —4F 9
Mill La. Ong —3A 10
Mill La. Orp —1D 33
Mill La. Ors —4C 18
Mill La. Oxt —4C 32
Mill La. Romf —2E 17
Mill La. Stock —4D 11
Mill La. Tap —4C 12
Mill La. Toot —3F 9
Mill La. Under —4A 34
Mill La. Yald —4E 35
Mill Meads. —4C 16
Mill Pond Rd. Dart —2A 26
Mill Rd. Ave —4A 18
Mill Rd. Bill —1D 19
Mill Rd. Cobh —2B 30
Mill Rd. Eps —1D 31
Mill Rd. Gill —3F 27
Mill Rd. Good E —1C 10
Mill Rd. Stock —4D 11
Mill Rd. Tad —3E 31
Mill Rd. W Dray —1F 21
Mill Street. —2D 35
Mill St. E Mal —2D 35
Mill St. H'low —1E 9
Mill St. Loose —3F 35
Mill St. Red —4F 31
Millwall. —1B 24
Millwall F.C. —1B 24
Mill Way. Dork —3D 31
Milman Rd. NW6 —4E 15
Milton. —2C 26
Milton Rd. Cat —2A 32
Milton Rd. Grav —2C 26 (in two parts)
Milton Rd. Swans —2B 26
Milton St. Swans —2B 26
Mimbridge. —1E 29
Mimms Hall Rd. Pot B —3E 7
Mimms La. Shenl & Pot B —3D 7
Mincing La. Chob —1D 29
Minley. —2A 28
Minley La. B'water —2A 28
Minley Link Rd. Farn —3A 28
Minley Rd. B'water & Farn —2A 28
Minley Rd. Farn —2A 28
Minley Rd. Fleet —2A 28
Minnow End. —1D 11
Minories. EC3 —4A 16
Missenden Rd. Che —3D 5
Missenden Rd. Gt Kin —4B 4
Miswell La. Tring —1C 4
Mitcham. —3F 23
Mitcham La. SW16 —3F 23
Mitcham Rd. SW17 —3F 23
Mitcham Rd. Croy —4A 24
Mitchley Av. Purl & S Croy —1A 32
Mitchley Hill. S Croy —1A 32
Moat La. P'wd —3B 4
Mobwell. —3B 4
Moby Dick. (Junct.) —2E 17
Mockbeggar. —4E 35
(nr. Marden)
Mockbeggar. —2E 27
(nr. Wainscott)
Mogador. —3E 31
Mogador Rd. Tad —3E 31
Mogden La. Iswth —2C 22
Molesey Rd. W on T & W Mol —4B 22
Molesworth St. SE13 —2C 24
Mollison Av. Enf —4B 8
Mollison Dri. Wall —1A 32
Mollison Way. Edgw —2D 15
Molrams La. Gt Bad —2E 11
Monarchs Way. Chesh —3B 8
Moneyhill. —1F 13
Moneyrow Green. —1B 20
Moneyrow Grn. Holyp —1B 20
Monkham's La. Wfd G —1C 16 (in two parts)
Monks La. Eden —4C 32
Monks Orchard. —4B 24
Monks Orchard Rd. Beck —4B 24
Monks Risborough. —2A 4
Monkswell La. Coul —3E 31
Monkton Hadley. —4E 7
Monkton La. Farnh —4A 28
Monmouth Rd. N9 —1B 16
Monmouth St. WC2 —4A 16
Montague Pl. WC1 —4F 15
Montague Waye. S'hall —1B 22
Montagu Rd. N18 & N9 —1B 16
Montem La. Slou —4D 13
Montpelier Row. SE3 —1C 24
Montrose Av. Edgw —2D 15
Monument Hill. Wey —4A 22
Monument La. Chal P —2E 13
Monument Rd. Wok —1E 29
Monument Way. N15 —2A 16
Moore's Rd. Dork —4C 30
Moorfield Rd. Den —3F 13
Moorgate. EC2 —4A 16
Moor Hall La. E Han —3F 11
Moorhall Rd. Hare —2F 13
Moor Hall Rd. H'low —1E 9
Moorhouse. —3D 33
Moorhouse Bank. —3D 33
Moorhouse Rd. Oxt & W'ham —4D 33
Moor Junction. (Junct.) —1F 21
Moor La. Chess —4D 23
Moor La. Rick —1A 14
Moor La. Sarr —4F 5
Moor Park. —1A 14
Moors Wlk. Wel G —1F 7
Morants Ct. Rd. Dun G —2F 33
Morden. —3E 23
Morden Hall Rd. Mord —3F 23
Morden Park. —4E 23
Morden Rd. SW19 —3E 23
Morden Rd. Mitc —3F 23
Moreland St. EC1 —4A 16
More La. Esh —4B 22
Mores La. Pil H —1A 18
Moreton. —2F 9
Moreton Bri. More —2F 9
Moreton Mill. —1F 9
Moreton Rd. Fyf —2A 10
Moreton Rd. More —2F 9
Moreton Rd. Ong —2A 10
Morgan's La. Hay —4A 14
Morland Rd. Croy —4A 24
Morley Hill. Stan H —3D 19
Morley's Rd. Weald —4F 33
Morning La. E9 —3B 16
Mornington Rd. Gnfd —4B 14
Morris Rd. E3 —4B 16
Mortimer Rd. NW10 —4E 15
Mortimer St. W1 —4F 15
Mortlake. —2D 23
Mortlake High St. SW14 —2D 23
Mortlake Rd. Rich —1D 23
Morton Way. N14 —1F 15
Morval Rd. SW2 —2A 24
Moss End. —2B 20
Moss La. Pinn —2B 14
Mote Rd. Maid —3F 35
Mote Rd. S'brne & Ivy H —3A 34
Motherwell Way. Grays —1B 26
Motspur Park. —4E 23
Motspur Pk. N Mald —4D 23
Mottingham. —2C 24
Mottingham La. SE9 —2C 24
Mottingham Rd. SE9 —2D 25
Mott St. E4 & Lou —4C 8
Moulsham. —2E 11
Moulsham St. Chelm —2E 11 (in two parts)
Mount Av. W5 —4C 14
Mount End. —3E 9
Mount End. They M —3E 9
Mountgrove Rd. N5 —3A 16
Mt. Harry Rd. Sev —3F 33
Mount La. Den —3F 13
Mountnessing. —4C 10
Mountnessing By-Pass. Mount & Ing —4C 10
Mountnessing La. Dodd —4B 10
Mountnessing Postmill. —4C 10
Mountnessing Rd. Bill —1D 19
Mountnessing Rd. B'more & Brtwd —3B 10
Mt. Nugent. Che —2D 5
Mount Pleasant. —2F 13
Mt. Pleasant. Barn —4F 7
Mt. Pleasant. Wemb —4D 15
Mt. Pleasant La. Brick —3B 6
Mt. Pleasant Rd. N17 —2A 16
Mount Rd. They G —3E 9
Mounts Hill. Wink —2C 20
Mounts Rd. Grnh —2B 26
Movers Lane. (Junct.) —4D 17
Movers La. Bark —4D 17
Mowden. —1F 11
Mowden Hall La. Hat P —1F 11
Mucking. —4D 19
Muckingford. —1D 27
Muckingford Rd. W Til —1C 26
Mucking Wharf Rd. Stan H —4D 19
Mugswell. —3E 31
Mulberry Grn. H'low —1E 9
Mulberry Way. E18 —2C 16
Mulgrave Rd. Sutt —1E 31
Mumfords La. Chal P —2E 13
Mundaydean La. Mar —2A 12
Mungo Pk. Rd. Rain —3F 17
Munster Rd. SW6 —1E 23
Murchison Av. Bex —2E 25
Murdoch Rd. Wokgm —3A 20
Murray Rd. Ott —1F 29
Murrellhill La. Binf —3A 20
Murthering La. Romf —1F 17
Museum of Kent Life. —2F 35
Mussenden La. Hort K & Dart —4A 26
Muswell Hill. —2F 15
Muswell Hill. N10 —2F 15
Muswell Hill B'way. N10 —2F 15
Muswell Hill Rd. N6 & N10 —2F 15
Mutton La. Pot B —3E 7
Mutton Row. Ong —3F 9
Myddelton Av. Enf —4A 8
Myddelton Pk. N20 —1F 15
Myddleton Rd. N22 —2A 16
Myrke. —1D 21
Mytchett. —3B 28
Mytchett Pl. Rd. Myt —3B 28
Mytchett Rd. Myt —3B 28

Nag's Head. (Junct.) —3A 16
Nag's Head La. Gt Miss —4B 4
Nags Head La. Upm & Brtwd —2A 18
Nags Head Rd. Enf —4B 8
Nairdwood La. P'wd —3B 4
Nallhead Rd. Felt —3B 22
Naphill. —4A 4
Napier Rd. Gill —4F 27
Napsbury. —2C 6
Napsbury La. St Alb —2C 6
Nap, The. K Lan —3A 6
Narcot La. Chal G —1E 13
Narrow La. Warl —2B 32
Nascott Wood Rd. Wat —4A 6
Nash. —4C 24
Nash Bank. Meop —3C 26
Nashdom La. Burn —3C 12
Nash La. Kes —1C 32
Nash Lee. —1A 4
Nash Lee Rd. Terr & Wen —1A 4
Nashleigh Hill. Che —3D 5
Nash Mills. —2A 6
Nash Mills La. Hem H —2A 6
Nash Street. —3C 26
Nast Hyde. —2D 7
Nathan's La. Hghwd —2C 10
Nathan Way. SE28 —1D 25
National Maritime Museum. —1C 24
National Motorboat Museum. —3E 19
National Recreation Centre. (Crystal Palace) —3B 24
Navestock Heath. —4F 9
Navestock Side. —4A 10
Navestockside. Brtwd —4A 10
Nazaire Rd. Chelm —1D 11
Nazeing. —2C 8
Nazeing Comn. Naze —2C 8
Nazeing Glass Works. —2B 8
Nazeing New Rd. Brox —2B 8
Nazeing Rd. Naze —2C 8
Neasden. —3D 15
Neasden Junction. (Junct.) —3D 15
Neasden La. NW10 —3D 15
Neasden La. N. NW10 —3D 15
Nelson Rd. E4 —2B 16
Nelson Rd. Gill —4F 27
Nelson Rd. Houn & Twic —2B 22
Nelson Rd. H'row A —1A 22
Nene Rd. H'row A —1A 22
Nepicar Farm. —2C 34
Nepicar La. Wro —2C 34
Netherlands Rd. Barn & N20 —1F 15
Nether Mayne. Bas —2E 19
Netherne La. Coul —3F 31
Nether Street. —1B 10
Nether St. N3 & N12 —2E 15
Nether St. Ab R —1B 10
Nettleden. —1F 5
Nettleden Rd. Lit H —1E 5
Nettleden Rd. L Gad & Wat E —1E 5
Nettlestead. —3D 35
Nettlestead Green. —4D 35
Nettlestead La. Mere —3D 35
Nettleswell. —1D 9
Nevedon. —2E 19
Nevendon Rd. Bas & W'fd —2E 19
Nevendon Rd. By-Pass. W'fd —1F 19
New Addington. —1C 32
Newark La. Wok —2F 29
Newarks Rd. Good E —1C 10
New Ash Green. —4B 26
New Barn. —3C 26
New Barnet. —4F 7
Newbarn La. Seer —1D 13
New Barn La. W'ham & Sev —2D 33
New Barn Rd. Long & Grav —3C 26
New Barn Rd. Swan —3F 25
New Barn St. E13 —4C 16
New Beckenham. —3B 24
New Bond St. W1 —4F 15
New Bowers Way. Chelm —1E 11
New Bri. St. EC4 —4A 16
Newbury Av. Enf —4B 8
Newbury Park. —2D 17
Newbury Rd. H'row A —1A 22
New Cavendish St. W1 —4F 15
New Charlton. —1C 24
New Chu. Rd. SE5 —1A 24
New City Rd. E13 —4C 16
New College of Cobham. —3D 27
New Cross. —1B 24
New Cross. (Junct.) —1B 24
New Cross Gate. —1B 24
New Cross Gate. (Junct.) —1B 24
New Cross Rd. SE14 —1B 24
New Cut. E Far —3F 35
New Cut Rd. Weav —3F 35
New Denham. —3F 13
Newell Green. —3B 20
New Eltham. —2D 25
New Forest Ride. Brack —4B 20
Newgate Street. —2A 8
Newgate St. Hert —2F 7
Newgatestreet Rd. G Oak —2A 8
Newgate St. Village. Hert —2A 8
New Greens. —1C 6
New Ground. —1D 5
Newground Rd. New G —1D 5
Newham Way. E16 & E6 —4C 16
New Haw. —1F 29
New Haw Rd. Add —4F 21
New Heston Rd. Houn —1B 22
Newhouse. —1A 10
(nr. Moreton)
New House. —2C 26
(nr. Northfleet)
New Ho. La. Grav —2C 26
New Hythe. —2E 35
New Hythe La. Lark —2E 35
Newington. —1A 24
Newington Butts. SE11 —1A 24
Newington Causeway. SE1 —1A 24
Newington Grn. N1 —3A 16
Newington Grn. Rd. N1 —3A 16
New Inn La. Guild —4E 29
New Kent Rd. SE17 —1A 24
New King's Rd. SW6 —1E 23
Newlands. —1C 14
Newlands La. Meop —1C 34
Newlands Pk. SE26 —3B 24
New La. Wok & Guild —2E 29
New Lodge Chase. L Bad —2F 11
New London Rd. Chelm (in two parts) —2E 11
New Malden. —3D 23
Newman's End. —1F 9
New Mile Rd. Asc —3C 20
New Mill. —1C 4
New Nabbotts Way. Chelm —1E 11
Newney Green. —2C 10
New N. Rd. N1 —3A 16
New N. Rd. Ilf —2D 17
New Oxford St. WC1 —4F 15
New Pk. Rd. SW2 —2A 24
New Plaistow Rd. E15 —4C 16
New Pond Rd. Holm G —4C 4
Newport Rd. H'row A —1A 22
New Pound La. Mere —3C 34
New Rd. E1 —4B 16
New Rd. E4 —1B 16
New Rd. SE2 —1E 25
New Rd. Abr —1E 17
New Rd. Alb —4F 29
New Rd. Asc —3C 20
New Rd. Bag & W'sham —1C 28
New Rd. Berk —1E 5
New Rd. Bur —4F 27
New Rd. Chat —4F 27
New Rd. Cher —4F 21
New Rd. Chil —4E 29
New Rd. Coles —4D 5
New Rd. Crox G —1A 14
New Rd. Dag & Rain —4E 17
New Rd. Dit —2E 35
New Rd. E Mal —2E 35
New Rd. Felt —2A 22
New Rd. Grays —1B 26 (in two parts)
New Rd. High W —1A 12
New Rd. Lac G & Walt H —4A 4
New Rd. Limp —3C 32
New Rd. N'chu —1D 5
New Rd. Penn —1C 12
New Rd. P Ris —3A 4
New Rd. Rad —4C 6
New Rd. Sarr —4F 5
New Rd. Shep —3A 22
New Rd. Sund —3E 33
New Rd. Tad —3E 31
New Rd. Tand —4B 32
New Rd. Uxb —4A 14
New Rd. W Mol —3B 22
New Rd. W'ton T —1A 4
New Rd. Av. Chat —4F 27
New Rd. Hill. Kes & Brom —1D 33
New Southgate. —2F 15
New Street. —4C 26
New St. Chelm —2E 11
New St. Rd. Meop & Sev —4C 26
New Thundersley. —2F 19
Newtown. —3D 5
(nr. Chesham)
New Town. —2A 26
(nr. Dartford)
Newtown Rd. Mar —3A 12
New Wanstead. E11 —2C 16
New Way La. Thr B —1F 9
New Wickham La. Egh —3E 21
New Windsor. —2D 21
New Windsor St. Uxb —4F 13
New Wokingham Rd. Crowt —4A 20
Newyears Green. —3A 14
Newyears Grn. La. Hare —2A 14
New Years La. Knock & Orp —2D 33
New Zealand Av. W on T —4A 22
Nightingale La. SW12 & SW4 —2F 23
Nightingale La. Brom —3C 24
Nightingale La. Ide H —4E 33
Nightingale La. St Alb —2C 6
Nightingale Pl. SE18 —1D 25
Nightingale Rd. N9 —1B 16
Nightingale Rd. Cars —4F 23
Nightingale Rd. Rick —1F 13
Nightingales La. Chal G —4E 5
Nine Ashes. —3B 10
Nine Ashes Rd. B'more & Brtwd —3B 10
Nine Elms. —1F 23
Nine Elms La. SW8 —1F 23
Ninehams Rd. Cat —2A 32
Nine Mile Ride. Brack —4A 20
Nine Mile Ride. Wokgm & Crowt —4A 20
Nizels. —4A 34
Nizels La. Hild —4A 34
Noah's Ark. —2A 34
Noah's Ark. Kems —2A 34
Noak Bridge. —2D 19
Noak Hill. —1A 18
(nr. Harold Hill)
Noak Hill. —2D 19
(nr. Steeple View)
Noak Hill Rd. Bill & Bas —1D 19
Noak Hill Rd. Romf —1F 17
Noble Tree Rd. Hild —4A 34
Noel Park. —2A 16
Noel Rd. W3 —4D 15
Noke La. St Alb —2B 6
Norbiton. —3D 23
Norbury. —3A 24
Norbury Av. SW16 & T Hth —3A 24
Norbury Cres. SW16 —3A 24
Norden Rd. M'head —4B 12
Norfolk Rd. M'head —4B 12
Norheads La. Warl & Big H —2C 32
Nork. —2E 31
Norlands La. Egh —3F 21
Normandy. —4C 28
Normandy Rd. St Alb —1C 6
Norman Rd. SE8 —1B 24
Norman Rd. W Mal —2D 35
Normansland. —1C 6
Norreys Dri. M'head —1B 20
Norris Hill Rd. Fleet —3A 28
Norsey Rd. Bill —1D 19
Norsted La. Prat B —1E 33
North Acton. —4D 15
N. Acton Rd. NW10 —4D 15
Northall Rd. Bexh —1F 25
North App. Wat —3B 6
North Ascot. —3C 20
N. Ash Rd. New Ash —4B 26
N. Audley St. W1 —4F 15
North Av. Chelm —1D 11
Northaw. —3F 7
Northaw Rd. E. Cuff —3F 7
Northaw Rd. W. N'thaw —3F 7
North Benfleet. —2F 19
N. Birkbeck Rd. E11 —3C 16
Northborough Rd. Slou —4D 13
Northbrook Rd. Ilf —3D 17
North Camp. —3B 28
North Cheam. —4E 23
Northchurch. —1D 5
N. Circular Rd. N2, N3 & N12 —2E 15
N. Circular Rd. N13 —1A 16
N. Circular Rd. NW2 —3D 15
N. Circular Rd. NW4 —3E 15
N. Circular Rd. NW10 —4D 15

46 A-Z London Motorists Atlas

N. Circular Rd.—Plaistow Rd.

N. Circular Rd. NW11 —2E 15
Northcote Rd. SW11 —2F 23
Northcote Rd. Croy —4A 24
Northcote Rd. Roch —3E 27
North Cray. —3E 25
N. Cray Rd. Sidc & Bex —3E 25
Northcroft Rd. Egh —3E 21
N. Dane Way. Chat —4F 27
Northdown Rd. Wold —3B 32
North End. —1F 25 **(nr. Erith)**
North End. —3F 15 **(nr. Hampstead)**
North End. W14 —1E 23
Northend. Hem H —2A 6
N. End La. Orp —1D 33
N. End Rd. NW11 —3E 15
Northend Rd. Eri —1F 25
N. End Way. NW3 —3F 15
Northern Perimeter Rd. H'row A —1A 22
Northern Perimeter Rd. W. H'row A —1A 22
Northern Rd. Slou —4D 13
Northern Woods. F Hth —2C 12
Northey Av. Sutt —1E 31
North Farnborough. —3B 28
North Feltham. —2B 22
Northfield Av. W13 & W5 —4C 14
Northfields. —1C 22
North Finchley. —1F 15
Northfleet. —2C 26
Northfleet Green. —3C 26
Northfleet Grn. Rd. S'fleet —3C 26
N. Folly Rd. E Far —4E 35
North Ga. Roch —3F 27
North Halling. —4E 27
North Harrow. —2B 14
North Hill. N6 —2F 15
North Hill. Horn H —3D 19
North Hill. L Bad —1F 11
North Hill. Rick —4F 5
N. Hill Dri. Romf —1F 17
North Hillingdon. —3A 14
North Holmwood. —4C 30
N. Hyde La. S'hall & Houn —1B 22
N. Hyde Rd. Hay —1A 22
Northiam. N12 —1E 15
North Kensington. —4E 15
North La. Alder —4B 28
North Lee. —1A 4
N. Lee La. Terr —1A 4
North Looe. —1E 31
N. Meadow. Off —2C 34
North Mymms. —2D 7
North Ockendon. —3B 18
Northolt. —3B 14
Northolt Rd. Harr —3B 14
N. Orbital Rd. Wat & St Alb —3B 6
Northover. Brom —2C 24
N. Park Rd. Iver —1F 21
N. Pole La. Kes —1C 32
N. Pole Rd. W10 —4E 15
N. Pole Rd. E Mal & Barm —3D 35
Northridge Way. Hem H —2F 5
North Rd. N6 —3F 15
North Rd. N7 —3A 16
North Rd. Ches B —4D 5
North Rd. Hav —1F 17
North Rd. Hert —1A 8
North Rd. S'hall —4B 14
North Rd. S Ock & Upm —4B 18
North Rd. Wid E —1B 12
North Sheen. —2D 23
North Stifford. —4B 18
North St. SW4 —2F 23
North St. Barm —3E 35
North St. Cars —4F 23
North St. Guild —4E 29
North St. Horn —3F 17
North St. Naze —2C 8
North St. Romf —2F 17
North St. Strood —3E 27
North St. Wink —3C 20
North Town. —4B 28 **(nr. Aldershot)**
North Town. —4B 12 **(nr. Maidenhead)**
Northumberland Av. WC2 —4A 16
Northumberland Heath. —1F 25
Northumberland Pk. N17 —2B 16
Northumberland Rd. Maid —3F 35
North View. Pinn —3B 14
North Watford. —4B 6
North Weald Airfield. —2E 9
North Weald Airfield Memorial Museum. —3E 9
North Weald Bassett. —2F 9
North Wembley. —3C 14
N. Western Av. Wat —4A 6
N. Western Way. Bush —4B 6
Northwick. —4F 19
Northwick Rd. Can I —4F 19
Northwold Rd. N16 & E5 —3A 16
Northwood. —2A 14
Northwood Hills. —2A 14
Northwood Rd. Hare —2F 13
Northwood Rd. T Hth & SE19 —3A 24
Northwood Way. N'wd —2B 14
North Woolwich. —4D 17
N. Woolwich Rd. E16 —4C 16
Norton Heath. —2B 10
Norton Heath Rd. Will —2B 10
Norton La. H Ong —2B 10
Norton Mandeville. —2B 10
Norwich Rd. N'wd —2A 14
Norwood. —3A 24
Norwood End. —1A 10
Norwood End. Fyf —1A 10
Norwood Green. —1B 22
Norwood High St. SE27 —3A 24
Norwood La. Iver —4F 13
Norwood La. Meop —4C 26
Norwood New Town. —3A 24
Norwood Rd. SE27 & SE24 —2A 24
Norwood Rd. S'hall —1B 22
Notting Hill. —4E 15
Notting Hill Ga. W11 —4E 15
Nower Hill. Pinn —2B 14
Nower, The. W'ham —2D 33
Nunhead. —2B 24
Nunhead La. SE15 —2B 24
Nuper's Hatch. —1F 17
Nupton Dri. Barn —1E 15
Nuptown. —2B 20
Nuptown La. Nup —2B 20
Nursery Rd. Lou —4C 8
Nursery Rd. Sun —3A 22
Nurstead Chu. La. Meop —3C 26
Nurstead La. Long —3C 26
Nutfield. —4A 32
Nutfield Marsh Rd. Nutf —4F 31
Nutfield Rd. Mers —3F 31
Nutfield Rd. Red —4F 31
Nuxley Rd. Belv —1E 25

Oak Av. Hamp —3B 22
Oakcroft Rd. W Byf —1F 29
Oakdene Rd. Cobh —1B 30
Oakenden Rd. Ludd —4C 26
Oak End Way. Ger X —2E 13
Oaken La. Clay —4C 22
Oak Farm La. Fair —1C 34
Oakfield La. Dart —2F 25
Oakfield Rd. SE20 —3B 24
Oakfield Rd. Croy —4A 24
Oak Hill. Wfd G —2C 16
Oak Hill. Wood S —4D 29
Oak Hill Rd. Stap A —1F 17
Oakhurst. —4A 34
Oakington Av. Wemb —3D 15
Oaklands La. Big H —1C 32
Oaklands La. Smal —1D 7
Oak La. Sev —3F 33
Oak La. St L —2C 4
Oaklawn Rd. Lea —2C 30
Oakleigh Park. —1F 15
Oakleigh Pk. N. N20 —1F 15
Oakleigh Pk. S. N20 —1F 15
Oakleigh Rd. N. N20 —1F 15
Oakleigh Rd. S. N11 —1F 15
Oakley Green. —1C 20
Oakley Grn. Rd. Oak G —1C 20
Oakley Rd. Brom —4D 25
Oakley Sq. NW1 —4F 15
Oakley St. SW3 —1F 23
Oakridge La. Ald —4C 6
Oak Rd. Cray H —2E 19
Oaks Rd. Croy —4B 24
Oaks Rd. Stai —2F 21
Oakthorpe Rd. N13 —1A 16
Oakwood. —1A 16
Oakwood Av. Beck —3C 24
Oakwood Hill. Lou —1D 17
Oakwood Rd. Brick —3B 6
Oakwood Rd. Maid —3F 35
Oatlands Av. Wey —4A 22
Oatlands Chase. Wey —4A 22
Oatlands Dri. Slou —4D 13
Oatlands Dri. Wey —4A 22
Oatlands Park. —4A 22
Occam Rd. Guild —4D 29
Ockendon Rd. Upm & N Ock —3A 18
Ockham. —2A 30
Ockham La. Ock & Cob —2A 30
Ockham Rd. N. Ock & Lea —2A 30
Ockham Rd. S. E Hor —3A 30
Ockwells Rd. M'head —1B 20
Odiham Rd. Farnh —4A 28
Offham. —2C 34
Offham Rd. W Mal —2D 35
Offord Rd. N1 —3A 16
Okehampton Cres. Well —1E 25
Old Bethnal Grn. Rd. E2 —4B 16
Old Bexley. —2E 25
Old Bexley La. Bex & Dart (in two parts) —2F 25
Old Bisley Rd. Frim —2B 28
Old Brentford. —1C 22
Old Brompton Rd. SW5 & SW7 —1E 23
Oldbury. —2B 34
Oldbury La. Igh —2B 34
Old Chapel Rd. Swan —4F 25
Old Chatham Rd. Blue B —2F 35
Old Chatham Rd. S'ing —1F 35
Old Chertsey Rd. Chob —1E 29
Old Chu. Hill. Lang H —3D 19
Old Chu. La. NW9 —3D 15
Old Chu. La. E Peck —3D 35
Old Chu. La. Mount —4C 10
Old Chu. La. Stan —1C 14
Old Chu. Rd. E4 —1B 16
Old Chu. Rd. Burh —1E 35
Old Chu. Rd. E Han —3F 11
Old Chu. Rd. Mount —4C 10 (in three parts)
Oldchurch Rd. Romf —2F 17
Old Chu. Rd. Ton —3C 34
Old Coach Rd., The. Col G —1F 7
Old Coulsdon. —2A 32
Old Dover Rd. SE3 —1C 24
Old Farley Rd. S Croy & Warl —1B 32
Oldfield La. N. Gnfd —4C 14
Oldfield La. S. Gnfd —4C 14
Oldfield Rd. M'head —4B 12
Oldfields Rd. Sutt —4E 23
Old Ford. —4B 16
Old Ford. (Junct.) —4B 16
Old Ford Rd. E2 & E3 —4B 16
Old Gorhambury House. —2B 6
Old Harlow. —1E 9
Old Highway. Hod —1B 8
Old Hill. Chst —3D 25
Old Hill. Orp —1D 33
Oldhouse La. K Lan —4A 6
Old Isleworth. —2C 22
Old Kent Rd. SE1 & SE15 —1A 24
Old La. Tats —2C 32
Old La. Wok & Cob —2A 30
Old Lodge La. Purl —1A 32
Old London Rd. Badg M —1E 33
Old London Rd. Eps —2E 31
Old London Rd. H'low —1E 9
Old London Rd. Knock —2E 33
Old London Rd. Mick —3C 30
Old London Rd. Raw —1F 19
Old London Rd. St Alb —2C 6
Old London Rd. Wro —2B 34
Old Loose Hill. Loose —4F 35
Old MacDonalds Educational Farm Park. —1A 18
Old Maidstone Rd. Sidc —3E 25
Old Malden. —4D 23
Old Malden La. Wor Pk —4D 23
Old Marylebone Rd. NW1 —4F 15
Old Mill La. Uxb —4F 13
Old Mill Rd. Den —3F 13
Old Mill Rd. K Lan —3A 6
Old Nazeing Rd. Brox —2B 8
Old Oak Common. —4D 15
Old Oak Common. La. NW10 & W3 —4D 15
Old Oak La. NW10 —4D 15
Old Oak Rd. W3 —4D 15
Old Oxford Rd. Pid —1A 12
Old Oxted. —4C 32
Old Pk. Av. Enf —1A 16
Old Pk. Ridings. N21 —1A 16
Old Portsmouth Rd. Art —4E 29
Old Rectory La. Den —3F 13
Old Rectory Rd. Ong —3F 9
Old Redding. Harr —1B 14
Old Reigate Rd. Bet —4D 31
Old Rd. Bkld —4D 31
Old Rd. Dart —2F 25
Old Rd. E Peck —4D 35
Old Rd. H'low —1E 9
Old Rd. Nave & Brtwd —4F 9
Old Rd. W'bury —3D 35
Old Rd. E. Grav —2C 26
Old Rd. W. Grav —2C 26
Old Roxwell Rd. Writ —2D 11
Old School La. Brock —4D 31
Old Soar Rd. Plax —3B 34
Old Southend Rd. H Grn —3F 11
Old Sta. Rd. Lou —1D 17
Old Street. (Junct.) —4A 16
Old St. EC1 —4A 16
Old Terry's Lodge Rd. Sev —2A 34
Old Tilburstow Rd. S God —4B 32
Old Tovil Rd. Maid —3F 35
Old Town. SW4 —2F 23
Old Town. Croy —4A 24
Old Tree La. Bou M —4F 35
Old Uxbridge Rd. Rick —1F 13
Old Watling St. Roch —3E 27
Old Windsor. —2E 21
Old Woking. —2E 29
Old Wokingham Rd. Wokgm & Crowt —4A 20
Old Woking Rd. Wok & W Byf —2F 29
Oliver Rd. E10 —3B 16
Oliver Rd. Grays —1B 26
Oliver Way. Chelm —1D 11
Olleberrie La. Sarr —3F 5
Olympia. —1E 23
One Pin La. Farn C —3D 13
One Tree Hill. Stan H & Bas —3D 19
One Tree Hill Rd. Guild —4E 29
Ongar Castle. —3A 10
Ongar Greensted Saxon Wooden Church. —3F 9
Ongar Hill. Add —1F 29
Ongar Rd. Abr —4E 9
Ongar Rd. Fyf —2A 10
Ongar Rd. Ing & Cook G —2C 10
Ongar Rd. Kel H & Brtwd —3A 10
Ongar Rd. Mar R —1B 10
Ongar Rd. Ston M —3A 10
Ongar Rd. Writ —2D 11
Onslow Sq. SW7 —1F 23
Onslow St. Guild —4E 29
Onslow Village. —4D 29
Opladen Way. Brack —4B 20
Orange Hill Rd. Edgw —2D 15
Orange Tree Hill. Hav —1F 17
Orchard Av. Bill —4D 11
Orchard Av. Croy —4B 24
Orchard Gdns. Chess —4D 23
Orchard Leigh. —3E 5
Orchard Rd. Beac —1D 13
Orchard Rd. King T —3D 23
Orchard Way. Croy —4B 24
Ordnance Cres. SE10 —1C 24
Ordnance Rd. Alder —4B 28
Ordnance Rd. Enf —4B 8
Organ Crossroads. (Junct.) —1E 31
Oriental Rd. Wok —2E 29
Orphanage Rd. Wat —4B 6
Orpington. —4E 25
Orpington By-Pass Rd. Orp & Bad M —1E 33
Orpington Rd. Chst —3D 25
Orsett. —4C 18
Orsett Heath. —4C 18
Orsett Rd. Grays —1B 26
Orsett Rd. Ors & Stan H —4C 18
Orwell Dri. Ayl —1A 4
Osborne La. Warf —3B 20
Osborne Rd. Wind —2D 21
Osidge. —1F 15
Osidge La. N14 —1F 15
Ossulton Way. N2 —2F 15
Osterley. —1C 22
Osterley Rd. Iswth —1C 22
Otford. —2F 33
Otford La. Hals —1E 33
Otford Rd. Sev —2F 33
Ottershaw. —1F 29
Otterspool Way. Wat —4B 6
Ottways La. Asht —2C 30
Outing's La. Dodd —4B 10
Outram Rd. Croy —4A 24
Outwood Comn. Rd. Bill —1D 19
Outwood Farm Rd. Bill —1D 19
Outwood La. Blet —4A 32
Outwood La. Red —4A 32
Outwood La. Tad & Coul —2E 31
Oval Cricket Ground, The. —1A 24
Oval Rd. N. Dag —4E 17
Ovenden Rd. Sund —2E 33
Overcliffe. Grav —2C 26
Overton Dri. E11 —3C 16
Overy St. Dart —2A 26
Owletts. —3D 27
Owlsmoor. —1A 28
Owlsmoor Rd. Camb —1A 28
Oxenden Rd. Tong —4B 28
Oxenhoath Rd. Hdlw —4C 34
Oxestall's Rd. SE8 —1B 24
Oxford Rd. Den & Uxb —3F 13
Oxford Rd. Ger X —2D 13
Oxford Rd. High W —1A 12
Oxford Rd. Mar —3A 12
Oxford Rd. Stok —1A 12
Oxford St. W1 —4F 15
Oxford St. High W —1B 12
Oxford St. Lee C —2C 4
Oxgate La. NW2 —3E 15
Oxhey. —1B 14
Oxhey Dri. N'wd & Wat —1B 14
Oxhey La. Wat & Pinn —1B 14
Oxhey Rd. Wat —1B 14
Oxlease. —1E 7
Oxlease Dri. Hat —2E 7
Oxlow La. Dag —3E 17
Oxshott. —1C 30
Oxshott Rd. Lea —2C 30
Oxted. —3C 32
Oxted Rd. God —4B 32
Oyster La. Byfl —1F 29

Pachesham Park. —2C 30
Packet Boat La. Uxb —4F 13
Packhorse La. Ridge —3D 7
Packhorse Rd. Ger X —2E 13
Paddenswick Rd. W6 —1E 23
Paddington. —4F 15
Paddlesworth. —1D 35
Paddlesworth Rd. Snod —1D 35
Paddocks, The. Wemb —3D 15
Padham's Green. —4C 10
Padham's Grn. Rd. Ing —4C 10
Page Heath La. Brom —3C 24
Pages La. N10 —2F 15
Page St. NW7 —2E 15
Paines La. Pinn —2B 14
Pains Hill. —4C 32
Painshill. (Junct.) —1A 30
Pains Hill. Oxt —4C 32
Painters Rd. Ilf —2E 17
Palace Av. Maid —3F 35
Palace Gdns. Ter. W8 —4E 15
Palace Ga. W8 —1F 23
Palace Gates Rd. N22 —2F 15
Palermo Rd. NW10 —4E 15
Paley Street. —1B 20
Paley St. M'head —1B 20
Pall Mall. SW1 —4F 15
Palmers Av. Grays —1C 26
Palmers Green. —1A 16
Palmers Hill. Epp —3E 9
Palmerston Rd. E17 —2B 16
Palmerston Rd. N22 —2A 16
Palmerston Rd. Buck H —1C 16
Pampisford Rd. Purl & S Croy —1A 32
Pancake La. Hem H —2A 6
Pancras Rd. NW1 —4F 15
Pan La. E Han —3F 11
Panshanger Dri. Wel G —1E 7
Papercourt La. Rip —2F 29
Parade, The. Bour E —3B 12
Paradise Rd. Rich —2D 23
Paradise Wildlife Park. —2A 8
Parchmore Rd. T Hth —3A 24
Paringdon Rd. H'low —2D 9
Parish La. SE20 —3B 24
Parish La. Farn C —3D 13
Park Av. N22 —2A 16
Park Av. Bush —4B 6
Park Av. Chelm —2D 11
Park Av. Enf —1A 16
Park Av. S'hall —1B 22
Park Barn. —4D 29
Park Corner Rd. S'fleet —3B 26
Park Cres. W1 —4F 15
Parker's Farm Rd. Ors —3C 18
Parker's Green. —4B 34
Parker's Hill. Asht —2D 31
Park Farm Rd. Upm —3A 18
Park Fields. Roch —3E 27
Parkfields. Wel G —1E 7
Parkgate Rd. SW11 —1F 23
Parkgate Rd. Orp —4F 25
Parkgate Rd. Wall —4F 23
Park Hall Rd. SE21 —2A 24
Park Hill. Cars —1F 31
Park Hill. Meop —3C 26
Park Hill Rd. NW3 —3F 15
Parkhill Rd. Bex —2E 25
Pk. Hill Rd. Croy —4A 24
Parkhurst Rd. N7 —3A 16
Parklands. Wal A —3C 8
Park La. W1 —4F 15
Park La. Asht —2D 31
Park La. Beac —2D 13
Park La. Bou M —4F 35
Park La. Brox —2B 8
Park La. Cars —4F 23
Park La. Chesh —2A 8
Park La. Croy —4A 24
Park La. Guild —4F 29
Park La. Hare —2F 13
Park La. Hay —4A 14
Park La. Horn —2F 17
Park La. Houn —1B 22
Park La. L End —1A 12
Park La. Rams H —1E 19
Park La. Reig —4E 31
Park La. Sev —2A 34
Park La. Slou —3D 13
Park La. Wemb —3D 15
Park La. E. Reig —4E 31
Park La. Paradise. Chesh —2B 8
Park Langley. —3C 24
Parkpale La. Brock —4D 31
Park Pde. NW10 —4D 15
Park Rd. N8 —2F 15
Park Rd. N12 —1F 15
Park Rd. N18 —1B 16
Park Rd. NW1 —4F 15
Park Rd. NW4 —3E 15
Park Rd. SE25 —3A 24
Park Rd. Alb —4A 30
Park Rd. Bans —2F 31
Park Rd. Brack —3B 20
Park Rd. Camb —2B 28
Park Rd. Che —3D 5
Park Rd. Chst —3D 25
Park Rd. Crow —4C 32
Park Rd. Dart —2A 26
Park Rd. E Peck —3D 35
Park Rd. Farn —3B 28
Park Rd. Hdlw —3C 34
Park Rd. Hamp H —3B 22
Park Rd. Hamp W —3C 22
Park Rd. Kenl —2A 32
Park Rd. King T —3D 23
Park Rd. Leyb —2D 35
Park Rd. Rad —4C 6
Park Rd. Rick —1A 14
Park Rd. Slou —4D 13
Park Rd. Stai —2F 21
Park Rd. Sun —3B 22
Park Rd. Tedd —3C 22
Park Rd. Tring —1C 4
Park Rd. Uxb —3A 14
Park Rd. Warl —1C 32
Park Rd. W Mal —2C 34
Park Royal. —4D 15
Park Royal Junction. (Junct.) —4D 15
Park Royal Rd. NW10 —4D 15
Parkside. SW19 —2E 23
Parkside. Mat T —1F 9 (off Rainbow Rd.)
Parkside Av. Bexh —1F 25
Parkside Av. Til —1C 26
Parkside Gdns. Barn —1F 15
Parkside Way. Harr —2B 14
Park Street. —2C 6
Park St. SW8 —1A 24
Park St. W1 —4F 15
Park St. Camb —1B 28
Park St. Coln —1F 21
Park St. St Alb —2C 6
Park St. La. Park —3B 6
Park View Rd. N17 —2B 16
Park View Rd. Uxb —4A 14
Park View Rd. Well —2E 25
Parkway. NW1 —4F 15
Parkway. Chelm —2E 11
Parkway. Guild —4E 29
Parkway. New Ad —1C 32
Park Way. Ruis —3B 14
Parkway. Wel G —1E 7
Parkway, The. Houn —1B 22
Parkway, The. S'hall & Hay —1B 22
Park Wood. —4F 35
Parlaunt Rd. Slou & Iver —1E 21
Parley Dri. Wok —2E 29
Parliament La. Burn —3C 12
Parnall Rd. H'low —1D 9
Parnell Rd. E3 —4B 16 (in two parts)
Parrock Rd. Grav —2C 26
Parrock St. Grav —2C 26
Parrott's La. C'bry & Buck C —2C 4
Parsloe Rd. Epp G & H'low —2D 9
Parsloes Av. Dag —3E 17
Parslow's Hillock. —3A 4
Parsonage Green. —1E 11
Parsonage La. Enf —4A 8
Parsonage La. Marg —3D 11
Parsonage La. Sidc —3E 25
Parsonage La. Slou —3D 13
Parsonage La. Wind —1D 21
Parsonage Manorway. Belv —1E 25
Parsonage Rd. Egh —3E 21
Parsons Green. —1E 23
Parson's Grn. La. SW6 —1E 23
Parsons La. Dart —2F 25
Parsons Mead. Croy —4A 24
Parson St. NW4 —2E 15
Partingdale La. NW7 —1E 15
Partridge Av. Chelm —1D 11
Partridge Green. —1D 11
Partridge Rd. H'low —1D 9
Parvilles. —1F 9
Parvis Rd. W Byf —1F 29
Paslow Wood Common. —3B 10
Passingford Bridge. —4F 9
Passmores. —1D 9
Pastures, The. High W —1A 12
Patchetts Green. —4C 6
Patching Hall La. Chelm —1D 11
Paternoster Hill. Wal A —3C 8
Patmos Rd. SW9 —1A 24
Pattens La. Roch —4F 27
Pauls Hill. Penn —1C 12
Paul St. EC1 —4A 16
Pawsons Rd. Croy —4A 24
Peach St. Wokgm —3A 20
Peacock La. Wokgm & Brack —4A 20
Peakes La. Chesh —3A 8
Peakes Way. Chesh —3A 8
Pea La. Upm —3B 18
Peartree. —1E 7
Peartree Green. —4B 10
Peartree La. Dan —3F 11
Pear Tree La. H'std —4F 27
Peartree La. Shorne & High —3D 27
Peartree La. Wel G —1E 7
Peasbody Rd. Farn —3B 28
Peascod St. Wind —1D 21
Peascroft Rd. Hem H —2A 6
Pease Hill. As —1B 34
Pebble Hill Rd. Bet —4D 31
Peckham. —1B 24
Peckham Bush. —4C 34
Peckham High St. SE15 —1B 24
Peckham Hill St. SE15 —1B 24
Peckham Hurst Rd. W Peck —3C 34
Peckham Pk. Rd. SE15 —1B 24
Peckham Rd. SE5 & SE15 —1A 24
Peckham Rye. SE22 —2B 24 (in two parts)
Peck's Hill. Naze —2C 8
Pedlars End. —2F 9
Pednor Bottom. Chart —3C 4
Pednormead End. —3D 5
Pednor Rd. Che —3C 4
Peeble Hill. Lea —4A 30
Peens La. Bou M —4F 35
Pegmire La. Ald —4C 6
Pegs La. Hert —1A 8
Pelham Rd. Grav —2C 26
Pelham Rd. S. Grav —2C 26
Pelham St. SW7 —1F 23
Pells La. W King —1B 34
Pembridge La. Brox —2A 8
Pembridge Rd. W11 —4E 15
Pembridge Vs. W11 & W2 —4E 15
Pembroke B'way. Camb —1B 28
Pembroke Rd. W8 —1E 23
Pembroke Rd. Chat —3F 27
Pembroke Rd. Eri —1F 25
Pembroke Rd. Ruis —3A 14
Pembroke Rd. Sev —3F 33
Pembroke Rd. Wemb —3C 14
Pembury Rd. E8 —3B 16
Pendell Rd. Blet —4A 32
Pendleton Rd. Reig —4F 31
Penenden Heath. —2F 35
Penenden Heath Rd. Maid —2F 35
Penfold La. Holm G & L Mis —4C 4
Penge. —3B 24
Penge Rd. SE25 & SE20 —3B 24
Penhill Rd. Bex —2E 25
Penn. —1C 12
Penn Bottom. Penn —1C 12
Penn Rd. Beac —1C 12
Penn Rd. Hasl —1B 12
Penn Rd. Knot —1C 12
Penn St. —4C 4
Penn St. Amer —1C 12
Penny Pot. —1D 29
Pennypot La. Chob —1D 29
Penny Royal Rd. Dan —2F 11
Penrhyn Rd. King T —3D 23
Penton St. N1 —4A 16
Pentonville Rd. N1 —4A 16
Penwith Rd. SW18 —2E 23
Pepper Hill. Gt Amw —1B 8
Pepper's Green. —1C 10
Pepys Rd. SE14 —1B 24
Percival St. EC1 —4A 16
Percy Rd. N21 —1A 16
Percy Rd. Hamp —3B 22
Percy Rd. Twic —2B 22
Perivale. —4C 14
Perks La. P'wd —4B 4
Perry Hall Rd. Orp —4D 25
Perry Hill. SE23 —2B 24
Perry Hill. Cli —2F 27
Perry Hill. Worp —3D 29
Perry Rise. SE23 —2B 24
Perrys La. Prat B —1E 33
Perry Street. —2C 26
Perry St. Bill —1D 19
Perry St. Chst —3D 25
Perry St. Dart —2F 25
Perry St. N'fleet —2C 26
Perry Vale. SE23 —2B 24
Perth Rd. N22 —2A 16
Perth Rd. Ilf —2D 17
Pested Bars Rd. Bou M —3F 35
Peterborough Rd. Harr —3C 14
Peterley. Gt Miss —4B 4
Petersfield Av. Romf —2A 18
Petersham. —2D 23
Petersham Rd. Rich —2C 22
Peters La. Mon R —3A 4
Petherton Rd. N5 —3A 16
Pettings. —1B 34
Pettits La. Dodd —4B 10
Pettits La. Romf —2F 17
Pettits La. N. Romf —2F 17
Pettman Cres. SE28 —1D 25
Pett's Hill. N'holt —3B 14
Petts Wood. —4D 25
Petts Wood Rd. Orp —4D 25
Pheasant Hill. Chal G —1E 13
Pheasant La. Maid —3F 35
Philanthropic Rd. Red —4F 31
Philip La. N15 —2A 16
Philpot La. Chob —1E 29
Philpots La. Leigh —4F 33
Phipps Hatch La. Enf —4A 8
Picardy Manorway. Belv —1E 25
Picardy Rd. Belv —1E 25
Picardy St. Belv —1E 25
Piccadilly. W1 —4F 15
Piccotts End. —1F 5
Piccotts End. Hem H —1F 5
Piccotts End Rd. Hem H —1F 5
Pickford La. Bexh —1E 25
Pickhurst La. W Wick & Brom —4C 24
Pield Heath Rd. Uxb —4A 14
Pierce Mill Rd. Hdlw —4C 34
Piercing Hill. They B —4D 9
Pier Rd. E16 —1D 25
Pier Rd. Gill —3F 27
Pigeonhouse La. Wink —2C 20
Piggott's Hill. N Dean —4A 4
Pigstye Green. —2B 10
Pigstye Grn. Rd. Will —2B 10
Pike Fish La. Pad W & Ladd —4D 35
Pike La. Upm —3A 18
Pikey La. E Mal —2D 35
Pilgrims Hatch. —1B 18
Pilgrims La. N Stif —4B 18
Pilgrims La. T'sey & W'ham —3C 32
Pilgrims Way. Ayle —1E 35
Pilgrims Way. Boxl —2F 35
Pilgrims Way. Cux —1D 35
Pilgrims Way. Guild —4E 29
Pilgrims Way. Sev —2B 34
Pilgrims Way. Sund & Sev —2A 34
Pilgrims Way. Tros —1C 34
Pilgrims Way. W'ham & Sev —3D 33
Pilgrims Way E. Otf —2F 33
Pilgrims Way W. Sev & Otf —2F 33
Pillar Box Rd. Sev —2A 34
Pimlico. —2A 6 **(nr. Bedmond)**
Pimlico. —1F 23 **(nr. Westminster)**
Pimlico Rd. SW1 —1F 23
Pinesfield La. Tros —1C 34
Pines Rd. Brom —3D 25
Pine Tree La. Ivy H —3B 34
Pinewood Rd. Iver —3E 13
Pinkham Way. N11 —2F 15
Pink Hill. Par H —3A 4
Pink La. Burn —4C 12
Pinkneys Dri. M'head —4A 12
Pinkneys Green. —4A 12
Pinkneys Rd. M'head —4B 12
Pink Rd. Lac G —3A 4
Pinnacles. —1D 9
Pinner. —2B 14
Pinner Green. —2B 14
Pinner Grn. Pinn —2B 14
Pinner Hill Rd. Pinn —2B 14
Pinner Rd. Harr —2B 14
Pinner Rd. N'wd —2A 14
Pinner Rd. Pinn —2B 14
Pinner Rd. Wat —1B 14
Pinner View. Harr —2C 14
Pinnerwood Park. —2B 14
Piper's Hill. Gt Gad —1F 5
Pipers La. Gt Kin —4B 4
Pipers La. Hpdn —1C 6
Pipps Hill. —2D 19
Pipps Hill Rd. N. Cray H —2E 19
Pirbright. —2D 29
Pirbright Camp. —2C 28
Pirbright Grn. Wok —3D 29
Pirbright Rd. Norm —4C 28
Pitch Place. —3D 29
Pitfield St. EC1 —4A 16
Pitsea. —3E 19
Pitsea Hall La. Pits —3E 19
Pitsea Rd. Pits —2E 19
Pitshanger La. W5 —4C 14
Pittswood. —4B 34
Pix Farm La. Hem H —2E 5
Pixham. —4C 30
Pixham La. Dork —4C 30
Pizien Well. —3D 35
Pizien Well Rd. W'bury —3D 35
Place Farm La. Dodd —4B 10
Place Farm Rd. Blet —4A 32
Placehouse La. Coul —2A 32
Plain, The. Epp —3E 9
Plaistow. —3C 24 **(nr. Bromley)**
Plaistow. —4C 16 **(nr. West Ham)**
Plaistow La. Brom —3C 24 (in two parts)
Plaistow Rd. E15 —4C 16

Plantagenet Rd.—Rye La.

Plantagenet Rd. Barn —4F 7
Plantation Rd. Amer —4D 5
Plantation Rd. Bore —1F 11
Plashet. —3C 16
Plashet Gro. E6 —4C 16
Plashet Rd. E13 —4C 16
Platt Ho. La. Fair —1C 34
Platts La. NW3 —3E 15
Plaxdale Grn. Rd. Stans —1B 34
Plaxtol. —3B 34
Plaxtol La. Plax —3B 34
Pleasure Pit Rd. Asht —2D 31
Plevna Rd. N9 —1B 16
Plomer Grn. La. D'ley —1A 12
Plomer Hill. High W —1A 12
Plough Hill. Cuff —3A 8
Plough Hill. Igh —3B 34
Plough La. SW19 & SW17 —3F 23
Plough La. D'side —2B 30
Plough La. Purl —1A 32
Plough La. Sarr —3F 5
Plough La. Stoke P —4E 13
Plough La. Wall —4A 24
Plough La. Wokgm —3A 20
Plough Rd. SW11 —2F 23
Plough Way. SE16 —1B 24
Ployters Rd. H'low —2D 9
Plug La. Meop —4C 26
Plumstead. —1D 25
Plumstead Common. —1D 25
Plumstead Comn. Rd. SE18 —1D 25
Plumstead High St. SE18 —1D 25
Plumstead Rd. SE18 —1D 25
Pococks La. Eton —1D 21
Pointers Green. —2A 30
Polehanger La. Hem H —1F 5
Pole Hill Rd. Uxb —4A 14
Polesden Lacey. —3B 30
Polesden La. Wok —3F 29
Poles Hill. Sarr —3F 5
Polesteeple Hill. Big H —2C 32
Polhill. Hals —2F 33
Polish War Memorial. (Junct.) —3B 14
Pollard Rd. N20 —1F 15
Pollards Wood Hill. Oxt —3C 32
Pollards Wood Rd. Oxt —4C 32
Polsted La. Comp —4D 29
Pomeroy St. SE15 —1B 24
Pond App. Holm G —4C 4
Ponders End. —1B 16
Pondfield La. Brtwd —1B 18
Pond La. Ivy H —3A 34
Pond Park. —3D 5
Pond Pk. Rd. Che —3D 5
Ponds Rd. Chelm —3E 11
Pond St. NW3 —3F 15
Pondtail. —3A 28
Pont St. SW1 —1F 23
Poole St. N1 —4A 16
Pooley Green. —3F 21
Pooley Grn. Rd. Egh —3E 21
Pool Rd. W Mol —4B 22
Pootings. —4D 33
Pootings Rd. Four E —4D 33
Popes La. W5 —1C 22
Popes La. Cook —3B 12
Popes La. Oxt —4C 32
Popeswood. —3A 20
Popeswood Rd. Binf —3A 20
Poplar. —4B 16
Poplar High St. E14 —4B 16
Poplar Way. Felt —2B 22
Porchester Rd. W2 —4E 15
Porlock Av. Harr —3C 14
Porters Av. Dag —3E 17
Porters Way. W Dray —1A 22
Port Hill. Hert —1A 8
Port Hill. Prat B —1E 33
Portland Pl. W1 —4F 15
Portland Rd. SE25 —3B 24
Portman Sq. W1 —4F 15
Portnalls Rd. Coul —2F 31
Portsmouth Rd. Esh —1B 30
Portsmouth Rd. Frim & Camb —2B 28
Portsmouth Rd. Guild —4E 29
Portsmouth Rd. King T —3C 22
Portsmouth Rd. Rip & Cobh —2F 29
Portsmouth Rd. Th Dit, Surb & King T —4C 22
Portsmouth Rd. Wok —3F 29
Portway. E15 —4C 16
Potash La. Platt —2C 34
Potash Rd. Bill —4D 11
Potash Rd. Mat G —1F 9
Potkiln La. Jor —2D 13
Potley Hill Rd. B'water —1A 28
Potten End. —1F 5
Potten End Hill. Wat E —1F 5
Potter Row. Gt Miss —3B 4
Potters Bar. —3E 7
Potters Crouch. —2B 6
Potterscrouch La. Pot C —2B 6
Potters La. Borwd —4D 7
Potters La. Send —3E 29
Potter's Rd. Barn —4E 7
Potter Street. —1E 9
Potter St. H'low —1E 9
Potter St. N'wd & Pinn —2B 14
Pouchen End. —2F 5
Pouchen End La. Hem H —2F 5
Pound Farm La. Ash —4C 28
Pound La. NW10 —3E 15
Pound La. Eps —1D 31
Pound La. Knock —2E 33
Pound La. Pits & N Ben —2F 19
Pound La. W'sham —1C 28
Pound Rd. E Peck —4D 35
Pound St. Cars —4F 23
Pound St. Wen —2B 4
Pound, The. Cook —3B 12
Poverest. —4E 25
Poverest Rd. Orp —4D 25
Powder Mill La. Twic —2B 22
Powder Mills. —4A 34
Powerscroft Rd. E5 —3B 16
Powys La. N13 & N14 —1A 16
Poyle. —1F 21
Poyle La. Burn —4C 12
Poyle Rd. Coln —2F 21
Poyle Rd. Tong —4B 28
Poynders Rd. SW4 —2F 23
Praed St. W2 —4F 15
Pratling Street. —2E 35
Pratling St. Ayle —2E 35
Pratt's Bottom. —1E 33
Pratt's Bottom. (Junct.) —1E 33
Pratts Farm La. L Walt —1E 11
(in two parts)
Pratt St. NW1 —4F 15
Prebendal Av. Ayl —1A 4
Prebend St. N1 —4A 16
Preston. —3D 15
Preston Hill. Harr —3D 15
Preston La. Tad —2E 31
Preston Rd. Harr & Wemb —3D 15
Prestons Rd. Brom —4C 24
Prestwick Rd. Wat —1B 14
Prestwood. —3B 4
Pretoria Rd. N17 & N18 —2A 16
Pretoria Rd. N. N18 —2A 16
Prey Heath Rd. Wok —3E 29
Prices La. Reig —4E 31
Priestfield. Roch —4E 27
Priest Hill. Egh & Wind —2E 21
Priestley Rd. Sur R —4D 29
Priests Bri. SW14 & SW15 —2D 23
Priests La. Brtwd —1B 18
Priestwood. —3B 20
(nr. Bracknell)
Priestwood. —4C 26
(nr. Meopham Green)
Priestwood Green. —4C 26
Priestwood Rd. Meop —1C 34
Primrose Hill. K Lan —3A 6
Primrose Hill. Wid E —4B 4
Primrose Hill. —4F 15
Primrose Hill Rd. NW3 —3F 15
Prince Albert Rd. NW8 & NW1 —4F 15
Prince Arthur Rd. Gill —3F 27
Prince Charles Av. Chat —1F 35
Prince Charles Av. Ors —4C 18
Prince Charles Rd. SE3 —1C 24
Prince George Av. N14 —1F 15
Prince Imperial Rd. Chst —3D 25
Prince of Wales Dri. SW11 —1F 23
Prince of Wales Rd. NW5 —3F 15
Prince of Wales Rd. SE3 —1C 24
Prince of Wales Rd. Out —4A 32
Prince Regent La. E13 & E16 —4C 16
Prince's Av. Alder —3B 28
Princes Av. Chat —1F 35
Princes Park. —1F 35
Princes Risborough. —3A 4
Prince's Rd. Brtwd —4A 10
Princes Rd. Chelm —2E 11
Princes Rd. Dart —2F 25
Princes Road Interchange. (Junct.) —2A 26
Princess Margaret Rd. Linf & E Til —1D 27
Princess Way. Red —4F 31
Printinghouse La. Hay —1A 22
Prior Rd. Camb —1B 28
Priorsfield Rd. Comp —4D 29
Priory La. SW15 —2D 23
Priory La. Warf —3B 20
Priory Rd. N8 —2F 15
Priory Rd. NW6 —4E 15
Priory Rd. Burn —4C 12
Priory Rd. Roch —3E 27
Priory Rd. S'dale —3B 20
Priory Rd. Sutt —4E 23
Pritchard's Rd. E2 —4B 16
Prospect Av. Farn —2B 28
Prospect Hill. E17 —2B 16
Prospect Rd. Ash V —3B 28
Prospect Rd. Farn —3B 28
Prospect Rd. St Alb —2C 6
Prune Hill. Egh —3E 21
Pudding La. Chig —1D 17
Puddledock. —4E 33
Puddledock La. Dart —3F 25
Puddledock La. W'ham —4D 33
Pudds Cross. —3E 5
Pumpkin Hill. Slou —3D 13
Pump La. Hay —1B 22
Pump La. Spri —1E 11
Pump La. N. Mar —2A 12
Pump St. Horn H —4D 19
Punchbowl La. Dork —4C 30
Punch Bowl La. Hem H & St Alb —1A 6
Purfleet. —1A 26
Purfleet By-Pass. Purf —1A 26
Purfleet Rd. Ave —1A 26
Purley. —1A 32
Purley Cross. (Junct.) —1A 32
Purley Downs Rd. Purl & S Croy —1A 32
Purley Way. Croy & Kenl —4A 24
Pursley Rd. NW7 —2E 15
Purton La. Farn R —3D 13
Putney. —2E 23
Putney Bri. SW15 & SW6 —2E 23
Putney Bri. Rd. SW15 & SW18 —2E 23
Putney Heath. —2E 23
Putney Heath. SW15 —2E 23
Putney High St. SW15 —2E 23
Putney Hill. SW15 —2E 23
Puttenden Rd. S'brne —4B 34
Puttenham. —4C 28
Puttenham Heath Rd. Putt —4C 28
Puttenham Hill. Putt —4C 28
Puttenham Rd. Seale —4B 28
Pye Corner. —1D 9
Pyenest Rd. H'low —1D 9
Pyestock. —3A 28
Pyle Hill. —3E 29
Pynest Grn. La. Wal A —4C 8
Pyrcroft Rd. Cher —4F 21
Pyrford. —2F 29
Pyrford Comn. Rd. Wok —2F 29
Pyrford Green. —2F 29
Pyrford Rd. W Byf & Wok —1F 29
Pyrford Village. —2F 29
Pyrles La. Lou —4D 9

Quadrant, The. Rich —2D 23
Quaker La. Wal A —3C 8
Quakers Hall La. Sev —2F 33
Quarries, The. Bou M —4F 35
Quarry Hill Rd. Bor G —2B 34
Quarry St. Guild —4E 29
Quarry St. Guild —4E 29
Quarry Wood Rd. Mar & Cook D —3A 12
Quebec House. —3D 33
Queen Alexandra Rd. High W —1B 12
Queen Anne Av. Brom —3C 24
Queen Elizabeth Rd. King T —3D 23
Queen's Av. Alder —4B 28
Queen's Av. Wat —1A 14
Queensbridge Rd. E8 & E2 —3A 16
Queensbury. —2D 15
Queen's Club. —1E 23
Queens Dri. W3 —4D 15
Queens Farm Rd. Shorne —2D 27
Queens Ga. SW7 —1F 23
Queens Mead Rd. Brom —3C 24
Queen's Pk. —4D 11
Queens Pk. Av. Bill —4D 11
Queens Park Rangers F.C. —4E 15
Queens Ride. SW13 & SW15 —2E 23
Queens Rd. E17 —2B 16
Queens Rd. NW4 —2E 15
Queens Rd. SE15 & SE14 —1B 24
Queens Rd. SW19 —3E 23
Queen's Rd. Alder —4A 28
Queens Rd. Bisl —2D 29
Queens Rd. Brtwd —1B 18
Queens Rd. Buck H —1C 16
Queens Rd. Croy —4A 24
Queen's Rd. Dat —1E 21
Queens Rd. Eri —1F 25
Queen's Rd. Farn —3B 28
Queen's Rd. King T —3D 23
Queen's Rd. Maid —3E 35
Queen's Rd. Rich —2D 23
Queen's Rd. Tedd —3C 22
Queens Rd. Wat —4B 6
Queens Rd. Wey & W on T —4A 22
Queenstown Rd. SW8 —1F 23
Queen St. Gom —4A 30
Queen St. M'head —4B 12
Queensway. W2 —4E 15
Queensway. Hat —1E 7
Queensway. Hem H —2F 5
Queensway. Orp —4D 25
Queen Victoria. (Junct.) —4E 23
Queen Victoria St. EC4 —4A 16
Quex Rd. NW6 —4E 15
Quickley La. Rick —1F 13
Quickmoor La. K Lan —3F 5
Quinta Dri. Barn —1E 15

Rabbits Rd. S Dar —3A 26
Rabies Heath Rd. Blet —4A 32
Rabley. —3D 7
Rackstraw Rd. Camb —1A 28
Radford Way. Bill —1D 19
Radlett. —3C 6
Radlett La. Shenl —3C 6
Radlett Rd. Ald —4B 6
Radlett Rd. Frog —3C 6
Radlett Rd. Wat —4B 6
Radley Green. —2C 10
Radley Grn. Rd. Rox —2B 10
Radwater Av. W'fd —1F 19
Raeburn Av. Surb —4D 23
RAF Halton Airfield. —1B 4
RAF Northolt Airfield. —3A 14
Ragged Hall La. St Alb —2B 6
Rag Hill Rd. Tats —2C 32
Raglan Rd. Reig —4E 31
Ragmans La. Mar —2A 12
Rags La. Chesh —3A 8
Ragstone Rd. Slou —1D 21
Raikes La. Ab H —4B 30
Railton Rd. SW2 —2A 24
Railway App. Cher —4F 21
Railway App. Harr —2C 14
Railway St. Chat —4F 27
Railway St. Gill —3F 27
Railway Ter. K Lan —3A 6
Rainbow La. Stan H —4D 19
Rainham. —4F 17
Rainham Hall. —4F 17
Rainham Rd. Gill —4F 27
Rainham Rd. Horn & Rain —3F 17
Rainham Rd. N. Dag —3E 17
Rainham Rd. S. Dag —3F 17
Rainsford La. Chelm —2D 11
Rainsford Rd. Chelm —2D 11
Ralph's Ride. Brack —3B 20
Ramsden. —4E 25
Ramsden Bellhouse. —1E 19
Ramsden Heath. —1E 19
Ramsden Pk. Rd. Bill —1E 19
Ram St. SW18 —2E 23
Rances La. Wokgm —3A 20
Rancliffe Rd. E6 —4D 17
Randalls Rd. Lea —2C 30
Randles La. Sev —2E 33
Ranger's Rd. E4 & Lou —1C 16
Ranmore Common. —4C 30
Ranmore Comn. Rd. Westh —4B 30
Ranmore Rd. Dork —4C 30
Ratcliffe Highway. Chatt —2F 27
Ravensbourne Pk. SE6 —2B 24
Ravenscourt Gro. Horn —3A 18
Ravens La. Berk —2E 5
Ravensworth Rd. W Wick —4C 24
Rawlings La. Seer —1D 13
Rawreth. —1F 19
Rawreth La. Raw —1F 19
Rawreth Shot. —1F 19
Rayleigh Rd. Hut —1B 18
Rayley La. N Wea —2E 9
Ray Mead Rd. M'head —4C 12
Ray Mill Rd. E. M'head —4B 12
Ray Mill Rd. W. M'head —4B 12
Raymouth Rd. SE16 —1B 24
Rayners Lane. —3B 14
Rayners La. Pinn —2B 14
Raynes Park. —3E 23
Ray Pk. Av. M'head —4B 12
Ray Pk. Rd. M'head —4B 12
Ray's Hill. Braz E —2C 4
Rays Hill. Hort K —3A 26
Ray St. M'head —4B 12
Reading Rd. Farn —3B 28
Reading Rd. S. Fleet —3A 28
Rectory Hill. Amer —4D 5
Rectory La. SW17 —3F 23
Rectory La. Asht —2D 31
Rectory La. Bans —2F 31
Rectory La. Barm —3E 35
Rectory La. Bookh —3B 30
Rectory La. Brack —4B 20
Rectory La. Bras —3E 33
Rectory La. Byfl —1A 30
Rectory La. Chelm —2E 11
Rectory La. Igh —2B 34
Rectory La. K Lan —3A 6
Rectory La. Lou —4D 9
Rectory La. Shenl —3D 7
Rectory La. Sidc —3E 25
Rectory La. Surb —4C 22
Rectory La. W'ham —3D 33
Rectory Pk. S Croy —1A 32
Rectory Rd. N16 —3A 16
Rectory Rd. As —4B 26
Rectory Rd. Beck —3B 24
Rectory Rd. Cli —2E 27
Rectory Rd. Coul —3F 31
Rectory Rd. Farn —3B 28
Rectory Rd. Grays —1C 26
Rectory Rd. L Bur —2D 19
Rectory Rd. Ors —4C 18
Rectory Rd. Pits —2F 19
(in three parts)
Rectory Rd. Rick —1F 13
Rectory Rd. Tap —4C 12
Rectory Rd. W Til —1C 26
Rectory Rd. Wokgm —3A 20
Redan Rd. Alder —4B 28
Redbourn. —1B 6
Redbourn La. Hpdn —1B 6
Redbourn Rd. Hem H —1A 6
Redbourn Rd. St Alb —1B 6
Redbridge. —2D 17
Redbridge La. E. Ilf —2D 17
Redbridge La. W. E11 —2C 16
Redbridge Roundabout. (Junct.) —2C 16
Redcliffe Gdns. SW10 —1E 23
Rede Ct. Rd. Strood —3E 27
Redhall La. Chan X —4A 6
Redhill. —4F 31
(nr. Reigate)
Red Hill. —3D 35
(nr. Wateringbury)
Red Hill. Chst —3D 25
Red Hill. W'bury —3D 35
Redhill Aerodrome. —4A 32
Redhill Rd. Cobh —1A 30
Redhill Rd. New Ash —4B 26
Redland End. —3A 4
Red La. Clay —1C 30
Red La. Oxt —4C 32
Red Lion La. SE18 —1D 25
Red Lion La. Sarr —4F 5
Red Lion Rd. Chob —1D 29
Red Lion Rd. Surb —4D 23
Red Lion St. WC1 —4A 16
Red Lion St. Che —3D 5
Red Lion St. Rich —2C 22
Red Lodge Rd. W Wick —4C 24
Redmans La. Sev —1F 33
Red Post Hill. SE24 —2A 24
Redricks La. E'wck —1D 9
Redriff Rd. SE16 —1B 24
Red Rd. Light —1C 28
Red Rover. (Junct.) —2D 23
Redstone Hill. Red —4F 31
Redstone Hollow. Red —4F 31
Red St. S'fleet —3B 26
Redvers. Alder —3B 28
Redwall La. Hunt & Lint —4E 35
Redwell La. Igh —3B 34
Reede Rd. Dag —3E 17
Reed's Hill. Brack —4B 20
Reeds La. S'brne —3B 34
Reed St. Cli —1E 27
Reeves La. Roy —2C 8
Regent's Park. —4F 15
Regents Pk. Rd. N3 —2E 15
Regent's Pk. Rd. NW1 —4F 15
Regent St. W1 & SW1 —4F 15
Regina Rd. S'hall —1B 22
Reigate. —4E 31
Reigate Av. Sutt —4E 23
Reigate Hill. Reig —4E 31
Reigate Hill Interchange. (Junct.) —3E 31
Reigate Rd. Dork & Bet —4C 30
Reigate Rd. Eps & Tad —1E 31
Reigate Rd. Lea —3C 30
Reigate Rd. Reig & Red —4F 31
Renfree Rd. Shep —4A 22
Renwick Rd. Bark —4E 17
Replingham Rd. SW18 —2E 23
Repository Rd. SE18 —1D 25
Reservoir Rd. Lou —4C 8
Rettendon. —4F 11
Rettendon Rd. E Han —3F 11
Rhodeswell Rd. E1 —4B 16
Richings Park. —1F 21
Richings Way. Iver —1F 21
Richmond. —2C 22
Richmond Bri. Twic & Rich —2C 22
Richmond Circus. (Junct.) —2D 23
Richmond Hill. Rich —2D 23
Richmond Rd. E8 —3A 16
Richmond Rd. Gill —3F 27
Richmond Rd. Iswth —2C 22
Richmond Rd. King T —3C 22
Richmond Rd. Twic —2C 22
Ricketts Hill Rd. Tats —2C 32
Rickford. Guild —3D 29
Rickmansworth. —1F 13
Rickmansworth La. Chal P —2E 13
Rickmansworth Rd. Amer —4D 5
Rickmansworth Rd. Chor —4F 5
Rickmansworth Rd. Hare —2F 13
Rickmansworth Rd. N'wd —1A 14
Rickmansworth Rd. Pinn —2B 14
Rickmansworth Rd. Wat —4A 6
Riddlesdown. —1A 32
Riddlesdown Rd. Purl —1A 32
Ridge. —3D 7
Ridge Av. N21 —1A 16
Ridge La. Wat —4A 6
Ridgemead Rd. Egh —2E 21
Ridge Rd. N21 —1A 16
Ridge Rd. Sutt —4E 23
Ridge, The. L Bad —2F 11
Ridge, The. Wold & Warl —3B 32
Ridgeway. High W —1B 12
Ridgeway. Wel G —1E 7
Ridgeway Rd. Iswth —1C 22
Ridgeway, The. E4 —1B 16
Ridgeway, The. NW7 —1E 15
Ridgeway, The. Chat —4F 27
Ridgeway, The. Cuff —3F 7
Ridgeway, The. Enf —4A 8
Ridgeway, The. Lea —3C 30
Ridgeway, The. N Har —2B 14
Ridgeway, The. Pot B & Enf —4F 7
Ridgeway, The. Shorne —3D 27
Ridgeway, The. St Alb —1C 6
Ridgeway, The. Tonb —4B 34
Ridgway. —2F 29
Ridgway. SW19 —3E 23
Riding Ct. Rd. Dat —1E 21
Riding La. Hild —4A 34
Ridlands La. Oxt —3C 32
Ridley. —1B 34
Riefield Rd. SE9 —2D 25
Riffhams Chase. L Bad —2F 11
Riffhams La. Dan —2F 11
Rignall Rd. Gt Miss —3B 4
Rignals La. Chelm —3E 11
Ringlestone. —2F 35
Ringmead. Brack —4A 20
Rings Hill. Hild —4A 34
Ring, The. Brack —3B 20
Ripley. —2F 29
Ripley By-Pass. Rip —3F 29
Ripley La. Wok & Lea —3A 30
Ripley Rd. Send & Guild —3F 29
Ripley Springs. —3E 21
Ripon Way. Borwd —1D 15
Ripple Rd. Bark & Dag —4D 17
Ripple Road Junction. (Junct.) —4E 17
Risborough Rd. Stoke M —1A 4
Rise Park. —2F 17
Rise Rd. Asc —4D 21
Rise, The. Gnfd & Wemb —3C 14
River Bank. E Mol —3C 22
Riverhead. —2F 33
River Hill. Sev —3A 34
Riverhill House Gardens. —3A 34
River Rd. Bark —4D 17
Riverside. Eyns —4F 25
Riverside Dri. Rich —2C 22
Riverside Dri. Rick —1F 13
Riverside Rd. Stanw —2F 21
Riverside Wlk. Iswth —2C 22
Riverside Way. Camb —2B 28
River View. Grays —1C 26
Riverview Park. —3D 27
Roberts La. Chal P —1E 13
Robert St. NW1 —4F 15
Robert Way. W'fd —1F 19
Robin Hood. (Junct.) —2D 23
Robin Hood La. Sut G —3E 29
Robin Hood La. W'slde —1F 35
Robin Hood Rd. Wok —2D 29
Robin Hood Way. SW15 & SW20 —2D 23
Robins Nest Hill. L Berk —1F 7
Robinsway. W on T —4B 22
Robson Av. NW10 —4E 15
Robson Rd. SE27 —2A 24
Rocfort Rd. Snod —1E 35
Rochester. —3F 27
Rochester Airport. —4F 27
Rochester Av. Brom —3C 24
Rochester Castle. —3E 27
Rochester Rd. Ayle —2E 35
Rochester Rd. Burh —1E 35
Rochester Rd. Cux —4E 27
(in two parts)
Rochester Rd. Grav —2D 27
Rochester Rd. Roch & Chat —4F 27
Rochester Rd. Woul —4E 27
Rochester Row. SW1 —1F 23
Rochester Way. SE3 & SE9 —2C 24
Rochester Way. Dart —2F 25
Rochester Way Relief Rd. SE3 & SE9 —1C 24
Rock Av. Gill —4F 27
Rockfield Rd. Oxt —3C 32
Rock Hill. Orp —1E 33
Rockingham Rd. Uxb —4F 13
Rock Rd. Bor G —2B 34
Rockshaw Rd. Red —3F 31
Rocks La. SW13 —2E 23
Rocks Rd., The. E Mal —2E 35
Rocky La. Reig —3F 31
Rodborough Rd. NW11 —3E 15
Roding La. Buck H & Chig —1D 17
Roding La. N. Wfd G —2D 17
Roding La. S. Ilf & Wfd G —2C 16
Roding Rd. Lou —1D 17
Rodney Rd. SE17 —1A 24
Roe Green. —1E 7
(nr. Hatfield)
Roe Green. —2D 15
(nr. Hendon)
Roe Grn. NW9 —2D 15
Roehampton. —2E 23
Roehampton High St. SW15 —2E 23
Roehampton Lane. (Junct.) —2E 23
Roehampton La. SW15 —2E 23
Roehampton Vale. SW15 —2D 23
Roehyde Way. Hat —2D 7
Roestock La. Col H —2D 7
Roffe's La. Cat —3A 32
Rogers La. Stoke P —3D 13
Rogers Wood La. Fawk —4B 26
Rokesly Av. N8 —2A 16
Rolls Rd. SE1 —1A 24
Roman Rd. E2 & E3 —4B 16
Roman Rd. Mount —4C 10
Roman Villa Rd. Dart —3A 26
Roman Way. Croy —4A 24
Romford. —2F 17
Romford Rd. E15 & E12 —3C 16
Romford Rd. Ave —4A 18
Romford Rd. Chig —1E 17
Romford Rd. Ong —3A 10
Romford Rd. Romf —2E 17
Romney Rd. SE10 —1C 24
Romney Street. —1A 34
Romney St. Knat —1A 34
Rom Valley Way. Romf —3F 17
Ron Leighton Way. E6 —4D 17
Roodlands La. Four E —4E 33
Rookery Hill. Corr —4E 19
Rookery Rd. B'more —3B 10
Rookery Rd. Orp —1D 33
Rookery, The. —1B 14
Rook La. Cat —3A 32
Roothill Rd. Bet —4D 31
Roper's La. H Hals —2F 27
Rosebay Av. Bill —4D 11
Rosebery Av. EC1 —4A 16
Rosedale. —3B 8
Rosedale Way. Chesh —3B 8
Rosehill. —4F 23
Rose Hill. Burn —4C 12
Rose Hill. Sutt —4E 23
Rose Hill Roundabout. (Junct.) —4F 23
Rose La. Rip —2F 29
Rose La. Romf —2E 17
Rosemary La. B'water —1A 28
Rosemary La. Hods —1C 34
Rosendale Rd. SE24 —2A 24
Rose St. Wokgm —3A 20
Rosherville. —2C 26
Rosslyn Hill. NW3 —3F 15
Rossmore Rd. NW1 —4F 15
Rossway. Berk —2D 5
Rossway La. Wig —1D 5
Rothbury Rd. E9 —3B 16
Rotherhithe. —1B 24
Rotherhithe New Rd. SE1 —1B 24
Roughetts Rd. Rya —2D 35
Roughway. —3B 34
Roughway La. D Grn & Rough —3B 34
Roughwood La. Chal G —1E 13
Round Acre. Bas —2D 19
Round Bush. —4C 6
Round Clo. B'water —1A 28
Roundshaw. —1A 32
Round Street. —3C 26
Round St. Sole S —3C 26
Roundway, The. N17 —2A 16
Roundwood Rd. NW10 —3D 15
Rowan Rd. SW16 —3F 23
Rowdow. Otf —2A 34
Rowdow La. Sev —1F 33
Rowhill. —1F 29
Rowley Green. —4D 7
Rowley Grn. Rd. Barn —1E 15
Rowley La. Borwd & Barn —4D 7
Rowley La. Wex —4E 13
Rowley Rd. Ors —4C 18
Row Town. —1F 29
Rowtown. Add —1F 29
Roxeth. —3C 14
Roxeth Grn. Av. Harr —3B 14
Roxeth Hill. Harr —3C 14
Roxwell. —1C 10
Roxwell Rd. Chelm —1D 11
Royal Air Force Museum. —2D 15
Royal Albert Way. E16 —4C 16
Royal British Legion Village. —2E 35
Royal Docks Rd. E6 & Bark —4D 17
Royal Engineers Museum. —3F 27
Royal Engineers Way. Maid —2F 35
Royal Hill. SE10 —1C 24
Royal Horticultural Society (Wisley) Gardens. —2A 30
Royal Hospital Rd. SW3 —1F 23
Royal La. W Dray & Uxb —4A 14
Royal Mint St. E1 —4A 16
Royal Pde. SE3 —1C 24
Royal Pde. Chst —3D 25
Royal Windsor Racecourse. —1D 21
Roydon. —1C 8
Roydon Hall Rd. E Peck —4D 35
Roydon Hamlet. —2C 8
Roydon Rd. H'low —1D 9
Roydon Rd. Stan A —1C 8
Royds La. Kel H —4A 10
Roystons, The. Surb —4D 23
Ruckholt Rd. E10 —3B 16
Rucklers Lane. —3F 5
Rucklers La. K Lan —3F 5
Ruddlesway. Wind —1C 20
Rugby Rd. Twic —2C 22
Ruislip. —3A 14
Ruislip Common. —2A 14
Ruislip Gardens. —3A 14
Ruislip Manor. —3B 14
Ruislip Rd. N'holt & Gnfd —4B 14
Ruislip Rd. E. UB6 & W13 —4C 14
Runfold. —4B 28
Running Waters. Brtwd —1B 18
Runnymede. —2E 21
Runnymede. —2E 21
Runsell La. Dan —2F 11
Runwell. —1F 19
Runwell Rd. W'fd & Runw —1F 19
Rushbottom La. Ben —2F 19
(in two parts)
Rushett. —4D 33
Rushett La. Chess —1C 30
Rushetts Farm. —4F 31
Rush Green. —3F 17
Rushey Grn. SE6 —2B 24
Rush Grn. Rd. Romf —3F 17
Rushgrove Av. NW9 —2D 15
Rushley. Bas —2F 19
Rushmere La. Orch —3E 5
Rushmoor Arena. —4A 28
Rushmoor Rd. Alder —4A 28
Rushmore Hill. Orp & Sev —1E 33
Rushworth Rd. Reig —4E 31
Ruskin Rd. Cars —4F 23
Russell Gdns. W'fd —1F 19
Russell Green. —1F 11
Russell La. N20 —1F 15
Russell Rd. Enf —4A 8
Russell Rd. Shep —4A 22
Russell St. WC1 —4A 16
Rutts, The. Bush —1C 14
Ruxbury Rd. Cher —4F 21
Ruxley. —3E 25
Ruxley La. Eps —1D 31
Ryarsh. —2D 35
Ryarsh Rd. Birl —1D 35
Rycroft La. Sev —3F 33
Rydens. —4B 22
Rydens Rd. W on T —4B 22
Ryde's Hill. Guild —4D 29
Ryde, The. —1E 7
Rye Gro. Wok —1D 29
Rye Hill. —2D 9
Rye Hill Rd. H'low —2D 9
Rye House Gatehouse. —1C 8
Ryehurst La. Binf —3A 20
Rye La. SE15 —1B 24
Rye La. Dun G & Otf —2F 33

48 A-Z London Motorists Atlas

Rye Park—Spriggs La.

Rye Park. —1B 8
Rye Rd. *Hod* —1B 8

Sabine's Green. —4A 10
Sabine's Rd. *Nave & Brtwd* —4F 9
Saffron Green. —4E 7
St Agnells La. *Hem H* —1A 6
St Albans. —2C 6
St Albans Hill. *Hem H* —2A 6
St Albans La. *Ab L* —2B 6
St Albans Rd. *Barn* —4E 7
St Albans Rd. *Hpdn* —1B 6
St Albans Rd. *Hem H* —2F 5
St Albans Rd. *Redb* —1B 6
St Albans Rd. *Sandr & Pot B* —3D 7
St Albans Rd. *St Alb* —1C 6
St Albans Rd. *Wat* —4B 6
St Albans Rd. E. *Hat* —1E 7
St Albans Rd. W. *Hat* —1D 7
St Andrew's Dri. *Stan* —2C 14
St Andrew's Rd. *Til* —1C 26
St Andrew St. *Hert* —1A 8
St Andrew's Way. *Slou* —4C 12
St Anne's Rd. *Lon C* —3C 6
St Anne's Rd. *Mount* —4C 10
St Ann's Hill. *SW18* —2E 23
St Ann's Hill Rd. *Cher* —4F 21
St Ann's Rd. *N15* —2A 16
St Anns Rd. *Cher* —4F 21
St Asaph Rd. *SE15* —2B 24
St Augustine's Rd. *Belv* —1E 25
St Barnabas Rd. *Sutt* —4F 23
St Barnabas Rd. *Wfd G* —2C 16
St Blaise Av. *Brom* —3C 24
St Botolphs Rd. *Sev* —3F 33
St Bride's Av. *Edgw* —2D 15
St Catherines Rd. *Frim G* —2B 28
St Chads Rd. *Til* —1C 26
St Clements Way. *Grnh* —2B 26
St Clere Hill Rd. *W King* —1A 34
St Cloud Way. *M'head* —4B 12
St Davids Rd. *Swan* —3F 25
St Dunstan's. (Junct.) —1E 31
St Dunstans Av. *W3* —4D 15
St Dunstan's Hill. *Sutt* —1E 31
St Dunstan's Rd. *Felt* —2A 22
St Edith's Rd. *Kems* —2A 34
St Edwards Way. *Romf* —2F 17
St George's Av. *Wey* —1A 30
St George's Dri. *SW1* —1F 23
St George's Hill. —1A 30
St George's Rd. *SE1* —1A 24
St Georges Rd. *Bad L & Runf* —4B 28
St Helens La. *E Far* —3E 35
St Helier. —4F 23
St Helier Av. *Mord* —4F 23
St Hubert's La. *Ger X* —3E 13
St James La. *Grnh* —2A 26
St James Rd. *Chesh* —3A 8
St James's. —4F 15
St James's Dri. *SW17* —2F 23
St James's Rd. *SE1 & SE16* —1B 24
St James's Rd. *Croy* —4A 24
St James's St. *SW1* —4F 15
St James St. *E17* —2B 16
St Johns. —1B 24
(nr. Lewisham)
St John's. —2F 33
(nr. Sevenoaks)
St Johns. —2E 29
(nr. Woking)
St John's Gro. *N19* —3F 15
St John's Hill. *SW11* —2F 23
St John's Hill. *Sev* —2F 33
St John's Hill Rd. *Wok* —2E 29
St John's Jerusalem Garden. —3A 26
St John's Rd. *Farn* —2A 28
St John's Rd. *Harr* —2C 14
St John's Rd. *Hem H* —2F 5
St John's Rd. *Iswth* —1C 22
St John's Rd. *Uxb* —4F 13
St John's Rd. *Wemb* —3D 15
St John's Rd. *Wok* —2E 29
St John St. *EC1* —4A 16
St John's Way. *N19* —3F 15
St John's Wood. —4F 15
St John's Wood Rd. *NW8* —4F 15
St Judes Rd. *Egh* —3E 21
St Julians. —2C 6
St Julians Rd. *Sev* —3A 34
St Katherine's La. *Snod* —1D 35
St Leonards. —2C 4
St Leonards Hamlet. —3F 17
St Leonard's Rd. *Clay* —1C 30
St Leonards Rd. *Naze* —2C 8
St Leonard's Rd. *Th Dit* —4C 22
St Leonard's Rd. *Wind* —2D 21
St Leonard's St. *W Mal* —2D 35
St Luke's Rd. *Old Win* —2E 21
St Margaret's. —1E 5
(nr. Great Gaddesden)
St Margarets. —1C 8
(nr. Hoddesdon)
St Margarets. —2C 22
(nr. Richmond)
St Margarets Rd. *S Dar & Dart* —3A 26
St Margarets Rd. *Twic* —2C 22
St Margarets Roundabout. (Junct.) —2C 22
St Margaret's St. *Roch* —4E 27
St Margaret St. *SW1* —1A 24
St Mark's Cres. *M'head* —4B 12
St Mark's Hill. *Surb* —4D 23
St Mark's Rd. *W10* —4E 15
St Mark's Rd. *Binf* —3A 20
St Marks Rd. *Enf* —1A 16
St Mark's Rd. *M'head* —4B 12
St Marks Rd. *Mitc* —3F 23
St Martins La. *WC2* —4A 16
St Mary Cray. —3E 25
St Mary's Hill. *Asc* —4C 20
St Mary's Island. —3F 27
St Mary's La. *Hert* —1A 8
St Mary's La. *Upm & Brtwd* —3A 18
St Marys Platt. —2C 34
St Mary's Rd. *SW19* —3E 23
St Marys Rd. *W5* —1C 22
St Mary's Rd. *Slou* —4E 13
St Mary's Rd. *Surb* —4C 22
St Mary's Rd. *Wey* —4A 22
St Mary's Way. *Che* —3D 5
St Matthews Rd. *SW2* —2A 24
St Michael's St. *St Alb* —2B 6
St Mildreds Rd. *SE12 & SE6* —2C 24
St Nicholas La. *Bas* —2D 19
St Nicholas Way. *Sutt* —4E 23
St Norbert Rd. *SE4* —2B 24
St Pancras. —4A 16
St Pancras Way. *NW1* —3F 15
St Paul's Av. *NW2* —3E 15
St Paul's Cray. —3E 25
St Paul's Cray Rd. *Chst* —3D 25
St Paul's Rd. *N1* —3A 16
St Pauls Rd. *Bark* —4D 17
St Paul's Way. *E14* —4B 16
St Paul's Wood Hill. *Orp* —3D 25
St Peter's Rd. *Croy* —4A 24
St Peter's St. *St Alb* —2C 6
St Peter St. *Maid* —3F 35
St Peter's Way. *Cher & Add* —4F 21
St Philip's Av. *Maid* —3F 35
St Quintin Av. *W10* —4E 15
St Stephens. —2C 6
St Stephen's Hill. *St Alb* —2C 6
St Thomas' Dri. *Pinn* —2B 14
St Thomas St. *SE1* —1A 24
St Vincents Av. *Dart* —2A 26
St Vincent's Hamlet. —1A 18
St Vincents La. *Adtn* —2C 34
St Vincents Rd. *Dart* —2A 26
St William's Way. *Roch* —4F 27
Salcott Cres. *W'fd* —1F 19
Salisbury Rd. *Wor Pk* —4D 23
Salmon La. *E1* —4B 16
Salmons La. *Whyt* —2A 32
Salmons La. W. *Cat* —2A 32
Salmon St. *NW9* —3D 15
Saltbox Hill. *Big H* —1C 32
Salt Box Rd. *Guild* —3E 29
Salter Rd. *SE16* —1B 24
Salters Hill. *SE19* —3A 24
Salt La. *Cli* —2E 27
Salts La. *Loose* —4F 35
Salusbury Rd. *NW6* —4E 15
Sampleoak La. *Chil* —4F 29
Sandbanks Hill. *Bean* —3B 26
Sandcross La. *Reig* —4E 31
Sanders La. *NW7* —2E 15
Sanderstead. —1B 32
Sanderstead Hill. *S Croy* —1A 32
Sanderstead Rd. *S Croy* —1A 32
Sandford Mill Rd. *Chelm* (in three parts) —2E 11
Sandford Rd. *Chelm* —2E 11
Sandhill La. *High* —2E 27
Sandhills La. *Vir W* —4E 21
Sandhurst. —1A 28
Sandhurst La. *B'water* —1A 28
Sandhurst Rd. *SE6* —2C 24
Sandhurst Rd. *Crowt* —1A 28
Sandhurst Rd. *Finch* —4A 20
Sandhurst Rd. *Sand* —1A 28
Sandling. —2F 35
Sandling La. *S'ing* —2F 35
Sandling Rd. *Maid* —2F 35
(in two parts)
Sandon. —2F 11
Sandown Park Racecourse. —4C 22
Sandpit Hall Rd. *Chob* —1E 29
Sandpit La. *Brtwd & Pil H* —1A 18
Sandpit La. *St Alb & M'wck* —2C 6
Sandpit Rd. *Red* —4F 31
Sandridge. —1C 6
Sandridgebury La. *St Alb* —1C 6
Sandridge Rd. *St Alb* —1C 6
Sandringham Cres. *St Alb* —1C 6
Sandringham Rd. *E8* —3A 16
Sands. —1A 12
Sands End. —1F 23
Sands Rd. *Seale* —4B 28
Sandycombe Rd. *Rich* —2D 23
Sandy Cross. —4B 28
Sandy La. *Ave* —4A 18
Sandy La. *Bean* —2B 26
Sandy La. *Bet* —4D 31
Sandy La. *B'water* —1A 28
Sandy La. *Blet* —4A 32
Sandy La. *Bush* —4C 6
Sandy La. *C Crook* —4A 28
Sandy La. *Cobh & Lea* —1B 30
Sandy La. *Farn* —2A 28
Sandy La. *Guild* —4E 29
Sandy La. *N'wd* —1A 14
Sandy La. *Nutf* —4A 32
Sandy La. *Oxt* —3C 32
Sandy La. *Red* —4A 32
Sandy La. *Rya* —2D 35
Sandy La. *Sev* —3B 34
Sandy La. *Shere* —4A 30
Sandy La. *S Nut* —4A 32
Sandy La. *St M & Sidc* —3E 25
Sandy La. *Sutt* —1E 31
Sandy La. *Tedd & King T* —3C 22
Sandy La. *Wall* —1F 31
Sandy La. *W Mal* —2C 34
Sandy La. N. *Wall* —1F 31
Sandy La. S. *Wall* —1F 31
Sandy Lodge Way. *N'wd* —1A 14
Sanford St. *SE14* —1B 24
Sangley Rd. *SE6* —2B 24
Santers La. *Pot B* —4B 6
Saracens R.U.F.C. —1F 15
Sarratt. —4F 5
Sarratt Bottom. —4F 5
Sarratt La. *Rick* —4F 5
Sarratt Rd. *Rick* —4F 5
Saunders La. *Wok* —2D 29
Savernake Way. *Brack* —4B 20
Savill Garden, The. —3D 21
Sawpit Hill. *Hasl* —4B 4
Sawyers La. *Pot B* —3E 7
Saxbys Rd. *Sev* —2A 34
Scabharbour La. *Hild* —4F 33
Scabharbour Rd. *Weald* —4F 33
Scarborough. —1E 35
Scarborough La. *Burh* —1E 35
Scarletts La. *Kiln G* —1A 20
School Clo. *Bisl* —2D 29
School Hill. *Red* —3F 31
School La. *Ab R* —1A 10
School La. *Add* —4F 21
School La. *Amer* —4D 5
School La. *Bean* —3B 26
School La. *Beau R* —1B 10
School La. *Broom* —1E 11
School La. *Bush* —1B 14
School La. *Fet* —2C 30
School La. *High* —3E 27
School La. *Hort K & Dart* —3A 26
School La. *Knat* —1A 34
School La. *Mar* —2B 12
School La. *Norm* —4C 28
School La. *Ors* —4C 18
School La. *Penn S* —4C 4
School La. *Pirb* —2D 29
School La. *Plax* —3B 34
School La. *Seal* —2A 34
School La. *Seer* —2D 13
School La. *Stock* —4D 11
School La. *Swan* —3F 25
School La. *Tros* —2C 34
School La. *Woul* —4E 27
School La. *W'ton T* —1A 4
School Rd. *Ashf* —3A 22
School Rd. *D'ham* —4E 11
School Rd. *Good E* —1C 10
School Rd. *Kel H* —4A 10
School Rd. *Ong* —3F 9
School Rd. *Penn* —1C 12
School Rd. *Wal L* —2A 20
School Rd. *W'sham* —4C 20
School Road Junction. (Junct.) —3A 22
Scilly Isles. (Junct.) —4C 22
Scotch Comn. *W13* —4C 14
Scotch House. (Junct.) —1F 23
Scotland Bri. Rd. *New Haw* —1F 29
Scotland Grn. Rd. *Enf* —1B 16
Scotshall La. *Warl* —2C 32
Scots Hill. *Rick* —1A 14
Scott's Gro. Rd. *Chob* —1D 29
Scott's La. *Brom* —3C 24
Scratchers La. *Fawk* —4A 26
Scrubbs La. *NW10* —4E 15
Scudders Hill. *Fawk* —4B 26
Seal. —2A 34
Seal Chart. —3A 34
Seale. —4B 28
Seale La. *Putt* —4C 28
Seale La. *Seale* —4B 28
Seal Hollow Rd. *Sev* —3F 33
Seal Rd. *Sev* —2F 33
Second Av. *H'low* —1D 9
Sedge Grn. *Naze* —2C 8
Seer Green. —2D 13
Selhurst. —4A 24
Selhurst Rd. *SE25* —4A 24
Selsdon. —1B 32
Selsdon Pk. Rd. *S Croy & Croy* —1B 32
Selsdon Rd. *S Croy* —4A 24
Selvage La. *NW7* —1D 15
Selwyn Av. *E4* —2C 16
Send. —3F 29
Send Barns La. *Send* —3F 29
Send Hill. *Send* —3F 29
Sendmarsh. —3F 29
Send Marsh Rd. *Wok* —3F 29
Send Rd. *Send* —3F 29
Sergehill La. *Bedm* —2B 6
Seven Arches Rd. *Brtwd* —1B 18
Seven Hills Rd. *Iver* —3E 13
Seven Hills Rd. *W on T & Cob* —1A 30
Seven Kings. —3D 17
Seven Kings Rd. *Ilf* —3D 17
Seven Mile La. *Wro H, Sev & Mere* —2C 34
Sevenoaks. —3F 33
Sevenoaks By-Pass. *Sev* —3F 33
Sevenoaks Common. —3F 33
Sevenoaks Museum & Art Gallery. —3F 33
(off Buckhurst La.)
Sevenoaks Rd. *Grn St & Hals* —4D 25
Sevenoaks Rd. *Igh* —3A 34
(in two parts)
Sevenoaks Rd. *Otf* —2F 33
Sevenoaks Way. *Orp* —3E 25
Sevenoaks Weald. —4F 33
Seven Sisters. (Junct.) —2A 16
Seven Sisters Rd. *N7 & N15* —3A 16
Sewardstone. —4C 8
Sewardstonebury. —4C 8
Sewardstone Rd. *E2* —4B 16
Sewardstone Rd. *E4 & Wal A* —1B 16
Seymour Ct. Rd. *Mar* —2A 12
Seymour Pl. *W1* —4F 15
Seymour St. *W1* —4F 15
Shacklands Rd. *Sev* —1F 33
Shacklegate La. *Tedd* —3C 22
Shackleton Way. *Wel G* —1F 7
Shacklewell. —3B 16
Shacklewell La. *N16* —3A 16
Shadwell. —4B 16
Shaftesbury Av. *W1 & WC2* —4F 15
Shaftesbury Av. *Harr* —3B 14
Shaggy Calf La. *Slou* —4E 13
Shalford. —4E 29
Shalford Rd. *Guild & Shalf* —4E 29
Shannon Corner. (Junct.) —3E 23
Shantock Hall La. *Bov* —3E 5
Shantock La. *Bov* —3E 5
Shardeloes Rd. *SE4* —2B 24
Sharnal Street. —2F 27
Sharpes La. *Hem H* —2E 5
Shawfield Rd. *Ash* —4B 28
Shawstead Rd. *Gill* —4F 27
Sheal's Cres. *Maid* —3F 35
Shears, The. (Junct.) —3A 22
Sheen Comn. Dri. *Rich* —2D 23
Sheen La. *SW14* —2D 23
Sheen Rd. *Rich* —2D 23
Sheepbarn La. *Warl* —1C 32
Sheepcote Dell Rd. *Holm G & Beam* —4C 4
Sheepcote La. *M'head* —2B 20
Sheepcote La. *Orp* —4E 25
Sheepcote La. *Wbrn G* —3C 12
Sheepcote Rd. *Harr* —2C 14
Sheepcot La. *Wat* —3B 6
(in two parts)
Sheephouse La. *Wott* —4B 30
Sheephouse Rd. *M'head* —4B 12
Sheepridge La. *Mar & F Hth* —2B 12
Sheep Wlk. *Shep* —4A 22
Sheering Lwr. Rd. *H'low* —1E 9
Sheering Rd. *H'low* —1E 9
Sheerwater. —1F 29
Sheerwater Rd. *Wdhm & W Byf* —1F 29
Sheet Hill. —3B 34
Sheet Hill. *Plax* —3B 34
Sheet St. *Wind* —1D 21
Sheet St. Rd. *Wind* —3C 20
Sheffield Rd. *Slou* —4D 13
Shelbourne Rd. *N17* —2B 16
Shellbank La. *Dart* —3B 26
Shelley. —2A 10
Shelleys La. *Knock* —2E 33
Shellow Bowells. —2B 10
Shellow Rd. *Will* —2B 10
Shelvers Way. *Tad* —2E 31
Shendish Airfield. —2F 5
Shenfield. —1B 18
Shenfield Rd. *Brtwd* —1B 18
Shenley. —3D 7
Shenleybury. —3D 7
Shenleybury. *Shenl* —3D 7
Shenley Hill. *Rad* —4C 6
Shenley La. *Lon C* —2C 6
Shenley Rd. *Borwd* —4D 7
Shenley Rd. *Hem H* —1A 6
Shenley Rd. *Rad* —3C 6
Shepherdess Wlk. *N1* —4A 16
Shepherd & Flock Roundabout. *Farnh* —4A 28
Shepherds Bush. —4E 15
Shepherd's Bush Grn. *W12* —1E 23
Shepherd's Bush Rd. *W6* —1E 23
Shepherd's Hill. *N6* —2F 15
Shepherd's Hill. *Red* —3F 31
Shepherds Hill. *Romf* —2A 18
Shepherd's La. *Brack* —3B 20
Shepherd's La. *Dart* —2F 25
Shepherd's La. *Guild* —4D 29
Shepherds La. *Hur* —4A 12
Shepherd's La. *Rick* —1F 13
Shepherds Way. *Brk P* —3F 7
Shepiston La. *Hay* —1A 22
Shepperton. —4A 22
Shepperton Green. —3A 22
Shepperton Rd. *N1* —4A 16
Shepperton Rd. *Stai & Shep* —3F 21
Shepway. —3F 35
Sherard Rd. *SE9* —2D 25
Sherbourne. *Alb* —4F 29
Shere. —4A 30
Shere La. *Shere* —4A 30
Shere Rd. *W Cla & Shere* —4F 29
Shere Rd. *W Hor* —3A 30
(in two parts)
Sherfield Rd. *Grays* —1B 26
Shernhall St. *E17* —2C 16
Sherwood Pk. Rd. *Mitc* —3F 23
Shillitoe Av. *Pot B* —3E 7
Shingle Barn La. *W Far* —4E 35
Shipbourne. —3B 34
Shipbourne Rd. *Tonb & Ship* —4B 34
Ship Hill. *Slou & Beac* —3D 13
Ship Hill. *Tats* —2C 32
Ship La. *Ave & Purf* —4A 18
Ship La. *Farn* —2B 28
Ship La. *Swan & S at H* —3A 26
Shipley Hills Rd. *Meop* —4C 26
Ship Rd. *W Han* —3E 11
Shirehall Rd. *Dart* —3F 25
Shire La. *Chal P* —1E 13
(in two parts)
Shire La. *C'bry* —1C 4
Shire La. *Chor* —1E 13
Shire La. *Kes & Orp* —1D 33
(in two parts)
Shirland Rd. *W9* —4E 15
Shirley. —4B 24
Shirley Chu. Rd. *Croy* —4B 24
Shirley Hills Rd. *Croy* —4B 24
Shirley Oaks. —4B 24
Shirley Rd. *Croy* —4B 24
Shirley Way. *Croy* —4B 24
Shoe La. *Alder* —3B 28
Shonks Mill Rd. *Nave* —4F 9
Shooters Hill. —1D 25
Shooters Hill. *SE18 & Well* —1D 25
Shooters Hill Rd. *SE10 & SE18* —1C 24
Shootersway. —2D 5
Shootersway. *Berk* —1D 5
Shoot Up Hill. *NW2* —3E 15
Shoppenhangers Rd. *M'head* —1B 20
Shoreditch. —4A 16
Shoreditch High St. *E1* —4A 16
Shoreham. —1F 33
Shoreham La. *Hals* —1E 33
Shoreham La. *Orp* —1E 33
Shoreham Rd. *Eyns* —1F 33
Shoreham Rd. *Shor* —1F 33
Shores Rd. *Wok* —1E 29
Shorne. —3D 27
Shorne Ifield Rd. *Shorne* —3D 27
Shorne Ridgeway. —3D 27
Shortlands. —3C 24
Shortlands Rd. *Brom* —3C 24
Short La. *Oxt* —4C 32
Short La. *Rams H* —1E 19
Short La. *Stai* —2A 22
Shorts Way. *Roch* —4E 27
Shotgate. —1F 19
Shreding Green. —4F 13
Shrubbery Rd. *S Dar* —3A 26
Shrublands Rd. *Berk* —1E 5
Shrubs Hill. —4D 21
Shrubs Rd. *Rick* —2A 14
Shurlock Row. —2A 20
Sidcup. —2E 25
Sidcup By-Pass. *Chst & Sidc* —3D 25
Sidcup Hill. *Sidc* —3E 25
Sidcup Rd. *SE12 & SE9* —2C 24
Sidlow. —4E 31
Sidmouth Dri. *Ruis* —3B 14
Sidmouth Rd. *NW2* —3E 15
Sidmouth St. *WC1* —4A 16
Sidney St. *E1* —4B 16
Silver Hill. *Chal G* —1E 13
Silver La. *Will* —2B 10
Silverstead La. *W'ham* —2D 33
Silver St. *Chesh* —3A 8
Silver St. *Enf* —4A 8
Silverthorne Rd. *SW8* —1F 23
Silvertown. —1C 24
Silvertown Way. *E16* —4C 16
Silwood Rd. *Asc* —3D 21
Simmons La. *E4* —1C 16
Singles Cross La. *Knock* —1E 33
Single Street. —2D 33
Single St. *Berr G & Orp* —2D 33
Singlewell. —3C 26
Singlewell Rd. *Grav* —2C 26
Sipson. —1A 22
Sipson La. *W Dray & Hay* —1A 22
Sipson Rd. *Harm* —1A 22
Sipson Rd. *W Dray* —1A 22
Sittingbourne Rd. *Maid* —2F 35
(in two parts)
Siviter Way. *Dag* —3E 17
Sixth Cross Rd. *Twic* —2C 22
Skeet Hill La. *Orp* —4E 25
Skibbs La. *Orp* —4E 25
Skid Hill La. *Warl* —1C 32
Skimped Hill La. *Brack* —3B 20
Skinner St. *EC1* —4A 16
Skinney La. *Hort K* —3A 26
Skreens Pk. Rd. *Will & Rox* —1C 10
Slade Green. —1F 25
Slade Grn. Rd. *Eri* —1F 25
Slade Oak La. *Ger X & Uxb* —2E 13
Slade Rd. *Ott* —1F 29
Slades Hill. *Enf* —4A 8
Slade's La. *Chelm* —3E 11
Slade, The. *SE18* —1D 25
Slad La. *Lac G & Speen* —4A 4
Sleapshyde. —2D 7
Sleapshyde La. *Smal* —2D 7
Slewins La. *Horn* —2F 17
Slines New Rd. *Wold* —2B 32
Slines Oak Rd. *Wold & Warl* —3B 32
Slipshatch Rd. *Reig* —4E 31
Sloane St. *SW1* —1F 23
Slough. —1E 21
Slough La. *H'ley* —3D 31
Slough La. *S'ton* —4A 4
Slough Rd. *Dat* —1E 21
Slough Rd. *Iver* —4F 13
Slough Rd. *Wind* —1D 21
Slyfield Green. —3E 29
Smalldean La. *S'ton & Lac G* —4A 4
Smallford. —2D 7
Smallford La. *Smal* —2D 7
Smallgains La. *Stock* —4D 11
Small Profits. *Yald* —4D 35
Smallshoes Hill. *Mash* —1C 10
Smart's Heath La. *Wok* —3E 29
Smart's Heath Rd. *Wok* —3D 29
Smewins Rd. *White* —1A 20
Smitham Bottom La. *Purl* —1F 31
Smitham Downs Rd. *Purl* —1A 32
Smiths Hill. *W Far* —4E 35
Smiths La. *Chesh* —2A 8
Smith's La. *Wind* —1D 21
Smokey Row. —2A 4
Smug Oak. —3B 6
Smug Oak La. *Brick* —3B 6
Snag La. *Cud* —1D 33
Snakes Hill. *N'side* —4A 10
Snakes La. E. *Wfd G* —2C 16
Snakes La. W. *Wfd G* —1C 16
Snaresbrook. —2C 16
Snaresbrook Rd. *E11* —2C 16
Snatts Hill. *Oxt* —3C 32
Snodland. —1E 35
Snodland By-Pass. *Snod* —1E 35
Snodland Rd. *Birl & Snod* —1D 35
Snoll Hatch Rd. *E Peck* —4D 35
Snowerhill Rd. *Bet* —4D 31
Snow's Ride. *W'sham* —4C 20
Soho. —4F 15
Solefields Rd. *Sev* —3F 33
Solesbridge La. *Rick* —4F 5
Sole Street. —4C 26
Sole St. *Meop & Grav* —4C 26
Solway. *Hem H* —1A 6
Somerset Rd. *Red* —4F 31
Somerset Rd. *S'hall* —4B 14
Somers Town. —4F 15
Somnes Av. *Can I* —3F 19
Sopwell. —2C 6
Sopwith Dri. *Brook P* —1A 30
Sorrells, The. *Stan H* —4D 19
South Acton. —1D 23
Southall. —4B 14
Southall Green. —1B 22
Southall La. *Houn & S'hall* —1B 22
Southampton Rd. *NW5* —3F 15
Southampton Row. *WC1* —4A 16
Southampton Way. *SE5* —1A 24
South Ascot. —4C 20
S. Ash Rd. *As* —1B 34
S. Audley St. *W1* —4F 15
South Beddington. —1F 31
South Benfleet. —3F 19
Southborough. —4D 25
(nr. Bromley)
Southborough. —4C 22
(nr. Surbiton)
Southborough La. *Brom* —4D 25
Southborough Rd. *Brom* —4D 25
Southbridge Rd. *Croy* —4A 24
Southbrook Rd. *SE12* —2C 24
Southbury Rd. *Enf* —4A 8
South Camp. —4B 28
South Chingford. —1B 16
Southcroft Rd. *SW17 & SW16* —3F 23
S. Croxted Rd. *SE21* —2A 24
South Croydon. —1A 32
S. Dagenham Rd. *Dag & Rain* —3F 17
South Darenth. —3A 26
S. Ealing Rd. *W5* —1C 22
S. Eden Pk. Rd. *Beck* —4B 24
Southend. —3C 24
South End. *Croy* —4A 24
Southend Arterial Rd. *Bas & W'fd* —2D 19
Southend Arterial Rd. *Ray & Lgh S* —2F 19
Southend Arterial Rd. *Romf & L War* —2A 18
Southend Arterial Rd. *Upm & Bas* —2B 18
Southend Arterial Rd. *W Horn* —2B 18
Southend Cres. *SE9* —2D 25
Southend La. *SE26 & SE6* —3B 24
Southend Rd. *E4 & E17* —2B 16
Southend Rd. *E18 & Wfd G* —2C 16
S. End Rd. *NW3* —3F 15
Southend Rd. *Beck* —3B 24
Southend Rd. *Bill & Cray H* —1D 19
Southend Rd. *Corr* —3E 19
Southend Rd. *Grays* —1C 26
Southend Rd. *H Grn & Ret C* —3F 11
S. End Rd. *Rain & Horn* —4F 17
Southend Rd. *W'fd* —1F 19
(in two parts)
Souther Cross Rd. *Good E* —1C 10
Southernhay. *Bas* —2E 19
(in two parts)
Southern Perimeter Rd. *H'row A* —2F 21
Southerns La. *Coul* —3F 31
Southern Way. *H'low* —1D 9
South Farnborough. —3B 28
Southfield Rd. *W4* —1D 23
Southfields. —2D 19
(nr. Basildon)
Southfields. —2E 23
(nr. Wandsworth)
Southfleet. —3B 26
Southfleet Rd. *Bean* —3B 26
Southfleet Rd. *Swans* —2B 26
Southgate. —1F 15
Southgate Rd. *N1* —4A 16
Southgate Rd. *Pot B* —3F 7
South Godstone. —4B 32
South Green. —1D 19
South Gro. *E17* —2B 16
South Gro. *N6* —3F 15
South Hackney. —4B 16
South Hampstead. —3F 15
South Hanningfield. —4E 11
S. Hanningfield Rd. *S Han* —4E 11
South Harefield. —2F 13
South Harrow. —3C 14
South Hatfield. —2E 7
South Heath. —3C 4
South Hill. *Guild* —4E 29
South Hill. *Horn H* —4D 19
South Hill. *Lang H* —3D 19
S. Hill Rd. *Brack* —4B 20
South Hornchurch. —4F 17
Southill La. *Pinn* —2B 14
South Kensington. —1F 23
South Lambeth. —1A 24
S. Lambeth Rd. *SW8* —1A 24
Southlands La. *Oxt* —4B 32
Southlands Rd. *Brom* —3C 24
Southlands Rd. *Den* —3F 13
South La. *N Mald* —3D 23
S. Lane W. *N Mald* —3D 23
Southlea. —2E 21
Southlea Rd. *Wind & Slou* —1E 21
S. Lodge Av. *Mitc* —3A 24
S. Mayne. *Pits* —2E 19
S. Meadow La. *Wind* —1D 21
South Merstham. —3F 31
South Mimms. —3E 7
South Norwood. —3B 24
S. Norwood Hill. *SE25* —3A 24
South Nutfield. —4A 32
South Ockendon. —4B 18
Southover. *N12* —1E 15
South Oxhey. —1B 14
South Pde. *W4* —1D 23
South Park. —4E 31
S. Park Dri. *Ilf & Bark* —3D 17
S. Park Hill Rd. *S Croy* —4A 24
S. Park La. *Blet* —4B 32
South Rd. *S'hall* —1B 22
South Rd. *S Ock* —4B 18
South Rd. *Twic* —2C 22
South Rd. *Wok* —2E 29
South Ruislip. —3B 14
Southside Comn. *SW19* —3E 23
South Stifford. —1B 26
South Street. —1C 34
(nr. Meopham)
South Street. —2D 33
(nr. Westerham Hill)
South St. *Barm* —3E 35
South St. *Dork* —4C 30
South St. *Enf* —1B 16
South St. *Eps* —1D 31
South St. *Farnh* —4A 28
South St. *Iswth* —2C 22
South St. *Meop* —1C 34
South St. *Romf* —2F 17
South St. *Stai* —3F 21
South St. *Wen* —2B 4
South Tottenham. —2A 16
Southwark. —4A 16
Southwark Bri. *SE1* —4A 16
Southwark Bri. Rd. *SE1* —1A 24
Southwark Pk. Rd. *SE16* —1B 24
Southwark St. *SE1* —4A 16
South Way. *Ab L* —3A 6
Southway. *Guild* —4D 29
South Way. *Hat* —2E 7
South Way. *Wemb* —3D 15
South Weald. —1A 18
Southwell Pk. Rd. *Camb* —1B 28
South Wimbledon. —3E 23
Southwood. —3A 28
South Woodford. —2C 16
S. Woodford to Barking Relief Rd. *E11 & Bark* —2C 16
Southwood La. *N6* —3F 15
Southwood Rd. *SE9* —2D 25
Southwood Rd. *Farn* —3A 28
Spa Hill. *SE19* —3A 24
Spains Hall Rd. *Will* —2B 10
Spaniards Rd. *NW3* —3F 15
Sparepenny La. *Eyns* —4F 25
Sparrow Row. —1D 29
Sparrow Row. *Wok* —1D 29
Sparrow's Herne. *Bas* —3E 19
Sparrows Herne. *Bush* —1B 14
Sparrows La. *Hat H* —1A 10
Speedgate Hill. *Fawk* —4B 26
Speen. —4A 4
Speen Rd. *N Dean* —4A 4
Speer Rd. *Th Dit* —4C 22
Spelthorne La. *Ashf* —3A 22
Spencer Pk. *SW18* —2F 23
Spencers Rd. *M'head* —4B 12
Spencer St. *EC1* —4A 16
Spendiff. —2F 27
Spinfield La. *Mar* —3A 12
Spinney Hill. *Add* —4F 21
Spital. —2D 21
Spitalbrook. —1B 8
Spitalfields. —4B 16
Spitals Cross. —4D 33
Spital St. *Mar* —3A 12
Spook Hill. *N Holm* —4C 30
Sporehams La. *Dan* —3F 11
Spout Hill. *Croy* —4B 24
Spout La. *Crock H* —4D 33
Spriggs La. *B'more* —3B 10

Spring Bottom La.—Torrington Pl.

Spring Bottom La. Blet —3A 32
Springbridge Rd. W5 —4C 14
Spring Coppice La. Speen —4A 4
Spring Elms La. L Bad —2F 11
Springfield. —1E 11
Springfield Grn. Chelm —1E 11
Springfield Rd. Chelm —2E 11 (in two parts)
Spring Grove. —1C 22
Spring Gro. Rd. Houn & Iswth —1B 22
Springhead Rd. N'fleet —2C 26
Springhouse La. Corr —4E 19
Springhouse Rd. Corr —4D 19
Spring La. SE25 —4B 24
Spring La. Farn R —3D 13
Spring La. F Hth —2B 12
Spring La. Igh —2B 34
Spring La. M'head —3B 12
Spring La. Oxt —4C 32
Spring Park. —4B 24
Spring St. W2 —4F 15
Spring St. Eps —1D 31
Spring Wlk. Worm —2B 8
Springwell La. Rick & Uxb —1F 13
Spurlands End Rd. Gt Kin —4B 4
Spur Rd. Edgw —1D 15
Spur Rd. Iswth —1C 22
Spur Rd. Orp —4E 25
Square Hill Rd. Maid —3F 35
Squerryes Court. —3D 33
Squire's Bri. Rd. Shep —3A 22
Squires La. N3 —2E 15
Squirrel's Heath. —2F 17
Squirrels Heath La. Romf & Horn —2F 17
Squirrels Heath Rd. Romf —2A 18
Stablebridge Rd. Ast C —1B 4
Stack La. Hort K —3A 26
Staffhurst Wood La. Eden —4C 32
Staffordlake. —2D 29
Stafford Rd. Cat —3A 32
Stafford Rd. Wall & Croy —1F 31
Stagg Hill. Barn —4F 7
Stag Lane. (Junct.) —2D 23
Stag La. Chor —1F 13
Stag La. Edgw & NW9 —2D 15
Stag La. Gt Kin —4B 4
Staines. —3F 21
Staines By-Pass. Stai —2F 21
Staines Green. —1A 8
Staines Rd. Cher —4F 21
Staines Rd. Felt & Houn —2A 22
Staines Rd. Hamp & Twic —2B 22
Staines Rd. Stai —3F 21
Staines Rd. Wray —2E 21
Staines Rd. E. Sun —3B 22
Staines Rd. W. Ashf & Sun —3A 22
Stallion's Green. —4B 34
Stamford Brook Rd. W6 —1D 23
Stamford Hill. —2A 16
Stamford Hill. N16 —3A 16
Stamford Rd. N1 —3A 16
Stamford St. SE1 —4A 16
Stanborough. —1E 7
Stanborough Rd. Wel G —1E 7
Staneway. Bas —3D 19
Stanford La. Hdlw —4C 34
Stanford-le-Hope. —4D 19
Stanford Rivers. —3F 9
Stanford Rivers Rd. Ong —3A 10
Stanford Rd. Grays —1C 26
Stangate Rd. Birl —1D 35
Stanhope Gdns. SW7 —1F 23
Stanhope Rd. St Alb —2C 6
Stanhope Rd. Swans —2B 26
Stan La. W Peck —3C 34
Stanley Hill. Amer —4D 5
Stanley Hill. Pirb —2C 28
Stanley Pk. Rd. Cars & Wall —1F 31
Stanley Rd. Grays —1B 26
Stanley Rd. Twic & Tedd —3C 22
Stanmore. —2C 14
Stanmore Hill. Stan —1C 14
Stanners Hill. —1E 29
Stansfeld Rd. E16 —4C 16
Stanstead Abbots. —1C 8
Stanstead Rd. SE23 & SE6 —2B 24
Stanstead Rd. Cat —3A 32
Stanstead Rd. Hert & Gt A —1B 8
Stanstead Rd. Hod —1B 8
Stansted. —1B 34
Stansted Hill. Sev —1B 34
Stansted La. Sev —1B 34
Stanwell. —2F 21
Stanwell Moor. —2F 21
Stanwell Moor Rd. Stai & W Dray —2F 21
Stanwell Rd. Ashf —2A 22
Stanwell Rd. Felt —2A 22
Stanwell Rd. Hort —2E 21
Stapleford Abbotts. —1F 17
Stapleford Rd. Romf —1E 17
Stapleford Tawney. —4F 9
Stapleford Tawney Airfield. —4E 9
Staple Hill Rd. Wok —1D 29
Staplehurst Rd. Cars —1F 31
Staplehurst Rd. S'hrst —4F 35
Staple La. Guild —4F 29
Staples Corner. (Junct.) —3E 15
Stapleton Hall Rd. N4 —3A 16
Stapleton Rd. Borwd —4D 7
Star & Garter Hill. Rich —2D 23
Star Hill. Roch —3F 27
Star Hill. Wok —2E 29
Star Hill Rd. Dun G —2E 33
Star La. Coul —2F 31
Star La. Orp —3E 25
Startins La. Cook —3B 12
Starts Hill Rd. Orp —4D 25
Station App. Gt Miss —3B 4
Station App. Hay —4C 24
Station App. Oxt —3C 32
Station App. Rick —4F 5
Station App. Ruis —3B 14
Station App. Wok —2E 29
Station App. Rd. Tad —2E 31
Station Av. Cat —3B 32
Station Av. W on T —4B 22
Station Hall La. Ing —4C 10
Station Hill. Asc —3C 20
Station Hill. Brom —4C 24
Station Hill. Cook —3B 12
Station Hill. E Far —3E 35
Station La. Horn —3A 18
Station Rd. E4 —1C 16
Station Rd. N11 —1F 15
Station Rd. N21 —1A 16
Station Rd. N22 —2A 16
Station Rd. NW4 —2E 15
Station Rd. NW10 —4D 15
Station Rd. SW13 —1D 23
Station Rd. Add —4F 21
Station Rd. Amer —4D 5
Station Rd. Asc —4D 21
Station Rd. Barn —1E 15
Station Rd. Beac —2C 12
Station Rd. Bet —4D 31
Station Rd. Bor G —2B 34
Station Rd. Bour E —3B 12
Station Rd. Bras —3E 33
Station Rd. Brick —3B 6
Station Rd. Brk P —2E 7
Station Rd. Brox —2B 8
Station Rd. Cat —2B 32
Station Rd. Chob —1D 29
Station Rd. Cipp —4D 13
Station Rd. Cli —2E 27
Station Rd. Cray —2F 25
Station Rd. Cux —4E 27
Station Rd. Dag & Romf —3E 17
Station Rd. Dit —2E 35
Station Rd. Dork —4C 30
Station Rd. Dun G —2F 33
Station Rd. E Til —1D 27
Station Rd. Eden —4D 33
Station Rd. Edgw —2D 15
Station Rd. Epp —3E 9
Station Rd. Esh —4C 22
Station Rd. Eyns —4F 25
Station Rd. Gid P —2F 17
Station Rd. Gom —4A 30
Station Rd. Grnh —2B 26 (in two parts)
Station Rd. Hals —1E 33
Station Rd. H'low —1E 9
Station Rd. Harr —2C 14
Station Rd. Hay —1A 22
Station Rd. Hem H —2F 5
Station Rd. K Lan —3A 6
Station Rd. Langl —1E 21
Station Rd. Lea —2C 30
Station Rd. Let G —1F 7
Station Rd. Loud —2C 12
Station Rd. Lou —1D 17
Station Rd. Mar —3A 12
Station Rd. Meop —3B 26
Station Rd. Nett —4D 35
Station Rd. N Har —2B 14
Station Rd. Orp —4D 25
Station Rd. Otf —2F 33
Station Rd. Pot B —3A 8
Station Rd. Red —4F 31
Station Rd. Shor —1F 33
Station Rd. Short —3C 24
Station Rd. Sidc —2E 25
Station Rd. Smal —2D 7
Station Rd. Stoke M —1A 4
Station Rd. Stan A —1C 8
Station Rd. Stoke D —2B 30
Station Rd. St P —3E 25
Station Rd. Strood —3E 27
Station Rd. Sutt —1E 31
Station Rd. S at H —3A 26
Station Rd. Tap —4C 12
Station Rd. Th Dit —4C 22
Station Rd. Tring & A'bry —1C 4
Station Rd. Upm —3A 18
Station Rd. Uxb —4F 13
Station Rd. Wal X —3B 8
Station Rd. Wat —4B 6
Station Rd. W Dray —1A 22
Station Rd. W H'dn —2C 18
Station Rd. W Wick —4C 24
Station Rd. Wray —2E 21
Station Rd. E. Oxt —3C 32
Station Rd. W. Oxt —3C 32
Station Way. Buck H —1C 16
Station Way. Sutt —1E 31
Staveley Rd. W4 —1D 23
Staverton Rd. NW2 —3E 15
Steel's La. Oxs —1B 30
Steep Hill. Chob —1D 29
Steeple View. —2D 19
Stembridge Rd. SE20 —3B 24
Stephenson St. E16 —4C 16
Stephenson Way. Wat —4B 6
Stepney. —4B 16
Stepney Grn. E1 —4B 16
Stepney Way. E1 —4B 16
Sterling Way. N18 —1A 16
Sternhold Av. SW2 —2A 24
Stevens Hill. B'water —1A 28
Stevens La. Clay —1C 30
Stewards. —2D 9
Stewards Green. —3E 9
Stewards Grn. Rd. Epp —3E 9
Stewart's Dri. Farn C —3D 13
Steyne Rd. W3 —4D 15
Stickens La. E Mal —2D 35
Stifford Clays Rd. N Stif —4B 18 (in three parts)
Stifford Hill. S Ock & Grays —4B 18
Stifford Rd. S Ock —4A 18
Stilebridge. —4F 35
Stilebridge La. Mard —4F 35 (in two parts)
Stirling Corner. (Junct.) —1D 15
Stites Hill Rd. Cat —2A 32
Stoats Nest Rd. Coul —1A 32
Stock. —4D 11
Stockett La. Cox & L'se —4F 35
Stockett La. E Far —3F 35
Stock Hill. Big H —2C 32
Stocking La. Nap —4A 4
Stock La. Ing —4C 10
Stockley Park. —4A 14
Stockley Rd. W Dray —4A 14
Stock Rd. Bill —1D 19
Stock Rd. Gall —3E 11
Stock Rd. Stock —4D 11
Stocks Green. —4A 34
Stocks Grn. Rd. Hild —4A 34
Stocks La. Kel H —4A 10
Stocks Rd. Ald —1D 5
Stockton Rd. N18 —2B 16
Stock Towermill. —4D 11
Stockwell. —1A 24
Stockwell Rd. SW9 —1A 24
Stoke Common. —3E 13
Stoke Comn. Rd. Ful —3E 13
Stoke D'Abernon. —2B 30
Stoke Green. —4E 13
Stoke Grn. Stoke P —4E 13
Stoke Mandeville. —1A 4
Stoke Newington. —3A 16
Stoke Newington Chu. St. N16 —3A 16
Stoke Newington High St. N16 —3A 16
Stoke Newington Rd. N16 —3A 16
Stoke Poges. —4D 13
Stoke Poges La. Slou —4D 13
Stoke Rd. Ayl —1A 4
Stoke Rd. Cobh —2B 30
Stoke Rd. Guild —4E 29
Stoke Rd. Hoo —2F 27
Stoke Rd. Slou —4D 13
Stompond La. W on T —4B 22
Stomp Rd. Burn —4C 12
Stonard Rd. N13 —1A 16
Stonards Hill. Epp —3E 9
Stondon Massey. —3B 10
Stondon Pk. SE23 —2B 24
Stondon Rd. Ong —3A 10
Stone. —2A 26
Stonebridge. —4D 15
Stonebridge Rd. N'fleet —2B 26
Stonecot Hill. Sutt —4E 23
Stonecross. St Alb —2C 6
Stonegrove. —1D 15
Stonegrove. Edgw —1D 15
Stonehill. —1E 29
Stonehill Rd. Chob & Cher —1E 29
Stonehill Rd. Rox —2C 10
Stonehouse La. Hals —1E 33
Stonehouse La. Purf —1A 26
Stoneings La. Knock —2D 33
Stoneleigh. —4E 23
Stoneness Rd. Grays —1B 26
Stone Pk. Av. Beck —3B 24
Stone Pl. Rd. Grnh —2A 26
Stones Cross Rd. Swan —4F 25
Stone Street. —3A 34
Stone St. Rd. Ivy H —3A 34
Stoney Rd. Brack —3B 20
Stony Corner. Meop —3C 26
Stony Green. —4B 4
Stony Hill. Esh —1B 30
Stony La. Amer —4E 5
Stony La. Ong —2F 9
Stopford Rd. E13 —4C 16
Stotford Rd. Lea R —1A 10
Stoughton. —4E 29
Stoughton Rd. Guild —4E 29
Straight Bit. F Hth —2B 12
Straight Mile, The. Shur R —2A 20
Straight Rd. Old Win —2E 21
Straight Rd. Romf —1F 17
Strait Rd. E6 —4D 17
Strand. WC2 —4A 16
Stratford. —3C 16
Stratford Marsh. —4B 16
Stratford New Town. —3C 16
Stratford Rd. Ash V —3B 28
Stratford Rd. Wat —4B 6
Strathearn Rd. SW19 —3E 23
Stratheden Rd. SE3 —1C 24
Strath Ter. SW11 —2F 23
Strathyre Av. SW16 —3A 24
Stratton. —4B 32
Strawberry Hill. —2C 22
Strawberry Hill. Warf —3B 20
Strawberry Vale. Twic —2C 22
Straw Mill Hill. Maid —3F 35
Streatfield Rd. Harr —2C 14
Streatham. —3A 24
Streatham Common. —3A 24
Streatham Comn. N. SW16 —3A 24
Streatham High Rd. SW16 —2A 24
Streatham Hill. —2F 23
Streatham Hill. SW2 —2A 24
Streatham Park. —3F 23
Streatham Pl. SW2 —2A 24
Streatham Rd. Mitc & SW16 —3F 23
Streatham Vale. —3F 23
Streatham Vale. SW16 —3F 23
Street End Rd. Chat —4F 27
Streets Heath. W End —1D 29
Street, The. Alb —4F 29
Street, The. As —4B 26
Street, The. Asht —2D 31
Street, The. Bet —4D 31
Street, The. Bore —1F 11
Street, The. Boxl —2F 35
Street, The. Chfd —3F 5
Street, The. Cob —3D 27
Street, The. Comp —4D 29
Street, The. Eff —3B 30
Street, The. Fet —2C 30
Street, The. Grav —3D 27
Street, The. Guild —3F 29
Street, The. H Hals —2F 27
Street, The. H Ong —3A 10
Street, The. Hort K —3A 26
Street, The. Igh —2B 34
Street, The. L Walt —1E 11
Street, The. Maid —3C 34
Street, The. Meop —4C 26
Street, The. Plax —3B 34
Street, The. Putt —4C 28
Street, The. Rox —1C 10
Street, The. Rya —2D 35
Street, The. Shalf —4E 29
Street, The. Shorne —3D 27
Street, The. Shur R —2A 20
Street, The. Tstn —3E 35
Street, The. Tong —4B 28
Street, The. Up H'ing —1D 35
Street, The. W Hor —3A 30
Strood. —3E 27
Strood Green. —4D 31
Stroude. —3E 21
Stroude Rd. Egh —3E 21
Stroude Rd. Vir W & Egh —3E 21
Stroud Green. —3A 16
Stroud Grn. Rd. N4 —3A 16
Stuart Rd. Grav —2C 26
Stubbers La. Upm —3A 18
Stubbles La. Cook —3B 12
Stubbs Hill. Brack —3A 20
Stubbs Hill. Orp —1E 33
Stubbs La. Lwr K —3E 31
Stud Green. —1B 20
Studio Way. Borwd —4D 7
Studland St. W6 —1E 23
Studridge La. Speen —4A 4
Stumble Hill. S'brne —4B 34
Stump La. Chelm —2E 11
Sturt Grn. Holyp —1B 20
Sturt Rd. Frim G —2B 28
Styants Bottom. —2A 34
Styants Bottom Rd. Sev —2A 34
Succombs Hill. Warl —2B 32
Sudbury. —3C 14
Sudbury Ct. Dri. Harr —3C 14
Sudbury Hill. Harr —3C 14
Sudbury Rd. D'ham —4E 11
Suffield La. Putt —4C 28
Suffield Rd. High W —1A 12
Suffolk Rd. Harr —2B 14
Sugden Rd. Th Dit —4C 22
Summer Hill. Chst —3D 25
Summerhouse Dri. Bex & Dart —2F 25
Summerhouse La. Ald —4C 6
Summerleaze Rd. M'head —4B 12
Summer Rd. Th Dit —4C 22
Summers La. N12 —2F 15
Summerstown. —2F 23
Summerstown. SW17 —2F 23
Summerswood La. Borwd —3D 7
Summit Av. Farn —3A 28
Sumner Rd. Croy —4A 24
Sumners. —2D 9
Sunbury. —3B 22
Sunbury Common. —3A 22
Sunbury Cross. (Junct.) —3B 22
Sunbury Rd. Felt —2A 22
Sunbury Way. Felt —3B 22
Sunderland Rd. SE23 —2B 24
Sundridge. —3C 24 (nr. Bromley)
Sundridge. —3E 33 (nr. Sevenoaks)
Sundridge Av. Brom & Chst —3C 24
Sundridge Hill. Cux —4E 27
Sundridge Hill. Sev —2E 33
Sundridge La. Sev —2E 33
Sundridge Rd. Ide H —2E 33
Sun Hill. Fawk —4B 26
Sun-in-the-Sands. (Junct.) —1C 24
Sunningdale. —4D 21
Sunningdale Golf Course. —4D 21
Sunninghill. —4C 20
Sunninghill Rd. Asc —4C 20
Sunninghill Rd. W'sham —4C 20
Sunninghill Rd. Wind & Asc —3C 20
Sunnings La. Upm —3A 18
Sunningvale Av. Big H —2C 32
Sunnybank. Warl —2B 32
Sunnymeads. —2E 21
Sunnymede. —1D 19
Sunnyside Rd. Che —3D 5
Sunray Av. SE24 —2A 24
Sun St. EC2 —4A 16
Surbiton. —4C 22
Surbiton Cres. King T —3C 22
Surbiton Hill Pk. Surb —4D 23
Surbiton Hill Rd. Surb —4D 23
Surbiton Rd. King T —3C 22
Surrey Canal Rd. SE15 & SE14 —1B 24
Sussex Gdns. W2 —4F 15
Sussex Pl. W2 —4F 15
Sussex Pl. Slou —1E 21
Sussex Ring. N12 —1E 15
Sutherland Av. W9 —4E 15
Sutton. —4E 23 (nr. Ewell)
Sutton. —1F 21 (nr. Slough)
Sutton at Hone. —3A 26
Sutton Comn. Rd. Sutt —4E 23
Sutton Ct. Rd. W4 —1D 23
Sutton Green. —3E 29
Sutton Grn. Rd. Guild —3E 29
Sutton La. Houn —1B 22
Sutton La. Slou —1E 21
Sutton La. Sutt & Bans —1E 31
Sutton Pk. Rd. Sutt —1E 31
Sutton Rd. Cook —3B 12
Sutton Rd. Houn —1B 22
Sutton Rd. Maid —3F 35
Suttons Av. Horn —3F 17
Suttons La. Horn —3F 17
Swains La. F Hth —2B 12
Swakeleys Rd. Uxb —3A 14
Swakeleys Roundabout. (Junct.) —3A 14
Swallowdale La. Hem I —1A 6
Swallows Cross. —4B 10
Swallows Cross Rd. Mount —4B 10
Swallow St. Iver —4F 13
Swan Bottom. Lee —2C 4
Swandon Way. SW18 —2E 23
Swanland Rd. Pot B & Hat —3E 7
Swan La. B'water —1A 28
Swan La. Dart —2F 25
Swan La. Eden —4D 33
Swan La. Lee —2C 4
Swan La. Runw —1F 19
Swan La. Stock —3D 11
Swanley. —3F 25
Swanley Bar. —3E 7
Swanley Bar La. Pot B —3E 7
Swanley By-Pass. Sidc & Swan —3E 25
Swanley Interchange. (Junct.) —4F 25
Swanley La. Swan —3F 25
Swanley Village. —3F 25
Swanley Village Rd. Swan —3F 25
Swan Rd. Felt —3B 22
Swan Rd. W Dray —1F 21
Swanscombe. —2B 26
Swanscombe St. Swans —2B 26
Swansea Rd. Felt —2A 22
Swan St. W Mal —2D 35
Swan, The. (Junct.) —4C 24
Swanton. —3C 34
Swanton Rd. W Peck —3C 34
Swanton Valley La. W Peck —3C 34
Swaynesland Rd. Eden —4D 33
Sweeps La. Orp —4E 25
Sweetcroft La. Uxb —3A 14
Sweets La. E Mal —3E 35
Swift Cres. Chat —4F 27
Swillet, The. —1E 13
Swingate La. SE18 —1D 25
Swinley Rd. Asc —4C 20
Swiss Cottage. (Junct.) —3F 15
Switchback Rd. N. M'head —4B 12
Switchback Rd. S. M'head —4B 12
Swyncombe Av. W5 —1C 22
Sycamore Rd. Amer —4D 5
Sycamore Rd. Farn —3B 28
Sydenham. —3B 24
Sydenham Hill. SE26 & SE23 —3B 24
Sydenham Rd. SE26 —3B 24
Sydenham Rd. Croy —4A 24
Sydenham Rd. Guild —4E 29
Sydney Rd. Enf —4A 8
Sydney Rd. Guild —4E 29
Sydney St. SW3 —1F 23
Sylvan Hill. SE19 —3A 24
Sylvan Way. Wel G —1F 7
Symonds La. Yald —4D 35
Syon House. —1C 22
Syon La. Iswth —1C 22
Sythwood. Wok —2E 29

Taddington. W'slde —1F 35
Tadpole La. Ews —4A 28
Tadworth. —2E 31
Tadworth St. Tad —3E 31
Talgarth Rd. W14 —1E 23
Tally Rd. Oxt —4D 33
Tamworth La. Mitc —3F 23
Tamworth Rd. Croy —4A 24
Tandridge. —4B 32
Tandridge Hill La. God —3B 32
Tandridge La. Ling —4B 32
Tandridge La. Oxt —4B 32
Tanfield Av. NW2 —3D 15
Tangley La. Guild —3D 29
Tan Ho. La. N'side —4A 10
Tanhouse Rd. Oxt —4C 32
Tank Hill Rd. Purf —1A 26
Tank Rd. Camb —1A 28
Tanner's Hill. Brock —4D 31
Tanners La. Ilf —2D 17
Tanner St. SE1 —1A 24
Tannery La. Send —3F 29
Tanyard Hill. Shorne —3D 27
Taplow. —4C 12
Taplow Comn. Rd. Burn —3C 12
Taplow Rd. Tap —4C 12
Tapner's Rd. Bet —4D 31
Target Roundabout. (Junct.) —4B 14
Tarpots. —2F 19
Tate Rd. Sutt —4E 23
Tatling End. —3E 13
Tatsfield. —2C 32
Tatsfield Green. —2D 33
Tatsfield La. W'ham —2D 33
Tattenham Corner. —2E 31
Tattenham Corner Rd. Eps —2D 31
Tattenham Cres. Eps —2E 31
Tattenham Way. Tad —2E 31
Taunton Way. Stan & Edg —2D 15
Tavistock Pl. WC1 —4A 16
Tavistock Sq. WC1 —4F 15
Tawney Common. —3E 9
Tawney Comn. They M —3E 9
Tawneys Rd. H'low —1D 9
Taylor's La. High —3E 27
Taylor's La. Tros —1C 34
Teasaucer. Tovil —3F 35
Teddington. —3C 22
Tees Dri. Romf —1F 17
Teignmouth Gdns. Gnfd —4C 14
Telegraph Hill. High —3E 27
Telford Dri. Slou —1D 21
Telford Rd. N11 —1F 15
Temple. —3A 12
Temple End. High W —1B 12
Temple Fields. —1E 9
Temple Fortune. —2E 15
Temple Fortune La. NW11 —2E 15
Temple Hill. Dart —2A 26
Temple Hill. —2A 26
Temple Hill Sq. Dart —2A 26
Temple La. Bish —3A 12
Temple Mill La. E10 & E15 —3C 16
Temple Mills. —3B 16
Temple Rd. Eps —1D 31
Temple St. High W —1B 12
Temple Way. Binf —3A 20
Templewood La. Slou —3D 13
Ten Acre La. Egh —3F 21
Tendring Rd. H'low —1D 9 (in two parts)
Tennison Rd. SE25 —4A 24
Tentelow La. S'hall —1B 22
Terling Hall Rd. Terl —1F 11
Terling Rd. Hat P —1F 11
Terrace Rd. W on T —4B 22
Terrace Rd. N. Binf —3A 20
Terrace Rd. S. Binf —3A 20
Terrace, The. SW13 —1D 23
Terrace, The. Grav —2C 26 (in three parts)
Terrace, The. Wfd G —2C 16
Terrick. —1A 4
Terriers. —1B 12
Terry's La. Cook —3B 12
Terry's Lodge Rd. Wro —1B 34
Teston. —3E 35
Teston La. Tstn —3E 35
Teston Rd. Off —2C 34
Teston Rd. W Mal —2C 34
Tetherdown. N10 —2F 15
Thames Barrier Visitor Centre. —1C 24
Thames Ditton. —4C 22
Thames Haven. —4E 19
Thamesmead. —4E 17
Thames Rd. Bark —4D 17
Thames Rd. Dart —1F 25
Thames Side. Stai & Cher —3F 21
Thames St. Hamp —3B 22
Thames St. Stai —3F 21
Thames St. Sun —3B 22
Thames St. Wey —4A 22
Thames St. Wind —1D 21
Thames Way. Grav —2C 26 (in two parts)
Theberton St. N1 —4A 16
Theobalds La. Chesh —3B 8
Theobalds Pk. Rd. Enf —4A 8
Theobalds Rd. WC1 —4A 16
Theobald St. Rad & Borwd —4C 6
Thesiger Rd. SE20 —3B 24
Theydon Bois. —4D 9
Theydon Garnon. —4E 9
Theydon Mt. They M —3E 9
Theydon Mount. —4E 9
Theydon Rd. Epp —4D 9
Thicket Rd. SE20 —3B 24
Thieves La. Hert —1A 8
Third Av. H'low —1D 9
Thoby La. Mount —4C 10
Thomas More St. E1 —4B 16
Thompkins La. Farn R —3D 13
Thong. —3D 27
Thong La. Grav —3D 27
Thong La. Sev —2B 34
Thorkhill Rd. Th Dit —4C 22
Thornbury Rd. Iswth —1C 22
Thorncliffe Rd. S'hall —1B 22
Thorndon Av. W H'dn —2C 18
Thorndown La. W'sham —1C 28
Thorney. —1F 21
Thorney Bay Rd. Can I —4F 19
Thorney La. N. Iver —4F 13
Thorney La. S. Iver —1F 21
Thorney Mill Rd. Iver & W Dray —1F 21
Thornhill Av. SE18 —1D 25
Thornhill Rd. N1 —3A 16
Thornhill Rd. Alder —4B 28
Thornhill Rd. Surb —4D 23
Thornton Av. SW2 —2F 23
Thornton Heath. —3A 24
Thornton Heath Pond. (Junct.) —4A 24
Thornton Rd. SW12 —2F 23
Thornton Rd. Croy & T Hth —4A 24
Thornwood Common. —2E 9
Thornwood Rd. Epp —3E 9
Thorpe. —3F 21
Thorpe By-Pass. Egh —3E 21
Thorpe Green. —3E 21
Thorpe Lea. —3E 21
Thorpe Lea Rd. Egh —3E 21
Thorpe Park. —3F 21
Thorpe Rd. Cher —4F 21
Thorpe Rd. Stai —3F 21
Thrale Rd. SW16 —3F 23
Three Arch Rd. Red —4F 31
Three Cherry Trees La. Hem H —1A 6
Three Colts La. E2 —4B 16
Three Elm La. Gold G —4B 34
Three Gates Rd. Fawk —4A 26
Three Households. Chal G —1D 13
Three Mile Hill. Ing —3D 11
Threshers Bush. —1F 9
Threshers Bush. H'low —1E 9
Throwley Way. Sutt —4E 23
Thundersley. —2F 19
Thurloe Gdns. Romf —2F 17
Thurlow Pk. Rd. SE27 —2A 24
Thurlow St. SE17 —1A 24
Thurrock Lakeside. —1B 26
Thurrock Museum. —1B 26
Thurston Rd. SE13 —1B 24
Tibbet's Corner. (Junct.) —2E 23
Tibbet's Ride. SW15 —2E 23
Tibbs Hill Rd. Ab L —3A 6
Tickleback Row. —2B 20
Tideway, The. Roch —4F 27
Tiepigs La. W Wick & Brom —4C 24
Tilburstow Hill Rd. God —4B 32
Tilburstow Hill Rd. S God —4B 32
Tilbury. —2C 26
Tilbury Fort. —2C 26
Tilbury Rd. W H'dn —2C 18
Tilden La. Mard —4F 35
Tilegate Green. —1F 9
Tilehouse La. Den & Rick —2F 13
Tilehurst La. Binf —3A 20
Tilehurst La. Dork —4D 31
Tile Kiln La. Bex —2F 25 (in two parts)
Tilley La. H'ley —2D 31
Tilling Rd. NW2 —3E 15
Tillwicks Rd. H'low —1D 9
Tilt Rd. Cobh —2B 30
Timbercroft La. SE18 —1D 25
Timberden Bottom. —1F 33
Timberlog La. Bas —2E 19
Tinker Pot La. W King —1A 34
Tinkers La. Wind —2C 20
Tippendell La. St Alb —2B 6
Tipps Cross La. Hook E —3B 10
Tip's Cross. —3B 10
Tite Hill. Egh —3E 21
Tithebarns La. Send —3F 29
Tithepit Shaw La. Warl —2B 32
Titsey. —3C 32
Titsey Hill. T'sey —3C 32
Titsey Place. —3C 32
Titsey Rd. Oxt —3C 32
Tittle Row. —4B 12
Tiverton Rd. NW10 —4E 15
Tofts Chase. L Bad —1F 11
Tokyngton. —3D 15
Tollgate Rd. E16 & E6 —4C 16
Tollgate Rd. Col H —2D 7
Tollington Pk. N4 —3A 16
Tollington Rd. N7 —3A 16
Tollington Way. N7 —3A 16
Tolpits La. Wat —1A 14
Tolworth. —4D 23
Tolworth Junction (Toby Jug). (Junct.) —4D 23
Tolworth Rise N. Surb —4D 23
Tolworth Rise S. Surb —4D 23
Tomkyns La. Upm —2A 18
Toms Hill Rd. Ald —1D 5
Tom's La. K Lan & Abb L —3A 6
Tomswood Hill. Ilf —2D 17
Tomswood Rd. Chig —2D 17
Tonbridge. —4B 34
Tonbridge By-Pass. Sev & Tonb —4A 34
Tonbridge Rd. Barm —3E 35
Tonbridge Rd. Bough B —4E 33
Tonbridge Rd. E Peck —4C 34
Tonbridge Rd. Hdlw —4B 34
Tonbridge Rd. Hild —4A 34
Tonbridge Rd. Ivy H —3B 34
Tonbridge Rd. Maid —3C 34
Tonbridge Rd. Sev —3F 33
Tonbridge Rd. S'brne —4B 34
Tonbridge Rd. Tstn & W'bury —3D 35
Tongham. —4B 28
Tooley St. SE1 —4A 16
Toot Hill. —3F 9
Toot Hill Rd. Ong —3F 9
Tooting. —3F 23
Tooting Bec. —2F 23
Tooting Bec Gdns. SW16 —3F 23
Tooting Bec Rd. SW17 & SW16 —2F 23
Tooting Graveney. —3F 23
Tooting High St. SW17 —3F 23
Top Dartford Rd. Swan & Dart —3F 25
Torriano Av. NW5 —3F 15
Torridon Rd. SE6 —2C 24 (in two parts)
Torrington Pk. N12 —1F 15
Torrington Pl. WC1 —4F 15

Torrington Rd.—West Farleigh

Torrington Rd. *Ruis* —3B 14
Tottenham. —2A 16
Tottenham Ct. Rd. *W1* —4F 15
Tottenham Hale. —2B 16
Tottenham Hale Gyratory. (Junct.) —2A 16
Tottenham Hotspur F.C. —2B 16
Tottenham La. *N8* —2A 16
Totteridge. —1B 12
(nr. High Wycombe)
Totteridge. —1E 15
(nr. Mill Hill)
Totteridge Comn. *N20* —1E 15
Totteridge La. *N20* —1E 15
Totteridge La. *High W* —1B 12
Totteridge Rd. *High W* —1B 12
Totteridge Village. *N20* —1E 15
Touchen End. —1B 20
Touchen End Rd. *Holyp* —1B 20
Tovil. —3F 35
Tovil Hill. *Maid* —3F 35
Tovil Rd. *Maid* —3F 35
Tower Bri. *SE1* —4A 16
Tower Bri. Rd. *SE1* —1A 24
Tower Hill. —3F 5
(nr. Chipperfield)
Tower Hill. —4C 30
(nr. Dorking)
Tower Hill. (Junct.) —4A 16
Tower Hill. *Chfd* —3F 5
Tower Hill La. *Sandr* —1D 7
Tower Rd. *Coles* —1D 13
Tower Rd. *Orp* —4D 25
Tower Rd. *Twic* —2C 22
Tower View. *King H* —2D 35
Towncourt La. *Orp* —4D 25
Townend. *Cat* —2A 32
Town Hill. *W Mal* —2D 35
Town La. *Stai* —2F 21
Town La. *Wbrn G* —3C 12
Townley Rd. *Bexh* —2E 25
Townmead Rd. *SW6* —1F 23
Town Rd. *N9* —1B 16
Town Rd. *Cli* —2E 27
Townsend. —1C 6
Town, The. *Enf* —4A 8
Towpath. *Shep* —4A 22
Toy's Hill. —4E 33
Toy's Hill. *Four E* —4E 33
Trafalgar Av. *SE15* —1A 24
Trafalgar Rd. *SE10* —1C 24
Trafalgar Sq. *WC2* —4F 15
Tranquil Vale. *SE3* —1C 24
Trap's Hill. *Lou* —4D 9
Traps La. *N Mald* —3D 23
Travellers La. *Hat* —2E 7
Treadaway Rd. *F Hth* —2B 12
Tredegar Rd. *E3* —4B 16
Tree La. *Plax* —3B 34
Trelawney Av. *Slou* —1E 21
Trenches La. *Slou* —4E 13
Trench Wood. —4B 34
Treve Av. *Harr* —3C 14
Trevor Rd. *Hay* —1A 22
Trevthick Dri. *Dart* —2A 26
Trigg's La. *Wok* —2E 29
Tring. —1C 4
Tring Ford Rd. *Tring* —1C 4
Tring Hill. *Tring* —1B 4
Tring Rd. *N'chu* —1D 5
Tring Rd. *Wen* —2B 4
Tring Wharf. —1C 4
Trinity Rd. *SW18 & SW17* —2F 23
Tripton Rd. *H'low* —1D 9
Trodd's La. *Guild* —4F 29
Trooper Rd. *Ald* —1D 5
Trotters Bottom. *Barn* —4E 7
Trotters Rd. *H'low* —1E 9
Trottiscliffe. —1C 34
Trottiscliffe Rd. *Adtn* —2C 34
Trott Rd. *N10* —2F 15
Troy Town. —4D 33
Trueloves La. *Ing* —4C 10
Trumpetshill Rd. *Reig* —4E 31
Trumps Green. —4E 21
Trumpsgreen Rd. *Vir W* —4E 21
Trundleys Rd. *SE8* —1B 24
Trunk Rd. *Farn* —3A 28
Truro Rd. *N22* —2A 16
Tubbenden La. *Orp* —4D 25
Tubbs Rd. *NW10* —4D 15
Tudor Dri. *King T* —3C 22
Tudor Dri. *Mord* —4E 23
Tudor Gdns. *NW9* —3D 15
Tudor Way. *Orp* —4D 25
Tufnell Park. —3F 15
Tulse Hill. —2A 24
Tulse Hill. *SW2* —2A 24
Tumber St. *H'ley* —3D 31
Tumblefield Rd. *Stans* —1B 34
Tunnel App. *SE16* —1B 24
Tunnel Av. *SE10* —1C 24
(in two parts)
Tuns La. *Slou* —1D 21
Tupwood La. *Cat* —3B 32
Tupwood Scrubs Rd. *Cat* —3B 32
Turkey St. *Enf* —4B 8
Turner Rd. *Edgw* —2D 15
Turner's Hill. *Chesh* —3B 8
Turney Rd. *SE21* —2A 24
Turnford. —2B 8
Turnfurlong La. *Ayl* —1A 4
Turnham Green. —1D 23
Turnham Grn. Ter. *W4* —1D 23
Turnpike La. *N8* —2A 16
Turnpike La. *W Til* —1C 26
Turpington La. *Brom* —4D 25
Tweedy Rd. *Brom* —3C 24
Tweseldown Rd. *C Crook* —4A 28
Twickenham. —2C 22
Twickenham Bri. *Twic & Rich* —2C 22
Twickenham Rd. *Felt* —3B 22
Twickenham Rd. *Iswth* —2C 22
Twickenham Rd. *Rich* —2C 22
Twickenham Rd. *Tedd* —3C 22
Twickenham Rugby Ground. —2C 22
Twist, The. *Wig* —1C 4
Twitchell La. *Ast C* —1B 4
Twitchells La. *Jor* —1D 13
Twitton. —2F 33
Twitton La. *Otf* —2F 33
Two Dells La. *Ash G* —2D 5
Twogates Hill. *Cli* —2E 27
Two Waters. —2F 5
Two Waters Rd. *Hem H* —2F 5
Twyford Abbey Rd. *NW10* —4D 15
Twyford Av. *W3* —4D 15
Tye Comn. Rd. *Bill* —1C 18
Tyefields. *Pits* —2F 19
Tye Green. —1C 10
(nr. Good Easter)
Tye Green. —1D 9
(nr. Harlow)
Tye Green. —4D 11
(nr. Stock)
Tye, The. *E Han* —3F 11
Tye, The. *Marg* —3D 11
Tyland Barn. —2F 35
Tyland La. *S'lng* —2F 35
Tylers Causeway. —2F 7
Tylers Causeway. *New S* —2F 7
Tylers Green. —1C 12
(nr. Beaconsfield)
Tyler's Green. —3B 32
(nr. Godstone)
Tyler's Green. —2F 9
(nr. North Weald Bassett)
Tylers Grn. Rd. *Swan* —4F 25
Tylers Rd. *Roy* —2C 8
Tylers Way. *Wat* —4C 6
Tylney Rd. *E7* —3C 16
Tylney Rd. *Brom* —3C 24
Tyrell's Wood. —3D 31
Tysea Hill. *Stap A* —1F 17
Tysea Rd. *H'low* —1D 9
Tyttenhanger. —2D 7
Tyttenhanger Grn. *Tyngr* —2C 6

Underhill. —1E 15
Underling Green. —4F 35
Underriver. —3A 34
Underriver Ho. Rd. *Under* —4A 34
Union St. *SE1* —1A 24
Union St. *Farn* —3B 28
University Way. *Dart* —2F 25
Upchat Rd. *Upnor & C'den* —3F 27
Updown Hill. *W'sham* —1C 28
Upland Rd. *Thorn* —2D 9
Uplands Pk. Rd. *Enf* —4A 8
Upminster. —3A 18
Upminster Rd. *Horn & Upm* —3A 18
Upminster Rd. N. *Rain* —4F 17
Upminster Rd. S. *Rain* —4F 17
Upminster Smockmill. —3A 18
Upney La. *Bark* —3D 17
Upnor Castle. —3F 27
Upnor Rd. *Lwr U* —3F 27
Up. Austin Lodge Rd. *Eyns* —4F 25
Up. Barn Hill. *Hunt* —4E 35
Up. Beulah Hill. *SE19* —3A 24
Up. Bray Rd. *Bray* —1C 20
Up. Brentwood Rd. *Romf* —2F 17
Up. Brighton Rd. *Surb* —4C 22
Up. Chobham Rd. *Camb* —2B 28
Upper Clapton. —3B 16
Up. Clapton Rd. *E5* —3B 16
Up. College Ride. *Camb* —1B 28
Upper Dunsley. —1C 4
Upper Edmonton. —1B 16
Upper Elmers End. —4B 24
Up. Elmers End Rd. *Beck* —3B 24
Up. Fant Rd. *Maid* —3F 35
Up. Green Rd. *S'brne* —3B 34
Up. Green W. *Mitc* —3F 23
Up. Grosvenor St. *W1* —4F 15
Upper Hale. —4A 28
Up. Hale Rd. *Farnh* —4A 28
Upper Halliford. —4A 22
Up. Halliford By-Pass. *Shep* —4A 22
Up. Halliford Rd. *Shep* —3A 22
Upper Halling. —4D 27
Up. Ham Rd. *Rich* —3C 22
Up. High St. *Eps* —1D 31
Up. Highway. *K Lan & Abb L* —3A 6
Upper Holloway. —3F 15
Up. Hunton Hill. *E Far* —4E 35
Up. Icknield Way. *Ast C* —1B 4
Up. Icknield Way. *P Ris* —2A 4
Up. Luton Rd. *Chat* —4F 27
Up. Mayne. *Bas* —2D 19
Up. Mulgrave Rd. *Sutt* —1E 31
Upper North Dean. —4A 4
Up. North St. *E14* —4B 16
Upper Norwood. —3A 24
Up. Park Rd. *Belv* —1E 25
Up. Park Rd. *Camb* —1B 28
Up. Rainham Rd. *Horn* —3F 17
Up. Richmond Rd. *SW15* —2D 23
Up. Richmond Rd. W. *Rich & SW14* —2D 23
Upper Rd. *E13* —4C 16
Up. Selsdon Rd. *S Croy* —1A 32
Upper Shirley. —4B 24
Up. Shirley Rd. *Croy* —4B 24
Up. Stone St. *Maid* —3F 35
Upper St. *N1* —4A 16
Upper St. *Shere* —4A 30
Up. Sunbury Rd. *Hamp* —3B 22
Up. Sutton La. *Houn* —1B 22
Upper Sydenham. —3B 24
Up. Teddington Rd. *King T* —3C 22
Up. Thames St. *EC4* —4A 16
Up. Tollington Pk. *N4* —3A 16
Upper Tooting. —3F 23
Up. Tooting Rd. *SW17* —3F 23
Upper Upnor. —3F 27
Upper Walthamstow. —2C 16
Up. Weybourne La. *Farnh* —4A 28
Up. Wickham La. *Well* —1E 25
Upshire. —3C 8
Upshire Rd. *Wal A* —3C 8
Upshott La. *Wok* —2F 29
Upton. —3C 16
(nr. Plaistow)
Upton. —1E 21
(nr. Slough)
Upton Ct. Rd. *Slou* —1E 21
Upton La. *E7* —3C 16
Upton Park. —4C 16
Upton Rd. *Bexh* —2E 25
Urswick Rd. *E9* —3B 16
Uxbridge. —3F 13
Uxbridge Rd. *W3* —4D 15
Uxbridge Rd. *W5 & W7* —4C 14
Uxbridge Rd. *W12* —4E 15
Uxbridge Rd. *W13* —4C 14
Uxbridge Rd. *Felt* —2B 22
Uxbridge Rd. *Hamp* —3B 22
Uxbridge Rd. *Harr & Stan* —1C 14
Uxbridge Rd. *King T* —4C 22
Uxbridge Rd. *Pinn* —2B 14
Uxbridge Rd. *Rick* —1F 13
Uxbridge Rd. *Slou* —1E 21
Uxbridge Rd. *S'hall* —4B 14
Uxbridge Rd. *Uxb & Hay* —4A 14

Vache La. *Chal G* —1E 13
Valence Av. *Dag* —3E 17
Valence House Museum & Art Gallery. —3E 17
Vale of Heath. —3F 15
Vale Pk. View. *Hod* —1B 8
Vale Rd. *Ash V* —3B 28
Vale Rd. *Bush* —1B 14
Vale Rd. *Che* —3D 5
Vale Rd. *N'fleet* —2C 26
Vale Rd. *Wind* —1D 21
Vale, The. *NW11* —3E 15
Vale, The. *W3* —4D 15
Vale, The. *Che* —2D 5
Vale, The. *Hawr* —2D 5
Vallance Rd. *E2 & E1* —4B 16
Vallentin Rd. *E17* —2C 16
Valley Bri. *Chelm* —1E 11
Valley Dri. *Grav* —3C 26
Valley End. —1D 29
Valley End Rd. *Wok* —1D 29
Valley Hill. *Lou* —1D 17
Valley Rd. *SW16* —3A 24
Valley Rd. *Bill* —1D 19
Valley Rd. *Fawk* —4B 26
Valley Rd. *Hugh V* —4B 4
Valley Rd. *Kenl* —2A 32
Valley Rd. *Rick* —1F 13
Valley Rd. *Short* —3C 24
Valley Rd. *St Alb* —1C 6
Valley Rd. *Wel G* —1E 7
Vanbrugh Hill. *SE10 & SE3* —1C 24
Vanbrugh Pk. *SE3* —1C 24
Van Dieman's Rd. *Chelm* —2E 11
Vange. —3E 19
Vange By-Pass. *Bas* —3E 19
Vanity La. *Lint* —4F 35
Vansittart Rd. *Wind* —1D 21
Vapery La. *Pirb* —2C 28
Vaughan Rd. *Harr* —3C 14
Vauxhall. —1A 24
Vauxhall Bri. *SW1 & SE1* —1A 24
Vauxhall Bri. Rd. *SW1* —1F 23
Vauxhall Cross. (Junct.) —1A 24
Venus Hill. —3E 5
Venus Hill. *Bov* —3E 5
Verdant La. *SE6* —2C 24
Vernon Pl. *WC1* —4A 16
Verulamium Roman Town. —2B 6
Verulam Rd. *St Alb* —2B 6
Vesta Rd. *SE14* —1B 24
Vestry House Museum. —2B 16
Vicarage Causeway. *Hert H* —1B 8
Vicarage Cres. *SW11* —1F 23
Vicarage Farm Rd. *Houn* —1B 22
Vicarage Hill. *Ben* —3F 19
Vicarage Hill. *W'ham* —3D 33
Vicarage La. *E15* —3C 16
Vicarage La. *B'water* —1A 28
Vicarage La. *Bov* —2E 5
Vicarage La. *Chig* —1D 17
Vicarage La. *E Far* —3E 35
Vicarage La. *Grav* —2D 27
Vicarage La. *Gt Bad* —3E 11
Vicarage La. *Hoo* —3F 27
Vicarage La. *K Lan* —3A 6
Vicarage La. *N Wea* —2E 9
Vicarage La. *Send* —3F 29
Vicarage Rd. *Bex* —2E 25
Vicarage Rd. *B'water* —1A 28
Vicarage Rd. *B'water* —2A 28
Vicarage Rd. *Egh* —3E 21
Vicarage Rd. *Hall* —4D 27
Vicarage Rd. *Pott E* —1E 5
Vicarage Rd. *Rox* —1C 10
Vicarage Rd. *Sun* —3A 22
Vicarage Rd. *Wat* —1B 14
Vicarage Rd. *Wig* —1C 4
Vicarage Rd. *Wok* —2E 29
Vicarage Rd. *Yald* —4E 35
Victoria Dock Rd. *E16* —4C 16
Victoria Dri. *SW19* —2E 23
Victoria Embkmt. *SW1, WC2 & EC4* —1A 24
Victoria Pk. Rd. *E8* —4B 16
Victoria Rd. *N18 & N9* —1A 16
Victoria Rd. *NW10* —4D 15
Victoria Rd. *W3* —4D 15
Victoria Rd. *Alder* —4B 28
Victoria Rd. *Buck H* —1C 16
Victoria Rd. *Chelm* —2E 11
(in two parts)
Victoria Rd. *Dart* —2A 26
Victoria Rd. *Farn* —3B 28
Victoria Rd. *Gold G* —4C 34
Victoria Rd. *Romf* —2F 17
Victoria Rd. *Ruis* —3B 14
Victoria Rd. *Surb* —4C 22
Victoria Rd. *Wok* —2E 29
Victoria Rd. *Writ* —2D 11
Victoria Rd. S. *Chelm* —2E 11
Victoria St. *SW1* —1F 23
Victoria St. *Egh* —3E 21
Victoria St. *Roch* —3F 27
Victoria St. *St Alb* —2C 6
Victoria St. *Wind* —1D 21
Victoria Way. *Wok* —2E 29
View Rd. *Cli* —2E 27
Vigilant Way. *Grav* —3D 27
Vigo Hill. *Tros* —1C 34
Vigo La. *B'water* —1A 28
Vigo Rd. *Sev* —1B 34
Vigo Village. —1C 34
Village La. *Hedg* —3D 13
Village Rd. *Coles* —1D 13
Village Rd. *Den* —3F 13
Village Rd. *Dor* —1C 20
Village Rd. *Egh* —3E 21
Village Rd. *Enf* —1A 16
Village, The. —2D 21
Village, The. *SE7* —1C 24
Village, The. *Will* —2B 10
Village Way. *SE21* —2A 24
Village Way. *Beck* —3B 24
Village Way. *Pinn* —3B 14
Villa Rd. *High* —3E 27
Villiers Av. *Surb* —4D 23
Villiers Rd. *King T* —3D 23
Villiers Rd. *Slou* —4D 13
Villiers Rd. *Wat* —1B 14
Vincent La. *Dork* —4C 30
Vine La. *Uxb* —3A 14
Vines La. *Hild* —4A 34
Vines La. *Roch* —3F 27
Vineyards Rd. *N'thaw* —3F 7
Vinters Park. —2F 35
Violet Rd. *E3* —4B 16
Virginia Rd. *T Hth* —3A 24
Virginia Water. —4E 21
Vivian Av. *NW4* —2E 15

Waddon. —4A 24
Waddon New Rd. *Croy* —4A 24
Waddon Rd. *Croy* —4A 24
Waddon Way. *Croy* —1A 32
Wades Hill. *N21* —1A 16
Wadham Rd. *E17* —2B 16
Waggoners Roundabout. (Junct.) —1B 22
Waggon Rd. *Barn* —4E 7
Wainscott. —3F 27
Wainscott Eastern By-Pass. *Wain* —3F 27
Wainscott Northern By-Pass. *Strood & Wain* —3E 27
Wainscott Rd. *Wain* —3F 27
Wake Rd. *Lou* —4C 8
Waldegrave Rd. *Tedd & Twic* —3C 22
Waldens Rd. *Orp* —4E 25
Walderslade. —1F 35
Walderslade Rd. *Chat & Wald* —4F 27
Walderslade Woods. *Chat* —1F 35
Waldram Pk. Rd. *SE23* —2B 24
Wales Farm Rd. *W3* —4D 15
Walham Green. —1E 23
Walk, The. *Pot B* —3E 7
Wallend. —4D 17
Wallington. —1F 31
Wallington Green. (Junct.) —4F 23
Wallis Av. *Maid* —3F 35
Wall's Green. —2B 10
Walm La. *NW2* —3E 15
Walnut Hill Rd. *Grav* —3C 26
Walnut Tree Clo. *Guild* —4E 29
Walnut Tree Rd. *Dag* —3E 17
Walpole Rd. *N17* —2A 16
Walter's Ash. —4A 4
Walterton Rd. *W9* —4E 15
Waltham Abbey. —3C 8
Waltham Cross. —3B 8
Waltham Rd. *Bore* —1F 11
Waltham Rd. *Naze* —3C 8
Waltham Rd. *White* —1A 20
Waltham St Lawrence. —1A 20
Walthamstow. —2B 16
Waltham Way. *E4* —1B 16
Walton Bri. Rd. *Shep* —4A 22
Walton Hall Farm Museum. —4D 19
Walton Heath Golf Course. —3E 31
Walton La. *Farn R* —4D 13
Walton La. *Shep* —4A 22
Walton La. *Wey* —4A 22
Walton-on-Thames. —4B 22
Walton on the Hill. —3E 31
Walton Rd. *Eps* —2D 31
Walton Rd. *W on T & W Mol* —4B 22
Walton's Hall Rd. *Stan H* —1D 27
Walton St. *Tad* —3E 31
Walworth. —1A 24
Walworth Rd. *SE1* —1A 24
Wanborough. —4C 28
Wanborough Hill. *Wanb* —4C 28
Wandle Rd. *Mord* —3F 23
Wandsworth. —2E 23
Wandsworth Bri. *SW6 & SW18* —2E 23
Wandsworth Bri. Rd. *SW6* —1E 23
Wandsworth Gyratory. (Junct.) —2E 23
Wandsworth High St. *SW18* —2E 23
Wandsworth Rd. *SW8* —2F 23
Wanstead. —3C 16
Wantz Rd. *Marg* —3D 11
Wapping. —4B 16
Wapping High St. *E1* —4B 16
Wapping La. *E1* —4B 16
Wapping Way. *E1* —4B 16
Wapses Roundabout. (Junct.) —2B 32
Warbury La. *Knap* —2D 29
War Coppice Rd. *Cat* —3A 32
Wardour St. *W1* —4F 15
Wardrobes La. *L Row* —3A 4
Ware Rd. *Gt Amw & Hail* —1B 8
Ware Rd. *Hert* —1A 8
Wares Rd. *Good E* —1C 10
Warfield. —2B 20
Warfield Rd. *Brack* —3B 20
Warfield St. *Brack* —3B 20
Warham Rd. *S Croy* —4A 24
Warley. —1B 18
Warley Gap. *L War* —2B 18
Warley Hill. *Gt War & War* —2B 18
Warley Rd. *Upm & Gt War* —2A 18
Warley St. *Gt War & Upm* —2B 18
Warlingham. —2B 32
Warner Pl. *E2* —4B 16
Warners End. —2F 5
Warners End Rd. *Hem H* —2F 5
Warners Hill. *Cook* —3B 12
Warren Av. *Brom* —3C 24
Warren Corner. —4A 28
Warrendene Rd. *Hugh V* —4B 4
Warrengate Rd. *N Mym* —2E 7
Warren Ho. Rd. *Wokgm* —3A 20
Warren Ho. Rd. *Wokgm* —3A 20
Warren La. *Dodd* —4A 10
Warren La. *Grays* —1B 26
Warren La. *Oxs* —1C 30
Warren La. *Oxt* —4C 32
Warren La. *Wok* —2F 29
Warren Rd. *E10* —3C 16
Warren Rd. *Blue B* —1F 35
Warren Rd. *Brom* —4C 24
Warren Rd. *Chels* —4D 25
Warren Rd. *Guild* —4E 29
Warren Rd. *Ludd* —4D 27
Warren Rd. *Purl* —1A 32
Warren Rd. *S'fleet* —3B 26
Warren Rd. *S Han* —4E 11
Warren Rd. *Twic* —2C 22
Warren Row. —4A 12
Warren Row Rd. *Know H* —4A 12
Warwick Av. *W9* —4E 15
Warwick Gdns. *W14* —1E 23
Warwick La. *Rain & Upm* —4A 18
Warwick Rd. *W5* —1C 22
Warwick Rd. *W14 & SW5* —1E 23
Warwicks Bench. *Guild* —4E 29
Warwick's Bench Rd. *Guild* —4E 29
Warwick Ter. *SE18* —1D 25
Warwick Way. *SW1* —1F 23
Warwick Wold. —3A 32
Warwick Wold Rd. *Red* —3A 32
Wash Hill. *Wbrn G* —3C 12
Washington Av. *Hem H* —1A 6
Washneys Rd. *Orp* —1E 33
Washpond La. *Warl* —2C 32
Wash Rd. *Bas* —2D 19
(in two parts)
Wash Rd. *Hut* —1C 18
Wasps R.U.F.C. —3C 14
Watchet La. *Holm G & L Kin* —4B 4
Watchouse Rd. *Chelm* —3E 11
Watercroft Rd. *Hals* —1E 33
Waterdale. —3B 6
Waterdale. (Junct.) —3B 6
Waterden Rd. *E15* —3B 16
Waterden Rd. *Guild* —4E 29
Water End. —1F 5
(nr. Hemel Hempstead)
Water End. —2E 7
(nr. Welham Green)
Water End Rd. *Pott E* —1F 5
Waterfall Rd. *N11 & N14* —1F 15
Waterfields Way. *Wat* —4B 6
Waterhales. —1F 17
Waterhouse La. *Blet* —4B 32
Waterhouse La. *Chelm* —2D 11
Waterhouse La. *Kgswd* —2E 31
Wateringbury. —3D 35
Wateringbury Rd. *E Mal* —3D 35
Water La. *E15* —3C 16
Water La. *Alb* —4F 29
Water La. *Bov* —3E 5
Water La. *Cobh* —1B 30
Water La. *Farnh* —4A 28
Water La. *Ilf* —3D 17
Water La. *K Lan* —3A 6
Water La. *Roy* —2D 9
Water La. *Wat* —4B 6
Water La. *W Mal* —2D 35
Waterloo Bri. *SE1* —4A 16
Waterloo Rd. *SE1* —1A 24
Waterloo Rd. *Crowt* —1A 28
Waterloo Rd. *Eps* —1D 31
Waterloo Rd. *Romf* —2F 17
Waterloo Rd. *Uxb* —4F 13
Waterloo Rd. *Wokgm* —3A 20
Waterlow Rd. *Meop* —1C 34
Watermead Way. *N17* —2B 16
Water Oakley. —1C 20
Waterside. *Che* —3D 5
Waterside. —3D 5
Waterside. *K Lan* —3A 6
Waterside Dri. *W on T* —4B 22
Watersplash La. *Asc* —3C 20
Waterway Rd. *Lea* —2C 30
Waterworks Corner. (Junct.) —2C 16
Watery La. *Kems* —2A 34
Watery La. *Mat G* —1F 9
Watery La. *Sidc* —3E 25
Watery La. *Wbrn G* —2C 12
Watford. —4B 6
Watford By-Pass. *Borwd* —1C 14
Watford F.C. —1B 14
Watford Heath. —1B 14
Watford Heath. *Wat* —1B 14
Watford Rd. *Crox G* —1A 14
Watford Rd. *Els* —1C 14
Watford Rd. *Harr & Wemb* —3C 14
Watford Rd. *K Lan* —3A 6
Watford Rd. *N'wd* —2A 14
Watford Rd. *Rad* —4C 6
Watford Rd. *St Alb* —3B 6
Watford Way. *NW7 & NW4* —1D 15
Watling. —2D 15
Watling Av. *Edgw* —2D 15
Watling St. *Bexh* —2E 25
Watling St. *Chat* —4F 27
Watling St. *Cob & Strd* —3D 27
Watling St. *Dart & Grav* —2A 26
Watling St. *Rad & Borwd* —3C 6
Watling St. *St Alb* —2C 6
Watney's Rd. *Mitc* —4F 23
Watson's Wlk. *St Alb* —2C 6
Watton's Green. —1F 17
Watts Av. *Roch* —4F 27
Watt's Cross. —4A 34
Watt's Cross Rd. *Hild* —4A 34
Watts La. *Chst* —3D 25
Watts Rd. *Th Dit* —4C 22
Wat Tyler Rd. *SE13* —1C 24
Wat Tyler Way. *Maid* —3F 35
Waverley Cres. *SE18* —1D 25
Waverley Rd. *St Alb* —1C 6
Wayfield. —4F 27
Wayfield Rd. *Chat* —4F 27
Wayside. *NW11* —3E 15
Weald Bri. Rd. *N Wea* —2F 9
Weald Hall La. *Thorn* —2E 9
Weald Pk. Way. *S Wea* —1A 18
Weald Rd. *Brtwd* —1A 18
Weald Rd. *Sev* —3F 33
Wealdstone. —2C 14
Weald Way. *Cat* —3A 32
Weavering. —2F 35
Weavering St. *Weav* —3F 35
Weedon Hill. *Hyde H* —3C 4
Weeds Wood. —1F 35
Weigall Rd. *SE12* —2C 24
Weir Rd. *Cher* —4F 21
Welder's La. *Jor* —2D 13
Welham Green. —2E 7
Wellbrook Rd. *Orp* —4D 25
Well End. —4D 7
(nr. Borhamwood)
Well End. —2B 12
(nr. Bourne End)
Well End Rd. *Borwd* —4D 7
Weller Av. *Roch* —4F 27
Weller's La. *Nup* —2B 20
Wellesley Rd. *W4* —1D 23
Wellesley Rd. *Alder* —4A 28
Wellesley Rd. *Croy* —4A 24
Wellesley Rd. *Twic* —2C 22
Welley Rd. *Wray & Slou* —2E 21
Wellfield Rd. *Hat* —1E 7
Well Hall Rd. *SE9* —2D 25
Well Hall Roundabout. (Junct.) —2D 25
Well Hill. —1E 33
Well Hill. *Orp* —1E 33
Wellhouse Rd. *Str G* —4D 31
Welling. —1E 25
Welling High St. *Well* —2E 25
Wellington Av. *Alder* —4A 28
Wellington Av. *Vir W* —4E 21
Wellington Hill. *Lou* —4C 8
Wellingtonia Av. *Crowt* —1A 28
Wellington Rd. *NW8* —4F 15
Wellington Rd. *Hamp* —3C 22
Wellington Rd. N. *Houn* —2B 22
Wellington Rd. S. *Houn* —2B 22
Wellington St. *SE18* —1D 25
Wellington St. *WC2* —4A 16
Wellington St. *Grav* —2C 26
Wellington St. *Slou* —1D 21
Welling Way. *SE9 & Well* —2D 25
Well La. *Dan* —2F 11
Well La. *Stock* —4D 11
Well La. *Wok* —2E 29
Well Rd. *Maid* —2F 35
Well Rd. *N'thaw* —3F 7
Well Row. *B'frd* —1A 8
Wells Pk. Rd. *SE26* —3B 24
Well Street. —2D 35
Well St. *E8* —3B 16
Well St. *E Mal* —2D 35
Well St. *Loose* —4F 35
Wells Way. *SE5* —1A 24
Welwyn Garden City. —1E 7
Wembley. —3D 15
Wembley Hill Rd. *Wemb* —3D 15
Wembley Park. —3D 15
Wembley Pk. Dri. *Wemb* —3D 15
Wembley Stadium. —3D 15
Wemborough Rd. *Stan* —2C 14
Wendover. —2B 4
Wendover By-Pass. *Wen* —1A 4
Wendover Dean. —2B 4
Wendover Rd. *Ayl & Wen* —1A 4
Wendover Way. *Ayl* —1A 4
Wendover Way. *Well* —2E 25
Wenlock's La. *Ing* —3B 10
Wennington. —4A 18
Wennington Rd. *Rain* —4F 17
Wensleydale Rd. *Hamp* —3B 22
Wentworth. —4D 21
Wentworth Golf Course. —4D 21
Wessex Way. *M'head* —1B 20
West Acton. —4D 15
West Barnes. —4E 23
W. Barnes La. *N Mald* —3E 23
West Bedfont. —2A 22
Westbere Rd. *NW2* —3E 15
Westbourne Green. —4E 15
Westbourne Gro. *W2* —4E 15
Westbourne Gro. *W11* —4E 15
Westbourne Pk. *W11* —4E 15
Westbourne Rd. *N7* —3A 16
Westbourne Ter. *W2* —4F 15
Westbridge Rd. *SW11* —1F 23
Westbrook Rd. *Houn* —1B 22
Westbury Av. *N22* —2A 16
W. Bury St. *N9* —1A 16
West Byfleet. —1F 29
Westcar La. *W on T* —1B 30
West Clandon. —3F 29
Westcombe Hill. *SE3* —1C 24
West Comn. *Ger X* —2E 13
W. Common Rd. *Brom* —4C 24
Westcote Rd. *SW16* —3F 23
Westcott. —4C 30
Westcott Rd. *Dork* —4C 30
Westcott St. *Westc* —4B 30
Westcourt. —2D 27
West Drayton. —1A 22
W. Drayton Rd. *Uxb* —4A 14
West Dri. *SW16* —3F 23
West Dulwich. —2A 24
West Ealing. —4C 14
Wested La. *Swan* —4F 25
West End. —1D 29
(nr. Bisley)
West End. —4B 22
(nr. Esher)
West End. —3B 20
(nr. Newell Green)
West End. —4B 14
(nr. Northolt)
West End. —2A 20
(nr. Waltham St Lawrence)
West End. —1E 7
(nr. Welwyn Garden City)
West End. —4F 15
(nr. Westminster)
West End. *Ess* —2F 7
West End. *Kems* —2A 34
W. End La. *NW6* —3E 15
W. End La. *Esh* —4B 22
W. End La. *Pinn* —2B 14
W. End La. *Stoke P* —4D 13
W. End Rd. *N'holt* —3B 14
W. End Rd. *Ruis* —3A 14
W. End Rd. *Worm* —2A 8
Westerham. —3D 33
Westerham Hill. —2D 33
Westerham Hill. *W'ham* —2D 33
Westerham Rd. *Kes* —4D 25
Westerham Rd. *Oxt & W'ham* —3C 32
Westerham Rd. *Sev* —3E 33
Westerham Rd. *W'ham* —3E 33
Westerhill Rd. *Cox* —4F 35
Western Av. *UB6, W5 & W3* —4C 14
Western Av. *Brtwd* —1B 18
Western Av. *Den & Uxb* —3F 13
Western Av. *Gnfd* —4B 14
Western Av. *Ruis & N'holt* —3A 14
Western Circus. (Junct.) —4D 15
Western Dene. *Hasl* —4B 4
Western Perimeter Rd. *W Dray & H'row A* —1F 21
Western Rd. *SW19 & Mitc* —3F 23
Western Rd. *Bill* —1D 19
Western Rd. *Bor G* —2B 34
Western Rd. *Brack* —3A 20
Western Rd. *Brtwd* —1B 18
Western Rd. *Romf* —2F 17
Western Rd. *S'hall* —1B 22
Western Rd. *Tring* —1C 4
Western Way. *SE28* —1D 25
West Ewell. —1D 31
West Farleigh. —3E 35

CENTRAL LONDON

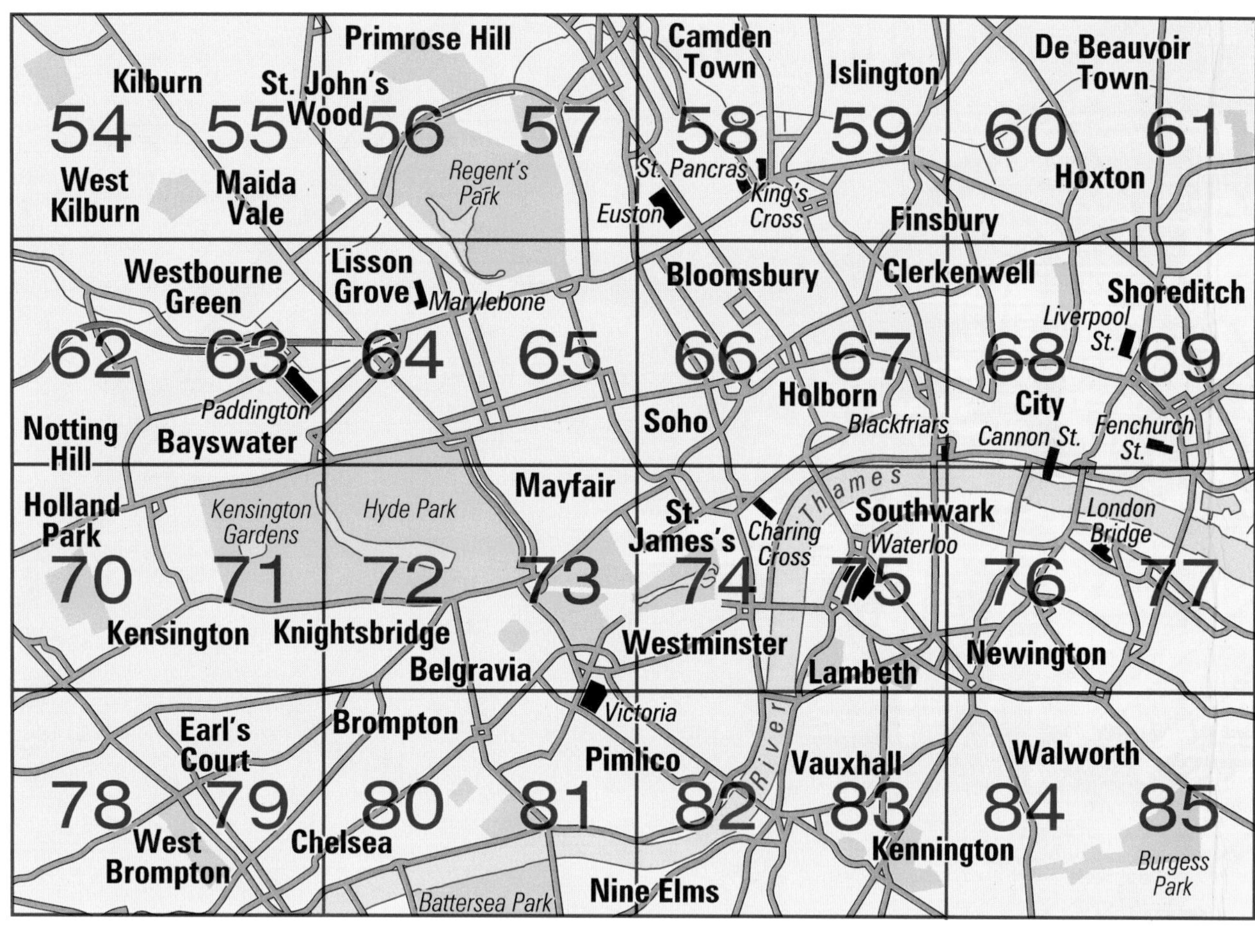

REFERENCE

Motorway	A40(M)
A Road	A10
B Road	B326
Dual Carriageway	
One Way Street	
Restricted Access	
Pedestrianized Road	
House Numbers (A & B Roads Only)	34 62
Parking Meters	
Car Park	P
Junction Name	MARBLE ARCH
Police Car Pound	
Borough Boundary	
Postal Boundary	
Map Continuation	75

Buildings	Educational Establishment	
	Hospital or Health Centre	
	Leisure or Recreational Facility	
	Open to the Public	
	Place of Interest	
	Shopping Centre or Market	
	Other Selected Buildings	
Cinema		🎞
Fire Station		■
Information Centre		🅸
National Grid Reference		¹78
Police Station		▲
Post Office		★
Railway Station		
Railway Station Entrance		
Railway Station		⮀
Underground		⊖
Docklands Light Railway		DLR
Theatre		
Toilet		▽
Toilet with Disabled Facilities		♿

Scale: 1:7,040   9 inches (22.86 cm) to 1 mile   or   14.2 cm to 1 kilometre

0	50	100	200	300 Yards	¼		½ Mile	
0	50	100	200	300	400	500	750 Metres	1 Kilometre

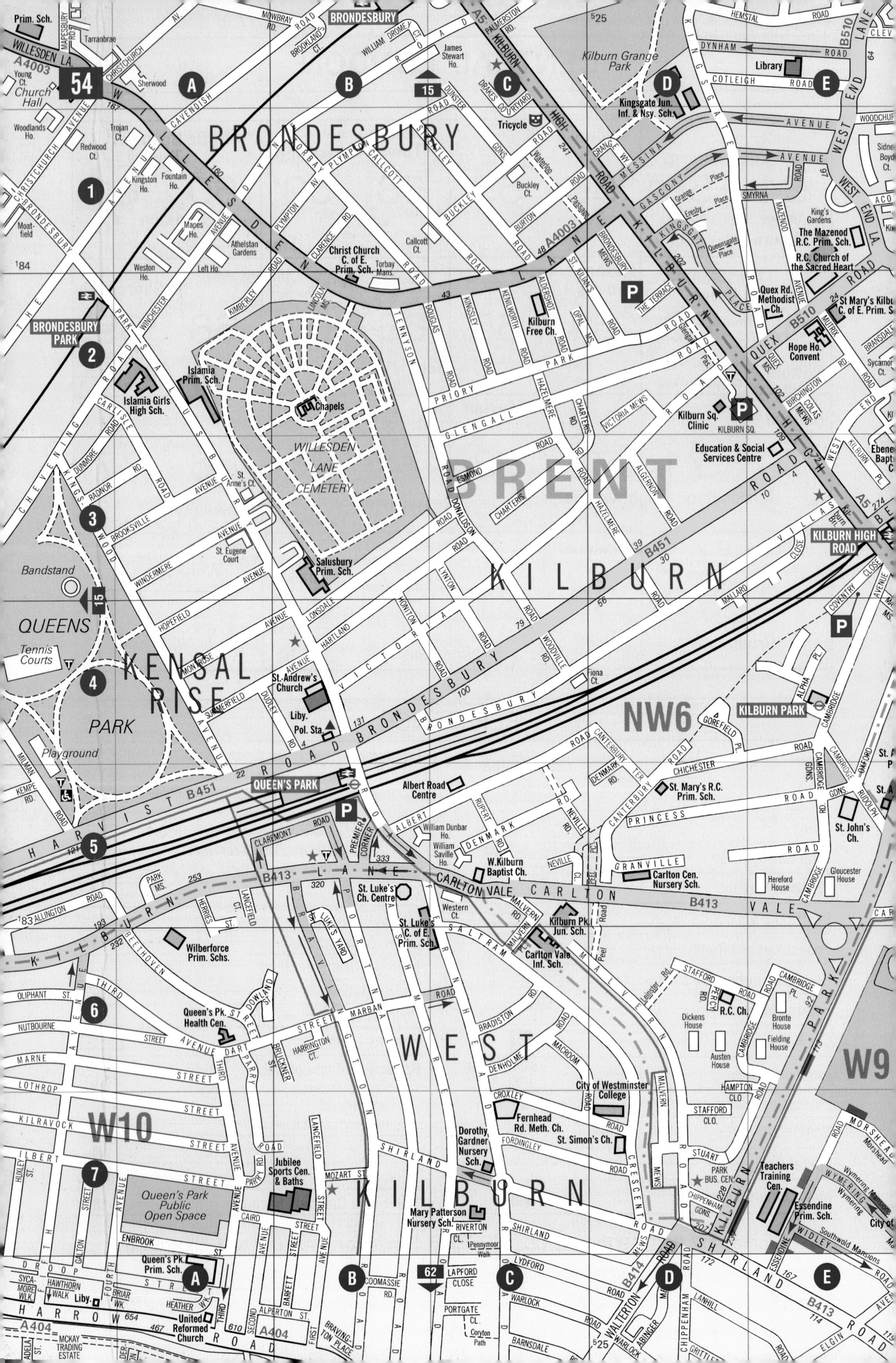
54
BRONDESBURY
BRONDESBURY PARK
KENSAL RISE
QUEENS PARK
KILBURN
BRENT
NW6
W10
W9
WEST KILBURN
KILBURN HIGH ROAD
KILBURN PARK
QUEEN'S PARK
WILLESDEN LANE CEMETERY
Kilburn Grange Park
Queen's Park Public Open Space
Prim. Sch.
Tarranbrae
Young Ct.
Church Hall
Woodlands Ho.
Redwood Ct.
Sherwood
Trojan Ct.
Kingston Ho.
Fountain Ho.
Moatfield
Mapes Ho.
Athelstan Gardens
Weston Ho.
Left Ho.
James Stewart Ho.
Tricycle
Buckley Ct.
Callcott Ct.
Christ Church C. of E. Prim. Sch.
Torbay Mans.
Kingsgate Jun. Inf. & Nsy. Sch.
Library
Kilburn Free Ch.
Islamia Prim. Sch.
Islamia Girls High Sch.
Chapels
St. Anne's Ct.
St. Eugene Court
Salusbury Prim. Sch.
St. Andrew's Church
Liby.
Pol. Sta.
Fiona Ct.
Bandstand
Tennis Courts
Playground
Kilburn Sq. Clinic
Education & Social Services Centre
Quex Rd. Methodist Ch.
The Mazenod R.C. Prim. Sch.
R.C. Church of the Sacred Heart
St Mary's Kilburn C. of E. Prim. Sch.
Hope Ho. Convent
King's Gardens
Albert Road Centre
William Dunbar Ho.
William Saville Ho.
W. Kilburn Baptist Ch.
St. Mary's R.C. Prim. Sch.
St. John's Ch.
Carlton Cen. Nursery Sch.
Hereford House
Gloucester House
St. Luke's Ch. Centre
St. Luke's C. of E. Prim. Sch.
Western Ct.
Kilburn Pk. Jun. Sch.
Carlton Vale Inf. Sch.
Wilberforce Prim. Schs.
Queen's Pk. Health Cen.
Harrington Ct.
R.C. Ch.
Dickens House
Bronte House
Austen House
Fielding House
City of Westminster College
Fernhead Rd. Meth. Ch.
St. Simon's Ch.
Dorothy Gardner Nursery Sch.
Mary Patterson Nursery Sch.
Jubilee Sports Cen. & Baths
Queen's Pk. Prim. Sch.
Liby.
United Reformed Church
Teachers Training Cen.
Essendine Prim. Sch.
Park Bus. Cen.
Wymering Mansions
Southwold Mansions
MCKAY TRADING ESTATE
WILLESDEN LA.
A4003
A5
B510
B451
B413
B414
A404
15
62

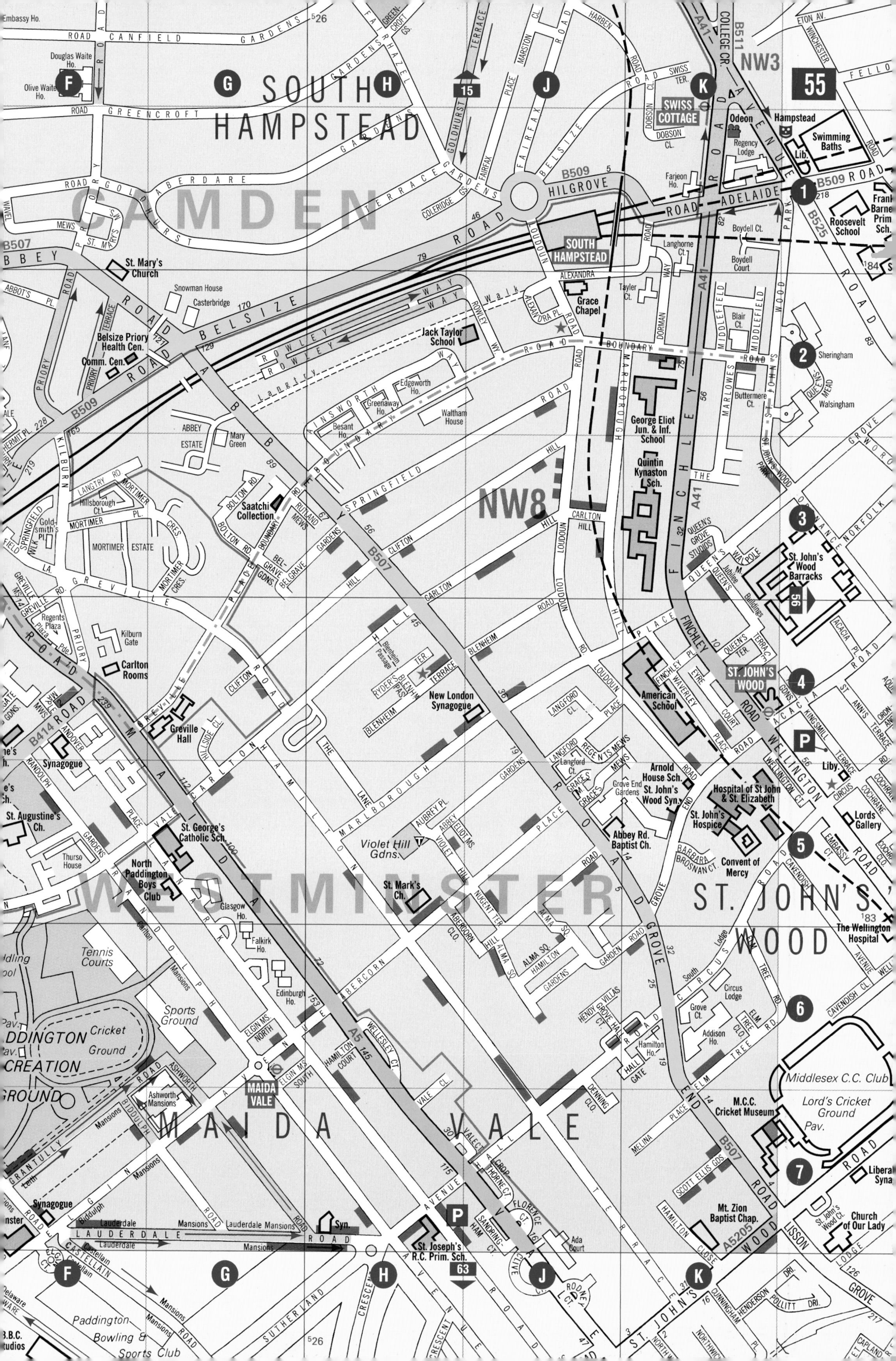
SOUTH HAMPSTEAD
CAMDEN
NW3
NW8
WESTMINSTER
ST. JOHN'S WOOD
MAIDA VALE
SWISS COTTAGE
SOUTH HAMPSTEAD
ST. JOHN'S WOOD
MAIDA VALE
Embassy Ho.
CANFIELD GARDENS
Douglas Waite Ho.
Olive Waite Ho.
GREENCROFT GARDENS
FAIRHAZEL GARDENS
GOLDHURST TERRACE
MARSTON CL.
HARBEN ROAD
COLLEGE CR.
ETON AV.
WINCHESTER ROAD
FELLOWS ROAD
Odeon
Hampstead
Swimming Baths
Lib.
Regency Lodge
Farjeon Ho.
DOBSON CL.
SWISS TER.
BELSIZE ROAD
HILGROVE ROAD
ADELAIDE ROAD
B509 ROAD
Frank Barnes Prim. Sch.
Roosevelt School
Boydell Ct.
Boydell Court
Langhorne Ct.
ABERDARE GARDENS
COLERIDGE GDNS.
FAIRFAX PLACE
FAIRFAX ROAD
ABBEY ROAD
ST. MARY'S MEWS
PRIORY ROAD
ABBOT'S PL.
St. Mary's Church
Snowman House
Casterbridge
Belsize Priory Health Cen.
Comm. Cen.
ROWLEY WAY
Langtry Walk
Jack Taylor School
ALEXANDRA PL.
ALEXANDRA ROAD
Grace Chapel
Tayler Ct.
DORMAN WAY
BOUNDARY ROAD
MIDDLEFIELD
Blair Ct.
Sheringham
Walsingham
QUEEN'S MEAD
MARLOWES
Buttermere Ct.
ST. JOHN'S WOOD PARK
Edgeworth Ho.
Greenaway Ho.
Besant Ho.
Waltham House
AINSWORTH WAY
ABBEY ESTATE
Mary Green
George Eliot Jun. & Inf. School
Quintin Kynaston Sch.
MARLBOROUGH HILL
FINCHLEY ROAD
KILBURN PRIORY
LANGTRY RD.
Hillsborough Ct.
MORTIMER PL.
MORTIMER CRES.
MORTIMER ESTATE
Goldsmith's Pl.
SPRINGFIELD WLK.
SPRINGFIELD ROAD
BOLTON RD.
Saatchi Collection
RUTLAND MEWS
BELGRAVE GARDENS
CLIFTON HILL
CARLTON HILL
LOUDOUN ROAD
QUEEN'S GROVE STUDIOS
WALPOLE M.
Jubilee Buildings
St. John's Wood Barracks
ORDNANCE HILL
NORFOLK ROAD
ACACIA PL.
ACACIA ROAD
QUEEN'S TERRACE
GREVILLE ROAD
Regents Plaza
Kilburn Gate
Carlton Rooms
BLENHEIM TERRACE
Blenheim Passage
RYDER'S TER.
BLENHEIM PAS.
New London Synagogue
BLENHEIM ROAD
LANGFORD CL.
LANGFORD PLACE
REGENTS MEWS
American School
FINCHLEY PL.
WAVERLEY PLACE
ST. JOHN'S WOOD
KINGSMILL TERRACE
ST. ANN'S TERRACE
B414 ROAD
ANDOVER
Synagogue
Greville Hall
HILLSIDE CL.
CARLTON VALE
HAMILTON TERRACE
THE LANE
MARLBOROUGH PLACE
GRACE'S MEWS
Grove End Gardens
Arnold House Sch.
St. John's Wood Syn.
WELLINGTON ROAD
WELLINGTON CT.
Hospital of St John & St. Elizabeth
St. John's Hospice
Liby.
CIRCUS ROAD
Lords Gallery
COCHRANE ST.
RANDOLPH
St. Augustine's Ch.
Thurso House
St. George's Catholic Sch.
North Paddington Boys Club
AUBREY PL.
ABBEY GARDENS
ELIOT MS.
Violet Hill Gdns.
VIOLET HILL
Abbey Rd. Baptist Ch.
BARBARA BROSNAN CT.
Convent of Mercy
CAVENDISH
EMBASSY CT.
The Wellington Hospital
St. Mark's Ch.
Glasgow Ho.
Falkirk Ho.
NUGENT TER.
ABERCORN CLO.
ALMA SQ.
HAMILTON GARDENS
GARDEN ROAD
GROVE END ROAD
Lodge
NEW COURT
South
Circus Lodge
Grove Ct.
Addison Ho.
ELM TREE CLO.
ELM TREE RD.
CAVENDISH CL.
Tennis Courts
Sports Ground
PADDINGTON RECREATION GROUND
Cricket Ground
ELGIN MS. NORTH
Edinburgh Ho.
ABERCORN PLACE
HAMILTON COURT
WELLESLEY CT.
HENDY VILLAS
GROVE HALL CT.
Hamilton Ho.
HALL GATE
ELM TREE ROAD
Middlesex C.C. Club
Lord's Cricket Ground
Pav.
M.C.C. Cricket Museum
ASHWORTH ROAD
Ashworth Mansions
ELGIN MS. SOUTH
MAIDA VALE
VALE CL.
DENNING CLO.
MELINA PLACE
BIDDULPH ROAD
GRANTULLY ROAD
ELGIN AVENUE
Mansions
Leith
Synagogue
LAUDERDALE ROAD
Lauderdale Mansions
Syn.
St. Joseph's R.C. Prim. Sch.
SANDRINGHAM CT.
HORNET CT.
CROFT
FLORENCE CT.
Ada Court
SCOTT ELLIS GDS.
Mt. Zion Baptist Chap.
HAMILTON CLOSE
Liberal Syna.
Church of Our Lady
St John's Wood Ct.
LISSON GROVE
LODGE
CASTELLAIN ROAD
ELGIN CT.
Paddington Bowling & Sports Club
B.B.C. Studios
DELAWARE
SUTHERLAND AVENUE
CRESCENT
RODNEY CT.
ST. JOHN'S WOOD
CUNNINGHAM PL.
HENDERSON DR.
POLLITT DR.
NORTHWICK
CAPLAND
A41
A5
A5205
B507
B509
B511
B525
F
G
H
J
K
1
2
3
4
5
6
7
15
56
63

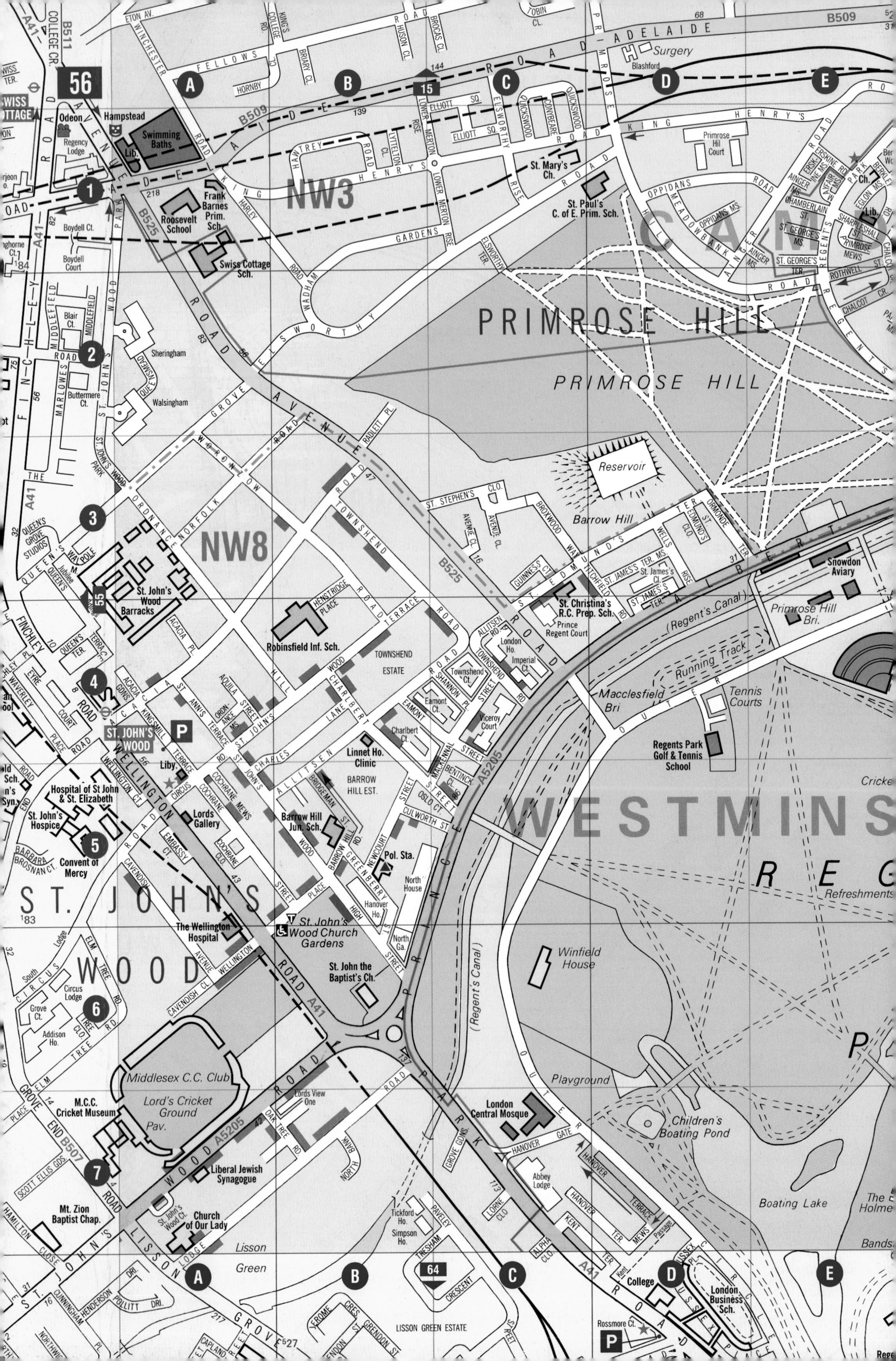
56
NW3
NW8
PRIMROSE HILL
ST. JOHN'S WOOD
WESTMINSTER
CAMDEN
Hampstead Swimming Baths
Swiss Cottage Sch.
Roosevelt School
Frank Barnes Prim. Sch.
St. Paul's C. of E. Prim. Sch.
St. Mary's Ch.
Primrose Hill Court
Reservoir
Barrow Hill
St. John's Wood Barracks
Robinsfield Inf. Sch.
Townshend Estate
St. Christina's R.C. Prep. Sch.
Snowdon Aviary
Primrose Hill Bri.
Running Track
Macclesfield Bri
Regents Park Golf & Tennis School
Linnet Ho. Clinic
Barrow Hill Est.
Barrow Hill Jun. Sch.
Pol. Sta.
Hospital of St John & St. Elizabeth
St. John's Hospice
Convent of Mercy
Lords Gallery
The Wellington Hospital
St. John's Wood Church Gardens
St. John the Baptist's Ch.
Winfield House
Middlesex C.C. Club
Lord's Cricket Ground
M.C.C. Cricket Museum
Liberal Jewish Synagogue
Mt. Zion Baptist Chap.
Church of Our Lady
London Central Mosque
Children's Boating Pond
Boating Lake
Playground
Abbey Lodge
College
London Business Sch.
Lisson Green Estate
15
55
64

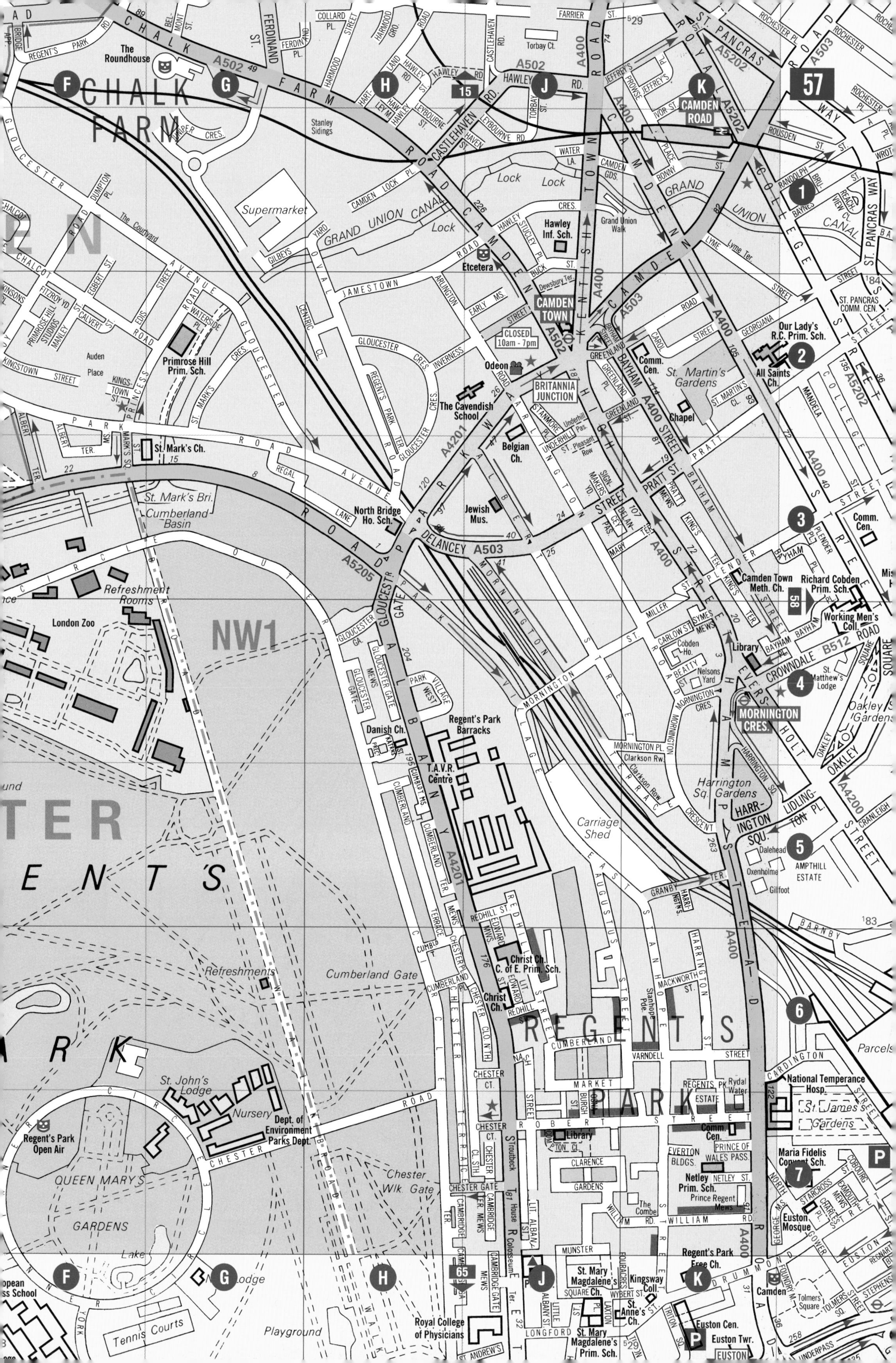

57
15
58
65
F
G
H
J
K
1
2
3
4
5
6
7
CHALK FARM
The Roundhouse
CHALK FARM ROAD
A502
REGENT'S PARK RD.
BRIDGE APP.
BEL-MONT ST.
FERDINAND ST.
FERDINAND PL.
COLLARD PL.
HARMOOD STREET
HARMOOD GRO.
HARTLAND RD.
HAWLEY RD.
HAWLEY CRES.
LEYBOURNE ST.
LEYBOURNE RD.
CASTLEHAVEN RD.
HAWLEY RD.
FARRIER ST.
Torbay Ct.
TORBAY ST.
JEFFREY'S PL.
JEFFREY'S ST.
PROWSE PL.
IVOR ST.
ROYAL COLLEGE ST.
ST. PANCRAS WAY
A5202
ROCHESTER PL.
ROCHESTER RD.
ROCHESTER SQ.
ROCHESTER WAY
ROUSDEN ST.
CAMDEN ROAD
A400
CAMDEN GDS.
WATER LA.
BONNY ST.
Stanley Sidings
ADELAIDE RD.
GLOUCESTER AVENUE
DUMPTON PL.
The Courtyard
CHALCOT ROAD
EGBERT ST.
FITZROY YD.
PRIMROSE HILL STUDIOS
CALVERT ST.
MANLEY ST.
EDIS STREET
KINGSTOWN STREET
Auden Place
KINGS-TOWN ST.
PRINCESS ROAD
Primrose Hill Prim. Sch.
WATERSIDE PL.
ST. MARK'S CRES.
PARK ROAD
ALBERT TER.
ALBERT TER. MS.
ST. MARK'S SQ.
St. Mark's Ch.
St. Mark's Bri.
Cumberland Basin
REGAL LANE
PRINCE ALBERT ROAD
A5205
Supermarket
CAMDEN LOCK PL.
GRAND UNION CANAL
Lock
GILBEYS YARD
OVAL ROAD
JAMESTOWN RD.
ARLINGTON ROAD
CENTRIC CL.
GLOUCESTER CRES.
INVERNESS STREET
REGENT'S PARK TER.
CAMDEN HIGH STREET
Hawley Inf. Sch.
STUCLEY PL.
BUCK ST.
Dewsbury Ter.
Grand Union Walk
Etcetera
EARLY MS.
CLOSED 10am - 7pm
CAMDEN TOWN
KENTISH TOWN ROAD
Odeon
Britannia Junction
The Cavendish School
North Bridge Ho. Sch.
Belgian Ch.
Jewish Mus.
STANMORE PL.
UNDERHILL ST.
Underhill Pas.
Pleasant Row
SIGNMAKERS YD.
PARKWAY
A4201
DELANCEY A503
DELANCEY PAS.
MARY TER.
CAMDEN STREET
A400
A503
BAYHAM STREET
GREENLAND PL.
GREENLAND RD.
Comm. Cen.
CAROL STREET
GEORGIANA STREET
St. Martin's Gardens
ST. MARTIN'S CL.
Chapel
Our Lady's R.C. Prim. Sch.
All Saints Ch.
MANDELA ST.
LYME ST.
Lyme Ter.
RANDOLPH ST.
BAYNES ST.
REACH VIEW CL.
GRAND UNION CANAL
St. Pancras Comm. Cen.
PRATT ST.
PRATT MEWS
KING'S TER.
PLENDER ST.
BAYHAM PL.
Camden Town Meth. Ch.
Richard Cobden Prim. Sch.
Working Men's Coll.
CROWNDALE ROAD
B512
Library
OAKLEY SQUARE
St. Matthew's Lodge
Oakley Gardens
EVERSHOLT ST.
MORNINGTON CRES.
MILLER ST.
CARLOW ST.
SYMES MEWS
Cobden Ho.
BEATTY ST.
Nelsons Yard
MORNINGTON ST.
MORNINGTON PL.
Clarkson Rw.
Clarkson Row
MORNINGTON TERRACE
MORNINGTON CRESCENT
HARRINGTON SQ.
Harrington Sq. Gardens
LIDLINGTON PL.
HARRINGTON SQU.
HAMPSTEAD ROAD
A4200
Dalehead
Oxenholme
Gillfoot
AMPTHILL ESTATE
CRANLEIGH ST.
Carriage Shed
GRANBY TER.
HARRINGTONS.
BARNBY ST.
NW1
OUTER CIRCLE
Refreshment Rooms
London Zoo
GLOUCESTER GATE
GLOUCESTER GATE MEWS
PARK VILLAGE WEST
PARK VILLAGE EAST
Danish Ch.
Regent's Park Barracks
T.A.V.R. Centre
CUMBERLAND MS.
CUMBERLAND TER.
CUMBERLAND TERRACE MEWS
CUMBERLAND PL.
ALBANY STREET
A4201
REDHILL ST.
EDWARD MEWS
Christ Ch. C. of E. Prim. Sch.
Christ Ch.
AUGUSTUS ST.
STANHOPE ST.
Stanhope Pde.
MACKWORTH ST.
HARRINGTON ST.
VARNDELL STREET
CUMBERLAND
MARKET
REGENT'S PARK
REGENT'S PARK ESTATE
Rydal Water
ROBERT STREET
Comm. Cen.
Library
CLARENCE GARDENS
EVERTON BLDGS.
PRINCE OF WALES PASS.
Netley Prim. Sch.
NETLEY ST.
Prince Regent Mews
WILLIAM RD.
The Combe
MUNSTER SQUARE
St. Mary Magdalene's Ch.
Kingsway Coll.
WYBERT ST.
St. Anne's Ch.
St. Mary Magdalene's Prim. Sch.
LONGFORD ST.
LAXTON PL.
Regent's Park Free Ch.
DRUMMOND ST.
Euston Cen.
Euston Twr.
EUSTON RD.
TRITON SQ.
National Temperance Hosp.
St. James's Gardens
CARDINGTON STREET
Parcels
Maria Fidelis Convent Sch.
Euston Mosque
STARCROSS ST.
CHARLES PL.
EXMOUTH MEWS
COBOURG ST.
GEORGE MS.
NORTH GOWER ST.
EVERSHOLT ST.
Camden
Tolmers Square
TOLMERS SQ.
STEPHENSON WAY
EUSTON UNDERPASS
Cumberland Gate
Refreshments
Chester Wlk. Gate
CHESTER GATE
CHESTER TERRACE
CHESTER CLO. N'TH
CHESTER CT.
CHESTER CL. STH.
CHESTER PL.
CHESTER RD.
CAMBRIDGE TER.
CAMBRIDGE TER. MEWS
CAMBRIDGE GATE MEWS
NASH STREET
Troutbeck
House
Colosseum Ter.
LIT. ALBANY ST.
ALBANY ST.
Royal College of Physicians
ST. ANDREW'S PL.
St. John's Lodge
Nursery
Dept. of Environment Parks Dept.
Regent's Park Open Air
QUEEN MARY'S GARDENS
INNER CIRCLE
Lake
Lodge
Tennis Courts
Playground
BROAD WALK
YORK
European Business School
REGENT'S PARK

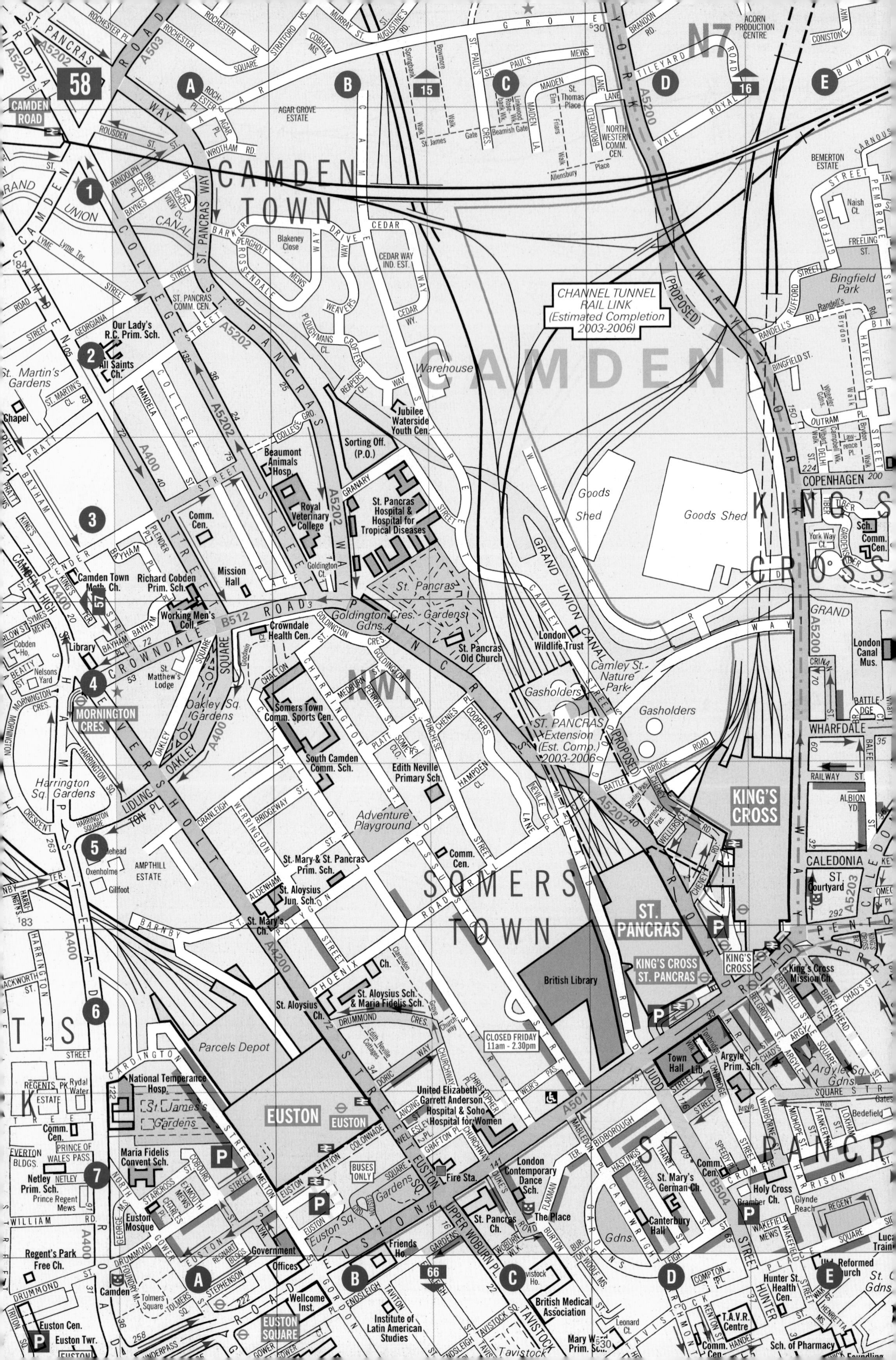
58
CAMDEN ROAD
CAMDEN TOWN
CAMDEN
SOMERS TOWN
KING'S CROSS
ST. PANCRAS
N7
NW1
15
16
57
66
CHANNEL TUNNEL RAIL LINK (Estimated Completion 2003-2006)
ST. PANCRAS Extension (Est. Comp.) 2003-2006
(PROPOSED)
AGAR GROVE ESTATE
ACORN PRODUCTION CENTRE
BEMERTON ESTATE
AMPTHILL ESTATE
REGENTS PK ESTATE
EVERTON BLDGS.
NORTH WESTERN COMM. CEN.
Blakeney Close
CEDAR WAY IND. EST.
Warehouse
Jubilee Waterside Youth Cen.
Sorting Off. (P.O.)
St. Pancras Hospital & Hospital for Tropical Diseases
Beaumont Animals Hosp.
Royal Veterinary College
Our Lady's R.C. Prim. Sch.
All Saints Ch.
St. Martin's Gardens
Chapel
Comm. Cen.
Mission Hall
Camden Town Meth. Ch.
Richard Cobden Prim. Sch.
Working Men's Coll.
Library
Crowndale Health Cen.
St. Pancras Gardens
St. Pancras Old Church
Goldington Cres. Gdns.
London Wildlife Trust
Camley St. Nature Park
Gasholders
Goods Shed
Bingfield Park
York Way Ct.
Sch.
Comm. Cen.
London Canal Mus.
MORNINGTON CRES.
Harrington Sq. Gardens
Oakley Sq. Gardens
St. Matthew's Lodge
Somers Town Comm. Sports Cen.
South Camden Comm. Sch.
Edith Neville Primary Sch.
Adventure Playground
St. Mary & St. Pancras Prim. Sch.
St. Aloysius Jun. Sch.
St. Mary's Ch.
St. Aloysius Sch. & Maria Fidelis Sch.
St. Aloysius Ch.
British Library
KING'S CROSS ST. PANCRAS
KING'S CROSS
King's Cross Mission Ch.
Parcels Depot
National Temperance Hosp.
St. James's Gardens
EUSTON
CLOSED FRIDAY 11am - 2.30pm
United Elizabeth Garrett Anderson Hospital & Soho Hospital for Women
Town Hall
Lib.
Argyle Prim. Sch.
Argyle Sq. Gdns
Maria Fidelis Convent Sch.
Netley Prim. Sch.
Euston Mosque
Regent's Park Free Ch.
Government Offices
Fire Sta.
London Contemporary Dance Sch.
The Place
St. Pancras Ch.
Friends Ho.
Euston Sq. Gardens
BUSES ONLY
St. Mary's German Ch.
Canterbury Hall
Comm. Cen.
Holy Cross Ch.
Utd. Reformed Church
Hunter St. Health Cen.
Wellcome Inst.
Institute of Latin American Studies
British Medical Association
Tavistock Ho.
T.A.V.R. Centre
Sch. of Pharmacy
Euston Cen.
Euston Twr.
EUSTON SQUARE
Camden
Tolmers Square
A5202
A503
A5200
A400
A4200
A501
B512
B504
A5203
ROCHESTER SQUARE
AGAR GROVE
ST. PANCRAS WAY
COLLEGE ST.
CAMDEN ST.
PRATT ST.
GEORGIANA ST.
CROWNDALE ROAD
EVERSHOLT ST.
CHARRINGTON ST.
PANCRAS ROAD
YORK WAY
GOODS WAY
CAMLEY ST.
MIDLAND ROAD
OSSULSTON ST.
CHALTON ST.
POLYGON ROAD
PHOENIX ST.
DRUMMOND CRES.
HAMPSTEAD ROAD
EUSTON ROAD
UPPER WOBURN PL.
GORDON ST.
JUDD ST.
HASTINGS ST.
CARTWRIGHT GARDENS
ARGYLE SQUARE
GRAY'S INN ROAD
COPENHAGEN ST.
CALEDONIAN ROAD
WHARFDALE RD.
RAILWAY ST.
CALEDONIA ST.
PENTONVILLE RD.
GRAND UNION CANAL
A B C D E
1 2 3 4 5 6 7

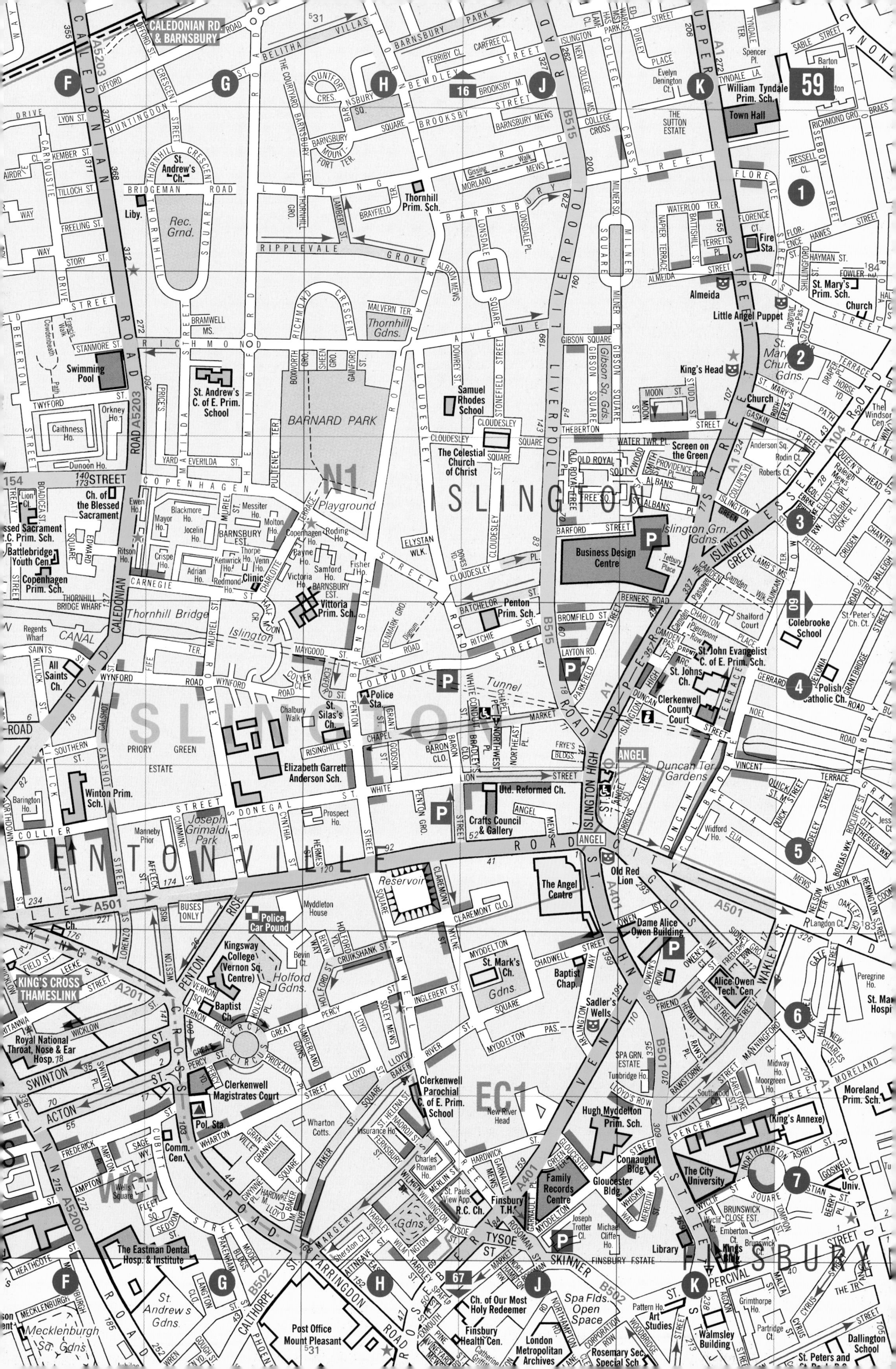

59
CALEDONIAN RD. & BARNSBURY
F
G
H
J
K
16
William Tyndale Prim. Sch.
Town Hall
THE SUTTON ESTATE
St. Andrew's Ch.
Liby.
Rec. Grnd.
Thornhill Prim. Sch.
Thornhill Gdns.
Almeida
Fire Sta.
St. Mary's Prim. Sch.
Church
Little Angel Puppet
King's Head
St. Mary's Church Gdns.
Swimming Pool
St. Andrew's C. of E. Prim. School
BARNARD PARK
Samuel Rhodes School
The Celestial Church of Christ
Screen on the Green
N1
Playground
ISLINGTON
Ch. of the Blessed Sacrament
Blessed Sacrament R.C. Prim. Sch.
Battlebridge Youth Cen.
Copenhagen Prim. Sch.
Business Design Centre
Islington Grn. Gdns.
Colebrooke School
Clinic
Vittoria Prim. Sch.
Penton Prim. Sch.
Thornhill Bridge
Regents Canal
Islington Tunnel
All Saints Ch.
St. John Evangelist C. of E. Prim. Sch.
St. Johns Ch.
Polish Catholic Ch.
Clerkenwell County Court
Police Sta.
St. Silas's Ch.
Elizabeth Garrett Anderson Sch.
Winton Prim. Sch.
ANGEL
Duncan Ter. Gardens
Utd. Reformed Ch.
Crafts Council & Gallery
Joseph Grimaldi Park
PENTONVILLE ROAD
Reservoir
The Angel Centre
Old Red Lion
Dame Alice Owen Building
Alice Owen Tech. Cen.
Police Car Pound
Kingsway College (Vernon Sq. Centre)
Holford Gdns.
St. Mark's Ch.
Baptist Chap.
Sadler's Wells
Baptist Ch.
KING'S CROSS THAMESLINK
Royal National Throat, Nose & Ear Hosp.
Clerkenwell Magistrates Court
Pol. Sta.
Comm. Cen.
Clerkenwell Parochial C. of E. Prim. School
EC1
New River Head
Hugh Myddelton Prim. Sch.
Moreland Prim. Sch.
(King's Annexe)
The City University
Connaught Bldg.
Gloucester Bldg.
Family Records Centre
Finsbury T.H.
St. Pauls View App. R.C. Ch.
WC1
The Eastman Dental Hosp. & Institute
St. Andrew's Gdns.
Mecklenburgh Sq. Gdns.
Post Office Mount Pleasant
67
Ch. of Our Most Holy Redeemer
Finsbury Health Cen.
London Metropolitan Archives
Spa Flds. Open Space
Rosemary Sec. Special Sch.
Art Studies
Walmsley Building
Library
FINSBURY
Dallington School
St. Peters and
Univ.
1
2
3
4
5
6
7
60

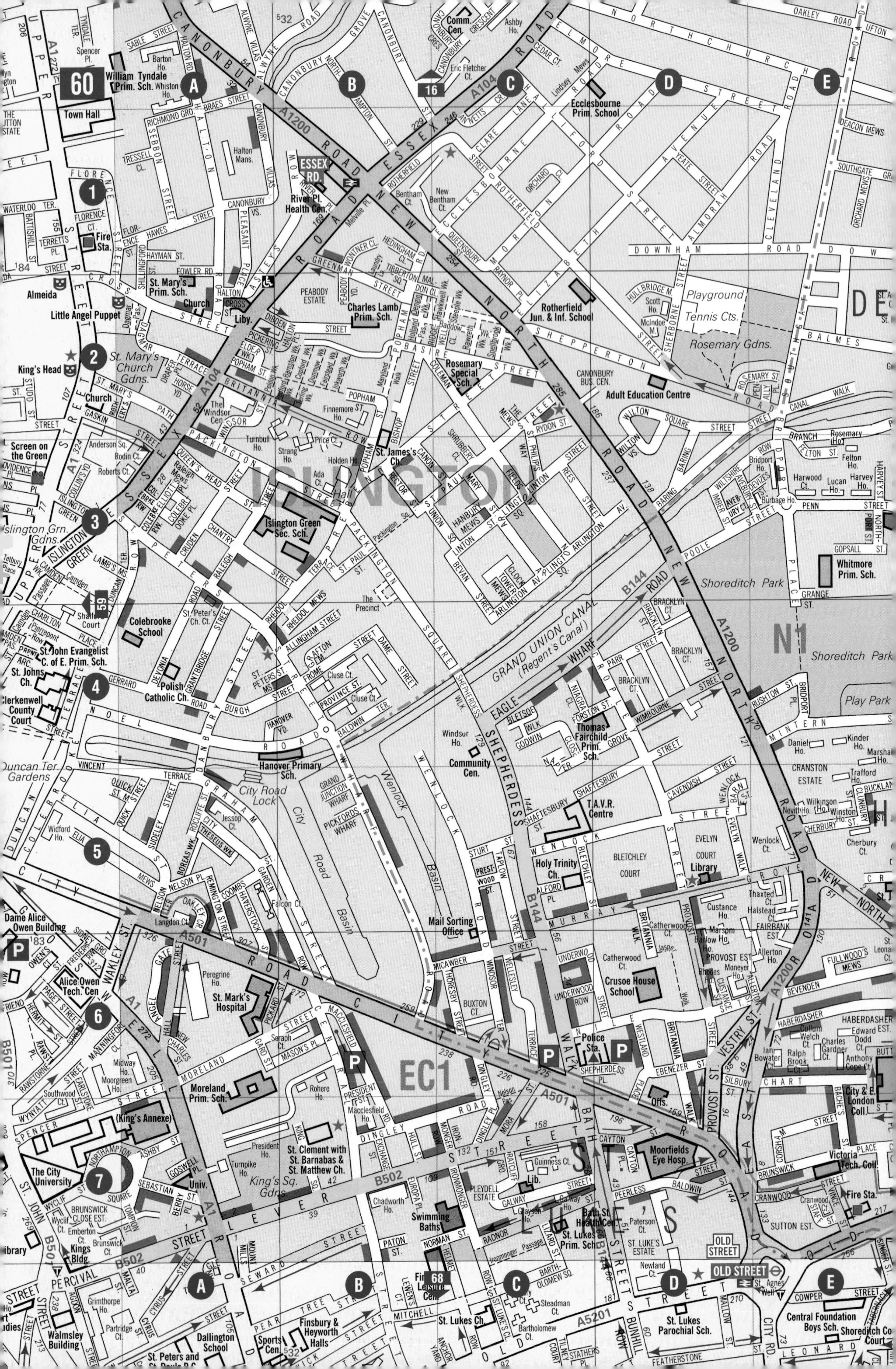

60
16
59
68
A
B
C
D
E
1
2
3
4
5
6
7
ISLINGTON
N1
EC1
CANONBURY ROAD
ESSEX ROAD
NEW NORTH ROAD
CITY ROAD
OLD STREET
UPPER STREET
GOSWELL ROAD
SHEPHERDESS WALK
BALDWIN STREET
GRAND UNION CANAL
(Regent's Canal)
City Road Basin
City Road Lock
Wenlock Basin
Shoreditch Park
Play Park
Rosemary Gdns.
Playground
Tennis Cts.
St. Mary's Church Gdns.
Islington Grn. Gdns.
Duncan Ter. Gardens
King's Sq. Gdns.
William Tyndale Prim. Sch.
Town Hall
Fire Sta.
Almeida
Little Angel Puppet
King's Head
Screen on the Green
St. Mary's Prim. Sch.
Church
Liby.
Charles Lamb Prim. Sch.
Peabody Estate
River Pl. Health Cen.
Essex Rd.
Ecclesbourne Prim. School
Rotherfield Jun. & Inf. School
Canonbury Bus. Cen.
Adult Education Centre
Rosemary Special Sch.
St. James's Ch.
Islington Green Sec. Sch.
Colebrooke School
Polish Catholic Ch.
St. John Evangelist C. of E. Prim. Sch.
St. Johns Ch.
Clerkenwell County Court
Hanover Primary Sch.
Community Cen.
Thomas Fairchild Prim. Sch.
T.A.V.R. Centre
Whitmore Prim. Sch.
Holy Trinity Ch.
Library
Mail Sorting Office
Crusoe House School
Police Sta.
Offs.
Dame Alice Owen Building
Alice Owen Tech. Cen
St. Mark's Hospital
Moreland Prim. Sch.
St. Clement with St. Barnabas & St. Matthew Ch.
(King's Annexe)
The City University
Univ.
Swimming Baths
Lib.
Bath St. Health Cen.
St. Lukes Prim. Sch.
Moorfields Eye Hosp.
St. Luke's Estate
Old Street
Victoria Tech. Coll.
City & E. London Coll.
Fire Sta.
Fire Leisure Cen.
St. Lukes Ch.
Finsbury & Heyworth Halls
Sports Cen.
Dallington School
St. Lukes Parochial Sch.
Central Foundation Boys Sch.
Shoreditch Co. Court
Walmsley Building
Kings Bldg.
Library
Cranston Estate
Bletchley Court
Evelyn Court
Provost Est.
A1200
A104
A1
A501
A5201
B144
B502
B501

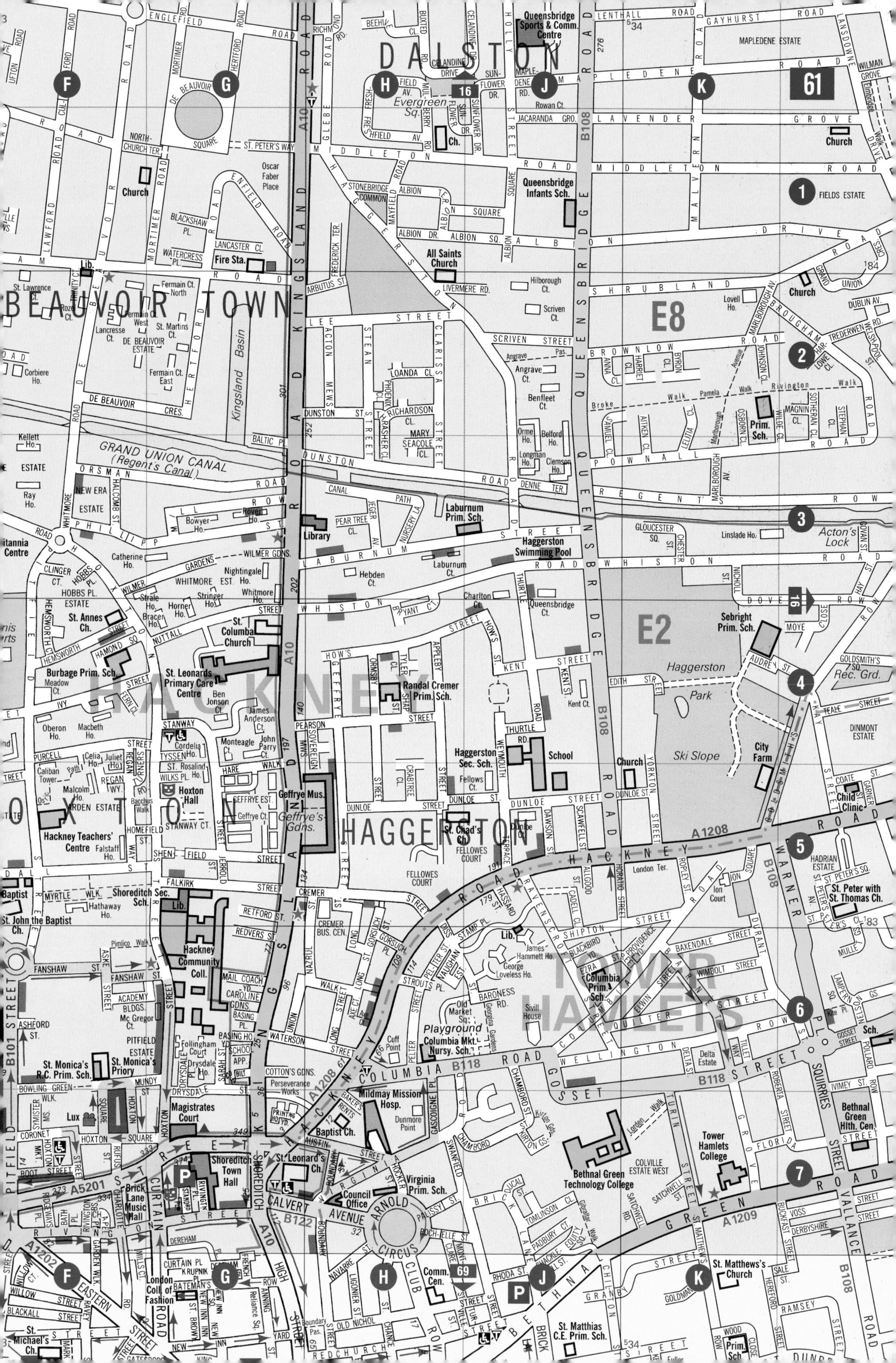
61
DALSTON
DE BEAUVOIR TOWN
HACKNEY
HOXTON
HAGGERSTON
TOWER HAMLETS
E8
E2
16
69
Queensbridge Sports & Comm. Centre
LENTHALL ROAD
GAYHURST ROAD
MAPLEDENE ESTATE
MAPLEDENE ROAD
LAVENDER GROVE
MIDDLETON ROAD
FIELDS ESTATE
SHRUBLAND ROAD
BROWNLOW ROAD
POWNALL ROAD
REGENT'S ROW
WHISTON ROAD
DOVE ROW
HACKNEY ROAD
COLUMBIA ROAD
GOSSET STREET
BETHNAL GREEN ROAD
QUEENSBRIDGE ROAD
KINGSLAND ROAD
ENGLEFIELD ROAD
DE BEAUVOIR SQUARE
DE BEAUVOIR ESTATE
DE BEAUVOIR CRES.
MORTIMER ROAD
ENFIELD ROAD
HERTFORD ROAD
LAWFORD ROAD
Kingsland Basin
GRAND UNION CANAL (Regent's Canal)
ORSMAN ROAD
PHILLIPP ST
WHITMORE ROAD
WHITMORE EST.
NUTTALL STREET
HEMSWORTH ST
St. Annes Ch.
Burbage Prim. Sch.
St. Columba Church
St. Leonards Primary Care Centre
Hoxton Hall
Geffrye Mus.
Geffrye's Gdns.
Hackney Teachers' Centre
Shoreditch Sec. Sch.
Hackney Community Coll.
St. John the Baptist Ch.
St. Monica's R.C. Prim. Sch.
St. Monica's Priory
Magistrates Court
Shoreditch Town Hall
Brick Lane Music Hall
London Coll. of Fashion
OLD STREET
HOXTON SQUARE
PITFIELD STREET
CURTAIN ROAD
SHOREDITCH HIGH STREET
CALVERT AVENUE
ARNOLD CIRCUS
St. Leonard's Ch.
Council Office
Virginia Prim. Sch.
Comm. Cen.
Mildmay Mission Hosp.
Baptist Ch.
Columbia Mkt. Nursy. Sch.
Columbia Prim. Sch.
Bethnal Green Technology College
Tower Hamlets College
St. Matthews's Church
St. Matthias C.E. Prim. Sch.
Haggerston Park
Ski Slope
City Farm
Sebright Prim. Sch.
Haggerston Swimming Pool
Laburnum Prim. Sch.
Library
Randal Cremer Prim. Sch.
Haggerston Sec. Sch.
School
St. Chad's Ch.
FELLOWES COURT
Queensbridge Infants Sch.
All Saints Church
Church
Prim. Sch.
Acton's Lock
Rec. Grd.
DINMONT ESTATE
Child Clinic
HADRIAN ESTATE
St. Peter with St. Thomas Ch.
Bethnal Green Hlth. Cen.
Fire Sta.
Lib.
Evergreen Sq.
Oscar Faber Place
A10
A1208
A1209
A5201
A1202
B108
B118
B122
B101

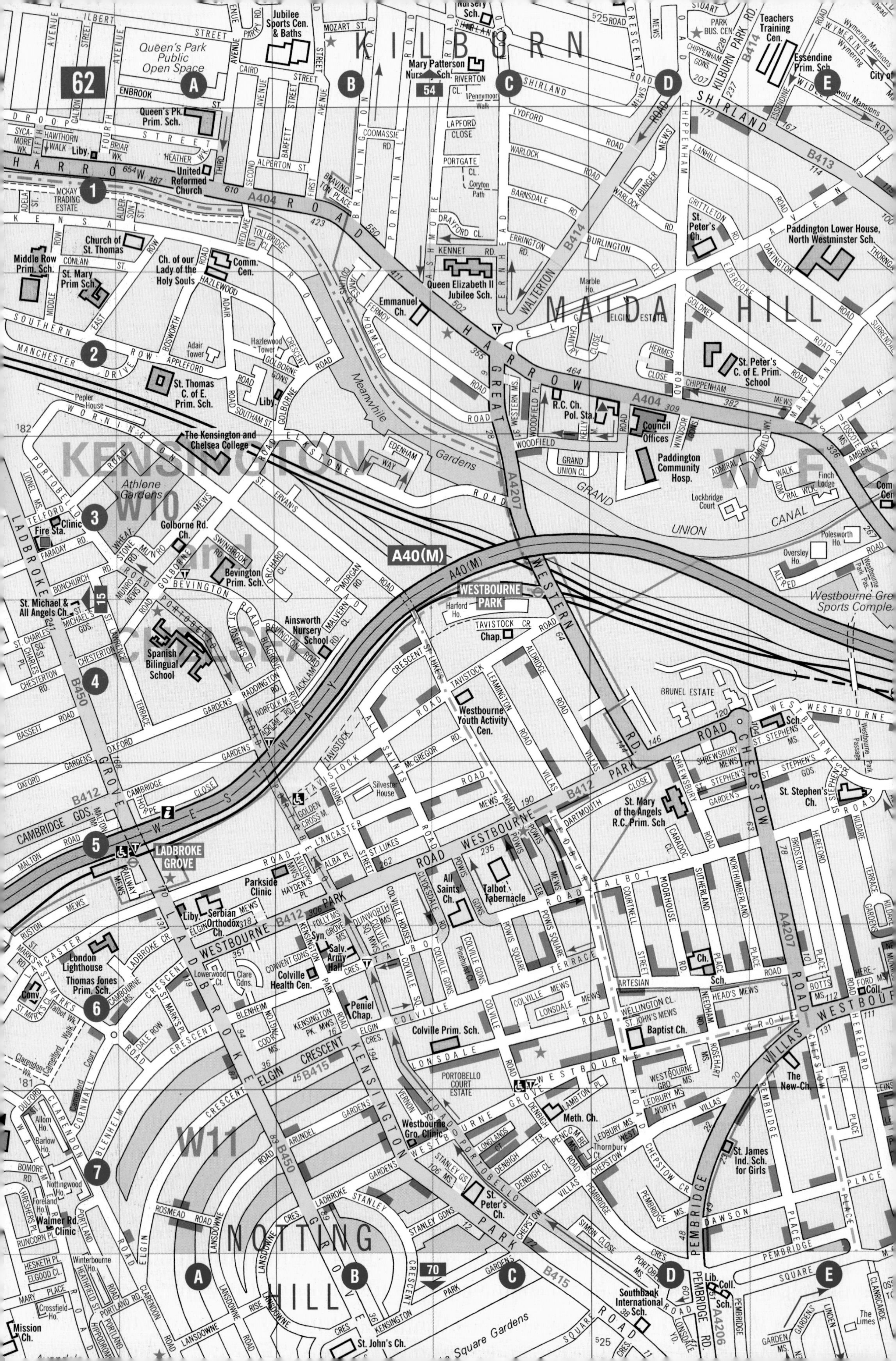
62
KILBURN
MAIDA HILL
KENSINGTON and CHELSEA
W10
W11
NOTTING HILL
WESTMINSTER
Queen's Park Public Open Space
Jubilee Sports Cen. & Baths
Mary Patterson Nurs. Sch.
54
Teachers Training Cen.
Essendine Prim. Sch.
Queen's Pk. Prim. Sch.
United Reformed Church
HARROW ROAD
A404
MCKAY TRADING ESTATE
Church of St. Thomas
Middle Row Prim. Sch.
St. Mary Prim Sch.
Ch. of our Lady of the Holy Souls
Comm. Cen.
Queen Elizabeth II Jubilee Sch.
Emmanuel Ch.
St. Peter's Ch.
Paddington Lower House, North Westminster Sch.
St. Peter's C. of E. Prim. School
ELGIN ESTATE
R.C. Ch.
Pol. Sta.
Council Offices
Paddington Community Hosp.
Adair Tower
Hazlewood Tower
St. Thomas C. of E. Prim. Sch.
Liby.
Pepler House
The Kensington and Chelsea College
Meanwhile Gardens
GRAND UNION CANAL
Athlone Gardens
Clinic
Fire Sta.
Golborne Rd. Ch.
Bevington Prim. Sch.
A40(M)
WESTWAY
WESTBOURNE PARK
Harford Ho.
Chap.
Ainsworth Nursery School
St. Michael & All Angels Ch.
15
Spanish Bilingual School
Westbourne Youth Activity Cen.
BRUNEL ESTATE
Westbourne Green Sports Complex
Sch.
St. Stephen's Ch.
St. Mary of the Angels R.C. Prim. Sch
Silvester House
LADBROKE GROVE
B450
B412
Parkside Clinic
All Saints' Ch.
Talbot Tabernacle
Serbian Orthodox Ch.
Syn.
Salv. Army Hall
Colville Health Cen.
London Lighthouse
Thomas Jones Prim. Sch.
Conv.
Peniel Chap.
Colville Prim. Sch.
Baptist Ch.
Ch.
Sch.
Coll.
PORTOBELLO COURT ESTATE
Meth. Ch.
The New Ch.
Westbourne Gro. Clinic
St. Peter's Ch.
St. James Ind. Sch. for Girls
Walmer Rd. Clinic
Mission Ch.
70
Southbank International Sch.
Lib.
Coll. Sch.
St. John's Ch.
The Limes
Square Gardens
B415
A4207
A4206
B413
B414
PEMBRIDGE RD.
KENSINGTON PARK ROAD
ELGIN CRESCENT
WESTBOURNE GROVE
WESTBOURNE PARK ROAD
CHEPSTOW ROAD
PORTOBELLO ROAD
GREAT WESTERN RD.
LANSDOWNE CRES.
ARUNDEL GARDENS
LADBROKE GARDENS
STANLEY GDNS
CHIPPENHAM ROAD
SHIRLAND ROAD
ELGIN AVENUE
SOUTHERN ROW
KENSAL ROAD
GOLBORNE ROAD
ST. ERVANS ROAD
TAVISTOCK CRESCENT
ST. LUKES ROAD
LANCASTER ROAD
BASSETT ROAD
OXFORD GARDENS
CAMBRIDGE GDS.
CHESTERTON RD.
ST. CHARLES SQ.
BLENHEIM CRESCENT
CORNWALL CRESCENT
CLARENDON ROAD
POWIS SQUARE
COLVILLE TERRACE
TALBOT ROAD
LEDBURY ROAD
HEREFORD ROAD
PEMBRIDGE VILLAS
PEMBRIDGE SQUARE
DAWSON PLACE

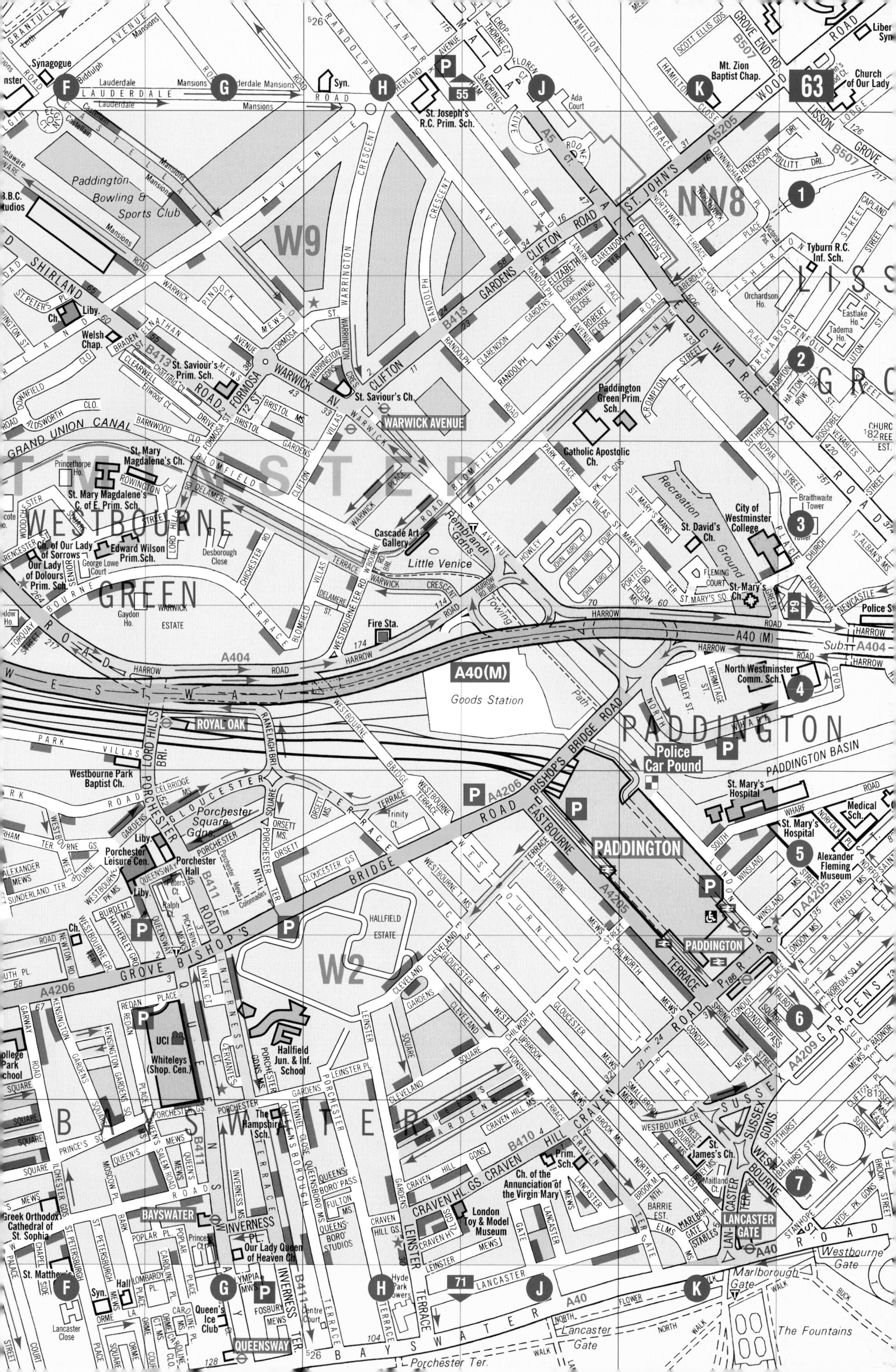

63
F
G
H
J
K
1
2
3
4
5
6
7
55
64
71
NW8
W9
W2
WESTBOURNE
GREEN
PADDINGTON
BAYSWATER
Synagogue
Lauderdale Mansions
Paddington Bowling & Sports Club
Syn.
St. Joseph's R.C. Prim. Sch.
Mt. Zion Baptist Chap.
Church of Our Lady
Ada Court
Tyburn R.C. Inf. Sch.
Liby.
Welsh Chap.
St. Saviour's Prim. Sch.
St. Saviour's Ch.
WARWICK AVENUE
GRAND UNION CANAL
St. Mary Magdalene's Ch.
St. Mary Magdalene's C. of E. Prim. Sch.
Ch. of Our Lady of Sorrows
Our Lady of Dolours Prim. Sch.
Edward Wilson Prim.Sch.
Desborough Close
Cascade Art Gallery
Little Venice
Rembrandt Gdns.
Paddington Green Prim. Sch.
Catholic Apostolic Ch.
Recreation Ground
St. David's Ch.
City of Westminster College
Braithwaite Tower
St. Mary's Ch.
Police Sta.
Fire Sta.
WARWICK ESTATE
Gaydon Ho.
HARROW ROAD
A404
A40 (M)
A40(M)
Goods Station
WESTWAY
North Westminster Comm. Sch.
ROYAL OAK
Westbourne Park Baptist Ch.
Police Car Pound
PADDINGTON BASIN
St. Mary's Hospital
Medical Sch.
Alexander Fleming Museum
Porchester Square Gdns.
Porchester Leisure Cen.
Porchester Hall
Trinity Ct.
HALLFIELD ESTATE
PADDINGTON
BISHOP'S BRIDGE ROAD
A4206
A4205
A4209
A5
A5205
B413
B411
B410
B507
UCI
Whiteleys (Shop. Cen.)
Hallfield Jun. & Inf. School
The Hampshire Sch.
Prim. Sch.
Ch. of the Annunciation of the Virgin Mary
London Toy & Model Museum
St. James's Ch.
Greek Orthodox Cathedral of St. Sophia
St. Matthew's Ch.
Our Lady Queen of Heaven Ch.
Queen's Ice Club
QUEENSWAY
LANCASTER GATE
Hyde Park Towers
Lancaster Close
Westbourne Gate
Marlborough Gate
The Fountains
BAYSWATER ROAD
A40
Porchester Ter.

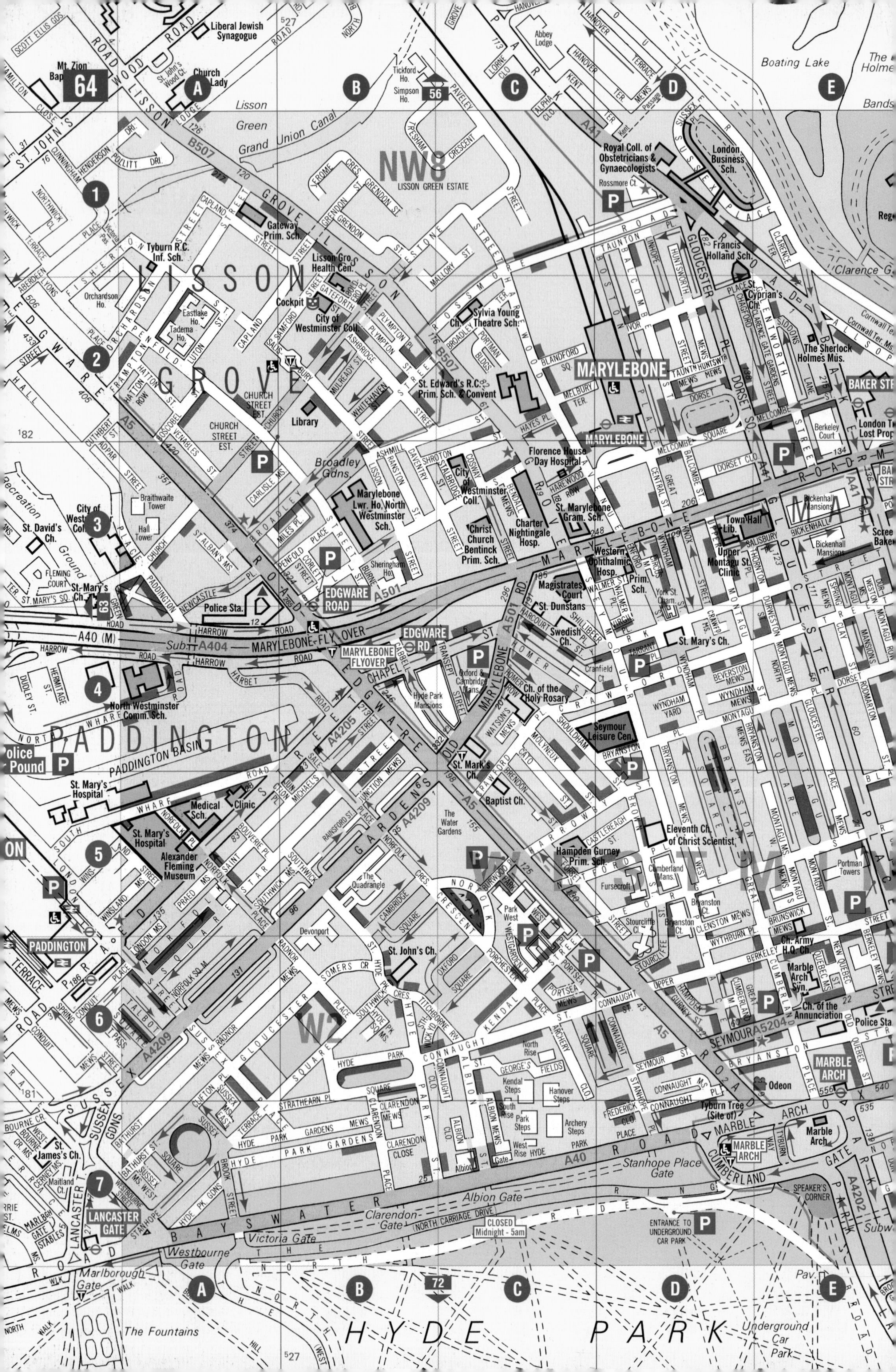

64
56
63
72
NW8
W2
LISSON GROVE
PADDINGTON
MARYLEBONE
HYDE PARK
Liberal Jewish Synagogue
Mt. Zion Bap.
Church Lady
Lisson Green
Grand Union Canal
LISSON GREEN ESTATE
Tickford Ho.
Simpson Ho.
Abbey Lodge
Boating Lake
The Holme
Bands
Royal Coll. of Obstetricians & Gynaecologists
London Business Sch.
Rossmore Ct.
Francis Holland Sch.
St. Cyprian's Ch.
The Sherlock Holmes Mus.
BAKER ST
London Lost Prop.
Berkeley Court
Clarence G
Gateway Prim. Sch.
Tyburn R.C. Inf. Sch.
Lisson Gro. Health Cen.
Cockpit
City of Westminster Coll.
Sylvia Young Theatre Sch.
St. Edward's R.C. Prim. Sch. & Convent
Orchardson Ho.
Eastlake Ho.
Tadema Ho.
CHURCH STREET EST.
Library
Broadley Gdns.
Florence House Day Hospital
St. Marylebone Gram. Sch.
Charter Nightingale Hosp.
Christ Church Bentinck Prim. Sch.
City of Westminster Coll.
Marylebone Lwr. Ho. North Westminster Sch.
Sheringham Ho.
Braithwaite Tower
Hall Tower
City of Westminster Coll.
St. David's Ch.
Recreation Ground
FLEMING COURT
St. Mary's Ch.
Police Sta.
EDGWARE ROAD
EDGWARE RD.
MARYLEBONE FLYOVER
Western Ophthalmic Hosp.
Prim. Sch.
York St. Cham.
Magistrates Court
St. Dunstans
Swedish Ch.
Town Hall Lib.
Upper Montagu St. Clinic
Bickenhall Mansions
Scree Bake
St. Mary's Ch.
Cranfield Ct.
Oxford & Cambridge Mans.
Hyde Park Mansions
Ch. of the Holy Rosary
Seymour Leisure Cen.
North Westminster Comm. Sch.
Police Pound
PADDINGTON BASIN
St. Mary's Hospital
Medical Sch.
Clinic
St. Mary's Hospital
Alexander Fleming Museum
St. Mark's Ch.
Baptist Ch.
The Water Gardens
Eleventh Ch. of Christ Scientist
Hampden Gurney Prim. Sch.
Cumberland Mans.
Fursecroft
Bryanston Ct.
Stourcliffe Cl.
Portman Towers
Ch. Army H.Q. Ch.
Marble Arch Syn.
Ch. of the Annunciation
Police Sta.
PADDINGTON
The Quadrangle
Devonport
St. John's Ch.
North Rise
Kendal Steps
Hanover Steps
South Rise
Park Steps
Archery Steps
West Rise
Albion
Odeon
MARBLE ARCH
Tyburn Tree (Site of)
Marble Arch
Stanhope Place Gate
Albion Gate
Clarendon Gate
NORTH CARRIAGE DRIVE
CLOSED Midnight - 5am
ENTRANCE TO UNDERGROUND CAR PARK
SPEAKER'S CORNER
Victoria Gate
Westbourne Gate
Marlborough Gate
St. James's Ch.
Maitland Ct.
LANCASTER GATE
The Fountains
Underground Car Park
Pav.
A40 (M)
A404
A5
A501
A4205
A4209
A41
A5204
A4202
B507
A40
BAYSWATER ROAD
MARYLEBONE ROAD
EDGWARE ROAD
SUSSEX GARDENS
PARK LANE
GLOUCESTER PLACE
A B C D E
1 2 3 4 5 6 7

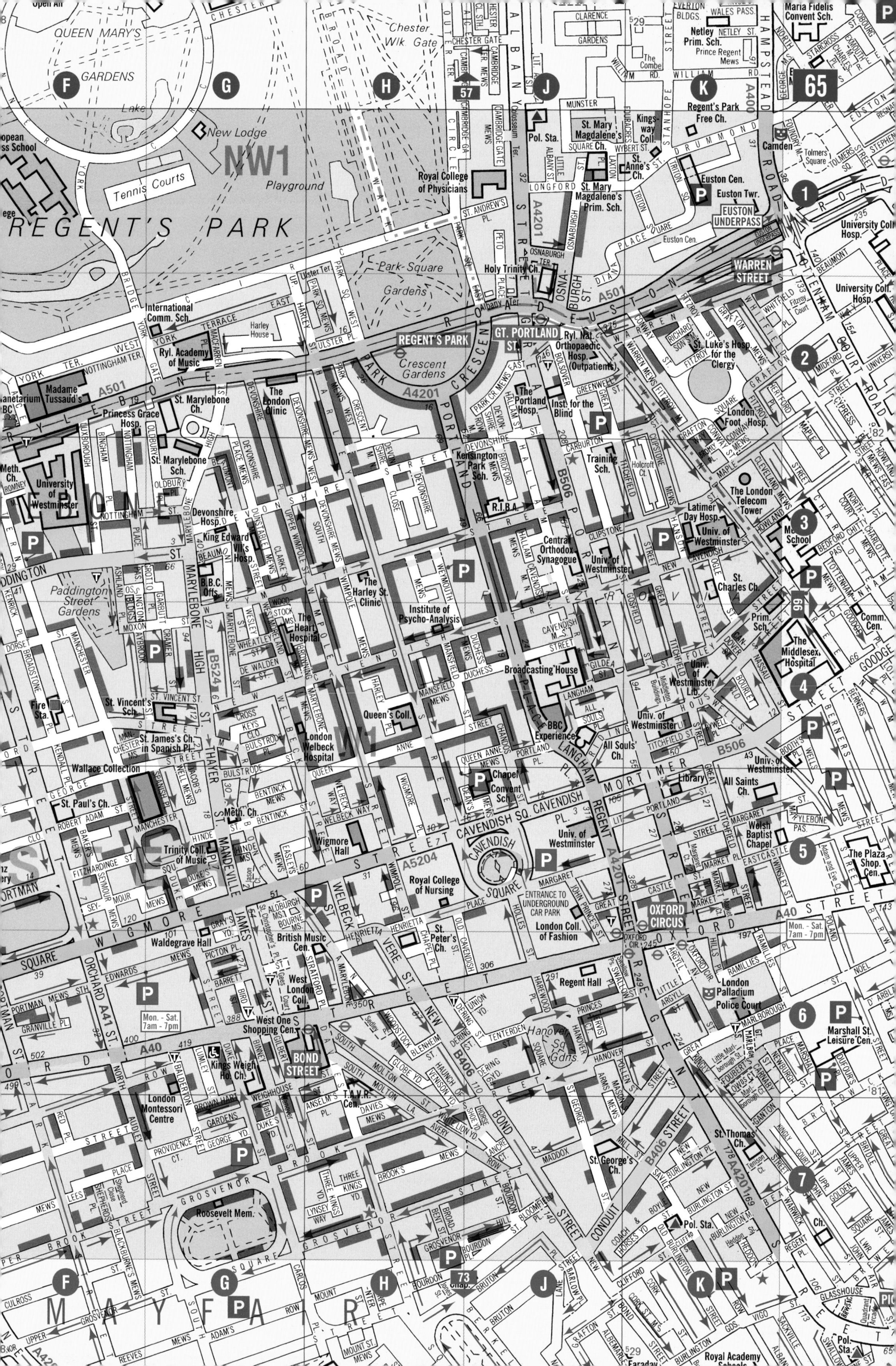
65
F
G
H
J
K
1
2
3
4
5
6
7
57
73
NW1
W1
QUEEN MARY'S GARDENS
REGENT'S PARK
Tennis Courts
Playground
New Lodge
Lake
Park Square Gardens
Crescent Gardens
REGENT'S PARK
GT. PORTLAND ST.
WARREN STREET
EUSTON UNDERPASS
OXFORD CIRCUS
BOND STREET
Royal College of Physicians
Madame Tussaud's
Ryl. Academy of Music
International Comm. Sch.
St. Marylebone Ch.
Princess Grace Hosp.
The London Clinic
University of Westminster
Paddington Street Gardens
The Harley St. Clinic
Institute of Psycho-Analysis
The Heart Hospital
Broadcasting House
BBC Experience
All Souls' Ch.
Queen's Coll.
London Welbeck Hospital
Wallace Collection
St. Paul's Ch.
Trinity Coll. of Music
Wigmore Hall
Royal College of Nursing
CAVENDISH SQUARE
London Coll. of Fashion
The London Telecom Tower
The Middlesex Hospital
All Saints Ch.
Welsh Baptist Chapel
The Plaza Shop. Cen.
London Palladium
Marshall St. Leisure Cen.
Regent Hall
Hanover Sq. Gdns
St. George's Ch.
St. Thomas Ch.
Roosevelt Mem.
West One Shopping Cen.
British Music Cen.
West London Coll.
Waldegrave Hall
London Montessori Centre
Kings Weigh Ho. Ch.
Euston Cen.
Euston Twr.
Camden
University Coll. Hosp.
Holy Trinity Ch.
St. Mary Magdalene's Ch.
St. Luke's Hosp. for the Clergy
London Foot Hosp.
Ryl. Nat. Orthopaedic Hosp. (Outpatients)
The Portland Hosp.
Inst. for the Blind
Central Orthodox Synagogue
Latimer Day Hosp.
St. Charles Ch.
Mon. - Sat. 7am - 7pm
MAYFAIR
Royal Academy Schools
EUSTON ROAD
MARYLEBONE ROAD
OXFORD STREET
REGENT STREET
PORTLAND PLACE
WIGMORE STREET
TOTTENHAM COURT ROAD
NEW BOND STREET
GROSVENOR SQUARE
A501
A4201
A5204
A40
A41
B506
B524
B406
A400

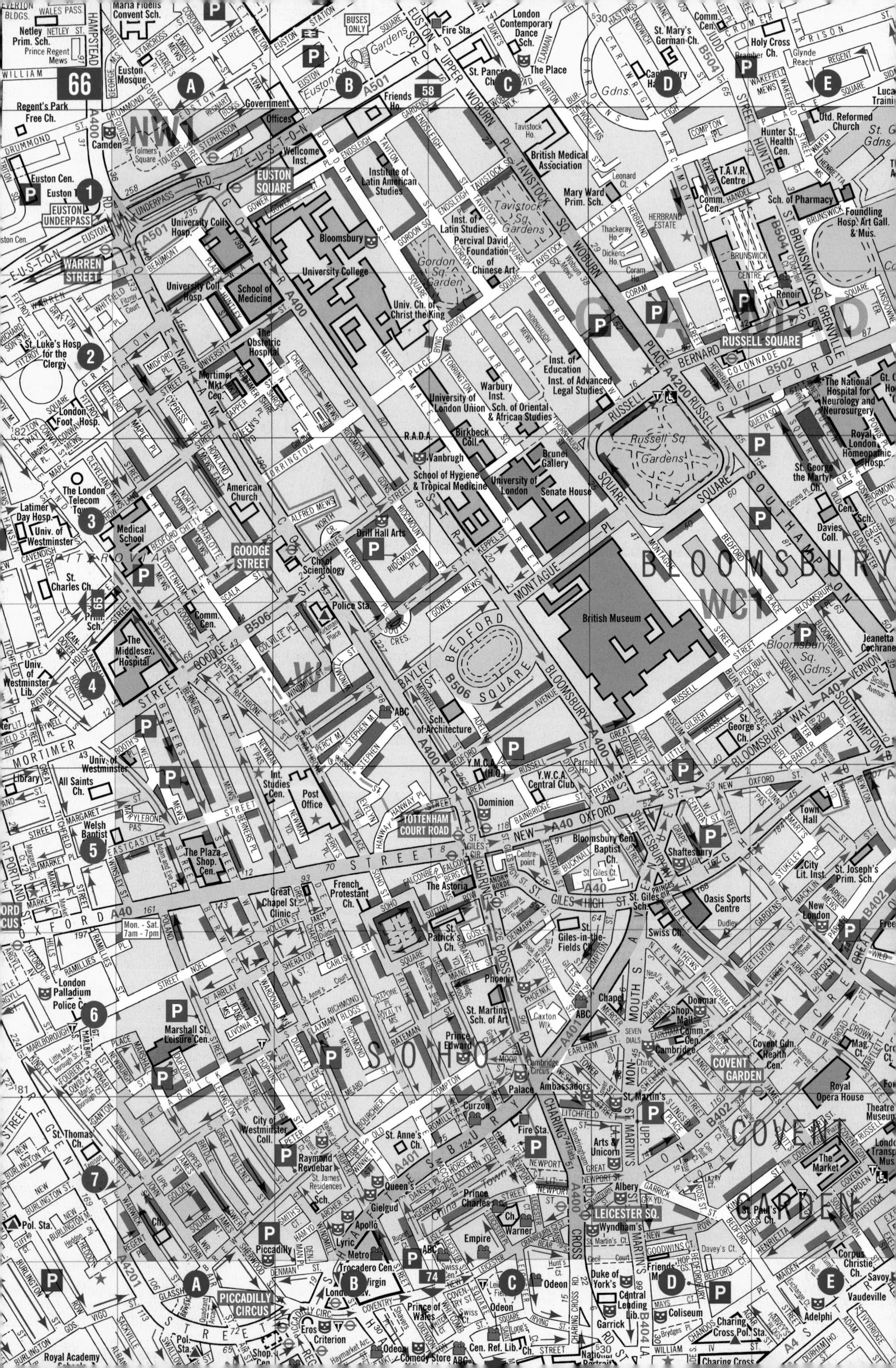
66
NW1
WC1
W1
BLOOMSBURY
SOHO
COVENT GARDEN
FITZROVIA
A
B
C
D
E
1
2
3
4
5
6
7
58
65
74
EUSTON SQUARE
EUSTON UNDERPASS
WARREN STREET
GOODGE STREET
TOTTENHAM COURT ROAD
RUSSELL SQUARE
COVENT GARDEN
LEICESTER SQ.
PICCADILLY CIRCUS
BUSES ONLY
Maria Fidelis Convent Sch.
Netley Prim. Sch.
Prince Regent Mews
Euston Mosque
Regent's Park Free Ch.
Camden
Tolmers Square
Government Offices
Euston Cen.
Wellcome Inst.
Friends Ho.
Fire Sta.
London Contemporary Dance Sch.
St. Pancras Ch.
The Place
St. Mary's German Ch.
Canterbury Ho.
Comm. Cen.
Holy Cross Ch.
Utd. Reformed Church
Hunter St. Health Cen.
T.A.V.R. Centre
Sch. of Pharmacy
Foundling Hosp. Art Gall. & Mus.
Tavistock Ho.
British Medical Association
Mary Ward Prim. Sch.
Leonard Ct.
Herbrand Estate
Thackeray Ho.
Dickens Ho.
Coram Ho.
Institute of Latin American Studies
Inst. of Latin Studies
Percival David Foundation of Chinese Art
Tavistock Sq. Gardens
Gordon Sq. Garden
University Coll. Hosp.
Bloomsbury
University College
Univ. Ch. of Christ the King
School of Medicine
The Obstetric Hospital
Mortimer Mkt. Cen.
St. Luke's Hosp. for the Clergy
London Foot Hosp.
The London Telecom Tower
Latimer Day Hosp.
Univ. of Westminster
Medical School
American Church
Drill Hall Arts
Ch. of Scientology
Police Sta.
R.A.D.A.
Vanbrugh
School of Hygiene & Tropical Medicine
Birkbeck Coll.
University of London Union
University of London
Senate House
Brunei Gallery
Warbury Inst.
Sch. of Oriental & African Studies
Inst. of Education
Inst. of Advanced Legal Studies
Russell Sq. Gardens
Renoir
Brunswick Centre
The National Hospital for Neurology and Neurosurgery
Royal London Homeopathic Hosp.
St. George the Martyr Ch.
Davies Coll.
British Museum
Bloomsbury Sq. Gdns.
Jeanetta Cochrane
St. Charles Ch.
Prim. Sch.
The Middlesex Hospital
Comm. Cen.
Univ. of Westminster Lib.
Bedford Square
Sch. of Architecture
ABC
Y.M.C.A. (H.Q.)
Y.W.C.A. Central Club
Dominion
Parnell Ho.
St. George's Ch.
Town Hall
Univ. of Westminster
All Saints Ch.
Library
Int. Studies Cen.
Post Office
Welsh Baptist
The Plaza Shop. Cen.
Bloomsbury Cen. Baptist Ch.
Centre-point
St. Giles Ct.
Shaftesbury
City Lit. Inst.
St. Joseph's Prim. Sch.
Oasis Sports Centre
New London
Mon. - Sat. 7am - 7pm
London Palladium
Police
French Protestant Ch.
Great Chapel St. Clinic
The Astoria
St. Patrick's Ch.
St. Giles Sch.
St. Giles-in-the-Fields Ch.
Swiss Ch.
Phoenix
Chapel
St. Martins Sch. of Art
Seven Dials
Donmar
Shop. Mall
Comm. Cen.
Cambridge
Covent Gdn. Health Cen.
Mag. Ct.
Royal Opera House
Theatre Museum
Marshall St. Leisure Cen.
City of Westminster Coll.
Prince Edward
Cambridge Circus
Palace
Ambassadors
St. Martin's
Fire Sta.
Curzon
St. Anne's Ch.
Raymond Revuebar
St. James Residences
Sch.
Queen's
Gielgud
Apollo
Lyric
Metro
Prince Charles
Ch.
Warner
Empire
Arts & Unicorn
Albery
Wyndham's
St. Thomas' Ch.
Pol. Sta.
Piccadilly
Trocadero Cen.
Virgin
London Pav.
Prince of Wales
Swiss Cen.
Odeon
Cen. Ref. Lib.
Comedy Store
Criterion
Eros
Duke of York's
Central Lending Lib.
Garrick
Coliseum
Friends
Charing Cross Pol. Sta.
St. Paul's Ch.
The Market
Corpus Christie Ch.
Savoy
Vaudeville
Adelphi
Royal Academy
Shop. Cen.
Pol. Sta.
National Portrait
EUSTON ROAD
GOWER STREET
TOTTENHAM COURT ROAD
OXFORD STREET
NEW OXFORD ST.
SHAFTESBURY AVENUE
CHARING CROSS ROAD
REGENT STREET
GREAT PORTLAND STREET
WOBURN PLACE
SOUTHAMPTON ROW
BLOOMSBURY WAY
HIGH HOLBORN
LONG ACRE
GUILFORD ST.
RUSSELL SQUARE
MONTAGUE PL.
GOODGE STREET
WARDOUR ST.
DEAN ST.
SOHO SQUARE
OLD COMPTON ST.
BREWER ST.
BROADWICK ST.
GT. MARLBOROUGH ST.
CARNABY ST.
GERRARD ST.
COVENTRY ST.
PICCADILLY CIRC.
A400
A40
A501
A4200
B506
B502
B504
B402
A401
A4201
B404
A4

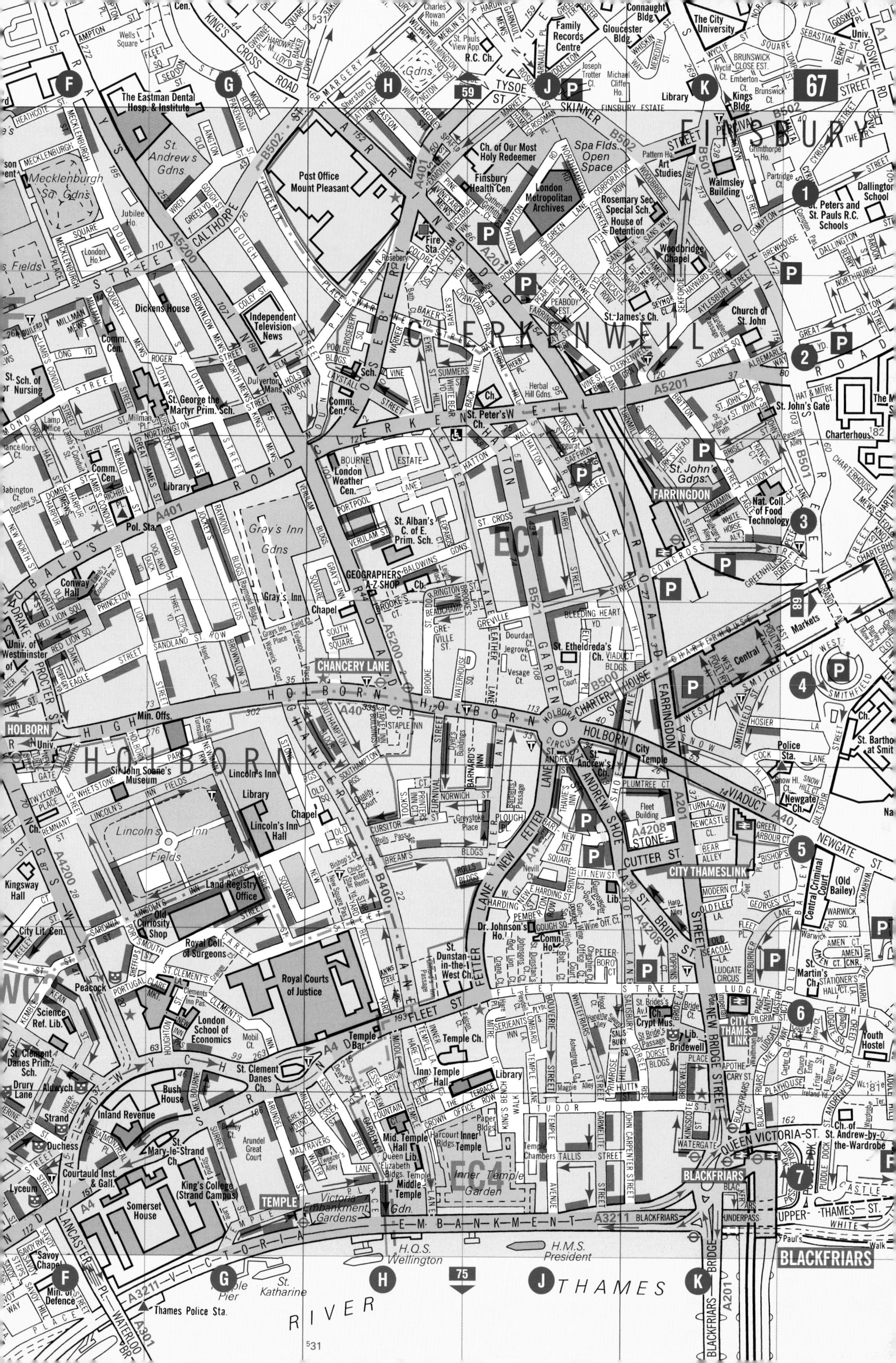

67
59
68
75
F
G
H
J
K
1
2
3
4
5
6
7
FINSBURY
CLERKENWELL
HOLBORN
EC1
EC4
WC2
RIVER THAMES
The Eastman Dental Hosp. & Institute
Post Office Mount Pleasant
Mecklenburgh Sq. Gdns.
St. Andrew's Gdns.
Dickens House
Independent Television News
Family Records Centre
Connaught Bldg.
Gloucester Bldg.
The City University
Ch. of Our Most Holy Redeemer
Finsbury Health Cen.
London Metropolitan Archives
Spa Flds. Open Space
Art Studies
Walmsley Building
Rosemary Sec. Special Sch.
House of Detention
Woodbridge Chapel
Church of St. John
St. Peters and St. Pauls R.C. Schools
Dallington School
St. George the Martyr Prim. Sch.
Library
Pol. Sta.
Conway Hall
Gray's Inn Gdns
Gray's Inn
London Weather Cen.
St. Alban's C. of E. Prim. Sch.
GEOGRAPHERS' A-Z SHOP
St. Etheldreda's Ch.
St. John's Gate
Charterhouse
FARRINGDON
Nat. Coll. of Food Technology
Central Markets
CHANCERY LANE
HOLBORN
HOLBORN CIRCUS
City Temple
Fleet Building
Sir John Soane's Museum
Lincoln's Inn
Lincoln's Inn Fields
Lincoln's Inn Hall
Land Registry Office
Old Curiosity Shop
Royal Coll. of Surgeons
Royal Courts of Justice
London School of Economics
St. Dunstan-in-the-West Ch.
Dr. Johnson's Ho.
CITY THAMESLINK
Central Criminal Court (Old Bailey)
Police Sta.
Newgate Ch.
St. Martin's Ch.
Youth Hostel
Temple Bar
Temple Ch.
Inner Temple Hall
Mid. Temple Hall
Middle Temple
Inner Temple Garden
Bush House
Inland Revenue
St. Clement Danes Ch.
St. Mary-le-Strand Ch.
Somerset House
King's College (Strand Campus)
Courtauld Inst. & Gall.
Kingsway Hall
City Lit. Cen.
Science Ref. Lib.
Peacock
Aldwych
Strand
Duchess
Lyceum
Savoy Chapel
Min. of Defence
Victoria Embankment Gardens
TEMPLE
BLACKFRIARS
H.Q.S. Wellington
H.M.S. President
Temple Pier
Thames Police Sta.
St. Andrew-by-the-Wardrobe
Bridewell
Crypt Mus.
VICTORIA EMBANKMENT
HOLBORN VIADUCT
FLEET ST
LUDGATE CIRCUS
QUEEN VICTORIA ST.
UPPER THAMES ST.
BLACKFRIARS BRIDGE
NEW BRIDGE STREET
FARRINGDON ROAD
CLERKENWELL ROAD
THEOBALD'S ROAD
GRAY'S INN ROAD
KINGSWAY
CHANCERY LANE
FETTER LANE
STRAND
ALDWYCH
NEWGATE ST.
HIGH HOLBORN

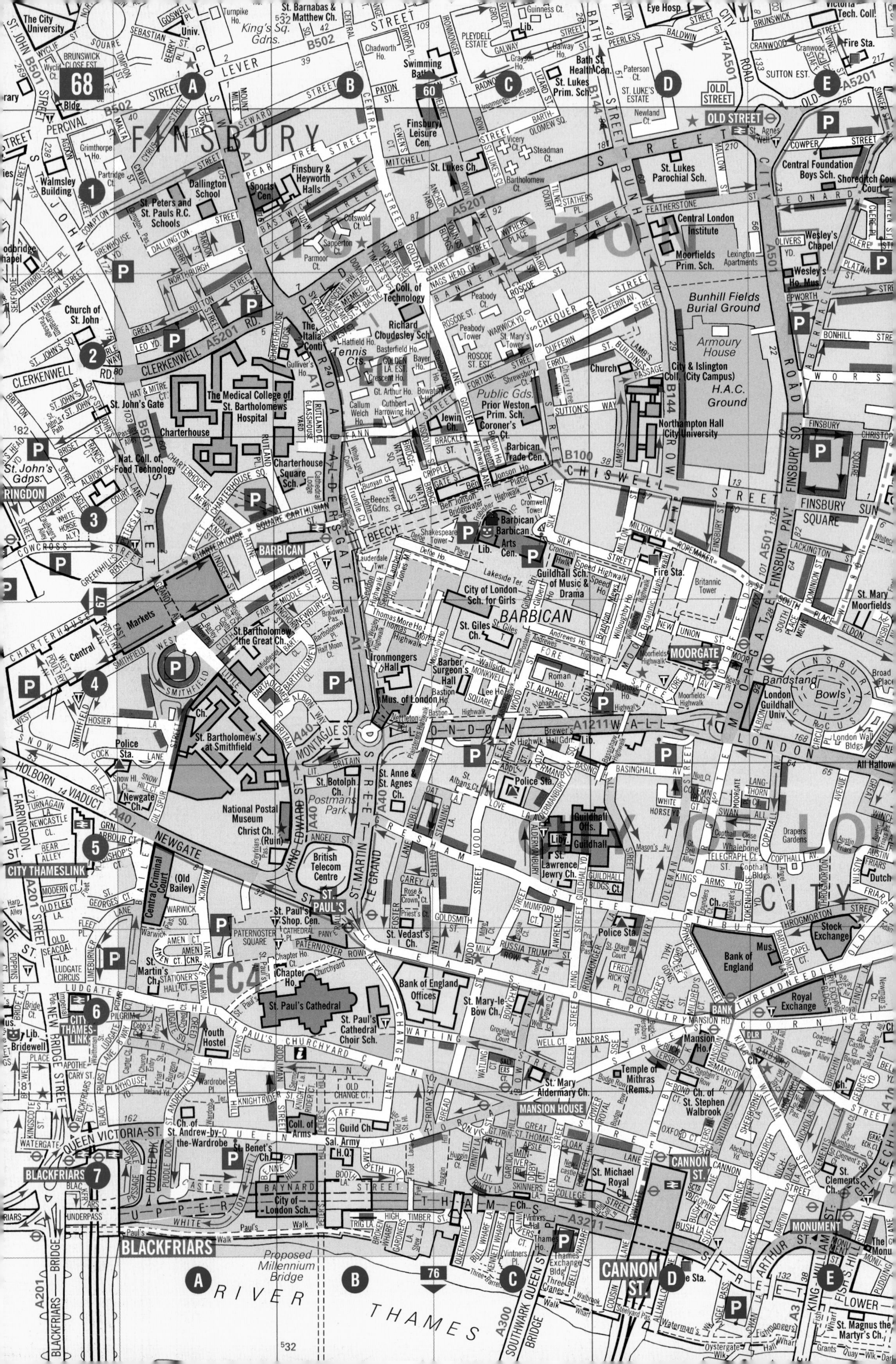
68
FINSBURY
ISLINGTON
BARBICAN
CITY
EC4
The City University
Finsbury Leisure Cen.
Swimming Bath
St. Lukes Ch.
Bath St. Health Cen.
St. Lukes Prim. Sch.
OLD STREET
Central Foundation Boys Sch.
St. Lukes Parochial Sch.
Central London Institute
Moorfields Prim. Sch.
Wesley's Chapel
Wesley's Ho. Mus.
Bunhill Fields Burial Ground
Armoury House
City & Islington Coll. (City Campus)
H.A.C. Ground
Northampton Hall City University
Finsbury & Heyworth Halls
Dallington School
St. Peters and St. Pauls R.C. Schools
Walmsley Building
Church of St. John
St. John's Gate
The Medical College of St. Bartholomews Hospital
Charterhouse
Nat. Coll. of Food Technology
Charterhouse Square Sch.
Coll. of Technology
Richard Cloudesley Sch.
Prior Weston Prim. Sch.
Coroner's Ct.
Barbican Trade Cen.
Barbican Arts Cen.
Guildhall Sch. of Music & Drama
City of London Sch. for Girls
St. Giles Ch.
BARBICAN
Markets
Central
SMITHFIELD
St. Bartholomew the Great Ch.
St. Bartholomew's at Smithfield
Ironmongers Hall
Mus. of London
Barber Surgeon's Hall
MOORGATE
London Guildhall Univ.
Bandstand
Bowls
FINSBURY CIRCUS
FINSBURY SQUARE
Police Sta.
St. Anne & St. Agnes Ch.
St. Botolph Ch.
Postmans Park
National Postal Museum
Christ Ch. (Ruin)
British Telecom Centre
ST. PAUL'S
Central Criminal Court (Old Bailey)
CITY THAMESLINK
St. Paul's Shop. Cen.
Paternoster Square
Chapter Ho.
St. Paul's Cathedral
St. Paul's Cathedral Choir Sch.
Bank of England Offices
St. Vedast's Ch.
St. Mary-le-Bow Ch.
Guildhall Offs.
Guildhall
St. Lawrence Jewry Ch.
Bank of England
Stock Exchange
Royal Exchange
BANK
Mansion Ho.
Temple of Mithras (Rems.)
St. Mary Aldermary Ch.
MANSION HOUSE
Ch. of St. Stephen Walbrook
Youth Hostel
Coll. of Arms
Guild Ch.
Sal. Army H.Q.
St. Andrew-by-the-Wardrobe
St. Benet's Ch.
City of London Sch.
BLACKFRIARS
St. Michael Royal Ch.
CANNON ST.
St. Clements Ch.
MONUMENT
St. Magnus the Martyr's Ch.
Proposed Millennium Bridge
RIVER THAMES
76
67
60
CLERKENWELL RD.
CHARTERHOUSE ST.
HOLBORN VIADUCT
NEWGATE ST.
ALDERSGATE ST.
LONDON WALL
CHISWELL STREET
CITY ROAD
MOORGATE
FARRINGDON ST.
NEW BRIDGE STREET
QUEEN VICTORIA ST.
UPPER THAMES ST.
CHEAPSIDE
CANNON ST.
GRESHAM ST.
KING WILLIAM ST.
SOUTHWARK BRIDGE
BLACKFRIARS BRIDGE
A B C D E
1 2 3 4 5 6 7

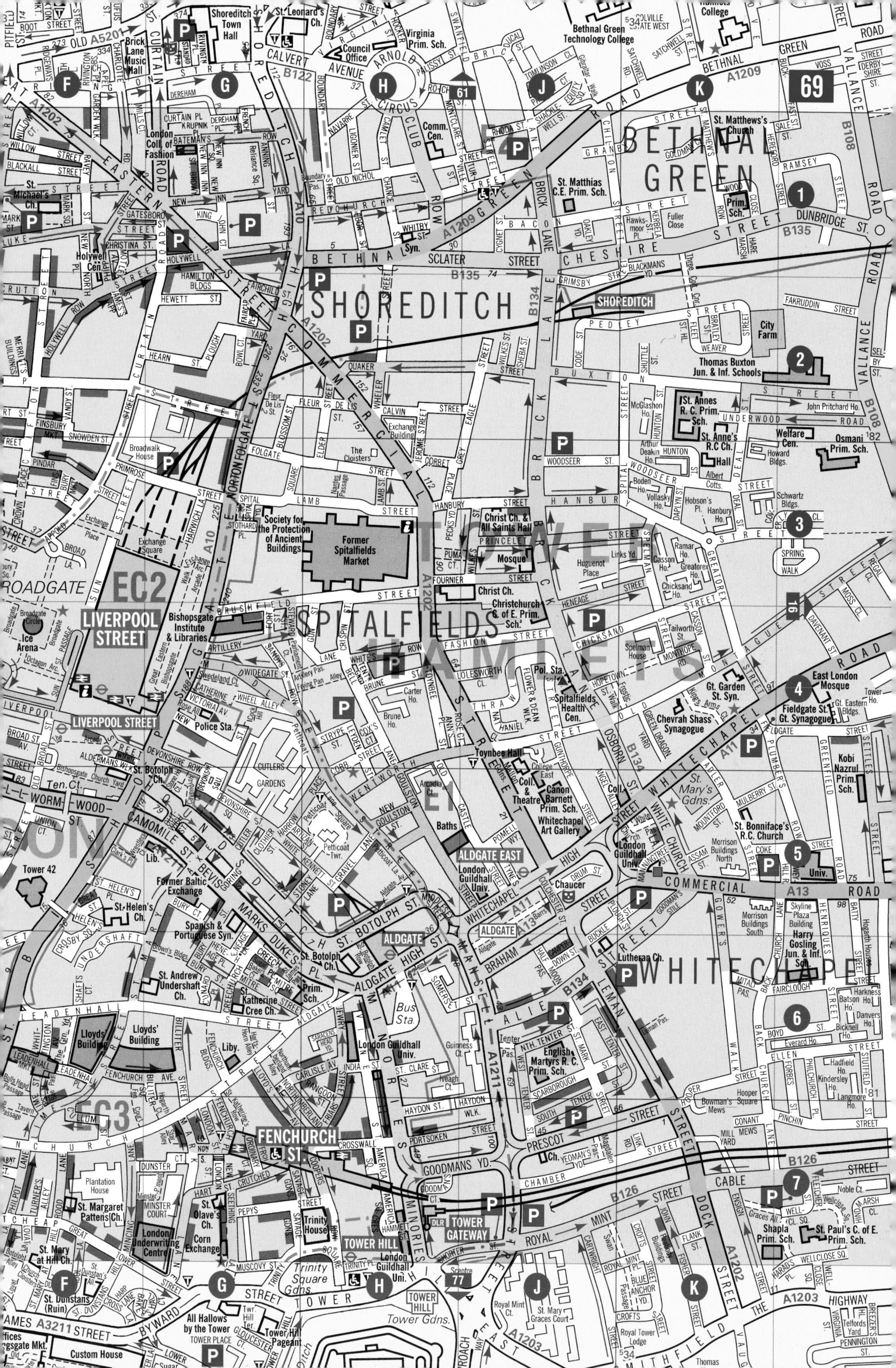
69
BETHNAL GREEN
SHOREDITCH
SPITALFIELDS
TOWER HAMLETS
WHITECHAPEL
EC2
EC3
E1
LIVERPOOL STREET
SHOREDITCH
ALDGATE EAST
ALDGATE
FENCHURCH ST.
TOWER HILL
TOWER GATEWAY
BROADGATE
Shoreditch Town Hall
St. Leonard's Ch.
Virginia Prim. Sch.
Council Office
Bethnal Green Technology College
Brick Lane Music Hall
London Coll. of Fashion
St. Matthew's Church
St. Matthias C.E. Prim. Sch.
Comm. Cen.
Syn.
City Farm
Thomas Buxton Jun. & Inf. Schools
St. Annes R. C. Prim. Sch.
St. Anne's R.C Ch.
Welfare Cen.
Osmani Prim. Sch.
Former Spitalfields Market
Society for the Protection of Ancient Buildings
Christ Ch. & All Saints Hall
Mosque
Christ Ch.
Christchurch & of E. Prim. Sch.
Bishopsgate Institute & Libraries
Broadwalk House
Ice Arena
Police Sta.
Pol. Sta.
Spitalfields Health Cen.
Gt. Garden St. Syn.
Chevrah Shass Synagogue
East London Mosque
Fieldgate St. Gt. Synagogue
Kobi Nazrul Prim. Sch.
Toynbee Hall
Coll. & Theatre
Canon Barnett Prim. Sch.
Whitechapel Art Gallery
London Guildhall Univ.
St. Boniface's R.C. Church
Univ.
Baths
Tower 42
Former Baltic Exchange
Spanish & Portuguese Syn.
St. Helen's Ch.
St. Andrew Undershaft Ch.
St. Katherine Cree Ch.
St. Botolph Ch.
Prim. Sch.
Lloyds Building
Lloyds' Building
Liby.
Lutheran Ch.
Chaucer
English Martyrs R. C. Prim. Sch.
Harry Gosling Jun. & Inf. Sch.
Skyline Plaza Building
Plantation House
St. Margaret Pattens Ch.
London Underwriting Centre
St. Olave's Ch.
Corn Exchange
Trinity House
St. Mary at Hill Ch.
St. Dunstans (Ruin)
All Hallows by the Tower
Custom House
Tower Hill Pageant
Trinity Square Gdns.
Tower Gdns.
Royal Mint Ct.
St. Mary Graces Court
Royal Tower Lodge
Shapla Prim. Sch.
St. Paul's C. of E. Prim. Sch.
Bus Sta.
COMMERCIAL ROAD
WHITECHAPEL HIGH STREET
COMMERCIAL STREET
BISHOPSGATE
SHOREDITCH HIGH STREET
BETHNAL GREEN ROAD
BRICK LANE
OLD STREET
GREAT EASTERN STREET
LEMAN STREET
MINORIES
ALDGATE HIGH ST.
LEADENHALL STREET
FENCHURCH STREET
GREAT TOWER STREET
THE HIGHWAY
ROYAL MINT STREET
CABLE STREET
CHESHIRE STREET
HANBURY STREET
VALLANCE ROAD
A1202
A1209
A10
A11
A13
A1211
A1203
A3211
B134
B135
B126
B108

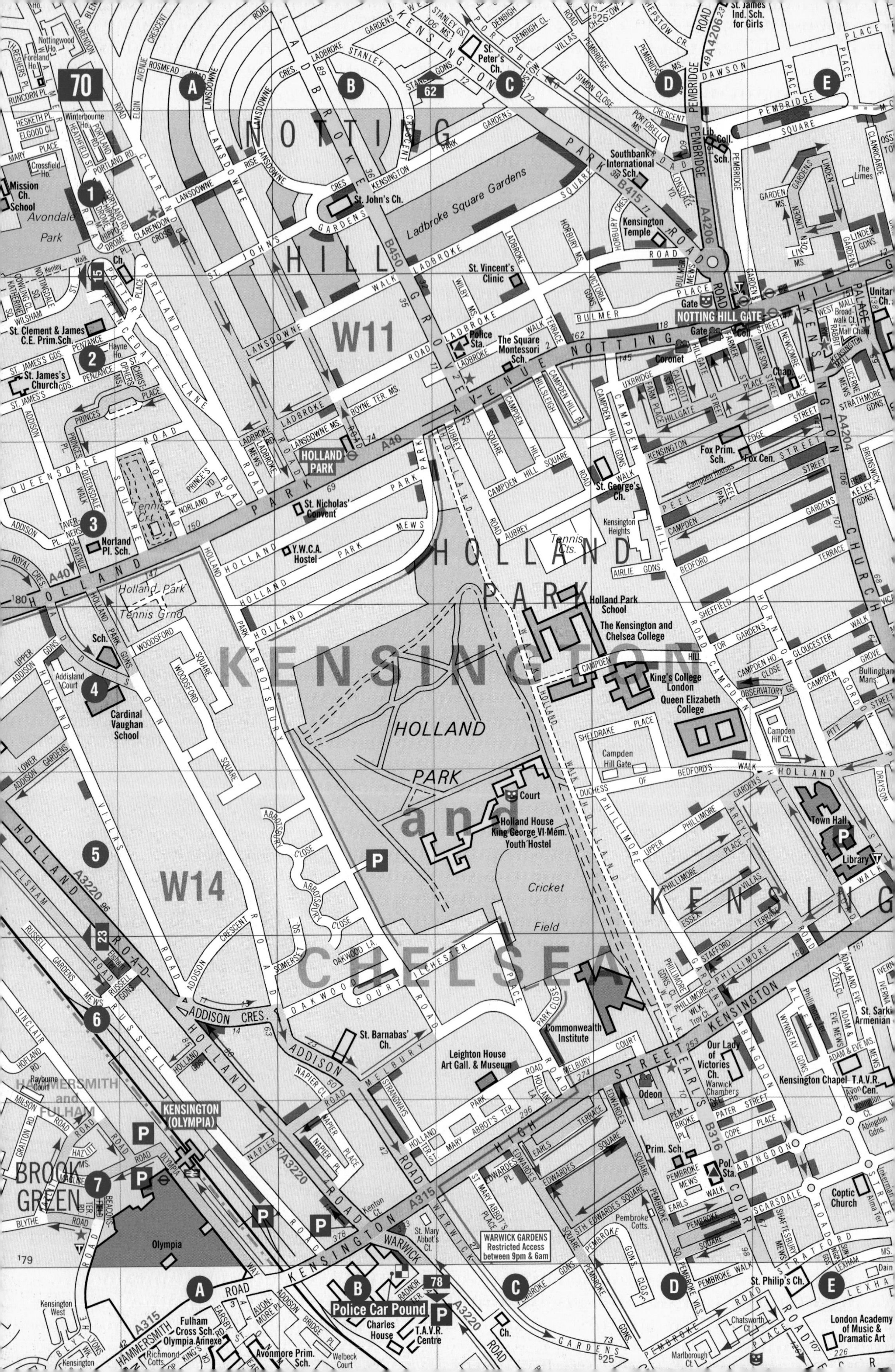

NOTTING HILL
W11
HOLLAND PARK
KENSINGTON and CHELSEA
W14
HOLLAND PARK
NOTTING HILL GATE
HOLLAND PARK
KENSINGTON (OLYMPIA)
HAMMERSMITH and FULHAM
BROOK GREEN
Olympia
Avondale Park
Ladbroke Square Gardens
Mission Ch. School
St. John's Ch.
St. Peter's Ch.
St. Vincent's Clinic
Police Sta.
The Square Montessori Sch.
Southbank International Sch.
Kensington Temple
Coronet
Fox Prim. Sch.
Fox Cen.
St. George's Ch.
Kensington Heights
St. Clement & James C.E. Prim.Sch.
St. James's Church
Hayne Ho.
St. Nicholas' Convent
Y.W.C.A. Hostel
Norland Pl. Sch.
Holland Park Tennis Grnd
Holland Park School
The Kensington and Chelsea College
King's College London
Queen Elizabeth College
Campden Hill Gate
Campden Hill Ct.
Town Hall
Library
Court
Holland House King George VI Mem. Youth Hostel
Cricket Field
Cardinal Vaughan School
Addisland Court
Commonwealth Institute
Leighton House Art Gall. & Museum
St. Barnabas' Ch.
Odeon
Our Lady of Victories Ch.
Warwick Chambers
Kensington Chapel
T.A.V.R. Cen.
St. Sarkis Armenian
Coptic Church
Prim. Sch.
Pol. Sta.
Pembroke Cotts.
WARWICK GARDENS Restricted Access between 9pm & 6am
St. Philip's Ch.
London Academy of Music & Dramatic Art
Police Car Pound
Charles House
T.A.V.R. Centre
Fulham Cross Sch. Olympia Annexe
Avonmore Prim. Sch.
Kensington West
Richmond Cotts.
Welbeck Court
Ch.
St. Mary Abbot's Ct.
Kenton Ct.
St. James Ind. Sch. for Girls
Lib. Coll.
Sch.
The Limes
Bullingham Mans.
Unitarian Ch.
LADBROKE GROVE
KENSINGTON PARK ROAD
PORTOBELLO ROAD
PEMBRIDGE ROAD
NOTTING HILL GATE
HOLLAND PARK AVENUE
KENSINGTON CHURCH STREET
CAMPDEN HILL ROAD
HOLLAND WALK
ABBOTSBURY ROAD
ADDISON ROAD
HOLLAND ROAD
KENSINGTON HIGH STREET
EARLS COURT ROAD
WARWICK GARDENS
PHILLIMORE GARDENS
ADDISON CRES.
MELBURY ROAD
HOLLAND PARK ROAD
EDWARDES SQUARE
PEMBROKE ROAD
HAMMERSMITH ROAD
A40
A315
A3220
A4206
A4204
B450
B415
B316
A B C D E
1 2 3 4 5 6 7

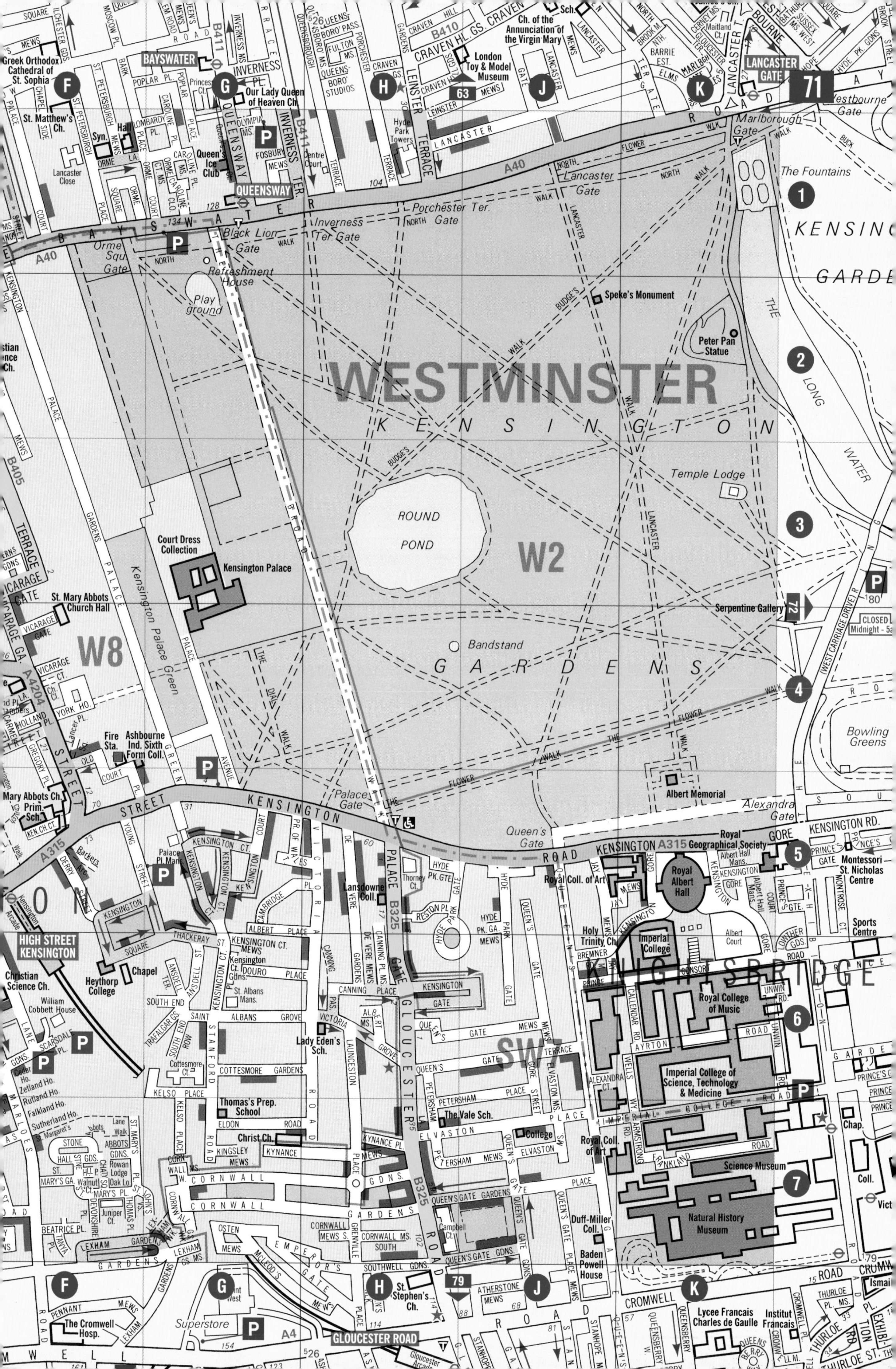

71
WESTMINSTER
KENSINGTON GARDENS
W2
W8
SW7
KNIGHTSBRIDGE
BAYSWATER
QUEENSWAY
LANCASTER GATE
HIGH STREET KENSINGTON
GLOUCESTER ROAD
BAYSWATER ROAD
KENSINGTON ROAD
CROMWELL ROAD
Greek Orthodox Cathedral of St. Sophia
St. Matthew's Ch.
Our Lady Queen of Heaven Ch.
Queen's Ice Club
Ch. of the Annunciation of the Virgin Mary
London Toy & Model Museum
Hyde Park Towers
Lancaster Close
The Fountains
Marlborough Gate
Westbourne Gate
North Lancaster Gate
Porchester Ter. Gate
Inverness Ter. Gate
Black Lion Gate
Orme Squ. Gate
Refreshment House
Play ground
Speke's Monument
Peter Pan Statue
THE LONG WATER
ROUND POND
Temple Lodge
Court Dress Collection
Kensington Palace
Kensington Palace Green
Serpentine Gallery
Bandstand
THE FLOWER WALK
Albert Memorial
Alexandra Gate
Queen's Gate
Palace Gate
Bowling Greens
St. Mary Abbots Church Hall
Mary Abbots Ch. Prim. Sch.
Fire Sta.
Ashbourne Ind. Sixth Form Coll.
Barkers
Kensington Arcade
Christian Science Ch.
William Cobbett House
Heythorp College
Chapel
Lansdowne Coll.
Lady Eden's Sch.
Thomas's Prep. School
Christ Ch.
The Vale Sch.
College
Royal Geographical Society
Royal Coll. of Art
Royal Albert Hall
Albert Court
Holy Trinity Ch.
Imperial College
Royal College of Music
Imperial College of Science, Technology & Medicine
Science Museum
Natural History Museum
Duff-Miller Coll.
Baden Powell House
Montessori St. Nicholas Centre
Sports Centre
Chap.
Lycee Francais Charles de Gaulle
Institut Francais
St. Stephen's Ch.
The Cromwell Hosp.
Superstore
CLOSED Midnight - 5a
63
72
79

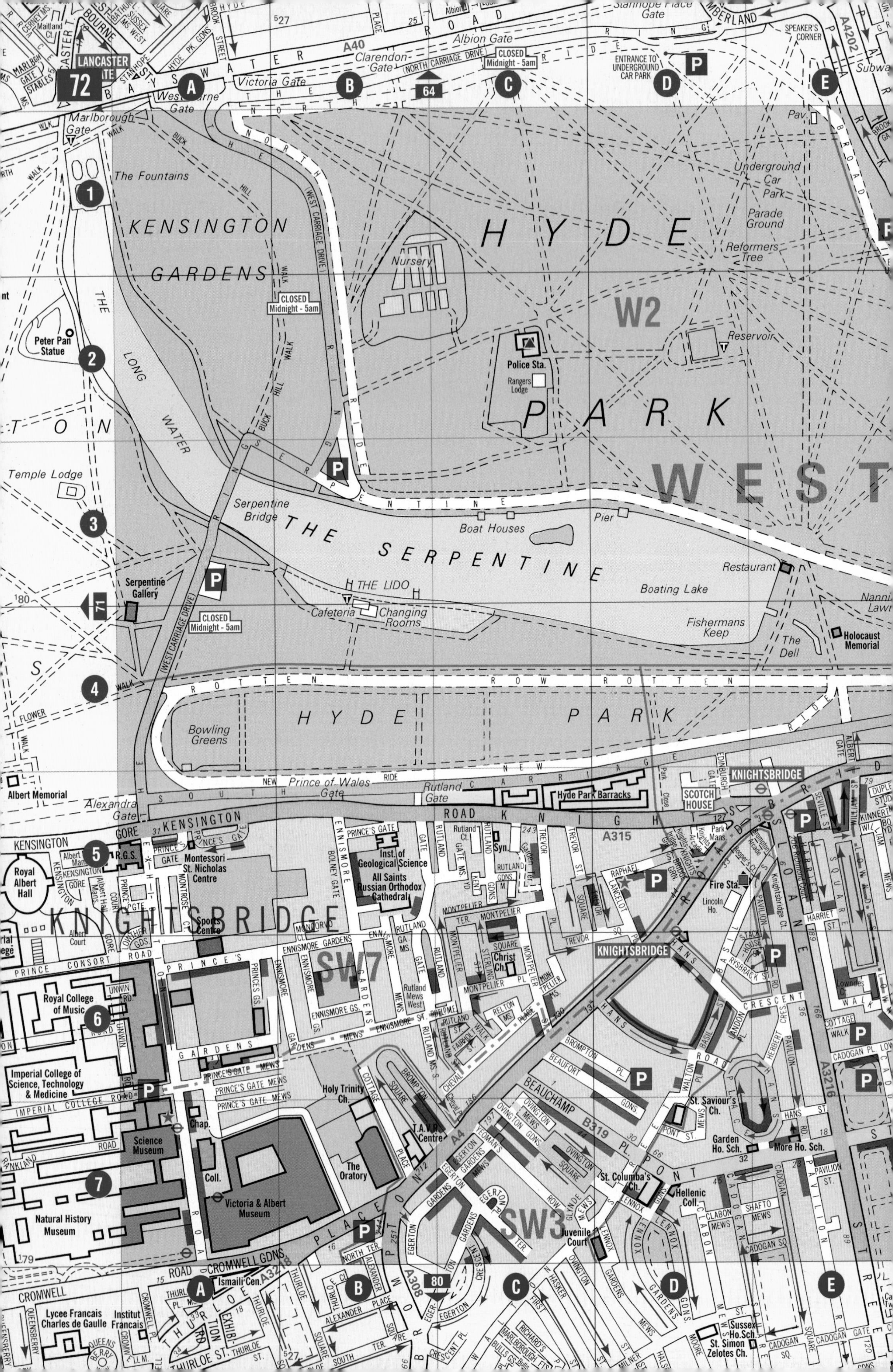
72
LANCASTER GATE
BAYSWATER ROAD
A40
Victoria Gate
Clarendon Gate
Albion Gate
Stanhope Place Gate
Westbourne Gate
Marlborough Gate
NORTH CARRIAGE DRIVE
CLOSED Midnight - 5am
64
ENTRANCE TO UNDERGROUND CAR PARK
SPEAKER'S CORNER
A4202
The Fountains
KENSINGTON GARDENS
HYDE PARK
Nursery
Police Sta.
Rangers Lodge
W2
Reservoir
Underground Car Park
Parade Ground
Reformers Tree
Peter Pan Statue
LONG WATER
BUCK HILL WALK
WEST CARRIAGE DRIVE
Temple Lodge
Serpentine Bridge
THE SERPENTINE
Boat Houses
Pier
WEST
Restaurant
Boating Lake
Serpentine Gallery
71
THE LIDO
Cafeteria
Changing Rooms
Fishermans Keep
The Dell
Holocaust Memorial
ROTTEN ROW
FLOWER WALK
Bowling Greens
SOUTH CARRIAGE DRIVE
Prince of Wales Gate
Rutland Gate
Hyde Park Barracks
Albert Memorial
Alexandra Gate
KENSINGTON ROAD
KNIGHTSBRIDGE
SCOTCH HOUSE
A315
Royal Albert Hall
R.G.S.
Montessori St. Nicholas Centre
Inst. of Geological Science
All Saints Russian Orthodox Cathedral
Syn.
Sports Centre
ENNISMORE GARDENS
Christ Ch.
SW7
Fire Sta.
Lincoln Ho.
Royal College of Music
PRINCE CONSORT ROAD
Imperial College of Science, Technology & Medicine
IMPERIAL COLLEGE ROAD
Holy Trinity Ch.
BROMPTON SQUARE
T.A.V.R. Centre
The Oratory
Science Museum
Chap.
Coll.
Victoria & Albert Museum
Natural History Museum
BROMPTON ROAD
A4
BEAUCHAMP PL.
B319
St. Saviour's Ch.
Garden Ho. Sch.
More Ho. Sch.
St. Columba's Ch.
Hellenic Coll.
SW3
Juvenile Court
SLOANE STREET
A3216
CADOGAN SQ.
CADOGAN GATE
CROMWELL ROAD
CROMWELL GDNS.
A3218
Ismaili Cen.
Lycee Francais Charles de Gaulle
Institut Francais
THURLOE PL.
A308
80
Sussex Ho. Sch.
St. Simon Zelotes Ch.

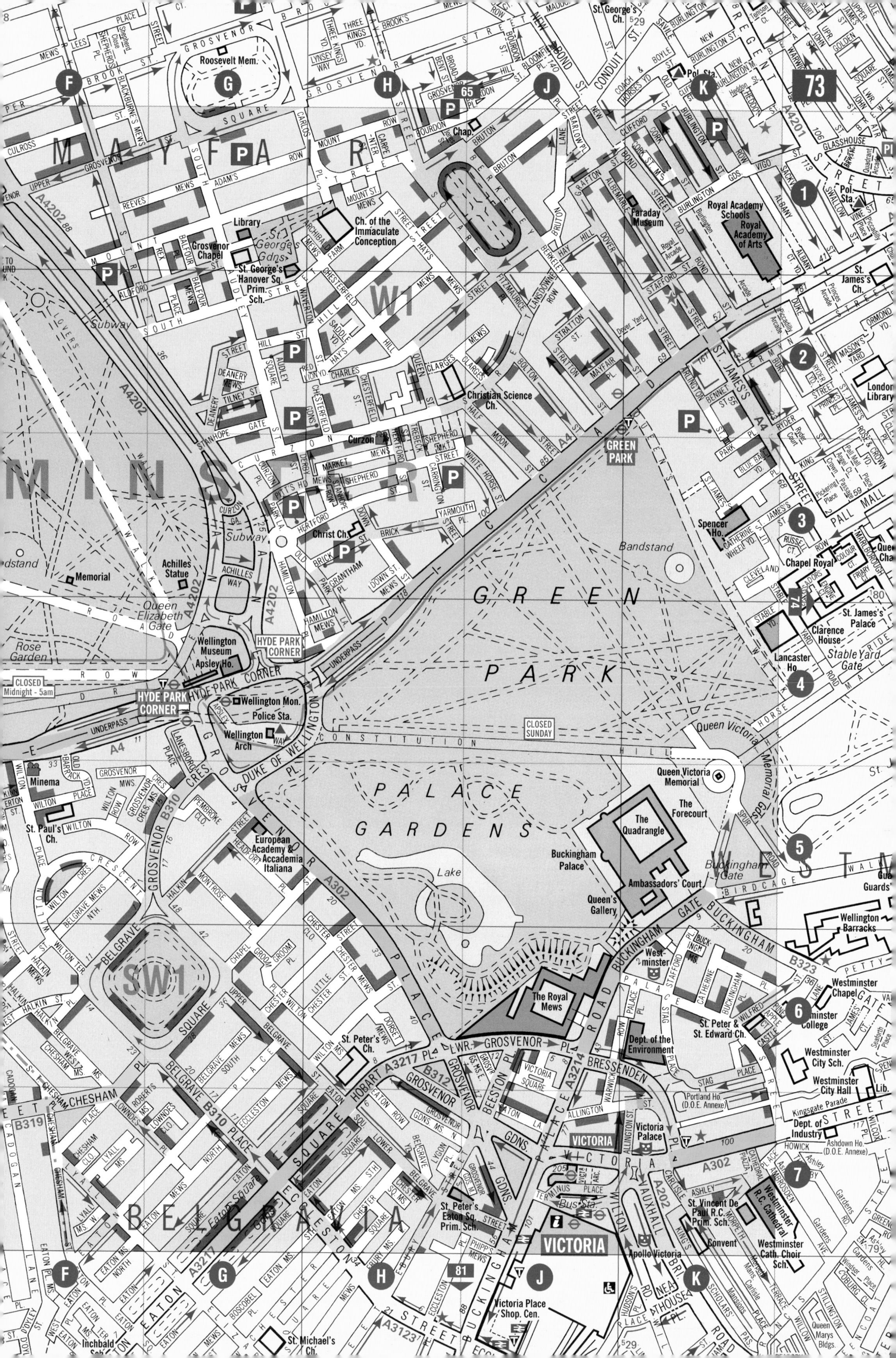
73
MAYFAIR
W1
SW1
BELGRAVIA
GREEN PARK
PALACE GARDENS
Roosevelt Mem.
Grosvenor Square
Library
Grosvenor Chapel
St. George's Gdns.
St. George's Hanover Sq. Prim. Sch.
Ch. of the Immaculate Conception
Berkeley Square
Faraday Museum
Royal Academy Schools
Royal Academy of Arts
Burlington Arcade
Royal Arcade
Pol. Sta.
St. James's Ch.
Princes Arcade
Piccadilly Arcade
London Library
Christian Science Ch.
Curzon
Christ Ch.
Spencer Ho.
Chapel Royal
Clarence House
St. James's Palace
Lancaster Ho.
Stable Yard Gate
Bandstand
Memorial
Achilles Statue
Queen Elizabeth Gate
Rose Garden
Wellington Museum Apsley Ho.
HYDE PARK CORNER
CLOSED Midnight - 5am
Wellington Mon.
Police Sta.
Wellington Arch
CLOSED SUNDAY
CONSTITUTION HILL
Queen Victoria Memorial
The Forecourt
The Quadrangle
Buckingham Palace
Ambassadors' Court
Queen's Gallery
Lake
Buckingham Gate
BIRDCAGE WALK
Guards' Chapel
Wellington Barracks
Minema
St. Paul's Ch.
European Academy & Accademia Italiana
The Royal Mews
Westminster Chapel
Westminster College
St. Peter & St. Edward Ch.
Dept. of the Environment
Westminster City Sch.
Westminster City Hall
Lib.
Kingsgate Parade
Portland Ho. (D.O.E. Annexe)
Dept. of Industry
Ashdown Ho. (D.O.E. Annexe)
Victoria Palace
VICTORIA
Bus Sta.
Apollo Victoria
St. Vincent De Paul R.C. Prim. Sch.
Convent
Westminster R.C. Cathedral
Westminster Cath. Choir Sch.
St. Peter's Ch.
St. Peter's Eaton Sq. Prim. Sch.
Victoria Place Shop. Cen.
St. Michael's Ch.
Queen Marys Bldgs.
PICCADILLY
PALL MALL
GROSVENOR PLACE
BELGRAVE SQUARE
EATON SQUARE
BUCKINGHAM PALACE ROAD
VICTORIA STREET
VAUXHALL BRIDGE ROAD
PARK LANE
A4
A4202
A302
A3214
A3217
A202
B310
B312
B319
B323
A4201
A3123
65
74
81
F
G
H
J
K
1
2
3
4
5
6
7

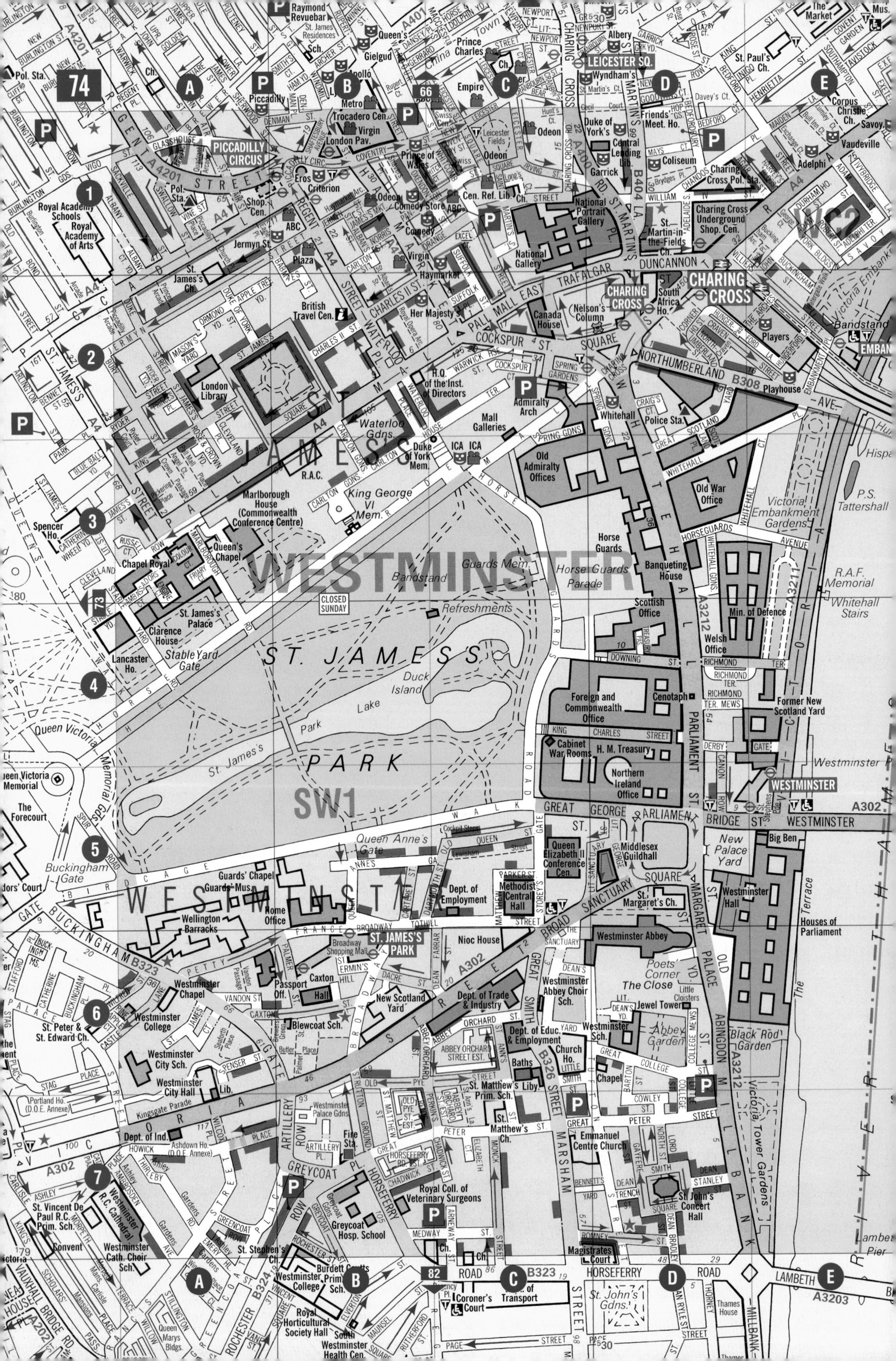
74
66
73
82
30
PICCADILLY CIRCUS
LEICESTER SQ.
CHARING CROSS
ST. JAMES'S PARK
WESTMINSTER
WC2
SW1
ST. JAMES'S PARK
Royal Academy of Arts
National Gallery
National Portrait Gallery
St. Martin-in-the-Fields Ch.
Nelson's Column
Admiralty Arch
Horse Guards Parade
Banqueting House
Foreign and Commonwealth Office
Cenotaph
H. M. Treasury
Cabinet War Rooms
Min. of Defence
Big Ben
Houses of Parliament
Westminster Hall
Westminster Abbey
St. Margaret's Ch.
Middlesex Guildhall
Queen Elizabeth II Conference Cen.
Methodist Central Hall
Wellington Barracks
St. James's Palace
Clarence House
Lancaster Ho.
Marlborough House (Commonwealth Conference Centre)
Queen Victoria Memorial
Westminster R.C. Cathedral
Victoria Tower Gardens
Victoria Embankment Gardens
Duck Island
CLOSED SUNDAY
A4
A302
A3212
A3203
B323
B326
B404
B308

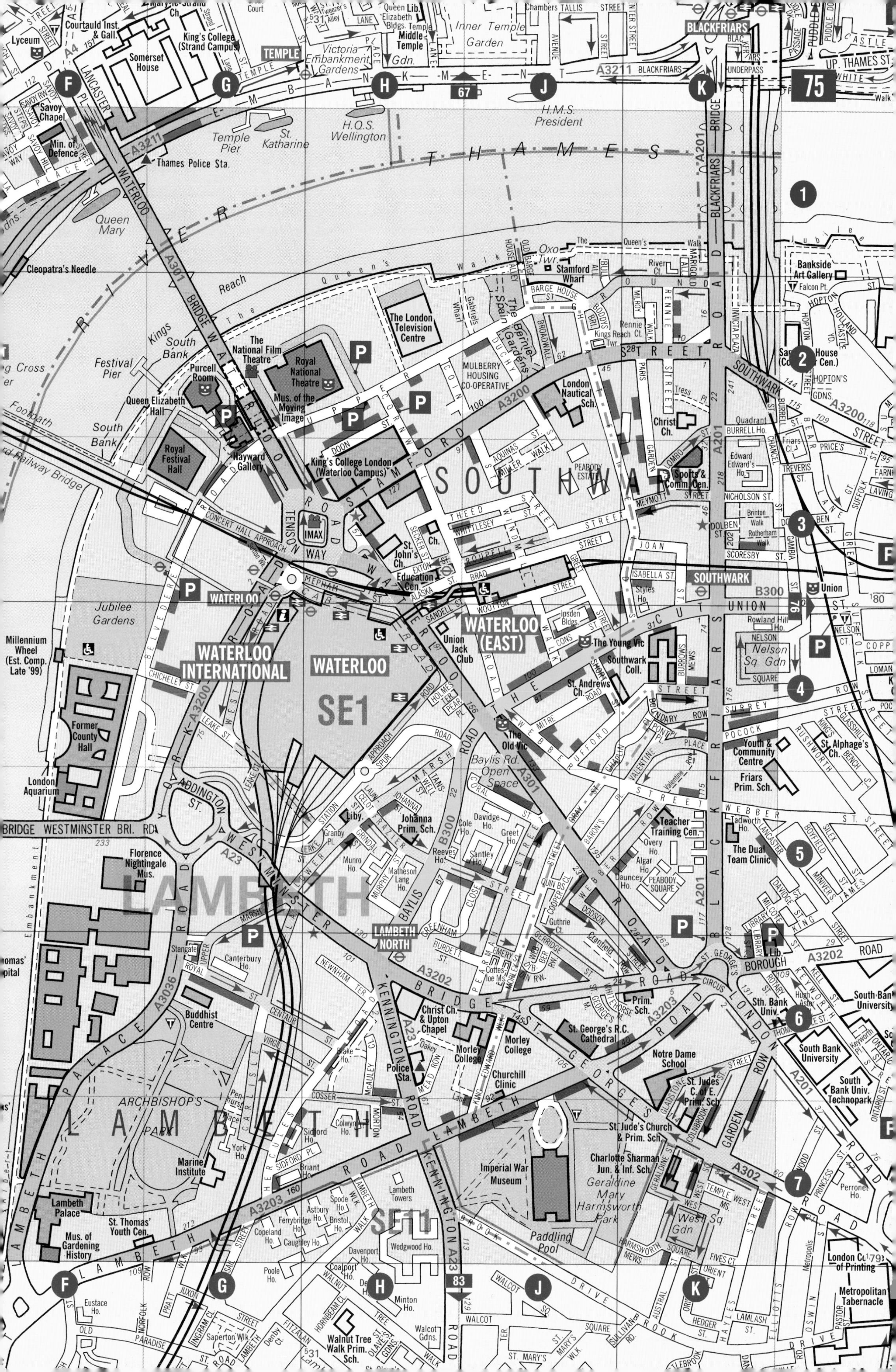

75
TEMPLE
BLACKFRIARS
SOUTHWARK
WATERLOO
WATERLOO INTERNATIONAL
WATERLOO (EAST)
LAMBETH NORTH
SE1
SE11
SOUTHWARK
LAMBETH
LAMBETH
THAMES
RIVER
Courtauld Inst. & Gall.
Lyceum
Somerset House
King's College (Strand Campus)
Middle Temple Gdn.
Inner Temple Garden
Victoria Embankment Gardens
Savoy Chapel
Min. of Defence
Thames Police Sta.
Temple Pier
St. Katharine
H.Q.S. Wellington
H.M.S. President
Queen Mary
Cleopatra's Needle
Reach
Kings Reach
Festival Pier
South Bank
Queen Elizabeth Hall
Purcell Room
The National Film Theatre
Royal National Theatre
Mus. of the Moving Image
Royal Festival Hall
Hayward Gallery
The London Television Centre
Oxo Twr.
Stamford Wharf
Gabriels Wharf
The Bernie Spain Gardens
MULBERRY HOUSING CO-OPERATIVE
London Nautical Sch.
King's College London (Waterloo Campus)
IMAX
Christ Ch.
PEABODY ESTATE
Sports & Comm. Cen.
St. John's Ch.
Education Cen.
Union Jack Club
The Young Vic
Southwark Coll.
St. Andrews Ch.
The Old Vic
Baylis Rd. Open Space
Jubilee Gardens
Millennium Wheel (Est. Comp. Late '99)
Former County Hall
London Aquarium
Florence Nightingale Mus.
Liby.
Johanna Prim. Sch.
Teacher Training Cen.
The Dual Team Clinic
Bankside Art Gallery
Union
Nelson Sq. Gdn
Youth & Community Centre
Friars Prim. Sch.
St. Alphage's Ch.
Lib.
South Bank University
Sth. Bank Univ.
South Bank Univ. Technopark
Christ Ch. & Upton Chapel
Morley College
Police Sta.
St. George's R.C. Cathedral
Notre Dame School
St. Judes C. of E. Prim. Sch.
St. Jude's Church & Prim. Sch.
Charlotte Sharman Jun. & Inf. Sch.
Geraldine Mary Harmsworth Park
Imperial War Museum
Paddling Pool
Churchill Clinic
Buddhist Centre
Marine Institute
ARCHBISHOP'S PARK
Lambeth Palace
Mus. of Gardening History
St. Thomas' Youth Cen.
Lambeth Towers
Wedgwood Ho.
Walnut Tree Walk Prim. Sch.
London College of Printing
Metropolitan Tabernacle
A3211 A3200 A201 A301 A3202 A23 A3203 A3036 A302 B300
1 2 3 4 5 6 7
F G H J K
67 76 83

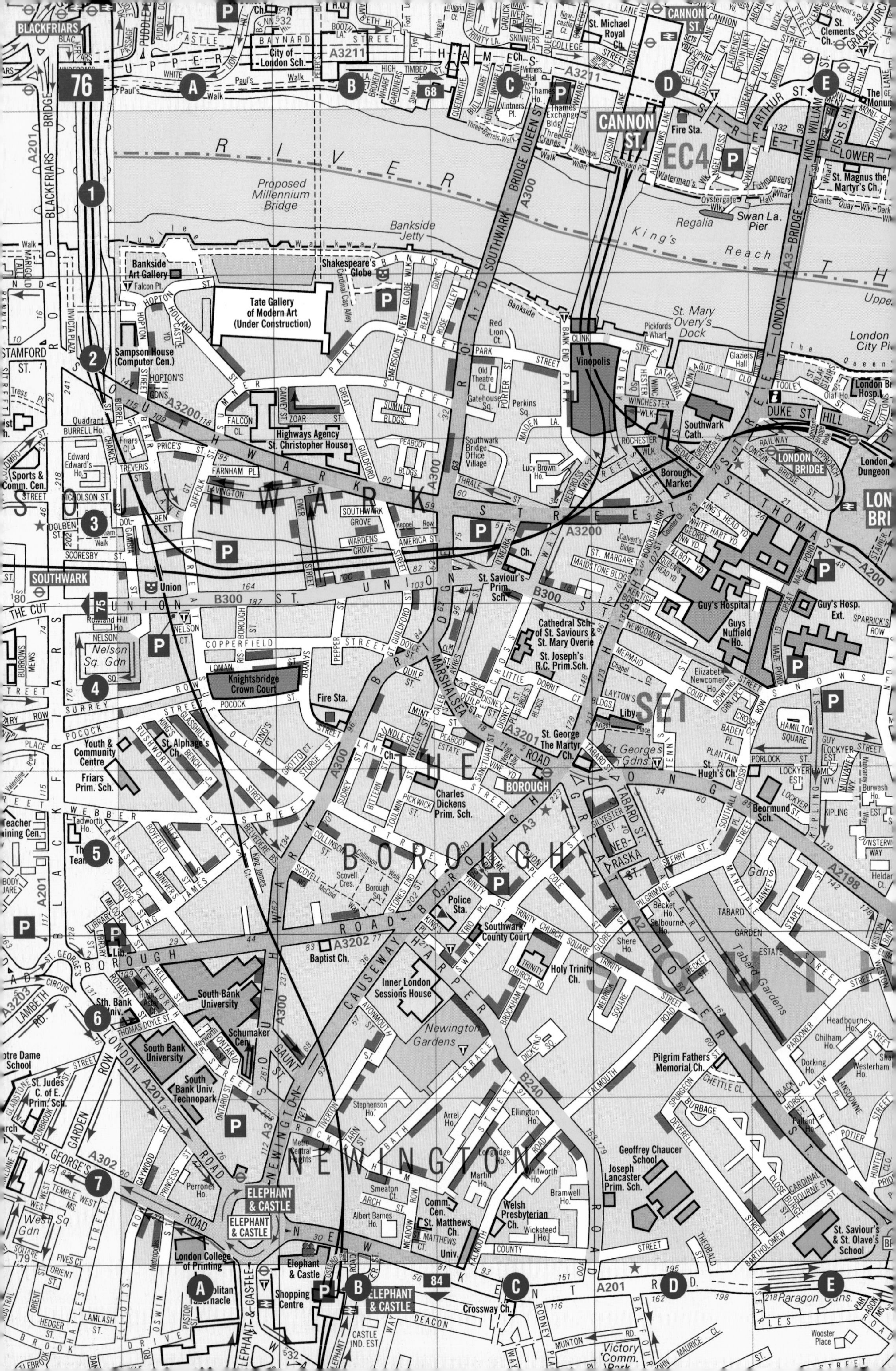
BLACKFRIARS
UPPER THAMES STREET
BAYNARD
City of London Sch.
A3211
Paul's Walk
TIMBER
68
QUEENHITHE
Vintners Pl.
Thames Ho.
Thames Exchange Bldg.
Three Cranes Walk
St. Michael Royal Ch.
CANNON ST.
COLLEGE
DOWGATE
CANNON ST.
Fire Sta.
EC4
ALLHALLOWS LANE
SWAN LA.
ARTHUR ST.
KING WILLIAM
FISH ST. HILL
LOWER
St. Magnus the Martyr's Ch.
Swan La. Pier
Regalia
St. Clements Ch.
GRACECHURCH
The Monument
R I V E R
T H A M E S
Proposed Millennium Bridge
Bankside Jetty
King's Reach
Jubilee Walkway
BLACKFRIARS BRIDGE
A201
Bankside Art Gallery
Falcon Pt.
Shakespeare's Globe
BANKSIDE
Tate Gallery of Modern Art (Under Construction)
HOPTON
HOLLAND
SOUTHWARK BRIDGE
A300
Red Lion Ct.
PARK STREET
Old Theatre Ct.
Gatehouse Sq.
Perkins Sq.
CLINK
Vinopolis
STONEY
St. Mary Overy's Dock
Pickfords Wharf
Glaziers Hall
MONTAGUE CLO.
WINCHESTER WLK.
Southwark Cath.
ROCHESTER WLK.
Borough Market
TOOLEY
London Bridge Hosp.
DUKE ST. HILL
LONDON BRIDGE
London Dungeon
LONDON BRI
London City Pier
Upper
STAMFORD ST.
Sampson House (Computer Cen.)
HOPTON'S GDNS.
SOUTHWARK
SUMNER
SUMNER BLDGS.
ZOAR ST.
Highways Agency St. Christopher House
GUILDFORD
PEABODY BLDGS.
Southwark Bridge Office Village
Lucy Brown Ho.
MAIDEN LA.
REDCROSS WAY
Quadrant
BURRELL Ho.
Edward Edward's Ho.
Sports & Comm. Cen.
NICHOLSON ST.
FARNHAM PL.
LAVINGTON
SOUTHWARK GROVE
WARDENS GROVE
AMERICA ST.
THRALE ST.
A3200
O'MEARA ST.
Ch.
ST. MARGARET'S CT.
MAIDSTONE BLDGS.
KING'S HEAD YD.
WHITE HART YD.
GEORGE INN YD.
TALBOT YD.
ST. THOMAS
A200
DOLBEN ST.
SCORESBY ST.
SOUTHWARK
Union
UNION ST.
B300
75
St. Saviour's Prim. Sch.
Guy's Hospital
Guy's Hosp. Ext.
Guys Nuffield Ho.
THE CUT
Rowland Hill Ho.
NELSON SQ.
Nelson Sq. Gdn
NELSON CT.
COPPERFIELD
PEPPER STREET
Cathedral Sch. of St. Saviours & St. Mary Overie
St. Joseph's R.C. Prim. Sch.
NEWCOMEN
MERMAID
Elizabeth Newcomen Ho.
SPARRICK'S ROW
LOMAN
Knightsbridge Crown Court
SAWYER
SURREY ROW
POCOCK ST.
Fire Sta.
QUILP ST.
MARSHALSEA
LITTLE DORRIT CT.
LAYTON'S BLDGS.
Liby.
SE1
SNOWSFIELDS
HAMILTON SQUARE
Youth & Community Centre
St. Alphage's Ct.
Friars Prim. Sch.
Ch.
PEABODY ESTATE
Charles Dickens Prim. Sch.
St. George The Martyr Ch.
BOROUGH
A3201
TABARD ST.
St. George's Gdns
St. Hugh's Ch.
LONG LANE
PORLOCK ST.
Beormund Sch.
KIPLING
WEBBER STREET
Tadworth Ho.
Teacher Training Cen.
TOULMIN ST.
PICKWICK ST.
COLLINSON ST.
Scovell Cres.
Borough Sq.
THE BOROUGH
A3
SILVESTER ST.
NEBRASKA ST.
SOUTHALL PL.
A2198
Police Sta.
Southwark County Court
TRINITY CHURCH SQUARE
Holy Trinity Ch.
PILGRIMAGE ST.
Becket Ho.
Selbourne Ho.
Shere Ho.
TABARD GARDEN ESTATE
Tabard Gardens
A3202
Baptist Ch.
BOROUGH ROAD
Lib.
South Bank University
Inner London Sessions House
MERRICK SQUARE
HARPER
GREAT DOVER STREET
A2
Sth. Bank Univ.
THOMAS DOYLE ST.
Schumaker Cen.
South Bank University
South Bank Univ. Technopark
Newington Gardens
DICKENS SQ.
B240
Pilgrim Fathers Memorial Ch.
CHETTLE CL.
Headbourne Ho.
Chilham Ho.
Dorking Ho.
Westerham Ho.
Notre Dame School
St. Judes C. of E. Prim. Sch.
LONDON ROAD
A201
ST. GEORGE'S CIRCUS
LAMBETH RD.
A3203
GAYWOOD
Perronet Ho.
ELEPHANT & CASTLE
NEWINGTON
Stephenson Ho.
Arrel Ho.
Ellington Ho.
Whitworth Ho.
Bramwell Ho.
Geoffrey Chaucer School
Joseph Lancaster Prim. Sch.
BURBAGE
DEVERELL
St. Saviour's & St. Olave's School
A302
ST. GEORGE'S RD.
West Sq. Gdn
London College of Printing
Metropolitan Tabernacle
Elephant & Castle Shopping Centre
Smeaton Ct.
Albert Barnes Ho.
Comm. Cen.
St. Matthews Ch.
Univ.
Welsh Presbyterian Ch.
Wicksteed Ho.
COUNTY STREET
NEW KENT ROAD
A201
Crossway Ch.
84
BALFOUR ST.
Paragon Gdns.
DEACON WAY
CASTLE IND. EST.
MUNTON RD.
Victory Comm. Park
Wooster Place
BROOK DRIVE
A B C D E
1 2 3 4 5 6 7

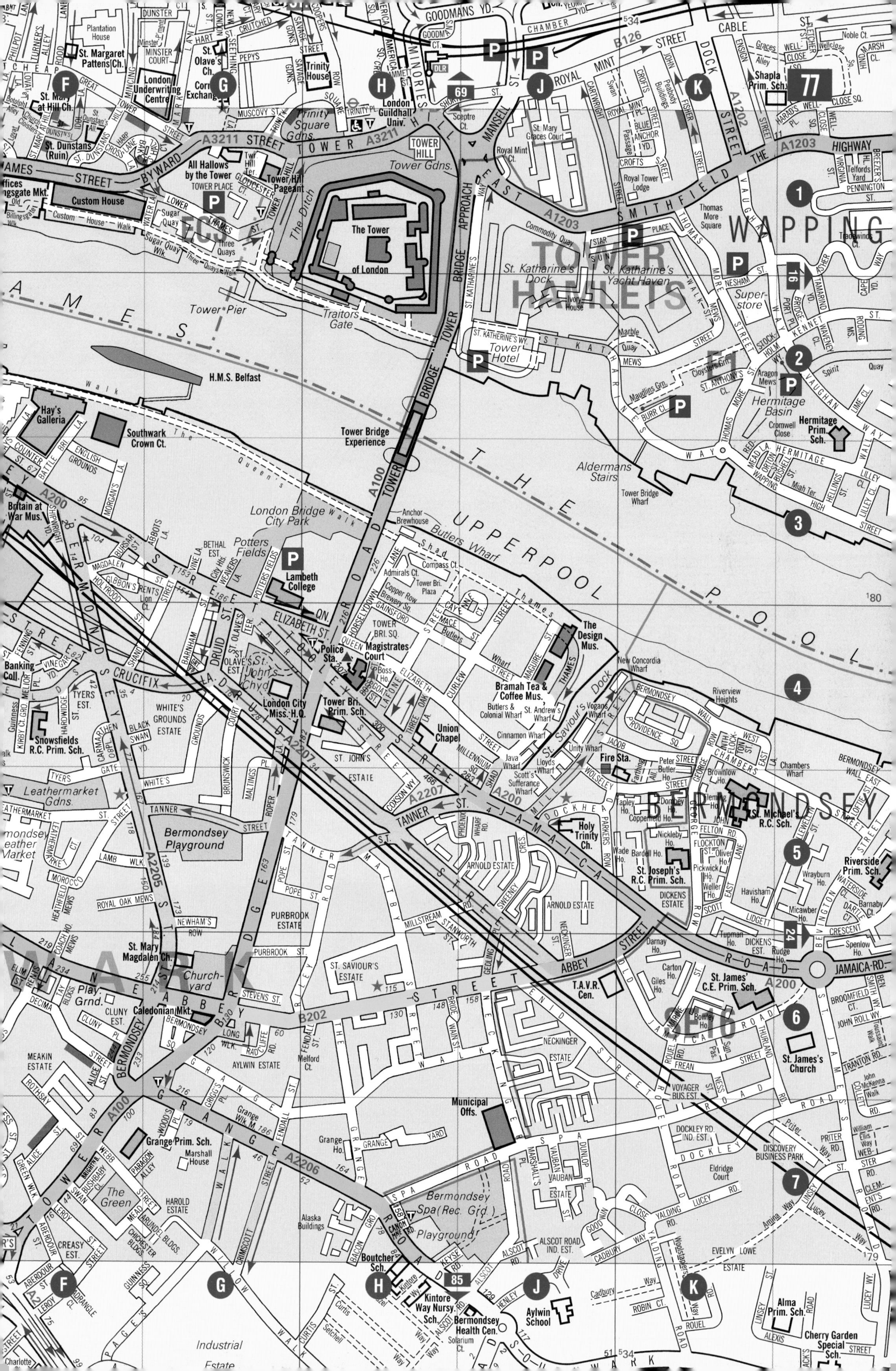
77
69
85
F
G
H
J
K
1
2
3
4
5
6
7
WAPPING
TOWER HAMLETS
BERMONDSEY
SOUTHWARK
EC3
E1
SE16
THE UPPER POOL
THAMES
The Tower of London
Tower Gdns.
The Ditch
Traitors Gate
Tower Pier
Tower Hill
Tower Hill Pageant
All Hallows by the Tower
Custom House
St. Dunstans (Ruin)
St. Mary at Hill Ch.
St. Margaret Pattens Ch.
St. Olave's Ch.
Corn Exchange
London Underwriting Centre
Trinity House
Trinity Square Gdns.
London Guildhall Univ.
Royal Mint Ct.
St. Katharine's Dock
St. Katharine's Yacht Haven
Tower Hotel
Tower Bridge Experience
H.M.S. Belfast
Hay's Galleria
Southwark Crown Ct.
Britain at War Mus.
London Bridge City Park
Potters Fields
Lambeth College
Magistrates Court
Police Sta.
London City Miss. H.Q.
Tower Bri. Prim. Sch.
Union Chapel
The Design Mus.
Bramah Tea & Coffee Mus.
Butlers Wharf
Holy Trinity Ch.
Fire Sta.
St. Michael's R.C. Sch.
St. Joseph's R.C. Prim. Sch.
Riverside Prim. Sch.
St. James' C.E. Prim. Sch.
St. James's Church
Hermitage Prim. Sch.
Hermitage Basin
Shapla Prim. Sch.
Snowsfields R.C. Prim. Sch.
Leathermarket Gdns.
Bermondsey Playground
St. Mary Magdalen Ch.
Caledonian Mkt.
Grange Prim. Sch.
Municipal Offs.
Bermondsey Spa (Rec. Grd.)
Boutcher Sch.
Kintore Way Nursy. Sch.
Bermondsey Health Cen.
Aylwin School
Alma Prim. Sch.
Cherry Garden Special Sch.
T.A.V.R. Cen.
Discovery Business Park
TOWER BRIDGE
TOWER BRIDGE ROAD
TOWER BRIDGE APPROACH
TOWER HILL
EAST SMITHFIELD
THE HIGHWAY
ROYAL MINT STREET
CABLE STREET
TOOLEY STREET
JAMAICA ROAD
ABBEY STREET
GRANGE ROAD
SPA ROAD
BERMONDSEY STREET
LONG LANE
A100
A200
A1203
A3211
A2206
A2207
A2205
A1202
B202
B126

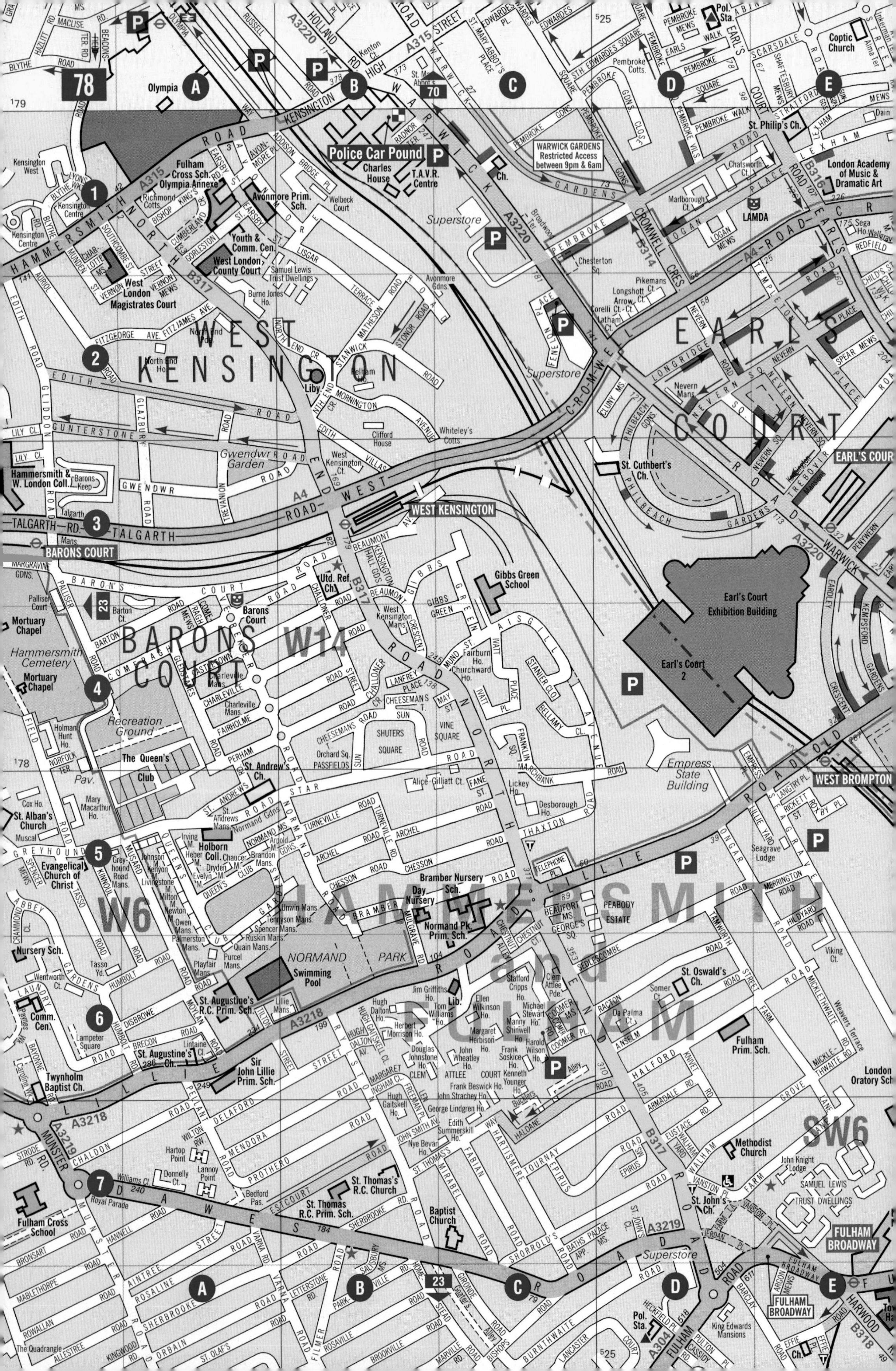

78
Olympia
WEST KENSINGTON
EARLS COURT
BARONS COURT
HAMMERSMITH and FULHAM
W14
W6
SW6
HAMMERSMITH ROAD
NORTH END ROAD
CROMWELL ROAD
WEST CROMWELL ROAD
TALGARTH RD.
LILLIE ROAD
DAWES ROAD
FULHAM ROAD
WARWICK ROAD
EARLS COURT ROAD
OLD BROMPTON ROAD
Police Car Pound
Charles House
T.A.V.R. Centre
WARWICK GARDENS Restricted Access between 9pm & 6am
Fulham Cross Sch. Olympia Annexe
Avonmore Prim. Sch.
Youth & Comm. Cen.
West London County Court
West London Magistrates Court
Kensington Centre
Superstore
LAMDA
London Academy of Music & Dramatic Art
St. Philip's Ch.
Coptic Church
St. Cuthbert's Ch.
WEST KENSINGTON
BARONS COURT
EARL'S COURT
WEST BROMPTON
FULHAM BROADWAY
Earl's Court Exhibition Building
Earl's Court 2
Empress State Building
Gibbs Green School
Hammersmith & W. London Coll.
Hammersmith Cemetery
Mortuary Chapel
Recreation Ground
The Queen's Club
St. Andrew's Ch.
St. Alban's Church
Evangelical Church of Christ
Holborn Coll.
Bramber Nursery Sch.
Normand Pk. Prim. Sch.
NORMAND PARK
Swimming Pool
St. Augustine's R.C. Prim. Sch.
St. Augustine's Ch.
Sir John Lillie Prim. Sch.
Twynholm Baptist Ch.
Fulham Cross School
St. Thomas's R.C. Church
St. Thomas R.C. Prim. Sch.
Baptist Church
St. Oswald's Ch.
Fulham Prim. Sch.
Methodist Church
St. John's Ch.
King Edwards Mansions
London Oratory Sch.
PEABODY ESTATE
SAMUEL LEWIS TRUST DWELLINGS
A B C D E
1 2 3 4 5 6 7

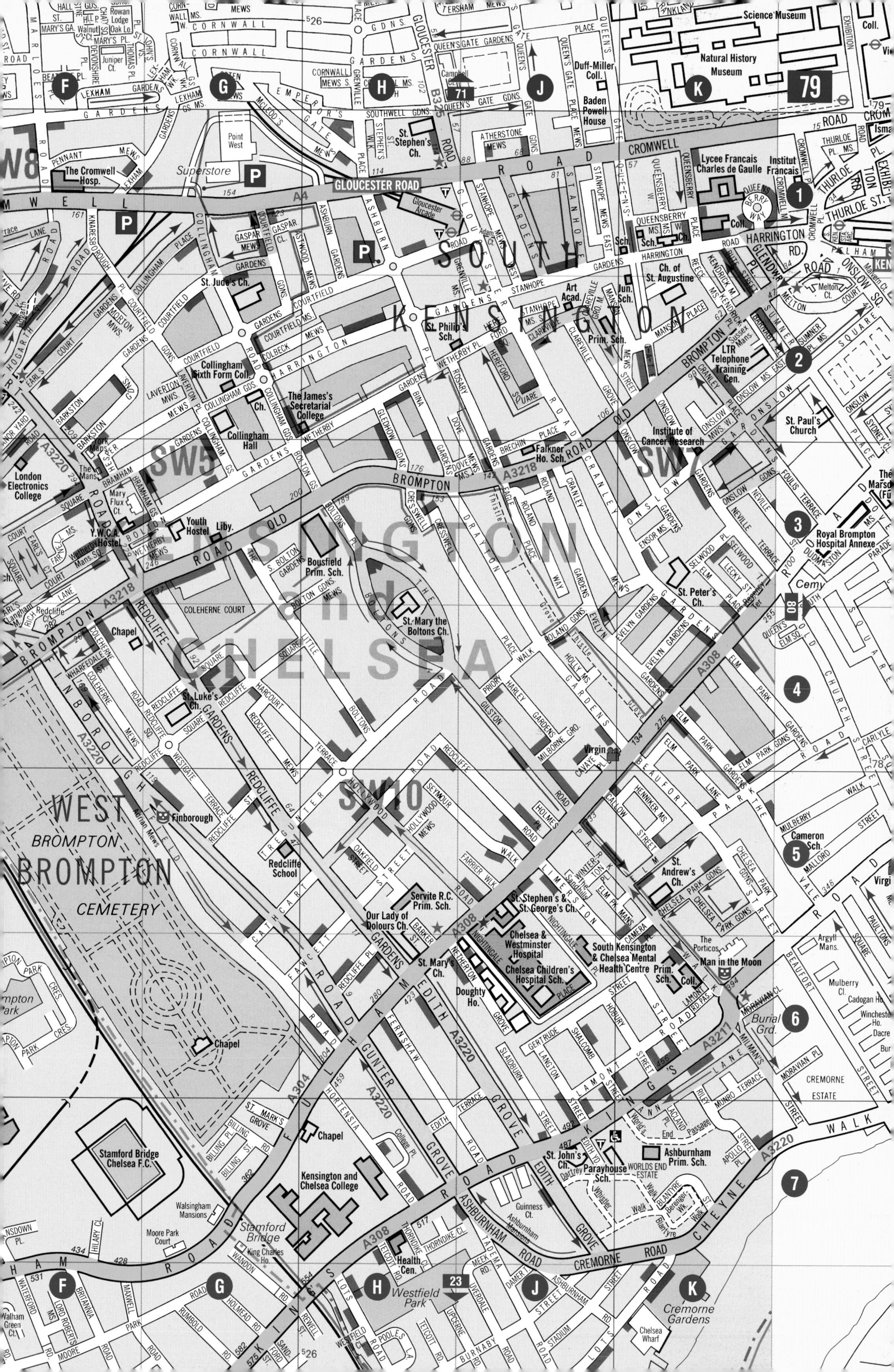

79
Science Museum
Natural History Museum
Duff-Miller Coll.
Baden Powell House
Lycee Francais Charles de Gaulle
Institut Francais
The Cromwell Hosp.
Point West
Superstore
GLOUCESTER ROAD
CROMWELL ROAD
Gloucester Arcade
St. Stephen's Ch.
SOUTH KENSINGTON
St. Jude's Ch.
St. Philip's Sch.
Ch. of St. Augustine
Art Acad.
Jun. Sch.
Prim. Sch.
LTR Telephone Training Cen.
Institute of Cancer Research
St. Paul's Church
Collingham Sixth Form Coll.
The James's Secretarial College
Collingham Hall
London Electronics College
Falkner Ho. Sch.
Royal Brompton Hospital Annexe
SW5
SW7
SW10
OLD BROMPTON ROAD
Youth Hostel
Liby.
Y.W.C.A. Hostel
Bousfield Prim. Sch.
KENSINGTON and CHELSEA
St. Mary the Boltons Ch.
St. Peter's Ch.
Coleherne Court
Chapel
St. Luke's Ch.
Redcliffe School
Finborough
WEST BROMPTON
BROMPTON CEMETERY
Servite R.C. Prim. Sch.
Our Lady of Dolours Ch.
St. Mary's Ch.
Doughty Ho.
St. Stephen's & St. George's Ch.
Chelsea & Westminster Hospital
Chelsea Children's Hospital Sch.
South Kensington & Chelsea Mental Health Centre
St. Andrew's Ch.
Cameron Sch.
Man in the Moon
The Porticos
Burial Grd.
CREMORNE ESTATE
Stamford Bridge Chelsea F.C.
Kensington and Chelsea College
Walsingham Mansions
Moore Park Court
Stamford Bridge
Health Cen.
Westfield Park
Guinness Ct.
St. John's Ch.
Parayhouse Sch.
WORLDS END ESTATE
Ashburnham Prim. Sch.
Cremorne Gardens
Chelsea Wharf
FULHAM ROAD
KING'S ROAD
CHEYNE WALK

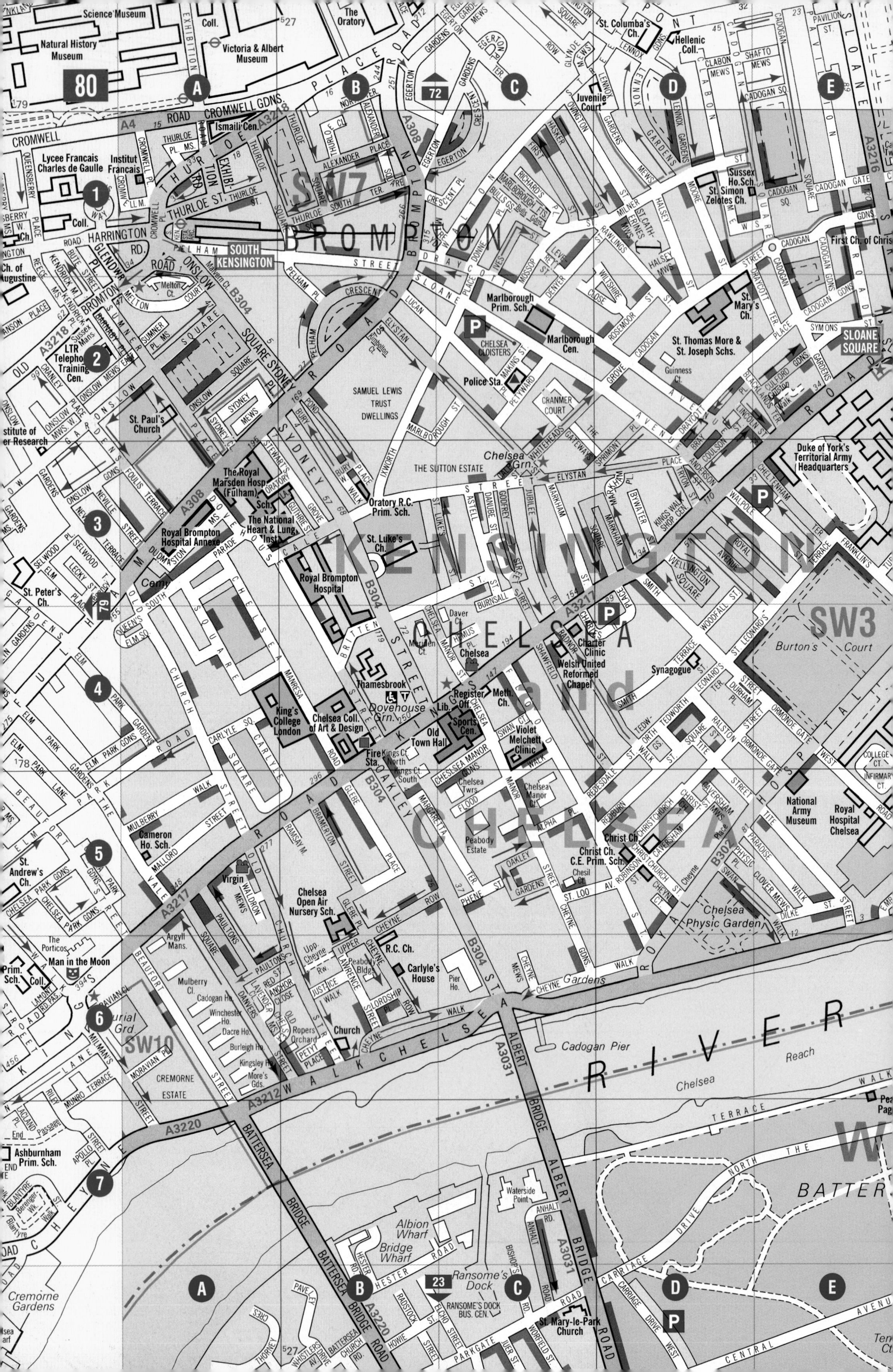
80
72
79
23
A
B
C
D
E
1
2
3
4
5
6
7
SW7
SW3
SW10
BROMPTON
KENSINGTON
and
CHELSEA
RIVER
Chelsea Reach
BATTER
Science Museum
Natural History Museum
Victoria & Albert Museum
The Oratory
Coll.
Ismaili Cen.
Lycee Francais Charles de Gaulle
Institut Francais
SOUTH KENSINGTON
St. Columba's Ch.
Hellenic Coll.
Juvenile Court
Sussex Ho.Sch.
St. Simon Zelotes Ch.
First Ch. of Chris
Marlborough Prim. Sch.
Marlborough Cen.
St. Mary's Ch.
St. Thomas More & St. Joseph Schs.
Guinness Ct.
SLOANE SQUARE
CHELSEA CLOISTERS
Police Sta.
SAMUEL LEWIS TRUST DWELLINGS
CRANMER COURT
THE SUTTON ESTATE
Chelsea Grn.
Duke of York's Territorial Army Headquarters
KINGS WALK SHOP CEN.
St. Paul's Church
The Royal Marsden Hosp. (Fulham)
The National Heart & Lung Inst.
Oratory R.C. Prim. Sch.
Royal Brompton Hospital Annexe
St. Luke's Ch.
Royal Brompton Hospital
St. Peter's Ch.
Burton's Court
Charter Clinic
Welsh United Reformed Chapel
Synagogue
Thamesbrook
Dovehouse Grn.
King's College London
Chelsea Coll. of Art & Design
Fire Sta.
Lib.
Register Off.
Sports Cen.
Old Town Hall
Meth. Ch.
Violet Melchett Clinic
Chelsea Manor Ct.
Peabody Estate
National Army Museum
Royal Hospital Chelsea
Cameron Ho. Sch.
Virgin
St. Andrew's Ch.
Christ Ch.
Christ Ch. C.E. Prim. Sch.
Chelsea Open Air Nursery Sch.
Chelsea Physic Garden
R.C. Ch.
Carlyle's House
Pier Ho.
The Porticos
Man in the Moon
Argyll Mans.
Mulberry Cl.
Cadogan Ho.
Winchester Ho.
Dacre Ho.
Burleigh Ho.
Kingsley Ho.
More's Gds.
CREMORNE ESTATE
Burial Grd.
Ropers Orchard
Church
Cadogan Pier
Ashburnham Prim. Sch.
Cremorne Gardens
Albion Wharf
Bridge Wharf
Ransome's Dock
RANSOME'S DOCK BUS. CEN.
Waterside Point
St. Mary-le-Park Church
CROMWELL ROAD
A4
A3218
A308
A3216
A3217
A3212
A3220
A3031
B304
B302
BROMPTON ROAD
FULHAM ROAD
KING'S ROAD
SLOANE STREET
SYDNEY STREET
OLD CHURCH STREET
OAKLEY STREET
ROYAL HOSPITAL ROAD
CHELSEA EMBANKMENT
CHEYNE WALK
BATTERSEA BRIDGE
ALBERT BRIDGE
BATTERSEA BRIDGE ROAD
ALBERT BRIDGE ROAD
CARRIAGE DRIVE NORTH
CARRIAGE DRIVE WEST
CENTRAL AVENUE
LOTS ROAD
HESTER ROAD
PARKGATE ROAD

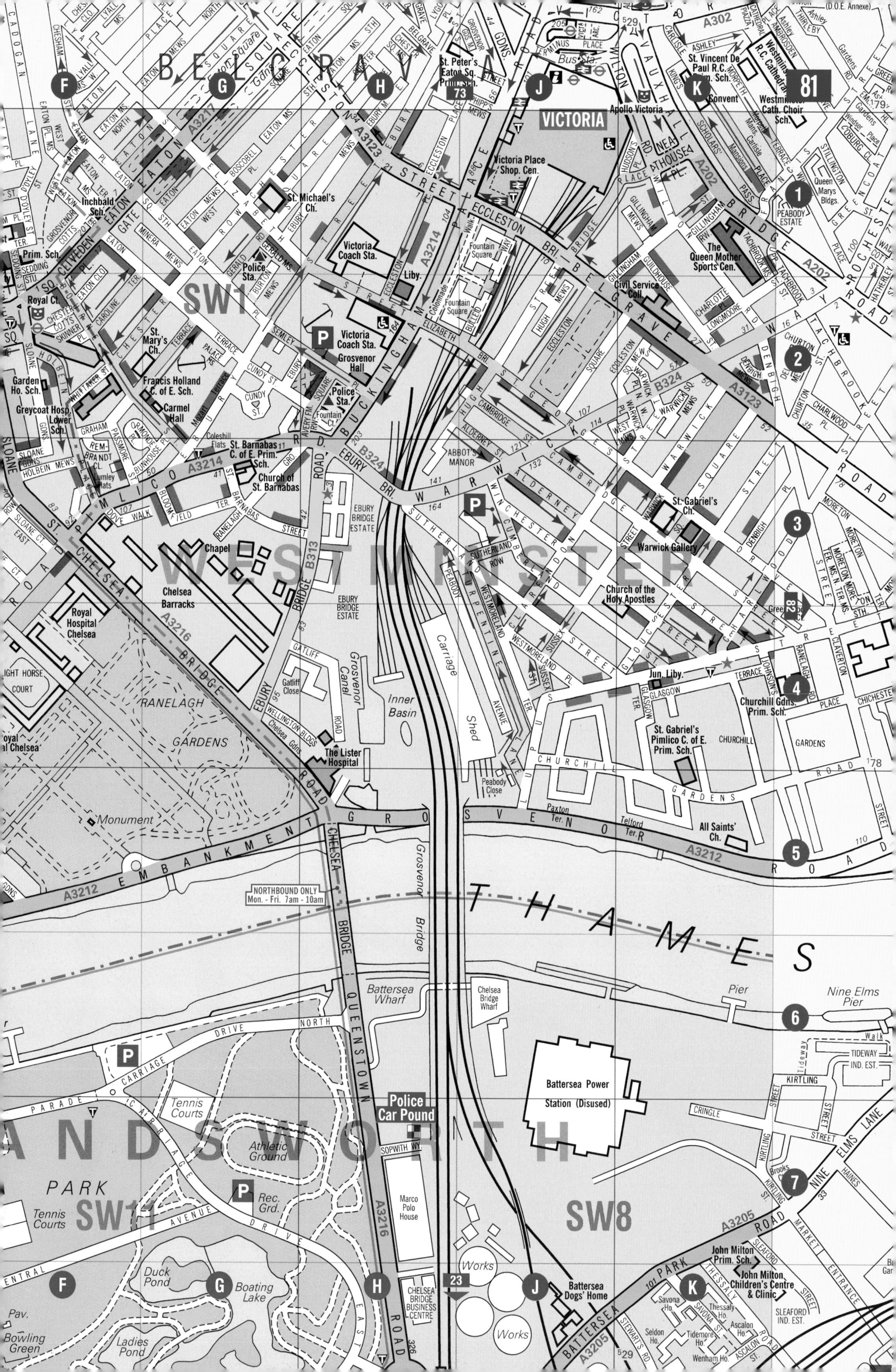
81
BELGRAVIA
WESTMINSTER
SW1
SW8
SW11
VICTORIA
THAMES
Chelsea Barracks
Royal Hospital Chelsea
Battersea Power Station (Disused)
Battersea Dogs' Home
Victoria Coach Sta.
Victoria Place Shop. Cen.
Apollo Victoria
Westminster R.C. Cathedral
The Queen Mother Sports Cen.
Church of the Holy Apostles
Warwick Gallery
St. Gabriel's Ch.
The Lister Hospital
Ebury Bridge Estate
Police Car Pound
Marco Polo House
Chelsea Bridge Business Centre
Grosvenor Canal
Inner Basin
Carriage Shed
Chelsea Bridge Wharf
Battersea Wharf
Nine Elms Pier
Ranelagh Gardens
Monument
Athletic Ground
Boating Lake
Duck Pond
Ladies Pond
Bowling Green
Tennis Courts
NORTHBOUND ONLY Mon. - Fri. 7am - 10am
A3212
A3216
A3214
A3123
A3205
A202
B324
B313
73
82
23

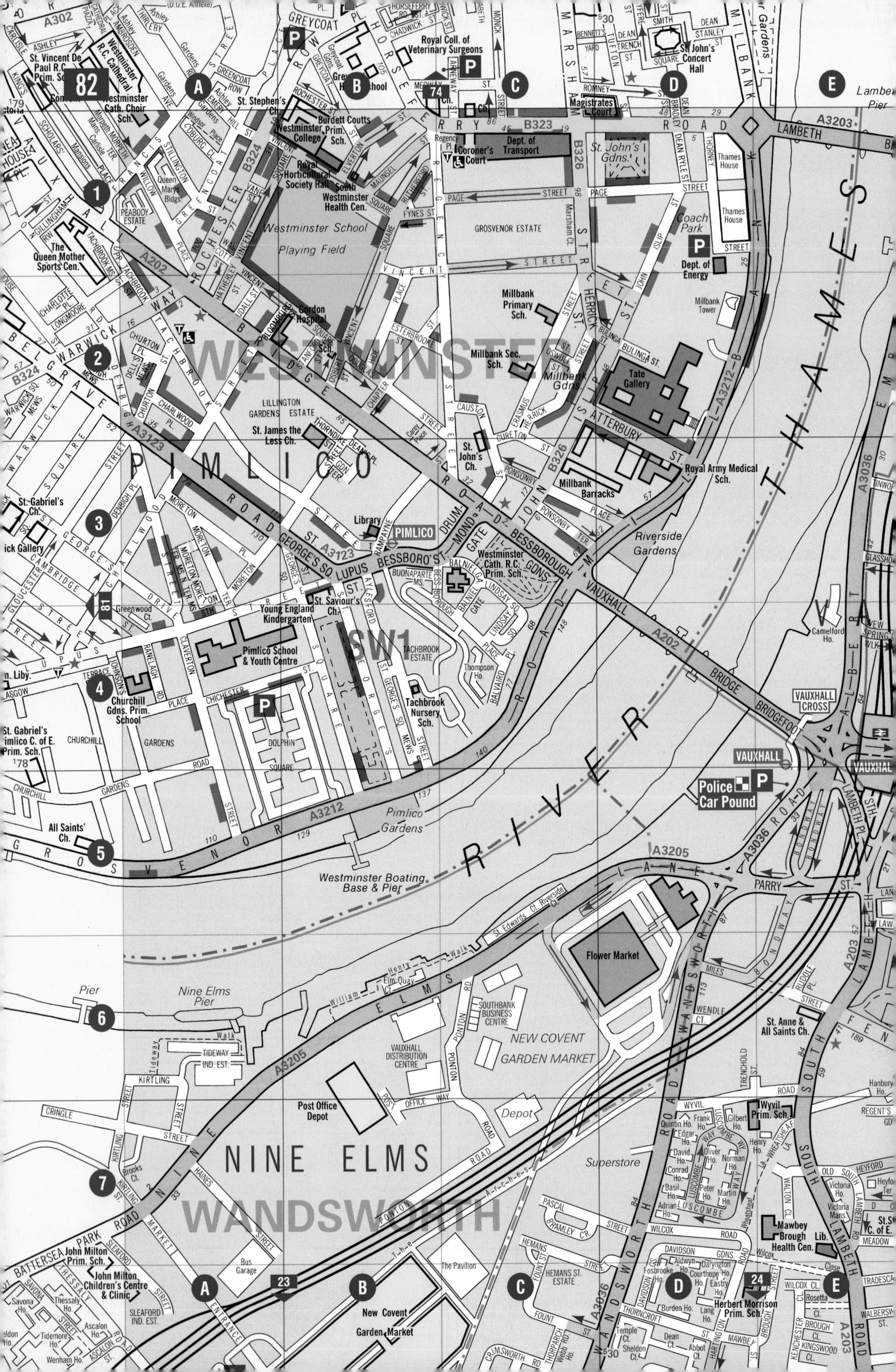
82
74
81
23
24
WESTMINSTER
PIMLICO
SW1
NINE ELMS
WANDSWORTH
RIVER THAMES
Westminster R.C. Cathedral
Westminster Cath. Choir Sch.
St. Vincent De Paul R.C. Prim. Sch.
Greycoat
Grey Coat Hospital School
Royal Coll. of Veterinary Surgeons
St. John's Concert Hall
Magistrates Court
St. Stephen's Ch.
Burdett Coutts Prim. Sch.
Westminster College
Royal Horticultural Society Hall
South Westminster Health Cen.
Coroner's Court
Dept. of Transport
St. John's Gdns.
Thames House
Westminster School Playing Field
Grosvenor Estate
Coach Park
Dept. of Energy
Millbank Tower
Millbank Primary Sch.
Millbank Sec. Sch.
Millbank Gdns.
Tate Gallery
Gordon Hospital
Queen Mary's Bldgs.
Peabody Estate
The Queen Mother Sports Cen.
Lillington Gardens Estate
St. James the Less Ch.
St. John's Ch.
Millbank Barracks
Royal Army Medical Sch.
Riverside Gardens
Library
Pimlico
Westminster Cath. R.C. Prim. Sch.
St. Gabriel's Ch.
Young England Kindergarten
St. Saviour's Ch.
Pimlico School & Youth Centre
Tachbrook Estate
Thompson Ho.
Tachbrook Nursery Sch.
Churchill Gdns. Prim. School
St. Gabriel's Pimlico C. of E. Prim. Sch.
Churchill Gardens
Dolphin Square
All Saints' Ch.
Pimlico Gardens
Westminster Boating Base & Pier
Vauxhall Cross
Vauxhall
Police Car Pound
Camelford Ho.
Nine Elms Pier
Tideway Ind. Est.
Flower Market
Southbank Business Centre
New Covent Garden Market
Vauxhall Distribution Centre
Post Office Depot
Depot
Superstore
St. Anne & All Saints Ch.
Wyvil Prim. Sch.
Mawbey Brough Health Cen.
Lib.
Herbert Morrison Prim. Sch.
Hemans St. Estate
Bus Garage
The Pavilion
New Covent Garden Market
John Milton Prim. Sch.
John Milton Children's Centre & Clinic
Sleaford Ind. Est.
Vauxhall Bridge Road
Horseferry Road
Lambeth Bridge
Millbank
Grosvenor Road
Belgrave Road
Lupus St.
St. George's Sq.
Bessborough Gdns.
Nine Elms Lane
Battersea Park Road
Wandsworth Road
South Lambeth Road
Kirtling Street
Ponton Road
Parry St.
Bondway
Wilcox Road
Luscombe Way
A202
A3212
A3205
A3036
A203
A3203
B323
B324
B326
A3123
A302

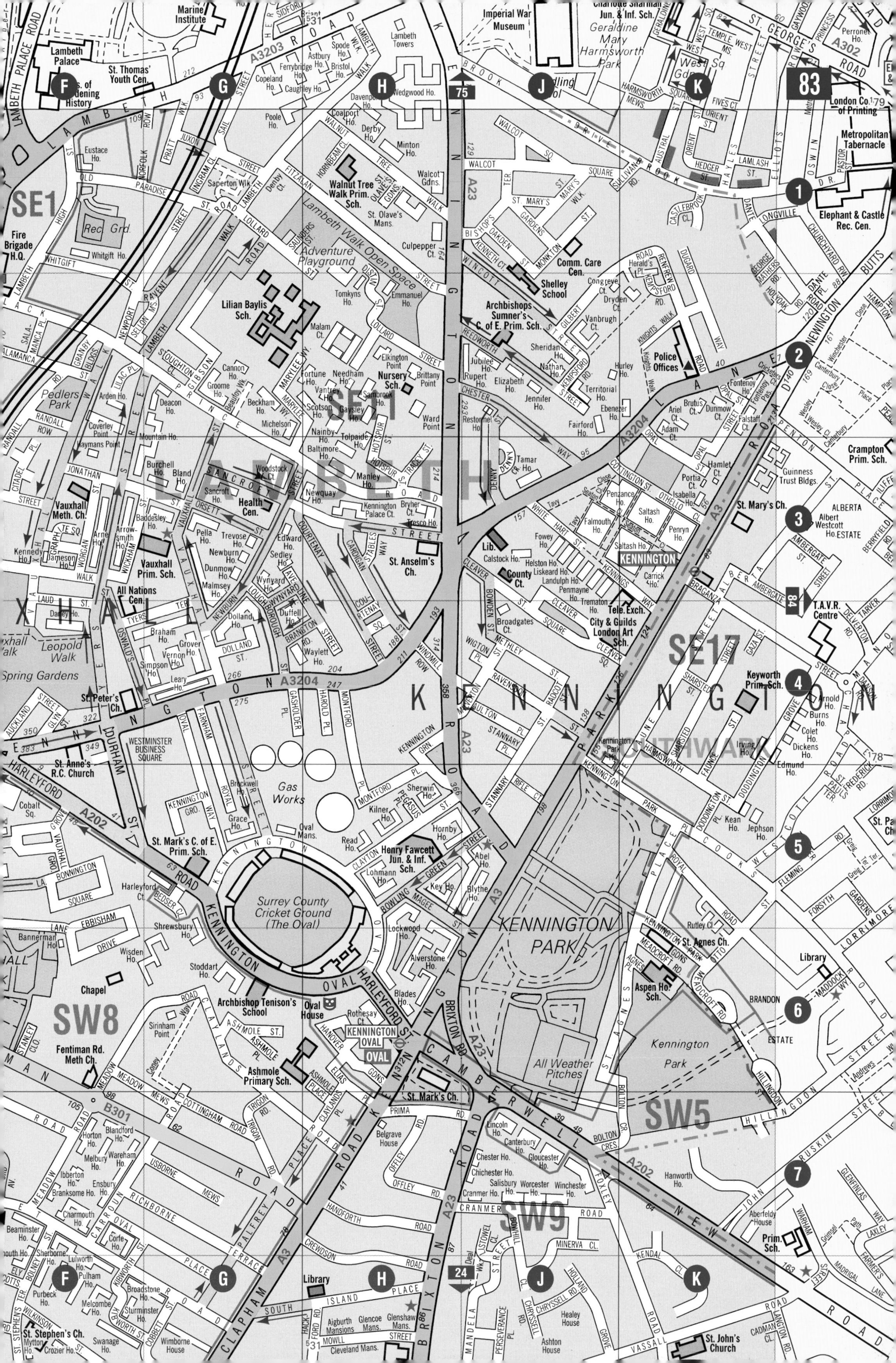
83
75
84
24
SE1
SE11
SE17
SW8
SW9
SW5
LAMBETH
VAUXHALL
KENNINGTON
SOUTHWARK
LAMBETH PALACE ROAD
Lambeth Palace
Mus. of Gardening History
Marine Institute
St. Thomas' Youth Cen.
Imperial War Museum
Geraldine Mary Harmsworth Park
Charlotte Sharman Jun. & Inf. Sch.
Lambeth Towers
A3203 ROAD
LAMBETH WALK
Wedgwood Ho.
West Sq. Gdns.
ST. GEORGE'S ROAD
A302
London Co. of Printing
Metropolitan Tabernacle
Elephant & Castle Rec. Cen.
Fire Brigade H.Q.
Rec. Grd.
Whitgift Ho.
Eustace Ho.
Saperton Wlk.
Walnut Tree Walk Prim. Sch.
Lambeth Walk Open Space
Adventure Playground
St. Olave's Mans.
Culpepper Ct.
Walcot Gdns.
Lilian Baylis Sch.
Comm. Care Cen.
Shelley School
Archbishops Sumner's C. of E. Prim. Sch.
Police Offices
Pedlers Park
Nursery Sch.
Health Cen.
Vauxhall Meth. Ch.
Vauxhall Prim. Sch.
All Nations Cen.
St. Anselm's Ch.
Lib.
County Ct.
KENNINGTON
Tele. Exch.
City & Guilds London Art Sch.
St. Mary's Ch.
Albert Westcott Ho. ESTATE
Crampton Prim. Sch.
Guinness Trust Bldgs.
T.A.V.R. Centre
Keyworth Prim. Sch.
Leopold Walk
Spring Gardens
St. Peter's Ch.
St. Anne's R.C. Church
A3204
KENNINGTON LANE
HARLEYFORD
A202
WESTMINSTER BUSINESS SQUARE
Gas Works
Oval Mans.
St. Mark's C. of E. Prim. Sch.
Henry Fawcett Jun. & Inf. Sch.
Surrey County Cricket Ground (The Oval)
KENNINGTON PARK
All Weather Pitches
Kennington Park
St. Agnes Ch.
Aspen Ho. Sch.
Library
BRANDON ESTATE
Chapel
Archbishop Tenison's School
Oval House
KENNINGTON OVAL
OVAL
Ashmole Primary Sch.
Fentiman Rd. Meth Ch.
St. Mark's Ch.
CAMBERWELL NEW ROAD
BRIXTON ROAD
A23
A3
CLAPHAM ROAD
B301
Library
Prim. Sch.
St. Stephen's Ch.
St. John's Church
F G H J K
1 2 3 4 5 6 7

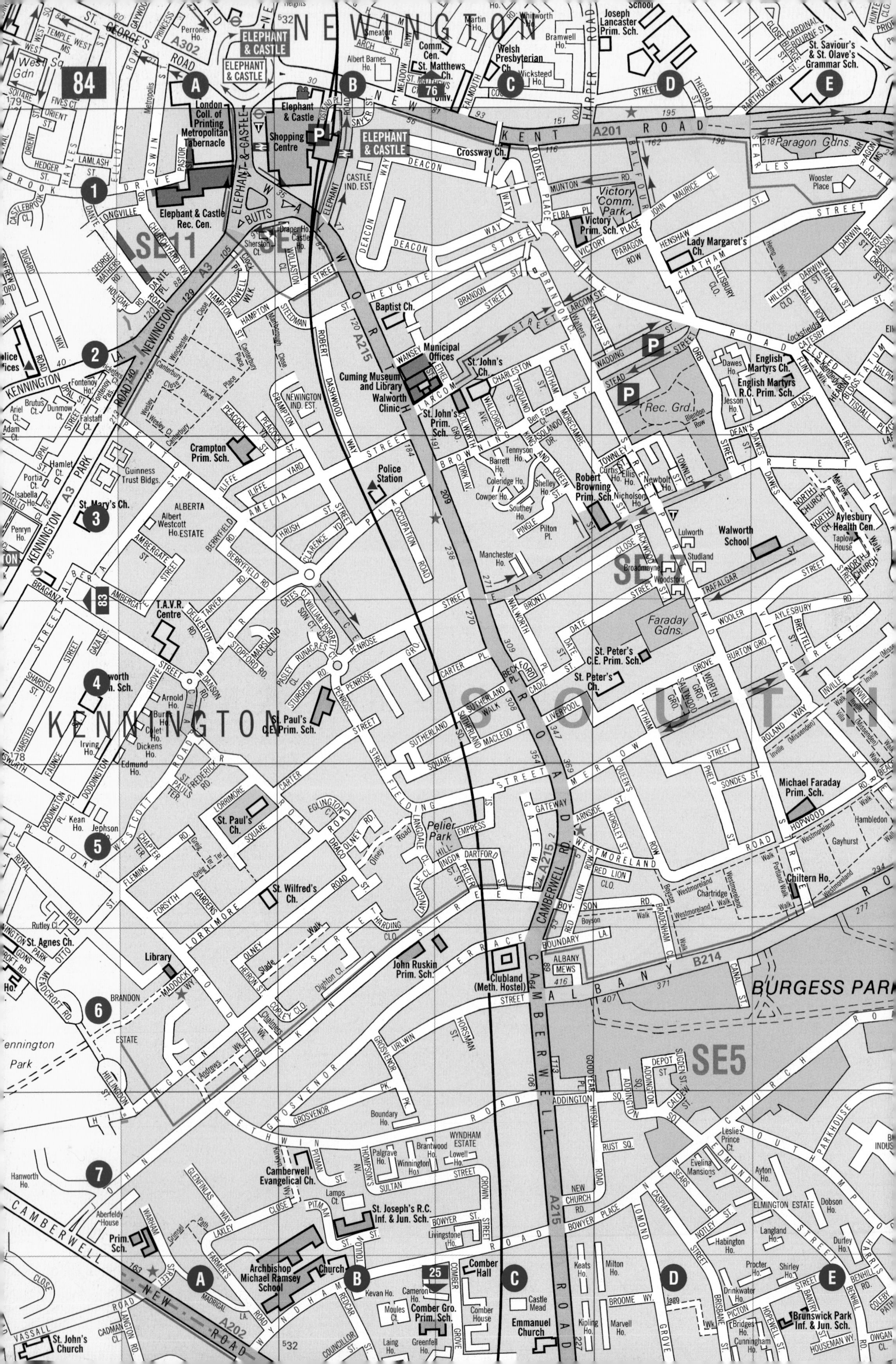

84
NEWINGTON
ELEPHANT & CASTLE
London Coll. of Printing
Metropolitan Tabernacle
Elephant & Castle Shopping Centre
Elephant & Castle Rec. Cen.
SE11
SE1
SE17
SE5
KENT ROAD
A201
A215
A3
A202
A302
B214
KENNINGTON
KENNINGTON PARK ROAD
NEWINGTON BUTTS
WALWORTH ROAD
CAMBERWELL ROAD
CAMBERWELL NEW ROAD
ALBANY ROAD
BURGESS PARK
Kennington Park
Welsh Presbyterian Ch.
Joseph Lancaster Prim. Sch.
St. Saviour's & St. Olave's Grammar Sch.
Crossway Ch.
Victory Comm. Park
Victory Prim. Sch.
Lady Margaret's Ch.
Baptist Ch.
Wansey Municipal Offices
Cuming Museum and Library
Walworth Clinic
St. John's Ch.
St. John's Prim. Sch.
English Martyrs Ch.
English Martyrs R.C. Prim. Sch.
Crampton Prim. Sch.
Guinness Trust Bldgs.
St. Mary's Ch.
Police Station
Robert Browning Prim. Sch.
Walworth School
Aylesbury Health Cen.
T.A.V.R. Centre
ALBERTA ESTATE
Faraday Gdns.
St. Peter's C.E. Prim. Sch.
St. Peter's Ch.
St. Paul's C.E. Prim. Sch.
St. Paul's Ch.
Pelier Park
Michael Faraday Prim. Sch.
Chiltern Ho.
St. Wilfred's Ch.
John Ruskin Prim. Sch.
Clubland (Meth. Hostel)
St. Agnes Ch.
Library
Camberwell Evangelical Ch.
St. Joseph's R.C. Inf. & Jun. Sch.
Archbishop Michael Ramsey School
Church
Comber Hall
Comber Gro. Prim. Sch.
Emmanuel Church
Brunswick Park Inf. & Jun. Sch.
St. John's Church
WYNDHAM ESTATE
ELMINGTON ESTATE
Prim. Sch.
76
83
25

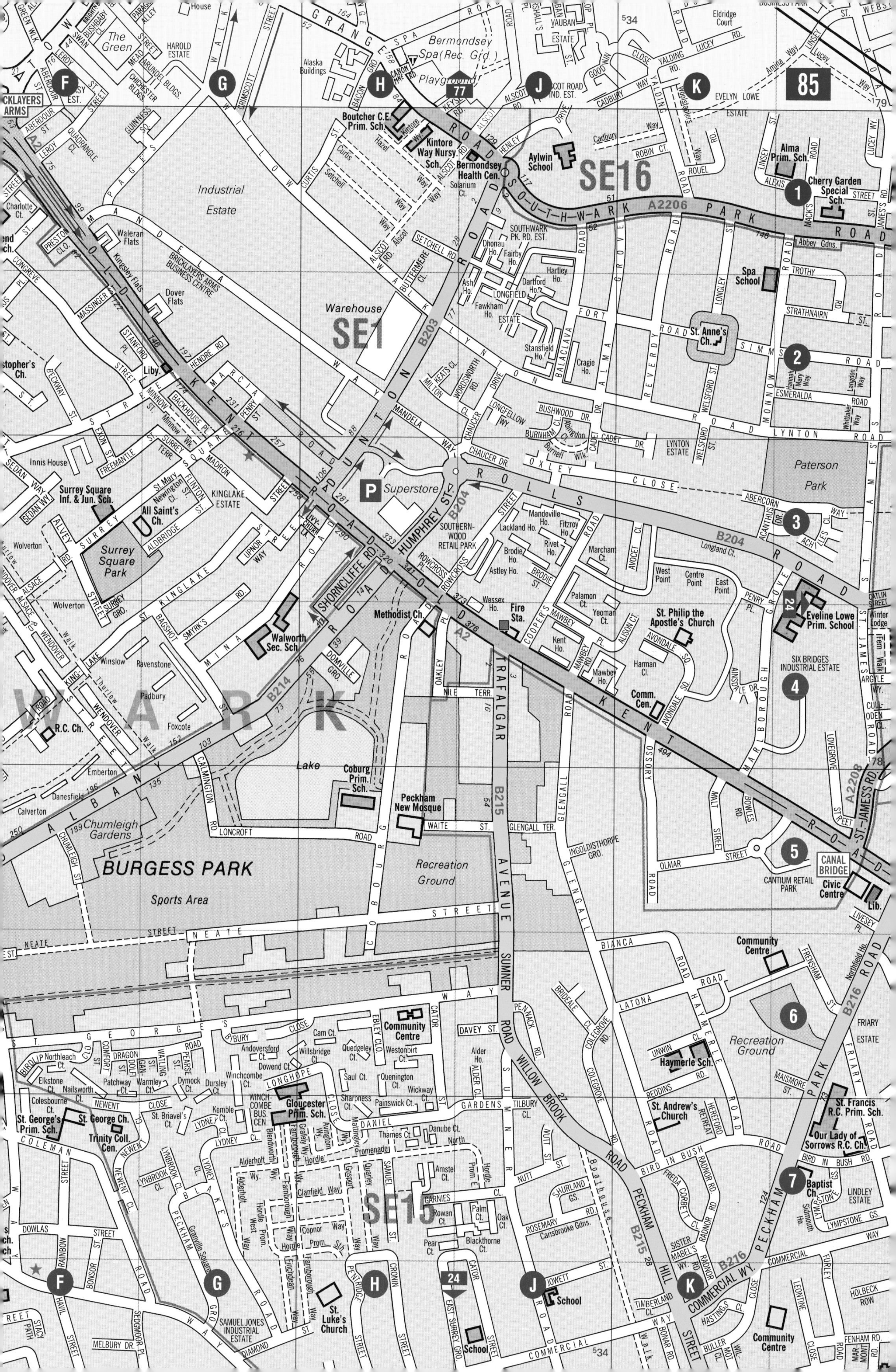
SE16
SE1
SE15
Bermondsey Spa (Rec. Grd.)
Playground
Industrial Estate
Warehouse
Superstore
SOUTHWARK PARK ROAD
A2206
OLD KENT ROAD
A2
B203
B204
B214
B215
B216
A2208
ALBANY ROAD
ROLLS ROAD
LYNTON ROAD
DUNTON ROAD
MANDELA WAY
GRANGE
WILLOW WALK
CANAL BRIDGE
Paterson Park
Surrey Square Park
BURGESS PARK
Chumleigh Gardens
Sports Area
Lake
Recreation Ground
Alma Prim. Sch.
Cherry Garden Special Sch.
Spa School
St. Anne's Ch.
Eveline Lowe Prim. School
SIX BRIDGES INDUSTRIAL ESTATE
St. Philip the Apostle's Church
Comm. Cen.
Fire Sta.
Methodist Ch.
Walworth Sec. Sch.
Surrey Square Inf. & Jun. Sch.
All Saint's Ch.
Boutcher C.E. Prim. Sch.
Kintore Way Nursy. Sch.
Bermondsey Health Cen.
Aylwin School
Coburg Prim. Sch.
Peckham New Mosque
Community Centre
Haymerle Sch.
St. Andrew's Church
St. Francis R.C. Prim. Sch.
Our Lady of Sorrows R.C. Ch.
Baptist Ch.
Gloucester Prim. Sch.
St. George's Prim. Sch.
St. George Ch.
Trinity Coll. Cen.
St. Luke's Church
School
SAMUEL JONES INDUSTRIAL ESTATE
CANTIUM RETAIL PARK
Civic Centre
Lib.
SOUTHERNWOOD RETAIL PARK
KINGLAKE ESTATE
LYNTON ESTATE
FRIARY ESTATE
LINDLEY ESTATE
HAROLD ESTATE
EVELYN LOWE ESTATE
SOUTHWARK PK. RD. EST.
BRICKLAYERS ARMS BUSINESS CENTRE
SUMNER ROAD
TRAFALGAR AVENUE
PECKHAM HILL STREET
PECKHAM PARK ROAD
WILLOWBROOK ROAD
COMMERCIAL WAY
ST. GEORGE'S WAY
NEATE STREET
GLENGALL ROAD
COBOURG ROAD
ST. JAMES'S ROAD
77
24
F
G
H
J
K
1
2
3
4
5
6
7

INDEX TO STREETS

HOW TO USE THIS INDEX

1. Each street name is followed by its Postal District and then by its map reference; e.g. Abbey Rd. *NW6 & NW8* —1F **55** is in the North West 6 and North West 8 Postal District and is to be found in square 1F on page **55**.
The page number being shown in bold type.
A strict alphabetical order is followed in which Av., Rd., St., etc. (though abbreviated) are read in full and as part of the street name; e.g. Alderholt Way appears after Alder Clo. but before Alder Ho.

2. Streets and a selection of Subsidiary names not shown on the Maps, appear in the index in *Italics* with the thoroughfare to which it is connected shown in brackets; e.g. *Almondsbury Ct. SE15 7F **85** (off Lynbrook Clo.)*

3. With the now general usage of Postcodes for addressing mail, it is not recommended that this index is used for such a purpose.

GENERAL ABBREVIATIONS

All : Alley	Cvn : Caravan	Cres : Crescent	Gt : Great	Mnr : Manor	Pas : Passage	St : Street
App : Approach	Cen : Centre	Cft : Croft	Grn : Green	Mans : Mansions	Pl : Place	Ter : Terrace
Arc : Arcade	Chu : Church	Dri : Drive	Gro : Grove	Mkt : Market	Quad : Quadrant	Trad : Trading
Av : Avenue	Chyd : Churchyard	E : East	Ho : House	Mdw : Meadow	Res : Residential	Up : Upper
Bk : Back	Circ : Circle	Embkmt : Embankment	Ind : Industrial	M : Mews	Ri : Rise	Va : Vale
Boulevd : Boulevard	Cir : Circus	Est : Estate	Junct : Junction	Mt : Mount	Rd : Road	Vw : View
Bri : Bridge	Clo : Close	Fld : Field	La : Lane	N : North	Shop : Shopping	Vs : Villas
B'way : Broadway	Comn : Common	Gdns : Gardens	Lit : Little	Pal : Palace	S : South	Wlk : Walk
Bldgs : Buildings	Cotts : Cottages	Gth : Garth	Lwr : Lower	Pde : Parade	Sq : Square	W : West
Bus : Business	Ct : Court	Ga : Gate	Mc : Mac	Pk : Park	Sta : Station	Yd : Yard

INDEX TO STREETS

Bidborough St.—Chesil Ct.

Bidborough St. WC1 —7D 58
Biddulph Mans. W9 —7F 55
Biddulph Rd. W9 —7F 55
Billing Pl. SW10 —7G 79
Billing Rd. SW10 —7G 79
Billing St. SW10 —7G 79
Billiter Sq. EC3 —6G 69
Billiter St. EC3 —6G 69
Bina Gdns. SW5 —2H 79
Bingfield St. N1 —2E 58
(in two parts)
Bingham Pl. W1 —3F 65
Binney St. W1 —6G 65
Birchington Rd. NW6 —2E 54
Birchin La. EC3 —6E 68
Birdcage Wlk. SW1 —5K 73
Bird in Bush Rd. SE15 —7K 85
Birdlip Clo. SE15 —6F 85
Bird St. W1 —6G 65
Birkenhead St. WC1 —6E 58
Bishop King's Rd. W14 —1A 78
Bishop's Bri. Rd. W2 —6G 63
Bishop's Ct. EC4 —5K 67
Bishop's Ct. WC2 —5H 67
Bishopsgate. EC2 —6F 69
Bishopsgate Arc. EC2 —4G 69
Bishopsgate Chu. Yd. EC2 —5F 69
Bishops Rd. SW6 —7C 78
Bishop's Rd. SW11 —7C 80
Bishop's Ter. SE11 —1J 83
Bishop St. N1 —2B 60
Bittern St. SE1 —5B 76
Blackall St. EC2 —1F 69
Blackbird Yd. E2 —6J 61
Blackburne's M. W1 —7F 65
Blackfriars Bri. SE1 & EC4 —1K 75
Blackfriars Ct. EC4 —7K 67
Black Friars La. EC4 —7K 67
Blackfriars Pas. EC4 —7K 67
Blackfriars Rd. SE1 —5K 75
Blackfriars Underpass. EC4 —7K 67
Black Horse Ct. SE1 —7E 76
Blacklands Ter. SW3 —2E 80
Blackmans Yd. E2 —1K 69
Blackmore Ho. N1 —3G 59
Black Prince Rd. SE1 & SE11 —2F 83
Blackshaw Pl. N1 —1G 61
Black Swan Yd. SE1 —4F 77
Blackthorne Ct. SE15 —7H 85
Blackwood St. SE17 —3D 84
Blades Ho. SE11 —6H 83
Blagrove Rd. W10 —4A 62
Blair Ct. NW8 —2K 55
Blake Ho. SE1 —6H 75
Blakeney Clo. NW1 —1B 58
Blake's Rd. SE15 —7G 85
Blandford Ho. SW8 —7F 83
Blandford Sq. NW1 —2C 64
Blandford St. W1 —5E 64
Bland Ho. SE11 —3G 83
Blantyre St. SW10 —7K 79
Blantyre Wlk. SW10 —7K 79
Blashford. NW3 —1D 56
Bleeding Heart Yd. EC1 —4J 67
Blendon Row. SE17 —2D 84
Blendworth Way. SE15 —7G 85
Blenheim Cres. W11 —7A 62
Blenheim Pas. NW8 —4H 55
Blenheim Rd. NW8 —4J 55
Blenheim St. W1 —6H 65
Blenheim Ter. NW8 —4H 55
Bletchley St. N1 —5C 60
Bletsoe Wlk. N1 —4C 60
Blithfield St. W8 —7F 71
Blomfield Rd. W9 —3G 63
Blomfield St. EC2 —4E 68
Blomfield Vs. W2 —4G 63
Bloomburg St. SW1 —2A 82
Bloomfield Pl. W1 —7J 65
Bloomfield Ter. SW1 —3G 81
Bloomsbury Ct. WC1 —4E 66
Bloomsbury Pl. WC1 —4E 66
Bloomsbury Sq. WC1 —4E 66
Bloomsbury St. WC1 —4C 66
Bloomsbury Way. WC1 —4D 66
Blore Ct. W1 —7B 66
Blossom St. E1 —3G 69
Bloxworth Gro. N1 —2G 59
Blue Anchor Yd. E1 —1K 77
Blue Ball Yd. SW1 —3K 73
Blythe Ho. SE11 —5J 83
Blythe Rd. W14 —7A 70
Boadicea St. N1 —3F 59
Boathouse Wlk. SE15 —7J 85
Boddy's Bri. SE1 —2J 75
Boden Ho. E1 —3K 69
Boldero Pl. NW8 —2B 64
Bolney Ga. SW7 —5B 72
Bolney St. SW8 —7F 83
Bolsover St. W1 —2J 65
Bolt Ct. EC4 —6J 67
Bolton Cres. SE5 —7J 83
Bolton Gdns. SW5 —3F 79
Bolton Gdns. M. SW10 —3H 79
Bolton Rd. NW8 —3G 55
Boltons Pl. SW10 —3H 79
Boltons, The. SW10 —3H 79
Bolton St. W1 —2J 73
Bomore Rd. W11 —7A 62
Bonar Rd. SE15 —7K 85
Bonchurch Rd. W10 —3A 62
Bond Ct. EC4 —6D 68
Bondway. SW8 —6E 82
Bonhill St. EC2 —2E 68
Bonnington Sq. SW8 —5F 83
Bonny St. NW1 —1K 57
Bonsor St. SE5 —7F 85
Book M. WC2 —6C 66
Booth La. EC4 —7B 68
Booth's Pl. W1 —4A 66
Boot St. N1 —7F 61
Boreas Wlk. N1 —5A 60
Borough High St. SE1 —5C 76
Borough Rd. SE1 —6K 75
Borough Sq. SE1 —5B 76
Borrett Clo. SE17 —4B 84
Boscobel Pl. SW1 —1G 81
Boscobel St. NW8 —2A 64
Boss Ho. SE1 —4H 77
Boss St. SE1 —4H 77
Boston Pl. NW1 —1D 64
Boswell Ct. WC1 —3E 66
Boswell St. WC1 —3E 66
Bosworth Rd. W10 —2A 62
Botolph All. EC3 —1F 77
Botolph La. EC3 —1F 77
Botts M. W2 —6E 62
Bounaparte M. SW1 —3B 82
Boundary Ho. SE5 —7B 84
Boundary La. SE5 & SE17 —6C 84
Boundary Pas. E2 —1H 69
Boundary Rd. NW8 —3G 55
Boundary Row. SE1 —4K 75
Boundary St. E2 —7H 61
(in two parts)
Bourchier St. W1 —7B 66
Bourdon Pl. W1 —7J 65
Bourdon St. W1 —1H 73
Bourlet Clo. W1 —4K 65
Bourne Est. EC1 —3H 67
Bourne M. W1 —5G 65
Bourne St. SW1 —2F 81
Bourne Ter. W2 —3F 63
Bouverie Pl. W2 —5A 64
Bouverie St. EC4 —6J 67
Bowater Ho. EC1 —2B 68
Bow Chyd. EC4 —6C 68
Bowden St. SE11 —3J 83
Bowhill Clo. SW9 —7J 83
Bowland Yd. SW1 —5E 72
Bow La. EC4 —6C 68
Bowl Ct. EC2 —2G 69
Bowles Rd. SE1 —5K 85
Bowley Ho. SE16 —6K 77
Bowling Grn. La. EC1 —1J 67
Bowling Grn. Pl. SE1 —4D 76
Bowling Grn. St. SE11 —5H 83
Bowling Grn. Wlk. N1 —6F 61
Bowman's M. E1 —7K 69
Bowmore Wlk. NW1 —1C 58
Bow St. WC2 —6E 66
Bowyer Ho. N1 —3G 61
Bowyer Pl. SE5 —7C 84
Bowyer St. SE5 —7C 84
Boxworth Gro. N1 —2G 59
Boydell Ct. NW8 —1K 55
Boyd St. E1 —6K 69
Boyfield St. SE1 —5A 76
Boyle St. W1 —7K 65
Boyne Ter. M. W11 —2B 70
Boyson Rd. SE17 —5C 84
Boyson Wlk. SE17 —5D 84
Brabant Ct. EC3 —7F 69
Bracer Ho. N1 —4G 61
Brackley St. EC1 —3C 68
Bracklyn Ct. N1 —4D 60
Bracklyn St. N1 —4D 60
Bradenham Clo. SE17 —6D 84
Braden St. W9 —2F 63
Bradiston Rd. W9 —6C 54
Bradley's Clo. N1 —4J 59
Brad St. SE1 —3J 75
Braes St. N1 —1A 60
Braganza St. SE17 —3K 83
Braham Ho. SE11 —4G 83
Braham St. E1 —6J 69
Braidwood Pas. EC1 —4B 68
Braithwaite Tower. W2 —3A 64
Bramber. WC1 —7D 58
Bramber Rd. W14 —5B 78
Bramerton St. SW3 —5B 80
Bramham Gdns. SW5 —3F 79
Bramley Cres. SW8 —7C 82
Bramwell Ho. SE1 —7C 76
Bramwell M. N1 —2G 59
Branch Pl. N1 —3E 60
Brandon Est. SE17 —6K 83
Brandon Mans. W14 —5A 78
Brandon M. EC2 —4D 68
Brandon Rd. N7 —1D 58
Brandon St. SE17 —2C 84
(in three parts)
Brangton Rd. SE11 —4G 83
Branksome Ho. SW8 —7F 83
Bransdale Clo. NW6 —2E 54
Brantwood Ho. SE5 —7B 84
Bratley St. E1 —2K 69
Bravington Pl. W9 —1B 62
Bravington Rd. W9 —5B 54
Brayfield Ter. N1 —1H 59
Bray Pl. SW3 —3D 80
Bread St. EC4 —7C 68
(in two parts)
Bream's Bldgs. EC4 —5H 67
Brechin Pl. SW7 —3J 79
Brecon Rd. W6 —6A 78
Breezer's Hill. E1 —1K 77
Bremner Rd. SW7 —6J 71
Brendon St. W1 —5C 64
Bressenden Pl. SW1 —6J 73
Breton Highwalk. EC2 —3C 68
Breton Ho. EC1 —3C 68
Brettell St. SE17 —4E 84
Brewers Grn. SW1 —6A 74
Brewer's Hall Garden. EC2 —4C 68
Brewer St. W1 —1A 74
Brewery Sq. SE1 —3H 77
Brewhouse Yd. EC1 —1K 67
Briant Ho. SE1 —7G 75
Briar Wlk. W10 —1A 62
Briary Clo. NW3 —1B 56
Brick Ct. EC4 —6H 67
Brick La. E2 & E1 —7J 61
Bricklayers Arms. (Junct.) —7E 76
Bricklayers Arms Bus. Cen. SE1 —1G 85
Brick St. W1 —3H 73
Brideale Clo. SE15 —6J 85
Bride Ct. EC4 —6K 67
Bride La. EC4 —6K 67
Bridewain St. SE1 —6H 77
Bridewell Pl. EC4 —6K 67
Bridford M. W1 —3J 65
Bridge App. NW1 —1F 57
Bridgefoot. SE1 —4E 82
Bridgeman Rd. N1 —1F 59
Bridgeman St. NW8 —5B 56
Bridge Pl. SW1 —1J 81
Bridgeport Pl. E1 —2K 77
Bridges Ho. SE5 —7D 84
Bridge St. SW1 —5D 74
Bridgewalk Heights. SE1 —4E 76
Bridgewater Highwalk. EC2 —3C 68
Bridgewater Sq. EC2 —3B 68
Bridgewater St. EC2 —3B 68
Bridgeway St. NW1 —5A 58
Bridge Yd. SE1 —2E 76
Bridle La. W1 —7A 66
Bridport Ho. N1 —3E 60
Bridport Pl. N1 —2E 60
(in two parts)
Bridstow Pl. W2 —5E 62
Brighton Bldgs. SE1 —7F 77
Brill Pl. NW1 —5C 58
Brinklow Ho. W2 —4F 63
Brinton Wlk. SE1 —3K 75
Brisbane St. SE5 —7D 84
Briset St. EC1 —3K 67
Bristol Gdns. W9 —2G 63
Bristol Ho. SE11 —7H 75
Bristol M. W9 —2G 63
Britannia Junction. (Junct.) —2J 57
Britannia Rd. SW6 —7F 79
Britannia Row. N1 —2A 60
Britannia St. WC1 —6F 59
Britannia Wlk. N1 —5D 60
(in two parts)
Britannic Highwalk. EC2 —4D 68
Britannic Tower. EC2 —3D 68
Brittany Point. SE11 —2H 83
Britten St. SW3 —4B 80
Britton St. EC1 —2K 67
Brixton Rd. SW9 & SE11 —7H 83
Broadbent St. W1 —7H 65
Broad Ct. WC2 —6E 66
Broadfield La. NW1 —1D 58
Broadgate. EC2 —3F 69
Broadgate Circ. EC2 —4F 69
Broadgate Cir. EC2 —4F 69
Broadgates Ct. SE11 —4J 83
Broad La. EC2 —3F 69
Broadley St. NW8 —3A 64
Broadley Ter. NW1 —2C 64
Broadmayne. SE17 —3D 84
Broad Sanctuary. SW1 —5C 74
Broadstone Ho. SW8 —7G 83
Broadstone Pl. W1 —4F 65
Broad St. Av. EC2 —4F 69
Broad St. Pl. EC2 —4E 68
Broad Wlk. NW1 —3G 57
Broad Wlk. W2 & W1 —1E 72
Broadwalk Ct. W8 —2E 70
Broadwalk Ho. EC2 —3F 69
Broad Wlk., The. W8 —3G 71
Broadwall. SE1 —2J 75
Broadway. SW1 —6B 74
Broadway Shop. Mall. SW1 —6B 74
Broadwick St. W1 —7A 66
Broadwood Ter. W8 —1C 78
Broad Yd. EC1 —2K 67
Brocas Clo. NW3 —1C 56
Brockham St. SE1 —6C 76
Brockwell Ho. SE11 —5G 83
Brodie Ho. SE1 —3J 85
Brodie St. SE1 —3J 85
Broken Wharf. EC4 —7B 68
Broke Wlk. E8 —2J 61
Bromfield St. N1 —4J 59
Bromley Pl. W1 —3K 65
Brompton Arc. SW3 —5E 72
Brompton Pk. Cres. SW6 —6F 79
Brompton Pl. SW3 —6C 72
Brompton Rd. SW3, SW7 & SW1 —1B 80
Brompton Sq. SW3 —6B 72
Brondesbury M. NW6 —1D 54
Brondesbury Pk. NW2 & NW6 —1A 54
Brondesbury Rd. NW6 —4B 54
Brondesbury Vs. NW6 —4C 54
Bronsart Rd. SW6 —7A 78
Bronte Ho. NW6 —6E 54
Bronti Clo. SE17 —4C 84
Brook Dri. SE11 —7J 75
Brooke's Ct. EC1 —4H 67
Brooke's Mkt. EC1 —3J 67
Brooke St. EC1 —4H 67
Brook Ga. W1 —1E 72
Brooklands Ct. NW6 —1B 54
Brook M. N. W2 —7J 63
Brooksby M. N1 —1J 59
Brooksby St. N1 —1H 59
Brooks Ct. SW8 —7A 82
Brooks M. W1 —7H 65
Brook St. W1 —7G 65
Brook St. W2 —7A 64
Brooksville Av. NW6 —3A 54
Brookville Rd. SW6 —7B 78
Broome Way. SE5 —7D 84
Broomfield Ct. SE16 —6K 77
Brougham Rd. E8 —2K 61
Brough Clo. SW8 —7E 82
Brough St. SW8 —7E 82
Brown Hart Gdns. W1 —7G 65
Browning Clo. W9 —2J 63
Browning M. W1 —4G 65
Browning St. SE17 —3C 84
Brownlow Ho. SE16 —6K 77
Brownlow M. WC1 —2G 67
Brownlow Rd. E8 —2J 61
Brownlow St. WC1 —4G 67
Browns Arc. W1 —1A 74
Brown's Bldgs. EC3 —6G 69
Brown St. W1 —5D 64
Broxwood Way. NW8 —3C 56
Bruckner St. W10 —6B 54
Bruges Pl. NW1 —1A 58
Brune Ho. E1 —4H 69
Brunel Est. W2 —4D 62
Brune St. E1 —4H 69
Brunswick Cen. WC1 —1D 66
Brunswick Clo. Est. EC1 —7K 59
Brunswick Ct. EC1 —7K 59
Brunswick Ct. SE1 —5G 77
Brunswick Gdns. W8 —3E 70
Brunswick M. W1 —5E 64
Brunswick Pl. N1 —7E 60
Brunswick Sq. WC1 —1E 66
Brushfield St. E1 —4G 69
Bruton La. W1 —1J 73
Bruton Pl. W1 —1J 73
Bruton St. W1 —1J 73
Brutus Ct. SE11 —2K 83
Bryanston Ct. W1 —5D 64
Bryanston M. E. W1 —4D 64
Bryanston M. W. W1 —4D 64
Bryanston Pl. W1 —4D 64
Bryanston Sq. W1 —4D 64
Bryanston St. W1 —6D 64
Bryant Ct. E2 —4H 61
Brydges Pl. WC2 —1D 74
Brydon Wlk. N1 —2E 58
Bryer Ct. EC2 —3B 68
Bryher Ct. SE11 —3H 83
Buckfast St. E2 —7K 61
Buck Hill Wlk. W2 —1A 72
Buckingham Arc. WC2 —1E 74
Buckingham Ga. SW1 —6K 73
Buckingham M. SW1 —6K 73
Buckingham Pal. Rd. SW1 —2H 81
Buckingham Pl. SW1 —6K 73
Buckingham St. WC2 —1E 74
Buckland Ct. N1 —4F 61
Buckland St. N1 —5E 60
Bucklers All. SW6 —7C 78
Bucklersbury. EC4 —6D 68
(in two parts)
Buckle St. E1 —6J 69
Buckley Ct. NW6 —1C 54
Buckley Rd. NW6 —1C 54
Bucknall St. WC2 —5C 66
Buck St. NW1 —1J 57
Budge Row. EC4 —7D 68
Budge's Wlk. W2 —3H 71
Bulinga St. SW1 —2D 82
Bull All. SE1 —1J 75
Bulleid Way. SW1 —2J 81
Buller Clo. SE15 —7K 85
Bullingham Mans. W8 —4E 70
Bull Inn Ct. WC2 —1E 74
Bulls Gdns. SW3 —1C 80
Bulls Head Pas. EC3 —6F 69
Bull Wharf La. EC4 —7C 68
Bulmer M. W11 —2D 70
Bulmer Pl. W11 —2C 70
Bulstrode Pl. W1 —4G 65
Bulstrode St. W1 —5G 65
Bunhill Row. EC1 —1D 68
Bunhouse Pl. SW1 —3G 81
Bunning Way. N7 —1E 58
Bunyan Ct. EC2 —3B 68
Buonaparte M. SW1 —3B 82
Burbage Clo. SE1 —7D 76
Burbage Ho. N1 —3E 60
Burchell Ho. SE11 —3G 83
Burden Ho. SW8 —7D 82
Burdett M. W2 —5F 63
Burdett St. SE1 —6H 75
Burgess Ind. Pk. SE5 —7E 84
Burge St. SE1 —7E 76
Burgh St. N1 —4A 60
Burgon St. EC4 —6A 68
Burleigh Ho. SW3 —6A 80
Burleigh St. WC2 —7F 67
Burlington Arc. W1 —1K 73
Burlington Clo. W9 —1D 62
Burlington Gdns. W1 —1K 73
Burnaby St. SW10 —7J 79
Burne Jones Ho. W14 —2A 78
Burnell Wlk. SE1 —3J 85
Burne St. NW1 —3B 64
Burnham Clo. SE1 —3J 85
Burnsall St. SW3 —3C 80
Burns Ho. SE17 —4A 84
Burnthwaite Rd. SW6 —7C 78
Burr Clo. E1 —2K 77
Burrell St. SE1 —2K 75
Burrows M. SE1 —4K 75
Bursar St. SE1 —3F 77
Burton Gro. SE17 —4D 84
Burton M. SW1 —2G 81
Burton Pl. WC1 —1C 66
Burton Rd. NW6 —1C 54
Burton St. WC1 —7C 58
Burwash Ho. SE1 —5E 76
Burwood Pl. W2 —5C 64
Bury Ct. EC3 —5G 69
Bury Pl. WC1 —4D 66
Bury St. EC3 —6G 69
Bury St. SW1 —2A 74
Bury Wlk. SW3 —2B 80
Bushbaby Clo. SE1 —7F 77
Bushell St. E1 —3K 77
Bush La. EC4 —7D 68
Bushwood Dri. SE1 —2J 85
Bute St. SW7 —1K 79
Butler Pl. SW1 —6B 74
Butlers & Colonial Wharf. SE1 —4J 77
Butlers Wharf. SE1 —4H 77
Buttermere Clo. SE1 —2H 85
Buttermere Ct. NW8 —2K 55
Buttesland St. N1 —6E 60
Buxted Rd. E8 —1H 61
Buxton Ct. N1 —6C 60
Buxton St. E1 —2J 69
Byng Pl. WC1 —2C 66
Byron Clo. E8 —2K 61
Byward St. EC3 —1G 77
Bywater St. SW3 —3D 80
Bywell Pl. W1 —4K 65
Cabbell St. NW1 —4B 64
Cable St. E1 —7K 69
Cab Rd. SE1 —4H 75
Cadbury Way. SE16 —1J 85
(in two parts)
Cadell Clo. E2 —5J 61
Cadet Dri. SE1 —3J 85
Cadiz St. SE17 —4C 84
Cadman Clo. SW9 —7K 83
Cadogan Gdns. SW3 —1E 80
Cadogan Ga. SW1 —1E 80
Cadogan Ho. SW3 —6A 80
Cadogan La. SW1 —7F 73
Cadogan Pl. SW1 —6E 72
Cadogan Sq. SW1 —7D 72
Cadogan St. SW3 —2D 80
Cahill St. EC1 —2D 68
Caird St. W10 —7A 54
Caithness Ho. N1 —3F 59
Caldew St. SE5 —7D 84
Caleb St. SE1 —4B 76
Caledonian Rd. N1 & N7 —1F 59
Caledonia St. N1 —5E 58
Cale St. SW3 —3B 80
Caliban Tower. N1 —5F 61
Callcott Ct. NW6 —1B 54
Callcott Rd. NW6 —1B 54
Callcott St. W8 —2D 70
Callendar Rd. SW7 —6K 71
Callow St. SW3 —5J 79
Callum Welch Ho. EC1 —2B 68
Calmington Rd. SE5 —5G 85
Calshot St. N1 —4F 59
Calstock Ho. SE11 —3J 83
Calthorpe St. WC1 —1G 67
Calvert Av. E2 —7G 61
Calverton. SE17 —5F 85
Calvert's Bldgs. SE1 —3D 76
Calvert St. NW1 —2F 57
Calvin St. E1 —2H 69
Camberwell New Rd. SE5 —6H 83
Camberwell Rd. SE17 & SE5 —5C 84
Cambourne M. W11 —6A 62
Cambridge Av. NW6 —4E 54
Cambridge Cir. WC2 —6C 66
Cambridge Gdns. NW6 —4E 54
Cambridge Gdns. W10 —5A 62
Cambridge Ga. NW1 —1H 65
Cambridge Ga. M. NW1 —1J 65
Cambridge Pl. NW6 —6E 54
Cambridge Pl. W8 —5G 71
Cambridge Rd. NW6 —5E 54
(in three parts)
Cambridge Sq. W2 —5B 64
Cambridge St. SW1 —2J 81
Cambridge Ter. NW1 —7H 57
Cambridge Ter. M. NW1 —7J 57
Cam Ct. SE15 —6H 85
Camden Gdns. NW1 —1J 57
Camden High St. NW1 —1J 57
Camden Lock Pl. NW1 —1H 57
Camden Pas. N1 —4K 59
Camden Rd. NW1 & N7 —2K 57
Camden St. NW1 —1J 57
Camden Wlk. N1 —3K 59
Camelford Ct. W11 —7A 62
Camelford Ho. SE1 —4E 82
Camelford Wlk. W11 —6A 62
Camera Pl. SW10 —6K 79
Cameron Ho. SE5 —7B 84
Camlet St. E2 —1H 69
Camley St. NW1 —1B 58
Camomile St. EC3 —5F 69
Campbell Ct. SW7 —7H 71
Campbell Wlk. N1 —3E 58
Campden Gro. W8 —4E 70
Campden Hill. W8 —4C 70
Campden Hill Ct. W8 —4E 70
Campden Hill Gdns. W8 —2D 70
Campden Hill Ga. W8 —5D 70
Campden Hill Pl. W11 —2C 70
Campden Hill Rd. W8 —2D 70
Campden Hill Sq. W8 —2C 70
Campden Ho. Clo. W8 —4E 70
Campden Houses. W8 —3D 70
Campden St. W8 —3D 70
Camperdown St. E1 —6J 69
Canal St. SE5 —6D 84
Canal Wlk. N1 —2E 60
Candover St. W1 —4K 65
Canfield Gdns. NW6 —1F 55
Canning Pas. W8 —6H 71
Canning Pl. W8 —6H 71
Canning Pl. M. W8 —6H 71
Cannon Ho. SE11 —2G 83
Cannon St. EC4 —6B 68
Canonbury Bus. Cen. N1 —2C 60
Canonbury Cres. N1 —1C 60
Canonbury Gro. N1 —1B 60
Canonbury Rd. N1 —1A 60
Canonbury St. N1 —1B 60
Canonbury Vs. N1 —1A 60
Canon Murnane Rd. SE1 —7H 77
Canon Row. SW1 —5D 74
Canon St. N1 —3B 60
Canterbury Ho. SE1 —6G 75
Canterbury Ho. SE5 —7J 83
Canterbury Pl. SE17 —2A 84
Canterbury Rd. NW6 —5D 54
Canterbury Ter. NW6 —4D 54
Canthus Dri. SE1 —3K 85
Cantium Retail Pk. SE1 —5K 85
Canvey St. SE1 —2B 76
Capel Ct. EC2 —6E 68
Capener's Clo. SW1 —5F 73
Cape Yd. E1 —2K 77
Capland St. NW8 —1A 64
Capper St. WC1 —2A 66
Caradoc Clo. W2 —5D 62
Carburton St. W1 —3J 65
Cardigan St. SE11 —3H 83
Cardinal Bourne St. SE1 —7E 76
Cardinal Cap All. SE1 —2B 76
Cardington St. NW1 —6A 58
Carey La. EC2 —5B 68
Carey Pl. SW1 —2B 82
Carey St. WC2 —6G 67
Carfree Clo. N1 —1J 59
Carisbrooke Gdns. SE15 —7J 85
Carlisle Av. EC3 —6H 69
Carlisle La. SE1 —7G 75
Carlisle Mans. SW1 —1K 81
Carlisle M. NW8 —3A 64
Carlisle Pl. SW1 —7K 73
Carlisle Rd. NW6 —2A 54
Carlisle St. W1 —6B 66
Carlos Pl. W1 —1G 73
Carlow St. NW1 —4K 57
Carlton Gdns. SW1 —3B 74
Carlton Hill. NW8 —5G 55
Carlton Ho. Ter. SW1 —3B 74
Carlton Mans. W9 —6F 55
Carlton St. SW1 —1B 74
Carlton Tower Pl. SW1 —1E 80
Carlton Va. NW6 —5C 54
Carlyle Sq. SW3 —4A 80
Carmarthen Pl. SE1 —4F 77
Carmel Ct. W8 —4F 71
Carmelite St. EC4 —7J 67
Carnaby St. W1 —6K 65
Carnegie St. N1 —3F 59
Carnoustie Dri. N1 —1C 58
Caroline Clo. W2 —1G 71
Caroline Gdns. E2 —6G 61
Caroline Pl. W2 —1G 71
Caroline Pl. M. W2 —1G 71
Caroline Ter. SW1 —2F 81
Caroline Wlk. W6 —6A 78
Carol St. NW1 —2K 57
Carpenter St. W1 —1H 73
Carriage Dri. E. SW11 —7F 81
Carriage Dri. N. SW11 —7D 80
(in two parts)
Carriage Dri. W. SW11 —7D 80
Carrick Ho. SE11 —3K 83
Carrington St. W1 —3H 73
Carroun Rd. SW8 —7F 83
Carter Ct. EC4 —6A 68
Carteret St. SW1 —5B 74
Carter Ho. E1 —4H 69
Carter La. EC4 —6A 68
Carter Pl. SE17 —4C 84
Carter St. SE17 —5B 84
Carthusian St. EC1 —3B 68
Carting La. WC2 —1E 74
Carton Ho. SE16 —6K 77
Cartwright Gdns. WC1 —7D 58
Cartwright St. E1 —7J 69
Caspian St. SE5 —7D 84
Cassidy Rd. SW6 —7D 78
Casson St. E1 —4K 69
Castellain Mans. W9 —1F 63
Castellain Rd. W9 —1F 63
Casterbridge. NW6 —2G 55
Castle Baynard St. EC4 —7A 68
Castlebrook Clo. SE11 —1K 83
Castle Ct. EC3 —6E 68
Castlehaven Rd. NW1 —1H 57
Castle Ho. SE1 —1B 84
Castle Ind. Est. SE17 —1B 84
Castle La. SW1 —6K 73
Castle Mead. SE5 —7C 84
Castlereagh St. W1 —5D 64
Castletown Rd. W14 —4A 78
Castle Yd. SE1 —2A 76
Catesby St. SE17 —2E 84
Cathcart Rd. SW10 —5G 79
Cathedral Lodge. EC1 —3B 68
Cathedral Piazza. SW1 —7K 73
Cathedral Pl. EC4 —6B 68
Cathedral St. SE1 —2D 76
Catherine Griffiths Ct. EC1 —1J 67
Catherine Ho. N1 —3G 61
Catherine Pl. SW1 —6K 73
Catherine St. WC2 —7F 67
Catherine Wheel All. E1 —4G 69
Catherine Wheel Yd. SW1 —3K 73
Catherwood Ct. N1 —6D 60
Catlin St. SE16 —3K 85
Cator St. SE15 —6H 85
(in two parts)
Cato St. W1 —4C 64
Catton St. WC1 —4F 67
Caughley Ho. SE11 —7H 75
Causton St. SW1 —2C 82
Cavaye Pl. SW10 —4J 79
Cavendish Av. NW8 —5A 56
Cavendish Clo. NW8 —6A 56
Cavendish Ct. EC3 —5G 69
Cavendish M. N. W1 —3J 65
Cavendish M. S. W1 —4J 65
Cavendish Pl. W1 —5J 65
Cavendish Rd. NW6 —1A 54
Cavendish Sq. W1 —5J 65
Cavendish St. N1 —5D 60
Caversham M. SW3 —5D 80
Caversham St. SW3 —5D 80
Caxton St. SW1 —6A 74
Caxton Wlk. WC2 —6C 66
Cayenne Ct. SE1 —4J 77
Cayton Pl. EC1 —7D 60
Cayton St. EC1 —7D 60
Cecil Ct. WC2 —1D 74
Cedar Ct. N1 —1C 60
Cedar Ho. W8 —6F 71
Cedarne Rd. SW6 —7F 79
Cedar Way. NW1 —1B 58
Cedar Way Ind. Est. NW1 —1B 58
Celandine Dri. E8 —1H 61
Celbridge M. W2 —5G 63
Celia Ho. N1 —5F 61
Centaur St. SE1 —6G 75
Central Av. SW11 —7D 80
Central Markets. EC1 —4K 67
Central St. EC1 —6B 60
Centre Ct. W2 —1H 71
Centre Point. SE1 —3K 85
Centrepoint. WC2 —5C 66
Centric Clo. NW1 —2G 57
Cerney M. W2 —7K 63
Cervantes Ct. W2 —6G 63
Chadwell St. EC1 —6J 59
Chadwick St. SW1 —7B 74
Chadworth Ho. EC1 —7B 60
Chagford St. NW1 —2D 64
Chalbury Wlk. N1 —4G 59
Chalcot Cres. NW1 —1E 56
Chalcot Rd. NW1 —1F 57
Chalcot Sq. NW1 —1F 57
Chaldon Rd. SW6 —7A 78
Chalk Farm Rd. NW1 —1F 57
Challoner Cres. W14 —4B 78
Challoner St. W14 —3B 78
Chalmer's Wlk. SE17 —6A 84
Chalton St. NW1 —4A 58
Chamberlain St. NW1 —1E 56
Chambers St. SE16 —4K 77
Chamber St. E1 —7J 69
Chambers Wharf. SE16 —4K 77
Chambord St. E2 —7J 61
Chancellors Ct. WC1 —3F 67
Chancel St. SE1 —3K 75
Chancery La. WC2 —4G 67
Chance St. E2 & E1 —1H 69
Chandos Pl. WC2 —1D 74
Chandos St. W1 —4J 65
Change All. EC3 —6E 68
Chantry Sq. W8 —7F 71
Chantry St. N1 —3A 60
Chapel Ct. SE1 —4D 76
Chapel Mkt. N1 —4H 59
Chapel Pl. EC2 —7F 61
Chapel Pl. N1 —4J 59
Chapel Pl. W1 —6H 65
Chapel Side. W2 —7F 63
Chapel St. NW1 —4B 64
Chapel St. SW1 —6G 73
Chaplin Clo. SE1 —4J 75
Chapone Pl. W1 —6B 66
Chapter Ho. Ct. EC4 —6B 68
Chapter Rd. SE17 —4A 84
Chapter St. SW1 —2B 82
Chapter Ter. SE17 —5A 84
Charfield Ct. W9 —2G 63
Charing Cross. SW1 —2D 74
Charing Cross Rd. WC2 —5C 66
Charing Ho. SE1 —4J 75
(off Windmill Wlk.)
Charlbert Ct. NW8 —4B 56
Charlbert St. NW8 —4B 56
Charles Gardner Ct. N1 —6E 60
Charles La. NW8 —5A 56
Charles Pl. NW1 —7A 58
Charles Rowan Ho. WC1 —7H 59
Charles II Pl. SW3 —4C 80
Charles II St. SW1 —2B 74
Charles Sq. N1 —7E 60
Charles Sq. Est. N1 —7E 60
Charles St. W1 —2H 73
Charleston St. SE17 —2C 84
Charleville Mans. W14 —4A 78
Charleville Rd. W14 —4A 78
Charlotte Ct. SE1 —1F 85
Charlotte Ct. SE17 —1F 85
Charlotte M. W1 —3A 66
Charlotte M. W14 —1A 78
Charlotte Pl. SW1 —2K 81
Charlotte Pl. W1 —4A 66
Charlotte Rd. EC2 —7F 61
Charlotte St. W1 —3A 66
Charlotte Ter. N1 —3G 59
Charlton Ct. E2 —3J 61
Charlton Pl. N1 —4K 59
Charlwood Pl. SW1 —2A 82
Charlwood St. SW1 —4K 81
(in two parts)
Charmouth Ho. SW8 —7F 83
Charrington St. NW1 —4B 58
Charterhouse Bldgs. EC1 —2B 68
Charterhouse M. EC1 —3A 68
Charterhouse Sq. EC1 —3A 68
Charterhouse St. EC1 —4J 67
Charteris Rd. NW6 —3C 54
Chartridge. SE17 —5D 84
Chart St. N1 —6E 60
Chatham St. SE17 —1D 84
Chatsworth Ct. W8 —1D 78
Chaucer Dri. SE1 —2J 85
Chaucer Mans. W14 —5E 78
Chaulden Ho. EC1 —7E 60
(off Cranwood St.)
Cheapside. EC2 —5B 68
Cheesemans Ter. W14 —4B 78
(in two parts)
Chelsea Bri. SW1 & SW8 —5H 81
Chelsea Bri. Bus. Cen. SW8 —7H 81
Chelsea Bri. Rd. SW1 —3F 81
Chelsea Bri. Wharf. SW8 —6J 81
Chelsea Cloisters. SW3 —2C 80
Chelsea Embkmt. SW3 —6B 80
Chelsea Gdns. SW1 —4G 81
Chelsea Mnr. Ct. SW3 —5C 80
Chelsea Mnr. Gdns. SW3 —4C 80
Chelsea Mnr. St. SW3 —4B 80
Chelsea Pk. Gdns. SW3 —5K 79
Chelsea Reach Tower. SW10
(off Worlds End Est.) —7K 79
Chelsea Sq. SW3 —3A 80
Chelsea Towers. SW3 —5C 80
Chelsea Wharf. SW10 —7K 79
Cheltenham Ter. SW3 —3E 80
Cheney Rd. N1 —5D 58
Chenies M. WC1 —2B 66
Chenies Pl. NW1 —4C 58
Chenies St. WC1 —3B 66
Cheniston Gdns. W8 —6F 71
Chepstow Cres. W11 —7D 62
Chepstow Pl. W2 —6E 62
Chepstow Rd. W2 —4D 62
Chepstow Vs. W11 —7C 62
Chequer St. EC1 —2C 68
(in two parts)
Cherbury Ct. N1 —5E 60
Cherbury St. N1 —5E 60
Cherry Tree Wlk. EC1 —2C 68
Chesham Clo. SW1 —7F 73
Chesham M. SW1 —6F 73
Chesham Pl. SW1 —7F 73
(in two parts)
Chesham St. SW1 —7F 73
Cheshire Ct. EC4 —6J 67
Cheshire St. E2 —1J 69
Chesil Ct. SW3 —5C 80

Chesson Rd.—Dulverton Mans.

Chesson Rd. W14 —5B 78
Chester Clo. SW1 —5H 73
Chester Clo. N. NW1 —6J 57
Chester Clo. S. NW1 —7J 57
Chester Cotts. SW1 —2F 81
Chester Ct. NW1 —6J 57
Chesterfield Gdns. W1 —2H 73
Chesterfield Hill. W1 —2H 73
Chesterfield St. W1 —2H 73
Chester Ga. NW1 —7H 57
Chester Ho. SW9 —7J 83
Chester M. SW1 —6H 73
Chester Pl. NW1 —6H 57
Chester Rd. NW1 —7G 57
Chester Row. SW1 —2F 81
Chester Sq. SW1 —1G 81
Chester Sq. M. SW1 —7H 73
Chester St. E2 —7K 61
(Vallance Rd.)
Chester St. E2 —3K 61
(Whiston Rd.)
Chester St. SW1 —6G 73
Chester Ter. NW1 —6H 57
Chesterton Rd. W10 —4A 62
Chesterton Sq. W8 —1C 78
Chester Way. SE11 —2J 83
Chestnut All. SW6 —6C 78
Chestnut Ct. SW6 —6C 78
Chettle Clo. SE1 —6D 76
Cheval Pl. SW7 —6C 72
Chevening Rd. NW6 —3A 54
Cheyne Ct. SW3 —5D 80
Cheyne Gdns. SW3 —5C 80
Cheyne M. SW3 —6C 80
Cheyne Pl. SW3 —5D 80
Cheyne Row. SW3 —6B 80
Cheyne Wlk. SW10 & SW3
(in three parts) —7K 79
Chicheley St. SE1 —4G 75
Chichester Bldgs. SE1 —7F 77
Chichester Ho. SW9 —7J 83
Chichester Rents. WC2 —5H 67
Chichester Rd. NW6 —5D 54
Chichester Rd. W2 —3G 63
Chichester St. SW1 —4A 82
Chicksand St. E1 —4J 69
Child's Pl. SW5 —2E 78
Child's St. SW5 —2E 78
Child's Wlk. SW5 —2E 78
Chilham Ho. SE1 —6E 76
Chiltern St. W1 —3F 65
Chilton St. E2 —1J 69
Chilworth M. W2 —6K 63
Chilworth St. W2 —6J 63
China Wharf. SE1 —5K 77
(off Mill St.)
Ching Ct. WC2 —6D 66
Chippenham Gdns. NW6 —7D 54
Chippenham M. W9 —2D 62
Chippenham Rd. W9 —1D 62
Chiswell St. EC1 —3C 68
Chitty St. W1 —3A 66
Christchurch Av. NW6 —1A 54
Christchurch St. SW3 —5D 80
Christchurch Ter. SW3 —5D 80
Christina St. EC2 —1F 69
Christopher Pl. NW1 —6C 58
Christophers M. W11 —2A 70
Christopher St. EC2 —3E 68
Chryssell Rd. SW9 —7J 83
Chumleigh St. SE5 —5F 85
Church Cloisters. EC3 —1F 77
Church Clo. W8 —4F 71
Church Entry. EC4 —6A 68
Churchill Gdns. SW1 —4K 81
Churchill Gdns. SW7 —7K 71
Churchill Gdns. Rd. SW1 —4J 81
Church Pas. EC2 —5C 68
(off Gresham St.)
Church Pl. SW1 —1A 74
Church St. W2 & NW8 —3A 64
Church St. Est. NW8 —2A 64
Churchward Ho. W14 —4C 78
Churchway. NW1 —6C 58
Churchyard Row. SE11 —1A 84
Churton Pl. SW1 —2A 82
Churton St. SW1 —2A 82
Cinnamon Wharf. SE1 —4J 77
Circus Lodge. NW8 —6K 55
Circus M. W1 —3D 64
Circus Pl. EC2 —4E 68
Circus Rd. NW8 —6K 55
Cirencester St. W2 —3F 63
Citadel Pl. SE11 —3F 83
City Garden Row. N1 —5A 60
City Heights. SE1 —3G 77
City Rd. EC1 —5K 59
Clabon M. SW1 —7D 72
Clanfield Way. SE15 —7H 85
Clanricarde Gdns. W2 —1E 70
Clapham Rd. SW9 —7G 83
Clare Gdns. W11 —6A 62
Clare La. N1 —1C 60
Clare Mkt. WC2 —6G 67
Claremont Clo. N1 —5J 59
Claremont Rd. W9 —5A 54
Claremont Sq. N1 —5H 59
Clarence Gdns. NW1 —7J 57
Clarence Ga. Gdns. NW1 —2E 64
Clarence Pas. NW1 —5D 58
Clarence Rd. NW6 —1B 54
Clarence Ter. NW1 —1E 64
Clarence Yd. SE17 —3B 84
Clarendon Clo. W2 —7B 64
Clarendon Cross. W11 —1A 70
Clarendon Gdns. W9 —2J 63
Clarendon Gro. NW1 —6B 58
Clarendon M. W2 —7B 64
Clarendon Pl. W2 —7B 64
Clarendon Rd. W11 —7A 62
Clarendon St. SW1 —4J 81
Clarendon Ter. W9 —1J 63
Clarendon Wlk. W11 —6A 62
Clareville Gro. SW7 —2J 79
Clareville Gro. M. SW7 —2J 79
Clareville St. SW7 —2J 79
Clarges M. W1 —2H 73
Clarges St. W1 —2J 73
Clarissa St. E8 —2H 61
Clarke's M. W1 —3G 65
Clark's La. WC2 —6F 67
Clarkson Row. NW1 —4K 57
Clark's Pl. EC2 —5F 69
Claverton St. SW1 —4A 82
Claylands Pl. SW8 —7H 83
Claylands Rd. SW8 —6G 83
Clay St. W1 —4E 64
Clayton St. SE11 —5H 83
Clearwell Dri. W9 —2F 63
Cleaver Sq. SE11 —4J 83
Cleaver St. SE11 —3J 83
Clem Attlee Ct. SW6 —6B 78
Clem Attlee Pde. SW6 —6C 78
Clement's Inn. WC2 —6G 67
Clement's Inn Pas. WC2 —6G 67
Clements La. EC4 —7E 68
Clement's Rd. SE16 —7K 77
Clemson Ho. E8 —3J 61
Clennam St. SE1 —4C 76
Clenston M. W1 —5D 64
Clere Pl. EC2 —1E 68
Clere St. EC2 —1E 68
Clerkenwell Clo. EC1 —1J 67
(in two parts)
Clerkenwell Grn. EC1 —2K 67
Clerkenwell Rd. EC1 —3H 67
Cleveland Gdns. W2 —6H 63
Cleveland Mans. SW9 —7H 83
(off Mowll St.)
Cleveland M. W1 —3K 65
Cleveland Pl. SW1 —2A 74
Cleveland Rd. N1 —1E 60
Cleveland Row. SW1 —3K 73
Cleveland Sq. W2 —6H 63
Cleveland St. W1 —2J 65
Cleveland Ter. W2 —6H 63
Cleve Rd. NW6 —1E 54
Clifford Ho. W14 —2B 78
Clifford's Inn Pas. EC4 —6H 67
Clifford St. W1 —1K 73
Clifton Ct. W9 —1K 63
Clifton Gdns. W9 —2H 63
Clifton Hill. NW8 —4G 55
Clifton Pl. W2 —6A 64
Clifton Rd. W9 —1J 63
Clifton St. EC2 —3F 69
Clifton Vs. W9 —3G 63
Clinger Ct. N1 —3F 61
Clink St. SE1 —2C 76
Clipstone M. W1 —3K 65
Clipstone St. W1 —3J 65
Clive Ct. W9 —1J 63
Cliveden Pl. SW1 —1F 81
Cloak La. EC4 —7C 68
Clock Pl. SE1 —1A 84
Clock Tower M. N1 —3C 60
Cloisters, The. E1 —3H 69
Cloth Ct. EC1 —4A 68
Cloth Fair. EC1 —4A 68
Clothier St. E1 —5G 69
Cloth St. EC1 —3B 68
Cloudesley Pl. N1 —3H 59
Cloudesley Rd. N1 —2H 59
Cloudesley Sq. N1 —2J 59
Cloudesley St. N1 —3J 59
Clover M. SW3 —5E 80
Cloysters Grn. E1 —2K 77
Club Row. E2 & E1 —1H 69
Clunbury St. N1 —5E 60
Cluny Est. SE1 —6F 77
Cluny M. SW5 —2D 78
Cluny Pl. SE1 —6F 77
Cluse Ct. N1 —4B 60
Clydesdale Rd. W11 —5B 62
Coach & Horses Yd. W1 —7K 65
Coach Ho. M. SE1 —6F 77
Coalport Ho. SE11 —1H 83
Coate St. E2 —5K 61
Cobalt Sq. SW8 —5F 83
Cobbett St. SW8 —7G 83
Cobb's Ct. EC4 —6A 68
Cobb St. E1 —4H 69
Cobden Ho. NW1 —4K 57
Cobham M. NW1 —1B 58
Cobourg Rd. SE5 —5H 85
Cobourg St. NW1 —7A 58
Coburg Clo. SW1 —1A 82
Cochrane Clo. NW8 —5A 56
Cochrane M. NW8 —5A 56
Cochrane St. NW8 —5A 56
Cock Hill. E1 —4G 69
Cock La. EC1 —4A 68
Cockpit Steps. SW1 —5C 74
Cockpit Yd. WC1 —3G 67
Cockspur Ct. SW1 —2C 74
Cockspur St. SW1 —2C 74
Code St. E1 —2J 69
Codrington M. W11 —6A 62
Coin St. SE1 —2H 75
Coke St. E1 —5K 69
Colas M. NW6 —2E 54
Colbeck M. SW7 —2G 79
Colchester St. E1 —5J 69
Coldbath Sq. EC1 —1H 67
Colebrooke Pl. N1 —3A 60
Colebrooke Row. N1 —5K 59
(in two parts)
Coleby Path. SE5 —7E 84
Colegrove Rd. SE15 —6J 85
Coleherne Ct SW5 —4G 79
Coleherne M. SW10 —4F 79
Coleherne Rd. SW10 —4F 79
Cole Ho. SE1 —5H 75
Coleman Fields. N1 —2C 60
Coleman Rd. SE5 —7F 85
Coleman St. EC2 —5D 68
Coleman St. Bldgs. EC2 —5D 68
Coleridge Gdns. NW6 —1H 55
Coleridge Ho. SE17 —3C 84
Colesbourne Ct. SE15 —7F 85
Coleshill Flats. SW1 —3G 81
Cole St. SE1 —5C 76
Colet Ho. SE17 —4A 84
Coley St. WC1 —2G 67
Collard Pl. NW1 —1H 57
College Ct. SW3 —4E 80
College Cres. NW3 —1K 55
(in two parts)
College Cross. N1 —1J 59
College E. E1 —4J 69
College Gro. NW1 —2B 58
College Hill. EC4 —7C 68
College M. SW1 —6D 74
College Pl. NW1 —2A 58
College Pl. SW10 —7H 79
College St. EC4 —7C 68
Collett Rd. SE16 —6K 77
Collier St. N1 —5F 59
Collingham Gdns. SW5 —2G 79
Collingham Pl. SW5 —2F 79
Collingham Rd. SW5 —1G 79
Collinson St. SE1 —5B 76
Collinson Wlk. SE1 —5B 76
Collin's Yd. N1 —3K 59
Colnbrook St. SE1 —7K 75
Colombo St. SE1 —3K 75
Colonnade. WC1 —2E 66
Colonnades, The. W2 —5G 63
Colonnade Wlk. SW1 —2H 81
Colosseum Ter. NW1 —7J 57
Colour Ct. SW1 —3A 74
Columbia Rd. E2 —6H 61
Colville Est. N1 —3F 61
Colville Est. W. E2 —7K 61
Colville Gdns. W11 —6C 62
(in two parts)
Colville Houses. W11 —5B 62
Colville M. W11 —6C 62
Colville Pl. W1 —4A 66
Colville Rd. W11 —6C 62
Colville Sq. W11 —6A 62
Colville Sq. M. W11 —6B 62
Colville Ter. W11 —6B 62
Colworth Gro. SE17 —2C 84
Colwyn Ho. SE1 —7H 75
Colyer Clo. N1 —4G 59
Comber Gro. SE5 —7C 84
Comber Ho. SE5 —7C 84
Combe, The. NW1 —7K 57
Comeragh M. W14 —4A 78
Comeragh Rd. W14 —4A 78
Comfort St. SE15 —6F 85
Commercial Rd. E1 & E14 —5K 69
Commercial St. E1 —2H 69
Commercial Way. SE15 —7J 85
Commodity Quay. E1 —1J 77
Compass Ct. SE1 —3H 77
Compton Clo. NW1 —7J 57
Compton Pas. EC1 —1A 68
Compton Pl. WC1 —1D 66
Compton St. EC1 —1K 67
Comus Pl. SE17 —2F 85
Conant M. E1 —7K 69
Concert Hall App. SE1 —3G 75
Conduit Ct. WC2 —7D 66
Conduit M. W2 —6K 63
Conduit Pas. W2 —6K 63
Conduit Pl. W2 —6K 63
Conduit St. W1 —7J 65
Coney Way. SW8 —6G 83
Congreve Ct. SE11 —2J 83
Congreve St. SE17 —1F 85
Conistone Way. N7 —1E 58
Conlan St. W10 —1A 62
Connaught Clo. W2 —6C 64
Connaught M. W2 —6D 64
Connaught Pl. W2 —7D 64
Connaught Sq. W2 —6D 64
Connaught St. W2 —6C 64
Conrad Ho. SW8 —7D 82
Cons St. SE1 —4J 75
Constitution Hill. SW1 —4H 73
Content St. SE17 —2D 84
Convent Gdns. W11 —6B 62
Conway M. W1 —2K 65
Conway St. W1 —2K 65
(in two parts)
Conybeare. NW3 —1C 56
Cook All. EC2 —5C 68
Cook's Rd. SE17 —5K 83
Coomassie Rd. W9 —1B 62
Coombs St. N1 —5A 60
Coomer M. SW6 —6C 78
Coomer Pl. SW6 —6C 78
Coomer Rd. SW6 —6C 78
Cooper Clo. SE1 —5J 75
Coopers La. NW1 —4C 58
Cooper's Rd. SE1 —3J 85
Cooper's Row. EC3 —7H 69
Copeland Ho. SE11 —7G 75
Copenhagen Ho. N1 —3H 59
Copenhagen St. N1 —3E 58
Cope Pl. W8 —7D 70
Copford Wlk. N1 —2B 60
Copley Clo. SE17 —6B 84
Copnor Way. SE15 —7H 85
Copperfield Ho. SE1 —5K 77
Copperfield St. SE1 —4A 76
Copper Row. SE1 —3H 77
Copthall Av. EC2 —5E 68
Copthall Bldgs. EC2 —5E 68
Copthall Clo. EC2 —5D 68
Coptic St. WC1 —4D 66
Coral St. SE1 —5J 75
Coram Ho. WC1 —1D 66
Coram St. WC1 —2D 66
Corbet Ct. EC3 —6E 68
Corbet Pl. E1 —3H 69
Cordelia Ho. N1 —4G 61
Corelli Ct. SW5 —2D 78
Corfe Ho. SW8 —7F 83
Cork St. W1 —1K 73
Cork St. M. W1 —1K 73
Corlett St. NW1 —3B 64
Corner Ho. St. WC2 —2D 74
Cornhill. EC3 —6E 68
Cornwall Cres. W11 —7A 62
Cornwall Gdns. SW7 —7G 71
Cornwall Gdns. Wlk. SW7 —7G 71
Cornwall M. S. SW7 —7H 71
Cornwall M. W. SW7 —7G 71
Cornwall Rd. SE1 —2H 75
Cornwall Ter. NW1 —2E 64
Cornwall Ter. M. NW1 —2E 64
Coronet St. N1 —7F 61
Corporation Row. EC1 —1J 67
Corsham St. N1 —7E 60
Coryton Path. W9 —1C 62
Cosmo Pl. WC1 —3E 66
Cosser St. SE1 —6H 75
Cosway St. NW1 —3C 64
Cotham St. SE17 —2C 84
Cotleigh Rd. NW6 —1D 54
Cotswold Ct. EC1 —1B 68
Cottage Grn. SE5 —7E 84
Cottage Pl. SW3 —6B 72
Cottage Wlk. SW1 —6E 72
Cottesloe M. SE1 —6J 75
Cottesmore Ct. W8 —6G 71
Cottesmore Gdns. W8 —6G 71
Cottingham Rd. SW8 —7G 83
Cottington St. SE11 —3J 83
Cottons Cen. SE1 —2F 77
Cotton's Gdns. E2 —6G 61
Cottons La. SE1 —2E 76
Coulson St. SW3 —3D 80
Councillor St. SE5 —7B 84
Counter Ct. SE1 —3D 76
Counter St. SE1 —3F 77
County St. SE1 —7C 76
Courtenay Sq. SE11 —4H 83
Courtenay St. SE11 —3H 83
Courtfield Gdns. SW5 —2F 79
Courtfield M. SW7 —2G 79
Courtfield Rd. SW7 —2H 79
Courthope Ho. SW8 —7D 82
Courtnell St. W2 —5D 62
Courtyard, The. N1 —1G 59
Courtyard, The. NW1 —1F 57
Cousin La. EC4 —1D 76
Covent Garden. WC2 —7E 66
Coventry Clo. NW6 —4E 54
Coventry St. W1 —1B 74
Coverley Clo. E1 —3K 69
Coverley Point. SE11 —2F 83
Cowcross St. EC1 —3K 67
Cowdenbeath Path. N1 —2F 59
Cowley St. SW1 —7D 74
Cowling Clo. W11 —2A 70
Cowper Ho. SE17 —3C 84
Cowper's Ct. EC3 —6E 68
Cowper St. EC2 —1E 68
Cox Ho. W6 —5A 78
Cox's Ct. E1 —4H 69
Coxson Way. SE1 —5H 77
Crabtree Clo. E2 —5H 61
Cragie Ho. SE1 —2J 85
Craig's Ct. SW1 —2D 74
Crail Row. SE17 —2E 84
Cramer St. W1 —4G 65
Crammond Clo. W6 —5A 78
Crampton St. SE17 —2B 84
Cranbourn All. WC2 —7C 66
Cranbourn St. WC2 —7C 66
Crane Ct. EC4 —6J 67
Cranfield Ct. W1 —4C 64
Cranfield Row. SE1 —6J 75
Cranleigh St. NW1 —5A 58
Cranley Gdns. SW7 —3J 79
Cranley M. SW7 —3J 79
Cranley Pl. SW7 —2K 79
Cranmer Ct. SW3 —2C 80
Cranmer Ho. SW9 —7J 83
Cranmer Rd. SW9 —7J 83
Cranston Est. N1 —5E 60
Cranwood Ct. EC1 —7E 60
Cranwood St. EC1 —7E 60
Craven Hill. W2 —7J 63
Craven Hill Gdns. W2 —7H 63
(in four parts)
Craven Hill M. W2 —7J 63
Craven Pas. WC2 —2D 74
Craven Rd. W2 —7J 63
Craven St. WC2 —2D 74
Craven Ter. W2 —7J 63
Crawford M. W1 —4D 64
Crawford Pas. EC1 —2J 67
Crawford Pl. W1 —5C 64
Crawford St. W1 —4C 64
Creasy Est. SE1 —7F 77
Creechurch La. EC3 —6G 69
Creechurch Pl. EC3 —6G 69
Creed Ct. EC4 —6A 68
Creed La. EC4 —6A 68
Cremer Bus. Cen. E2 —5H 61
Cremer St. E2 —5H 61
Cremorne Est. SW10 —6A 80
Cremorne Rd. SW10 —7J 79
Crescent. EC3 —7H 69
Crescent Ho. EC1 —2B 68
Crescent Pl. SW3 —1C 80
Crescent Row. EC1 —2B 68
Crescent St. N1 —1G 59
Cresswell Gdns. SW5 —3H 79
Cresswell Pl. SW10 —3H 79
Crestfield St. WC1 —6E 58
Crewdson Rd. SW9 —7H 83
Cricketer's Ct. SE11 —2K 83
Crimscott St. SE1 —7G 77
Crimsworth Rd. SW8 —7C 82
Crinan St. N1 —4E 58
Cringle St. SW8 —7K 81
Cripplegate St. EC2 —3C 68
Crispe Ho. N1 —3G 59
Crispin St. E1 —4H 69
Crofters Way. NW1 —2B 58
Crofts St. E1 —7K 69
Cromer St. WC1 —7D 58
Crompton St. W2 —2K 63
Cromwell Clo. E1 —2K 77
Cromwell Cres. SW5 —1D 78
Cromwell Gdns. SW7 —7A 72
Cromwell Highwalk. EC2 —3C 68
Cromwell M. SW7 —1A 80
Cromwell Pl. EC2 —3C 68
(off Barbican)
Cromwell Pl. SW7 —1A 80
Cromwell Rd. SW5 & SW7 —1E 78
Cromwell Tower. EC2 —3C 68
Crondall Ct. N1 —5E 60
Crondall St. N1 —5E 60
Cronin St. SE15 —7H 85
Crooked Billet Yd. E2 —6G 61
Cropley St. N1 —4D 60
Cropthorne Ct. W9 —7J 55
Crosby Ct. SE1 —4D 76
Crosby Row. SE1 —5D 76
Crosby Sq. EC3 —6F 69
Crossfield Ho. W11 —1A 70
Cross Keys Clo. W1 —4G 65
Cross Keys Sq. EC1 —4B 68
(off Lit. Britain)
Crosslet St. SE17 —1E 84
Cross St. N1 —2K 59
Crosswall. EC3 —7H 69
Crown Ct. EC2 —6C 68
Crown Ct. WC2 —6E 66
Crowndale Rd. NW1 —4A 58
Crown Office Row. EC4 —7H 67
Crown Pas. SW1 —3A 74
Crown Pl. EC2 —3F 69
Crown St. SE5 —7C 84
Croxley Rd. W9 —7C 54
Croydon Ho. SE1 —4J 75
(off Wootton St.)
Crozier Ho. SW8 —7F 83
Crucifix La. SE1 —4F 77
Cruden St. N1 —3A 60
Cruikshank St. WC1 —6H 59
Crutched Friars. EC3 —7G 69
Cubitt St. WC1 —7G 59
Cubitt's Yd. WC2 —7E 66
Cuff Point. E2 —6H 61
Culford Gdns. SW3 —2E 80
Culford Rd. N1 —1F 61
Culloden Clo. SE16 —4K 85
Cullum St. EC3 —7F 69
Cullum Welch Ct. N1 —6E 60
Culpeper Ct. SE11 —1H 83
Culross St. W1 —1F 73
Culworth St. NW8 —5B 56
Cumberland Cres. W14 —1A 78
(in two parts)
Cumberland Gdns. WC1 —6H 59
Cumberland Ga. W1 —7D 64
Cumberland Mans. W1 —5D 64
Cumberland Mkt. NW1 —6J 57
Cumberland Pl. NW1 —6H 57
Cumberland St. SW1 —3J 81
Cumberland Ter. NW1 —5H 57
Cumberland Ter. M. NW1 —5H 57
Cumming St. N1 —5G 59
Cunard Pl. EC3 —6G 69
Cundy St. SW1 —2G 81
Cunningham Ho. SE5 —7E 84
Cunningham Pl. NW8 —1K 63
Cureton St. SW1 —2C 82
Curlew St. SE1 —4J 77
Cursitor St. EC4 —5H 67
Curtain Pl. EC2 —1G 69
Curtain Rd. EC2 —7G 61
(in two parts)
Curtis Ho. SE17 —3D 84
Curtis St. SE1 —1H 85
Curtis Way. SE1 —1H 85
Curzon Ga. W1 —3G 73
Curzon Pl. W1 —3G 73
Curzon St. W1 —3G 73
Custance Ho. N1 —5D 60
Custance St. N1 —6D 60
Custom Ho. Wlk. EC3 —1F 77
Cuthbert Harrowing Ho. EC1 —2B 68
Cuthbert St. W2 —2K 63
Cutlers Gdns. E1 —5G 69
Cutler St. E1 —5G 69
Cut, The. SE1 —4K 75
Cygnet St. E1 —1J 69
Cynthia St. N1 —5G 59
Cypress Pl. W1 —2A 66
Cyrus St. EC1 —1A 68

Dabbs La. EC1 —2J 67
Dacre Ho. SW3 —6A 80
Dacre St. SW1 —6B 74
Dagmar Pas. N1 —2A 60
Dagmar Ter. N1 —2A 60
Dain Ct. W8 —1E 78
Dalehead. NW1 —5K 57
Dale Rd. SE17 —6A 84
Dale Row. W11 —6A 62
Dallington St. EC1 —1A 68
Damer Ter. SW10 —7J 79
Dame St. N1 —4B 60
Danbury St. N1 —4A 60
Danesfield. SE17 —5F 85
Dane St. WC1 —4F 67
Daniel Gdns. SE15 —7H 85
Daniel Ho. N1 —4E 60
Dansey Pl. W1 —7B 66
Danson Rd. SE17 —4A 84
Dante Pl. SE11 —2A 84
Dante Rd. SE11 —1K 83
Danube Ct. SE15 —7H 85
Danube St. SW3 —3C 80
Danvers Ho. E1 —6K 69
Danvers St. SW3 —6A 80
Da Palma Ct. SW6 —6D 78
Daplyn St. E1 —3K 69
D'Arblay St. W1 —6A 66
Dark Ho. Wlk. EC3 —1E 76
Darley Ho. SE11 —4F 83
Darnay Ho. SE16 —6K 77
Dartford Ho. SE1 —2J 85
Dartford St. SE17 —5C 84
Dartle Ct. SE16 —5K 77
Dartmouth Clo. W11 —5C 62
Dartmouth St. SW1 —5C 74
Dartrey Tower. SW10 —7J 79
(off Worlds End Est.)
Dartrey Wlk. SW10 —7J 79
Dart St. W10 —6A 54
Darwin St. SE17 —1E 84
(in two parts)
Darytngton Ho. SW8 —7D 82
Date St. SE17 —4C 84
Dauncey Ho. SE1 —5K 75
Davenant St. E1 —4K 69
Davenport Ho. SE11 —1H 83
Daventry St. NW1 —3B 64
Daver Ct. SW3 —4C 80
Davey's Ct. WC2 —7D 66
Davey St. SE15 —6J 85
Davidge Ho. SE1 —5J 75
Davidge St. SE1 —5A 76
David Ho. SW8 —7D 82
David M. W1 —3F 65
Davidson Gdns. SW8 —7D 82
Davies M. W1 —7H 65
Davies St. W1 —6H 65
Dawes Ho. SE17 —2E 84
Dawes Rd. SW6 —7A 78
Dawes St. SE17 —3E 84
Dawson Pl. W2 —7D 62
Dawson St. E2 —5J 61
Deacon Ho. SE11 —2G 83
Deacon M. N1 —1E 60
Deacon Way. SE17 —1B 84
Deal St. E1 —3K 69
Deal Wlk. SW9 —7J 83
Demead Way. SE15 —7H 85
(off Pentridge St.)
Dean Bradley St. SW1 —7D 74
Dean Ct. SW8 —7D 82
Deanery M. W1 —2G 73
Deanery St. W1 —2G 73
Dean Farrar St. SW1 —6C 74
Dean Ryle St. SW1 —1D 82
Dean's Bldgs. SE17 —2D 84
Dean's Ct. EC4 —6A 68
Dean's M. W1 —5J 65
Dean's Pl. SW1 —3B 82
Dean Stanley St. SW1 —7D 74
Dean St. W1 —5B 66
Dean's Yd. SW1 —6C 74
Dean Trench St. SW1 —7D 74
De Beauvoir Cres. N1 —2F 61
De Beauvoir Est. N1 —2F 61
De Beauvoir Rd. N1 —2F 61
De Beauvoir Sq. N1 —1G 61
Decima St. SE1 —6F 77
Defoe Ho. EC2 —3B 68
Defoe Pl. EC2 —3C 68
Delaford St. SW6 —7A 78
Delamere St. W2 —3H 63
Delamere Ter. W2 —3G 63
Delancey Pas. NW1 —3J 57
Delancey St. NW1 —3H 57
De Laune St. SE17 —4K 83
Delaware Mans. W9 —1F 63
Delaware Rd. W9 —1F 63
Delhi St. N1 —3E 58
Dell's M. SW1 —2A 82
Delta Est. E2 —6K 61
Delta St. E2 —6K 61
Delverton Rd. SE17 —4A 84
Denbigh Clo. W11 —7C 62
Denbigh M. SW1 —2K 81
Denbigh Pl. SW1 —3K 81
Denbigh Rd. W11 —7C 62
Denbigh St. SW1 —2K 81
(in two parts)
Denbigh Ter. W11 —7C 62
Denby Ct. SE11 —1G 83
Dengie Wlk. N1 —2B 60
Denholme Rd. W9 —7C 54
Denman Pl. W1 —7B 66
Denman St. W1 —1B 74
Denmark Gro. N1 —4H 59
Denmark Pl. WC2 —5C 66
Denmark Rd. NW6 —5C 54
(in two parts)
Denmark St. WC2 —6C 66
Denne Ter. E8 —3J 61
Denning Clo. NW8 —7J 55
Denny Cres. SE11 —3J 83
Denny St. SE11 —3J 83
Denyer St. SW3 —2C 80
Depot St. SE5 —6D 84
Derby Ga. SW1 —4D 74
Derby Ho. SE11 —1H 83
Derbyshire St. E2 —7K 61
Derby St. W1 —3G 73
Dereham Pl. EC2 —7G 61
Dering St. W1 —6H 65
Dering Yd. W1 —6J 65
Derry St. W8 —5F 71
Desborough Clo. W2 —3G 63
Desborough Ho. W14 —5C 78
De Vere Gdns. W8 —5H 71
De Vere M. W8 —6H 71
Deverell St. SE1 —7D 76
Devereux Ct. WC2 —6H 67
Devonia Rd. N1 —4A 60
Devonport. W2 —6B 64
Devonshire Clo. W1 —3H 65
Devonshire M. N. W1 —3H 65
Devonshire M. S. W1 —3H 65
Devonshire M. W. W1 —2G 65
Devonshire Pl. W1 —2G 65
Devonshire Pl. W8 —7F 71
Devonshire Pl. M. W1 —3G 65
Devonshire Row. EC2 —4G 69
Devonshire Row M. W1 —2J 65
Devonshire Sq. E1 —5G 69
Devonshire Sq. EC2 —5G 69
Devonshire St. W1 —3G 65
Devonshire Ter. W2 —6J 63
De Walden St. W1 —4G 65
Dewey Rd. N1 —4H 59
Dewsbury Ter. NW1 —2J 57
Dhonau Ho. SE1 —1J 85
Diadem Ct. W1 —6B 66
Dial Wlk., The. W8 —4G 71
Diamond St. SE15 —7G 85
Diana Pl. NW1 —1J 65
Dibden St. N1 —2A 60
Dibdin Row. SE1 —6J 75
Dickens Est. SE1 —5K 77
Dickens Est. SE16 —6K 77
Dickens Ho. NW6 —1D 62
Dickens Ho. SE17 —4A 84
Dickens Ho. WC1 —1D 66
Dickens Sq. SE1 —6C 76
Dighton Ct. SE5 —6B 84
Dignum St. N1 —4H 59
Dilke St. SW3 —5E 80
Dingley Pl. EC1 —7C 60
Dingley Rd. EC1 —7B 60
Dinmont Est. E2 —4K 61
Disbrowe Rd. W6 —6A 78
Discovery Bus. Pk. SE16 —7K 77
Disney Pl. SE1 —4C 76
Disney St. SE1 —4C 76
Diss St. E2 —6H 61
Distaff La. EC4 —7B 68
Distin St. SE11 —2H 83
Dobson Clo. NW6 —1K 55
Dobson Ho. SE5 —7E 84
Doby Ct. EC4 —7C 68
Dockhead. SE1 —5J 77
Dockley Rd. SE16 —7K 77
Dockley Rd. Ind. Est. SE16 —7K 77
Dock St. E1 —7K 69
Doddington Gro. SE17 —5K 83
Doddington Pl. SE17 —5K 83
Dodson St. SE1 —5J 75
Dog and Duck Yd. WC1 —3G 67
Dolben St. SE1 —3K 75
(in two parts)
Dolland Ho. SE11 —4G 83
Dolland St. SE11 —4G 83
Dolphin Sq. SW1 —4A 82
Dombey Ho. SE1 —5K 77
Dombey St. WC1 —3F 67
Domingo St. EC1 —2B 68
Dominion St. EC2 —3E 68
Domville Gro. SE5 —4H 85
Donaldson Rd. NW6 —3C 54
Donegal St. N1 —5G 59
Donnelly Ct. SW6 —7A 78
Donne Pl. SW3 —1C 80
Doon St. SE1 —3H 75
Doric Way. NW1 —6B 58
Dorking Ho. SE1 —6E 76
Dorman Way. NW8 —2K 55
Dorrington St. EC1 —3H 67
Dorrit St. SE1 —4C 76
Dorset Bldgs. EC4 —6K 67
Dorset Clo. NW1 —3D 64
Dorset M. SW1 —6H 73
Dorset Ri. EC4 —6K 67
Dorset Rd. SW8 —7E 82
Dorset Sq. NW1 —2D 64
Dorset St. W1 —4E 64
Doughty Ho. SW10 —6J 79
Doughty M. WC1 —2F 67
Doughty St. WC1 —1F 67
Douglas Johnston Ho. SW6 —6B 78
Douglas Rd. NW6 —2C 54
Douglas St. SW1 —2B 82
Douglas Waite Ho. NW6 —1F 55
Dourdan Ct. EC1 —4J 67
Douro Pl. W8 —6G 71
Dove Ct. EC2 —6D 68
Dovehouse St. SW3 —3A 80
Dove M. SW5 —2H 79
Dover Flats. SE1 —2G 85
Dove Row. E2 —4K 61
Dover St. W1 —1J 73
Dover Yd. W1 —2K 73
Doves Yd. N1 —3H 59
Dove Wlk. SW1 —3F 81
Dowend Ct. SE15 —6G 85
Dowgate Hill. EC4 —7D 68
Dowland St. W10 —6A 54
Dowlas St. SE5 —7F 85
Downfield Clo. W9 —2F 63
Downham Rd. N1 —1D 60
Downing St. SW1 —4D 74
Down St. W1 —3H 73
Down St. M. W1 —3H 73
Dowrey St. N1 —2H 59
Doyce St. SE1 —4B 76
D'Oyley St. SW1 —1F 81
Draco St. SE17 —5B 84
Dragon Rd. SE15 —6F 85
Dragon Yd. WC1 —5E 66
Drakes Courtyard. NW6 —1C 54
Drake St. WC1 —4F 67
Draper Ho. SE1 —1B 84
Draper Pl. N1 —2A 60
Drapers Gdns. EC2 —5E 68
Draycott Av. SW3 —1C 80
Draycott Pl. SW3 —2D 80
Draycott Ter. SW3 —2E 80
Drayford Clo. W9 —1C 62
Drayson M. W8 —5E 70
Drayton Gdns. SW10 —3J 79
Drewett Ho. E1 —6K 69
Drinkwater Ho. SE5 —7D 84
Droop St. W10 —1A 62
Druid St. SE1 —4G 77
Drummond Cres. NW1 —6B 58
Drummond Ga. SW1 —3C 82
Drummond St. NW1 —1K 65
Drum St. E1 —5J 69
Drury La. WC2 —5E 66
Dryden Ct. SE11 —2K 83
Dryden Mans. W14 —5A 78
Dryden St. WC2 —6E 66
Drysdale Ho. N1 —6G 61
Drysdale Pl. N1 —6G 61
Drysdale St. N1 —7G 61
Dublin Av. E8 —2K 61
Ducal St. E2 —7J 61
Duchess M. W1 —4J 65
Duchess of Bedford's Wlk. W8 —5D 70
Duchess St. W1 —4J 65
Duchy St. SE1 —2J 75
Duck La. W1 —6B 66
Dudley Ct. WC2 —5D 66
Dudley Rd. NW6 —4A 54
Dudley St. W2 —4K 63
Dudmaston M. SW3 —3A 80
Duffell Ho. SE11 —4G 83
Dufferin Av. EC1 —2D 68
Dufferin St. EC1 —2C 68
Dufour's Pl. W1 —6A 66
Dugard Way. SE11 —2K 83
Duke of Wellington Pl. SW1 —5G 73
Duke of York St. SW1 —2A 74
Duke's La. W8 —4E 70
Duke's M. W1 —5G 65
Duke's Pl. EC3 —6G 69
Duke's Rd. WC1 —7C 58
Duke St. SW1 —2A 74
Duke St. W1 —5G 65
Duke St. Hill. SE1 —2E 76
Duke's Yd. W1 —7G 65
Dulford St. W11 —7A 62
Dulverton Mans. WC1 —2G 67

Dumpton Pl.—Gt. Tower St.

Dumpton Pl. NW1 —1F 57
Dunbridge St. E2 —1K 69
Duncannon St. WC2 —1D 74
Duncan St. N1 —4K 59
Duncan Ter. N1 —5K 59
Dunloe Ct. E2 —5J 61
Dunloe St. E2 —5H 61
Dunlop Pl. SE16 —7J 77
Dunmore Point. E2 —7H 61
Dunmore Rd. NW6 —3A 54
Dunmow Ct. SE11 —2K 83
Dunmow Ho. SE11 —3G 83
Dunmow Wlk. N1 —2B 60
Dunn's Pas. WC1 —5E 66
Dunoon Ho. N1 —3F 59
Dunraven St. W1 —7E 64
Dunstable M. W1 —3G 65
Dunstan Rd. E8 —3H 61
Dunster Ct. EC3 —7G 69
Dunster Gdns. NW6 —1C 54
Dunsterville Way. SE1 —5E 76
Dunston Rd. E8 —3H 61
Dunston St. E8 —2H 61
Dunton Rd. SE1 —3H 85
Dunworth M. W11 —5B 62
Duplex Ride. SW1 —5E 72
Durant St. E2 —5K 61
Durfey Ho. SE5 —7E 84
Durham Ho. St. WC2 —1E 74
Durham Pl. SW3 —4D 80
Durham St. SE11 —4F 83
Durham Ter. W2 —5F 63
Dursley Ct. SE15 —6G 85
Durweston M. W1 —3E 64
Durweston St. W1 —4E 64
Dyer's Bldgs. EC1 —4H 67
Dymock Ct. SE15 —6G 85
Dyne Rd. NW6 —1A 54
Dynham Rd. NW6 —1D 54
Dyott St. WC1 —5C 66
Dysart St. EC2 —2F 69

Eagle Ct. EC1 —3K 67
Eagle Pl. SW1 —1A 74
Eagle Pl. SW7 —3J 79
Eagle St. WC1 —4F 67
Eagle Wharf Rd. N1 —4C 60
Eamont Ct. NW8 —4C 56
Eamont St. NW8 —4B 56
Eardley Cres. SW5 —3E 78
Earlham St. WC2 —6C 66
Earls Ct. Gdns. SW5 —2F 79
Earls Ct. Rd. W8 & SW5 —6D 70
Earl's Ct. Sq. SW5 —3E 78
Earlsferry Way. N1 —1E 58
Earls Ter. W8 —7C 70
Earlstoke St. EC1 —6K 59
Earl St. EC2 —3F 69
Earls Wlk. W8 —7D 70
Early M. NW1 —2J 57
Earnshaw St. WC2 —5C 66
Earsby St. W14 —1A 78
(in two parts)
Easley's M. W1 —5G 65
Eastbourne M. W2 —5J 63
Eastbourne Ter. W2 —5J 63
Eastcastle St. W1 —5K 65
Eastcheap. EC3 —7E 68
E. Harding St. EC4 —5J 67
Eastlake Ho. NW8 —2A 64
East La. SE16 —5K 77
Easton St. WC1 —1H 67
East Pas. EC1 —3B 68
East Point. SE1 —3K 85
E. Poultry Av. EC1 —4K 67
East Rd. N1 —7D 60
East Row. W10 —2A 62
Eastry Ho. SW8 —7D 82
E. Smithfield. E1 —1J 77
East St. SE17 —3C 84
E. Surrey Gro. SE15 —7H 85
E. Tenter St. E1 —6J 69
Eaton Clo. SW1 —2F 81
Eaton Ga. SW1 —1F 81
Eaton La. SW1 —7J 73
Eaton M. N. SW1 —1F 81
Eaton M. S. SW1 —1G 81
Eaton M. W. SW1 —1G 81
Eaton Pl. SW1 —7F 73
Eaton Row. SW1 —7H 73
Eaton Sq. SW1 —1F 81
Eaton Ter. SW1 —1F 81
Eaton Ter. M. SW1 —1F 81
Ebbisham Dri. SW8 —5F 83
Ebenezer Ho. SE11 —2K 83
Ebenezer St. N1 —6D 60
Ebley Clo. SE15 —6H 85
Ebor St. E1 —1H 69
Ebury Bri. SW1 —3H 81
Ebury Bri. Est. SW1 —3H 81
Ebury Bri. Rd. SW1 —4G 81
Ebury M. SW1 —1G 81
Ebury M. E. SW1 —1H 81
Ebury Sq. SW1 —2G 81
Ebury St. SW1 —3G 81
Ecclesbourne Rd. N1 —1C 60
Eccleston Bri. SW1 —1J 81
Eccleston M. SW1 —7G 73
Eccleston Pl. SW1 —2H 81
Eccleston Sq. SW1 —2J 81
Eccleston Sq. M. SW1 —2K 81
Eccleston St. SW1 —7G 73
Eckford St. N1 —4H 59
Edbrooke Rd. W9 —2D 62
Eden Clo. W8 —6E 70
Edenham Way. W10 —3B 62
Edgar Ho. SW8 —7D 82
Edge St. W8 —2E 70
Edgeworth Ho. NW8 —2H 55
Edgware Rd. W2 —2K 63
Edinburgh Ga. SW1 —5D 72
Edinburgh Ho. W9 —2G 55
Edis St. NW1 —2F 57
Edith Gro. SW10 —6H 79
Edith Neville Cotts. NW1 —6B 58
Edith Rd. W14 —2A 78
Edith St. E2 —4J 61
Edith Summerskill Ho. SW6 —7C 78
Edith Ter. SW10 —7H 79
Edith Yd. SW10 —7J 79
Edmund Ho. SE17 —4A 84
Edmund St. SE5 —7D 84
Edward Dodd Ct. N1 —6E 60
Edward Edward's Ho. SE1 —3K 75
Edwardes Pl. W8 —7C 70
Edwardes Sq. W8 —7C 70
Edward Ho. SE11 —3G 83
Edward M. NW1 —6J 57
Edwards M. N1 —1K 59
Edwards M. W1 —6F 65
Edward Sq. N1 —3F 59
Effie Pl. SW6 —7E 78
Effie Rd. SW6 —7E 78
Egbert St. NW1 —2F 57
Egerton Cres. SW3 —1C 80
Egerton Gdns. SW3 —7B 72
Egerton Gdns. M. SW3 —7C 72
Egerton Pl. SW3 —7C 72
Egerton Ter. SW3 —7C 72
Eglington Ct. SE17 —5B 84
Eglon M. NW1 —1E 56
Elba Pl. SE17 —1C 84
Elcho St. SW11 —7B 80
Elder St. E1 —3H 69
Elder Wlk. N1 —2A 60
Eldon Rd. W8 —7G 71
Eldon St. EC2 —4E 68
Eldridge Ct. SE16 —7K 77
Elephant & Castle. (Junct.) —7A 76
Elephant & Castle. SE1 —1A 84
Elephant Rd. SE17 —1B 84
Elgin Av. W9 —2C 62
Elgin Ct. W9 —1F 63
Elgin Cres. W11 —7A 62
Elgin Est. W9 —2D 62
Elgin M. W11 —6A 62
Elgin M. N. W9 —6G 55
Elgin M. S. W9 —6G 55
Elgood Clo. W11 —1A 70
Elia M. N1 —5K 59
Elias Pl. SW8 —6H 83
Elia St. N1 —5K 59
Elim Est. SE1 —6E 76
Elim St. SE1 —6E 76
Eliot M. NW8 —5H 55
Elizabeth Av. N1 —2C 60
Elizabeth Bri. SW1 —2H 81
Elizabeth Clo. W9 —2J 63
Elizabeth Ct. SW1 —7C 74
Elizabeth Ho. SE11 —2J 83
Elizabeth Newcomen Ho. SE1 —4D 76
Elizabeth St. SW1 —1G 81
Elkington Point. SE11 —2H 83
Elkstone Ct. SE15 —6F 85
Elkstone Rd. W10 —3B 62
Ellen St. E1 —6K 69
Ellen Wilkinson Ho. SW6 —6C 78
Ellery Ho. SE17 —2E 84
Ellington Ho. SE1 —7C 76
Elliott's Pl. N1 —3A 60
Elliott Sq. NW3 —1B 56
Elliotts Row. SE11 —1A 84
Ellis Ho. SE17 —3D 84
Ellis St. SW1 —1E 80
Ellwood Ct. W9 —2G 63
Elmbridge Wlk. E8 —1K 61
Elm Ct. EC4 —7H 67
Elmfield Way. W9 —3E 62
Elm Friars Wlk. NW1 —1C 58
Elmington Est. SE5 —7E 84
Elmore St. N1 —1C 60
Elm Pk. Gdns. SW10 —4K 79
Elm Pk. La. SW3 —4K 79
Elm Pk. Mans. SW10 —5J 79
Elm Pk. Rd. SW3 —5K 79
Elm Pl. SW7 —3K 79
Elm Quay Ct. SW8 —6B 82
Elms M. W2 —7K 63
Elm St. WC1 —2G 67
Elm Tree Clo. NW8 —6K 55
Elm Tree Rd. NW8 —6K 55
Elnathan M. W9 —2G 63
Elsham Rd. W14 —5A 70
Elsham Ter. W14 —6A 70
Elsted St. SE17 —2E 84
Elsworthy Ri. NW3 —1C 56
Elsworthy Rd. NW3 —2A 56
Elsworthy Ter. NW3 —1C 56
Elvaston M. SW7 —6J 71
Elvaston Pl. SW7 —7H 71
Elverton St. SW1 —1B 82
Elwin St. E2 —6K 61
Ely Cotts. SW8 —7F 83
Ely Ct. EC1 —4J 67
Ely Pl. EC1 —4J 67
Elystan Pl. SW3 —3C 80
Elystan St. SW3 —2B 80
Elystan Wlk. N1 —3H 59
Embankment Gdns. SW3 —5E 80
Embankment Pl. WC2 —2E 74
Embassy Ct. NW8 —5A 56
Embassy Ho. NW6 —1F 55
Emberton. SE17 —5F 85
Emberton Ct. EC1 —7K 59
Emerald St. WC1 —3F 67
Emerson St. SE1 —2B 76
Emery Hill St. SW1 —7A 74
Emery St. SE1 —6J 75
Emmanuel Ho. SE11 —2H 83
Emperor's Ga. SW7 —7H 71
Empress Pl. SW6 —4D 78
Empress St. SE17 —5C 84
Enbrook St. W10 —7A 54
Endell St. WC2 —5D 66
Endsleigh Gdns. WC1 —1B 66
Endsleigh Pl. WC1 —1C 66
Endsleigh St. WC1 —1B 66
Enfield Rd. N1 —1G 61
Enford St. W1 —3D 64
Engine Ct. SW1 —3A 74
Englefield Rd. N1 —1G 61
English Grounds. SE1 —3F 77
Enid St. SE16 —6H 77
Ennismore Gdns. SW7 —5B 72
Ennismore Gdns. M. SW7 —6B 72
Ennismore M. SW7 —6B 72
Ennismore St. SW7 —6B 72
Ensbury Ho. SW8 —7F 83
Ensign Ind. Cen. E1 —7K 69
(off Ensign St.)
Ensign St. E1 —7K 69
Ensor M. SW7 —3K 79
Epirus M. SW6 —7D 78
Epirus Rd. SW6 —7C 78
Epworth St. EC2 —2E 68
Equity Sq. E2 —7J 61
Erasmus St. SW1 —2C 82
Eresby Pl. NW6 —1D 54
Eric Fletcher Ct. N1 —1C 60
Errington Rd. W9 —1C 62
Errol St. EC1 —2C 68
Erskine M. NW3 —1E 56
Erskine Rd. NW3 —1E 56
Esmeralda Rd. SE1 —2K 85
Esmond Rd. NW6 —3C 54
Essendine Rd. W9 —1E 62
Essex Ct. EC4 —6H 67
Essex Rd. N1 —3K 59
Essex St. WC2 —6H 67
Essex Vs. W8 —5D 70
Estcourt Rd. SW6 —7A 78
Esterbrooke St. SW1 —2B 82
Ethel St. SE17 —2C 84
Eton Av. NW3 —1A 56
Europa Pl. EC1 —7B 60
Eustace Ho. SE11 —1F 83
Eustace Rd. SW6 —7D 78
Euston Cen. NW1 —1K 65
Euston Gro. NW1 —7B 58
Euston Rd. NW1 & N1 —2J 65
Euston Sq. NW1 —7B 58
Euston Sta. Colonnade. NW1 —7B 58
Euston St. NW1 —1A 66
Euston Underpass. (Junct.) —1K 65
Evelina Mans. SE5 —7D 84
Evelyn Dennington Ct. N1 —1K 59
Evelyn Gdns. SW7 —4J 79
Evelyn Lowe Est. SE16 —7K 77
Evelyn Mans. W14 —5A 78
Evelyn Wlk. N1 —5D 60
Evelyn Yd. W1 —5B 66
Everard Ho. E1 —6K 69
Everilda St. N1 —3G 59
Eversholt St. NW1 —4K 57
Everton Bldgs. NW1 —7K 57
Ewen Ho. N1 —3G 59
Ewer St. SE1 —3B 76
Excel Ct. WC2 —1C 74
Exchange Arc. EC2 —3G 69
Exchange Building. E1 —2H 69
Exchange Ct. WC2 —1E 74
Exchange Pl. EC2 —3F 69
Exchange Sq. EC2 —3G 69
Exchange St. EC1 —7B 60
Exeter St. WC2 —7E 66
Exhibition Rd. SW7 —5A 72
Exmouth Mkt. EC1 —1H 67
Exmouth M. NW1 —7A 58
Exon St. SE17 —3F 85
Exton St. SE1 —3H 75
Eyre Ct. NW8 —4K 55
Eyre St. Hill. EC1 —2H 67
Ezra St. E2 —6J 61

Fabian Rd. SW6 —7C 78
Fairbank Est. N1 —6E 60
Fairburn Ho. W14 —4C 78
Fairby Ho. SE1 —1J 85
Fairchild Pl. EC2 —2G 69
Fairchild St. EC2 —2G 69
Fairclough St. E1 —6K 69
Fairfax Pl. NW6 —1J 55
Fairfax Rd. NW6 —1J 55
Fairford Ho. SE11 —2J 83
Fairhazel Gdns. NW6 —1H 55
Fairholme Rd. W14 —4A 78
Fairholt St. SW7 —6C 72
Fairstead Wlk. N1 —2B 60
Fair St. SE1 —4G 77
Fakruddin St. E1 —2K 69
Falconberg Ct. W1 —5C 66
Falconberg M. W1 —5B 66
Falcon Clo. SE1 —2A 76
Falcon Ct. EC4 —6J 67
Falcon Ct. N1 —5A 60
Falcon Point. SE1 —2A 76
Falkirk Ho. W9 —6G 55
Falkirk St. N1 —5G 61
Falkland Ho. W8 —7F 71
Falmouth Ho. SE11 —3J 83
Falmouth Rd. SE1 —7C 76
Falstaff Ct. SE11 —2K 83
Falstaff Ho. N1 —5F 61
Fane St. W14 —5C 78
Fann St. EC1 & EC2 —2B 68
Fanshaw St. N1 —6F 61
Faraday Rd. W10 —3A 62
Fareham St. W1 —5B 66
Farjeon Ho. NW6 —1K 55
Farmer's Rd. SE5 —7A 84
Farmer St. W8 —2D 70
Farm La. SW6 —6E 78
Farm La. Clo. SW6 —7E 78
(off Farm La.)
Farm Pl. W8 —2D 70
Farm St. W1 —1H 73
Farnborough Way. SE15 —7G 85
Farnell M. SW5 —3F 79
Farnham Pl. SE1 —3A 76
Farnham Royal. SE11 —4G 83
Farrier St. NW1 —1J 57
Farrier Wlk. SW10 —5J 79
Farringdon La. EC1 —2J 67
Farringdon Rd. EC1 —1H 67
Farringdon St. EC4 —4K 67
Farthing All. SE1 —5K 77
Fashion St. E1 —4H 69
Faulkners All. EC1 —3K 67
Faunce St. SE17 —5K 83
Fawcett St. SW10 —6H 79
Fawkham Ho. SE1 —2J 85
Featherstone St. EC1 —1D 68
Fellows Ct. E2 —5H 61
Fellows Rd. NW3 —1A 56
Felton Ho. N1 —3E 60
Felton St. N1 —3E 60
Fenchurch Av. EC3 —6F 69
Fenchurch Bldgs. EC3 —6G 69
Fenchurch Pl. EC3 —7G 69
Fenchurch St. EC3 —7F 69
Fen Ct. EC3 —6F 69
Fendall St. SE1 —7G 77
(in two parts)
Fenelon Pl. W14 —2C 78
Fenham Rd. SE15 —7K 85
Fenning St. SE1 —4F 77
Fentiman Rd. SW8 —6E 82
Ferdinand Pl. NW1 —1G 57
Ferdinand St. NW1 —1G 57
Fermain Ct. E. N1 —2G 61
Fermain Ct. N. N1 —2G 61
Fermain Ct. W. N1 —2F 61
Fermoy Rd. W9 —2B 62
Fern Clo. N1 —4F 61
Fernhead Rd. W9 —5C 54
Fernsbury St. WC1 —7H 59
Fernshaw Rd. SW10 —6H 79
Fern Wlk. SE16 —4K 85
Ferriby Clo. N1 —1H 59
Ferrybridge Ho. SE11 —7G 75
Fetter La. EC4 —6J 67
(in two parts)
Field Ct. WC1 —4G 67
Fieldgate St. E1 —4K 69
Fielding Ho. NW6 —6E 54
Fielding St. SE17 —5B 84
Field Rd. W6 —4A 78
Fields Est. E8 —1K 61
Field St. WC1 —6F 59
Fife Ter. N1 —4G 59
Fifth Av. W10 —1A 62
Filmer Rd. SW6 —7B 78
Finborough Rd. SW10 —4F 79
Finchdean Way. SE15 —7G 85
Finch La. EC3 —6E 68
Finchley Pl. NW8 —4K 55
Finchley Rd. NW8 —3K 55
Finch Lodge. W9 —3E 62
Finnemore Ho. N1 —2B 60
Finsbury Av. EC2 —4E 68
Finsbury Av. Sq. EC2 —3F 69
Finsbury Cir. EC2 —4E 68
Finsbury Est. EC1 —7J 59
Finsbury Mkt. EC2 —2F 69
(in two parts)
Finsbury Pavement. EC2 —3E 68
Finsbury Sq. EC2 —3E 68
Finsbury St. EC2 —3D 68
Fiona Ct. NW6 —4C 54
First Av. W10 —1B 62
First St. SW3 —1C 80
Fisher Ho. N1 —3H 59
Fisher St. WC1 —4F 67
Fisherton St. NW8 —2K 63
Fishmongers Hall Wharf. EC4 —1E 76
Fish St. Hill. EC3 —1E 76
Fish Wharf. EC3 —1E 76
Fitzalan St. SE11 —1G 83
Fitzgeorge Av. W14 —2A 78
Fitzhardinge St. W1 —5F 65
Fitzjames Av. W14 —2A 78
Fitzmaurice Pl. W1 —2J 73
Fitzroy Ct. W1 —2A 66
Fitzroy M. W1 —2K 65
Fitzroy Rd. NW1 —2E 56
Fitzroy Sq. W1 —2K 65
Fitzroy St. W1 —2K 65
(in two parts)
Fitzroy Yd. NW1 —2F 57
Fives Ct. SE11 —7K 75
Flank St. E1 —7K 69
Flaxman Ct. W1 —6B 66
Flaxman Ter. WC1 —7C 58
Fleet Bldgs. EC4 —5K 67
Fleet Pl. EC4 —5K 67
Fleet Sq. WC1 —7G 59
Fleet St. EC4 —6H 67
Fleet St. Hill. E1 —2K 69
Fleming Ct. W2 —3K 63
Fleming Ho. SE16 —5K 77
Fleming Rd. SE17 —5A 84
Fletcher St. E1 —7K 69
Fleur-de-Lis St. E1 —2G 69
Flinton St. SE17 —3G 85
Flint St. SE17 —2E 84
Flitcroft St. WC2 —6C 66
Flockton St. SE16 —5K 77
Flood St. SW3 —4C 80
Flood Wlk. SW3 —5C 80
Floral St. WC2 —7D 66
Florence Ct. N1 —1K 59
Florence Ct. W9 —7J 55
Florence St. N1 —1K 59
Florida St. E2 —7K 61
Flower & Dean Wlk. E1 —4J 69
Flower Wlk., The. SW7 —5H 71
Foley St. W1 —4K 65
Folgate St. E1 —3G 69
Follingham Ct. N1 —6G 61
Folly M. W11 —5B 62
Fontenoy Ho. SE11 —2K 83
Fontenoy Pas. SE11 —2K 83
Forbes St. E1 —6K 69
Fordham St. E1 —5K 69
Fordingley Rd. W9 —7C 54
Foreland Ho. W11 —7A 62
Fore St. EC2 —4C 68
Fore St. Av. EC2 —4D 68
Formosa St. W9 —3G 63
Forset St. W1 —5C 64
Forston St. N1 —4C 60
Forsyth Gdns. SE17 —5A 84
Fort Rd. SE1 —2J 85
Fort St. E1 —4G 69
Fortune Ho. SE11 —2H 83
Fortune St. EC1 —2C 68
Fosbrooke Ho. SW8 —7D 82
Fosbury M. W2 —1G 71
Foscote M. W9 —2E 62
Foster La. EC2 —5B 68
Foubert's Pl. W1 —6K 65
Foulis Ter. SW7 —3A 80
Founders Ct. EC2 —5D 68
Foundry M. NW1 —1A 66
Fountain Ct. EC4 —7H 67
Fountain Ct. SW1 —2H 81
Fountain Ho. NW6 —1A 54
Fountain Sq. SW1 —1J 81
Fount St. SW8 —7C 82
Fournier St. E1 —3H 69
Fourth Av. W10 —1A 62
Fowey Ho. SE11 —3J 83
Fowler Rd. N1 —1A 60
Fox & Knot St. EC1 —3A 68
Foxcote. SE17 —4G 85
Foxley Rd. SW9 —7J 83
Frampton St. NW8 —2K 63
Francis Ct. EC1 —3K 67
Francis St. SW1 —1K 81
Francis Wlk. N1 —2F 59
Frank Beswick Ho. SW6 —6C 78
Frank Ho. SW8 —7D 82
Frankland Rd. SW7 —7K 71
Franklin Sq. W14 —4C 78
Franklin's Row. SW3 —3E 80
Frank Soskice Ho. SW6 —6C 78
Frazier St. SE1 —5H 75
Frean St. SE16 —6K 77
Freda Corbett Clo. SE15 —7K 85
Frederick Clo. W2 —7D 64
Frederick Rd. SE17 —5A 84
Frederick's Pl. EC2 —6D 68
Frederick's Row. EC1 —6K 59
Frederick St. WC1 —7F 59
Frederick Ter. E8 —1H 61
Frederic M. SW1 —5E 72
Freeling St. N1 —1E 58
(in two parts)
Freemantle St. SE17 —3F 85
French Ordinary Ct. EC3 —7G 69
French Pl. E1 —1G 69
Frensham St. SE15 —6K 85
Freshfield Av. E8 —1H 61
Friars Clo. SE1 —3A 76
Friar St. EC4 —6A 68
Friary Ct. SW1 —3A 74
Friary Est. SE15 —6K 85
Friary Rd. SE15 —6K 85
Friday St. EC4 —7B 68
Friend St. EC1 —6K 59
Frith St. W1 —6B 66
Frobisher Cres. EC2 —3C 68
Frome St. N1 —4B 60
Frostic Wlk. E1 —4K 69
Frye's Bldgs. N1 —4J 59
Frying Pan All. E1 —4H 69
Fulham Broadway. (Junct.) —7E 78
Fulham B'way. SW6 —7E 78
Fulham Rd. SW6 —7D 78
Fulham Rd. SW10 & SW3 —6H 79
Fuller Clo. E2 —1K 69
Fullwood's M. N1 —6E 60
Fulton M. W2 —7H 63
Fulwood Pl. WC1 —4G 67
Furley Rd. SE15 —7K 85
Furnival St. EC4 —5H 67
Fursecroft. W1 —5D 64
Fye Foot La. EC4 —7B 68
Fynes St. SW1 —1B 82

Gabriel's Wharf. SE1 —2J 75
Gaddesden Ho. EC1 —7E 60
Gage St. WC1 —3E 66
Gainford St. N1 —2H 59
Gainsford St. SE1 —4H 77
Galen Pl. WC1 —4D 66
Galton St. W10 —1A 62
Galway Ho. EC1 —7C 60
Galway St. EC1 —7C 60
Gambia St. SE1 —3A 76
Gandolfi St. SE15 —6F 85
Ganton St. W1 —7K 65
Garbutt Pl. W1 —4G 65
Garden Ct. EC4 —7H 67
Garden M. W2 —1G 71
Garden Rd. NW8 —6J 55
Garden Row. SE1 —7K 75
Garden Ter. SW1 —3B 82
Garden Ter. SW7 —5C 72
Garden Wlk. EC2 —7F 61
Gardners La. EC4 —7B 68
Gard St. EC1 —6A 60
Garlick Hill. EC4 —7C 68
Garnault M. EC1 —7J 59
Garnault Pl. EC1 —7J 59
Garner St. E2 —5K 61
Garnies Clo. SE15 —7H 85
Garrett St. EC1 —1C 68
Garrick St. WC2 —7D 66
Garrick Yd. WC2 —7D 66
Garway Rd. W2 —6F 63
Gascoigne Pl. E2 —7H 61
(in two parts)
Gascony Av. NW6 —1D 54
Gasholder Pl. SE11 —4G 83
Gaskin St. N1 —2K 59
Gaspar Clo. SW5 —1G 79
Gaspar M. SW5 —1G 79
Gateforth St. NW8 —2B 64
Gatehouse Sq. SE1 —2C 76
Gate M. SW7 —5C 72
Gatesborough St. EC2 —1F 69
Gates Ct. SE17 —4B 84
Gatesden. WC1 —7E 58
Gate St. WC2 —5F 67
Gateway. SE17 —5C 84
Gateways, The. SW3 —3C 80
Gatliff Clo. SW1 —4G 81
Gatliff Rd. SW1 —4H 81
Gattis Wharf. N1 —4E 58
Gaunt St. SE1 —6B 76
Gavel St. SE17 —1E 84
Gaydon Ho. W2 —3F 63
Gayfere St. SW1 —7D 74
Gayhurst. SE17 —5E 84
Gayhurst Rd. E8 —1K 61
Gaysley Ho. SE11 —2H 83
Gaywood St. SE1 —7A 76
Gaza St. SE17 —4K 83
Gedling Pl. SE1 —6J 77
Gees Ct. W1 —6G 65
Gee St. EC1 —1B 68
Geffrye Ct. N1 —5G 61
Geffrye Est. N1 —5G 61
Geffrye St. E2 —4H 61
George Ct. WC2 —1E 74
George Inn Yd. SE1 —3D 76
George Lindgren Ho. SW6 —7C 78
George Loveless Ho. E2 —6J 61
George Lowe Ct. W2 —3F 63
George Mathers Rd. SE11 —1K 83
George M. NW1 —7A 58
George Row. SE16 —5K 77
George's Sq. SW6 —5C 78
George St. W1 —5D 64
George Yd. EC3 —6E 68
George Yd. W1 —7G 65
Georgiana St. NW1 —2K 57
Georgina Gdns. E2 —6J 61
Geraldine St. SE11 —7K 75
Gerald M. SW1 —1G 81
Gerald Rd. SW1 —1G 81
Gerrard Pl. W1 —7C 66
Gerrard Rd. N1 —4K 59
Gerrard St. W1 —7B 66
Gerridge St. SE1 —6J 75
Gertrude St. SW10 —6J 79
Gibbon's Rents. SE1 —3F 77
Gibbs Grn. W14 —3B 78
Gibraltar Wlk. E2 —7J 61
Gibson Rd. SE11 —2G 83
Gibson Sq. N1 —2J 59
Gifford St. N1 —1E 58
Gilbert Bri. EC2 —4C 68
Gilbert Ho. EC2 —3C 68
Gilbert Ho. SW8 —7D 82
Gilbert Pl. WC1 —4D 66
Gilbert Rd. SE11 —2J 83
Gilbert St. W1 —6G 65
Gilbeys Yd. NW1 —1G 57
Gildea St. W1 —4J 65
Giles Ho. SE16 —6K 77
Gillfoot. NW1 —5K 57
Gillingham M. SW1 —1K 81
Gillingham Row. SW1 —1K 81
Gillingham St. SW1 —1K 81
Gilston Rd. SW10 —4J 79
Giltspur St. EC1 —5A 68
Gironde Rd. SW6 —7C 78
Gissing Wlk. N1 —1J 59
Gladstone St. SE1 —7K 75
Glasgow Ho. W9 —5G 55
Glasgow Ter. SW1 —4K 81
Glasshill St. SE1 —4A 76
Glasshouse St. W1 —1A 74
Glasshouse Wlk. SE11 —3E 82
Glasshouse Yd. EC1 —2B 68
Glazbury Rd. W14 —2A 78
Glaziers Hall. SE1 —2D 76
Glebe Pl. SW3 —5B 80
Glebe Rd. E8 —1H 61
Gledhow Gdns. SW5 —2H 79
Gledstanes Rd. W14 —4A 78
Glencoe Mans. SW9 —7H 83
Glendower Pl. SW7 —1K 79
Glenfinlas Way. SE5 —7A 84
Glengall Pas. NW6 —2D 54
Glengall Rd. NW6 —2C 54
Glengall Rd. SE15 —5J 85
Glengall Ter. SE15 —5J 85
Glenshaw Mans. SW9 —7H 83
Glentworth St. NW1 —2E 64
Gliddon Rd. W14 —2A 78
Globe St. SE1 —6D 76
Globe Yd. W1 —6H 65
Gloucester Arc. SW7 —1H 79
Gloucester Av. NW1 —1F 57
Gloucester Ct. EC3 —1G 77
Gloucester Cres. NW1 —2H 57
Gloucester Gdns. W2 —5H 63
Gloucester Ga. NW1 —4H 57
Gloucester Ga. M. NW1 —4H 57
Gloucester Ho. NW6 —5E 54
Gloucester Ho. SW9 & SE5 —7J 83
Gloucester M. W2 —6J 63
Gloucester M. W. W2 —6H 63
Gloucester Pl. NW1 & W1 —1D 64
Gloucester Pl. M. W1 —4E 64
Gloucester Rd. SW7 —6H 71
Gloucester Sq. E2 —3K 61
Gloucester Sq. W2 —6A 64
Gloucester St. SW1 —4K 81
Gloucester Ter. W2 —5G 63
Gloucester Wlk. W8 —4E 70
Gloucester Way. EC1 —7J 59
Glynde M. SW3 —7C 72
Glynde Reach. WC1 —7E 58
Glyn St. SE11 —4F 83
Goater's All. SW6 —7C 78
Goat St. SE1 —4H 77
Godfrey St. SW3 —3C 80
Goding St. SE11 —3E 82
Godliman St. EC4 —6B 68
Godson St. N1 —4H 59
Godwin Clo. N1 —4C 60
Golborne Gdns. W10 —2A 62
Golborne Rd. W10 —3A 62
Golden Cross M. W11 —5B 62
Golden La. EC1 —1B 68
Golden La. Est. EC1 —2B 68
Golden Sq. W1 —7A 66
Goldhurst Ter. NW6 —1F 55
Goldington Ct. NW1 —3B 58
Goldington Cres. NW1 —4B 58
Goldington St. NW1 —4B 58
Goldman Clo. E2 —1K 69
Goldney Rd. W9 —2D 62
Goldsmith's Pl. NW6 —3F 55
Goldsmith's Row. E2 —5K 61
Goldsmith's Sq. E2 —4K 61
Goldsmith St. EC2 —5C 68
Goodge Pl. W1 —4A 66
Goodge St. W1 —4A 66
Goodman's Ct. E1 —7H 69
Goodman's Stile. E1 —5K 69
Goodmans Yd. E1 —7H 69
Goods Way. NW1 —5D 58
Goodwin Clo. SE16 —7J 77
Goodwin Ct. NW1 —4A 58
Goodwins Ct. WC2 —7D 66
Goodyear Pl. SE5 —6C 84
Gophir La. EC4 —7D 68
Gopsall St. N1 —3E 60
Gordon Mans. WC1 —2B 66
Gordon Pl. W8 —4E 70
Gordon Sq. WC1 —1B 66
Gordon St. WC1 —1B 66
Gorefield Pl. NW6 —4D 54
Gore St. SW7 —6J 71
Goring St. EC3 —5G 69
Gorleston St. W14 —1A 78
Gorsuch Pl. E2 —6H 61
Gorsuch St. E2 —6H 61
Gosfield St. W1 —3K 65
Goslett Yd. WC2 —6C 66
Gosport Way. SE15 —7H 85
Gosset St. E2 —6J 61
Goswell Pl. EC1 —7A 60
Goswell Rd. EC1 —5K 59
Gough Sq. EC4 —5J 67
Gough St. WC1 —1G 67
Goulston St. E1 —5H 69
Govan St. E2 —3K 61
Gower Ct. WC1 —1B 66
Gower M. WC1 —4C 66
Gower Pl. WC1 —1A 66
Gower St. WC1 —1A 66
Gower's Wlk. E1 —5K 69
Gracechurch Ct. EC3 —7E 68
Gracechurch St. EC3 —7E 68
Grace Ho. SE11 —5G 83
Graces All. E1 —7K 69
Graces M. NW8 —5J 55
Grafton M. N1 —4B 60
Grafton M. W1 —2K 65
Grafton Pl. NW1 —7C 58
Grafton St. W1 —1J 73
Grafton Way. W1 & WC1 —2K 65
Graham St. N1 —5A 60
Graham Ter. SW1 —2F 81
Granary St. NW1 —3B 58
Granby Bldgs. SE11 —2F 83
Granby Pl. SE1 —5H 75
Granby St. E2 —1J 69
Granby Ter. NW1 —5K 57
Grand Av. EC1 —3A 68
Grand Junct. Wharf. N1 —5B 60
Grand Union Clo. W9 —3C 62
Grand Union Cres. E8 —1K 61
Grand Union Wlk. NW1 —1J 57
Grange Ct. WC2 —6G 67
Grange Ho. SE1 —7H 77
Grange Pl. NW6 —1D 54
Granger Gro. SE1 —4E 76
Grange Rd. SE1 —7G 77
Grange St. N1 —3E 60
Grange, The. SE1 —7H 77
Grange Wlk. SE1 —6G 77
Grange Wlk. M. SE1 —7G 77
Grange Way. NW6 —1D 54
Grange Yd. SE1 —7H 77
Grantbridge St. N1 —4A 60
Grantham Pl. W1 —3H 73
Grants Quay Wharf. EC3 —1E 76
Grant St. N1 —4H 59
Grantully Rd. W9 —7F 55
Granville Ct. N1 —2F 61
Granville Pl. W1 —6F 65
Granville Rd. NW6 —5D 54
(in two parts)
Granville Sq. SE15 —7G 85
Granville Sq. WC1 —7G 59
Granville St. WC1 —7G 59
Grape St. WC2 —5D 66
Graphite Sq. SE11 —3F 83
Grately Way. SE15 —7H 85
Gratton Rd. W14 —7A 70
Gravel La. E1 —5H 69
Gray's Inn Pl. WC1 —4G 67
Gray's Inn Rd. WC1 —6E 58
Gray's Inn Sq. WC1 —3H 67
Grayson Ho. EC1 —7C 60
Gray St. SE1 —5J 75
Gray's Yd. W1 —5G 65
Gt. Arthur Ho. EC1 —2B 68
Gt. Bell All. EC2 —5D 68
Gt. Castle St. W1 —5J 65
Gt. Central St. NW1 —3D 64
Gt. Chapel St. W1 —5B 66
Gt. College St. SW1 —6D 74
Gt. Cumberland M. W1 —6D 64
Gt. Cumberland Pl. W1 —5D 64
Gt. Dover St. SE1 —5C 76
Gt. Eastern Bldgs. E1 —4K 69
Gt. Eastern St. EC2 —7F 61
Gt. Eastern Wlk. EC2 —4G 69
Gt. George St. SW1 —5C 74
Gt. Guildford St. SE1 —2B 76
Gt. James St. WC1 —3F 67
Gt. Marlborough St. W1 —6K 65
Gt. Maze Pond. SE1 —4E 76
(in two parts)
Gt. Newport St. WC2 —7D 66
Gt. New St. EC4 —5J 67
Greatorex Ho. E1 —3K 69
Greatorex St. E1 —3K 69
Gt. Ormond St. WC1 —3E 66
Gt. Percy St. WC1 —6G 59
Gt. Peter St. SW1 —7B 74
Gt. Portland St. W1 —2J 65
Gt. Pulteney St. W1 —7A 66
Gt. Queen St. WC2 —6E 66
Gt. Russell St. WC1 —5C 66
Gt. St Helen's. EC3 —5F 69
Gt. St Thomas Apostle. EC4 —7C 68
Gt. Scotland Yd. SW1 —3D 74
Gt. Smith St. SW1 —6C 74
Gt. Suffolk St. SE1 —3A 76
Gt. Sutton St. EC1 —2A 68
Gt. Swan All. EC2 —5D 68
Gt. Titchfield St. W1 —2J 65
Gt. Tower St. EC3 —7G 69

Gt. Trinity La.—Keppel Row.

Gt. Trinity La. EC4 —7C 68
Gt. Turnstile. WC1 —4G 67
Gt. Western Rd. W9, W11 & W2 —2C 62
Gt. Winchester St. EC2 —5E 68
Gt. Windmill St. W1 —7B 66
Great Yd. SE1 —4G 77
Greaves Tower. SW10 —7J 79 (off Worlds End Est.)
Greek Ct. W1 —6C 66
Greek St. W1 —6C 66
Green Arbour Ct. EC1 —5K 67
Greenaway Ho. NW8 —2H 55
Greenberry St. NW8 —5B 56
Greencoat Pl. SW1 —1A 82
Greencoat Row. SW1 —7A 74
Greencroft Gdns. NW6 —1F 55
Green Dragon Ct. SE1 —3D 76
Green Dragon Yd. E1 —4K 69
Greenfell Ho. SE5 —7B 84
Greenfield Rd. E1 —4K 69
Greenham Clo. SE1 —5H 75
Greenhill's Rents. EC1 —3K 67
Green Hundred Rd. SE15 —6K 85
Greenland Pl. NW1 —2J 57
Greenland Rd. NW1 —2J 57
Greenland St. NW1 —2J 57
Greenman St. N1 —1B 60
Green's Ct. W1 —7B 66
Green St. W1 —7E 64
Green Ter. EC1 —7J 59
Green Wlk. SE1 —7F 77
Greenwell St. W1 —2J 65
Greenwood Ct. SW1 —4A 82
Green Yd. WC1 —1G 67
Green Yd., The. EC3 —6F 69
Greet Ho. SE1 —5J 75
Greet St. SE1 —3J 75
Gregory Pl. W8 —4F 71
Greig Ter. SE17 —5A 84
Grendon St. NW8 —1B 64
Grenfell Ho. SE5 —7B 84
Grenville M. SW7 —2J 79
Grenville Pl. SW7 —7H 71
Grenville St. WC1 —2E 66
Gresham St. EC2 —5B 68
Gresse St. W1 —4B 66
Greville Pl. NW6 —4G 55
Greville M. NW6 —3F 55
Greville Rd. NW6 —4F 55
Greville St. EC1 —4H 67 (in two parts)
Greycoat Gdns. SW1 —7B 74
Greycoat Pl. SW1 —7B 74
Greycoat St. SW1 —7B 74
Grey Eagle St. E1 —2J 69
Greyfriars Pas. EC1 —5A 68
Greyhound Ct. WC2 —7G 67
Greyhound Rd. W6 & W14 —5A 78
Greyhound Rd. Mans. W6 —5A 78
Greystoke Pl. EC4 —5H 67
Grigg's Pl. SE1 —7G 77
Grimsby St. E2 —2J 69
Grimsel Path. SE5 —7A 84
Grimthorpe Ho. EC1 —1A 68
Grindal St. SE1 —5H 75
Grittleton Rd. W9 —1D 62
Grocer's Hall Ct. EC2 —6D 68
Grocer's Hall Gdns. EC2 —6D 68
Groome Ho. SE11 —2G 83
Groom Pl. SW1 —6G 73
Grosvenor Cotts. SW1 —1F 81
Grosvenor Cres. SW1 —5G 73
Grosvenor Cres. M. SW1 —5F 73
Grosvenor Est. SW1 —1C 82
Grosvenor Gdns. SW1 —6H 73
Grosvenor Gdns. M. E. SW1 —6J 73
Grosvenor Gdns. M. N. SW1 —7H 73
Grosvenor Gdns. M. S. SW1 —7J 73
Grosvenor Ga. W1 —1F 73
Grosvenor Hill. W1 —7H 65
Grosvenor Pk. SE5 —6B 84
Grosvenor Pl. SW1 —4G 73
Grosvenor Rd. SW1 —5H 81
Grosvenor Sq. W1 —7G 65
Grosvenor St. W1 —7H 65
Grosvenor Ter. SE5 —7B 84
Grotto Ct. SE1 —4B 76
Grotto Pas. W1 —3G 65
Grove Ct. NW8 —6K 55
Grove End Gdns. NW8 —2K 63
Grove End Rd. NW8 —5K 55
Grove Gdns. NW8 —7C 56
Grove Hall Ct. NW8 —6J 55
Groveland Ct. EC4 —6C 68
Grove M. W11 —6B 62
Grover Ho. SE11 —4G 83
Guildhall Bldgs. EC2 —5D 68
Guildhall Yd. EC2 —5C 68
Guildhouse St. SW1 —1K 81
Guilford Pl. WC1 —2F 67
Guilford St. WC1 —2D 66
Guinness Ct. E1 —6J 69
Guinness Ct. EC1 —7C 60
Guinness Ct. NW8 —3C 56
Guinness Ct. SE1 —4F 77
Guinness Ct. SW3 —2D 80
Guinness Ct. SW10 —7J 79
Guinness Sq. SE1 —1F 85
Guinness Trust Bldgs. SE17 —3K 83
Gulliver's Ho. EC1 —2B 68
Gulston Wlk. SW3 —2E 80
Gunpowder Sq. EC4 —5J 67
Gun St. E1 —4H 69
Gunter Gro. SW10 —6H 79
Gunterstone Rd. W14 —2A 78
Gunthorpe St. E1 —4J 69
Guthrie Ct. SE1 —5J 75
Guthrie St. SW3 —3B 80
Gutter La. EC2 —5C 68
Guy St. SE1 —4E 76
Gwendwr Rd. W14 —3A 78
Gwynne Pl. WC1 —7G 59

Haberdasher Est. N1 —6E 60
Haberdasher Pl. N1 —6F 61 (in two parts)
Haberdasher St. N1 —6E 60
Habington Ho. SE5 —7D 84
Hackford Rd. SW9 —7H 83
Hackney Rd. E2 —7G 61
Hadfield Ho. E1 —6K 69
Hadrian Est. E2 —5K 61
Haggerston Rd. E8 & E2 —1H 61
Haines St. SW8 —7A 82
Halcomb St.. N1 —3F 61
Haldane Rd. SW6 —7C 78
Half Moon Ct. EC1 —4B 68
Half Moon Cres. N1 —4G 59
Half Moon Pas. E1 —6J 69
Half Moon St. W1 —2J 73
Halford Rd. SW6 —6D 78
Halkin Arc. SW1 —6E 72
Halkin M. SW1 —6F 73
Halkin Pl. SW1 —6F 73
Halkin St. SW1 —5G 73
Hallam M. W1 —3J 65
Hallam St. W1 —2J 65
Hallfield Est. W2 —5H 63
Hall Ga. NW8 —6K 55
Halliford St. N1 —1C 60
Hall Pl. W2 —2K 63
Hall Rd. NW8 —7J 55
Hall St. EC1 —6A 60
Hall Tower. W2 —3A 64
Halpin Pl. SE17 —2E 84
Halsey M. SW3 —1D 80
Halsey St. SW3 —1D 80
Halstead Ct. N1 —5E 60
Halton Cross St. N1 —2A 60
Halton Mans. N1 —1A 60
Halton Pl. N1 —2B 60
Halton Rd. N1 —1A 60
Hambledon. SE17 —5E 84
Hambury Ho. SW8 —7E 82
Hamilton Bldgs. EC2 —2G 69
Hamilton Clo. NW8 —7K 55
Hamilton Ct. W9 —6H 55
Hamilton Gdns. NW8 —6J 55
Hamilton Ho. NW8 —6K 55
Hamilton M. W1 —3H 73
Hamilton Pl. W1 —3G 73
Hamilton Sq. SE1 —4E 76
Hamilton Ter. NW8 —5G 55
Hamlet Ct. SE11 —3K 83
Hamlet Way. SE1 —4E 76
Hammersmith Rd. W6 & W14 —1A 78
Hammett St. EC3 —7H 69
Hamond Sq. N1 —4F 61
Hampden Clo. NW1 —5C 58
Hampden Gurney St. W1 —6D 64
Hampstead Rd. NW1 —4K 57
Hampton Clo. NW6 —6D 54
Hampton St. SE17 & SE1 —2A 84
Hamsworth M. SE11 —7K 75
Ham Yd. W1 —7B 66
Hanbury Ho. E1 —3K 69
Hanbury M. N1 —3C 60
Hanbury St. E1 —3H 69
Hand Ct. WC1 —4G 67
Handel St. WC1 —1D 66
Handforth Rd. SW9 —7H 83
Hanging Sword All. EC4 —6J 67
Hankey Pl. SE1 —5E 76
Hannah Mary Way. SE1 —2K 85
Hannell Rd. SW6 —7A 78
Hanover Flats. W1 —7G 65
Hanover Gdns. SE11 —6H 83
Hanover Ga. NW1 —7C 56
Hanover Ho. NW8 —5B 56
Hanover Pl. WC2 —6E 66
Hanover Sq. W1 —6J 65
Hanover Steps. W2 —6C 64
Hanover St. W1 —6J 65
Hanover Ter. NW1 —7D 56
Hanover Ter. M. NW1 —7C 56
Hanover Yd. N1 —4B 60
Hans Cres. SW1 —6D 72
Hanson St. W1 —3K 65
Hans Pl. SW1 —6E 72
Hans Rd. SW3 —6D 72
Hans St. SW1 —7E 72
Hanway Pl. W1 —5B 66
Hanway St. W1 —5B 66
Hanworth Ho. SE5 —7K 83
Harad's Pl. E1 —1K 77
Harben Rd. NW6 —1J 55
Harbet Rd. W2 —4A 64
Harcourt Bldgs. EC4 —7H 67
Harcourt St. W1 —4C 64
Harcourt Ter. SW10 —4G 79
Harding Clo. SE17 —5B 84
Hardwicke M. WC1 —7G 59
Hardwick St. EC1 —7J 59
Hardwidge St. SE1 —4F 77
Hare Ct. EC4 —6H 67
Hare Marsh. E2 —1K 69
Hare Pl. EC4 —6J 67
Hare Wlk. N1 —5G 61
Harewood Av. NW1 —2C 64
Harewood Pl. W1 —6J 65
Harewood Row. NW1 —3C 64
Harfleur Ct. SE11 —2K 83 (off Opal St.)
Harford Ho. W11 —3C 62
Harkness Ho. E1 —6K 69
Harleyford Ct. SW8 —5G 83
Harleyford Rd. SE11 —5F 83
Harleyford St. SE11 —6H 83
Harley Gdns. SW10 —4J 79
Harley Ho. NW1 —2G 65
Harley Pl. W1 —4H 65
Harley Rd. NW3 —1A 56
Harley St. W1 —2H 65
Harlowe Clo. E8 —2K 61
Harman Clo. SE1 —4K 85
Harmood Gro. NW1 —1H 57
Harmood St. NW1 —1H 57
Harmsworth M. SE11 —7K 75
Harmsworth St. SE17 —4K 83
Harold Est. SE1 —7G 77
Harold Pl. SE11 —4H 83
Harold Wilson Ho. SW6 —6C 78
Harp All. EC4 —5K 67
Harper Rd. SE1 —6B 76
Harp La. EC3 —1F 77
Harpur M. WC1 —3F 67
Harpur St. WC1 —3F 67
Harriet Clo. E8 —2K 61
Harriet St. SW1 —5E 72
Harriet Wlk. SW1 —5E 72
Harrington Ct. W10 —6B 54
Harrington Gdns. SW7 —2G 79
Harrington Rd. SW7 —1K 79
Harrington Sq. NW1 —4K 57
Harrington St. NW1 —5K 57
Harrison St. WC1 —7E 58
Harris St. SE5 —7E 84
Harrowby St. W1 —5C 64
Harrow Pl. E1 —5G 69
Harrow Rd. W2 —3F 63
Harrow Rd. W10 —1A 62
Harrow Rd. Bri. W2 —3J 63
Hartington Rd. SW8 —7D 82
Hartismere Rd. SW6 —7C 78
Hartland Rd. NW1 —1H 57
Hartland Rd. NW6 —4B 54
Hartley Ho. SE1 —1J 85
Hartop Point. SW6 —7A 78
Hartshorn All. EC3 —6G 69
Hart St. EC3 —7G 69
Harvey Ho. N1 —3E 60
Harvey's Bldgs. WC2 —1E 74
Harvey St. N1 —3E 60
Harvist Rd. NW6 —5A 54
Harwich La. EC2 —3G 69
Harwood Ct. N1 —3E 60
Harwood Rd. SW6 —7E 78
Hasker St. SW3 —1C 80
Haslam Clo. N1 —1J 59
Hassard St. E2 —5J 61
Hastings Clo. SE15 —7K 85
Hastings St. WC1 —7D 58
Hatfield Ho. EC1 —2B 68
Hatfields. SE1 —2J 75
Hathaway Ho. N1 —5F 61
Hatherley Gro. W2 —5F 63
Hatherley St. SW1 —2A 82
Hat & Mitre Ct. EC1 —2A 68
Hatton Garden. EC1 —3J 67
Hatton Pl. EC1 —3J 67
Hatton Row. NW8 —2A 64
Hatton St. NW8 —2A 64
Hatton Wall. EC1 —3J 67
Haunch of Venison Yd. W1 —6H 65
Havelock St. N1 —2E 58
Haven St. NW1 —1J 57
Haverstock St. N1 —5A 60
Havil St. SE5 —7F 85
Havisham Ho. SE16 —5K 77
Hawes St. N1 —1A 60
Hawksmoor Pl. E2 —1K 69
Hawkwell Wlk. N1 —2C 60
Hawley Cres. NW1 —1J 57
Hawley M. NW1 —1H 57
Hawley Rd. NW1 —1H 57 (in three parts)
Hawley St. NW1 —1H 57
Hawthorn Wlk. W10 —1A 62
Hawtrey Rd. NW3 —1B 56
Hayden's Pl. W11 —5B 62
Haydon St. EC3 —7H 69
Haydon Wlk. E1 —7J 69
Hayes Pl. NW1 —2C 64
Hay Hill. W1 —1J 73
Hayles St. SE11 —1K 83
Haymans Point. SE11 —3F 83
Hayman St. N1 —1A 60
Haymarket. SW1 —1B 74
Haymarket Arc. SW1 —1B 74
Haymerle Rd. SE15 —6K 85
Hayne Ho. W11 —2A 70
Hayne St. EC1 —3A 68
Hay's Galleria. SE1 —2F 77
Hay's La. SE1 —3F 77
Hay's M. W1 —1H 73
Hay St. E2 —3K 61
Hayward's Pl. EC1 —2K 67
Hazelmere Rd. NW6 —2C 54
Hazel Way. SE1 —1H 85
Hazlewood Cres. W10 —2A 62
Hazlewood Tower. W10 —2B 62
Hazlitt M. W14 —7A 70
Hazlitt Rd. W14 —7A 70
Headbourne Ho. SE1 —6E 76
Headfort Pl. SW1 —5G 73
Head's M. W11 —6D 62
Healey Ho. SW9 —7J 83
Hearn's Bldgs. SE17 —2E 84
Hearn St. EC2 —2G 69
Heathcote St. WC1 —1F 67
Heather Wlk. W10 —1A 62
Heathfield St. W11 —1A 70
Hebden Ct. E2 —3H 61
Heber Mans. W14 —5A 78
Heckfield Pl. SW6 —7D 78
Heddon St. W1 —7K 65
Hedger St. SE11 —1K 83
Hedingham Clo. N1 —1B 60
Heiron St. SE17 —6A 84
Heldar Ct. SE1 —5E 76
Hellings St. E1 —3K 77
Helmet Row. EC1 —7C 60
Helston Ho. SE11 —3J 83
Hemans St. SW8 —7C 82
Hemans St. Est. SW8 —7C 82
Hemingford Rd. N1 —3G 59
Hemming St. E1 —2K 69
Hemp Wlk. SE17 —1E 84
Hemstal Rd. NW6 —1D 54
Hemsworth Ct. N1 —4F 61
Hemsworth St. N1 —4F 61
Hemus Pl. SW3 —4C 80
Henderson Dri. NW8 —1K 63
Hendre Rd. SE1 —2G 85
Heneage La. EC3 —6G 69
Heneage Pl. EC3 —6G 69
Heneage St. E1 —3J 69
Henley Dri. SE1 —1J 85
Henniker M. SW3 —5K 79
Henrietta M. WC1 —1E 66
Henrietta Pl. W1 —6H 65
Henrietta St. WC2 —7E 66
Henriques St. E1 —5K 69
Henry Ho. SW8 —7E 82
Henshaw St. SE17 —1D 84
Henstridge Pl. NW8 —4B 56
Herald's Pl. SE11 —1K 83
Herbal Hill. EC1 —2J 67
Herbal Hill Gdns. EC1 —2J 67
Herbal Pl. EC1 —2J 67
Herbert Cres. SW1 —6E 72
Herbert Morrison Ho. SW6 —6B 78
Herbrand Est. WC1 —1D 66
Herbrand St. WC1 —1D 66
Hercules Rd. SE1 —7G 75
Hereford Ho. NW6 —5E 54
Hereford M. W2 —6E 62
Hereford Retreat. SE15 —7K 85
Hereford Rd. W2 —5E 62
Hereford Sq. SW7 —2J 79
Hereford St. E2 —1K 69
Hermes Clo. W9 —2D 62
Hermes St. N1 —5H 59
Hermitage St. W2 —4K 63
Hermitage Wall. E1 —3K 77
Hermit Pl. NW6 —3F 55
Hermit St. EC1 —6K 59
Herrick St. SW1 —2C 82
Herries St. W10 —5A 54
Herring St. SE5 —5G 85
Hertford Pl. W1 —2K 65
Hertford Rd. N1 —2G 61 (in two parts)
Hertford St. W1 —3H 73
Hesketh Pl. W11 —1A 70
Hesper M. SW5 —3F 79
Hester Rd. SW11 —7B 80
Hewett St. EC2 —2G 69
Heyford Av. SW8 —7E 82
Heyford Ter. SW8 —7E 82
Heygate St. SE17 —2B 84
Hide Pl. SW1 —2B 82
High Dalton Av. SW6 —6B 78
High Holborn. WC1 —5D 66
High Timber St. EC4 —7B 68
Highway, The. E1 & E14 —1K 77
Hilary Clo. SW6 —7F 79
Hilborough Ct. E8 —2J 61
Hildyard Rd. SW6 —5E 78
Hilgrove Rd. NW6 —1J 55
Hillery Clo. SE17 —2E 84
Hillgate Pl. W8 —2D 70
Hillgate St. W8 —2D 70
Hillingdon St. SE5 & SE17 —7K 83
Hill Rd. NW8 —6J 55
Hillsborough Ct. NW6 —3F 55
Hillside Clo. NW8 —4G 55
Hillsleigh Rd. W8 —2C 70
Hills Pl. W1 —6K 65
Hill St. W1 —2G 73
Hind Ct. EC4 —6J 67
Hinde M. W1 —5G 65
Hinde St. W1 —5G 65
Hindmarsh Clo. E1 —7K 69
Hippodrome M. W11 —1A 70
Hippodrome Pl. W11 —1A 70
Hobart Pl. SW1 —7H 73
Hobbs Pl. N1 —3F 61
Hobbs Pl. Est. N1 —3F 61
Hobson's Pl. E1 —3K 69
Hobury St. SW10 —6J 79
Hocker St. E2 —7H 61
Hofland Rd. W14 —6A 70
Hogan M. W2 —3K 63
Hogarth Ct. EC3 —6G 69
Hogarth Houses. E1 —5K 69
Hogarth Pl. SW5 —2F 79
Hogarth Rd. SW5 —2F 79
Holbeck Row. SE15 —7K 85
Holbein M. SW1 —3F 81
Holbein Pl. SW1 —2F 81
Holborn. EC1 —4H 67
Holborn Cir. EC1 —4J 67
Holborn Pl. WC1 —4F 67
Holborn Viaduct. EC1 —4J 67
Holcroft Ct. W1 —3K 65
Holden Ho. N1 —3B 60
Holford Pl. WC1 —6G 59
Holford St. WC1 —6H 59
Holford Yd. WC1 —6H 59
Holland Gdns. W14 —6A 70
Holland Gro. SW9 —7J 83
Holland La. W14 —6C 70
Holland Pk. W11 —3A 70
Holland Pk. Av. W11 —3A 70
Holland Pk. Gdns. W14 —3A 70
Holland Pk. M. W11 —3A 70
Holland Pk. Rd. W14 —7B 70
Holland Pas. N1 —2B 60
Holland Pl. W8 —4F 71
Holland Pl. Chambers. W8 —4F 71
Holland Rd. W14 —5A 70
Holland St. SE1 —2A 76
Holland St. W8 —5E 70
Holland Vs. Rd. W14 —4A 70
Holland Wlk. W8 —3C 70
Hollen St. W1 —5B 66
Holles St. W1 —5J 65
Holly M. SW10 —4J 79
Holly St. E8 —1J 61
Hollywood M. SW10 —5H 79
Hollywood Rd. SW10 —5H 79
Holman Hunt Ho. W6 —4A 78
Holmead Rd. SW6 —7G 79
Holmes Pl. SW10 —5J 79
Holmes Ter. SE1 —4H 75
Holsworthy Sq. WC1 —2G 67
Holyoak Rd. SE11 —2A 84
Holyrood St. SE1 —3F 77
Holywell La. EC2 —1G 69
Holywell Row. EC2 —2F 69
Homefield St. N1 —5F 61
Homer Row. W1 —4C 64
Homer St. W1 —4C 64
Homestead Rd. SW6 —7B 78
Honduras St. EC1 —1B 68
Honey La. EC2 —6C 68
Honiton Rd. NW6 —4B 54
Hood Ct. EC4 —6J 67
Hooper's Ct. SW3 —5D 72
Hooper Sq. E1 —6K 69
Hooper St. E1 —6K 69
Hopefield Av. NW6 —4A 54
Hopetown St. E1 —4J 69
Hopewell St. SE5 —7E 84
Hop Gdns. WC2 —1D 74
Hopkinsons Pl. NW1 —2F 57
Hopkins St. W1 —6A 66
Hopton's Gdns. SE1 —2A 76
Hopton St. SE1 —2A 76
Hopwood Rd. SE17 —5E 84
Horatio St. E2 —5J 61
Horbury Cres. W11 —1D 70
Horbury M. W11 —1C 70
Hordle Promenade E. SE15 —7J 85
Hordle Promenade N. SE15 —7H 85
Hordle Promenade S. SE15 —7G 85
Hordle Promenade W. SE15 —7G 85
Hormead Rd. W9 —2B 62
Hornbeam Clo. SE11 —1H 83
Hornby Clo. NW3 —1A 56
Hornby Ho. SE11 —5H 83
Horner Ho. N1 —4G 61
Hornton Pl. W8 —5E 70
Hornton St. W8 —4E 70
Horse & Dolphin Yd. W1 —7C 66
Horseferry Rd. SW1 —7B 74
Horseferry Rd. Est. SW1 —7B 74
Horseguards Av. SW1 —3D 74
Horse Guards Rd. SW1 —3C 74
Horselydown La. SE1 —4H 77
Horse Ride. SW1 —4K 73
Horse Shoe Yd. W1 —7J 65
Horse Yd. N1 —2A 60
Horsley St. SE17 —5D 84
Horsman St. SE5 —6C 84
Hortensia Rd. SW10 —7H 79
Horton Ho. SW8 —7F 83
Horton Ho. W6 —4A 78 (off Field Rd.)
Hosier La. EC1 —4K 67
Hotspur St. SE11 —3H 83
Houghton St. WC2 —6G 67
Houndsditch. EC3 —5G 69
Houseman Way. SE5 —7E 84
Howard Bldgs. E1 —3K 69
Howell Wlk. SE17 —2A 84
Howick Pl. SW1 —7A 74
Howie St. SW11 —7B 80
Howland M. E. W1 —3A 66
Howland St. W1 —3K 65
Howley Pl. W2 —3J 63
How's St. E2 —4H 61
Hoxton Mkt. N1 —7F 61
Hoxton Sq. N1 —7F 61
Hoxton St. N1 —3F 61
Hudson's Pl. SW1 —1K 81
Huggin Ct. EC4 —7C 68
Huggin Hill. EC4 —7C 68
Hugh Astor Ct. SE1 —6A 76
Hugh Dalton Ho. SW6 —6B 78
Hugh Gaitskell Clo. SW6 —6B 78
Hugh Gaitskell Ho. SW6 —7B 78
Hugh M. SW1 —2J 81
Hugh St. SW1 —2J 81
Huguenot Pl. E1 —3J 69
Hullbridge M. N1 —2D 60
Hull St. EC1 —7B 60
Hulme Pl. SE1 —5C 76
Humbolt Rd. W6 —6A 78
Humphrey St. SE1 —3H 85
Hungerford La. WC2 —2D 74
Hunter Clo. SE1 —7E 76
Hunter St. WC1 —1E 66
Huntingdon St. N1 —1F 59
Huntley St. WC1 —2A 66
Hunton St. E1 —2K 69
Hunt's Ct. WC2 —1C 74
Huntsman St. SE17 —2F 85
Huntsworth M. NW1 —1D 64
Hurdwick Pl. NW1 —4K 57 (off Harrington Sq.)
Hurley Ho. SE11 —2J 83
Huson Clo. NW3 —1B 56
Hutton St. EC4 —6K 67
Huxley St. W10 —7A 54
Hyde Park Corner. (Junct.) —4G 73
Hyde Pk. Corner. W1 —4G 73
Hyde Pk. Cres. W2 —6B 64
Hyde Pk. Gdns. W2 —7A 64
Hyde Pk. Gdns. M. W2 —7A 64
Hyde Pk. Ga. SW7 —5H 71 (in two parts)
Hyde Pk. Ga. M. SW7 —5J 71
Hyde Pk. Mans. NW1 —4B 64
Hyde Pk. Pl. W2 —7C 64
Hyde Pk. Sq. W2 —6B 64
Hyde Pk. Sq. M. W2 —6B 64
Hyde Pk. St. W2 —6B 64
Hyde Pk. Towers. W2 —1H 71
Hyde Rd. N1 —3E 60

Ian Bowater Ct. N1 —6E 60
Ibberton Ho. SW8 —7F 83
Idol La. EC3 —1F 77
Ifield Rd. SW10 —5G 79
Ilbert St. W10 —7A 54
Ilchester Gdns. W2 —7F 63
Ilchester Pl. W14 —6B 70
Iliffe St. SE17 —3A 84
Iliffe Yd. SE17 —3A 84
Imber St. N1 —3D 60
Imperial College Rd. SW7 —7K 71
Imperial Ct. NW8 —4C 56
Imperial Pde. EC4 —6K 67
India Pl. WC2 —7F 67
India St. EC3 —6H 69
Infirmary Ct. SW3 —5E 80
Ingestre Pl. W1 —6A 66
Inglebert St. EC1 —6H 59
Ingoldisthorpe Gro. SE15 —5J 85
Ingram Clo. SE11 —1G 83
Inigo Pl. WC2 —7E 66
Inkerman Ter. W8 —7E 70
Inner Circ. NW1 —7F 57
Inner Temple La. EC4 —6H 67
Innis Ho. SE17 —3F 85
Insurance Ho. WC1 —7H 59
Inver Ct. W2 —6G 63
Inverness Gdns. W8 —3F 71
Inverness M. W2 —7G 63
Inverness Pl. W2 —7G 63
Inverness St. NW1 —2H 57
Inverness Ter. W2 —6G 63
Invicta Plaza. SE1 —2K 75
Inville Rd. SE17 —4E 84
Inville Wlk. SE17 —5E 84
Inworth Wlk. N1 —2B 60
Ion Ct. E2 —5K 61
Ion Sq. E2 —5K 61
Ipsden Bldgs. SE1 —4J 75
Ireland Yd. EC4 —6A 68
Ironmonger La. EC2 —6C 68
Ironmonger Pas. EC1 —7C 60
Ironmonger Row. EC1 —7C 60
Irving Ho. SE17 —4K 83
Irving Mans. W14 —5A 78
Irving St. WC2 —1C 74
Isabella Ho. SE11 —3K 83
Isabella St. SE1 —3K 75
Islington Grn. N1 —3K 59
Islington High St. N1 —5J 59
Islington Pk. St. N1 —1J 59
Ivatt Pl. W14 —4C 78
Iveagh Ct. E1 —6H 69
Iverna Ct. W8 —6E 70
Iverna Gdns. W8 —6E 70
Ives St. SW3 —1C 80
Ivimey St. E2 —6K 61
Ivor Pl. NW1 —2D 64
Ivor St. NW1 —1K 57
Ivory Ho. E1 —2J 77
Ivybridge La. WC2 —1E 74
Ivychurch La. SE17 —3H 85
Ivy St. N1 —4F 61
Ixworth Pl. SW3 —3B 80

Jacaranda Gro. E8 —1J 61
Jacob St. SE1 —4J 77
Jacob's Well M. W1 —5G 65
Jago Wlk. SE5 —7D 84
Jamaica Rd. SE1 & SE16 —5J 77
James Anderson Ct. E2 —4G 61
James Collins Clo. W9 —2B 62
James Hammett Ho. E2 —6J 61
Jameson Ho. SE11 —3F 83
Jameson St. W8 —2E 70
James Stewart Ho. NW6 —1C 54
James St. W1 —5G 65
James St. WC2 —6E 66
Jamestown Rd. NW1 —2H 57
Jason Ct. W1 —5G 65
Jasper Wlk. N1 —6D 60
Java Wharf. SE1 —4J 77
Jay M. SW7 —5J 71
Jeffrey's Pl. NW1 —1K 57
Jeffrey's St. NW1 —1J 57
Jeger Av. E2 —3H 61
Jegrove Ct. EC1 —4J 67
Jennifer Ho. SE11 —2J 83
Jephson Ho. SE17 —5K 83
Jerdan Pl. SW6 —7D 78
Jermyn St. SW1 —2K 73 (in two parts)
Jerome Cres. NW8 —1B 64
Jerome St. E1 —3H 69
Jerrold St. N1 —5G 61
Jerusalem Pas. EC1 —2K 67
Jervis Ct. W1 —6J 65
Jesson Ho. SE17 —2D 84
Jessop Ct. N1 —5A 60
Jewry St. EC3 —6H 69
Jim Griffiths Ho. SW6 —6B 78
Joan St. SE1 —3K 75
Jocelin Ho. N1 —3G 59
Jockey's Fields. WC1 —3G 67
Johanna St. SE1 —5H 75
John Adam St. WC2 —1E 74
John Aird Ct. W2 —3J 63
John Carpenter St. EC4 —7K 67
John Felton Rd. SE16 —5K 77
John Fisher St. E1 —7K 69
John Islip St. SW1 —3C 82
John Knight Lodge. SW6 —7E 78
John Maurice Clo. SE17 —1D 84
John McKenna Wlk. SE16 —6K 77
John Parry Ct. N1 —4G 61
John Prince's St. W1 —5J 65
John Pritchard Ho. E1 —2K 69
John Roll Way. SE16 —6K 77
John Ruskin St. SE5 —7K 83
John's M. WC1 —2G 67
John Smith Av. SW6 —7B 78
Johnson Clo. E8 —2K 61
Johnson Mans. W14 —5A 78
Johnson's Ct. EC4 —6J 67
Johnson's Pl. SW1 —4K 81
John Strachey Ho. SW6 —6C 78
John St. WC1 —2G 67
John Trundle Ct. EC2 —3B 68
John Trundle Highwalk. EC2 —3B 68
John Wesley Highwalk. EC2 —4B 68
John Wheatley Ho. SW6 —6C 78
Jonathan St. SE11 —3F 83
Jones St. W1 —1H 73
Jordan Ho. N1 —3E 60
Joseph Pas. SE1 —3G 77
Joseph Trotter Clo. EC1 —7J 59
Jowett St. SE15 —7J 85
Jubilee Bldgs. NW8 —3K 55
Jubilee Ho. SE11 —2J 83
Jubilee Ho. WC1 —1F 67
Jubilee Pl. SW3 —3C 80
Jubilee Walkway. SE1 —1A 76
Judd St. WC1 —6D 58
Juer St. SW11 —7C 80
Juliet Ho. N1 —5F 61
Junction M. W2 —5B 64
Junction Pl. W2 —5B 64
Juniper Ct. W8 —7F 71
Juniper Cres. NW1 —1G 57
Justice Wlk. SW3 —6B 80
Juxon St. SE11 —1G 83

Katherine Sq. W11 —2A 70
Kay St. E2 —4K 61
Kean Ho. SE17 —5K 83
Kean St. WC2 —6F 67
Keats Clo. SE1 —2H 85
Keats Ho. SE5 —7C 84
Keats Pl. EC2 —4D 68
Keeley St. WC2 —6F 67
Kellett Ho. N1 —3F 61
Kell St. SE1 —6A 76
Kelly M. W9 —3C 62
Kelso Pl. W8 —6G 71
Kember St. N1 —1F 59
Kemble Ct. SE15 —7G 85
Kemble St. WC2 —6F 67
Kempe Rd. NW6 —5A 54
Kempsford Gdns. SW5 —4E 78
Kempsford Rd. SE11 —2J 83 (in two parts)
Kenchester Clo. SW8 —7E 82
Kendal Clo. SW9 —7K 83
Kendall Pl. W1 —4F 65
Kendal Steps. W2 —6C 64
Kendal St. W2 —6C 64
Kendrick M. SW7 —1K 79
Kendrick Pl. SW7 —2K 79
Kenilworth Rd. NW6 —2C 54
Kenley Wlk. W11 —2A 70
Kennedy Ho. SE11 —3F 83
Kennedy Wlk. SE17 —2E 84
Kenneth Ct. SE11 —1J 83
Kenneth Younger Ho. SW6 —6C 78
Kennet Rd. W9 —1C 62
Kennet St. E1 —2K 77
Kennett Wharf La. EC4 —7C 68
Kennings Way. SE11 —3J 83
Kennington Grn. SE11 —4H 83
Kennington Gro. SE11 —5G 83
Kennington La. SE11 —4F 83
Kennington Oval. (Junct.) —6H 83
Kennington Oval. SE11 —5G 83
Kennington Pal. Ct. SE11 —3H 83
Kennington Pk. Gdns. SE11 —5K 83
Kennington Pk. Ho. SE11 —4J 83
Kennington Pk. Pl. SE11 —5J 83
Kennington Pk. Rd. SE11 —7H 83
Kennington Rd. SE1 & SE11 —6H 75
Kenrick Pl. W1 —3F 65
Kensal Rd. W10 —1A 62
Kensington Arc. W8 —5F 71
Kensington Cen. W14 —1A 78 (in two parts)
Kensington Chu. Ct. W8 —5F 71
Kensington Chu. St. W8 —2E 70
Kensington Chu. Wlk. W8 —5F 71
Kensington Ct. W8 —5G 71
Kensington Ct. Gdns. W8 —6G 71
Kensington Ct. M. W8 —6G 71
Kensington Ct. Pl. W8 —6G 71
Kensington Gdns. Sq. W2 —6F 63
Kensington Ga. W8 —6H 71
Kensington Gore. SW7 —5J 71
Kensington Hall Gdns. W14 —3B 78
Kensington Heights. W8 —3D 70
Kensington High St. W14 & W8 —1B 78
Kensington Mall. W8 —2E 70
Kensington Mans. SW5 —3E 78
Kensington Pal. Gdns. W8 —2F 71
Kensington Pk. Gdns. W11 —1B 70
Kensington Pk. M. W11 —6B 62
Kensington Pk. Rd. W11 —6B 62
Kensington Pl. W8 —3D 70
Kensington Rd. W8 & SW7 —5J 71
Kensington Sq. W8 —5F 71
Kensington W. W14 —1A 78
Kensworth Ho. EC1 —7E 60
Kent Ct. E2 —4J 61
Kent Ho. SE1 —4J 85
Kentish Bldgs. SE1 —3D 76
Kentish Town Rd. NW1 & NW5 —2J 57
Kenton Ct. W14 —7B 70
Kenton St. WC1 —1D 66
Kent Pas. NW1 —1D 64
Kent St. E2 —4J 61
Kent Ter. NW1 —7C 56
Kent Yd. SW7 —5C 72
Kenway Rd. SW5 —2F 79
Kenwrick Ho. N1 —3G 59
Kenyon Mans. W14 —5A 78
Keppel Row. SE1 —3B 76

Keppel St.—Mill St.

Keppel St. WC1 —3C 66
Kerbela St. E2 —1K 69
Kevan Ho. SE5 —7B 84
Key Ho. SE11 —5H 83
Keyse Rd. SE1 —7H 77
Keystone Cres. N1 —5E 58
Keyworth Pl. SE1 —6A 76
Keyworth St. SE1 —6A 76
Kibworth St. SW8 —7F 83
Kiffen St. EC2 —1E 68
Kilburn Bri. NW6 —3E 54
Kilburn Ga. NW6 —4F 55
Kilburn High Rd. NW6 —1C 54
Kilburn La. W10 & W9 —6A 54
Kilburn Pk. Rd. NW6 —7D 54
Kilburn Pl. NW6 —3E 54
Kilburn Priory. NW6 —3F 55
Kilburn Sq. NW6 —2D 54
Kilburn Va. NW6 —3F 55
Kilburn Va. Est. NW6 —2E 54
Kildare Gdns. W2 —5E 62
Kildare Ter. W2 —5E 62
Killick St. N1 —4F 59
Kilner Ho. SE11 —5H 83
Kilravock St. W10 —7A 54
Kimberley Rd. NW6 —2A 54
Kimbolton Ct. SW3 —2B 80
Kincardine Gdns. W9 —2D 62
Kinder Ho. N1 —4E 60
Kindersley Ho. E1 —6K 69
King & Queen St. SE17 —3C 84
King Charles Ho. SW6 —7G 79
(off Wandon Rd.)
King Charles St. SW1 —4C 74
King Edward Mans. SW6 —7D 78
King Edward St. EC1 —5B 68
King Edward Wlk. SE1 —6J 75
King Henry's Rd. NW3 —1A 56
Kinghorn St. EC1 —4B 68
King James Ct. SE1 —5A 76
King James St. SE1 —5A 76
King John Ct. EC2 —1G 69
Kinglake Est. SE17 —3G 85
Kinglake St. SE17 —4F 85
Kingly Ct. W1 —7A 66
Kingly St. W1 —6K 65
Kings Arms Ct. E1 —4K 69
Kings Arms Yd. EC2 —5D 68
King's Bench St. SE1 —4A 76
King's Bench Wlk. EC4 —7J 67
King's College Rd. NW3 —1B 56
Kingscote St. EC4 —7K 67
King's Ct. SE1 —4A 76
Kings Ct. N. SW3 —4B 80
Kings Ct. S. SW3 —4B 80
Kings Cross. (Junct.) —6D 58
King's Cross Bri. N1 —6E 58
King's Cross Rd. WC1 —6F 59
King's Gdns. NW6 —1E 54
Kingsgate Pde. SW1 —7A 74
Kingsgate Pl. NW6 —1D 54
Kingsgate Rd. NW6 —1D 54
King's Head Yd. SE1 —3D 76
Kings Ho. SW8 —7E 82
(off S. Lambeth Rd.)
Kingsland Rd. E2 & E8 —7G 61
Kingsley Flats. SE1 —1F 85
Kingsley Ho. SW3 —6A 80
Kingsley M. W8 —7G 71
Kingsley Rd. NW6 —2C 54
King's M. WC1 —2G 67
Kingsmill Ter. NW8 —4A 56
King's Pl. SE1 —5B 76
King Sq. EC1 —7B 60
Kings Reach Tower. SE1 —2K 75
King's Rd. SW3 —4C 80
King's Rd. SW6 & SW10 —7G 79
King's Scholars' Pas. SW1 —7K 73
King's Ter. NW1 —3K 57
Kingston Ho. NW6 —1A 54
Kingstown St. NW1 —2F 57
(in two parts)
King St. EC2 —6C 68
King St. SW1 —3A 74
King St. WC2 —7D 66
Kings Wlk. Shop. Cen. SW3 —3D 80
Kingsway. WC2 —5F 67
Kingswood Av. NW6 —3A 54
Kingswood Clo. SW8 —7E 82
Kingswood Ct. NW6 —1E 54
King William St. EC4 —7E 68
Kingwood Rd. SW6 —7A 78
Kinnerton Pl. N. SW1 —5E 72
Kinnerton Pl. S. SW1 —5E 72
Kinnerton St. SW1 —5F 73
Kinnerton Yd. SW1 —5F 73
Kinnoul Rd. W6 —5A 78
Kintore Way. SE1 —1H 85
Kipling Est. SE1 —5E 76
Kipling Ho. SE5 —7C 84
Kipling St. SE1 —5E 76
Kirby Gro. SE1 —4F 77
Kirby St. EC1 —3J 67
Kirkman Pl. W1 —4B 66
Kirk St. WC1 —2G 67
Kirtling St. SW8 —7A 82
Kirton Gdns. E2 —7J 61
Kirwyn Way. SE5 —7B 84
Kite Pl. E2 —6K 61
Kitson Rd. SE5 —7C 84
Knaresborough Pl. SW5 —1F 79
Knightrider Ct. EC4 —7B 68
Knightrider St. EC4 —7A 68
Knight's Arc. SW1 —5D 72
Knightsbridge. SW7 & SW1 —5C 72
Knightsbridge Ct. SW1 —5E 72
Knightsbridge Grn. SW1 —5D 72
Knights Wlk. SE11 —2K 83
Knivet Rd. SW6 —6D 78
Knox St. W1 —3D 64
Kramer M. SW5 —4E 78
Krupnik Pl. EC2 —1G 69
Kynance M. SW7 —7G 71
Kynance Pl. SW7 —7H 71
Laburnum Ct. E2 —3H 61
Laburnum St. E2 —3H 61
Lackington St. EC2 —3E 68
Lackland Ho. SE1 —3J 85
Lacland Pl. SW10 —7K 79
Ladbroke Cres. W11 —6A 62
Ladbroke Gdns. W11 —7B 62
Ladbroke Gro. W10 & W11 —3A 62
Ladbroke M. W11 —3A 70
Ladbroke Rd. W11 —2A 70
Ladbroke Sq. W11 —1C 70
Ladbroke Ter. W11 —1C 70
Ladbroke Wlk. W11 —2C 70
Lafone St. SE1 —4H 77
Laing Ho. SE5 —7B 84
Lakeside Ter. EC2 —3C 68
Lambert Jones M. EC2 —3B 68
Lambert St. N1 —1H 59
Lambeth Bri. SW1 & SE1 —1E 82
Lambeth High St. SE1 —2F 83
Lambeth Hill. EC4 —7B 68
Lambeth Pal. Rd. SE1 —7F 75
Lambeth Rd. SE1 & SE11 —1F 83
Lambeth Towers. SE11 —7H 75
Lambeth Wlk. SE11 —1G 83
Lamb's Bldgs. EC1 —2D 68
Lamb's Conduit Pas. WC1 —3F 67
Lamb's Conduit St. WC1
(in three parts) —2F 67
Lamb's M. N1 —3K 59
Lamb's Pas. EC1 —3D 68
Lamb St. E1 —3H 69
Lambton Pl. W11 —7C 62
Lamb Wlk. SE1 —5F 77
Lamlash St. SE11 —1K 83
Lamont Rd. SW10 —6J 79
Lamont Rd. Pas. SW10 —6K 79
Lampern Sq. E2 —6K 61
Lampeter Sq. W6 —6A 78
Lamp Office Ct. WC1 —2F 67
Lamps Ct. SE5 —7B 84
Lanark Ho. SE1 —4K 85
(off Old Kent Rd.)
Lanark Pl. W9 —1J 63
Lanark Rd. W9 —5G 55
Lancashire Ct. W1 —7J 65
Lancaster Clo. N1 —1G 61
Lancaster Clo. W2 —1F 71
Lancaster Ct. SW6 —7C 78
Lancaster Ga. W2 —1H 71
Lancaster M. W2 —7J 63
Lancaster Pl. WC2 —7F 67
Lancaster Rd. W11 —6A 62
Lancaster St. SE1 —5K 75
Lancaster Ter. W2 —7K 63
Lancaster Wlk. W2 —1J 71
Lancefield Ct. W10 —5A 54
Lancefield St. W10 —7B 54
Lancelot Pl. SW7 —5D 72
Lancer Sq. W8 —4F 71
Lancing St. NW1 —7B 58
Lancresse Ct. N1 —2F 61
Landon Pl. SW1 —6D 72
Landulph Ho. SE11 —3J 83
Lanesborough Pl. SW1 —4G 73
Lane, The. NW8 —5H 55
Lanfrey Pl. W14 —4B 78
Langdale Clo. SE17 —5B 84
Langdon Ct. EC1 —5A 60
Langdon Way. SE1 —2K 85
Langford Clo. NW8 —4J 55
Langford Ct. NW8 —5J 55
Langford Pl. NW8 —4J 55
Langham Mans. SW5 —4F 79
Langham Pl. W1 —4J 65
Langham St. W1 —4J 65
Langhorne Ct. NW8 —1K 55
Lang Ho. SW8 —7D 82
Langland Ho. SE5 —7E 84
Langley Ct. WC2 —7D 66
Langley La. SW8 —5E 82
Langley Mans. SW8 —5F 83
Langley St. WC2 —6D 66
Langmore Ho. E1 —6K 69
Langthorn Ct. EC2 —5E 68
Langton Clo. WC1 —1G 67
Langton Rd. SW9 —7A 84
Langton St. SW10 —6J 79
Langtry Pl. SW6 —5E 78
Langtry Rd. NW8 —3F 55
Langtry Wlk. NW8 —2G 55
Lanhill Rd. W9 —1D 62
Lannoy Point. SW6 —7A 78
Lansdowne Cres. W11 —1A 70
Lansdowne Dri. E8 —1K 61
Lansdowne M. W11 —3B 70
Lansdowne Pl. SE1 —6E 76
Lansdowne Ri. W11 —1A 70
Lansdowne Rd. W11 —1A 70
Lansdowne Row. W1 —2J 73
Lansdowne Ter. WC1 —2E 66
Lansdowne Wlk. W11 —2A 70
Lant St. SE1 —4B 76
Lapford Clo. W9 —1C 62
Larcom St. SE17 —2B 84
Larissa St. SE17 —4E 84
Latham Ct. SW5 —2D 78
Latona Rd. SE15 —6K 85
Lauderdale Mans. W9 —7F 55
Lauderdale Pl. EC2 —3B 68
(off Barbican)
Lauderdale Rd. W9 —7F 55
Lauderdale Tower. EC2 —3B 68
Laud St. SE11 —3F 83
Launcelot St. SE1 —5H 75
Launceston Pl. W8 —6H 71
Laundry La. N1 —1B 60
Laundry Rd. W6 —6A 78
Laurence Pountney Hill. EC4 —7D 68
Laurence Pountney La. EC4 —1D 76
Lavender Clo. SW3 —6A 80
Lavender Gro. E8 —1J 61
Laverton M. SW5 —2G 79
Laverton Pl. SW5 —2G 79
Lavina Gro. N1 —4F 59
Lavington St. SE1 —3A 76
Lawford Rd. N1 —1F 61
Lawn La. SW8 —5E 82
Lawrence La. EC2 —6C 68
Lawrence Pl. N1 —3E 58
Lawrence St. SW3 —6B 80
Law St. SE1 —6E 76
Laxley Clo. SE5 —7A 84
Laxton Pl. NW1 —1J 65
Laystall St. EC1 —2H 67
Layton Rd. N1 —4J 59
Layton's Bldgs. SE1 —4D 76
Lazenby Ct. WC2 —7D 66
Leadenhall Mkt. EC3 —6F 69
Leadenhall Pl. EC3 —6F 69
Leadenhall St. EC3 —6F 69
Leake Ct. SE1 —5G 75
Leake St. SE1 —4G 75
Leamington Rd. Vs. W11 —4C 62
Leary Ho. SE11 —4G 83
Leather La. EC1 —3H 67
(in two parts)
Leathermarket Ct. SE1 —5F 77
Leathermarket St. SE1 —5F 77
Lecky St. SW7 —3K 79
Ledbury M. N. W11 —7D 62
Ledbury M. W. W11 —7D 62
Ledbury Rd. W11 —5C 62
Lee Ho. EC2 —4C 68
Leeke St. WC1 —6F 59
Lees Pl. W1 —7F 65
Lee St. E8 —2H 61
Left Ho. NW6 —1A 54
Leicester Ct. WC2 —7C 66
Leicester Pl. WC2 —7C 66
Leicester Sq. WC2 —1C 74
Leicester St. WC2 —7C 66
Leigh Pl. EC1 —3H 67
Leigh St. WC1 —1D 66
Leinster Gdns. W2 —6H 63
Leinster M. W2 —1H 71
Leinster Pl. W2 —6H 63
Leinster Rd. NW6 —6D 54
Leinster Sq. W2 —6E 62
Leinster Ter. W2 —7H 63
Leith Mans. W9 —7F 55
Leitia Clo. E8 —3K 61
Leman Pas. E1 —6K 69
Leman St. E1 —6J 69
Len Freeman Pl. SW6 —7B 78
Lennox Gdns. SW1 —7D 72
Lennox Gdns. M. SW1 —7D 72
Lenthall Rd. E8 —1J 61
Leonard Ct. WC1 —1D 66
Leonard St. EC2 —1E 68
Leontine Clo. SE15 —7K 85
Leopards Ct. EC1 —3H 67
Leo Yd. EC1 —2A 68
Leroy St. SE1 —1F 85
Leslie Prince Ct. SE5 —7D 84
Letterstone Rd. SW6 —7B 78
Leverett St. SW3 —1C 80
Leverington Pl. N1 —7F 61
Lever St. EC1 —7A 60
Lewen's Ct. EC1 —1B 68
Lewisham St. SW1 —5C 74
Lexham Gdns. W8 —1E 78
Lexham Gdns. M. W8 —7G 71
Lexham M. W8 —1E 78
Lexham Wlk. W8 —7G 71
Lexington Apartments. EC1 —1E 68
Lexington St. W1 —6A 66
Leybourne Rd. NW1 —1J 57
Leybourne St. NW1 —1H 57
Leyden St. E1 —4H 69
Library St. SE1 —5K 75
Lickey Ho. W14 —5C 78
Lidlington Pl. NW1 —5A 58
Light Horse Ct. SW3 —4F 81
Ligonier St. E2 —1H 69
Lilac Pl. SE11 —2F 83
Lilestone St. NW8 —1B 64
Lilley Clo. E1 —3K 77
Lillie Mans. SW6 —6A 78
Lillie Rd. SW6 —7A 78
Lillie Yd. SW6 —5E 78
Lillington Gdns. Est. SW1 —2A 82
Lily Clo. W14 —3A 78
Lily Pl. EC1 —3J 67
Limeburner La. EC4 —6K 67
Lime Clo. E1 —2K 77
Limerston St. SW10 —5J 79
Limes, The. W2 —1E 70
Lime St. EC3 —7F 69
Lime St. Pas. EC3 —7F 69
Lincoln Ho. SW3 —5D 72
Lincoln Ho. SW9 & SE5 —7J 83
Lincoln M. NW6 —2B 54
Lincoln's Inn Fields. WC2 —5F 67
Lincoln St. SW3 —2D 80
Linden Gdns. W2 —1E 70
Linden M. W2 —1E 70
Lindley Est. SE15 —7K 85
Lindsay Sq. SW1 —3C 82
Lindsey M. N1 —1C 60
Lindsey St. EC1 —3A 68
Linhope St. NW1 —1D 64
Link Rd. E1 —7K 69
Links Yd. E1 —3K 69
Linkwood Wlk. NW1 —1C 58
Linsey St. SE16 —7K 77
(in two parts)
Linslade Ho. E2 —3K 61
Lintaine Clo. W6 —6A 78
Linton St. N1 —3C 60
Lion Ct. N1 —3F 59
Lion Ct. SE1 —3G 77
Lionel M. W10 —3A 62
Lisgar Ter. W14 —1B 78
Liskeard Ho. SE11 —3J 83
Lisle St. WC2 —7C 66
Lisson Grn. Est. NW8 —1B 64
Lisson Gro. NW8 & NW1 —7A 56
Lisson St. NW1 —3B 64
Listowel Clo. SW9 —7J 83
Litchfield St. WC2 —7C 66
Lit. Albany St. NW1 —7J 57
(in two parts)
Lit. Argyll St. W1 —6K 65
Lit. Britain. EC1 —4A 68
Lit. Boltons, The. SW5 & SW10 —3G 79
Lit. Chester St. SW1 —6H 73
Lit. Cloisters. SW1 —6D 74
Lit. College La. EC4 —7D 68
Lit. College St. SW1 —7D 74
Lit. Dean's Yd. SW1 —6D 74
Lit. Dorrit Ct. SE1 —4C 76
Lit. Edward St. NW1 —6J 57
Lit. Essex St. WC2 —7H 67
Lit. George St. SW1 —5D 74
Lit. Marlborough St. W1 —6K 65
Lit. Newport St. WC2 —7C 66
Lit. New St. EC4 —5J 67
Lit. Portland St. W1 —5J 65
Lit. Russell St. WC1 —4D 66
Lit. St James's St. SW1 —3K 73
Lit. Sanctuary. SW1 —5D 74
Lit. Smith St. SW1 —6C 74
Lit. Somerset St. E1 —6H 69
Lit. Titchfield St. W1 —4K 65
Lit. Trinity La. EC4 —7C 68
Lit. Turnstile. WC1 —4F 67
Livermere Rd. E8 —2H 61
Liverpool Gro. SE17 —4C 84
Liverpool Rd. N7 & N1 —2J 59
Liverpool St. EC2 —4F 69
Livesey Pl. SE15 —5K 85
Livingstone Ho. SE5 —7C 84
Livingstone Mans. W14 —5A 78
Livonia St. W1 —6A 66
Lizard St. EC1 —7C 60
Llewellyn St. SE16 —5K 77
Lloyd Baker M. WC1 —7G 59
Lloyd Baker St. WC1 —7G 59
Lloyd's Av. EC3 —6G 69
Lloyd Sq. WC1 —6H 59
Lloyd's Row. EC1 —6K 59
Lloyd St. WC1 —6H 59
Lloyds Wharf. SE1 —5J 77
Loanda Clo. E8 —2H 61
Lockbridge Ct. W9 —3D 62
Locksfields. SE17 —2E 84
Lockwood Ho. SE11 —6H 83
Lockyer Est. SE1 —5E 76
Lockyer St. SE1 —5E 76
Lodge Rd. NW8 —1A 64
Loftie St. SE16 —5K 77
Lofting Rd. N1 —1G 59
Logan M. W8 —1D 78
Logan Pl. W8 —1D 78
Lohmann Ho. SE11 —5H 83
Lolesworth Clo. E1 —4J 69
Lollard St. SE11 —1G 83
(in two parts)
Loman St. SE1 —4A 76
Lombard Ct. EC3 —7E 68
Lombard La. EC4 —6J 67
Lombard St. EC3 —6D 68
Lombardy Pl. W2 —1G 71
Lomond Gro. SE5 —7D 84
Loncroft Rd. SE5 —5G 85
London Bri. SE1 & EC4 —2E 76
London Bri. St. SE1 —3E 76
London Bri. Wlk. SE1 —2E 76
London Ho. NW8 —4C 56
London Ho. WC1 —1F 67
London M. W2 —6A 64
London Rd. SE1 —6K 75
London St. EC3 —7G 69
London St. W2 —5K 63
London Ter. E2 —5K 61
London Wall. EC2 —4B 68
London Wall Bldgs. EC2 —4E 68
Long Acre. WC2 —7D 66
Longfellow Way. SE1 —2J 85
Longfield Est. SE1 —2J 85
Longford St. NW1 —1J 65
Longhope Clo. SE15 —6H 85
Longland Ct. SE1 —3K 85
Longlands Ct. W11 —7C 62
Long La. EC1 —4A 68
Long La. SE1 —5D 76
Longley St. SE1 —2K 85
Longman Ho. E8 —3J 61
Longmoore St. SW1 —2K 81
Longridge Ho. SE1 —7C 76
Longridge Rd. SW5 —2D 78
Long's Ct. WC2 —1C 74
Longshott Ct. SW5 —2D 78
Long St. E2 —6H 61
(in two parts)
Longville Rd. SE11 —1K 83
Long Wlk. SE1 —6G 77
Long Yd. WC1 —2F 67
Lonsdale M. W11 —6C 62
Lonsdale Pl. N1 —1J 59
Lonsdale Rd. NW6 —4B 54
Lonsdale Rd. W11 —6B 62
Lonsdale Sq. N1 —1J 59
Lonsdale Yd. W11 —1D 70
Lorden Wlk. E2 —7K 61
Lord Hills Bri. W2 —4G 63
Lord Hills Rd. W2 —3G 63
Lord N. St. SW1 —7D 74
Lord Roberts M. SW6 —7F 79
Lordship Pl. SW3 —6B 80
Lords Vw. One. NW8 —7B 56
Lorenzo St. WC1 —6F 59
Lorne Clo. NW8 —7C 56
Lorrimore Rd. SE17 —6A 84
Lorrimore Sq. SE17 —5A 84
Lothbury. EC2 —5D 68
Lothrop St. W10 —6A 54
Lots Rd. SW10 —7H 79
Loudoun Rd. NW8 —3J 55
Loughborough St. SE11 —3G 83
Lovat La. EC3 —1F 77
Lovegrove St. SE1 —4K 85
Love La. EC2 —5C 68
Lovell Ho. E8 —2K 61
Lovers' Wlk. W1 —2F 73
Lowell Ho. SE5 —7C 84
Lwr. Addison Gdns. W14 —5A 70
Lwr. Belgrave St. SW1 —7H 73
Lwr. Clarendon Wlk. W11 —6A 62
Lwr. Grosvenor Pl. SW1 —6J 73
Lwr. James St. W1 —7A 66
Lwr. John St. W1 —7A 66
Lwr. Marsh. SE1 —5H 75
Lwr. Merton Ri. NW3 —1B 56
Lwr. Robert St. WC2 —1E 74
Lwr. Sloane St. SW1 —2F 81
Lwr. Thames St. EC3 —1E 76
Lowerwood Ct. W11 —6A 62
Lowndes Clo. SW1 —7G 73
Lowndes Ct. SW1 —6E 72
Lowndes Ct. W1 —6K 65
Lowndes Pl. SW1 —7F 73
Lowndes Sq. SW1 —5E 72
Lowndes St. SW1 —6E 72
Lowther Gdns. SW7 —6A 72
Loxham St. WC1 —7E 58
Lucan Ho. N1 —3E 60
Lucan Pl. SW3 —2B 80
Lucerne M. W8 —2E 70
Lucey Rd. SE16 —7K 77
Lucey Way. SE16 —7K 77
(in two parts)
Lucy Brown Ho. SE1 —3C 76
Ludgate B'way. EC4 —6K 67
Ludgate Cir. EC4 —6K 67
Ludgate Hill. EC4 —6K 67
Ludgate Sq. EC4 —6A 68
Ludlow St. EC1 —1B 68
Luke St. EC2 —1F 69
Lulworth. SE17 —3D 84
Lulworth Ho. SW8 —7F 83
Lumley Ct. WC2 —1E 74
Lumley Flats. SW1 —3F 81
Lumley St. W1 —6G 65
Lupus St. SW1 —5J 81
Luscombe Way. SW8 —7D 82
Luton St. NW8 —2A 64
Luxborough St. W1 —2F 65
Lyall M. SW1 —7F 73
Lyall M. W. SW1 —7F 73
Lyall St. SW1 —7F 73
Lydford Rd. W9 —1C 62
Lydney Clo. SE15 —7G 85
Lygon Pl. SW1 —7H 73
Lyme St. NW1 —1K 57
Lyme Ter. NW1 —1K 57
Lympstone Gdns. SE15 —7K 85
Lynbrook Clo. SE15 —7G 85
Lynton Est. SE1 —3K 85
Lynton Rd. NW6 —3C 54
Lynton Rd. SE1 —2H 85
Lyons Pl. NW8 —2K 63
Lyon St. N1 —1F 59
Lyons Wlk. W14 —1A 78
Lytham St. SE17 —4D 84
Lyttelton Clo. NW3 —1B 56
Mabledon Pl. WC1 —7C 58
Mablethorpe Rd. SW6 —7A 78
McAuley Clo. SE1 —6H 75
Macbeth Ho. N1 —4F 61
Macclesfield Ho. EC1 —7B 60
Macclesfield Rd. EC1 —6B 60
Macclesfield St. W1 —7C 66
McCoid Way. SE1 —5B 76
McConnell M. NW1 —7B 58
Mace St. SE1 —4H 77
Macfarren Pl. NW1 —2G 65
McGarvey Clo. NW8 —7J 55
McGlashon Ho. E1 —2K 69
McGregor Ct. N1 —6G 61
McGregor Rd. W11 —4B 62
Mcindoe M. N1 —2D 60
McKay Trad. Est. W10 —1A 62
Mackennal St. NW8 —5C 56
Macklin St. WC2 —5E 66
Mack's Rd. SE16 —1K 85
Mackworth St. NW1 —6K 57
McLeod's M. SW7 —7G 71
Macleod St. SE17 —4C 84
Maclise Rd. W14 —7A 70
Macroom Rd. W9 —6C 54
Maddock Way. SE17 —6A 84
Maddox St. W1 —7J 65
Madrigal La. SE5 —7A 84
Madron St. SE17 —3G 85
Magdalen Pas. E1 —7J 69
Magdalen St. SE1 —3F 77
Magee St. SE11 —5H 83
Magnin Clo. E8 —2K 61
Magpie All. EC4 —6J 67
Maguire St. SE1 —4J 77
Maida Av. W2 —3J 63
Maida Va. W9 —4F 55
Maiden La. NW1 —1C 58
Maiden La. SE1 —2C 76
Maiden La. WC2 —1E 74
Maidstone Bldgs. SE1 —3C 76
Mail Coach Yd. E2 —6G 61
Maismore St. SE15 —6K 85
Maitland Ct. W2 —7K 63
Makins St. SW3 —2C 80
Malcolm Ct. SE11 —2H 83
Malcolm Ho. N1 —5F 61
Maldon Clo. N1 —2B 60
Malet Pl. WC1 —2B 66
Malet St. WC1 —2B 66
Mallard Clo. NW6 —3D 54
Mall Chambers. W8 —2E 70
Mall Gallery. WC2 —6D 66
Mallon Gdns. E1 —5J 69
Mallord St. SW3 —5A 80
Mallory St. NW8 —1C 64
Mallow St. EC1 —1D 68
Mall, The. SW1 —3C 74
Malmsey Ho. SE11 —3G 83
Malta St. EC1 —1A 68
Maltby St. SE1 —5H 77
Maltings Pl. SE1 —5G 77
Malton M. W10 —5A 62
Malton Rd. W10 —5A 62
Maltravers St. WC2 —7H 67
Malt St. SE1 —5K 85
Malvern Clo. W10 —4B 62
Malvern Ct. SW7 —2B 80
Malvern M. NW6 —6D 54
Malvern Pl. NW6 —6C 54
Malvern Rd. E8 —1K 61
Malvern Rd. NW6 —5C 54
(in two parts)
Malvern Ter. N1 —2H 59
Manchester Dri. W10 —2A 62
Manchester Ho. SE17 —3C 84
Manchester M. W1 —4F 65
Manchester Sq. W1 —5G 65
Manchester St. W1 —4F 65
Manciple St. SE1 —5D 76
Mandela St. NW1 —2A 58
Mandela St. SW9 —7J 83
Mandela Way. SE1 —1F 85
Mandeville Pl. W1 —5G 65
Manette St. W1 —6C 66
Manley Ho. SE11 —3H 83
Manley St. NW1 —2F 57
Manneby Prior. N1 —5G 59
Manningford Clo. EC1 —6K 59
Manningtree St. E1 —5K 69
Manny Shinwell Ho. SW6 —6C 78
Manor M. NW6 —4E 54
Manor Pl. SE17 —4A 84
Manresa Rd. SW3 —4B 80
Mansell St. E1 —6J 69
Mansfield M. W1 —4H 65
Mansfield St. W1 —4H 65
Mansford St. E2 —5K 61
Mansion Ho. Pl. EC4 —6D 68
Mansion Ho. St. EC4 —6D 68
Mansions, The. SW5 —3F 79
Manson M. SW7 —2J 79
Manson Pl. SW7 —2K 79
Mapesbury Rd. NW2 —1A 54
Mapes Ho. NW6 —1A 54
Mapledene Est. E8 —1K 61
Mapledene Rd. E8 —1J 61
Maple M. NW6 —4F 55
Maple Pl. W1 —2A 66
Maple St. W1 —3K 65
Marban Rd. W9 —6B 54
Marble Arch. (Junct.) —7E 64
Marble Arch. W1 —7D 64
Marble Ho. W9 —2C 62
Marble Quay. E1 —2K 77
Marchant Ct. SE1 —3J 85
Marchbank Rd. W14 —5C 78
Marchmont St. WC1 —1D 66
Marcia Rd. SE1 —2G 85
Marco Polo Ho. SW8 —7H 81
Margaret Ct. W1 —5K 65
Margaret Herbison Ho. SW6 —6C 78
Margaret Ingham Clo. SW6
(off Rylston Rd.) —7B 78
Margaret St. W1 —5J 65
Margaretta Ter. SW3 —5B 80
Margery St. WC1 —7H 59
Margravine Gdns. W6 —3A 78
Marian Pl. E2 —3K 61
Marigold All. SE1 —1K 75
Marine St. SE16 —6K 77
Market Ct. W1 —5K 65
Market Entrance. SW8 —7A 82
Market M. W1 —3H 73
Market Pl. W1 —5K 65
Markham Pl. SW3 —3D 80
Markham Sq. SW3 —3D 80
Markham St. SW3 —3C 80
Mark La. EC3 —7G 69
Mark Sq. EC2 —1F 69
Mark St. EC2 —1F 69
Marlborough Av. E8 —3K 61
(in two parts)
Marlborough Clo. SE17 —2A 84
Marlborough Ct. W1 —7K 65
Marlborough Ct. W8 —1D 78
Marlborough Flats. SW3 —1C 80
Marlborough Ga. Stables. W2 —7K 63
Marlborough Gro. SE1 —4K 85
Marlborough Hill. NW8 —2K 55
Marlborough Pl. NW8 —5H 55
Marlborough Rd. SW1 —3A 74
Marlborough St. SW3 —2B 80
Marloes Rd. W8 —7F 71
Marlowes, The. NW8 —2K 55
Marmont Rd. SE15 —7K 85
Marne St. W10 —6A 54
Marshall Ho. N1 —4E 60
Marshall Ho. SE1 —7G 77
Marshall's Pl. SE16 —7J 77
Marshall St. W1 —6A 66
Marshalsea Rd. SE1 —4C 76
Marsham Ct. SW1 —1C 82
Marsham St. SW1 —7C 74
Marsland Clo. SE17 —4A 84
Marsom Ho. N1 —6D 60
Marston Clo. NW6 —1J 55
Martin Ho. SE1 —7C 76
Martin Ho. SW8 —7D 82
Martin La. EC4 —7E 68
Martlett Ct. WC2 —6E 66
Mart St. WC2 —7E 66
Marvell Ho. SE5 —7D 84
Marville Rd. SW6 —7C 78
Mary Grn. NW8 —2G 55
Marylands Rd. W9 —2E 62
Maryland Wlk. N1 —2B 60
Marylebone Flyover. (Junct.) —4B 64
Marylebone Flyover. W2 —4B 64
Marylebone High St. W1 —3G 65
Marylebone La. W1 —4G 65
Marylebone M. W1 —4H 65
Marylebone Pas. W1 —5A 66
Marylebone Rd. NW1 —3C 64
Marylebone St. W1 —4G 65
Marylee Way. SE11 —2G 83
Mary Macarthur Ho. W6 —5A 78
Mary Pl. W11 —1A 70
Mary Seacole Clo. E8 —3H 61
Mary St. N1 —3C 60
Mary Ter. NW1 —3J 57
Mason's Arms M. W1 —6J 65
Mason's Av. EC2 —5D 68
Mason's Pl. EC1 —6B 60
Mason St. SE17 —1E 84
Mason's Yd. SW1 —2A 74
Massinger St. SE17 —2F 85
Matheson Lang Ho. SE1 —5H 75
Matheson Rd. W14 —2B 78
Mathews Yd. WC2 —6D 66
Matilda St. N1 —3G 59
Matthew Parker St. SW1 —5C 74
Mattingley Way. SE15 —7H 85
Maudlins Grn. E1 —2K 77
Maunsel St. SW1 —1B 82
Mawbey Ho. SE1 —4J 85
Mawbey Pl. SE1 —4J 85
Mawbey Rd. SE1 —4J 85
Mawbey St. SW8 —7D 82
Maxwell Rd. SW6 —7F 79
Mayfair M. NW1 —1E 56
Mayfair Pl. W1 —2J 73
Mayfield Rd. E8 —1H 61
Maygood St. N1 —4H 59
Mayor Ho. N1 —3G 59
Mays Ct. WC2 —1D 74
May St. W14 —4C 78
Mazenod Av. NW6 —1E 54
Meadcroft Rd. SE11 —6K 83
(in two parts)
Meadowbank. NW3 —1D 56
Meadow Ct. N1 —4F 61
Meadow M. SW8 —6F 83
Meadow Pl. SW8 —7E 82
Meadow Rd. SW8 —7F 83
Meadow Row. SE1 —7B 76
Mead Row. SE1 —6H 75
Meakin Est. SE1 —6F 77
Meard St. W1 —6B 66
Mecklenburgh Pl. WC1 —1F 67
Mecklenburgh Sq. WC1 —1F 67
Mecklenburgh St. WC1 —1F 67
Medburn St. NW1 —4B 58
Medway St. SW1 —7B 74
Meek Rd. SW10 —7J 79
Melbourne Pl. WC2 —7G 67
Melbury Ct. W8 —6C 70
Melbury Dri. SE5 —7F 85
Melbury Ho. SW8 —7F 83
Melbury Rd. W14 —6B 70
Melbury Ter. NW1 —2C 64
Melcombe Ho. SW8 —7F 83
Melcombe Pl. NW1 —3D 64
Melcombe St. NW1 —2E 64
Melford Ct. SE1 —6H 77
Melina Pl. NW8 —7K 55
Melior Pl. SE1 —4F 77
Melior St. SE1 —4F 77
Melon Pl. W8 —4E 70
Melton Ct. SW7 —2A 80
Melton St. NW1 —7A 58
Melville Pl. N1 —1B 60
Memel Ct. EC1 —2B 68
Memel St. EC1 —2B 68
Mendora Rd. SW6 —7A 78
Mepham St. SE1 —3H 75
Mercer St. WC2 —6D 66
Meredith St. EC1 —7K 59
Meriden Ct. SW3 —4B 80
Merlin St. WC1 —7H 59
Mermaid Ct. SE1 —4D 76
Merrick Sq. SE1 —6D 76
Merrington Rd. SW6 —5E 78
Merritt's Bldgs. EC2 —2F 69
Merrow St. SE17 —5C 84
Merrow Wlk. SE17 —3E 84
Messina Av. NW6 —1D 54
Messiter Ho. N1 —3G 59
Methley St. SE11 —4J 83
Metro Central Heights. SE1 —7B 76
Metropolis. SE11 —7A 76
Mews St. E1 —2K 77
Mews, The. N1 —2C 60
Meymott St. SE1 —3K 75
Miah Ter. E1 —3K 77
Micawber Ho. SE16 —5K 77
Micawber St. N1 —6C 60
Michael Cliffe Ho. EC1 —7J 59
Michael Faraday Ho. SE17 —4E 84
Michael Stewart Ho. SW6 —6C 78
Michelson Ho. SE11 —2G 83
Micklethwaite Rd. SW6 —6E 78
Middlefield. NW8 —2K 55
Middle Row. W10 —2A 62
Middlesex Pas. EC1 —4A 68
Middlesex St. E1 —4G 69
Middle St. EC1 —3B 68
Middle Temple La. EC4 —6H 67
Middleton Bldgs. W1 —4K 65
Middleton Rd. E8 —1H 61
Middle Yd. SE1 —2F 77
Midford Pl. W1 —2A 66
Midhope St. WC1 —7E 58
Midland Rd. NW1 —5C 58
Midway Ho. EC1 —6A 60
Milborne Gro. SW10 —4J 79
Milcote St. SE1 —5K 75
Miles Pl. NW8 —3B 64
Miles St. SW8 —6D 82
Milford La. WC2 —7H 67
Milk St. EC2 —6C 68
Millbank. SW1 —7D 74
Millbank Tower. SW1 —2D 82
Millbrook Pl. NW1 —4K 57
(off Hampstead Rd.)
Millennium Sq. SE1 —4J 77
Miller St. NW1 —4K 57
Miller Wlk. SE1 —3J 75
Millman M. WC1 —2F 67
Millman Pl. WC1 —2F 67
Millman St. WC1 —2F 67
Mill Row. N1 —3G 61
Mills Ct. EC2 —1F 69
Millstream Rd. SE1 —5H 77
Mill St. SE1 —5J 77

A-Z London Motorists Atlas 91

Mill St. W1 —7K 65
Mill Yd. E1 —7K 69
Milman Rd. NW6 —4A 54
Milman's St. SW10 —6K 79
Milner Pl. N1 —2J 59
Milner Sq. N1 —1J 59
Milner St. SW3 —1D 80
Milroy Wlk. SE1 —2K 75
Milson Rd. W14 —6A 70
Milton Clo. SE1 —2H 85
Milton Ct. EC2 —3D 68
Milton Ct. Highwalk. EC2 (off Barbican) —3D 68
Milton Ho. SE5 —7D 84
Milton Mans. W14 —5A 78
Milton St. EC2 —3D 68
Milverton St. SE11 —4J 83
Mina Rd. SE17 —4G 85
Mincing La. EC3 —7F 69
Minera M. SW1 —1G 81
Minerva Clo. SW9 —7J 83
Miniver Pl. EC4 —7C 68
Miniver St. SE1 —5A 76
Minnow St. SE17 —2G 85
Minnow Wlk. SE17 —2G 85
Minories. EC3 —6H 69
Minster Ct. EC3 —7G 69
Minster Pavement. EC3 —7G 69
Mintern St. N1 —4E 60
Minton Ho. SE11 —1H 83
Mint St. SE1 —4B 76
Mirabel Rd. SW6 —7C 78
Missenden. SE17 —4E 84
Mitali Pas. E1 —6K 69
Mitcheldean Ct. SE15 —7F 85 (off Newent Clo.)
Mitchell St. EC1 —1B 68
Mitre Ct. EC2 —5C 68
Mitre Ct. EC4 —6J 67
Mitre Rd. SE1 —4J 75
Mitre Sq. EC3 —6G 69
Mitre St. EC3 —6G 69
Mitre Yd. SW3 —1C 80
Moatfield. NW6 —1A 54
Mobil Ct. WC2 —6G 67
Model Bldgs. WC1 —7G 59
Modern Ct. EC4 —5K 67
Molton Ho. N1 —3G 59
Molyneux St. W1 —4C 64
Monck St. SW1 —7C 74
Moncorvo Clo. SW7 —5B 72
Moneyer Ho. N1 —6D 60
Monkton St. SE11 —1J 83
Monkwell Sq. EC2 —4C 68
Monmouth Pl. W2 —6F 63
Monmouth Rd. W2 —6E 62
Monmouth St. WC2 —6D 66
Monnow Rd. SE1 —2K 85
Montague Clo. SE1 —2D 76
Montague Pl. WC1 —3C 66
Montague St. EC1 —4B 68
Montague St. WC1 —3D 66
Montagu Mans. W1 —3E 64
Montagu M. N. W1 —4E 64
Montagu M. S. W1 —5E 64
Montagu M. W. W1 —5E 64
Montagu Pl. W1 —4D 64
Montagu Row. W1 —4E 64
Montagu Sq. W1 —4E 64
Montagu St. W1 —5E 64
Montclare St. E2 —7H 61
Monteagle Ct. N1 —4G 61
Montford Pl. SE11 —4H 83
Monthope Rd. E1 —4K 69
Montpelier M. SW7 —6C 72
Montpelier Pl. SW7 —6C 72
Montpelier Sq. SW7 —5C 72
Montpelier St. SW7 —6C 72
Montpelier Ter. SW7 —5C 72
Montpelier Wlk. SW7 —6C 72
Montreal Pl. WC2 —7F 67
Montrose Av. NW6 —4A 54
Montrose Ct. SW7 —5A 72
Montrose Pl. SW1 —5G 73
Monument St. EC3 —1E 76
Moon St. N1 —2K 59
Moore Pk. Ct. SW6 —7G 79
Moore Pk. Rd. SW6 —7F 79
Moore St. SW3 —1D 80
Moorfields. EC2 —4D 68
Moorfields Highwalk. EC2 —4D 68
Moorgate. EC2 —5D 68
Moorgate Pl. EC2 —5D 68
Moorgreen Ho. EC1 —6K 59
Moorhouse Rd. W2 —5D 62
Moor La. EC2 —4D 68
Moor Pl. EC2 —4D 68
Moor St. W1 —6D 66
Mora St. EC1 —7C 60
Moravian Clo. SW10 —6K 79
Moravian Pl. SW10 —6A 80
Morecambe St. SE17 —2C 84
Moreland St. EC1 —6A 60
More's Gdns. SW3 —6A 80
Moreton Pl. SW1 —3A 82
Moreton St. SW1 —3A 82
Moreton Ter. SW1 —3A 82
Moreton Ter. M. N. SW1 —3A 82
Moreton Ter. M. S. SW1 —3A 82
Morgan Rd. W10 —3B 62
Morgan's La. SE1 —3F 77
Morland M. N1 —1J 59
Morley St. SE1 —6J 75
Mornington Av. W14 —2B 78
Mornington Cres. NW1 —4K 57
Mornington Pl. NW1 —4K 57
Mornington St. NW1 —4J 57
Mornington Ter. NW1 —3J 57
Morocco St. SE1 —5F 77
Morpeth Mans. SW1 —1K 81
Morpeth Ter. SW1 —7K 73
Morrison Bldgs. N. E1 —5K 69
Morrison Bldgs. S. E1 —5K 69
Morshead Mans. W9 —7E 54
Morshead Rd. W9 —7E 54
Mortimer Cres. NW6 —3F 55
Mortimer Est. NW6 —3F 55
Mortimer Mkt. WC1 —2A 66
Mortimer Pl. NW6 —3F 55
Mortimer Rd. N1 —1G 61 (in two parts)
Mortimer St. W1 —5J 65
Morton M. SW5 —2F 79
Morton Pl. SE1 —7H 75
Morton Rd. N1 —1C 60
Morwell St. WC1 —4B 66
Moscow Pl. W2 —7F 63
Moscow Rd. W2 —7E 62
Moss Clo. E1 —3K 69
Mossop St. SW3 —1C 80
Motcomb St. SW1 —6F 73
Motley Av. EC2 —1F 69
Moules Ct. SE5 —7B 84
Mountain Ho. SE11 —3G 83
Mountford St. E1 —5K 69
Mountfort Cres. N1 —1H 59
Mountfort Ter. N1 —1H 59
Mountjoy Clo. EC2 —4C 68 (off Barbican)
Mountjoy Ho. EC2 —4C 68
Mt. Mills. EC1 —7A 60
Mt. Pleasant. WC1 —2H 67
Mount Row. W1 —1H 73
Mount St. W1 —1F 73
Mount St. M. W1 —1H 73
Mowbray Rd. NW6 —1B 54
Mowll St. SW9 —7H 83
Moxon St. W1 —4F 65
Moye Clo. E2 —4K 61
Moylan Rd. W6 —6A 78
Mozart St. W10 —7B 54
Mozart Ter. SW1 —2G 81
Mulberry Rd. E8 —1H 61
Mulberry St. E1 —5K 69
Mulberry Wlk. SW3 —5A 80
Mulgrave Rd. SW6 —5B 78
Mullet Gdns. E2 —6K 61
Mulready St. NW8 —2B 64
Mulvaney Way. SE1 —5E 76
Mumford Ct. EC2 —5C 68
Munden St. W14 —1A 78
Mund St. W14 —4C 78
Mundy St. N1 —6F 61
Munro Ho. SE1 —5H 75
Munro M. W10 —3A 62
Munro Ter. SW10 —6K 79
Munster Rd. SW6 —7A 78
Munster Sq. NW1 —7J 57
Munton Rd. SE17 —1C 84
Muriel St. N1 —4G 59 (in two parts)
Murphy St. SE1 —5H 75
Murray Gro. N1 —5C 60
Murray St. NW1 —1B 58
Musard Rd. W6 —5A 78
Muscal. W6 —5A 78
Muscovy St. EC3 —1G 77
Museum St. WC1 —4D 66
Mutrix Rd. NW6 —2E 54
Myddelton Pas. EC1 —6J 59
Myddelton Sq. EC1 —6J 59
Myddelton St. EC1 —7J 59
Myddleton Ho. WC1 —5H 59
Mylne St. EC1 —6H 59
Myrtle Wlk. N1 —5F 61
Mytton Ho. SW8 —7F 83

Nags Head Ct. EC1 —2C 68
Nailsworth Ct. SE15 —6F 85
Nainby Ho. SE11 —2H 83
Naish Ct. N1 —1E 58
Nantes Pas. E1 —3H 69
Naoroji St. WC1 —7H 59
Napier Clo. W14 —6B 70
Napier Gro. N1 —4C 60
Napier Pl. W14 —7B 70
Napier Rd. W14 —7A 70
Napier Ter. N1 —1K 59
Nash St. NW1 —6J 57
Nassau St. W1 —4K 65
Nathan Ho. SE11 —2J 83
Nathaniel Clo. E1 —4J 69
Navarre St. E2 —1H 69
Nazrul St. E2 —6H 61
Neal St. WC2 —6D 66
Neal's Yd. WC2 —6D 66
Neate St. SE5 —6F 85 (in three parts)
Neathouse Pl. SW1 —1K 81
Nebraska St. SE1 —5D 76
Neckinger. SE1 —6J 77
Neckinger Est. SE16 —6J 77
Neckinger St. SE1 —6J 77
Needham Ho. SE11 —2H 83
Needham Rd. W11 —6D 62
Nelson Ct. SE1 —4A 76
Nelson Gdns. E2 —6K 61
Nelson Pas. EC1 —7C 60
Nelson Pl. N1 —5A 60
Nelson Sq. SE1 —4K 75
Nelsons Yd. NW1 —4K 57
Nelson Ter. N1 —5A 60
Nesham St. E1 —2K 77
Ness St. SE16 —6K 77
Netherton Gro. SW10 —6J 79
Netley St. NW1 —7K 57
Nettleton Ct. EC2 —4B 68
Nevern Mans. SW5 —2D 78
Nevern Pl. SW5 —2E 78
Nevern Rd. SW5 —2D 78
Nevern Sq. SW5 —2D 78
Nevill Ct. EC4 —5J 67
Neville Clo. NW1 —5C 58
Neville Clo. NW6 —5C 54
Neville Rd. NW6 —5C 54
Neville St. SW7 —3K 79
Neville Ter. SW7 —3K 79
Nevitt Ho. N1 —5E 60
New Bentham Ct. N1 —1C 60
Newbolt Ho. SE17 —3D 84
New Bond St. W1 —6H 65
New Bri. St. EC4 —6K 67
New Broad St. EC2 —4E 68
Newburgh St. W1 —6K 65
New Burlington M. W1 —7K 65
New Burlington Pl. W1 —7K 65
New Burlington St. W1 —7K 65
Newburn Ho. SE11 —3G 83
Newburn St. SE11 —4G 83
Newbury St. EC1 —4B 68
Newcastle Clo. EC4 —5K 67
Newcastle Ct. EC4 —7C 68
Newcastle Pl. W2 —3A 64
Newcastle Row. EC1 —2J 67
New Cavendish St. W1 —4G 65
New Change. EC4 —6B 68
New Charles St. EC1 —6A 60
New Chu. Rd. SE5 —7C 84 (in two parts)
New College M. N1 —1J 59
Newcombe St. W8 —2E 70
Newcomen St. SE1 —4D 76
New Compton St. WC2 —6C 66
New Concordia Wharf. SE1 —4K 77
New Ct. EC4 —7H 67
Newcourt St. NW8 —5B 56
New Covent Garden Mkt. SW8 —7B 82
New Coventry St. W1 —1C 74
Newent Clo. SE15 —7F 85
New Era Est. N1 —3F 61
New Fetter La. EC4 —5J 67
Newgate St. EC1 —5A 68
New Globe Wlk. SE1 —2B 76
New Goulston St. E1 —5H 69
Newham's Row. SE1 —5G 77
Newington Butts. SE11 & SE1 —2A 84
Newington Causeway. SE1 —7A 76
Newington Ind. Est. SE17 —2B 84
New Inn B'way. EC2 —1G 69
New Inn Pas. WC2 —6G 67
New Inn Sq. EC2 —1G 69
New Inn St. EC2 —1G 69
New Inn Yd. EC2 —1G 69
New Kent Rd. SE1 —7B 76
Newland Ct. EC1 —1D 68
New London St. EC3 —7G 69
Newman Pas. W1 —4A 66
Newman's Ct. EC3 —6E 68
Newman's Row. WC2 —4G 67
Newman St. W1 —4A 66
Newman Yd. W1 —5B 66
Newnham Ter. SE1 —6H 75
New N. Pl. EC2 —1F 69
New N. Rd. N1 —1B 60
New N. St. WC1 —3F 67
New Oxford St. WC1 —5C 66
Newport Ct. WC2 —7C 66
Newport Pl. WC2 —7C 66
Newport St. SE11 —2F 83
Newquay Ho. SE11 —3H 83
New Quebec St. W1 —6E 64
New Ride. SW7 & SW1 —5A 72
New River Head. EC1 —7J 59
New Row. WC2 —7D 66
New Spring Gdns. Wlk. SE11 —4E 82
New Sq. WC2 —5H 67
New Sq. Pas. WC2 —5H 67
New St. EC2 —4G 69
New St. Sq. EC4 —5J 67
Newton Mans. W14 —5A 78
Newton Rd. W2 —6E 62
Newton St. WC2 —5E 66
New Turnstile. WC1 —4F 67
New Union St. EC2 —4D 68
New Wharf Rd. N1 —4E 58
Niagra Clo. N1 —4C 60
Nicholas La. EC4 —7E 68
Nicholas Pas. EC4 —7E 68
Nicholl St. E2 —3K 61
Nicholson Ho. SE17 —3D 84
Nicholson St. SE1 —3K 75
Nickleby Ho. SE16 —5K 77
Nightingale Ho. E1 —2K 77 (off Thomas More St.)
Nightingale Ho. N1 —3G 61
Nightingale Pl. SW10 —6J 79
Nile St. N1 —6C 60
Nile Ter. SE15 —4H 85
Nine Elms La. SW8 —7A 82
Noble Ct. E1 —7K 69
Noble St. EC2 —5B 68
Noel Rd. N1 —4K 59
Noel St. W1 —6A 66
Norfolk Cres. W2 —5B 64
Norfolk M. W10 —4B 62
Norfolk Pl. W2 —5A 64
Norfolk Rd. NW8 —3A 56
Norfolk Row. SE1 —1G 83
Norfolk Sq. W2 —6A 64
Norfolk Sq. M. W2 —6A 64
Norfolk Ter. W6 —4A 78
Norland Pl. W11 —3A 70
Norland Sq. W11 —3A 70
Normand Gdns. W14 —5A 78
Normand M. W14 —5A 78
Normand Rd. W14 —5B 78
Norman Ho. SW8 —7D 82
Norman St. EC1 —7B 60
Norris St. SW1 —1B 74
Northampton Rd. EC1 —1J 67
Northampton Row. EC1 —1J 67
Northampton Sq. EC1 —7K 59
Northampton St. N1 —1B 60
N. Audley St. W1 —6F 65
N. Bank. NW8 —7B 56
Northburgh St. EC1 —2A 68
N. Carriage Dri. W2 —7B 64
Northchurch. SE17 —3E 84 (in two parts)
Northchurch Rd. N1 —1D 60
Northchurch Ter. N1 —1F 61
North Ct. W1 —3A 66
North Cres. WC1 —3B 66
Northdown St. N1 —4E 58
Northeast Pl. N1 —4J 59
N. End Cres. W14 —2B 78
N. End Ho. W14 —2A 78
N. End Pde. W14 —2A 78
N. End Rd. W14 & SW6 —1A 78
Northfield Ho. SE15 —6K 85
N. Flockton St. SE16 —4K 77
N. Flower Wlk. W2 —1J 71
North Gate. NW8 —6B 56
N. Gower St. NW1 —7A 58
North Ho. NW8 —5B 56
Northington St. WC1 —2G 67
Northleach Ct. SE15 —6F 85
North M. WC1 —2G 67
Northport St. N1 —3E 60
N. Ride. W2 —1A 72
North Ri. W2 —6C 64
North Row. W1 —7E 64
N. Tenter St. E1 —6J 69
North Ter. SW3 —7B 72
Northumberland All. EC3 —6G 69
Northumberland Av. WC2 —2D 74
Northumberland Pl. W2 —5D 62
Northumberland St. WC2 —2D 74
North Wlk. W2 —1H 71
N. Western Commercial Cen. NW1 —1D 58
Northwest Pl. N1 —4J 59
N. Wharf Rd. W2 —4K 63
Northwick Clo. NW8 —1K 63
Northwick Ter. NW8 —1K 63
Norton Folgate. E1 —3G 69
Norwich St. EC4 —5H 67
Notley St. SE5 —7D 84
Nottingdale Sq. W11 —2A 70
Nottingham Ct. WC2 —6D 66
Nottingham Pl. W1 —2F 65
Nottingham St. W1 —3F 65
Nottingham Ter. NW1 —2F 65
Notting Hill Ga. W11 —2C 70
Nottingwood Ho. W11 —7A 62
Nugent Ter. NW8 —5J 55
Nun Ct. EC2 —5D 68
Nursery La. E2 —3H 61
Nutbourne St. W10 —6A 54
Nutford Pl. W1 —5C 64
Nuttall St. N1 —4G 61
Nutt St. SE15 —7J 85
Nye Bevan Ho. SW6 —7B 78

Oak Ct. SE15 —7J 85 (off Sumner Rd.)
Oakden St. SE11 —1J 83
Oakey La. SE1 —6H 75
Oakfield St. SW10 —5H 79
Oakington Rd. W9 —1E 62
Oakley Cres. EC1 —5A 60
Oakley Gdns. SW3 —5C 80
Oakley Pl. SE1 —4H 85
Oakley Rd. N1 —1E 60
Oakley Sq. NW1 —4A 58
Oakley St. SW3 —5B 80
Oakley Yd. E2 —1J 69
Oak Lodge. W8 —7F 71
Oak Tree Rd. NW8 —7A 56
Oakwood Ct. W14 —6B 70
Oakwood La. W14 —6B 70
Oat La. EC2 —5C 68
Oberon Ho. N1 —4F 61
Observatory Gdns. W8 —4D 70
Occupation Rd. SE17 —3B 84
Octagon Arc. EC2 —4F 69
Odhams Wlk. WC2 —6E 66
O'Donnell Ct. WC1 —1E 66
Offley Rd. SW9 —7H 83
Offord Rd. N1 —1F 59
Offord St. N1 —1F 59
Ogle St. W1 —3K 65
Old Bailey. EC4 —6A 68
Old Barge Ho. All. SE1 —1J 75
Old Barrack Yd. SW1 —5F 73
Old Billingsgate Wlk. EC3 —1F 77
Old Bond St. W1 —1K 73
Old Brewer's Yd. WC2 —6D 66
Old Broad St. EC2 —6E 68
Old Brompton Rd. SW5 & SW7 —4E 78
Old Bldgs. WC2 —5H 67
Old Burlington St. W1 —7K 65
Oldbury Pl. W1 —3G 65
Old Castle St. E1 —5H 69
Old Cavendish St. W1 —6J 65
Old Change Ct. EC4 —6B 68
Old Chelsea M. SW3 —6B 80
Old Chu. St. SW3 —3A 80
Old Compton St. W1 —7B 66
Old Ct. Pl. W8 —4F 71
Old Fish St. Hill. EC4 —7B 68
Old Fleet La. EC4 —5K 67
Old Gloucester St. WC1 —3E 66
Old Jamaica Rd. SE16 —6K 77
Old Jewry. EC2 —6D 68
Old Kent Rd. SE1 & SE15 —1F 85
Old Mnr. Yd. SW5 —2F 79
Old Mkt. Sq. E2 —6H 61
Old Marylebone Rd. NW1 —4C 64
Old Montague St. E1 —4K 69
Old Nichol St. E2 —1H 69
Old N. St. WC1 —3F 67
Old Pal. Yd. SW1 —6D 74
Old Paradise St. SE11 —1F 83
Old Pk. La. W1 —3G 73
Old Pye St. SW1 —6B 74
Old Pye St. Est. SW1 —7B 74
Old Quebec St. W1 —6E 64
Old Queen St. SW1 —5C 74
Old Royal Free Pl. N1 —3J 59
Old Royal Free Sq. N1 —3J 59
Old Seacoal La. EC4 —6K 67
Old S. Lambeth Rd. SW8 —7E 82
Old Sq. WC2 —5H 67
Old Street. (Junct.) —7D 60
Old St. EC1 —2B 68
Old Theatre Ct. SE1 —2C 76
Oliphant St. W10 —6A 54
Oliver Ho. SE16 —5K 77
Oliver Ho. SW8 —7D 82
Olivers Yd. EC1 —1E 68
Olive Waite Ho. NW6 —1F 55
Olmar St. SE1 —5K 85
Olney Rd. SE17 —6A 84 (in two parts)
Olympia M. W2 —1G 71
Olympia Way. W14 —7A 70
O'Meara St. SE1 —3C 76
Omega Pl. N1 —5E 58
Ongar Rd. SW6 —5D 78
Onslow Gdns. SW7 —2K 79
Onslow M. E. SW7 —2K 79
Onslow M. W. SW7 —2K 79
Onslow Sq. SW7 —1A 80
Onslow St. EC1 —2J 67
Ontario St. SE1 —6A 76
Opal M. NW6 —2C 54
Opal St. SE11 —3K 83
Oppidans M. NW3 —1D 56
Oppidans Rd. NW3 —1D 56
Orange St. WC2 —1C 74
Orange Yd. W1 —6C 66
Oratory La. SW3 —3A 80
Orbain Rd. SW6 —7A 78
Orb St. SE17 —2D 84
Orchard Clo. N1 —1C 60
Orchard Clo. W10 —3A 62
Orchard M. N1 —1E 60
Orchardson Ho. NW8 —2K 63
Orchardson St. NW8 —2K 63
Orchard Sq. W14 —4B 78
Orchard St. W1 —6F 65
Orde Hall St. WC1 —2F 67
Ordnance Hill. NW8 —3A 56
Ordnance M. NW8 —4A 56
Orient St. SE11 —1K 83
Orkney Ho. N1 —3F 59
Orme Ct. W2 —1G 71
Orme Ct. M. W2 —1G 71
Orme Ho. E8 —2J 61
Orme La. W2 —1F 71
Orme Sq. W2 —1F 71
Ormond Clo. WC1 —3E 66
Ormonde Ga. SW3 —4D 80
Ormonde Pl. SW1 —2F 81
Ormonde Ter. NW8 —3D 56
Ormond M. WC1 —2E 66
Ormond Yd. SW1 —2A 74
Ormsby St. E2 —4H 61
Orsett M. W2 —5G 63 (in two parts)
Orsett St. SE11 —3G 83
Orsett Ter. W2 —5G 63
Orsman Rd. N1 —3F 61
Orton St. E1 —3K 77
Osbert St. SW1 —2B 82
Osborn Clo. E8 —2K 61
Osborn St. E1 —4J 69
Oscar Faber Pl. N1 —1G 61
Oslo Ct. NW8 —5B 56
Osnaburgh St. NW1 —2J 65
Osnaburgh St. NW1 —7J 57
Osnaburgh Ter. NW1 —1J 65
Osric Path. N1 —5F 61
Ossington Bldgs. W1 —4F 65
Ossington Clo. W2 —1E 70
Ossington St. W2 —1F 71
Ossory Rd. SE1 —4K 85
Ossulston St. NW1 —5B 58
Ostend Pl. SE17 —1B 84
Osten M. SW7 —7G 71
Oswin St. SE11 —1A 84
Othello Clo. SE11 —3K 83
Otto St. SE17 —6K 83
Outer Circ. NW1 —4D 56
Outram Pl. N1 —2E 58
Outwich St. EC3 —5G 69
Oval Mans. SE11 —5G 83
Oval Pl. SW8 —7F 83
Oval Rd. NW1 —1H 57
Oval Way. SE11 —4G 83
Oversley Ho. W2 —3E 62
Overy Ho. SE1 —5K 75
Ovington Gdns. SW3 —7C 72
Ovington M. SW3 —7C 72
Ovington Sq. SW3 —7C 72
Ovington St. SW3 —1C 80
Owen Mans. W14 —5A 78
Owen's Ct. EC1 —6K 59
Owen's Row. EC1 —6K 59
Owen St. EC1 —5K 59
Owgan Clo. SE5 —7E 84
Oxendon St. SW1 —1B 74
Oxenholme. NW1 —5K 57
Oxford & Cambridge Mans. NW1 —4C 64
Oxford Cir. W1 —6K 65
Oxford Cir. Av. W1 —6K 65
Oxford Ct. EC4 —7D 68
Oxford Gdns. W10 —5A 62
Oxford Rd. NW6 —5E 54
Oxford Sq. W2 —6C 64
Oxford St. W1 —6E 64
Oxley Clo. SE1 —3J 85
Oystergate Wlk. EC4 —1D 76

Packington Sq. N1 —3B 60
Packington St. N1 —3A 60
Padbury. SE17 —4G 85
Padbury Ct. E2 —7J 61
Paddington Grn. W2 —3A 64
Paddington St. W1 —3F 65
Pageantmaster Ct. EC4 —6K 67
Page St. SW1 —1C 82
Page's Wlk. SE1 —1F 85
Paget St. EC1 —6K 59
Painswick Ct. SE15 —7H 85
Pakenham St. WC1 —7G 59
Palace Av. W8 —4G 71
Palace Ct. W2 —1F 71
Palace Gdns. M. W8 —2E 70
Palace Gdns. Ter. W8 —2E 70
Palace Ga. W8 —5H 71
Palace Grn. W8 —3F 71
Palace M. SW1 —2G 81
Palace M. SW6 —7C 78
Palace Pl. SW1 —6K 73
Palace Pl. Mans. W8 —5G 71
Palace St. SW1 —6K 73
Palamon Ct. SE1 —3J 85
Palfrey Pl. SW8 —7G 83
Palgrave Ho. SE5 —7B 84
Palissy St. E2 —7H 61
Pallant Ho. SE1 —7E 76
Palliser Ct. W14 —3A 78
Palliser Rd. W14 —3A 78
Pall Mall. SW1 —3A 74
Pall Mall E. SW1 —2C 74
Pall Mall Pl. SW1 —3A 74
Palm Ct. SE15 —7H 85 (off Garnies Clo.)
Palmerston Mans. W14 —6A 78
Palmerston Rd. NW6 —1C 54 (in two parts)
Palmer St. SW1 —6B 74
Pamela Wlk. E8 —2K 61
Pancras La. EC4 —6C 68
Pancras Rd. NW1 —4B 58
Panton St. SW1 —1B 74
Panyer All. EC4 —6B 68
Paper Bldgs. EC4 —7J 67
Parade, The. SW11 —7E 80
Paradise Wlk. SW3 —5E 80
Paragon All. SE1 —7F 77
Paragon M. SE1 —1E 84
Paragon Row. SE17 —1D 84
Pardoner St. SE1 —6E 76
Pardon St. EC1 —1A 68
Paris Garden. SE1 —2K 75
Park Bus. Cen. NW6 —7D 54
Park Clo. SW1 —5D 72
Park Clo. W14 —6C 70
Park Cres. W1 —2H 65
Park Cres. M. E. W1 —2J 65
Park Cres. M. W. W1 —2H 65
Parker M. WC2 —5E 66
Parkers Row. SE1 —5J 77
Parker St. WC2 —6E 66
Parkfield St. N1 —4J 59
Parkgate Rd. SW11 —7C 80
Parkhouse St. SE5 —7E 84
Park La. W1 —7E 64
Park Mans. SW1 —5D 72
Park Mans. SW8 —5E 82
Park M. W10 —5A 54
Park Pl. SW1 —3K 73
Park Pl. Gdns. W2 —3J 63
Park Pl. Vs. W2 —3J 63
Park Rd. NW8 & NW1 —6B 56
Park Sq. E. NW1 —1H 65
Park Sq. M. NW1 —2H 65
Park Sq. W. NW1 —1H 65
Park Steps. W2 —7C 64
Park St. SE1 —2B 76
Park St. W1 —6F 65
Park Village E. NW1 —3H 57
Park Village W. NW1 —4H 57
Parkville Rd. SW6 —7B 78
Park Wlk. SW10 —5J 79
Parkway. NW1 —3H 57
Park West. W2 —5C 64
Park W. Pl. W2 —5C 64
Parliament Ct. E1 —4G 69
Parliament Sq. SW1 —5D 74
Parliament St. SW1 —4D 74
Parmoor Ct. EC1 —1B 68
Parnell Ho. WC1 —5C 66
Parr St. N1 —4D 60
Parry Rd. W10 —6A 54 (in two parts)
Parry St. SW8 —5E 82
Partridge Ct. EC1 —1K 67
Pascal St. SW8 —7C 82
Pasley Clo. SE17 —4B 84
Passfields. W14 —4B 78
Passing All. EC1 —3A 68
Passmore St. SW1 —3F 81
Pastor St. SE11 —1A 84 (in two parts)
Patchway Ct. SE15 —6F 85
Paternoster Row. EC4 —6B 68
Paternoster Sq. EC4 —6A 68
Paterson Ct. EC1 —7D 60
Pater St. W8 —7D 70
Paton St. EC1 —7B 60
Pattern Ho. EC1 —1K 67
Paul St. EC2 —2F 69
Paul's Wlk. EC4 —7A 68
Paultons Sq. SW3 —5A 80
Paultons St. SW3 —6A 80
Paveley Dri. SW11 —7B 80
Paveley St. NW8 —7C 56
Pavilion Rd. SW1 —5E 72
Pavilion St. SW1 —7E 72
Pavilion, The. SW8 —7C 82
Paxton Ter. SW1 —5J 81
Payne Ho. N1 —3G 59
Paynes Wlk. W6 —6A 78
Peabody Av. SW1 —3H 81
Peabody Bldgs. E1 —7K 69
Peabody Bldgs. SE1 —3B 76
Peabody Bldgs. SW3 —6B 80
Peabody Clo. SW1 —5J 81
Peabody Ct. EC1 —2C 68
Peabody Est. EC1 —2J 67
Peabody Est. N1 —2B 60
Peabody Est. SE1 —3J 75 (Hatfield St.)
Peabody Est. SE1 —4C 76 (Mint St.)
Peabody Est. SW1 —1A 82
Peabody Est. SW3 —6C 80
Peabody Est. SW6 —5D 78
Peabody Sq. SE1 —5K 75
Peabody Tower. EC1 —2C 68
Peabody Yd. N1 —2B 60
Peacock St. SE17 —2A 84
Peacock Yd. SE17 —2A 84
Pear Ct. SE15 —7H 85
Pearman St. SE1 —6J 75
Pear Pl. SE1 —4H 75
Pearse St. SE15 —6G 85
Pearson St. E2 —4H 61
Pear Tree Clo. E2 —2H 61
Pear Tree Ct. EC1 —2J 67
Pear Tree St. EC1 —1A 68
Peckham Gro. SE15 —7G 85
Peckham Hill St. SE15 —7K 85
Peckham Pk. Rd. SE15 —7K 85
Pecks Yd. E1 —3H 69
Pedley St. E1 —2J 69
Peel Pas. W8 —3D 70
Peel Precinct. NW6 —5D 54
Peel Rd. NW6 —6D 54
Peel St. W8 —3D 70
Peerless St. EC1 —7D 60
Pegasus Pl. SE11 —5H 83
Peldon Wlk. N1 —2A 60
Pelham Cres. SW7 —2B 80
Pelham Ho. W14 —2B 78
Pelham Pl. SW7 —2B 80
Pelham St. SW7 —1A 80
Pelier St. SE17 —5C 84
Pella Ho. SE11 —3G 83
Pellant Rd. SW6 —6A 78
Pelter St. E2 —6H 61
Pemberton Row. EC4 —5J 67
Pembridge Cres. W11 —7D 62
Pembridge Gdns. W2 —1D 70
Pembridge M. W11 —7D 62
Pembridge Pl. W2 —7E 62
Pembridge Rd. W11 —1D 70
Pembridge Sq. W2 —1E 70
Pembridge Vs. W11 & W2 —7D 62
Pembroke Clo. SW1 —5G 73
Pembroke Cotts. W8 —7D 70
Pembroke Gdns. W8 —1C 78
Pembroke Gdns. Clo. W8 —7C 70
Pembroke M. W8 —7D 70
Pembroke Pl. W8 —7D 70
Pembroke Rd. W8 —1C 78
Pembroke Sq. W8 —7D 70
Pembroke St. N1 —1E 58
Pembroke Vs. W8 —1D 78
Pembroke Wlk. W8 —1D 78
Penally Pl. N1 —2E 60
Pencombe M. W11 —7C 62
Penfold Pl. NW1 —3B 64
Penfold St. NW8 & NW1 —2A 64
Penley Ct. WC2 —7G 67
Penmayne Ho. SE11 —3J 83
Pennack Rd. SE15 —6J 85
Pennant M. W8 —1F 79
Pennington St. E1 —1K 77
Penn St. N1 —3E 60
Pennymoor Wlk. W9 —1C 62
Penrose Gro. SE17 —4B 84
Penrose St. SE17 —4B 84
Penryn Ho. SE11 —3K 83
Penryn St. NW1 —4B 58
Penry Pl. SE1 —3K 85
Penry St. SE1 —2G 85
Penshurst Pl. SE1 —7G 75
Penton Gro. N1 —5H 59
Penton Pl. SE17 —2A 84
Penton Ri. WC1 —6G 59
Penton St. N1 —4H 59
Pentonville Rd. N1 —6E 58
Pentridge St. SE15 —7H 85
Penywern Rd. SW5 —3E 78
Penzance Ho. SE11 —3J 83
Penzance Pl. W11 —2A 70
Penzance St. W11 —2A 70
Pepler Ho. W10 —2A 62
Pepper St. SE1 —4B 76
Pepys St. EC3 —7G 69
Percival St. EC1 —1K 67
Percy Cir. WC1 —6G 59
Percy M. W1 —4B 66
Percy Pas. W1 —4B 66
Percy Rd. NW6 —6D 54
Percy St. W1 —4B 66
Percy Yd. WC1 —6G 59
Peregrine Ho. EC1 —6A 60
Perham Rd. W14 —4A 78
Perkin's Rents. SW1 —7C 74
Perkins Sq. SE1 —2C 76
Perronet Ho. SE1 —7A 76
Perry's Pl. W1 —5B 66
Perseverance Pl. SW9 —7J 83
Perseverance Works. E2 —7G 61
Peterborough Ct. EC4 —6J 67
Peter Butler Ho. SE1 —4K 77
Peters Ct. W2 —5G 63
Petersham La. SW7 —6H 71
Petersham M. SW7 —7H 71
Petersham Pl. SW7 —7H 71
Peters Hill. EC4 —7B 68
Peter's La. EC1 —3A 68
Peter St. W1 —7B 66
Peto Pl. NW1 —1J 65
Petticoat La. E1 —4H 69
Petticoat Sq. E1 —5H 69
Petticoat Tower. E1 —5H 69
Petty France. SW1 —6A 74
Petyt Pl. SW3 —6B 80
Petyward. SW3 —2C 80
Peveril Ho. SE1 —7E 76
Phelp St. SE17 —5D 84
Phene St. SW3 —5C 80
Philbeach Gdns. SW5 —3D 78
Philchurch Pl. E1 —6K 69
Phillimore Gdns. W8 —5D 70
Phillimore Gdns. Clo. W8 —6D 70
Phillimore Pl. W8 —5D 70
Phillimore Ter. W8 —6E 70
Phillimore Wlk. W8 —6D 70
Phillipp St. N1 —3F 61
Philpot La. EC3 —7F 69
Phipp's M. SW1 —7J 73
Phipp St. EC2 —1F 69
Phoenix Clo. E8 —2H 61
Phoenix Pl. WC1 —1G 67
Phoenix Rd. NW1 —6B 58
Phoenix St. WC2 —6C 66
Phoenix Wharf Rd. SE1 —5J 77
Physic Pl. SW3 —5D 80
Piazza, The. WC2 —7E 66
Piccadilly. W1 —4H 73
Piccadilly Arc. SW1 —2K 73
Piccadilly Cir. W1 —1B 74
Piccadilly Pl. W1 —1A 74
Pickard St. EC1 —6A 60
Pickering M. W2 —5G 63
Pickering Pl. SW1 —3A 74
Pickering St. N1 —2A 60
Pickfords Wharf. N1 —5B 60
Pickfords Wharf. SE1 —2D 76
Pickwick Ho. SE16 —5K 77
Pickwick St. SE1 —5B 76
Picton Pl. W1 —6G 65
Picton St. SE5 —7D 84
Pied Bull Yd. WC1 —4D 66
Pier Ho. SW3 —6C 80

Pierrepont Arc.—St Peters Chu.

Pierrepont Arc. N1 —4K 59
Pierrepont Row. N1 —4K 59
Pikemans Ct. SW5 —2D 78
Pilgrimage St. SE1 —5D 76
Pilgrim St. EC4 —6K 67
Pilton Pl. SE17 —3C 84
Pimlico Rd. SW1 —3F 81
Pimlico Wlk. N1 —6F 61
Pinchin St. E1 —7K 69
Pindar St. EC2 —3F 69
Pindock M. W9 —2G 63
Pineapple Ct. SW1 —6K 73
Pinehurst Ct. W11 —6C 62
Pine St. EC1 —1H 67
Pingle St. SE17 —3C 84
Pitfield Est. N1 —6F 61
Pitfield St. N1 —7F 61
Pitman St. SE5 —7B 84
(in two parts)
Pitt's Head M. W1 —3G 73
Pitt St. W8 —4E 70
Plaisterers Highwalk. EC2 —4B 68
Plantain Pl. SE1 —4D 76
Plantation Ho. EC3 —7F 69
Platina St. EC2 —1E 68
Platt St. NW1 —4B 58
Playfair Mans. W14 —6A 78
Playhouse Yd. EC4 —6K 67
Plaza Pde. NW6 —4F 55
Plaza, The. W1 —5A 66
Pleasant Pl. N1 —1A 60
Pleasant Row. NW1 —3J 57
Plender Pl. NW1 —3A 58
Plender St. NW1 —3K 57
Pleydell Ct. EC4 —6J 67
Pleydell Est. EC1 —7C 60
Pleydell St. EC4 —6J 67
Plough Ct. EC3 —7E 68
Ploughmans Clo. NW1 —2B 58
Plough Pl. EC4 —5J 67
Plough St. E1 —5J 69
Plough Yd. EC2 —2G 69
Plowden Bldgs. EC4 —7H 67
(off Temple)
Plumber's Row. E1 —4K 69
Plumtree Ct. EC4 —5K 67
Plympton Av. NW6 —1B 54
Plympton Pl. NW8 —2B 64
Plympton Rd. NW6 —1B 54
Plympton St. NW8 —2B 64
Pocock St. SE1 —4K 75
Point West. SW7 —1G 79
Poland St. W1 —5A 66
Polesworth Ho. W2 —3E 62
Pollard Row. E2 —6K 61
Pollard St. E2 —6K 61
Pollen St. W1 —6K 65
Pollitt Dri. NW8 —1A 64
Polygon Rd. NW1 —5B 58
Pomell Way. E1 —5J 69
Pond Pl. SW3 —2B 80
Ponsonby Pl. SW1 —3C 82
Ponsonby Ter. SW1 —3C 82
Ponton Rd. SW8 —6C 82
Pont St. SW1 —7D 72
Pont St. M. SW1 —7D 72
Pontypool Pl. SE1 —4K 75
Poole Ho. SE11 —1G 83
Pooles Bldgs. WC1 —2H 67
Pooles La. SW10 —7H 79
Poole St. N1 —3D 60
Pope's Head All. EC3 —6E 68
Pope St. SE1 —5G 77
Popham Rd. N1 —2B 60
Popham St. N1 —2A 60
(in two parts)
Poplar Pl. W2 —7F 63
Poppins Ct. EC4 —6K 67
Porchester Gdns. W2 —7G 63
Porchester Gdns. M. W2 —6G 63
Porchester M. W2 —5G 63
Porchester Pl. W2 —6C 64
Porchester Rd. W2 —5G 63
Porchester Sq. W2 —5G 63
Porchester Ter. W2 —6H 63
Porchester Ter. N. W2 —5G 63
Porlock St. SE1 —4E 76
Porter St. SE1 —2C 76
Porter St. W1 —3E 64
Porteus Rd. W2 —3K 63
Portgate Clo. W9 —1C 62
Portia Ct. SE11 —3K 83
Porticos, The. SW3 —6K 79
Portland M. W1 —6A 66
Portland Pl. W1 —2H 65
Portland Rd. W11 —7A 62
Portland St. SE17 —3D 84
Portland Wlk. SE17 —5E 84
Portman Bldgs. NW1 —2C 64
Portman Clo. W1 —5E 64
Portman M. S. W1 —6F 65
Portman Sq. W1 —5F 65
Portman St. W1 —6F 65
Portman Towers. W1 —5E 64
Portnall Rd. W9 —5B 54
Portobello Ct. Est. W11 —6C 62
Portobello M. W11 —1D 70
Portobello Rd. W10 —3A 62
Portobello Rd. W11 —5B 62
Portpool La. EC1 —3H 67
Portsea M. W2 —6C 64
Portsea Pl. W2 —6C 64
Portsmouth St. WC2 —6F 67
Portsoken St. E1 —7H 69
Portugal St. WC2 —6F 67
Postern, The. EC2 —4C 68
Post Office Ct. EC3 —6E 68
Post Office Way. SW8 —7B 82
Potier St. SE1 —7E 76
Potters Fields. SE1 —3G 77
Pottery La. W11 —1A 70
Poultry. EC2 —6D 68
Powis Gdns. W11 —5C 62
Powis M. W11 —5C 62
Powis Pl. WC1 —2E 66
Powis Sq. W11 —5C 62
Powis Ter. W11 —5C 62
Pownall Rd. E8 —3J 61
Poxon Ct. EC4 —6A 68
Praed M. W2 —5A 64
Praed St. W2 —6K 63
Pratt M. NW1 —3K 57
Pratt St. NW1 —3K 57
Pratt Wlk. SE11 —1G 83
Prebend St. N1 —3B 60
Precinct, The. N1 —3B 60
Premier Corner. W9 —5B 54
Prescot St. E1 —7J 69
President Ho. EC1 —7A 60
President St. EC1 —6B 60
Preston Clo. SE1 —1F 85
Prestwood St. N1 —5C 60
Price Ho. N1 —3B 60
Price's St. SE1 —3A 76
Price's Yd. N1 —2G 59
Prideaux Pl. WC1 —6G 59
Priest's Ct. EC2 —5B 68
Prima Rd. SW9 —7H 83
Primrose Hill. EC4 —6J 67
Primrose Hill Ct. NW3 —1D 56
Primrose Hill Rd. NW3 —1D 56
Primrose Hill Studios. NW1 —2F 57
Primrose M. NW1 —1E 56
(off Sharpleshall St.)
Primrose St. EC2 —3F 69
Prince Albert Rd. NW8 & NW1 —6B 56
Prince Consort Rd. SW7 —6J 71
Princedale Rd. W11 —2A 70
Princelet St. E1 —3J 69
Prince of Wales Pas. NW1 —7K 57
Prince of Wales Ter. W8 —5G 71
Prince Regent Ct. NW8 —4C 56
Prince Regent M. NW1 —7K 57
Prince's Arc. SW1 —2A 74
Princes Cir. WC2 —5D 66
Prince's Gdns. SW7 —6A 72
Prince's Ga. SW7 —5A 72
Prince's Ga. Ct. SW7 —5A 72
Prince's Ga. M. SW7 —6A 72
Prince's M. W2 —7F 63
Prince's Pl. SW1 —2A 74
Princes Pl. W11 —2A 70
Princess Ct. W2 —7G 63
Prince's Sq. W2 —7E 62
Princess Rd. NW1 —2G 57
Princess Rd. NW6 —5D 54
Princess St. SE1 —7A 76
Prince's St. EC2 —6D 68
Princes St. W1 —6J 65
Prince's Yd. W11 —3A 70
Princethorpe Ho. W2 —3F 63
Princeton St. WC1 —4F 67
Printers Inn Ct. EC4 —5H 67
Printer St. EC4 —5J 67
Printing Ho. Yd. E2 —7G 61
Prioress St. SE1 —7E 76
Priory Ct. EC4 —6A 68
Priory Grn. Est. N1 —4F 59
Priory Pk. Rd. NW6 —2C 54
(in two parts)
Priory Rd. NW6 —2F 55
Priory Ter. NW6 —2F 55
Priory Wlk. SW10 —4J 79
Priter Rd. SE16 —7K 77
Priter Way. SE16 —7K 77
Procter Ho. SE5 —7E 84
Procter St. WC1 —4F 67
Prospect Ho. N1 —5H 59
Prothero Rd. SW6 —7A 78
Providence Ct. W1 —7G 65
Providence Pl. N1 —3K 59
Providence Row. N1 —5F 59
Providence Sq. SE1 —4K 77
Providence Yd. E2 —6K 61
Province St. N1 —4B 60
Provost Est. N1 —6D 60
Provost St. N1 —5D 60
Prowse Pl. NW1 —1K 57
Prudent Pas. EC2 —6C 68
Pudding La. EC3 —1E 76
Puddledock. EC4 —7A 68
(in two parts)
Pulham Ho. SW8 —7F 83
Pulteney Ter. N1 —3G 59
Pulton Pl. SW6 —7D 78
Puma Ct. E1 —3H 69
Pump Ct. EC4 —6H 67
Purbeck Ho. SW8 —7F 83
Purbrook Est. SE1 —5G 77
Purbrook St. SE1 —6G 77
Purcell St. N1 —4F 61
Purchese St. NW1 —4C 58
Purley Pl. N1 —1K 59

Quadrangle Clo. SE1 —1F 85
Quadrangle, The. SW6 —7A 78
Quadrangle, The. W2 —5B 64
Quadrant Arc. W1 —1A 74
Quadrant Ho. SE1 —2K 75
Quaker St. E1 —2H 69
Quality Ct. WC2 —5H 67
Quebec M. W1 —6E 64
Quedgeley Ct. SE15 —6H 85
Queen Anne M. W1 —4J 65
Queen Anne's Ga. SW1 —5B 74
Queen Anne St. W1 —5H 65
Queen Anne's Wlk. WC1 —2E 66
Queen Elizabeth Bldgs. EC4 —7H 67
Queen Elizabeth St. SE1 —4G 77
Queenhithe. EC4 —7C 68
Queen Marys Bldgs. SW1 —1A 82
Queensberry M. W. SW7 —1K 79
Queensberry Pl. SW7 —1K 79
Queensberry Way. SW7 —1K 79
Queensborough M. W2 —7H 63
Queensborough Pas. W2 —7H 63
Queensborough Studios. W2 —7H 63
Queensborough Ter. W2 —7G 63
Queensbridge Ct. E2 —3J 61
Queensbridge Rd. E8 & E2 —2J 61
Queen's Club Gdns. W14 —5A 78
Queen's Ct. W2 —1G 71
Queensdale Rd. W11 —3A 70
Queensdale Wlk. W11 —3A 70
Queen's Elm Pde. SW3 —3A 80
(off Old Church St.)
Queen's Elm Sq. SW3 —4A 80
Queen's Gdns. W2 —7H 63
Queen's Ga. SW7 —5J 71
Queen's Ga. Gdns. SW7 —7H 71
Queen's Ga. M. SW7 —6H 71
Queensgate Pl. NW6 —1D 54
Queen's Ga. Pl. SW7 —7J 71
Queen's Ga. Pl. M. SW7 —7J 71
Queen's Ga. Ter. SW7 —6H 71
Queen's Gro. NW8 —3K 55
Queen's Gro. Studios. NW8 —3K 55
Queen's Head St. N1 —3A 60
Queen's Head Yd. SE1 —3D 76
Queensmead. NW8 —2A 56
Queen's M. W2 —7F 63
Queen Sq. WC1 —2E 66
Queen Sq. Pl. WC1 —2E 66
Queen's Row. SE17 —5D 84
Queen's Ter. NW8 —3K 55
Queenstown Rd. SW8 —6H 81
Queen St. EC4 —7C 68
Queen St. W1 —2H 73
Queen St. Pl. EC4 —1C 76
Queen's Wlk. SW1 —2K 73
Queen's Wlk., The. SE1 —2E 76
Queen's Wlk., The. SE1 —2G 75
Queensway. W2 —5G 63
Queen's Yd. WC1 —2A 66
Queen Victoria St. EC4 —7K 67
Quenington Ct. SE15 —6H 85
Quex M. NW6 —2E 54
Quex Rd. NW6 —2E 54
Quick St. N1 —5A 60
Quick St. M. N1 —5K 59
Quickswood. NW3 —1C 56
Quilp St. SE1 —4B 76
Quilter St. E2 —6K 61
Quin Bldgs. SE1 —5J 75
Quinton Ho. SW8 —7D 82

Rabbit Row. W8 —2E 70
Racton Rd. SW6 —6D 78
Radcliffe Rd. SE1 —6G 77
Radcot St. SE11 —4J 83
Raddington Rd. W10 —4A 62
Radlett Pl. NW8 —3B 56
Radley M. W8 —7E 70
Radnor M. W2 —6A 64
Radnor Pl. W2 —6B 64
Radnor Rd. NW6 —3A 54
Radnor Rd. SE15 —7K 85
Radnor St. EC1 —7C 60
Radnor Ter. W14 —1B 78
Radnor Wlk. SW3 —4C 80
Radstock St. SW11 —7B 80
Railway App. SE1 —3E 76
Railway M. W10 —5A 62
Railway St. N1 —5E 58
Rainbow St. SE5 —7F 85
Rainsford St. W2 —5B 64
Raleigh M. N1 —3A 60
Raleigh St. N1 —3A 60
Ralph Brook Ct. N1 —6E 60
Ralph Ct. W2 —5G 63
Ralston St. SW3 —4D 80
Ramar Ho. E1 —3K 69
Ramillies Pl. W1 —6K 65
Ramillies St. W1 —6K 65
Rampayne St. SW1 —3B 82
Ramsay M. SW3 —5B 80
Ramsey St. E2 —1K 69
Randall Rd. SE11 —3F 83
Randall Row. SE11 —2F 83
Randell's Rd. N1 —2E 58
Randolph Av. W9 —5F 55
Randolph Cres. W9 —2H 63
Randolph Gdns. NW6 —5F 55
Randolph M. W9 —2J 63
Randolph Rd. W9 —2H 63
Randolph St. NW1 —1A 58
Ranelagh Bri. W2 —4G 63
Ranelagh Gro. SW1 —3G 81
Ranelagh Rd. SW1 —4A 82
Rangoon St. EC3 —6H 69
Ransome's Dock Bus. Cen. SW11 —7C 80
Ranston St. NW1 —3B 64
Raphael St. SW7 —5D 72
Ratcliff Gro. EC1 —7C 60
Rathbone Pl. W1 —4B 66
Rathbone St. W1 —4A 66
Ravenscroft St. E2 —5J 61
Ravensdon St. SE11 —4J 83
Ravenstone. SE17 —4G 85
Ravent Rd. SE11 —2G 83
Ravey St. EC2 —1F 69
Rawlings St. SW3 —1D 80
Rawreth Wlk. N1 —2C 60
Rawstorne Pl. EC1 —6K 59
Rawstorne St. EC1 —6K 59
Rayburne Ct. W14 —6A 70
Ray Ho. N1 —3F 61
Raymond Bldgs. WC1 —3G 67
Raynor Pl. N1 —2C 60
Ray St. EC1 —2J 67
Ray St. Bri. EC1 —2J 67
Reachview Clo. NW1 —1A 58
Read Ho. SE11 —5H 83
Reapers Clo. NW1 —2B 58
Rector St. N1 —3B 60
Red Anchor Clo. SW3 —6A 80
Redan Pl. W2 —6F 63
Redburn St. SW3 —5D 80
Redcar St. SE5 —7B 84
Redchurch St. E2 —1H 69
Redcliffe Clo. SW5 —4F 79
Redcliffe Gdns. SW5 & SW10 —4G 79
Redcliffe M. SW10 —4G 79
Redcliffe Pl. SW10 —6H 79
Redcliffe Rd. SW10 —4H 79
Redcliffe Sq. SW10 —4G 79
Redcliffe St. SW10 —5G 79
Redcross Way. SE1 —4C 76
Reddins Rd. SE15 —6K 85
Rede Pl. W2 —6E 62
Redesdale St. SW3 —5D 80
Redfield La. SW5 —1E 78
Redfield M. SW5 —1E 78
Redford Wlk. N1 —2B 60
Redhill St. NW1 —5J 57
Red Lion Clo. SE17 —5D 84
Red Lion Ct. EC4 —6J 67
Red Lion Ct. SE1 —2C 76
Red Lion Row. SE17 —5C 84
Red Lion Sq. WC1 —4F 67
Red Lion St. WC1 —3F 67
Red Lion Yd. W1 —2H 73
Redmead La. E1 —3K 77
Redmond Ho. N1 —3G 59
Red Pl. W1 —7F 65
Redvers St. N1 —6G 61
Redwood Ct. NW6 —1A 54
Redwood Mans. W8 —7F 71
(off Chantry Sq.)
Reece M. SW7 —1K 79
Reedworth St. SE11 —2J 83
Rees St. N1 —3C 60
Reeves Ho. SE1 —5H 75
Reeves M. W1 —1F 73
Regal Clo. E1 —3K 69
Regal La. NW1 —3G 57
Regan Way. N1 —4F 61
Regency Lodge. NW3 —1K 55
Regency Pl. SW1 —1C 82
Regency St. SW1 —1C 82
Regency Ter. SW7 —3K 79
Regent Pl. W1 —7A 66
Regent's Bri. Gdns. SW8 —7E 82
Regents M. NW8 —4J 55
Regents Pk. Est. NW1 —6K 57
Regent's Pk. Gdns. M. NW1 —2E 56
Regent's Pk. Rd. NW1 —1E 56
(in two parts)
Regent's Pk. Ter. NW1 —2H 57
Regents Plaza. NW6 —4F 55
Regent Sq. WC1 —7E 58
Regent's Row. E8 —3J 61
Regent St. SW1 —1B 74
Regent St. W1 —5J 65
Regents Wharf. N1 —4F 59
Regnart Bldgs. NW1 —1A 66
Reliance Sq. EC2 —1G 69
Relton M. SW7 —6C 72
Rembrandt Clo. SW1 —3F 81
Remington St. N1 —5A 60
Remnant St. WC2 —5F 67
Renfrew Rd. SE11 —1K 83
Rennie Ct. SE1 —2K 75
Rennie St. SE1 —2K 75
Rephidim St. SE1 —7F 77
Reston Pl. SW7 —5H 71
Restormel Ho. SE11 —2J 83
Retford St. N1 —5G 61
Reverdy Rd. SE1 —2K 85
Rewell St. SW6 —7H 79
Rex Pl. W1 —1G 73
Rheidol M. N1 —4B 60
Rheidol Ter. N1 —4A 60
Rhoda St. E2 —1J 69
Rhodes Ho. N1 —6D 60
Richardson Clo. E8 —2H 61
Richardson's M. W1 —2K 65
Richard's Pl. SW3 —1C 80
Richbell Pl. WC1 —3F 67
Richborne Ter. SW8 —7F 83
Rich La. SW5 —4F 79
Richmond Av. N1 —2G 59
Richmond Bldgs. W1 —6B 66
Richmond Cotts. W14 —1A 78
Richmond Ct. SW1 —5E 72
Richmond Cres. N1 —2G 59
Richmond Gro. N1 —1A 60
Richmond M. W1 —6B 66
Richmond Rd. E8 —1H 61
Richmond Ter. SW1 —4D 74
Richmond Ter. M. SW1 —4D 74
Rickett St. SW6 —5E 78
Ridgeways Pl. EC2 —7F 61
Ridgewell Clo. N1 —2C 60
Ridgmount Gdns. WC1 —2B 66
Ridgmount Pl. WC1 —3B 66
Ridgmount St. WC1 —3B 66
Riding Ho. St. W1 —4J 65
Rifle Ct. SE11 —5J 83
Riley Rd. SE1 —6H 77
Riley St. SW10 —6K 79
Ring, The. W2 —2B 72
Ripplevale Gro. N1 —1G 59
Risborough St. SE1 —4A 76
Risinghill St. N1 —4H 59
Rising Sun Ct. EC1 —4A 68
Rita Rd. SW8 —6E 82
River Ct. SE1 —2K 75
River Pl. N1 —1B 60
Riverside Ct. SW8 —5C 82
River St. EC1 —6H 59
Riverton Clo. W9 —7C 54
Riverview Heights. SE16 —4K 77
Rivington Bldgs. EC2 —7F 61
Rivington Pl. EC2 —7G 61
Rivington St. EC2 —7F 61
Rivington Wlk. E8 —2K 61
Robert Adam St. W1 —5F 65
Roberta St. E2 —6K 61
Robert Clo. W9 —2J 63
Robert Dashwood Way. SE17 —2B 84
Roberts Ct. N1 —3A 60
Roberts M. SW1 —7F 73
Roberts Pl. EC1 —1J 67
Robert St. NW1 —7J 57
Robert St. WC2 —1E 74
Robin Ct. SE16 —1K 85
Robinson St. SW3 —5D 80
Rochelle St. E2 —7H 61
Rochester Pl. NW1 —1K 57
(in two parts)
Rochester Row. SW1 —1A 82
Rochester Sq. NW1 —1A 58
Rochester St. SW1 —7B 74
Rochester Wlk. SE1 —3D 76
Rockingham St. SE1 —7B 76
Rocliffe St. N1 —5A 60
Rocque Ho. SW6 —7B 78
(off Estcourt Rd.)
Rodin Ct. N1 —3A 60
Roding Ho. N1 —3H 59
Roding M. E1 —2K 77
Rodmarton St. W1 —4E 64
Rodney Ct. W9 —1J 63
Rodney Pl. SE17 —1C 84
Rodney Rd. SE17 —1C 84
Rodney St. N1 —4G 59
Roger St. WC1 —2G 67
Rohere Ho. EC1 —6B 60
Roland Gdns. SW7 —3J 79
Roland Way. SE17 —4E 84
Roland Way. SW7 —3J 79
Rolls Bldgs. EC4 —5J 67
Rolls Pas. EC4 —5H 67
Rolls Rd. SE1 —3J 85
Roman Ho. EC2 —4C 68
Romilly St. W1 —7C 66
Romney M. W1 —3F 65
Romney St. SW1 —7C 74
Rood La. EC3 —7F 69
Ropemaker St. EC2 —3D 68
Roper La. SE1 —5G 77
Ropers Orchard. SW3 —6B 80
Ropley St. E2 —5K 61
Rosalind Ho. N1 —5G 61
Rosaline Rd. SW6 —7A 78
Rosary Gdns. SW7 —2J 79
Rosaville Rd. SW6 —7B 78
Roscoe St. EC1 —2C 68
Roscoe St. Est. EC1 —2C 68
Rose All. EC2 —4G 69
Rose All. SE1 —2C 76
Rosebank Wlk. NW1 —1C 58
Rosebery Av. EC1 —2H 67
Rosebery Ct. EC1 —1H 67
Rosebery Sq. EC1 —2H 67
Rose Ct. E1 —4H 69
Rose & Crown Ct. EC2 —5B 68
Rose & Crown Yd. SW1 —3A 74
Rosehart M. W11 —6D 62
Rosemary Ho. N1 —3E 60
Rosemary St. N1 —2E 60
Rosemoor St. SW3 —2D 80
Rose St. WC2 —7D 66
Rosetta Clo. SW8 —7E 82
Rosewood Ho. SW8 —5F 83
Rosmead Rd. W11 —7A 62
Rosoman Pl. EC1 —1J 67
Rosoman St. EC1 —7J 59
Rossendale Way. NW1 —1A 58
Rossmore Ct. NW1 —1D 64
Rossmore Rd. NW1 —2C 64
Rotary St. SE1 —6K 75
Rotherfield St. N1 —1B 60
Rotherham Wlk. SE1 —3K 75
Rotherhithe New Rd. SE16 —4K 85
Rothery St. N1 —2A 60
Rothesay Ct. SE11 —6H 83
Rothsay St. SE1 —6F 77
Rothwell St. NW1 —2E 56
Rotten Row. SW7 & SW1 —4A 72
Rouel Rd. SE16 —6K 77
(in two parts)
Roundhouse, The. NW1 —1G 57
Roupell St. SE1 —3J 75
Rousden St. NW1 —1K 57
Rover Ho. N1 —3G 61
Rowallan Rd. SW6 —7A 78
Rowan Ct. E8 —1J 61
Rowan Ct. SE15 —7H 85
(off Garniers Clo.)
Rowcross Pl. SE1 —3H 85
Rowcross St. SE1 —3H 85
Rowington Clo. W2 —3F 63
Rowland Hill Ho. SE1 —4K 75
Rowley Way. NW8 —2G 55
Roxby Pl. SW6 —5E 78
Royal Arc. W1 —1K 73
Royal Av. SW3 —3D 80
Royal College St. NW1 —1K 57
Royal Ct. EC3 —6E 68
Royal Cres. W11 —3A 70
Royal Exchange Av. EC3 —6E 68
Royal Exchange Bldgs. EC3 —6E 68
Royal Hospital Rd. SW3 —6D 80
Royal Mews, The. —6J 73
Royal Mint Ct. EC3 —1J 77
Royal Mint Pl. E1 —1J 77
Royal Mint St. E1 —7J 69
Royal Oak M. SE1 —5F 77
Royal Opera Arc. SW1 —2B 74
Royal Pde. SW6 —7A 78
Royal Rd. SE17 —5K 83
Royal St. SE1 —6G 75
Royal Tower Lodge. E1 —1K 77
Royalty M. W1 —6B 66
Rozel Ct. N1 —2F 61
Rudge Ho. SE16 —6K 77
Rudolf Pl. SW8 —6E 82
Rudolph Rd. NW6 —5E 54
Rufford St. N1 —2E 58
Rufus St. N1 —7F 61
Rugby St. WC1 —2F 67
Rumbold Rd. SW6 —7G 79
Runacres Ct. SE17 —4B 84
Runcorn Pl. W11 —7A 62
Rupert Ct. W1 —7B 66
Rupert Ho. SE11 —2J 83
Rupert Rd. NW6 —5C 54
Rupert St. W1 —7B 66
Rushton St. N1 —4E 60
Rushworth St. SE1 —4A 76
Ruskin Mans. W14 —6A 78
Russell Ct. SW1 —3A 74
Russell Gdns. W14 —6A 70
Russell Gdns. M. W14 —5A 70
Russell Rd. W14 —6A 70
Russell Sq. WC1 —2D 66
Russell St. WC2 —7E 66
Russia Ct. EC2 —6C 68
Russia Row. EC2 —6C 68
Ruston M. W11 —6A 62
Rust Sq. SE5 —7D 84
Rutherford St. SW1 —1B 82
Rutland Ct. EC1 —2B 68
Rutland Ct. SW7 —5C 72
Rutland Gdns. SW7 —5C 72
Rutland Gdns. M. SW7 —5C 72
Rutland Ga. SW7 —5C 72
Rutland Ga. M. SW7 —5B 72
Rutland Ho. W8 —7F 71
Rutland M. NW8 —3G 55
Rutland M. E. SW7 —6C 72
Rutland M. S. SW7 —6B 72
Rutland M. W. SW7 —6B 72
Rutland Pl. EC1 —3A 68
Rutland St. SW7 —6C 72
Rutley Clo. SE17 —5K 83
Rydal Water. NW1 —7K 57
Ryder Ct. SW1 —2A 74
Ryder's Ter. NW8 —4H 55
Ryder St. SW1 —2A 74
Ryder Yd. SW1 —2A 74
Rydon St. N1 —2C 60
Rylston Rd. SW6 —6B 78
Rysbrack St. SW3 —6D 72

Sable St. N1 —1A 60
Sackville St. W1 —1A 74
Saddle Yd. W1 —2H 73
Saffron Hill. EC1 —2J 67
Saffron St. EC1 —3J 67
Sage Way. WC1 —7F 59
Sail St. SE11 —1G 83
St Agnes Pl. SE11 —6J 83
St Agnes Well. EC1 —1E 68
St Albans Ct. EC2 —5C 68
St Alban's Gro. W8 —6G 71
St Albans Mans. W8 —6G 71
St Alban's M. W2 —3A 64
St Alban's Pl. N1 —3K 59
St Alban's St. SW1 —1B 74
St Alphage Garden. EC2 —4C 68
St Alphage Highwalk. EC2 —4C 68
St Alphage Ho. EC2 —4D 68
St Andrew's Hill. EC4 —7A 68
St Andrews Mans. W14 —5A 78
St Andrew's Pl. NW1 —1J 65
St Andrew's Rd. W14 —5A 78
St Andrew St. EC4 —4J 67
St Andrews Wharf. SE1 —4J 77
St Anne's Ct. NW6 —3A 54
St Anne's Ct. W1 —6B 66
St Ann's La. SW1 —7C 74
St Ann's St. SW1 —6C 74
St Ann's Ter. NW8 —4A 56
St Anselm's Pl. W1 —7H 65
St Anthony's Clo. E1 —2K 77
St Aubins Ct. N1 —2F 61
St Augustine's Rd. NW1 —1B 58
St Barnabas St. SW1 —3G 81
St Benet's Pl. EC3 —7E 68
St Botolph Row. EC3 —6H 69
St Botolph St. EC3 —6H 69
St Brelades Ct. N1 —2F 61
St Briavel's Ct. SE15 —7G 85
St Bride's Av. EC4 —6K 67
St Bride's Pas. EC4 —6K 67
St Bride St. EC4 —5K 67
St Catherines M. SW3 —1D 80
St Chad's Pl. WC1 —6E 58
St Chad's St. WC1 —6E 58
St Charles Pl. W10 —4A 62
St Charles Sq. W10 —3A 62
St Christopher's Pl. W1 —5G 65
St Clare St. EC3 —6H 69
St Clement's Ct. EC4 —7E 68
St Clement's La. WC2 —6G 67
St Cross St. EC1 —3J 67
St Dunstans All. EC3 —1F 77
St Dunstans Ct. EC4 —6J 67
St Dunstans Hill. EC3 —1F 77
St Dunstans La. EC3 —1F 77
St Edmund's Clo. NW8 —3D 56
St Edmund's Ter. NW8 —3C 56
St Edwards Ct. SW8 —5C 82
St Ermin's Hill. SW1 —6B 74
St Ervan's Rd. W10 —3A 62
St Eugene Ct. NW6 —3A 54
St George's Bldgs. SE1 —4C 76
St George's Cir. SE1 —6K 75
St Georges Ct. EC4 —5K 67
St George's Dri. SW1 —2J 81
St George's Fields. W2 —6C 64
St Georges La. EC3 —1E 76
St George's M. NW1 —1E 56
St George's M. SE1 —6J 75
St George's Rd. SE1 —6J 75
St George's Sq. SW1 —3B 82
St George's Sq. M. SW1 —4B 82
St George's Ter. NW1 —1E 56
St George St. W1 —6J 65
St George's Way. SE15 —6F 85
St Giles Cir. W1 —5C 66
St Giles Ct. WC2 —5D 66
St Giles High St. WC2 —5C 66
St Giles Pas. WC2 —6C 66
St Giles Ter. EC2 —4C 68
St Helena St. WC1 —7H 59
St Helen's Pl. EC3 —5F 69
St James' Ct. SW1 —6A 74
St James Ga. NW1 —1C 58
St James Residences. W1 —7B 66
St James's. SW1 —2A 74
St James's App. EC2 —2F 69
St James's Clo. NW8 —3D 56
St James's Gdns. W11 —2A 70
St James's Mkt. SW1 —1B 74
St James's Pas. EC3 —6G 69
St James's Pl. SW1 —3K 73
St James's Rd. SE1 —5K 85
St James's Rd. SE16 —6K 77
St James's Row. EC1 —2K 67
St James's Sq. SW1 —2A 74
St James's St. SW1 —2K 73
St James's Ter. NW8 —4D 56
St James's Ter. M. NW8 —3D 56
St James's Wlk. EC1 —1K 67
St John's Clo. SW6 —7D 78
St John's Est. N1 —5E 60
St John's Est. SE1 —4H 77
St John's Gdns. W11 —1A 70
St John's La. EC1 —2K 67
St John's M. W11 —6D 62
St John's Path. EC1 —2K 67
St John's Pl. EC1 —2K 67
St John's Sq. EC1 —2K 67
(in two parts)
St John St. EC1 —5J 59
St John's Vs. W8 —7F 71
St John's Wood Ct. NW8 —7A 56
St John's Wood High St. NW8 —5A 56
St John's Wood Pk. NW8 —3K 55
St John's Wood Rd. NW8 —1K 63
St John's Wood Ter. NW8 —4A 56
St Joseph's Clo. W10 —4A 62
St Julian's Rd. NW6 —1C 54
St Katharine's Precinct. NW1 —4H 57
St Katharine's Way. E1 —2J 77
St Katherine's Row. EC3 —7G 69
St Lawrence Ct. N1 —2F 61
St Lawrence Ter. W10 —4A 62
St Leonard's Ct. N1 —6E 60
St Leonard's Ter. SW3 —4D 80
St Loo Av. SW3 —5C 80
St Luke's Clo. EC1 —1C 68
St Luke's Est. EC1 —1D 68
St Luke's M. W11 —5B 62
St Luke's Rd. W11 —4B 62
St Luke's St. SW3 —3C 80
St Luke's Yd. W9 —5B 54
St Margaret's Clo. EC2 —4D 68
St Margaret's Ct. SE1 —3D 76
St Margaret's La. W8 —7F 71
St Margaret St. SW1 —5D 74
St Mark's Clo. W11 —6A 62
St Mark's Cres. NW1 —2G 57
St Mark's Gro. SW10 —7G 79
St Mark's Pl. W11 —6A 62
St Mark's Rd. W10 & W11 —6A 62
St Mark's Sq. NW1 —3F 57
St Mark St. E1 —6J 69
St Martin's Clo. NW1 —2K 57
St Martins Ct. N1 —2G 61
St Martin's Ct. WC2 —7D 66
St Martin's La. WC2 —7D 66
St Martin's le Grand. EC1 —5B 68
St Martin's Pl. WC2 —1D 74
St Martin's St. WC2 —1C 74
St Mary Abbot's Ct. W14 —7B 70
St Mary Abbot's Pl. W8 —7C 70
St Mary Abbot's Ter. W14 —7B 70
St Mary at Hill. EC3 —1F 77
St Mary Axe. EC3 —6G 69
St Mary Graces Ct. E1 —1J 77
St Mary Newington Clo. SE17 —3G 85
St Mary's Gdns. SE11 —1J 83
St Mary's Ga. W8 —7F 71
St Mary's Mans. W2 —3K 63
St Mary's M. NW6 —1F 55
St Mary's Path. N1 —2K 59
St Mary's Pl. W8 —7F 71
St Mary's Sq. W2 —3K 63
St Mary's Ter. W2 —3J 63
St Mary's Tower. EC1 —2C 68
St Mary's Wlk. SE11 —1J 83
St Matthews Ct. SE1 —7B 76
St Matthew's Lodge. NW1 —4A 58
St Matthew's Row. E2 —7K 61
St Matthew St. SW1 —7B 74
St Michael's All. EC3 —6E 68
St Michael's Gdns. W10 —4A 62
St Michael's St. W2 —5A 64
St Mildred's Ct. EC2 —6D 68
St Olaf Ho. SE1 —2E 76
St Olaf's Rd. SW6 —7A 78
St Olaf Stairs. SE1 —2E 76
St Olave's Ct. EC2 —6D 68
St Olave's Est. SE1 —4G 77
St Olave's Gdns. SE11 —1H 83
St Olave's Mans. SE11 —1H 83
St Olave's Ter. SE1 —4G 77
St Oswald's Pl. SE11 —3F 83
St Oswulf St. SW1 —2C 82
St Pancras Commercial Cen. NW1 —2A 58
St Pancras Way. NW1 —1K 57
St Paul's All. EC4 —6A 68
St Paul's Chyd. EC4 —6A 68
St Paul's Cres. NW1 —1C 58
(in two parts)
St Paul's M. NW1 —1C 58
St Paul's Ter. SE17 —5A 84
St Paul St. N1 —3B 60
(in two parts)
St Paul's Studios. W14 —3A 78
(off Talgarth Rd.)
St Pauls Vw. Apartments. EC1 —7H 59
St Peter's All. EC3 —6E 68
St Peter's Av. E2 —5K 61
St Petersburgh M. W2 —7F 63
St Petersburgh Pl. W2 —7F 63
St Peters Chu. Ct. N1 —4A 60

St Peter's Clo.—Trafalgar Gdns.

St Peter's Clo. E2 —5K 61
St Peters Pl. W9 —2F 63
St Peter's Sq. E2 —5K 61
St Peter's St. N1 —3A 60
St Peter's St. M. N1 —4A 60
St Peter's Way. N1 —1G 61
St Philip's Way. N1 —3C 60
St Saviour's Est. SE1 —6H 77
St Stephen's Clo. NW8 —3C 56
St Stephen's Cres. W2 —5E 62
St Stephen's Gdns. W2 —5D 62 (in two parts)
St Stephen's M. W2 —4E 62
St Stephens Pde. SW1 —5E 74
St Stephen's St. EC4 —6D 68
St Stephen's Ter. SW8 —7F 83
St Stephen's Wlk. SW7 —1H 79
St Swithins La. EC4 —7D 68
St Thomas Pl. NW1 —1C 58
St Thomas St. SE1 —3D 76
St Thomas's Way. SW6 —7B 78
St Vincent St. W1 —4G 65
Salamanca Pl. SE1 —2F 83
Salamanca St. SE1 & SE11 —2E 82
Salem Rd. W2 —7G 63
Sale Pl. W2 —4B 64
Sale St. E2 —1K 69
Salisbury Clo. SE17 —2D 84
Salisbury Ct. EC4 —6K 67
Salisbury Ho. SW9 —7J 83
Salisbury M. SW6 —7B 78
Salisbury Pas. SW6 —7B 78 (off Dawes Rd.)
Salisbury Pl. W1 —3E 64
Salisbury Sq. EC4 —6J 67
Salisbury St. NW8 —2B 64
Saltash Ho. SE11 —3K 83
Salters Ct. EC4 —6C 68
Salter's Hall Ct. EC4 —7D 68
Saltram Cres. W9 —6C 54
Saltwood Gro. SE17 —4D 84
Salusbury Rd. NW6 —2A 54
Sambrook Ho. SE11 —2H 83
Samford Ho. N1 —3H 59
Samford St. NW8 —2B 64
Samuel Clo. E8 —2J 61
Samuel Jones Ind. Est. SE15 —7G 85
Samuel Lewis Trust Dwellings. SW3 —2B 80
Samuel Lewis Trust Dwellings. SW6 —7E 78
Samuel Lewis Trust Dwellings. W14 —1B 78
Samuel St. SE15 —7H 85
Sancroft Ho. SE11 —3G 83
Sancroft St. SE11 —3G 83
Sanctuary St. SE1 —4C 76
Sanctuary, The. SW1 —6C 74
Sandell St. SE1 —4H 75
Sandford St. SW6 —7G 79
Sandhills, The. SW10 —5J 79
Sandland St. WC1 —4G 67
Sandringham Ct. W9 —7J 55
Sandringham Flats. WC2 —7C 66
Sandwich St. WC1 —7D 58
Sandys Row. E1 —4G 69
Sans Wlk. EC1 —1J 67
Santley Ho. SE1 —5J 75
Saperton Wlk. SE11 —1G 83
Sapperton Ct. EC1 —1B 68
Saracens Head Yd. EC3 —6H 69
Sarah St. N1 —6G 61
Sardinia St. WC2 —6F 67
Satchwell Rd. E2 —7K 61
Satchwell St. E2 —7K 61
Saul Ct. SE15 —6H 85
Saunders St. SE11 —1G 83
Savage Gdns. EC3 —7G 69
Savile Row. W1 —7K 65
Savona Ho. SW8 —7K 81
Savona St. SW8 —7K 81
Savoy Bldgs. WC2 —1F 75
Savoy Ct. WC2 —1F 75
Savoy Hill. WC2 —1F 75
Savoy Pl. WC2 —1E 74
Savoy Row. WC2 —7F 67
Savoy Steps. WC2 —1F 75
Savoy St. WC2 —7F 67
Savoy Way. WC2 —1F 75
Sawyer St. SE1 —4B 76
Sayer St. SE17 —1B 84
Scala St. W1 —3A 66
Scarborough St. E1 —6J 69
Scarsdale Pl. W8 —6F 71
Scarsdale Vs. W8 —7E 70
Scawfell St. E2 —5J 61
Sceptre Ct. EC3 —1J 77
School App. E2 —6G 61
Schwartz Bldgs. E1 —3K 69
Sclater St. E1 —1H 69
Scoresby St. SE1 —3K 75
Scotch House. (Junct.) —5D 72
Scotland Pl. SW1 —3D 74
Scotson Ho. SE11 —2H 83
Scotswood St. EC1 —1J 67
Scott Ellis Gdns. NW8 —7K 55
Scott Ho. N1 —2D 60
Scott Lidgett Cres. SE16 —5K 77
Scott's Sufferance Wharf. SE1 —5J 77
Scott's Yd. EC4 —7D 68
Scovell Cres. SE1 —5B 76
Scovell Rd. SE1 —5B 76
Scriven Ct. E8 —2J 61
Scriven St. E8 —2J 61
Scrutton St. EC2 —2F 69
Seaford St. WC1 —7E 58
Seaforth Pl. SW1 —6A 74
Seagrave Lodge. SW6 —5E 78
Seagrave Rd. SW6 —5E 78
Searles Rd. SE1 —1E 84
Sears St. SE5 —7D 84
Seaton Clo. SE11 —3J 83
Sebastian St. EC1 —7A 60
Sebbon St. N1 —1A 60
Secker St. SE1 —3H 75
Second Av. W10 —1A 62
Sedan Way. SE17 —3F 85
Sedding St. SW1 —1F 81
Sedding Studios. SW1 —1F 81
Seddon Highwalk. EC2 —3B 68
Seddon Ho. EC2 —4B 68
Seddon St. WC1 —7G 59
Sedgmoor Pl. SE5 —7G 85
Sedlescombe Rd. SW6 —6C 78
Sedley Ho. SE11 —3G 83
Sedley Pl. W1 —6H 65
Seething La. EC3 —7G 69
Sega Ho. SW5 —1E 78
Sekforde St. EC1 —2K 67
Selbourne Ho. SE1 —5D 76
Selby St. E1 —2K 69
Seldon Ho. SW8 —7K 81
Sellon M. SE11 —2F 83
Selwood Pl. SW7 —3K 79
Selwood Ter. SW7 —3K 79
Semley Pl. SW1 —2G 81
Senior St. W2 —3F 63
Seraph Ct. EC1 —6B 60
Serjeant's Inn. EC4 —6J 67
Serle St. WC2 —5G 67
Sermon La. EC4 —6B 68
Serpentine Rd. W2 —3B 72
Setchell Rd. SE1 —1H 85
Setchell Way. SE1 —1H 85
Settles St. E1 —4K 69
Seven Dials. WC2 —6D 66
Seven Dials Ct. WC2 —6D 66
Seville M. N1 —1F 61
Seville St. SW1 —5E 72
Sevington St. W9 —2F 63
Seward St. EC1 —1A 68
Seymour Clo. EC1 —2K 67
Seymour M. W1 —5F 65
Seymour Pl. W1 —3C 64
Seymour St. W2 & W1 —6D 64
Seymour Wlk. SW10 —5H 79
Shacklewell St. E2 —1J 69
Shad Thames. SE1 —3H 77
Shaftesbury Av. W1 & WC2 —7B 66
Shaftesbury M. W8 —7E 70
Shaftesbury Pl. EC2 —4B 68 (off Barbican)
Shaftesbury St. N1 —5C 60 (in two parts)
Shafto M. SW1 —7E 72
Shafts Ct. EC3 —6F 69
Shakespeare Tower. EC2 —3C 68
Shalcomb St. SW10 —6J 79
Shalford Ct. N1 —4K 59
Shalford Ho. SE1 —6E 76
Shand St. SE1 —4F 77
Shannon Pl. NW8 —4C 56
Shap St. E2 —4H 61
Sharpleshall St. NW1 —1E 56
Sharpness Ct. SE15 —7H 85
Sharsted St. SE17 —4K 83
Shaver's Pl. SW1 —1B 74
Shawfield St. SW3 —4C 80
Sheba St. E1 —2J 69
Sheen Gro. N1 —2H 59
Sheffield St. WC2 —6F 67
Sheffield Ter. W8 —4D 70
Sheldon Ct. SW8 —7D 82
Sheldrake Pl. W8 —4C 70
Shelley Ho. SE17 —3C 84
Shelton St. WC2 —6D 66 (in two parts)
Shenfield St. N1 —5G 61
Shepherd Clo. W1 —7F 65
Shepherdess Pl. N1 —6D 60
Shepherdess Wlk. N1 —4C 60
Shepherd Mkt. W1 —3H 73
Shepherds Pl. W1 —7F 65
Shepherd St. W1 —3H 73
Shepperton Rd. N1 —2C 60
Sheraton St. W1 —6B 66
Sherborne Ho. SW8 —7F 83
Sherborne La. EC4 —7D 68
Sherborne St. N1 —2D 60
Sherbrooke Rd. SW6 —7A 78
Shere Ho. SE1 —5D 76
Sheridan Ho. SE11 —2J 83
Sheringham. NW8 —2A 56
Sheringham Ho. NW1 —3B 64
Sherlock M. W1 —3F 65
Sherston Ct. SE1 —1A 84
Sherston Ct. WC1 —7H 59
Sherwin Ho. SE11 —5H 83
Sherwood. NW6 —1A 54
Sherwood St. W1 —7A 66
Shillibeer Pl. W1 —4C 64
Shillingford St. N1 —2A 60
Ship & Mermaid Row. SE1 —4E 76
Ship Tavern Pas. EC3 —7F 69
Shipton St. E2 —6J 61
Shipwright Yd. SE1 —3F 77
Shirland M. W9 —7C 54
Shirland Rd. W9 —7B 54
Shirley Ho. SE5 —7E 84
Shoe La. EC4 —5J 67
Shoreditch Ct. E8 —2J 61 (off Queensbridge Rd.)
Shoreditch High St. E1 —7G 61
Shorncliffe Rd. SE1 —3H 85
Shorrold's Rd. SW6 —7C 78
Shorter St. E1 —1H 77
Shorts Gdns. WC2 —6D 66
Short St. SE1 —4J 75
Shouldham St. W1 —4C 64
Shrewsbury Ct. EC1 —2C 68
Shrewsbury Ho. SW8 —6G 83
Shrewsbury M. W2 —4D 62
Shrewsbury Rd. W2 —5D 62
Shropshire Pl. WC1 —2A 66
Shroton St. NW1 —3B 64
Shrubbary Clo. N1 —3C 60
Shrubland Rd. E8 —2J 61
Shurland Gdns. SE15 —7J 85
Shuters Sq. W14 —4B 78
Shuttle St. E1 —2K 69
Sicilian Av. WC1 —4E 66
Sidmouth La. NW1 —2E 64
Sidford Ho. SE1 —7G 75
Sidford Pl. SE1 —7G 75
Sidmouth Ho. SE15 —7K 85
Sidmouth St. WC1 —7E 58
Sidney Boyd Ct. NW6 —1E 54
Sidney Gro. EC1 —6K 59
Signmakers Yd. NW1 —3J 57
Silbury St. N1 —6D 60
Silex St. SE1 —5A 76
Silk St. EC2 —3C 68
Sillitoe Ho. N1 —3E 60
Silver Pl. W1 —7A 66
Silvester Ho. W11 —5B 62
Silvester St. SE1 —5D 76
Simla Ho. SE1 —5E 76
Simms Rd. SE1 —2K 85
Simon Clo. W11 —7C 62
Simpson Ho. NW8 —7B 56
Simpson Ho. SE11 —4G 83
Sinclair Rd. W14 —6A 70
Singer St. EC2 —7E 60
Sirinham Point. SW8 —6G 83
Sise La. EC4 —6D 68
Sister Mabel's Way. SE15 —7K 85
Sivill Ho. E2 —6J 61
Six Bridges Ind. Est. SE1 —4K 85
Skinner Pl. SW1 —2F 81
Skinners La. EC4 —7C 68
Skinner St. EC1 —1J 67
Skyline Plaza Building. E1 —5K 69
Slade Wlk. SE17 —6A 84
Slaidburn St. SW10 —6J 79
Sleaford Ind. Est. SW8 —7A 82
Sleaford St. SW8 —7K 81
Slingsby Pl. WC2 —7D 66
Sloane Av. SW3 —2B 80
Sloane Ct. E. SW3 —3F 81
Sloane Ct. W. SW3 —3F 81
Sloane Gdns. SW1 —2F 81
Sloane Sq. SW1 —2E 80
Sloane St. SW1 —5E 72
Sloane Ter. SW1 —1F 81
Smallbrook M. W2 —6K 63
Smart's Pl. WC2 —5E 66
Smeaton Ct. SE1 —7B 76
Smithfield St. EC1 —4K 67
Smith's Ct. W1 —7B 66
Smith Sq. SW1 —7D 74
Smith St. SW3 —3D 80
Smith Ter. SW3 —4D 80
Smyrk's Rd. SE17 —4G 85
Smyrna Rd. NW6 —1E 54
Snowden St. EC2 —3F 69
Snow Hill. EC1 —4K 67
Snow Hill Ct. EC1 —5A 68 (in two parts)
Snowman Ho. NW6 —2G 55
Snowsfields. SE1 —4E 76
Soho Sq. W1 —5B 66
Soho St. W1 —5B 66
Solarium Ct. SE1 —1H 85
Soley M. WC1 —6H 59
Somer Ct. SW6 —6D 78
Somers Clo. NW1 —4B 58
Somers Cres. W2 —6B 64
Somerset Sq. W14 —6B 70
Sondes St. SE17 —5D 84
Sopwith Way. SW8 —7H 81
Sotheran Clo. E8 —2K 61
Southall Pl. SE1 —5D 76
Southampton Bldgs. WC2 —4H 67
Southampton Pl. WC1 —4E 66
Southampton Row. WC1 —3E 66
Southampton St. WC2 —7E 66
Southampton Way. SE5 —7D 84
Southam St. W10 —2A 62
S. Audley St. W1 —1G 73
Southbank Bus. Cen. SW8 —6C 82
S. Bolton Gdns. SW5 —3G 79
S. Carriage Dri. SW7 & SW1 —5A 72
Southcombe St. W14 —1A 78
South Cres. WC1 —4B 66
S. Eaton Pl. SW1 —1G 81
S. Edwardes Sq. W8 —7C 70
South End. W8 —6G 71
S. End Row. W8 —6G 71
Southern Row. W10 —2A 62
Southern St. N1 —4F 59
Southernwood Retail Pk. SE1 —3H 85
Southey Ho. SE17 —3C 84
Southgate Gro. N1 —1E 60
Southgate Rd. N1 —2E 60
S. Island Pl. SW9 —7G 83
S. Kensington Sta. Arc. SW7 —1A 80
S. Lambeth Pl. SW8 —5E 82
S. Lambeth Rd. SW8 —7E 82
South Lodge. NW8 —6K 55
S. Molton La. W1 —6H 65
S. Molton St. W1 —6H 65
South Pde. SW3 —3A 80
South Pl. EC2 —4E 68
South Pl. M. EC2 —4E 68
South Ri. W2 —7C 64
South Sq. WC1 —4H 67
South St. W1 —2G 73
S. Tenter St. E1 —7J 69
South Ter. SW7 —1B 80
Southwark Bri. SE1 & EC4 —1C 76
Southwark Bri. Office Village. SE1 —3C 76
Southwark Bri. Rd. SE1 —6A 76
Southwark Gro. SE1 —3B 76
Southwark Pk. Rd. SE16 —1J 85
Southwark Pk. Rd. Est. SE1 —1J 85
Southwark St. SE1 —2K 75
Southwell Gdns. SW7 —1H 79
S. Wharf Rd. W2 —5K 63
Southwick M. W2 —5A 64
Southwick Pl. W2 —6B 64
Southwick St. W2 —5B 64
Southwick Yd. W2 —6B 64
Southwold Mans. W9 —7E 54
Southwood Ct. EC1 —7K 59
Southwood Smith St. N1 —3K 59
Sovereign M. E2 —4H 61
Spafield St. EC1 —1H 67
Spa Grn. Est. EC1 —6K 59
Spanish Pl. W1 —5G 65
Spa Rd. SE16 —7H 77
Sparrick's Row. SE1 —4E 76
Speaker's Corner. W2 —7E 64
Spear M. SW5 —2E 78
Speed Highwalk. EC2 —3C 68
Speed Ho. EC2 —3D 68
Speedy Pl. WC1 —7D 58
Spellbrook Wlk. N1 —2C 60
Spelman Ho. E1 —4K 69
Spelman St. E1 —3K 69
Spencer M. W6 —5A 78
Spencer Pl. N1 —1K 59
Spencer St. EC1 —7K 59
Spenlow Ho. SE16 —6K 77
Spenser St. SW1 —6A 74
Spirit Quay. E1 —2K 77
Spital Sq. E1 —3G 69
Spital St. E1 —3K 69
Spital Yd. E1 —3G 69
Spode Ho. SE11 —7H 75
Sprimont Pl. SW3 —3D 80
Springbank Wlk. NW1 —1B 58
Springfield La. NW6 —3F 55
Springfield Rd. NW8 —3H 55
Springfield Wlk. NW6 —3F 55
Spring Gdns. SW1 —2C 74
Spring M. W1 —3E 64
Spring St. W2 —6K 63
Spring Wlk. E1 —3K 69
Spurgeon St. SE1 —7D 76
Spur Rd. SE1 —5H 75
Spur Rd. SW1 —5K 73
Squirries St. E2 —6K 61
Stables Way. SE11 —3H 83
Stable Yd. SW1 —4K 73
Stable Yd. Rd. SW1 —3K 73
Stacey St. WC2 —6C 66
Stackhouse St. SW3 —6D 72
Stacy Path. SE5 —7F 85
Stadium St. SW10 —7J 79
Stafford Clo. NW6 —7D 54
Stafford Cripps Ho. SW6 —6C 78
Stafford Pl. SW1 —6K 73
Stafford Rd. NW6 —6D 54
Stafford St. W1 —2K 73
Stafford Ter. W8 —6D 70
Staff St. EC1 —7E 60
Stag Pl. SW1 —6K 73
Stainer St. SE1 —3E 76
Staining La. EC2 —5C 68
Stalbridge St. NW1 —3C 64
Stamford St. SE1 —3H 75
Stamford Wharf. SE1 —1J 75
Stamp Pl. E2 —6J 61
Standard Pl. EC2 —7G 61
Stanford Pl. SE17 —2F 85
Stanford Rd. W8 —6G 71
Stanford St. SW1 —2B 82
Stangate. SE1 —6G 75
Stanhope Gdns. SW7 —1J 79
Stanhope Ga. W1 —3G 73
Stanhope M. E. SW7 —1J 79
Stanhope M. S. SW7 —2J 79
Stanhope M. W. SW7 —1J 79
Stanhope Pde. NW1 —6K 57
Stanhope Pl. W2 —6D 64
Stanhope Row. W1 —3H 73
Stanhope Ter. W2 —7A 64
Stanier Clo. W14 —4C 78
Stanley Clo. SW8 —6F 83
Stanley Cohen Ho. EC1 —2C 68
Stanley Cres. W11 —7B 62
Stanley Gdns. W11 —7B 62
Stanley Gdns. M. W11 —7C 62
Stanley Pas. NW1 —5D 58
Stanley Sidings. NW1 —1H 57
Stanmore Pl. NW1 —2J 57
Stanmore St. N1 —2F 59
Stannary Pl. SE11 —4J 83
Stannary St. SE11 —5J 83
Stansfield Ho. SE1 —2J 85
Stanway Ct. N1 —5G 61
Stanway St. N1 —4G 61
Stanwick Rd. W14 —2B 78
Stanworth St. SE1 —5H 77
Staple Inn. WC1 —4H 67
Staple Inn Bldgs. WC1 —4H 67
Staple St. SE1 —5E 76
Star All. EC3 —7G 69
Starcross St. NW1 —7A 58
Star Pl. E1 —1J 77
Star Rd. W14 —5B 78
Star St. W2 —5A 64
Star Yd. WC2 —5H 67
Station App. Rd. SE1 —5H 75
Stationers' Hall Ct. EC4 —6A 68
Steadman Ct. EC1 —1C 68
Stead St. SE17 —2D 84
Stean St. E8 —2H 61
Stedham Pl. WC1 —5D 66
Steedman St. SE17 —2B 84
Steelyard Pas. EC4 —1D 76
Steeple Wlk. N1 —2C 60
Stephan Clo. E8 —2K 61
Stephen M. W1 —4B 66
Stephenson Ho. SE1 —7B 76
Stephenson Way. NW1 —1A 66
Stephen St. W1 —4B 66
Sterling St. SW7 —6C 72
Sterry St. SE1 —5D 76
Stevens St. SE1 —6G 77
Steward St. E1 —4G 69
Stewart's Gro. SW3 —3A 80
Stewart's Rd. SW8 —7K 81
Stew La. EC4 —7B 68
Stillington St. SW1 —1A 82
Stockholm Way. E1 —2K 77
Stoddart Ho. SW8 —6G 83
Stonebridge Comn. E8 —1H 61
Stone Bldgs. WC2 —4G 67
Stonecutter St. EC4 —5K 67
Stonefield St. N1 —2J 59
Stone Hall Gdns. W8 —7F 71
Stone Hall Pl. W8 —7F 71
Stone Ho. Ct. EC3 —5G 69
Stones End St. SE1 —5B 76
Stoney La. E1 —5G 69
Stoney St. SE1 —2D 76
Stonor Rd. W14 —2B 78
Stopford Rd. SE17 —4A 84
Store St. WC1 —4B 66
Storey's Ga. SW1 —5C 74
Story St. N1 —1F 59
Stothard Pl. EC2 —3G 69
Stoughton Clo. SE11 —2G 83
Stourcliffe Clo. W1 —5D 64
Stourcliffe St. W1 —6D 64
Strale Ho. N1 —3F 61
Strand. WC2 —2D 74
Strand La. WC2 —7G 67
Strang Ho. N1 —3B 60
Strangways Ter. W14 —6B 70
Stranraer Way. N1 —1E 58
Stratford Av. W8 —7E 70
Stratford Pl. W1 —6H 65
Stratford Rd. W8 —7E 70
Stratford Vs. NW1 —1B 58
Strathearn Pl. W2 —7B 64
Strathmore Gdns. W8 —2E 70
Strathnairn St. SE1 —2K 85
Stratton St. W1 —2J 73
Streatham St. WC1 —5D 66
Streatley Rd. NW6 —1B 54
Stringer Ho. N1 —3G 61
Strode Rd. SW6 —7A 78
Strouts Pl. E2 —6H 61
Strutton Ground. SW1 —6B 74
Strype St. E1 —4H 69
Stuart Rd. NW6 —7D 54 (in two parts)
Stucley Pl. NW1 —1J 57
Studd St. N1 —2K 59
Studio Pl. SW1 —5E 72
Studland. SE17 —3D 84
Stukeley St. WC2 —5E 66
Sturgeon Rd. SE17 —4B 84
Sturge St. SE1 —4B 76
Sturminster Ho. SW8 —7F 83
Sturt St. N1 —5C 60
Stutfield St. E1 —6K 69
Styles Ho. SE1 —3K 75
Sudeley St. N1 —5A 60
Sudrey St. SE1 —5B 76
Suffolk La. EC4 —7D 68
Suffolk Pl. SW1 —2C 74
Suffolk St. SW1 —1C 74
Sugar Bakers Ct. EC3 —6G 69
Sugar Quay. EC3 —1G 77
Sugar Quay Wlk. EC3 —1G 77
Sugden St. SE17 —6D 84
Sullivan Rd. SE11 —1K 83
Sultan St. SE5 —7B 84
Summerfield Av. NW6 —4A 54
Summers St. EC1 —2H 67
Sumner Bldgs. SE1 —2B 76
Sumner Pl. SW7 —2A 80
Sumner Pl. M. SW7 —2A 80
Sumner Rd. SE15 —6J 85 (in two parts)
Sumner St. SE1 —2A 76
Sun Ct. EC3 —6E 68
Sunderland Ter. W2 —5F 63
Sunflower Dri. E8 —1J 61
Sunningdale Gdns. W8 —7E 70
Sun Pas. SE16 —6K 77
Sun Rd. W14 —4B 78
Sun St. EC2 —3E 68 (in two parts)
Sun St. Pas. EC2 —4F 69
Sun Wlk. E1 —1J 77
Surrendale Pl. W9 —2E 62
Surrey Gro. SE17 —4F 85
Surrey Row. SE1 —4K 75
Surrey Sq. SE17 —3F 85
Surrey St. WC2 —7G 67
Surrey Ter. SE17 —3G 85
Sussex Gdns. W2 —7K 63
Sussex M. E. W2 —6A 64
Sussex M. W. W2 —7A 64
Sussex Pl. NW1 —1D 64
Sussex Pl. W2 —6A 64
Sussex Sq. W2 —7A 64
Sussex St. SW1 —4J 81
Sutherland Av. W9 —2E 62
Sutherland Ho. W8 —7F 71
Sutherland Pl. W2 —5D 62
Sutherland Row. SW1 —3J 81
Sutherland Sq. SE17 —4B 84
Sutherland St. SW1 —3H 81
Sutherland Wlk. SE17 —4C 84
Sutton Est. EC1 —7E 60
Sutton Est., The. N1 —1K 59
Sutton Est., The. SW3 —3C 80
Sutton Row. W1 —5C 66
Sutton's Way. EC1 —2C 68
Sutton Wlk. SE1 —1G 75
Swallow Pas. W1 —6J 65
Swallow Pl. W1 —6J 65
Swallow St. W1 —1A 74
Swanage Ho. SW8 —7F 83
Swan Ct. SW3 —4C 80
Swanfield St. E2 —7H 61
Swan La. EC4 —1E 76
Swan Mead. SE1 —7F 77
Swans Pas. E1 —7J 69
Swan St. SE1 —6C 76
Swan Wlk. SW3 —5D 80
Swedeland Ct. E1 —4G 69
Sweeney Cres. SE1 —5J 77
Swinbrook Rd. W10 —3A 62
Swinton Pl. WC1 —6F 59
Swinton St. WC1 —6F 59
Swiss Cen. W1 —7C 66
Swiss Cottage. (Junct.) —1K 55
Swiss Ct. WC2 —1C 74
Swiss Ter. NW6 —1K 55
Sycamore Ct. NW6 —2E 54
Sycamore St. EC1 —2B 68
Sycamore Wlk. W10 —1A 62
Sydney Clo. SW3 —2A 80
Sydney M. SW3 —2A 80
Sydney Pl. SW7 —2A 80
Sydney St. SW3 —2B 80
Symes M. NW1 —4K 57
Symister M. N1 —7F 61
Symons St. SW3 —2E 80

Tabard Garden Est. SE1 —5D 76
Tabard St. SE1 —4D 76
Tabernacle St. EC2 —2E 68
Tachbrook Est. SW1 —4B 82
Tachbrook M. SW1 —1K 81
Tachbrook St. SW1 —2A 82
Tadema Ho. NW8 —2A 64
Tadema Rd. SW10 —7J 79
Tadworth Ho. SE1 —5K 75
Tailworth St. E1 —4K 69
Talbot Ct. EC3 —7E 68
Talbot Rd. W11 & W2 —6C 62 (in two parts)
Talbot Sq. W2 —6A 64
Talbot Wlk. W11 —6A 62
Talbot Yd. SE1 —3D 76
Talgarth Mans. W14 —3A 78
Talgarth Mans. W14 —3A 78
Talgarth Rd. W6 & W14 —3A 78
Tallis St. EC4 —7J 67
Tamar Ho. SE11 —3J 83
Tamarind Yd. E1 —2K 77
Tamworth St. SW6 —5D 78
Tankerton St. WC1 —7E 58
Tanner St. SE1 —5G 77
Tanswell St. SE1 —5H 75
Tapley Ho. SE1 —5K 77
Taplow Ho. SE17 —3E 84
Taplow St. N1 —5C 60
Tarn St. SE1 —7B 76
Tarranbrae. NW6 —1A 54
Tarrant Pl. W1 —4D 64
Tarver Rd. SE17 —4A 84
Tasso Rd. W6 —5A 78
Tasso Yd. W6 —6A 78
Tatum St. SE17 —2E 84
Taunton M. NW1 —2D 64
Taunton Pl. NW1 —1D 64
Taverners Clo. W11 —3A 70
Tavistock Cres. W11 —4B 62 (in three parts)
Tavistock Ho. WC1 —1C 66
Tavistock M. W11 —5B 62
Tavistock Pl. WC1 —1D 66
Tavistock Rd. W11 —5B 62 (in two parts)
Tavistock Sq. WC1 —1C 66
Tavistock St. WC2 —7E 66 (in two parts)
Taviton St. WC1 —1B 66
Tavy Clo. SE11 —3J 83
Tay Bldgs. SE1 —6F 77
Tayler Ct. NW8 —2K 55
Tayport Clo. N1 —1E 58
Teale St. E2 —4K 61
Tedworth Gdns. SW3 —4D 80
Tedworth Sq. SW3 —4D 80
Telegraph St. EC2 —5D 68
Telephone Pl. SW6 —5C 78
Telford Rd. W10 —3A 62
Telfords Yd. E1 —1K 77
Telford Ter. SW1 —5K 81
Temple. EC4 —7H 67
Temple Av. EC4 —7J 67
Temple Chambers. EC4 —7J 67
Temple Ct. SW8 —7D 82
Temple La. EC4 —6J 67
Temple Pl. WC2 —7G 67
Templeton Pl. SW5 —2E 78
Temple W. M. SE11 —7K 75
Tenison Ct. W1 —7K 65
Tenison Way. SE1 —3G 75
Tenniel Clo. W2 —7H 63
Tennis St. SE1 —4D 76
Tennyson Ho. SE17 —3C 84
Tennyson Mans. W14 —5A 78
Tennyson Rd. NW6 —2C 54 (in two parts)
Tenterden St. W1 —6J 65
Tenter Ground. E1 —4H 69
Tenter Pas. E1 —6J 69
Terling Wlk. N1 —2B 60
Terminus Pl. SW1 —7J 73
Terrace, The. EC4 —6J 67
Terrace, The. NW6 —2D 54
Terrace Wlk. SW11 —7D 80
Terretts Pl. N1 —1K 59
Territorial Ho. SE11 —2J 83
Tetbury Pl. N1 —3K 59
Tetcott Rd. SW10 —7H 79 (in two parts)
Thackeray Ct. W14 —7A 70
Thackeray Ho. WC1 —1D 66
Thackeray St. W8 —6G 71
Thames Ct. SE15 —7H 85
Thames Exchange Building. EC4 —1C 76
Thames Ho. EC4 —1C 76
Thames Ho. SW1 —1D 82
Thanet St. WC1 —7D 58
Thavie's Inn. EC1 —5J 67
Thaxted Ct. N1 —5E 60
Thaxton Rd. W14 —5C 78
Thayer St. W1 —4G 65
Theberton St. N1 —2J 59
Theed St. SE1 —3H 75
Theobald's Rd. WC1 —4E 66
Theobald St. SE1 —7D 76
Theseus Wlk. N1 —5A 60
Thessaly Ho. SW8 —7K 81
Thessaly Rd. SW8 —7K 81
Third Av. W10 —6A 54
Thirleby Rd. SW1 —7A 74
Thistle Gro. SW10 —3J 79
Thomas Doyle St. SE1 —6A 76
Thomas More Highwalk. EC2 —4B 68
Thomas More Ho. EC2 —4B 68
Thomas More Sq. E1 —1K 77
Thomas More St. E1 —1K 77
Thomas Neals Shop. Mall. WC2 —6D 66
Thomas Pl. W8 —7F 71
Thompson's Av. SE5 —7B 84
Thomson Ho. SW1 —4C 82
Thoresby St. N1 —6C 60
Thornbury Ct. W11 —7D 62
Thorncroft St. SW8 —7D 82
Thorndike Clo. SW10 —7H 79
Thorndike St. SW1 —2B 82
Thorney Ct. W8 —5H 71
Thorney Cres. SW11 —7A 80
Thorney St. SW1 —1D 82
Thorngate Rd. W9 —1E 62
Thornhaugh M. WC1 —2C 66
Thornhaugh St. WC1 —2C 66
Thornhill Bri. Wharf. N1 —3F 59
Thornhill Cres. N1 —1G 59
Thornhill Gro. N1 —1G 59
Thornhill Rd. N1 —1H 59
Thornhill Sq. N1 —1G 59
Thornton Pl. W1 —3E 64
Thorparch Rd. SW8 —7C 82
Thorpe Clo. W10 —5A 62
Thorpe Ho. N1 —3G 59
Thrale St. SE1 —3C 76
Thrasher Clo. E8 —2H 61
Thrawl St. E1 —4J 69
Threadneedle St. EC2 —6E 68
Three Barrels Wlk. EC4 —1C 76
Three Colt Corner. E2 & E1 —1K 69
Three Cranes Wlk. EC4 —1C 76
Three Cups Yd. WC1 —4G 67
Three Kings Yd. W1 —7H 65
Three Oak La. SE1 —4H 77
Three Quays. EC3 —1G 77
Three Quays Wlk. EC3 —1G 77
Threshers Pl. W11 —7A 62
Throgmorton Av. EC2 —5E 68
Throgmorton St. EC2 —5E 68
Thrush St. SE17 —3B 84
Thurland Rd. SE16 —6K 77
Thurloe Clo. SW7 —1B 80
Thurloe Pl. SW7 —1A 80
Thurloe Pl. M. SW7 —1A 80
Thurloe Sq. SW7 —1A 80
Thurloe St. SW7 —1A 80
Thurlow St. SE17 —3E 84
Thurlow Wlk. SE17 —3F 85
Thurso Ho. NW6 —5F 55
Thurtle Rd. E2 —3J 61
Tibberton Sq. N1 —1B 60
Tiber Gdns. N1 —3E 58
Tickford Ho. NW8 —7B 56
Tidemore Ho. SW8 —7K 81
Tideway Ind. Est. SW8 —6A 82
Tideway Wlk. SW8 —6A 82
Tilbury Clo. SE15 —7J 85
Tileyard Rd. N7 —1D 58
Tillet Way. E2 —6K 61
Tilloch St. N1 —1F 59
Tilney Ct. EC1 —1C 68
Tilney St. W1 —2G 73
Tilton St. SW6 —6A 78
Timberland Clo. SE15 —7K 85
Timber St. EC1 —1B 68
Tinworth St. SE11 —3F 83
Tisbury Ct. W1 —7B 66
Tisdall Pl. SE17 —2E 84
Titchborne Row. W2 —6B 64
Titchfield Rd. NW8 —3D 56
Tite St. SW3 —4D 80
Tiverton St. SE1 —7B 76
Tobin Clo. NW3 —1C 56
Tokenhouse Yd. EC2 —5D 68
Tollbridge Clo. W10 —1A 62
Tollgate Gdns. NW6 —4F 55
Tolmers Sq. NW1 —1K 65
Tolpaide Ho. SE11 —3H 83
Tolpuddle St. N1 —4H 59
Tomkyns Ho. SE11 —2H 83
Tomlinson Clo. E2 —7J 61
Tompion St. EC1 —7A 60
Tom Williams Ho. SW6 —6C 78
Tonbridge St. WC1 —6D 58
Tonbridge Wlk. WC1 —6D 58
Took's Ct. EC4 —5H 67
Tooley St. SE1 —2E 76
Topham St. EC1 —1H 67
Torbay Ct. NW1 —1J 57
Torbay Man. NW6 —2B 54
Torbay Rd. NW6 —1B 54
Torbay St. NW1 —1J 57
Tor Gdns. W8 —4D 70
Torquay St. W2 —4F 63
Torrens St. EC1 —5K 59
Torrington Pl. WC1 —3B 66
Torrington Sq. WC1 —2C 66
Tothill St. SW1 —5B 74
Tottenham Ct. Rd. W1 —2A 66
Tottenham M. W1 —3A 66
Tottenham St. W1 —4A 66
Toulmin St. SE1 —5B 76
Toulon St. SE5 —7B 84
Tournay Rd. SW6 —7C 78
Toussaint Wlk. SE16 —6K 77
Tower Bri. SE1 & E1 —3H 77
Tower Bri. App. E1 —2H 77
Tower Bri. Bus. Complex. SE16 —7K 77
Tower Bri. Plaza. SE1 —3H 77
Tower Bri. Rd. SE1 —7F 77
Tower Bri. Sq. SE1 —4H 77
Tower Bri. Wharf. E1 —3K 77
Tower Ct. WC2 —6D 66
Tower Hill. (Junct.) —7J 69
Tower Hill. EC3 —1G 77
Tower Hill Ter. EC3 —1G 77
Tower Ho. E1 —4K 69
Tower Pl. EC3 —1G 77
Tower Royal. EC4 —7D 68
Tower St. WC2 —6C 66
Townley St. SE17 —3D 84 (in two parts)
Townsend St. SE17 —2E 84
Townshend Ct. NW8 —4C 56
Townshend Est. NW8 —4B 56
Townshend Rd. NW8 —3B 56
Toynbee St. E1 —4H 69
Tracey St. SE11 —3H 83
Tradescant Rd. SW8 —7E 82
Tradewinds Ct. E1 —1K 77
Trafalgar Av. SE15 —4J 85
Trafalgar Gdns. W8 —6G 71

Trafalgar Sq.—Zoar St.

Trafalgar Sq. WC2 —2C 74
Trafalgar St. SE17 —3D 84
Trafford Ho. N1 —5E 60
Transept St. NW1 —4C 64
Tranton Rd. SE16 —6K 77
Treasury Pas. SW1 —4D 74
Treaty St. N1 —3F 59
Trebeck St. W1 —2H 73
Trebovir Rd. SW5 —3E 78
Trederwen Rd. E8 —2K 61
Tregunter Rd. SW10 —5G 79
Trematon Ho. SE11 —3J 83
Trenchold St. SW8 —6D 82
Tresco Ho. SE11 —3H 83
Tresham Cres. NW8 —1B 64
Tressell Clo. N1 —1A 60
Tress Pl. SE1 —2K 75
Trevanion Rd. W14 —3A 78
Treveris St. SE1 —3A 76
Trevor Pl. SW7 —5C 72
Trevor Sq. SW7 —6C 72
Trevor St. SW7 —5C 72
Trevose Ho. SE11 —3G 83
Triangle, The. EC1 —1A 68
Trig La. EC4 —7B 68
Trigon Rd. SW8 —7G 83
Trinity Chu. Sq. SE1 —5C 76
Trinity Ct. N1 —2F 61
Trinity Ct. W2 —5H 63
Trinity Pl. EC3 —1H 77
Trinity Sq. EC3 —1G 77
Trinity St. SE1 —5C 76
Trio Pl. SE1 —5C 76
Triton Sq. NW1 —1K 65
Trojan Ct. NW6 —1A 54
Trothy Rd. SE1 —1K 85
Troutbeck Ho. NW1 —7J 57
Troy Ct. W8 —6D 70
Trump St. EC2 —6C 68
Trundle St. SE1 —4B 76
Tryon St. SW3 —3D 80
Tudor St. EC4 —7J 67
Tufton St. SW1 —6D 74
Tunbridge Ho. EC1 —6K 59
Tupman Ho. SE16 —5K 77
Turin St. E2 —7K 61
Turk's Head Yd. EC1 —3K 67
Turks Row. SW3 —3E 80
Turnagain La. EC4 —5K 67
Turner's All. EC3 —7F 69
Turners Rd. N1 —5F 61
Turneville Rd. W14 —5B 78
Turnmill St. EC1 —2K 67
Turnpike Ho. EC1 —7A 60
Turpentine La. SW1 —3J 81
Turquand St. SE17 —2C 84
Turville St. E2 —1J 69
Tutshill Ct. SE15 —7G 85 (off Lynbrook Clo.)
Tweezer's All. WC2 —7H 67
Twyford Pl. WC2 —5F 67
Twyford St. N1 —2F 59
Tyburn Way. W1 —7E 64
Tyers Est. SE1 —4F 77
Tyers Ga. SE1 —5F 77
Tyers St. SE11 —4F 83
Tyers Ter. SE11 —4F 83
Tyler Clo. E2 —4H 61
Tyler's Ct. W1 —6B 66
Tyndale La. N1 —1K 59
Tyndale Mans. N1 —1K 59 (off Upper St.)
Tyndale Ter. N1 —1K 59
Tyne St. E1 —5J 69
Tysoe St. EC1 —7J 59

Udall St. SW1 —2A 82
Ufford St. SE1 —4J 75
Ufton Gro. N1 —1E 60
Ufton Rd. N1 —1E 60 (in two parts)
Ulster Pl. NW1 —2H 65
Ulster Ter. NW1 —2H 65
Underhill Pas. NW1 —2J 57
Underhill St. NW1 —3J 57
Undershaft. EC3 —6F 69
Underwood Rd. E1 —2K 69
Underwood Row. N1 —6C 60
Underwood St. N1 —6C 60
Union Ct. EC2 —5F 69
Union Sq. N1 —3C 60
Union St. SE1 —4K 75
Union Wlk. E2 —6G 61
Union Yd. W1 —6J 65
Unity Wharf. SE1 —4J 77
University St. WC1 —2A 66
Unwin Clo. SE15 —6K 85
Unwin Mans. W14 —5A 78
Unwin Rd. SW7 —6K 71
Upbrook M. W2 —6J 63
Upcerne Rd. SW10 —7H 79
Upnor Way. SE17 —3G 85
Up. Addison Gdns. W14 —4A 70
Up. Belgrave St. SW1 —6G 73
Up. Berkeley St. W1 —6D 64
Up. Brook St. W1 —1F 73
Up. Camelford Wlk. W11 —6A 62 (off St Mark's Rd.)
Up. Cheyne Row. SW3 —6B 80
Up. Clarendon Wlk. W11 —6A 62 (off Clarendon Rd.)
Up. Dengie Wlk. N1 —2C 60 (off Basire St.)
Up. Grosvenor St. W1 —1F 73
Up. Ground. SE1 —2J 75
Up. Harley St. NW1 —2G 65
Up. Hawkwell Wlk. N1 —2C 60 (off Maldon Clo.)
Up. James St. W1 —7A 66
Up. John St. W1 —7A 66
Up. Marsh. SE1 —6G 75
Up. Montagu St. W1 —3D 64
Up. Phillimore Gdns. W8 —5D 70
Up. Rawreth Wlk. N1 —2C 60 (off Basire St.)
Up. St Martin's La. WC2 —7D 66
Upper St. N1 —5K 59
Up. Tachbrook St. SW1 —1K 81
Up. Thames St. EC4 —7A 68
Up. Wimpole St. W1 —3G 65
Up. Woburn Pl. WC1 —7C 58
Urlwin St. SE5 —6B 84
Usborne M. SW8 —7G 83
Uverdale Rd. SW10 —7J 79
Uxbridge St. W8 —2D 70

Vale Clo. W9 —7H 55
Vale Ct. W9 —7J 55
Valentine Pl. SE1 —5K 75
Valentine Row. SE1 —5K 75
Vale Royal. N7 —1D 58
Vale, The. SW3 —5A 80
Vallance Rd. E2 & E1 —7K 61
Vanbrugh Ct. SE11 —2J 83
Vandon Pas. SW1 —6A 74
Vandon St. SW1 —6A 74
Vandy St. EC2 —2F 69
Vane St. SW1 —1A 82
Vanston Pl. SW6 —7D 78
Vantrey Ho. SE11 —2H 83
Varna Rd. SW6 —7A 78
Varndell St. NW1 —6K 57
Vassall Rd. SW9 —7K 83
Vauban Est. SE16 —7J 77
Vauban St. SE16 —7J 77
Vaughan Est. E2 —6H 61
Vaughan Way. E1 —1K 77
Vauxhall Bri. SW1 & SE1 —3D 82
Vauxhall Bri. Rd. SW1 —7K 73
Vauxhall Cross. (Junct.) —4E 82
Vauxhall Cross. SE1 —4E 82
Vauxhall Distribution Cen. SW8 —6C 82
Vauxhall Gro. SW8 —5E 82
Vauxhall St. SE11 —3G 83
Vauxhall Wlk. SE11 —4F 83
Venables St. NW8 —2A 64
Venn Ho. N1 —3G 59
Vereker Rd. W14 —4A 78
Vere St. W1 —6H 65
Verney Rd. SE16 —5K 85
Vernon Ho. SE11 —4G 83
Vernon M. W14 —2A 78
Vernon Pl. WC1 —4E 66
Vernon Ri. WC1 —6G 59
Vernon Sq. WC1 —6G 59
Vernon St. W14 —2A 78
Vernon Yd. W11 —7B 62
Verulam Bldgs. WC1 —3G 67
Verulam St. WC1 —3H 67
Vesage Ct. EC1 —4J 67
Vestry St. N1 —6D 60
Viaduct Bldgs. EC1 —4J 67
Vibart Wlk. N1 —3E 58
Vicarage Ct. W8 —4F 71
Vicarage Gdns. W8 —3E 70
Vicarage Ga. W8 —4F 71
Viceroy Ct. NW8 —4C 56
Vicery Ct. EC1 —1C 68
Victoria Arc. SW1 —7J 73
Victoria Av. EC2 —4G 69
Victoria Embkmt. SW1, WC2 & EC4 —4E 74
Victoria Gdns. W11 —2D 70
Victoria Gro. W8 —6H 71
Victoria Gro. M. W2 —1E 70
Victoria Ho. N1 —3G 59
Victoria Ho. SW8 —7E 82
Victoria Mans. SW8 —7E 82
Victoria M. NW6 —2D 54
Victoria Pas. NW8 —1K 63
Victoria Pl. Shop. Cen. SW1 —1J 81
Victoria Rd. NW6 —4B 54
Victoria Rd. W8 —5H 71
Victoria Sq. SW1 —6J 73
Victoria St. SW1 —7J 73
Victory Pl. SE17 —1C 84
Vigo St. W1 —1K 73
Viking Ct. SW6 —6E 78
Villa St. SE17 —4E 84
Villa Wlk. SE17 —4E 84
Villiers St. WC2 —1D 74
Vincent Sq. SW1 —1A 82
Vincent St. SW1 —1A 82
Vincent Ter. N1 —4K 59
Vince St. EC1 —7E 60
Vine Ct. E1 —4K 69
Vinegar Yd. SE1 —4F 77
Vine Hill. EC1 —2H 67
Vine La. SE1 —3G 77
Vine Sq. W14 —4C 78
Vine St. EC3 —6H 69
Vine St. W1 —1A 74
Vine St. Bri. EC1 —2J 67
Vine Yd. SE1 —4C 76
Vineyard M. EC1 —1H 67
Vineyard Wlk. EC1 —1H 67
Vintners Ct. EC4 —1C 76
Vintners Hall. EC4 —1C 76
Vintner's Pl. EC4 —1C 76
Violet Hill. NW8 —5H 55
Virgil Pl. W1 —4D 64
Virgil St. SE1 —6G 75
Virginia Rd. E2 —7H 61
Virginia St. E1 —1K 77
Viscount St. EC1 —2B 68
Vogans Wharf. SE1 —4J 77
Vollasky Ho. E1 —3K 69
Voss St. E2 —7K 61
Voyager Bus. Est. SE16 —6K 77

Wadding St. SE17 —2D 84
Wade Ho. SE1 —5K 77
Wadham Gdns. NW3 —2B 56
Waite St. SE15 —5H 85
Waithman St. EC4 —6K 67
Wakefield M. WC1 —7E 58
Wakefield St. WC1 —7E 58
Wakley St. EC1 —6K 59
Walberswick St. SW8 —7E 82
Walbrook. EC4 —7D 68
Walbrook Wharf. EC4 —1C 76
Walcorde Av. SE17 —2C 84
Walcot Gdns. SE11 —1H 83
Walcot Sq. SE11 —1J 83
Walcott St. SW1 —1A 82
Waldron M. SW3 —5A 80
Waleran Flats. SE1 —1F 85
Walham Grn. Ct. SW6 —7F 79
Walham Gro. SW6 —7D 78
Walham Yd. SW6 —7D 78
Walker's Ct. W1 —7B 66
Wallgrave Rd. SW5 —1F 79
Wallgrave Ter. SW5 —1E 78
Wallis All. SE1 —4C 76
Wallside. EC2 —4C 68
Walmer Pl. W1 —3D 64
Walmer Rd. W11 —7A 62
Walmer St. W1 —3D 64
Walnut Ct. W8 —7F 71
Walnut Tree Wlk. SE11 —1H 83
Walpole M. NW8 —3K 55
Walpole St. SW3 —3D 80
Walsingham. NW8 —2A 56
Walsingham Mans. SW6 —7G 79
Walters Clo. SE17 —2C 84
Walterton Rd. W9 —2C 62
Waltham Ho. NW8 —2H 55
Walton Clo. SW8 —7E 82
Walton Pl. SW3 —6D 72
Walton St. SW3 —1C 80
Walworth Pl. SE17 —4C 84
Walworth Rd. SE1 & SE17 —1A 84
Wandon Rd. SW6 —7G 79
Wandsworth Rd. SW8 —7D 82
Wansdown Pl. SW6 —7F 79
Wansey St. SE17 —2B 84
Wapping High St. E1 —3K 77
Wardens Gro. SE1 —3B 76
Wardour M. W1 —6A 66
Wardour St. W1 —5A 66
Ward Point. SE11 —2H 83
Wardrobe Pl. EC4 —6A 68
Wardrobe Ter. EC4 —7A 68
Wareham Ho. SW8 —7F 83
Warham St. SE5 —7A 84
Warlock Rd. W9 —1C 62
Warmley Ct. SE15 —6G 85
Warner Pl. E2 —5K 61
Warner St. EC1 —2H 67
Warner Yd. EC1 —2H 67
Warren M. W1 —2K 65
Warren St. W1 —2K 65
Warrington Cres. W9 —2H 63
Warrington Gdns. W9 —2H 63
Warwick Av. W9 & W2 —2G 63
Warwick Chambers. W8 —6D 70
Warwick Ct. WC1 —4G 67
Warwick Cres. W2 —3H 63
Warwick Est. W2 —4G 63
Warwick Gdns. W14 —7C 70
Warwick Ho. St. SW1 —2C 74
Warwick La. EC4 —5A 68
Warwick Pas. EC4 —5A 68
Warwick Pl. W9 —3H 63
Warwick Pl. N. SW1 —2K 81
Warwick Rd. W14 & SW5 —7B 70
Warwick Row. SW1 —7J 73
Warwick Sq. EC4 —5A 68
Warwick Sq. SW1 —3K 81
Warwick Sq. M. SW1 —2K 81
Warwick St. W1 —7A 66
Warwick Way. SW1 —3H 81
Warwick Yd. EC1 —2C 68
Watercress Pl. N1 —1G 61
Waterford Rd. SW6 —7F 79
Water Gdns., The. W2 —5B 64
Watergate. EC4 —7K 67
Watergate Wlk. WC2 —2E 74
Waterhouse Sq. EC1 —4H 67
Water La. EC3 —1G 77
Water La. NW1 —1C 58
Waterloo Bri. WC2 & SE1 —1F 75
Waterloo Pas. NW6 —1C 54
Waterloo Pl. SW1 —2B 74
Waterloo Rd. SE1 —2G 75
Waterloo Ter. N1 —1K 59
Waterman's Wlk. EC4 —1D 76
Waterside Clo. SE16 —5K 77
Waterside Pl. NW1 —2G 57
Waterside Point. SW11 —7C 80
Waterson St. E2 —6G 61
Water St. WC2 —7H 67
Water Tower Pl. N1 —3K 59
Watling Ct. EC4 —6C 68
Watling St. EC4 —6B 68
Watling St. SE15 —6G 85
Watson's M. W1 —4C 64
Wavel M. NW6 —1F 55
Waveney Clo. E1 —2K 77
Waverley Pl. NW8 —4K 55
Waverton St. W1 —2G 73
Waylett Ho. SE11 —4G 83
Weavers La. SE1 —3G 77
Weavers Ter. SW6 —6E 78
Weaver St. E1 —2K 69
Weavers Way. NW1 —2B 58
Webber Row. SE1 —6J 75 (in two parts)
Webber St. SE1 —4J 75
Webb Ho. SW8 —7C 82
Webb St. SE1 —7F 77
Webster Rd. SE16 —7K 77
Wedgwood Ho. SE11 —7H 75
Wedgwood M. W1 —6C 66
Weighhouse St. W1 —7G 65
Weir's Pas. NW1 —6C 58
Welbeck Ct. W14 —1B 78
Welbeck St. W1 —4G 65
Welbeck Way. W1 —5H 65
Wellclose Sq. E1 —7K 69
Well Ct. EC4 —6C 68
Weller Ho. SE16 —5K 77
Wellers Ct. N1 —5D 58
Weller St. SE1 —4B 76
Wellesley Ct. W9 —6H 55
Wellesley Pl. NW1 —7B 58
Wellesley Ter. N1 —6C 60
Wellington Bldgs. SW1 —4G 81
Wellington Clo. W11 —6D 62
Wellington Ct. NW8 —5K 55
Wellington Pl. NW8 —6A 56
Wellington Rd. NW8 —5A 56
Wellington Row. E2 —6J 61
Wellington Sq. SW3 —3D 80
Wellington St. WC2 —7E 66
Wellington Ter. W2 —1F 71
Wells M. W1 —4A 66
Wells Ri. NW8 —3D 56
Wells Sq. WC1 —7F 59
Wells St. W1 —4K 65
Wells Way. SE5 —5E 84
Wells Way. SW7 —6K 71
Welsford St. SE1 —3K 85
Welshpool St. E8 —2K 61 (in two parts)
Wendle Ct. SW8 —6D 82
Wendover. SE17 —3F 85 (in two parts)
Wenham Ho. SW8 —7K 81
Wenlock Barn Est. N1 —5D 60
Wenlock Ct. N1 —5D 60
Wenlock Rd. N1 —5B 60
Wenlock St. N1 —5C 60
Wentworth Ct. W6 —6A 78
Wentworth St. E1 —5H 69
Werrington St. NW1 —5A 58
Wesley Clo. SE17 —2A 84
Wesley St. W1 —4G 65
Wessex Ho. SE1 —4J 85
Westbourne Bri. W2 —4H 63
Westbourne Cres. W2 —7K 63
Westbourne Cres. M. W2 —7K 63
Westbourne Gdns. W2 —5F 63
Westbourne Gro. W11 & W2 —7B 62
Westbourne Gro. M. W11 —6D 62
Westbourne Gro. Ter. W2 —5F 63
Westbourne Pk. M. W2 —5F 63
Westbourne Pk. Pas. W2 —4E 62
Westbourne Pk. Rd. W11 & W2 —6A 62
Westbourne Pk. Vs. W2 —4E 62
Westbourne St. W2 —7K 63
Westbourne Ter. W2 —5H 63
Westbourne Ter. M. W2 —5H 63
Westbourne Ter. Rd. W2 —4H 63
Westbourne Ter. Rd. Bri. W2 —3H 63
W. Carriage Dri. W2 —1B 72
W. Central St. WC1 —5D 66
Westcott Rd. SE17 —5K 83
W. Cromwell Rd. W14 & SW5 —3B 78
W. Eaton Pl. SW1 —1F 81
W. Eaton Pl. M. SW1 —1F 81
W. End La. NW6 —1E 54
Westerham Ho. SE1 —6E 76
Western Ct. NW6 —5C 54
Western M. W9 —2C 62
Westfield Clo. SW10 —7H 79
W. Garden Pl. W2 —6C 64
Westgate Ter. SW10 —4G 79
W. Halkin St. SW1 —6F 73
W. Harding St. EC4 —5J 67
W. Kensington Ct. W14 —3B 78
W. Kensington Mans. W14 —4B 78
Westland Pl. N1 —6D 60
West Mall. W8 —2E 70
West M. SW1 —2K 81
Westminster Bri. SW1 & SE1 —5E 74
Westminster Bri. Rd. SE1 —5F 75
Westminster Bus. Sq. SE11 —4F 83
Westminster Pal. Gdns. SW1 —7B 74
Westmoreland Pl. SW1 —4J 81
Westmoreland Rd. SE17 —5C 84
Westmoreland St. W1 —4G 65
Westmoreland Ter. SW1 —3J 81
Westmoreland Wlk. SE17 —5D 84
Westonbirt Ct. SE15 —6H 85
Weston Ho. NW6 —1A 54
Weston Ri. WC1 —6G 59
Weston St. SE1 —6E 76 (in three parts)
W. Point. SE1 —3K 85
W. Poultry Av. EC1 —4K 67
West Ri. W2 —7C 64
West Rd. SE1 —4G 75
West Rd. SW3 —4E 80
W. Smithfield. EC1 —4K 67
West Sq. SE11 —7K 75
West St. WC2 —6C 66
W. Tenter St. E1 —6J 69
W. Warwick Pl. SW1 —2K 81
Westway. W2 —4F 63
Westway. W12, W10 & W2 —5A 62
Wetherby Gdns. SW5 —2H 79
Wetherby Mans. SW5 —3F 79
Wetherby M. SW5 —3G 79
Wetherby Pl. SW7 —2H 79
Weyhill Rd. E1 —5K 69
Weymouth Ho. SW8 —7F 83
Weymouth M. W1 —3H 65
Weymouth St. W1 —4G 65
Weymouth Ter. E2 —4J 61
Whalebone Ct. EC2 —5D 68
Wharfdale Rd. N1 —4E 58
Wharfedale St. SW10 —4F 79
Wharf Rd. N1 —5B 60
Wharf Rd. NW1 —1B 58
Wharton Cotts. WC1 —7H 59
Wharton St. WC1 —7G 59
Wheatley St. W1 —4G 65
Wheatsheaf La. SW8 —7D 82 (in two parts)
Wheatstone Rd. W10 —3A 62
Wheeler Gdns. N1 —2E 58
Wheler St. E1 —2H 69
Whetstone Pk. WC2 —5F 67
Whidborne St. WC1 —7E 58
Whiskin St. EC1 —7K 59
Whistlers Av. SW11 —7B 80
Whistler Tower. SW10 —7J 79 (off Worlds End Est.)
Whistler Wlk. SW10 —7J 79
Whiston Rd. E2 —4H 61 (in two parts)
Whitby St. E1 —1H 69
Whitcomb Ct. WC2 —1C 74
Whitcomb St. WC2 —1C 74
White Bear Yd. EC1 —2H 67
Whitechapel High St. E1 —5J 69
Whitechapel Rd. E1 —5K 69
White Chu. La. E1 —5K 69
White Chu. Pas. E1 —5K 69
White Conduit St. N1 —4J 59
Whitecross Pl. EC2 —3E 68
Whitecross St. EC1 —1C 68
Whitefriars St. EC4 —6J 67
Whitehall. SW1 —2D 74
Whitehall Ct. SW1 —3D 74
Whitehall Gdns. SW1 —3D 74
Whitehall Pl. SW1 —3D 74
White Hart Ct. EC2 —4F 69
White Hart St. SE11 —3J 83
White Hart Yd. SE1 —3D 76
Whitehaven St. NW8 —2B 64
Whitehead's Gro. SW3 —3C 80
White Horse All. EC1 —3K 67
Whitehorse M. SE1 —6J 75
White Horse St. W1 —3J 73
White Horse Yd. EC2 —5D 68
White Kennett St. E1 —5G 69
Whiteley's Cotts. W14 —2C 78
Whiteleys Shop. Cen. W2 —6G 63
White Lion Ct. EC3 —6F 69
White Lion Hill. EC4 —7A 68
White Lion St. N1 —5H 59
White Lion Yd. W1 —7H 65
White Lyon Ct. EC2 —3B 68
White's Grounds. SE1 —5G 77
White's Grounds Est. SE1 —4G 77
White's Row. E1 —4H 69
Whitfield Pl. W1 —2K 65
Whitfield St. W1 —2K 65
Whitgift Ho. SE11 —1F 83
Whitgift St. SE11 —1F 83
Whitmore Est. N1 —3G 61
Whitmore Ho. N1 —4G 61
Whitmore Rd. N1 —3F 61
Whittaker St. SW1 —2F 81
Whittaker Way. SE1 —2K 85
Whittington Av. EC3 —6F 69
Whittlesey St. SE1 —3J 75
Whitworth Ho. SE1 —7C 76
Wickham St. SE11 —3F 83
Wicklow St. WC1 —6F 59
Wicksteed Ho. SE1 —7C 76
Wickway Ct. SE15 —6H 85
Widegate St. E1 —4G 69
Widford Ho. N1 —5K 59
Widley Rd. W9 —7E 54
Wigmore Pl. W1 —5H 65
Wigmore St. W1 —6F 65
Wigton Pl. SE11 —4J 83
Wilbraham Pl. SW1 —1E 80
Wilby M. W11 —2C 70
Wilcox Clo. SW8 —7E 82 (in two parts)
Wilcox Pl. SW1 —7A 74
Wilcox Rd. SW8 —7D 82
Wild Ct. WC2 —6F 67
Wilde Clo. E8 —2K 61
Wilds Rents. SE1 —6F 77
Wild St. WC2 —6E 66
Wilfred St. SW1 —6K 73
Wilkes St. E1 —3J 69 (in two parts)
Wilkinson Ho. N1 —5E 60
Wilkinson St. SW8 —7F 83
Wilks Pl. N1 —5G 61
Willesden La. NW2 & NW6 —1A 54
William Cobbett Ho. W8 —6F 71
William Dromey Ct. NW6 —1B 54
William Dunbar Ho. NW6 —5B 54
William Ellis Way. SE16 —7K 77
William IV St. WC2 —1D 74
William Henry Wlk. SW8 —6B 82
William M. SW1 —5E 72
William Rd. NW1 —7J 57
William Saville Ho. NW6 —5C 54
Williams Clo. SW6 —7A 78
Williamson Ct. SE17 —4B 84
William St. SW1 —5E 72
Willoughby Highwalk. EC2 —4D 68
Willoughby Ho. EC2 —4D 68
Willoughby St. WC1 —4D 66
Willow Brook Rd. SE15 —6J 85
Willow Ct. EC2 —1F 69
Willow Pl. SW1 —1A 82
Willow St. EC2 —1F 69
Willow Wlk. SE1 —1G 85
Willsbridge Ct. SE15 —6H 85
Wilman Gro. E8 —1K 61
Wilmcote Ho. W2 —3F 63
Wilmer Gdns. N1 —3F 61
Wilmington Sq. WC1 —7H 59
Wilmington St. WC1 —7H 59
Wilmot Clo. SE15 —7K 85
Wilsham St. W11 —2A 70
Wilson St. EC2 —4E 68
Wilton Cres. SW1 —5F 73
Wilton M. SW1 —6G 73
Wilton Pl. SW1 —5F 73
Wilton Rd. SW1 —7K 73
Wilton Row. SW1 —5F 73
Wilton Row. SW6 —7A 78
Wilton Sq. N1 —2D 60
Wilton St. SW1 —6H 73
Wilton Ter. SW1 —6F 73
Wilton Vs. N1 —3D 60
Wiltshire Clo. SW3 —2D 80
Wiltshire Row. N1 —3D 60
Wimbolt St. E2 —6K 61
Wimborne Ho. SW8 —7G 83
Wimborne St. N1 —4D 60
Wimpole M. W1 —3H 65
Wimpole St. W1 —3H 65
Winchcombe Bus. Cen. SE15 —7G 85
Winchcombe Ct. SE15 —6G 85
Winchester Av. NW6 —2A 54
Winchester Clo. SE17 —2A 84
Winchester Ho. SW3 —6A 80
Winchester Ho. SW9 —7J 83
Winchester Rd. NW3 —1A 56
Winchester Sq. SE1 —2D 76
Winchester St. SW1 —3J 81
Winchester Wlk. SE1 —2D 76
Wincott St. SE11 —1J 83
Windermere Av. NW6 —3A 54
Windmill Row. SE11 —4H 83
Windmill St. W1 —4B 66 (in two parts)
Windmill Wlk. SE1 —3J 75
Windsor Cen., The. N1 —2A 60
Windsor Gdns. W9 —3D 62
Windsor Ho. N1 —4C 60
Windsor Pl. SW1 —1A 82
Windsor St. N1 —2A 60
Windsor Ter. N1 —6C 60
Wine Office Ct. EC4 —6J 67
Winnett St. W1 —7B 66
Winnington Ho. SE5 —7B 84
Winsland M. W2 —5K 63
Winsland St. W2 —5K 63
Winsley St. W1 —5A 66
Winslow. SE17 —4F 85
Winston Ho. N1 —5E 60
Winterbourne Ho. W11 —1A 70
Winter Lodge. SE16 —4K 85
Winterton Pl. SW10 —5J 79
Wisden Ho. SW8 —6G 83
Withers Pl. EC1 —1C 68
Woburn M. WC1 —2C 66
Woburn Pl. WC1 —1C 66
Woburn Sq. WC1 —2C 66
Woburn Wlk. WC1 —7C 58
Wollaston Clo. SE1 —1B 84
Wolseley St. SE1 —5J 77
Wolverton. SE17 —3F 85
Wontner Clo. N1 —1B 60
Woodbridge St. EC1 —1K 67
Woodchester Sq. W2 —3F 63
Woodchurch Rd. NW6 —1E 54
Wood Clo. E2 —1K 69
Woodfall St. SW3 —4D 80
Woodfield Pl. W9 —2C 62
Woodfield Rd. W9 —3C 62
Woodlands Ho. NW6 —1A 54
Woodseer St. E1 —3J 69
Woodsford. SE17 —3D 84
Woodsford Sq. W14 —4A 70
Woods M. W1 —7E 64
Wood's Pl. SE1 —7G 77
Woodstock Ct. SE11 —3G 83
Woodstock M. W1 —4G 65
Woodstock St. W1 —6H 65
Wood St. EC2 —6C 68
Woodville Rd. NW6 —4C 54
Wooler St. SE17 —4D 84
Woolf M. WC1 —1C 66
Woolstaplers Way. SE16 —7K 77
Wooster Pl. SE1 —1E 84
Wootton St. SE1 —4J 75
Worcester Ho. SW9 —7J 83
Wordsworth Rd. SE1 —2J 85
Worfield St. SW11 —7C 80
Worgan St. SE11 —3F 83
Worlds End Est. SW10 —7K 79
World's End Pas. SW10 —7K 79
Wormwood St. EC2 —5F 69
Wornington Rd. W10 —2A 62
Woronzow Rd. NW8 —3A 56
Worship St. EC2 —2E 68
Worth Gro. SE17 —4D 84
Wrayburn Ho. SE16 —5K 77
Wren St. WC1 —1G 67
Wrestlers Ct. EC3 —5F 69
Wright's La. W8 —5E 70
Wrotham Rd. NW1 —1A 58
Wybert St. NW1 —1J 65
Wyclif Ct. EC1 —7K 59
Wyclif St. EC1 —7K 59
Wymering Mans. W9 —7E 54
Wymering Rd. W9 —7E 54
Wyndham Est. SE5 —7C 84
Wyndham M. W1 —4D 64
Wyndham Pl. W1 —4D 64
Wyndham Rd. SE5 —7A 84
Wyndham St. W1 —3D 64
Wyndham Yd. W1 —4D 64
Wynford Rd. N1 —4F 59
Wynnstay Gdns. W8 —6E 70
Wynyard Ho. SE11 —3G 83
Wynyard Ter. SE11 —3G 83
Wynyatt St. EC1 —7K 59
Wythburn Pl. W1 —6D 64
Wyvil Rd. SW8 —7D 82

Yalding Rd. SE16 —7K 77
Yardley St. WC1 —7H 59
Yarmouth Pl. W1 —3H 73
Yeate St. N1 —1D 60
Yeoman Ct. SE1 —4J 85
Yeoman's Row. SW3 —7C 72
Yeoman's Yd. E1 —7J 69
York Av. SE17 —3C 84
York Bri. NW1 —1F 65
York Bldgs. WC2 —1E 74
York Ga. NW1 —2F 65
York Ho. SE1 —7G 75
York Ho. Pl. W8 —4F 71
York Mans. SW5 —3F 79
York Pl. WC2 —1E 74
York Rd. SE1 —5G 75
Yorkshire Grey Yd. WC1 —4F 67
York St. W1 —4D 64
York St. Chambers. W1 —4D 64
York Ter. E. NW1 —2G 65
York Ter. W. NW1 —2F 65
Yorkton St. E2 —5K 61
York Way. N7 & N1 —1D 58
York Way Ct. N1 —3E 58
Young Ct. NW6 —1A 54
Youngs Bldgs. EC1 —1C 68
Young St. W8 —5F 71

Zetland Ho. W8 —6F 71
Ziggurat. EC1 —3J 67
Zoar St. SE1 —2B 76

INDEX TO SELECTED PLACES OF INTEREST, CINEMAS, THEATRES and HOSPITALS

with their map square reference